DIFFERENT VOICES

DIFFERENT VOICES

Women and the Holocaust

EDITED AND WITH INTRODUCTIONS BY

Carol Rittner AND *John K. Roth*

PARAGON HOUSE
New York

First edition, 1993

Published in the United States by

Paragon House
90 Fifth Avenue
New York, NY 10011

Grateful acknowledgment is made for permission to use the following items in this book:
Portions of Gertrud Kolmar's poetry as epigraphs. "The Woman Poet" and excerpts from
"Murder," "We Jews," and "Towers" are from Gertrud Kolmar, *Dark Soliloquy: The Selected
Poems of Gertrud Kolmar*, trans. Henry A. Smith. New York: The Seabury Press, 1975.
Copyright © 1975 by The Seabury Press. Reprinted by permission of HarperCollins
Publishers.
The map "Concentration Camps" by Martin Gilbert. This map is from Israel Gutman et
al., eds., *Encyclopedia of the Holocaust*, 4 vols. New York: Macmillan Publishing Company,
1990. Copyright © 1990 by Martin Gilbert and reprinted by his permission.
The maps of Auschwitz and Auschwitz–Birkenau from Anna Pawelczynska, *Values and
Violence in Auschwitz: A Sociological Analysis*, trans. Catherine S. Leach. Berkeley: University
of California Press, 1979. Copyright © 1979 by The Regents of the University of California. Reprinted by permission of the University of California Press.
Photographs from *The Auschwitz Album: A Book Based upon an Album Discovered by a
Concentration Camp Survivor, Lili Meier*, text by Peter Hellman. New York: Random House,
1981. The photographs are reprinted by permission of Yad Vashem, The Holocaust
Martyrs' and Heroes' Remembrance Authority, Jerusalem, Israel.

Library of Congress Cataloging-in-Publication Data

Different voices : women and the Holocaust / edited and with
introductions by Carol Rittner and John K. Roth.—1st ed.
p.   cm.
Includes bibliographical references and index.
ISBN 1-55778-503-1   —ISBN 1-55778-504-X (pbk.)
1. Holocaust, Jewish (1939–1945)—Personal narratives.   2. Jewish
women—Biography.   3. World War, 1939–1945—Women—Biography.
4. Holocaust, Jewish (1939–1945)—Literary collections.
I. Rittner, Carol Ann   II. Roth, John K.
D804.3D53   1993
940.53'18—dc20   92-28233
                                                          CIP

Manufactured in the United States of America

To
The Sisters of Mercy
Especially Those
In Dallas, Pennsylvania,
And Derry, Northern Ireland

And what does the Lord require of you? To act justly and to love mercy and to walk humbly with your God.

Micah 6:8

You hold me now completely in your hands.

My heart beats like a frightened little bird's
Against your palm. Take heed! You do not think
A person lives within the page you thumb.
To you this book is paper, cloth, and ink,

Some binding thread and glue, and thus is dumb,
And cannot touch you (though the gaze be great
That seeks you from the printed marks inside),
And is an object with an object's fate.

And yet it has been veiled like a bride,
Adorned with gems, made ready to be loved,
Who asks you bashfully to change your mind,
To wake yourself, and feel, and to be moved.

But still she trembles, whispering to the wind:
"This shall not be." And smiles as if she knew.
Yet she must hope. A woman always tries,
Her very life is but a single "You . . ."

With her black flowers and her painted eyes,
With silver chains and silks of spangled blue.
She knew more beauty when a child and free,
But now forgets the better words she knew.

A man is so much cleverer than we,
Conversing with himself of truth and lie,
Of death and spring and iron-work and time.
But I say "you" and always "you and I."

This book is but a girl's dress in rhyme,
Which can be rich and red, or poor and pale,
Which may be wrinkled, but with gentle hands,
And only may be torn by loving nails.

So then, to tell my story, here I stand.
The dress's tint, though bleached in bitter lye,
Has not all washed away. It still is real.
I call then with a thin, ethereal cry.

You hear me speak. But do you hear me feel?

GERTRUD KOLMAR, "The Woman Poet"

Contents

Part Three

VOICES OF REFLECTION

Maps and Photographs

Preface

"But where," she asked, "are the women?" The voice John Roth heard on the long-distance telephone line was Carol Rittner's. She had just received a copy of *Holocaust: Religious and Philosophical Implications*, which Roth and Michael Berenbaum edited for Paragon House in 1989. It reprinted classic Holocaust reflections by influential writers such as Elie Wiesel, Primo Levi, Yehuda Bauer, and Raul Hilberg. Rittner liked the book, but its contents were male-dominated. Her question was justified.

Different Voices: Women and the Holocaust is our joint response to the questions "Where were the women during the Holocaust?" and "How do the particularities of women's experiences in that event compare and contrast with those of men?" The Holocaust targeted and destroyed women—Jews especially but also non-Jews. The active or passive complicity of other women—Germans but also non-Germans—facilitated and legitimated the process of destruction that annihilated millions. During the Holocaust women lived in ghettos and in hiding. They struggled to survive in resistance units as well as in concentration camps and killing centers. Other women served in German offices and camps or made homes for the men who did the dirty, killing work that their Nazi oaths of loyalty required. Just as the Nazis tried to persuade German women that no duty was more important than bearing sons for the Third Reich, they also insisted with a vengeance that Jewish motherhood must be eradicated forever.

Despite all this, relatively little attention has been paid to women's experiences before, during, and after the Holocaust. Much of the best witness literature by women, the autobiographical accounts of those who survived the Holocaust, is out of print or not easily accessible. Much of the most widely read scholarship—historical, sociopolitical, philosophical, and religious—treats the Holocaust as if sexual and gender differences did not make a difference. A lot of significant detail has gone unmentioned if not unnoticed. Thus the particularities of women's experiences and reflections have been submerged and ignored.

Different Voices takes steps to repair that neglect. Although the book's introductory materials, as well as its bibliographical suggestions, include contributions by men, the primary principle that governed our selection of the book's contents is that they should exemplify the best writing by and about women who encountered the Holocaust. These women have done so either through direct experience or through the painstaking study and sustained reflection that confer authority even though the writer may not have reckoned with the Holocaust firsthand.

Picking what to include and what to leave out of this book required difficult choices. One kind, for example, involved Anne Frank. Born on June 12, 1929, she and her family left their native Germany for Holland soon after the Nazis took power in 1933. Her relatively carefree life changed on May 10, 1940, when Germany invaded and occupied the Netherlands. By early July 1942 conditions for Dutch Jews had drastically worsened—what the Germans called the "Final Solution" was under way—and the Franks went into hiding in Amsterdam. They were betrayed in early August 1944. Thus, on September 3, 1944, Anne Frank and her family boarded the last Auschwitz-bound transport that left the Dutch transit camp at Westerbork. They arrived at Auschwitz–Birkenau two days later. Until late October Anne was in the women's camp at Auschwitz. Then she was sent to Bergen-Belsen, where she perished from typhus on March 31, 1945.

Anne Frank's famous diary survived. It begins on her thirteenth birthday and ends shortly before the Franks were arrested in Amsterdam, not long after Anne turned fifteen. No part of the diary appears here. We reasoned, first, that the diary is readily available, and, second, that *Different Voices* ought to concentrate on writings by and about adult women. Full of feeling and wisdom though it is, Anne Frank's youthful voice speaks differently enough from those resounding in these pages that it seemed best not to expand the category "women and the Holocaust" so broadly as to include it. Even that restriction did not make the decision process much easier. There are so many women's voices that speak insightfully, eloquently, poignantly about the Holocaust. Fortunately, their numbers are increasing because of the many oral history projects that are recording the Holocaust testimonies of the former victims. In these pages, however, it is the written word that speaks.

As the Holocaust shows, there has been much darkness in the twentieth century. One encouraging sign, however, is the growing interest in and concern about the circumstances, identities, and prospects of women. We have experienced this interest and concern in our teaching about the Holocaust. In recent years, for example, the heavily enrolled Holocaust course that John Roth teaches annually at Claremont McKenna College has drawn a majority of women. Their desire to study what happened to women during the Holocaust helped to inspire this book. Carol Rittner has experienced similar reactions in her Holocaust explorations with the women she has been teaching. If *Different Voices* contributes to a better understanding of women's experience—understanding that is needed by men and women alike—then it will accomplish all that we hope for it.

A word about the book's three-part organization will help orient the reader. The first voices are those of experience. These women, most but not all of them Jewish, were trapped by the "Final Solution." Unlike the millions of women who lost their families and their lives in that catastrophe, most of these survived to bear witness for the living as well as for the dead. The selections we have chosen pivot around Auschwitz, the Nazi death camp in Poland whose name has rightly become almost synonymous with the Holocaust itself.

This part of the book could have had a different focus. It might have concentrated on the Warsaw ghetto or on the women's concentration camp at Ravensbrück, Germany. Conditions for women in those places were desperate, too, but Auschwitz offers a microcosm of extremity justifying its central position in this book.

The book's second major part accents voices of interpretation. Most of them belong to historians. They step back from the immediacy of personal experience to analyze the larger picture, and their perspectives assess the particular ways in which Nazi theory and practice made an impact on women. They also explore how the women targeted by that theory and practice responded to those threatening realities.

Voices of experience and interpretation are complemented by the voices of reflection in Part Three. These include Holocaust survivors and a child of survivors. The voices of poets, storytellers, philosophers, and religious thinkers as well as historians are heard here as they explore questions about memory and morality, fragmentation and faith, and the insights and implications that the experiences of women during the Holocaust provide for contemporary life, women's studies, and feminist thought.

In the book's diverse contents, it should be noted, there are occasional variations in note forms and in the spelling of some names, places, and terms, especially those that were peculiar to life in Auschwitz and other camps. We have let these variations stand. The authors' contributions remain as close as possible to their original styles. Carol Rittner and John Roth have introduced the contributors, their experiences, and the key issues they raise. We hope that the book's chronology, maps, photos, and glossary will prove helpful as well.

Opportunities to study women's experiences of the Holocaust, and then to share our findings by publishing this book, leave us indebted to many people. We are especially grateful for support from Maury Chandler, Cary Davidson, Charlotte Cordes, Jon Keates, Perry Lerner, Phil Minkin, Harold and Sallyann Rosenn, and Jack Stark. These individuals—along with institutional backing from Claremont McKenna College, Claremont, California; the Coolidge Research Colloquium, Cambridge, Massachusetts; the Religious Sisters of Mercy, Dallas, Pennsylvania; and Temple Israel, Wilkes-Barre, Pennsylvania—generously provided funds to cover permissions fees to publish copyrighted material.

We are grateful to all the authors and publishers who gave permission to reprint their work. Special thanks go to Rachel Altman, Mary Jo Leddy, Deborah Lipstadt, and Joan Ringelheim—good friends, each and all—who took the time to write original contributions for this volume. We also are deeply indebted to Rosette C. Lamont, who graciously shared her brilliant new translations of Charlotte Delbo's writings. Martin Gilbert helped us with maps. Judith Levin, Zvi Reiter, and Alan Rosen gave the assistance we needed for the book's photographs. Pat Padilla typed major portions of the manuscript.

For care, patience, and encouragement, no one tops Jo Glorie, our superb editor at Paragon House. Under her direction, H. L. Kirk, Ed Paige, Carla Sommerstein, and G. Nick Street helped us immensely along the way. Karen Attyah, Laura Cohen, and Kathleen O'Neill—three outstanding students at Claremont McKenna College—cheerfully handled countless details as the book developed from start to finish.

Carol Rittner and John Roth scarcely could have known all that awaited us as we began to hear the different voices that echo in the experience, interpretation, and reflection of women and the Holocaust. We encountered much that intensified despair, but especially the support and encouragement we received from friends such as those named above and countless others kept convincing us that this project was worthwhile. Our readers, we hope, will share that conviction as they explore what follows.

Prologue

WOMEN AND THE HOLOCAUST

So then, to tell my story, here I stand. . . .
You hear me speak. But do you hear me feel?

GERTRUD KOLMAR

The Holocaust was Nazi Germany's planned total destruction of the Jewish people and the actual murder of nearly six million of them.[1] This genocidal campaign—the most systematic, bureaucratic, and unrelenting ever—also destroyed millions of non-Jewish civilians because the Nazis believed their threat to the Third Reich approached, though it could never equal, that posed by Jews.[2] In German this destruction process became known as *die Endlösung*—the "Final Solution." The Hebrew word *Shoah*, meaning catastrophe, also is frequently used to name it. One result of the Shoah was that millions of women, the vast majority of them Jewish, perished during its devastation.

Among the women who did not return was a Jewish poet named Gertrud Kolmar. Her words provide the epigraph for this book and the thematic preludes for its various parts as well.[3] Kolmar wanted "to tell my story." Her poems made a brilliant start, but her life ended before she could finish the telling. The wound of this interrupted life stays unhealed, but not only because the exact date of Kolmar's death in Auschwitz, the camp to which she was almost certainly deported from Berlin during the winter of 1943, remains unknown. The disaster that ruined her life has even more to do with the immeasurable loss Nazi Germany inflicted by decreeing that women such as Gertrud Kolmar must be destroyed.

1

To explore what such decrees involved, note that antisemitism was at the heart of Nazi ideology. Nazi antisemitism meant that race—specifically the "purity" of German blood and culture—counted for everything. Nothing could be tolerated that might pollute the racial strength on which the Third Reich depended. According to Nazi theory, Jewish life posed this threat to a degree that surpassed every other. Germans could not afford to let Jews remain in their midst.

As the history of Nazi Germany so emphatically shows, racism's "logic" ultimately entails genocide. For if you take seriously the idea that one race endangers the well-being of another, the only way to remove that menace completely is to do away, once and for all, with everyone and everything that embodies it. Thus, the Holocaust took the lives of 1.5 million Jewish children who were not yet in their teens. If most forms of racism shy away from such extreme measures, Nazi Germany's antisemitism did not.

A connection can also be shown between antisemitism, racism, and sexism. Sexism, which divides social roles according to biological functions, can exist without racism, but whenever claims are made that one race is superior to any or all others, discrimination directed at women is unlikely to be far behind. Because women are the ones who bear children, they are put uniquely at risk as members of a group targeted as racially inferior.

The racism of Nazi ideology ultimately implied that the existence of Jewish women constituted a deadly obstacle to the racial purity and cultural superiority that Germany "deserved." What follows in this book will suggest and show that the Holocaust's killing operations, especially where the Jews were concerned, made explicit distinctions between men and women.[4] As Joan Ringelheim has argued in her important contribution to this volume, the Holocaust's deportation and death lists often included gender identification. Women and men were segregated in concentration and death camps. Traditional attitudes among German Nazis partly account for such separations, and early on they treated Jewish women more benignly than Jewish men, but once World War II began in 1939 and the "Final Solution" was fully under way in 1942, Jewish women were increasingly at risk.

In wartime elderly Jewish women were useless to the Nazis, and they were sentenced to death by starvation, disease, shooting, or gas. Of more troubling concern to Nazi Germany were Jewish women of child-bearing age. On one hand, their work for the Third Reich could be productive. On the other, their menace was especially acute because they could produce Jewish children. Hitler's war against the Jews was determined to prevent that outcome.

Any consistent Nazi plan had to target Jewish women specifically as women, for they were the only ones who would finally be able to ensure the continuity of Jewish life. Indeed, although the statistical data about the Holocaust will never be exact, there is sound evidence that the odds for surviving the Holocaust were worse for Jewish women than for Jewish men. For even though Jewish men often perished before and probably at a faster rate than

Jewish women until 1942, the loss of life overall during the Holocaust was apparently greater for Jewish women than for Jewish men. At Auschwitz, for example, the Jewish women selected for labor were mainly in their late teens and early twenties and without children. Auschwitz selection policy kept children, usually those under fourteen, with their mothers. Along with older women, those mothers were typically dispatched to the gas chambers on arrival. At the end of the war, more men than women could be found among the total of Jewish survivors, and more of the men were older, too. In sum, to use Ringelheim's telling phrase, the Holocaust put Jewish women in "double jeopardy." In less extreme ways, the same point could be made about the thousands of non-Jewish women who also found themselves trapped in the Holocaust's web because they were suspect politically or identified as belonging to other groups—Slavs, for example, or Gypsies—that the Nazi racial hierarchy classified as inferior.

Even though no book about the Holocaust has been more widely read than the diary of Anne Frank, most of the best-known accounts of the Holocaust tend to be by men—from survivors such as Primo Levi and Elie Wiesel, for example, to scholars such as Yehuda Bauer and Raul Hilberg and philosophical and religious interpreters such as Emil Fackenheim and Richard Rubenstein.[5] As this book shows, however, neither before, during, nor after the Shoah have women been silent about experiences that left them forever marked, if not destroyed, by the "Final Solution." Their experiences, interpretations, and reflections are not necessarily at odds with those of their male counterparts. Much that happened to men and women during the Holocaust was devastatingly alike. But much that happened was devastatingly different, too. Raul Hilberg states the point persuasively when he writes: "The Final Solution was intended by its creators to ensure the annihilation of all Jews. . . . Yet the road to annihilation was marked by events that specifically affected men as men and women as women."[6] Testimony and scholarship that reflect those differences deserve attention and respect.

No calculus of cruelty should be used to make the insidious wholesale judgment that what happened to one gender during the Holocaust was worse than what happened to the other or that one gender's reflections and memories are clearer or more truthful and important than the other's. Similar experiences are not identical, however, and in the Shoah differences between men and women made a significant difference. As Myrna Goldenberg aptly sums up the situation, the hell may have been the same for women and men during the Holocaust, but the horrors were different.[7]

How did women respond to their circumstances during the Holocaust? What was most important to women who had to live under conditions of deprivation, humiliation, terror, and death? Were there gender-related resources that women drew upon to sustain hope as well as life in the ghettos and camps? What particular vulnerabilities exposed them to extraordinary suffering and death? Does the study of women and the Holocaust highlight new or at least different questions that we should be asking—not just about women but about every human being who had to endure the Holocaust's darkness? The history of the Holocaust is incomplete without responses to such questions, and they have not received the attention they deserve. Not everyone, however, welcomes the emphasis on women that *Different Voices* and other recent studies provide. For example, Joan Ringelheim reports dissent by interpreters such as Helen Fagin and Cynthia Ozick. Focusing on the particularity of women's experiences, they have argued, involves two dangers: (1) It may denigrate the Holocaust's significance by turning the Shoah merely into an example of sexism. (2) It may detract from the much more fundamental fact that, as Ozick once put it, "the Holocaust happened to victims who were not seen as men, women, or children but *as Jews.*"8

The counterargument, however, is more compelling. Precisely because the Nazis targeted Jews and others in racial terms, they had to see those victims in their male and female particularity. Far from reducing the Shoah to an example of sexism, emphasis on what happened to women reveals what otherwise would remain hidden: a fuller picture of the unprecedented and unrelenting killing that the "Final Solution's" antisemitism and racism entailed. *Different Voices* helps make that case by increasing awareness about women's experiences during the Holocaust. Its contents, however, go further than that. In addition to building on Gertrud Kolmar's hope that someone will "hear me speak," they also resound versions of her aching question "But do you hear me feel?" Moved by voices like hers, we recognize that no good thing should be taken for granted. This sensitivity can strengthen determination against forces of the kind that silenced her and so many of her sisters.

Gertrud Kolmar's life was only one of the millions wasted by the Third Reich's destruction of the European Jews, and thus her story is only one of the many narratives contained in these pages. But beyond providing the indispensable reminder that people—children, men, and women; non-Jews as well as Jews—suffered and died one by one in the Shoah, her story can help to provide a historical context for contemplating what happened particularly to women during the Holocaust. So, with those considerations in mind, note that Gertrud Chodziesner was born in Berlin on December 10, 1894. Descended from Jewish merchants who had once lived in the Polish town of Chodziez (Kolmar, as the Germans called it) she would grow up in comfortable Berlin surroundings before adopting Kolmar as her pen name.

An influential and highly nationalistic German historian, Heinrich von Treitschke, died just two years after Gertrud Chodziesner's birth. In 1879 he had promoted a fateful phrase: *"Die Juden sind unser Unglück"* (The Jews are our misfortune). That slogan would be festooned at Nazi party rallies in the 1930s. During the 1890s, however, little approaching the ultimate virulence of Nazi antisemitism existed in Germany. As Treitschke's canard indicated, anti-Jewish feeling and politics were hardly strangers to Germany, but typically assimilated, bourgeois Jewish families like the Chodziesners had no reason to expect that a "Final Solution" shadowed their future. That fate was virtually unthinkable to anyone, anywhere, on the eve of the twentieth century.

Meanwhile Jews living in Poland, where pogroms were commonplace, or in Russia—there the official policy toward the Jews was that one third would be assimilated, one third would be forced out, and another third would die—had more to fear than their brothers and sisters in Germany. Even in France, where the "Jewish question" became a decisive political issue with the arrest of Captain Alfred Dreyfus for treason in 1894, the Jewish future was more problematic than in Germany. The same could be said of Austria, where a boy named Adolf Hitler had been born in 1889.

The relative safety of Jewish families like the Chodziesners would not last in the twentieth century, neither in Germany nor anywhere else in Europe, once that child grew from his obscure Austrian origins to become leader of a small antisemitic political party—the Nazis—in November 1921 and then battled his way to become the German chancellor on January 30, 1933. For as early as 1919, a few days before Hitler joined the fledgling Nazi party, he stated the following position: "Purely emotional antisemitism finds its final expression in the form of pogroms. Rational antisemitism, by contrast, must lead to a systematic and legal struggle against, and eradication of, what privileges the Jews enjoy over other foreigners. . . . Its final objective, however, must be the total removal [*Entfernung*] of all Jews from our midst."[9]

The road to the Holocaust had many twists and turns. Until World War II made the plan unworkable, Nazi policy equated "total removal" with forced Jewish emigration. But Hitler's speeches and writings—for example, *Mein Kampf* (1925)—revealed his unrelenting hatred for the Jews. The unthinkable was starting to be thought: Hitler and his followers would bring the "Final Solution" into view.

Meanwhile Gertrud Kolmar was growing up as an introverted, solitary girl who filled her life with history and nature, languages and writing. During World War I, while Hitler served in the trenches of the German army, she worked as an interpreter and a postal censor. But by the time Hitler, stunned by Germany's capitulation, was recovering at the war's end from a poison-gas attack his army unit had experienced, some of her poems were in print. Although she would never marry and have children, Kolmar had fallen in love during the war years. The relationship did not last, but the experience became a resource that informed her poetry, which often took love as its theme. In the meantime, not love but hate, revenge, and dreams of German "redemption" informed Hitler's politics.

In the summer of 1923, not long before Hitler's November attempt in Munich to bring down the government of the Weimar Republic he despised, the Chodziesner family moved from Berlin to a rural suburb named Finkenkrug. While Hitler served a mild and abbreviated prison sentence for his insurrection, composing *Mein Kampf* during the confinement, Kolmar wrote poetry about nature and animals. Four years later she spent a brief time in Hamburg as a private tutor. Her experiences with the sea in that port city would mark her poetry distinctively. Concurrently Hitler had made a mark of his own by calling into existence a personal bodyguard, the black-shirted *Schutzstaffel* (SS), which would have Heinrich Himmler at its head in January 1929. Under Himmler's leadership, the SS (only two hundred strong in 1929) would grow to number in the hundreds of thousands. Forming an awesome empire in the Nazi state, it eventually controlled the vast network of concentration, labor, and death camps that implemented the "Final Solution."

While Hitler and Himmler advanced their power and the Nazi party became a more formidable player in German politics, Gertrud Kolmar cared for her aging parents. Their health declined, but her poetry got better and better. In 1930, her mother died, Hitler's Nazi party got 18.3 percent of the total vote in the national Reichstag elections, and Kolmar began work on a long project that would result in a poetic cycle, *Weibliches Bildnis* (*Image of Woman*). Along with two other series of poems, *Kind* (*Child*) and *Tierträume* (*Animal Dreams*), it makes her bid for lasting literary fame. Kolmar's poems express love for the earth, her Jewish people, animals, children, men, her sexuality. This love, however, is shadowed by darker, tragic tones. Some of them anticipate losing what is loved; others acknowledge the impossibility of fulfillment for which Gertrud Kolmar yearned.

About the same time, toward the end of 1932, the rising tide of Hitler's political influence seemed to turn. Although the Nazis were never to win a majority in any freely contested national election, in late July 1932 they had tallied more than fourteen million votes, a total more than half a million higher than the combined results of the Nazis' two closest rivals, the Communists and the Social Democrats. But within a few months, when new elections were held in Germany's increasingly unstable political circumstances, the Nazi party received two million votes less than before and lost thirty-four seats in the Reichstag. Hitler was convinced that his dreams would not succeed. Nevertheless, on January 30, 1933, Hitler got the power he craved when Germany's president, Paul von Hindenburg, was persuaded to invoke emergency dictatorial power granted him under the Weimar constitution to prevent an overthrow of democratic order. Ironically, when Hindenburg used his authority to appoint Hitler chancellor, he ensured the very result his action was supposed to forestall. Six months later, the Nazis stood as the only legal political party in Germany, Hitler's decrees were as good as law, basic civil rights had been suspended, and thousands of the regime's suspected political opponents had been imprisoned. The destruction process that would send Gertrud Kolmar to Auschwitz had gotten under way.

In 1933, there were about 566,000 Jews in Germany—a little over half of them women. Most were highly assimilated. The German census of 1939 would show that figure shrinking to a little over 200,000—nearly 60 percent of them women. Single Jewish men had the best chances to emigrate. As a result, more German-Jewish women than men would be deported and killed in the "Final Solution."[10] Gertrud Kolmar, like so many of her Jewish sisters and brothers, did not—indeed, probably could not—imagine, let alone prepare for, what was coming. Yet she must have had premonitions. Two years earlier, for example, she had completed a short novel called *Eine Mutter* (*A Mother*). It is about Martha Jadassohn, a young Jewish woman who has grown up in Berlin. Her marriage to a Christian fails; her daughter, who has inherited her mother's dark looks, is brutally raped; and Martha, who poisons her daughter to end the child's misery, eventually takes her own life by drowning in the river Spree. The Berlin backdrop that Kolmar depicted for this tragedy was one rife with Nazi antisemitism.

Forebodings became more pronounced in Kolmar's 1933 poem cycle *Das Wort der Stummen* (*Words of Silent People*). One of them—it speaks about those who are "Cut off from human life, / Stiff, wounded, branded with official stamps"—is titled "Im Lager." It is about a concentration camp. Six months after Hitler became chancellor, some 27,000 political prisoners were being held under "protective custody" in Germany. At first such suspects were dispersed to a variety of detention centers, but gradually the model established at the Dachau camp, situated about ten miles northwest of Munich, became normative. Heinrich Himmler, head of the SS, was the Nazi leader who established Dachau, which received its first prisoners in late March 1933.

Dachau's prisoners were male, but it did not follow that women were exempt from the concentration camps. Although it did not emulate the Dachau model at first, an early women's camp functioned at Moringen from October 1933 to March 1938. Meanwhile Himmler and his associates consolidated SS control over all the camps, expanding them and systematizing their procedures. Run more along Dachau's lines, a second women's concentration camp opened in March 1938 at Lichtenburg, a former men's camp that became available when its inmates and SS guard units were transferred to Buchenwald, which had started operations in 1937. The Lichtenburg camp closed in May 1939, when a permanent installation for women opened at Ravensbrück. This camp stood about fifty miles north of Berlin, near the railway station at Fürstenberg.

Built on reclaimed swamp land, Ravensbrück was designed to hold about 15,000 prisoners. By 1944 it held 42,000 from twenty-three nations. On average about 15 percent of the camp population was Jewish. Along with Gypsies, who numbered about 5.5 percent of the prisoner population, the Jewish women were segregated from and treated more harshly than the other inmates. The camp was a forced-labor installation; it focused on textile work, including the production of SS uniforms. Ravensbrück also provided training for many of the 3,000 women who eventually served as administrators and guards at other camps, Auschwitz among them.[11] Maria Mandel, who became

SS Chief Supervisor at the women's camp in Auschwitz, got training at Ravensbrück. So did Irma Griese, one of the most notorious female guards at Auschwitz.

Ravensbrück would not be liberated until late April 1945. When the Soviet forces arrived, they found only 3,500 sick women still in the camp. Records in the Ravensbrück archives showed, however, that during the camp's overall existence a total of 132,000 women and children had been imprisoned there. The fact that children could be found in Ravensbrück should not be overlooked. Some arrived with their mothers. Others were born there—863 of them between 1943 and 1945. Lacking adequate food and health care, nearly all of them died there, too. In a pattern that would be widely replicated, the Nazi targeting at Ravensbrück could keep women and children together. But where Jews and other "inferior" lives were at stake, the mother-child relationship was ultimately one the Nazis were determined to destroy. Nothing about the "Final Solution" was more definite than that.

Early on, the mortality rate at Ravensbrück had been comparatively low, but after 1941 it worsened. Eventually death claimed 92,000 of Ravensbrück's total prisoner population. That number included some 32,000 who had been gassed in the camp's final months when the Germans evacuated to Ravensbrück prisoners from camps in the East made vulnerable as the Red Army forced Germany's retreat. In the end, no other concentration camp in Germany had such a high percentage of murdered prisoners.[12]

Gertrud Kolmar spent no time in Moringen, Lichtenburg, or Ravensbrück. She was neither a socialist or a communist, a political or religious dissident, nor a prostitute or criminal, nor had she violated any of Nazi Germany's race-defilement laws—all misdeeds sufficient to put a woman in such places. Of course, her Jewish identity could cause misfortune, too, but before 1939, as Sybil Milton points out, "Jewish women were incarcerated in the jails and concentration camps of Nazi Germany . . . *only if* they belonged to one of the other affected categories."[13] In addition, at least until World War II began with Germany's invasion of Poland on September 1, 1939, the Nazis' anti-Jewish policies aimed more at forced emigration than at incarceration or death. Instrumental in creating a climate of terror that would persuade Jews to leave Germany, certainly incarceration and death did occur, and thus Jewish women were always among the victims of the women's camps on German soil. Nevertheless, prior to 1939 and the outbreak of war, Kolmar's situation was similar to that of many German Jewish women. Living inside a vise that was closing, she experienced pariah status, but that condition was still moderated by "normal social inhibitions" that restrained Nazi violence toward Jewish women.[14] Slave labor or death in a camp were not yet the immediate threats they would later prove to be.

When the full Nazi assault on women did come, it was not restricted to slave labor or death. Especially in 1942–1943, Ravensbrück prisoners—many of them Polish women—could testify that tortuous medical "experiments" wasted women, too. Prior to testing a questionable array of treatments and remedies, infections were induced, limbs amputated, and wartime wounds replicated on the Ravensbrück "rabbits," as they were called by the SS experimenters. Also high on the list of priorities was the goal of finding ever more efficient ways to sterilize women. Surgical sterilization was slow, too expensive to use on a mass scale. So German doctors tried X-rays, injections, and drugs to find faster and more easily applicable procedures to control reproduction.

Thus, in practices brutal and bizarre, German medicine served genocidal interests at the expense of women as well as men. Nazi ideology and policy required such action, for it rested on the eugenic conviction—a "biomedical imperative," as Robert Jay Lifton calls it—that racial differences made all the difference.[15] According to these views, German racial superiority had to be protected, indeed enhanced, and therefore every inferior group was to be regarded as a cancerous threat and treated accordingly. Already laws decreed in 1933, during the earliest months of the Nazi regime, legalized race-hygiene sterilization to prevent the propogation of *lebensunwertes Leben* (lives unworthy of life).

Nazi logic entailed different policies for women who could bear the pure sons and daughters that the Third Reich craved. For this population, abortions were prohibited, and a miscarriage could make one suspect. The purpose of the *Lebensborn* (Spring of Life) program, established by Himmler in 1935 and financed by the SS, was to increase the quantity and quality of German life by encouraging German women to give birth to illegitimate children. Fathered by SS men and other racially valuable Germans, these children would be their mothers' gifts to Hitler and the Third Reich. The *Lebensborn* program provided pre- and postnatal care and adoption services. During the war years, it expanded into kidnapping, when Himmler directed *Lebensborn* authorities to import "racially acceptable" children from occupied countries such as Poland, France, and Norway. To sum up the situation for women, Nazi policy meant prohibition of motherhood and compulsory sterilization for "inferior" women, prohibition of sterilization or abortion, and expected, if not compulsory, motherhood for those deemed to be of good German stock.

Gertrud Kolmar had no children and experienced no concentration-camp medical experiments in Germany. By the summer of 1938, however, she did think about emigrating—perhaps to Palestine or, later that year, to England as a tutor. We know these things because Kolmar's sister, Hilde Wenzel, had fled Germany and found asylum in Switzerland. Nuancing their letters to pass them by the German censors, Gertrud and Hilde wrote to each other regularly. Hilde also received and cared for the unpublished stories and poems that Gertrud sent her. But if Kolmar's writings emigrated, duty to her father kept her in Germany to look after him. That decision enabled her to enjoy the Jewish press's glowing reviews of her book *Die Frau und die Tiere* (*The*

Woman and the Animals), which appeared in September. Just a few weeks later, however, her public recognition took a disheartening turn.

Following the assassination of Ernst vom Rath, a minor German diplomat in Paris, by a Jewish youth named Herschel Grynszpan, the largest pogrom in German history—*Kristallnacht*—broke out on November 9–10, 1938. Incited by Josef Goebbels, the Nazi minister of propaganda, mobs in Germany and Austria torched synagogues, looted Jewish businesses, and took Jewish lives. In the aftermath, some 30,000 Jewish men, but apparently no Jewish women, were interned in concentration camps. Jewish newspapers that had reviewed Gertrud Kolmar's new book were shut down. Unsold copies of *Die Frau und die Tiere* were destroyed. Laws affecting Jewish property also required Kolmar and her father to sell their house in Finkenkrug and relocate to a downtown Berlin tenement district apartment that had been allocated to them.

Two months later, on January 30, 1939, Hitler celebrated the sixth anniversary of his rise to power by making a speech to the Reichstag. He told his audience that a world war would mean "the annihilation of the Jewish race in Europe."[16] Before 1939 was over, that war was under way, and so was the fulfillment of Hitler's prophecy. As those events unfolded, Gertrud Kolmar kept doing what she knew best—writing. One project was a story called *Susanna*. Written in a maturing, confident style, it is about an adolescent girl who lives in the German-Polish East. Her world is one of fantasy and friendship but also of broken relationships and hopeless love. At the story's end, she is found dead along railroad tracks leading to Berlin.

By the late spring of 1940, the roads of Europe increasingly led to and from Berlin. In Poland, Hitler's forces controlled the western half of the country, including Warsaw, steps to ghettoize Polish Jewry were under way, and Himmler had ordered the establishment of a concentration camp at Oswiecim. Located conveniently at the junction of major European railway lines, it would become better known as Auschwitz. In western Europe, German troops were well on their way to conquering Denmark, Norway, Holland, Belgium, and France. Inside Germany, race-hygiene efforts got a new twist as the so-called Euthanasia Program, authorized by Hitler himself, implemented the gassing of mental patients and other "defectives" in German hospitals.

Meanwhile, poetry occupied Gertrud Kolmar. So did the study of Hebrew, which she began in early April. With increasing seriousness and intensity, she began to write in a different voice, as she explains in a letter dated November 24, 1940, only a few days after the Warsaw ghetto had been sealed: "I have just recently learned what a Hebrew poem should *not* be, and how I should not write, and feel now that I will soon know how I *must* write. This poem that does not yet exist . . . is already forming within me. Perhaps it will take months or years . . . but it will see the light. . . . Perhaps because of this I have written nothing more in German recently."[17] Unfortunately, Kolmar did not have months and years—at least not many of them—and no trace of her Hebrew poetry remains.

As the vise on Gertrud Kolmar's life continued to tighten, much of its pressure—not yet known to her—involved plans and places far away from Berlin. On March 1, 1941, for example, Himmler inspected Auschwitz and ordered its enlargement by construction of a new installation at Birkenau (Auschwitz II). A little more than three months later, Germany attacked the Soviet Union, unleashing mobile killing squads (*Einsatzgruppen*) that would murder hundreds of thousands of Jews at Babi Yar and other places before their work was taken over by killing centers such as those at Auschwitz–Birkenau and Treblinka. Closer to Kolmar's home, orders sent from Hermann Göring's Berlin office on July 31, 1941, charged Reinhard Heydrich with responsibility to plan the "final solution of the Jewish question."

Unlike the circumstances in many other European countries controlled by Germany, ghettos were not established in Germany. But the German Jews were increasingly crowded together, and so, a few weeks before Göring sent his "Final Solution" order to Heydrich, Kolmar and her father had been herded along with other Jews into closer Berlin quarters. She had also been ordered to report for factory labor. Three months later—in October—the deportation of German Jews eastward to ghettos in Poland, Lithuania, and Latvia began. If those ghettos were not always death traps themselves, they became staging areas for further deportations to camps that were.

For a time Gertrud Kolmar was spared. She continued her factory labor and was still able to get mail to her sister in Switzerland. She reports, for instance, her "romance" with a young medical student she met at the factory in Charlottenburg where they worked, and on March 5, 1942, she speaks about her efforts, against disheartening odds, to keep writing: "When I have made even a little progress with it," she says, referring to a story she had started, "and feel that what I have done is good and beautiful, then at times I am very happy."[18]

Times for happiness were running out in 1942, for, as historian Richard Breitman states, it would become "one of the most dreadful years in the long history of the Jewish people."[19] A case in point involved Reinhard Heydrich. Although Japan's bombing of Pearl Harbor had delayed the talks he originally scheduled for December 9, 1941, Heydrich convened on January 20, 1942, what has come to be known as the Wannsee Conference. Its purpose was not to discuss, let alone to question, whether there should be a "Final Solution." The aim instead was to inform key officials that it would occur and, accordingly, "to bring their general activities into line."[20] Thus, in a meeting of less than two hours, including lunch, the fifteen men—eight of them holders of university doctorates—who met in a comfortable lakeside villa outside Berlin could conclude their formal business and break up into small groups to discuss the details they would have to handle. Ten days later, in a speech at the Berlin Sportpalast, Adolf Hitler celebrated the ninth anniversary of his rise to power by predicting to the German people that "the result of this war will be the total annihilation of the Jews."[21]

The promised annihilation would occur by a combination of working Jews to death and murdering them outright. Thus, to make the "Final Solution" a reality, killing had to become more efficient than the *Einsatzgruppen* or ghettos could be. The "solution" to that problem was the killing center. Already during the summer of 1941, Himmler had authorized construction of such places, and during 1942 six of them—Chelmno, Majdanek, Belzec, Sobibor, and Treblinka along with Auschwitz–Birkenau—became fully operational as rail transports delivered Jews deported not only from the ghettos of Poland and other eastern European regions but from every place where the Nazis could capture them.

Each killing center had its particularities, but, as Breitman says, they all "practiced mass murder on assembly-line principles."[22] In 1942, moreover, mass murder practiced on assembly-line principles could go forward in these killing centers on Polish soil without much opposition. For the tides of war had by no means turned, and German domination of Europe was vast. That domination entailed depths of darkness such as the following in 1942:

February 15: At Auschwitz I, the first transport of Jews is killed with Zyklon B gas. **February 27:** Decisions are taken to upgrade and expand the killing capacity of Auschwitz by constructing four new gas chambers and crematoriums at Birkenau. **March 26:** A separate women's section—subordinate to Ravensbrück— is established at Auschwitz I, when a transport of 999 female prisoners arrives from the women's concentration camp at Ravensbrück. Mostly criminals or "asocials," these "founders" of the women's camp will become block leaders and labor supervisors when it is moved to Auschwitz–Birkenau. On this same date, 999 Jewish women from Proprad in Slovakia are also sent to the Auschwitz women's camp. Under the supervision of Adolf Eichmann, this registered transport is the first of its kind sent to Auschwitz by Section IV B 4 of the RSHA (*Reichssicherheitshauptamt*, Reich Security Main Office), which continued the Third Reich's extermination policies throughout World War II.[23] **May 4:** For the first time, a "selection" takes place among prisoners already at Auschwitz– Birkenau. Those found "unfit for work" go to the gas chambers. **June 12:** On her thirteenth birthday, about three weeks before her family goes into hiding in Amsterdam, Anne Frank begins writing in the diary she received as a gift from her father. **July 4:** For the first time at Auschwitz, the camp administration carries out a selection as a rail transport arrives. This transport contains Slovakian Jews. As these selections continue in the months and years to come, Nazi doctors determine on the spot who lives and dies. Young Jews who can perform heavy physical tasks have the best chance to be selected for work. Those virtually certain to be condemned to death include the sick, invalids, people over fifty, pregnant women, women with nursing children, and children under fourteen; the latter are often accompanied by their mothers. Often 90 percent or more of the arrivals are sent to the gas chambers. Rarely are more than 20 percent chosen for labor. Rarer still are occasions when women make up a majority of those spared for work. **July 7:** Himmler discusses the sterilization of Jewish women with Professor Dr. Carl Clauberg and informs him that Auschwitz is at his disposal for experiments.

July 10: The Reich Security Main Office directs that the women's section at Auschwitz shall be officially called Auschwitz Concentration Camp, Women's Section, Auschwitz East, Upper Silesia. **July 22:** Mass deportations of Jews from the Warsaw ghetto to Treblinka get under way. **August 5–10:** The women's section at Auschwitz I is moved to Section B-Ia in Birkenau. **Sometime in September:** Gertrud Kolmar's father is deported from Berlin to the so-called model ghetto at Theresienstadt. She never sees him again. **October 8:** Maria Mandel, formerly SS supervisor in Lichtenburg (1938–1939) and Ravensbrück (1939–1942) replaces Johanna Langefeldt as head supervisor at the Auschwitz–Birkenau women's camp. Mandel promotes an orchestra composed of women prisoners. Under the direction of prisoner Alma Rosé, a niece of the composer Gustav Mahler, it performs as labor squadrons leave and return to the camp each day.

Such notes offer only a few glimpses from 1942. There is much more that could be detailed, including the fact that on December 17 the United States, Great Britain, the Soviet Union, and the governments-in-exile of occupied European nations issued a jointly signed statement condemning Nazi Germany's "bestial policy of cold-blooded extermination." Nevertheless, the "Final Solution" continued its destructive work for more than two years. Meanwhile, by the time of the Allies' condemnation, 1942 had become, in Raul Hilberg's words, "the most lethal year in Jewish history."[24] By year's end the Third Reich had destroyed nearly four million European Jews. Of that number, at least two-thirds—about 2.7 million by Hilberg's reckoning—perished in 1942 alone.[25]

Gertrud Kolmar was still alive at the end of 1942. She may have sensed, however, that her days were numbered. One of her last letters—dated December 15, 1942—speaks about her sense of fate. It reflects the disposition of the Roman Stoics she admired: "Even though I do not know what [my fate] will be, I have accepted it in advance, I have given myself up to it, and know that it will not crush me, will not find me too small."[26]

In February 1943, the Germans made a special drive to deport the last Jews from Berlin, even those who worked in war-essential industries. The last letter from Gertrud Kolmar is dated February 20–21. She was most likely caught in the roundup of Jewish workers that occurred a few days later. Camp records indicate that from late February until mid-March 1943, numerous transports brought several thousand Jews from Berlin to Auschwitz–Birkenau. Most of the women and children were gassed on arrival.[27] The circumstances of Gertrud Kolmar's death are uncertain, but she probably was among those who were immediately killed. Berlin was declared *judenfrei* in June. The liquidation of German Jewry was officially completed in July.

Assuming that she perished at Auschwitz, Gertrud Kolmar was only one of the approximately 1.5 million men, women, and children—90 percent of them Jews—who shared that fate. Even as World War II turned decisively against Nazi Germany, Himmler and his colleagues became more determined than ever to win their war against the Jews. Relatively unscathed prior to 1944, for example, hundreds of thousands of Hungarian Jews were targeted after the Germans occupied the territory of their faltering Hungarian allies on March 19. More than half a million of them perished—mostly at Auschwitz–Birkenau—before November 1944, when Himmler ordered the discontinuation of killing with Zyklon B and the destruction of the crematoriums at Auschwitz. By that time European Jewry as it had existed before the Nazi era was virtually destroyed.

Auschwitz was liberated by the Red Army on January 27, 1945. Those troops found about 7,000 sick and exhausted prisoners—4,000 of them women. A much larger number, however, had been evacuated by the Nazis on January 17–18. The last roll call had included 31,894 prisoners—16,577 of them women. Most of these prisoners were force-marched westward until they dropped or arrived at camps where the Germans still planned to extract labor from them. In April most of the remaining camps were liberated by the Allies. Nazi Germany surrendered in early May, but even then the Holocaust did not end. Death continued to take its Jewish toll in the camps for "displaced persons." Other Jews lost their lives trying to enter Palestine clandestinely. All who survived had to cope with what Holocaust survivor Ida Fink so aptly calls "the ruins of memory."[28]

Having provided background that may help the different voices of women and the Holocaust to speak for themselves, this prologue has nearly said enough. Before it ends, however, consider a few things more. On the night of May 24, 1944, a transport of 3,500 Hungarian Jews departed the Carpathian city of Berehovo for Auschwitz–Birkenau. Arriving two days later, this transport rolled directly through the camp's gates, taking advantage of a special spur added to the rail network earlier that spring. The ensuing "selection" left the new arrivals just steps away from the barracks where some of them would live or from the gas chambers where most of them, especially the women and children, would die.

The handling of the Berehovo transport was routine—with one major exception. Usually photography was strictly forbidden at Auschwitz, but on this occasion, two SS cameramen were on the ramp where the cattle cars unloaded. They took nearly two hundred pictures of the Jews from Berehovo, documenting the selection process thoroughly. Many of the pictures—some of them reprinted in this book—show women, young and old, with children and without, selected to work and to die.

Lili Jacob, eighteen, was one of those selected to work. After being quarantined for several weeks, her left arm was tattooed with number A-10862 on July 25, 1944. The eldest of six children and the only daughter, she would be the sole survivor of her family. In December 1944, she was evacuated from Auschwitz–Birkenau and sent to Dora, a missile plant located underground near Nordhausen, Germany. Gravely ill from typhus and malnutrition as that labor camp was being liberated in April 1945, Jacob was carried into a recently vacated SS barrack by some fellow prisoners. There she not only began to recover but also discovered a brown clothbound album containing photographs. To her amazement, she recognized people in them. She recognized the place where the photographs had been taken, too. Lili Jacob possessed what has come to be known as *The Auschwitz Album*, the series of pictures taken by the SS cameramen who recorded the Auschwitz arrival and decimation of the Berehovo transport she had been on a year before.[29]

Thanks to Lili Jacob Meier, knowledge about the Holocaust, including awareness about women, has been enhanced. The same can be said of Danuta Czech. Born in Poland in 1922, she was an active member of the resistance during World War II. In 1955, she joined the research staff at the Auschwitz archives and eventually became head of the scientific research department. Her *Auschwitz Chronicle 1939–1945*, translated from Polish into English in 1990, is a vast, painstakingly assembled record of what happened in the camp day by day. The detail of its overwhelming 855 pages is possible because the Germans kept extensive records at Auschwitz. Beginning in the summer of 1944, they began to cover their tracks by erasing the incriminating evidence of their crimes, but there was more evidence than could be destroyed: original German documents, resistance-movement reports, testimony by former prisoners, trial records, even diaries unearthed from the ground where members of the *Sonderkommandos*, the doomed labor squads who operated the crematoriums, had buried them.

Czech's calendar makes a special effort to include the names of Auschwitz prisoners. "Not numbers," she contends, "but only real, specific human beings can touch the feelings and imagination of other human beings." The *Chronicle*, she rightly adds, "is not only a framework for research into the camp's history and the fate of the prisoners and an aid for criminal investigations, it is an epitaph, a memorial book for those who suffered and struggled in Auschwitz–Birkenau and its auxiliary camps, for those who did not survive Auschwitz, who died nameless—I am thinking especially of those who were killed in the gas chambers immediately after their arrival, without even being registered."[30]

The *Chronicle*'s entries are filled with references to women. For example, its record for January 6, 1945, names four Jewish female prisoners—Ella Gärtner, Roza Robota, Regina Safir, and Estera Wajsblum—who were hanged publicly on that date in the women's camp at Auschwitz–Birkenau.[31] They had been caught after resisting their fate by helping to smuggle explosives to other prisoners who sabotaged Auschwitz–Birkenau's Crematorium IV during the *Sonderkommando* revolt that occurred on October 7, 1944.

The four of them epitomize the valor of women who resisted the "Final Solution" in ghettos, partisan groups, and camps. The same can be said of a condemned Polish woman who figures in Czech's leap-year entry for February 29, 1944. In Birkenau's Crematorium IV, Czech reports,

A young woman steps forward from among the condemned and says, facing the SS men, that all those present are clear about the fact that they are about to die in the famous Auschwitz gas chambers and burn in the crematorium, but that the times in which these crimes can be committed in secret were now past. Today the entire world knows what is going on in Auschwitz, and for every person murdered here the Germans will have to pay dearly. Finally, she says she leaves this world convinced that an end to these crimes is not far away. While entering the crematorium the condemned sing "Poland is not yet lost" and "To the Barricades."[32]

That woman had a name. If she knew it, no doubt Danuta Czech would have included it, but probably no one knows that woman's name anymore. Yet the *Auschwitz Chronicle* contains her voice, and, like the photos in Lili Meier's *Auschwitz Album*, what it tells bears remembering because no one should assume that what went on in Auschwitz will never happen again.

"You hear me speak," Kolmar's "Woman Poet" says. "But do you hear me feel?" There is no photograph of Gertrud Kolmar in any Auschwitz album. Nor does the *Auschwitz Chronicle* identify her—except perhaps as a nameless number. It seems unlikely, moreover, that she resisted her fate in the ways embodied by the women in the specific entries just cited from Czech's reports. Nevertheless, her poetic question could caption the photographs in Lili Meier's *Album*. It speaks, in fact, for all of the Holocaust's victims—dead or alive.

In its own distinctive manner, Gertrud Kolmar's life and especially her question "But do you hear me feel?" echo protest and even resistance. Her question is the right one. Inflected in varied tones, it is raised by all the different voices who speak in the pages that follow. Listening for that question, hearing it, heeding it, responding to it—those acts could lead us, as the poet urges, to change our minds, to wake ourselves, and to move in ways that mend the world.

NOTES

1. We follow Yehuda Bauer's lead in defining the Holocaust. See his essay "Holocaust and Genocide: Some Comparisons," *Lessons and Legacies: The Meaning of the Holocaust in a Changing World*, ed. Peter Hayes (Evanston, Ill.: Northwestern University Press, 1991), 36.
2. The estimates vary, depending on how the statistics are compiled, but the numbers may go as high as nine to ten million, and the figure is unlikely to be less than that for the Jewish victims. For more on this subject, see Michael Berenbaum, ed., *A Mosaic of Victims: Non-Jews Persecuted and Murdered by the Nazis* (New York: New York University Press, 1990) and Bohdan Wytwycky, *The Other Holocaust: Many Circles of Hell* (Washington, D.C.: The Novak Report, 1980).
3. See Gertrud Kolmar, *Dark Soliloquy: The Selected Poems of Gertrud Kolmar*, trans.

Henry A. Smith (New York: Seabury Press, 1975), especially 55–57, 99, 113–15, 215, and 241. We have benefited from translator Henry Smith's substantial introduction to this book, which provides a helpful overview of Kolmar's life and work. See also Lawrence L. Langer's discussion of Kolmar in *Versions of Survival: The Holocaust and the Human Spirit* (Albany: State University of New York Press, 1982), 191–250.

4. In one way or another, all of the selections in this volume help to establish this point. Particularly important in this regard, however, is the work of Joan Ringelheim. Reprinted in this book, her "Women and the Holocaust: A Reconsideration of Research" and especially the updated postscript and appendices she has added to that 1985 article are of fundamental importance.

5. For a significant treatment of the use (and abuse) to which the diary of Anne Frank has been put, see Alvin H. Rosenfeld, "Popularization and Memory: The Case of Anne Frank," *Lessons and Legacies*, 243–278.

6. Raul Hilberg, *Perpetrators Victims Bystanders: The Jewish Catastrophe 1933–1945* (New York: HarperCollins, 1992), 126. In its section on Holocaust victims, Hilberg's book contains a brief chapter entitled "Men and Women" (see 126–130). His principal findings include the following points: (1) There were more women than men in the Jewish population of German-dominated Europe, and "in the final tally, women were most probably more than half of the dead, but men died more rapidly." (2) Mass executions by shooting typically targeted Jewish men first, because "there was a need to rationalize the infliction of death, and it was easier to do so when the victims were men." All too soon, however, "it was the turn of the Jewish women and children" as well. (3) Before the ghettos in eastern Europe were liquidated by the Nazis in 1942 and thereafter, hard labor and inadequate nourishment produced a death rate that was higher for Jewish men than for Jewish women. But when deportations from the ghettos to the death camps began, "there was a reversal of fortunes. . . . More women than men could now be considered 'surplus.' " (4) When labor selections were made at the death camps, "fewer women than men were spared from immediate gassing. Possibly a third of the Jews who survived Auschwitz were women."

    If Hilberg's judgments are more cautious and conservative than those of other writers who speak in *Different Voices*, his account nevertheless makes clear that gender differences were significant during the Holocaust and that attention to those differences is important in understanding what the Jewish catastrophe entailed.

7. See Myrna Goldenberg, "Different Horrors, Same Hell: Women Remembering the Holocaust," *Thinking the Unthinkable: Meanings of the Holocaust*, ed. Roger S. Gottlieb (New York: Paulist Press, 1991), 150–166. Goldenberg is a literary scholar who has concentrated on Jewish women's biographies as well as women's experiences during the Holocaust. "Narratives by women survivors," she is convinced, "form a group that differs significantly from those by men" (150). For related insights, see Ellen S. Fine, "Women Writers and the Holocaust: Strategies for Survival," *Reflections of the Holocaust in Art and Literature*, ed. Randolph L. Braham (Boulder, Colo.: Social Science Monographs, 1990), and Marlene Heinemann, *Gender and Destiny: Women Writers and the Holocaust* (Westport, Conn.: Greenwood Press, 1986).

8. See Joan Ringelheim, "Thoughts About Women and the Holocaust," *Thinking the*

Unthinkable, 144–145. The quotation from Ozick comes from a letter she wrote to Ringelheim in 1980.

9. Adolf Hitler, letter to Staff-Captain Karl Mayr, September 16, 1919, *Hitler's Letters and Notes*, ed. Werner Maser and trans. Arnold Pomerans (New York: Harper, 1973), 215.

10. For more on these points see Sybil Milton, "Women and the Holocaust: The Case of German-Jewish Women," *When Biology Became Destiny: Women in Weimar and Nazi Germany*, ed. Renate Bridenthal, Atina Grossman, and Marion Kaplan (New York: Monthly Review Press, 1984), 301. Milton's essay is reprinted in this book. See 218.

11. For more detail on this point, see ibid., 308. In this book see 224.

12. Konnilyn G. Feig, *Hitler's Death Camps: The Sanity of Madness* (New York: Holmes & Meier, 1981), 156. Very few books that provide historical overviews of the Holocaust, including those written by women such as Lucy Dawidowicz (*The War Against the Jews 1933–1945*), Nora Levin (*The Holocaust: The Destruction of European Jewry 1933–1945*), or Leni Yahil (*The Holocaust: The Fate of European Jewry, 1932–1945*), contain any extended discussions specifically about women. Feig's book offers a relatively early exception to that rule.

    Starting with the origins of Dachau and ending with the liberation of Bergen-Belsen, the major part of Feig's exploration concentrates on the nineteen most important and notorious of the German camps. Feig visited them all during her research. Her agenda included Ravensbrück, the sixth camp her book discusses. As she focused on that early women's camp, she apparently realized that its existence was symptomatic of more than might meet the eye at first glance. The result was an extended analysis that made Ravensbrück one part of a bigger topic: How did the Nazis' antisemitic and racial policies affect women?

    Feig is no feminist historian, but she does raise hard questions about the specificity of women's experiences during the Holocaust: "Did women suffer more than men; did they face worse conditions?" Feig finds that issue "complex and difficult to approach when evaluating the truly ghastly conditions for *all* human beings" in the camps. Nevertheless she does not shy away from the conclusion that her analysis of the facts leads her to draw: "Since the *core* of Nazi racial and population policy dealt with women, and since *anatomy was indeed destiny to the Nazis*, yes, women had it worse. It is fair to conclude that a pregnant woman in a camp suffers more than a man." The credibility of that judgment is arguable, but to dismiss Feig's view too easily would be, in her words, to "underestimate the central part played by sexism in Nazi thought and action." See *Hitler's Death Camps*, 133–190, especially 159, 171. The italics in the quotations are Feig's.

13. Milton, "Women and the Holocaust," *When Biology Became Destiny*, 300. The italics are Milton's. In this book see 216.

14. Ibid.

15. See Robert Jay Lifton, *The Nazi Doctors: Medical Killing and the Psychology of Genocide* (New York: Basic Books, 1986).

16. See "Extract from the Speech by Hitler, January 30, 1939," *Documents on the Holocaust: Selected Sources on the Destruction of the Jews of Germany and Austria, Poland, and the Soviet Union*, ed. Yitzhak Arad, Yisrael Gutman, and Abraham Margolit (Oxford: Pergamon Press, 1987), 135.

17. See Henry A. Smith, "Gertrud Kolmar's Life and Works," *Dark Soliloquy*, 47–48.

18. See *Dark Soliloquy*, 50.

19. Richard Breitman, "The 'Final Solution' in 1942," *Fifty Years Ago: In the Depths of Darkness* (Washington, D.C.: United States Holocaust Memorial Council, 1992), 13.

20. The quotation is from the Wannsee Protocol, the summary of the Wannsee Conference that was prepared by Adolf Eichmann, head of Department IV B 4, the Gestapo's Jewish section, and the man who would become responsible for coordinating rail transportation that brought Jews from all over Europe to the "Final Solution's" killing centers. Full of euphemistic language, the Wannsee Protocol was carefully edited by Eichmann's superiors. Thirty copies were made. Only the sixteenth carbon copy survived. See *Fifty Years Ago*, 39–57, which reprints the entire Wannsee Protocol.

21. See "Chronology of Events, 1942," *Fifty Years Ago*, 19.

22. Breitman, "The 'Final Solution' in 1942," *Fifty Years Ago*, 37.

23. This information, and much of the other data about women in Auschwitz, comes from lists that were secretly kept by prisoners employed in the Admissions Office of the Political Department at the camp. These lists record numbers—from 1 to 75697—that were given to women during the period from March 26, 1942, to February 26, 1944. The information was smuggled out of the camp in 1944. See Danuta Czech, *Auschwitz Chronicle 1939–1945*, trans. Barbara Harshav, Martha Humphreys, and Steven Shearier (New York: Holt, 1990), 148.

24. Raul Hilberg, "Opening Remarks: The Discovery of the Holocaust," *Lessons and Legacies*, 12.

25. Raul Hilberg, *The Destruction of the European Jews*, 3 vols., rev. and def. ed. (New York: Holmes & Meier), 3:1220.

26. *Dark Soliloquy*, 52.

27. Czech, *Auschwitz Chronicle 1939–1945*, 339–352.

28. Ida Fink, *A Scrap of Time and Other Stories*, trans. Madeline Levine and Francine Prose (New York: Schocken Books, 1987), 3. The story from which this phrase comes, "A Scrap of Time," is reprinted in this book. See 41.

29. See Peter Hellman, *The Auschwitz Album: A Book Based Upon an Album Discovered by a Concentration Camp Survivor, Lili Meier* (New York: Random House, 1981).

30. Czech, *Auschwitz Chronicle 1939–1945*, xiv.

31. Here we follow Danuta Czech's spelling of these women's names. In this book's contributions by Anna Heilman and Rose Meth, the spelling of three of the names varies (Alla Gaertner, Regina Saperstein, and Estusia Wajcblum).

32. Czech, *Auschwitz Chronicle 1939–1945*, 591.

General Suggestions for Further Reading

Arad, Yitzhak. *The Pictorial History of the Holocaust*. New York: Macmillan, 1990.

Arad, Yitzhak, Yisrael Gutman, and Abraham Margolit, eds. *Documents on the Holocaust: Selected Sources on the Destruction of the Jews of Germany and Austria, Poland, and the Soviet Union*. Oxford: Pergamon Press, 1981.

Bauer, Yehuda. *A History of the Holocaust*. New York: Franklin Watts, 1982.

Berenbaum, Michael, ed. *A Mosaic of Victims: Non-Jews Persecuted by the Nazis*. New York: New York University Press, 1990.

Bezwinska, Jadwiga, and Danuta Czech, eds. *KL Auschwitz Seen by the SS: Höss, Broad, Kremer*. Translated by Constantine Fitzgibbon, Krystyna Michalik, and Zbigniew Bezwinski. New York: Howard Fertig, 1984.

Bridenthal, Renate, Atina Grossman, and Marion Kaplan, eds., *When Biology Became Destiny: Women in Weimar and Nazi Germany*. New York: Monthly Review Press, 1984.

Czech, Danuta. *Auschwitz Chronicle, 1939–1945*. Translated by Barbara Harshav, Martha Humphreys, and Stephen Shearier. New York: Holt, 1990.

Dawidowicz, Lucy S. *The War Against the Jews*. New York: Holt, Rinehart and Winston, 1975.

Feig, Konnilyn G. *Hitler's Death Camps: The Sanity of Madness*. New York: Holmes & Meier, 1983.

Fishman, Ellen. "Why Women Are Writing Holocaust Memoirs Now." *Lilith* 15 (Spring 1990).

Gilbert, Martin. *The Holocaust: A History of the Jews of Europe during the Second World War*. New York: Holt, Rinehart and Winston, 1985.

Gottlieb, Roger S., ed. *Thinking the Unthinkable: Meanings of the Holocaust*. New York: Paulist Press, 1990.

Gutman, Israel, et al., eds., *Encyclopedia of the Holocaust*, 4 vols. New York: Macmillan, 1990.

Hayes, Peter, ed., *Lessons and Legacies: The Meaning of the Holocaust in a Changing World*. Evanston: Northwestern University Press, 1991.

Hellman, Peter. *The Auschwitz Album: A Book Based Upon an Album Discovered by a Concentration Camp Survivor, Lili Meier*. New York: Random House, 1981.

Hilberg, Raul. *The Destruction of the European Jews*, 3 vols., rev. and def. ed. New York: Holmes & Meier, 1985.

——. *Perpetrators Victims Bystanders: The Jewish Catastrophe 1933–1945*. New York: HarperCollins, 1992.

Jäckel, Eberhard. *Hitler's Weltanschauung: A Blueprint for Power*. Translated by Herbert Arnold. Middletown, Conn.: Wesleyan University Press, 1972.

Kolmar, Gertrud. *Dark Soliloquy: The Selected Poems of Gertrud Kolmar*. Translated and introduced by Henry A. Smith. New York: Seabury, 1975.

Koonz, Claudia. *Mothers in the Fatherland: Women, the Family, and Nazi Politics*. New York: St. Martin's, 1987.

Krausnick, Helmut, Hans Buchheim, Martin Broszat, and Hans-Adolf Jacobsen. *Anatomy of the SS State*. Translated by Richard Barry, Marian Jackson, and Dorothy Long. New York: Walker, 1968.

Langer, Lawrence L. *Holocaust Testimonies: The Ruins of Memory*. New Haven: Yale University Press, 1991.

——. *Versions of Survival: The Holocaust and the Human Spirit*. Albany State University of New York Press, 1982.

Laska, Vera, ed. *Women in the Resistance and in the Holocaust: The Voices of Eyewitnesses*. Westport, Conn.: Greenwood Press, 1983.

Levin, Nora. *The Holocaust: The Destruction of European Jewry 1933–1945*. New York: Schocken, 1973.

Lipstadt, Deborah E. *Beyond Belief: The American Press and the Coming of the Holocaust, 1933–1945*. New York: Free Press, 1986.

Miller, Judith. *One by One, by One: Facing the Holocaust*. New York: Simon & Schuster, 1990.

Rittner, Carol, and John K. Roth, eds. *Memory Offended: The Auschwitz Convent Controversy*. New York: Praeger, 1991.

Roth, John K., and Michael Berenbaum, eds. *Holocaust: Religious and Philosophical Implications*. New York: Paragon House, 1989.

Rubenstein, Richard L., and John K. Roth. *Approaches to Auschwitz: The Holocaust and Its Legacy*. Louisville: John Knox/Westminster Press, 1987.

Smolen, Kazimierz, Danuta Czech, et al. *From the History of KL-Auschwitz*. Translated by Krystyna Michalik. New York: Howard Fertig, 1982.

Wyman, David S. *The Abandonment of the Jews: America and the Holocaust, 1941–1945*. New York: Pantheon, 1984.

Wytwycky, Bohdan. *The Other Holocaust: Many Circles of Hell*. Washington, D.C.: The Novak Report, 1980.

Yahil, Leni. *The Holocaust: The Fate of European Jewry, 1932–1945*. Translated by Ina Friedman and Haya Galai. New York: Oxford University Press, 1990.

Chronology

In addition to noting major events during the Third Reich, World War II, and the Holocaust, this chronology pays attention to those that are particularly relevant to the subject of women and the Holocaust.

1933 January 30 Adolf Hitler becomes chancellor of Germany. German Jews soon feel the effects of the Nazis' anti-Jewish policies of segregation and forced emigration.

March 20 Dachau, one of the first concentration camps in Germany, is established about ten miles northwest of Munich.

May 10 The Nazis instigate public burnings of books by Jewish authors and authors opposed to Nazism.

May 26 Nazi legislation restricts abortion and prohibits voluntary sterilization but also legalizes race-hygiene sterilization.

July 14 The Law for the Prevention of Hereditarily Diseased Offspring is passed in Germany. Taking effect on January 1, 1934, it orders sterilization to prevent the propagation of *lebensunwertes Leben* (lives unworthy of life). Some 200,000 to 350,000 persons were sterilized by 1939.

July 20 The Vatican signs a concordat with Germany.

October The first centralized concentration camp for women opens at Moringen.

1934   January 26 Germany and Poland sign a ten-year non-aggression pact.

              February 24 Gertrud Scholtz-Klink becomes the leader (*Reichsführerin*) of the National Socialist Women's Union and the German Women's Agency. In November 1934 she receives the title Reich Women's *Führerin* (*Reichsfrauenführerin*).

                  July 3 Nazi Germany creates a centralized system of State Health Offices with departments for gene and race care. Laws prohibiting marriage with "alien races" and with the "defective" among the "German-blooded" are also passed.

                August 2 The German president, Paul von Hindenburg, dies. Subsequently Hitler combines the offices of chancellor and president and declares himself *Führer* of the Third Reich.

1935   September 15 The Nuremberg Laws are decreed at a Nazi party rally. They contain two especially important provisions: (1) The Reich Citizenship Law states that German citizenship belongs only to those of "German or related blood." (2) The Law for the Protection of German Blood and German Honor prohibits marriage and extramarital intercourse between Jews and persons of "German or related blood."

              November 14 The First Ordinance to the Reich Citizenship Law specifies that "a Jew cannot be a Reich citizen." It also enacts a classification system to define various degrees of Jewishness. One is defined as a full Jew if "descended from at least three grandparents who are fully Jewish by race," or if "descended from two fully Jewish grandparents" and subject to other conditions specified by the ordinance. A grandparent is defined as fully Jewish if he or she "belonged to the Jewish religious community."

1936   July 12 The concentration camp at Sachsenhausen is established.

              October 25 The Rome–Berlin Axis agreement is signed.

1937	July 16	The concentration camp at Buchenwald is established.
1938	March 13	*Anschluss*: The Third Reich annexes Austria.
	March 21	The women's concentration camp at Moringen closes. The last women imprisoned there are sent to a newly formed women's concentration camp at Lichtenburg, which becomes available when its male inmates and SS guard units are transferred to Buchenwald.
	June 15	Fifteen hundred German Jews are sent to concentration camps.
	July 6–15	Representatives from thirty-two nations attend the Evian Conference to discuss the German refugee problem, but no significant action toward solving it is taken.
	August 17	Jewish women in Nazi Germany are required to add "Sarah" to their names, and all Jewish men "Israel."
	September 29–30	Munich Conference parties agree to the German annexation of part of Czechoslovakia.
	October 5	The passports of German Jews are marked with a large red *J*, for *Jude*.
	October 28	Some 17,000 Polish Jews are expelled from Germany to Zbaszyn on the Polish border.
	November 9–10	Following the assassination of Ernst vom Rath, a minor German diplomat in Paris, by a Jewish youth named Herschel Grynszpan, the *Kristallnacht* pogrom—instigated by Josef Goebbels, the Nazi minister of propaganda—erupts in Germany and Austria. Synagogues are burned, Jewish businesses looted, and Jews are beaten by Nazi thugs. Some 30,000 Jews are interned in concentration camps.
	November 15	Jewish children are excluded from German schools.

1939　　January 30　Hitler tells the German Reichstag that a world war will mean "the annihilation of the Jewish race in Europe."

May 15　Situated some fifty miles north of Berlin and near the railway station at Fürstenberg, the Ravensbrück concentration camp for women is established. On May 18, the first prisoners— 867 women from Lichtenburg—are transferred there.

June 29　More than four hundred Gypsy women from Austria are deported to Ravensbrück.

August 23　The Nazi–Soviet nonaggression pact is signed.

September 1　World War II begins with Germany's invasion of Poland.

September 3　France and Great Britain declare war on Germany.

September 17　Soviet troops invade Poland and occupy the eastern half of the country.

September 21　Reinhard Heydrich, head of the Reich Security Main Office, orders the establishment of Jewish councils (*Judenräte*) in Poland and the concentration of Polish Jews.

September 28　Germany and the USSR partition Poland. German forces occupy Warsaw.

November 20　Heinrich Himmler, head of the SS, orders the arrest and incarceration of all Gypsy women, astrologers, and fortune tellers in areas controlled by the Nazis.

1940　　Early January　The first experimental gassing of mental patients, Jewish and others, occurs in German hospitals. The order for this so-called Euthanasia Program, code-named T4, was given by Hitler in October 1939 and backdated to September 1. More than 70,000 persons perished before protests, spurred by a few church leaders, brought about the program's official termination on September 1, 1941. In fact, however, the operation continued until the end of World War II.

February 8   The establishment of the Lodz ghetto is ordered. The ghetto is sealed on April 30.

April 9–June 22   Germany conquers Denmark, Norway, Holland, Belgium, and France.

April 27   Himmler orders the establishment of a concentration camp at Oswiecim (Auschwitz), Poland. Located about 40 miles west of Cracow, the camp has major railway lines nearby, a key factor in making Auschwitz the main killing center in the Nazi system.

Mid-October   The Jews of Warsaw are ghettoized. By mid-November the ghetto is sealed.

1941

March 1   Himmler inspects Auschwitz, orders the construction of an additional camp at Birkenau (Auschwitz II), and makes prisoners available to I. G. Farben for construction of an industrial plant near Auschwitz.

March 3   Adolf Eichmann is appointed head of the Gestapo's Section for Jewish Affairs, a position that gives him responsibility for deportation of Jews to the camps and killing centers in the East.

March 30   Hitler tells his military leaders that the forthcoming war against Russia will be one of "extermination."

June 22   Germany attacks the USSR. The *Einsatzgruppen* engage in mass killing. All of Poland falls under German domination.

July 31   Hermann Göring signs orders that give Heydrich authority to prepare "the final solution of the Jewish question."

September 3   Six hundred Soviet POWs are gassed with Zyklon B in Auschwitz as the Nazis experiment to find efficient methods of mass extermination.

September 29–30   More than 33,000 Jews from Kiev are murdered by *Einsatzkommando* 4a at the Babi Yar ravine.

October 6   Lobor detention camp in Yugoslavia, a camp for mostly Jewish women and children, opens.

October 15   The Nazis begin the deportation of 20,000 Jews from Germany, Austria, Luxembourg, and Czechoslovakia eastward to ghettos in Poland, Lithuania, and Latvia.

October 23   Emigration—but not deportation—of Jews from Germany is prohibited.

November 1   Construction of a killing center at Belzec begins in Poland. Killing operations start on March 17, 1942.

Late November   Following orders from Heydrich, the first Jews arrive at Theresienstadt, a ghetto/concentration camp established to serve as a "model Jewish settlement" suitable for Red Cross inspection.

December 7   Japan attacks Pearl Harbor. The United States declares war on Japan.

December 8   The first gassing of Jews in a killing center is carried out at Chelmno in Poland. About 320,000 Jews were killed there.

December 11   The United States declares war on Germany and Italy.

1942   January 20   At Wannsee, a Berlin suburb, Heydrich presides at a meeting of top Nazi officials to coordinate the "Final Solution."

February 15   First transport of Jews killed with Zyklon B gas at Auschwitz I.

March 1   Construction of the Sobibor killing center begins in Poland. Jews are first killed there in early May 1942. Russian POWs are moved from the main Auschwitz camp to become the first inmates of Auschwitz–Birkenau (Auschwitz II).

March 8   At Auschwitz I, a temporary fence that segregated the now-relocated Russian POWs is torn down and replaced by a concrete wall that isolates Blocks 1–10. Camp rumors say that female prisoners will be housed in this area.

March 20   In a farmhouse renovated for the purpose, gas chambers are put into operation at Auschwitz–Birkenau. Polish Jews from Upper Silesia are the first victims.

March 26   A separate women's camp is established at Auschwitz when 999 German female prisoners—classified as asocial, criminal, or political—arrive from Ravensbrück. Its director is SS Chief Supervisor Johanna Langefeldt. On this same date, 999 Jewish women from Slovakia are also sent to Auschwitz. This transport is the first of its kind under the supervision of Adolf Eichmann, director of Section IV B 4 of the Reich Security Main Office. The new arrivals from these transports occupy the blocks in Auschwitz I that formerly housed Russian POWs.

April 27   The first transport of female Polish political prisoners arrives at Auschwitz.

May 4   For the first time, a "selection" takes place among prisoners who have been at Auschwitz–Birkenau for several months. Those found "unfit for work" go to the gas chambers.

May 21   Operated by I. G. Farben, a synthetic rubber and petroleum plant opens at Monowitz (also known as Buna or Auschwitz III). It uses Jewish prisoners from Auschwitz I.

May 30   Professor Dr. Carl Clauberg solicits Himmler's help to carry out sterilization experiments on female prisoners in Auschwitz.

July 4   For the first time at Auschwitz, the camp administration carries out a selection at the railroad unloading platform. The transport involved contains Jews from Slovakia.

July 7   Himmler discusses the sterilization of Jewish women with Professor Dr. Carl Clauberg and others. Himmler informs Clauberg that Auschwitz is at his disposal for experiments on the prisoners.

July 10   Clauberg is informed that Himmler wants him to go to Ravensbrück to carry out sterilization procedures on Jewish women. Himmler specifically wants to learn how much time is required to sterilize 1,000 Jewish women.

July 15–16   Dutch Jews are first deported from Westerbork to Auschwitz.

July 17–18   Himmler inspects the Auschwitz camp complex, takes part in the killing of a transport of Jews, attends roll call in the women's camp, and approves the flogging of female prisoners. He also orders Rudolf Höss, the commandant of Auschwitz, to proceed faster with construction of the Birkenau camp.

July 19   Himmler orders the extermination of the Jews of the Government-General of Poland completed by the end of the year.

July 22   The killing center at Treblinka is operational. By August 1943, some 870,000 Jews have perished there.

July 22–
September 12   Mass deportations of Jews from the Warsaw ghetto are under way. Some 300,000 Jews are deported, 265,000 of them to Treblinka.

August 5–10   The women's section at Auschwitz I is moved to Section B-Ia in Birkenau.

August 8   Edith Stein (aka Sister Theresa Benedicta of the Cross), a German Jewish philosopher who converted to Catholicism and became a Carmelite nun, arrives in Auschwitz after deportation from Westerbork. After a "selection," she is murdered in the gas chambers with other Jews. In 1987, she is beatified by Pope John Paul II.

October 8   Maria Mandel, formerly SS supervisor in Lichtenburg (1938–1939) and Ravensbrück (1939–1942) concentration camps replaces Johanna Langefeldt as Head Supervisor in Auschwitz. She organizes the female orchestra in Birkenau. Langefeldt returns to her former post as Head Supervisor at Ravensbrück. Mandel was executed in December 1947 after a Polish court sentenced her to death.

November 19	Soviet troops launch a key counterattack against German forces near Stalingrad.
December 28	Professor Dr. Carl Clauberg begins sterilization "experiments" on female prisoners in Barracks 28 of the Birkenau women's camp. Other female prisoners are kept in Barracks 27 for his exclusive use. He performs experiments on approximately 700 women.

1943

January 18	The first Warsaw ghetto uprising breaks out.
February 2	Soviet forces defeat the German army at Stalingrad.
February 22	Sophie Scholl, a member of "The White Rose," a resistance group consisting of students from the University of Munich, is executed after being found guilty of treason by the Nazi People's Court.
February 26	The first transport of Gypsies from Germany arrives at Auschwitz. They are placed in a special Gypsy camp.
March 22–June 25	Construction is completed on four crematoriums and gas chambers, and they are made operational at Auschwitz–Birkenau.
April 19–30	American and British representatives meet in Bermuda to discuss rescue for European Jews, but no significant plans emerge.
April 19–May 16	The Warsaw ghetto uprising occurs, and the ghetto is destroyed.
April 30	The women's camp at Auschwitz–Birkenau contains 18,659 prisoners; 6,119 of the women are incapable of working.
June 8	A transport with 3,000 children and their mothers leaves the Netherlands for Sobibor. All are gassed on arrival.
Mid-June	Himmler orders the liquidation of remaining ghettos.
July 11	Hitler bans public reference to the "final solution of the Jewish question."

August 2   Prisoners in Treblinka revolt.

October 1–2   The Danes begin the rescue of 7,200 Danish Jews.

October 14   Prisoners in Sobibor revolt.

October 23   Some 1,800 Polish Jews arrive in Auschwitz from Bergen-Belsen. The women are taken to Crematorium II, where they are ordered to undress. One woman, a beautiful young dancer named Franceska Mann, flings part of her clothing at the head of SS Staff Sergeant Schillinger, grabs his revolver, and shoots him twice. She also shoots SS Sergeant Emmerich. Other women attack the SS men with their bare hands. Schillinger dies; Emmerich recovers; all the women are gassed. News of this resistance becomes legendary in the camp.

1944

March 19   Germany occupies Hungary and begins subjecting Hungary's Jewish population (some 825,000) to the Final Solution.

June 6   D-Day: Allied forces land at Normandy.

July 20   German officers attempt to assassinate Hitler.

August 2   The Gypsy family camp in Auschwitz–Birkenau is liquidated.

October 7   Revolt by a Jewish *Sonderkommando* in Auschwitz–Birkenau. With explosives smuggled by women prisoners, the men in the *Sonderkommando* wreck Crematorium IV before the uprising is crushed.

Early November   Killing with Zyklon B gas in the gas chambers of Auschwitz is discontinued.

November 7   Hannah Senesh, a twenty-three-year-old Jewish poet who volunteered in Palestine for a secret mission to aid the Hungarian Jews, is executed after her capture in Hungary.

November 26   Himmler orders the destruction of the crematoriums in Auschwitz–Birkenau.

1945   January 6   Four Jewish female prisoners—Ella Gärtner, Roza Robota, Regina Safir, and Estera Wajsblum—are hanged in the women's camp of Auschwitz. By smuggling explosives, they made the October 7, 1944, *Sonderkommando* uprising possible.

January 17–18   Forced SS evacuation of prisoners from Auschwitz gets under way. The last roll call includes 31,894 prisoners, among them 16,577 women.

January 27   The Red Army liberates Auschwitz.

April 11   Buchenwald concentration camp is liberated by American forces.

April 15   Bergen-Belsen concentration camp is liberated by British forces.

April 29–30   Ravensbrück concentration camp is liberated by Soviet forces, who find some 3,500 female prisoners.

April 30   Adolf Hitler and Eva Braun commit suicide in Hitler's Berlin bunker.

May 7–8   Germany surrenders; V-E Day, the war in Europe ends.

1945   September 17– November 17   Bergen-Belsen war crimes trials are held. About 20 women, including Irma Griese, are tried for assaulting and torturing prisoners. Found guilty, Griese is sentenced to death.

1946   October 25– August 20, 1947   Trial of Nazi doctors: Dr. Herta Oberheuser, the only female defendant at the doctors' trial, is found guilty of giving lethal injections and sentenced to twenty years in prison.

Main Camps in the Third Reich and the Nazi-Occupied Territories

Part One

VOICES OF EXPERIENCE

The murderers are loose! They search the world
All through the night, oh God, all through the night!
To find the fire kindled in me now,
This child so like a light, so still and mild.

GERTRUD KOLMAR

She called the poem "Murder." It comes from a series titled *Weibliches Bildnis* (*Image of Woman*). World War II had not yet begun, Hermann Göring had not yet told Reinhard Heydrich to prepare plans for the "Final Solution" when Gertrud Kolmar wrote "The murderers are loose!" Those words said more than she knew, but she was right. The murderers were loose. Searching the world night and day, they would find and kill their prey in ghettos, ravines, and camps.

If human history is divided into chapters, none has proved more brutal than the one burdened by the name *Holocaust*. Of all the places where the Holocaust's murderers were loose, none was worse than Auschwitz. Even the Nazis said so. Consider, for example, the testimony of Dr. Johann Paul Kremer. A man in his late fifties with doctorates in biology and medicine, this professor of anatomy at the University of Münster had joined the Nazi party in 1929 and the SS in 1935. Kremer kept a diary. It reports that on August 29, 1942, he received orders that sent him to Auschwitz, where he would spend the next three months replacing a surgeon who was said to be ill.

Arriving from Prague on August 30, Kremer took a room in the SS hotel that was situated near the town railway station in Oswiecim. His diary notes the poor climate—hot, humid weather, over 80 degrees in the shade. It remarks that there were "innumerable flies" in the area but also describes the good food he enjoyed. This note rings with irony because Kremer's research specialty involved hunger. So, in addition to selecting who would live and who would die as transports arrived at Auschwitz and beyond presiding over the gassing of prisoners as well—both of these were tasks Nazi policy required physicians to do—he studied, as he later put it, "the changes developing in the human organism as the result of starvation."[1] On numerous occasions Kremer would interview starving inmates before they died or were put to death by lethal injection. Then he would immediately remove organs from the corpses and examine them. Disregarding what he had done in 1942, Kremer would use some of his 1945 diary entries to chastise Allied pilots for inhumanity in bombing Germany. Meanwhile, Kremer had hardly been alone in doing "research" on Auschwitz prisoners. Scores of Nazi doctors, scientists, and pharmaceutical firms took advantage of the opportunities afforded by the vast prisoner population.

Within a week of Kremer's Auschwitz arrival, he was deeply involved in the camp's life and death. His diary's shorthand for September 5, 1942, tells the story in two brief sentences: "This noon was present at a special action in the women's camp ("Moslems")—the most horrible of all horrors. *Hschf.* Thilo, military surgeon, is right when he said today to me we were located here in '*anus mundi.*' "[2]

Holocaust scholar Walter Laqueur translates *anus mundi* as "the asshole of the world." Such description fits what Kremer saw on that September day in 1942, for the "special action" had been the gassing of some eight hundred women prisoners. During a war crimes interrogation in Cracow, Poland, on July 18, 1947, Kremer elaborated on that experience. Hideous though it is, his voice needs to be heard:

> Particularly unpleasant had been the action of gassing emaciated women from the women's camp. Such individuals were generally called "*Muselmänner*" ("*Moslems*"). I remember taking part in the gassing of such women in daylight. I am unable to state how numerous that group had been. When I came to the bunker they sat clothed on the ground. As the clothes were in fact worn out camp clothes they were not let into the undressing barracks but undressed in the open. I could deduce from the behavior of these women that they realized what was awaiting them. They begged the SS men to be allowed to live, they wept, but all of them were driven to the gas chamber and gassed. Being an anatomist I had seen many horrors, had to do with corpses, but what I then saw was not to be compared with anything seen ever before. It was under the influence of these impressions that I had noted in my diary, under the date of September 5, 1942: "The most horrible of all horrors. *Hauptsturmführer* Thilo . . . was right saying today to me that we were located here in '*anus mundi.*' " I had used this expression because I could not imagine anything more sickening and more horrible.[3]

Laqueur rightly calls Auschwitz an international death factory. Specifically, Jewish women, children, and men were brought there from all over Europe.

While no one knows for sure how many people perished in that place, the most careful estimates put the figure around 1.5 million, 90 percent of them Jews. Included in that number would be some 340,000 people who are known specifically to have died because they were among the more than 400,000 officially registered prisoners who received Auschwitz numbers. Records kept in the camp offices indicate that about 130,000 of that latter total were women. Unlike those who were killed on arrival, these prisoners were spared for forced labor. German registration policy ensured that no Auschwitz prisoner ever got the number of a deceased inmate. These accurate records were kept mostly by women prisoners who worked in Section II of the camp's administration. One of those secretaries, Lore Shelley, aptly calls these women "secretaries of death."[4] They thought of themselves as members of a *Himmelfahrtskommando* (an on-the-way-to-heaven squad) because they knew so many terrible secrets and thus assumed they would not be left alive. Not only did some of them survive but also they smuggled and preserved valuable information, including, in particular, information about women which otherwise would have been lost.

Auschwitz grew from modest beginnings to become a vast area whose "Interest Zone" covered nearly twenty-five square miles. Maps show plans for expansion at Auschwitz–Birkenau. The camp, however, was never equipped to house at once the 400,000 inmates who comprised the total spared for work. Nor was it necessary to do so. Disease—especially typhus and diarrhea—and hunger thinned the population. Typically prisoners got little more than 1,000 calories a day; most of the "food" was nearly inedible. Within three to six months, many prisoners succumbed to starvation. Periodic selections took thousands of others. The need for labor also fluctuated, and the prisoner population grew or declined accordingly.

Still, there were times when the prisoner population reached 120,000 to 150,000. In early October 1944 there were more than 40,000 registered women "living" in the camp. During the summer of 1944 the number may have been considerably higher, owing to a large population of unregistered Hungarian Jewish women who awaited decisions about their fate. The overcrowding of the barracks is something that virtually every survivor's memoir stresses. Many of those barracks were built to a standard design—OKH 260/9—that had been developed to stable fifty-two horses. At Auschwitz, the barracks "housed" hundreds of human beings in space that barely gave room to breathe.

On October 31, 1942, Kremer observed that Auschwitz had experienced "very beautiful autumn weather for the last 14 days, so that every day one has the opportunity of sun-bathing in the garden of the *Waffen SS* club house. Even the clear nights have been relatively mild."[5] This report is not one that any Auschwitz prisoner would have made. For example, one Jewish woman— her Holocaust experiences made her wonder, "Is there such a thing as love?"—calls Auschwitz "hell on earth" and remembers it this way:

The days. Let me tell you about the days. We got up at three o'clock in the morning to work, and by 4:00 or 4:30 in the summers the sun was up. I swear to you, the sun was not bright. The sun was red, or it was black to me. . . . The sun was never life to me. It was destruction. It was never beautiful. We almost forgot what life was all about.[6]

Many people know about the Holocaust through survivors such as Viktor Frankl, Primo Levi, and Elie Wiesel. The narratives of their experiences have gained a wide audience, and rightly so. Fewer people know about the Holocaust through survivors such as Charlotte Delbo, Ida Fink, and Isabella Leitner. It is fair to say that Holocaust memory has been shaped most decisively, and Holocaust scholarship has been influenced most frequently, by men. Remembering the Holocaust is an incomplete act, however, if the voices heard, and the silences commemorated, are predominantly male. What women and men remember is not identical. Biology and socialization both determine destiny, and during the Holocaust the paths of destiny were often different for women and men. Both women and men were subjected to certain similar kinds of torment in the ghettos and camps—filth, starvation, forced labor, sexual abuse, humiliation, death—but only women had to cope with pregnancy, for example, amenorrhea, abortion, or invasive gynecological examinations. Women who survived the Holocaust, and Auschwitz in particular, have left a record for future generations that should not be overlooked but instead explored and emphasized.

That exploration and emphasis should occur not because women's voices are necessarily clearer or better than men's—though in many individual cases they are—but because they are women's voices reflecting on their own particular experiences in ways that no one else can do for them. The need, however, is not just to let women speak for themselves. Of equal, if not greater, importance is the need for them to be heard. As Gertrud Kolmar put it in "The Woman Poet," "You hear me speak. But do you hear me feel?"

The twelve memoirs by women that make up the contents of this book's first part do not encompass every aspect of women's experience during the Holocaust. No voice, singular or collective, could do so. What these women describe is a journey that starts in an unnamed but typical Polish town, reaches Holland, France, and Hungary, and then heads for "hell on earth." Usually women who entered Auschwitz—mothers, daughters, sisters, aunts and cousins, friends, wives, and lovers—did not return. The ones who survived speak for the dead as much as for the living.

"We had baked pike," wrote Kremer in his Auschwitz diary on September 23, 1942, "as much of it as we wanted, real coffee, excellent beer and sandwiches."[7] In the memoirs that follow, there are no reports like that one. The contrast bears remembering.

NOTES

1. See "Diary of Johann Paul Kremer," *KL Auschwitz Seen by the SS: Höss, Broad, Kremer*, ed. Jadwiga Bezwinska and Danuta Czech and trans. Krystyna Michalik (New York: Howard Fertig, 1984), 221. We are indebted to Walter Laqueur for several references to Kremer and for other details about Auschwitz. See his foreword to Danuta Czech, *Auschwitz Chronicle 1939–1945*, trans. Barbara Harshav, Martha Humphries, and Stephen Shearier (New York: Holt, 1990), xv–xxi.

2. "Diary of Johann Paul Kremer," *KL Auschwitz Seen by the SS*, 215. Kremer's first direct involvement in Auschwitz gassings occurred on September 2, 1942. He was in attendance to revive SS men who might be affected by the Zyklon B. In comparison with what he witnessed, Kremer wrote, "Dante's Inferno seems to be almost a comedy. Auschwitz is justly called an extermination camp!" (214).

3. Ibid., 215. The *Muselmänner* to whom Kremer refers were walking skeletons who were beyond recovery because of acute starvation and psychic exhaustion. At the Ravensbrück women's camp, Sybil Milton notes, female inmates in this condition were called *Schmuckstücke* (literally, pieces of jewelry). She doubts that this gender-specific language was peculiar to Ravensbrück, although it probably originated there. See Sybil Milton, "Women and the Holocaust: The Case of German and German-Jewish Women," *When Biology Became Destiny: Women in Weimar and Nazi Germany*, ed. Renate Bridenthal, Atina Grossman, and Marion Kaplan (New York: Monthly Review Press, 1984), 308. Milton's essay is reprinted in this book. See 224.

4. See *Secretaries of Death: Accounts by Former Prisoners Who Worked in the Gestapo of Auschwitz*, ed. and trans. Lore Shelley (New York: Shengold, 1986), and also *Auschwitz—the Nazi Civilization: Twenty-three Women Prisoners' Accounts*, ed. and trans. Lore Shelley (Lanham, Md.: University Press of America, 1992).

5. "Diary of Johann Paul Kremer," *KL Auschwitz Seen by the SS*, 226.

6. Edith P., as she is identified by Lawrence L. Langer, is one of the many women who has given her oral history to the Fortunoff Video Archive for Holocaust Testimonies established at Yale University in 1982. The quotation is from Lawrence L. Langer, *Holocaust Testimonies: The Ruins of Memory* (New Haven: Yale University Press, 1991), 55, 105.

7. "Diary of Johann Paul Kremer, *KL Auschwitz Seen by the SS*, 220.

1

Ida Fink

I want to talk about a certain time not measured in months and years.

IDA FINK

Nazi Germany invaded Poland on September 1, 1939. Estimated at 1.7 million men, its troops—highly mechanized and with superior air power—rapidly overwhelmed the mobilized but outnumbered and ill-equipped Polish forces. By the end of September Poland surrendered, its army was demobilized, and Germany and its then-ally the Soviet Union divided up the devastated country. The Germans were determined to carry out their racial policies, to make the newly incorporated Polish territories judenrein *(Jew-free). They began a massive program of roundups, ghettoization, deportation, and mass murder. Poland still bears the scars.*

Excavating what she calls "the ruins of memory," Ida Fink remembers those events. So devastating that they cannot be "measured in months and years," her scraps of Holocaust time shatter the continuity of experience. Fink's voice merits hearing early on in this book because she reminds one of the difficulty and the importance of remembering.

Fink was born in Poland in 1921. German occupation of her country curtailed her study of music. Ghettoized in 1942, she survived the "Final Solution" in hiding. She emigrated to Israel in 1957 and went on to a distinguished writing career. In 1985 her book of autobiographical short stories, A Scrap of Time, *won the first Anne Frank Prize for Literature. More recently she published* The Journey, *a novel about the Holocaust.*

The issues Fink raises about memory and the Holocaust do not respect gender differences. And yet her writing makes it worth remembering that experience and

40

thus memory, too, are by no means identical for men and women. The story that follows, "A Scrap of Time," is about ordinary people who were forced to confront extraordinary evil. It is a muted scream, perhaps one might say a whisper in the face of the unspeakable. Fink describes an "action" that changed everything for her. She helps us see that the differences in human experience and memory are no less important than the similarities.

A Scrap of Time

I want to talk about a certain time not measured in months and years. For so long I have wanted to talk about this time, and not in the way I will talk about it now, not just about this one scrap of time. I wanted to, but I couldn't, I didn't know how. I was afraid, too, that this second time, which is measured in months and years, had buried the other time under a layer of years, that this second time had crushed the first and destroyed it within me. But no. Today, digging around in the ruins of memory, I found it fresh and untouched by forgetfulness. This time was measured not in months but in a word—we no longer said "in the beautiful month of May," but "after the first 'action,' or the second, or right before the third." We had different measures of time, we different ones, always different, always with that mark of difference that moved some of us to pride and others to humility. We, who because of our difference were condemned once again, as we had been before in our history, we were condemned once again during this time measured not in months nor by the rising and setting of the sun, but by a word—"action," a word signifying movement, a word you would use about a novel or a play.

I don't know who used the word first, those who acted or those who were the victims of their action; I don't know who created this technical term, who substituted it for the first term, "round-up"—a word that became devalued (or dignified?) as time passed, as new methods were developed, and "round-up" was distinguished from "action" by the borderline of race. Round-ups were for forced labor.

We called the first action—that scrap of time that I want to talk about—a round-up, although no one was rounding anyone up; on that beautiful, clear morning, each of us made our way, not willingly, to be sure, but under orders, to the marketplace in our little town, a rectangle enclosed by high, crooked buildings—a pharmacy, clothing stores, an ironmonger's shop—and framed by a sidewalk made of big square slabs that time had fractured and broken. I have never again seen such huge slabs. In the middle of the marketplace stood

From Ida Fink, *A Scrap of Time and Other Stories,* trans. Madeline Levine and Francine Prose. New York: Schocken Books, 1989. Copyright © 1987 by Random House, Inc. Reprinted by permission of Pantheon Books, a division of Random House, Inc.

the town hall, and it was right there, in front of the town hall, that we were ordered to form ranks.

I should not have written "we," for I was not standing in the ranks, although, obeying the order that had been posted the previous evening, I had left my house after eating a perfectly normal breakfast, at a table that was set in a normal way, in a room whose doors opened onto a garden veiled in morning mists, dry and golden in the rising sun.

Our transformation was not yet complete; we were still living out of habit in that old time that was measured in months and years, and on that lovely peaceful morning, filled with dry, golden mists, we took the words "conscription of labor" literally, and as mature people tend to read between the lines, our imaginations replaced the word "labor" with "labor camp," one of which, people said, was being built nearby. Apparently those who gave the order were perfectly aware of the poverty of our imaginations; that is why they saved themselves work by issuing a written order. This is how accurately they predicted our responses: after finishing a normal breakfast, at a normally set table, the older members of the family decided to disobey the order because they were afraid of the heavy physical labor, but they did not advise the young to do likewise—the young, who, if their disobedience were discovered, would not be able to plead old age. We were like infants.

This beautiful, clear morning that I am digging out of the ruins of my memory is still fresh; its colors and aromas have not faded: a grainy golden mist with red spheres of apples hanging in it, and the shadows above the river damp with the sharp odor of burdock, and the bright blue dress that I was wearing when I left the house and when I turned around at the gate. It was then, probably at that very moment, that I suddenly progressed, instinctively, from an infantile state to a still naive caution—instinctively, because I wasn't thinking about why I avoided the gate that led to the street and instead set off on a roundabout route, across the orchard, along the riverbank, down a road we called "the back way" because it wound through the outskirts of town. Instinctively, because at that moment I still did not know that I wouldn't stand in the marketplace in front of the town hall. Perhaps I wanted to delay that moment, or perhaps I simply liked the river.

Along the way, I stopped and carefully picked out flat stones, and skipped them across the water; I sat down for a while on the little bridge, beyond which one could see the town, and dangled my legs, looking at my reflection in the water and at the willows that grew on the bank. I was not yet afraid then, nor was my sister. (I forgot to say that my younger sister was with me, and she, too, skipped stones across the water and dangled her legs over the river, which is called the Gniezna—a pitiful little stream, some eight meters wide.) My sister, too, was not yet afraid; it was only when we went further along the street, beyond the bridge, and the view of the marketplace leapt out at us from behind the building on the corner, that we suddenly stopped in our tracks.

There was the square, thick with people as on a market day, only different, because a market-day crowd is colorful and loud, with chickens clucking, geese honking, and people talking and bargaining. This crowd was silent. In a way it resembled a rally—but it was different from that, too. I don't know what it was exactly. I only know that we suddenly stopped and my sister began to tremble, and then I caught the trembling, and she said, "Let's run away," and although no one was chasing us and the morning was still clear and peaceful, we ran back to the little bridge, but we no longer noticed the willows or the reflections of our running figures in the water; we ran for a long time until we were high up the steep slope known as Castle Hill—the ruins of an old castle stood on top of it—and on this hillside, the jewel of our town, we sat down in the bushes, out of breath and still shaking.

From this spot we could see our house and our garden—it was just as it always was, nothing had changed—and we could see our neighbor's house, from which our neighbor had emerged, ready to beat her carpets. We could hear the slap slap of her carpet beater.

We sat there for an hour, maybe two, I don't know, because it was then that time measured in the ordinary way stopped. Then we climbed down the steep slope to the river and returned to our house, where we heard what had happened in the marketplace, and that our cousin David had been taken, and how they took him, and what message he had left for his mother. After they were taken away, he wrote down again what he had asked people to tell her; he threw a note out of the truck and a peasant brought it to her that evening— but that happened later. First we learned that the women had been told to go home, that only the men were ordered to remain standing there, and that the path chosen by our cousin had been the opposite of ours. We had been horrified by the sight of the crowd in the marketplace, while he was drawn towards it by an enormous force, a force as strong as his nerves were weak, so that somehow or other he did violence to his own fate, he himself, himself, himself, and that was what he asked people to tell his mother, and then he wrote it down: "I myself am to blame, forgive me."

We would never have guessed that he belonged to the race of the Impatient Ones, doomed to destruction by their anxiety and their inability to remain still, never—because he was round-faced and chubby, not at all energetic, the sort of person who can't be pulled away from his book, who smiles timidly, girlishly. Only the end of the war brought us the truth about his last hours. The peasant who delivered the note did not dare to tell us what he saw, and although other people, too, muttered something about what they had seen, no one dared to believe it, especially since the Germans offered proofs of another truth that each of us grasped at greedily; they measured out doses of it sparingly, with restraint—a perfect cover-up. They went to such trouble, created so many phantoms, that only time, time measured not in months and years, opened our eyes and convinced us.

Our cousin David had left the house later than we did, and when he reached the marketplace it was already known—not by everyone, to be sure, but by the so-called Council, which in time became the *Judenrat*—that the words "conscription for labor" had nothing to do with a labor camp. One friend, a far-sighted older man, ordered the boy to hide just in case, and since it was too late to return home because the streets were blocked off, he led him to his own apartment in one of the houses facing the marketplace. Like us, not comprehending that the boy belonged to the race of the Impatient Ones, who find it difficult to cope with isolation and who act on impulse, he left David in a room that locked from inside. What our cousin experienced, locked up in that room, will remain forever a mystery. Much can be explained by the fact that the room had a view of the marketplace, of that silent crowd, of the faces of friends and relatives, and it may be that finally the isolation of his hiding place seemed to him more unbearable than the great and threatening unknown outside the window—an unknown shared by all who were gathered in the marketplace.

It was probably a thought that came in a flash: not to be alone, to be together with everyone. All that was needed was one movement of his hand.

I think it incorrect to assume that he left the hiding place because he was afraid that they would search the houses. That impatience of the heart, that trembling of the nerves, the burden of isolation, condemned him to extermination together with the first victims of our town.

He stood between a lawyer's apprentice and a student of architecture and to the question, "Profession?" he replied, "Teacher," although he had been a teacher for only a short time and quite by chance. His neighbor on the right also told the truth, but the architecture student lied, declaring himself a carpenter, and this lie saved his life—or, to be more precise, postponed the sentence of death for two years.

Seventy people were loaded into trucks; at the last moment the rabbi was dragged out of his house—he was the seventy-first. On the way to the trucks they marched past the ranks of all those who had not yet managed to inform the interrogators about the work they did. It was then that our cousin said out loud, "Tell my mother that it's my own fault and that I beg her forgiveness." Presumably, he had already stopped believing what all of us still believed later: that they were going to a camp. He had that horrifying clarity of vision that comes just before death.

The peasant who that evening brought us the note that said, "I myself am to blame, forgive me," was somber and didn't look us in the eye. He said he had found the note on the road to Lubianki and that he didn't know anything else about it; we knew that he knew, but we did not want to admit it. He left, but he came back after the war to tell us what he had seen.

A postcard from the rabbi arrived two days later, convincing everyone that those who had been taken away were in a labor camp. A month later, when the lack of any further news began to make us doubt the camp, another postcard arrived, this one written by someone else who had been deported—an accountant, I think. After the postcard scheme came the payment of contributions: the authorities let it be understood that kilos of coffee or tea—or gold— would provide a family with news of their dear ones. As a gesture of compassion they also allowed people to send food parcels to the prisoners, who, it was said, were working in a camp in the Reich. Once again, after the second action, a postcard turned up. It was written in pencil and almost indecipherable. After this postcard, we said, "They're done for." But rumors told a different story altogether—of soggy earth in the woods by the village of Lubianki, and of a bloodstained handkerchief that had been found. These rumors came from nowhere; no eyewitnesses stepped forward.

The peasant who had not dared to speak at the time came back after the war and told us everything. It happened just as rumor had it, in a dense, overgrown forest, eight kilometers outside of town, one hour after the trucks left the marketplace. The execution itself did not take long; more time was spent on the preparatory digging of the grave.

At the first shots, our chubby, round-faced cousin David, who was always clumsy at gymnastics and sports, climbed a tree and wrapped his arms around the trunk like a child hugging his mother, and that was the way he died.

2

Etty Hillesum

What is going on, what mysteries are these, in what sort of fatal mechanism have we become enmeshed? The answer cannot simply be that we are all cowards. We're not that bad. We stand before a much deeper question . . .

ETTY HILLESUM

In October 1939 the Dutch government established a camp in the peat bogs of northeastern Holland. Located near the German border, Westerbork's dismal wooden barracks were originally used to house Jewish refugees who had entered the Netherlands illegally. Westerbork was destined, however, to become a much more deadly place after the Germans invaded Holland on May 10, 1940. Westerbork was never an Auschwitz. Indeed, for a time it contained a more or less "permanent" population that led a relatively "normal" life. But before the war ended, Westerbork became for virtually all its Jewish inmates what it really was: a deportation assembly depot that organized Dutch Jews for transport to Nazi death camps.

Beginning in mid-July 1942, trains from Westerbork carried approximately 104,000 of Holland's 140,000 Jews to the East. Most of those transports went to Sobibor and Auschwitz. The victims included the Hillesum family—Etty, twenty-nine, her father, mother, and brother, Mischa, a brilliant young musician. They were deported from Westerbork on September 7, 1943. Upon arrival at Auschwitz—the most likely date is September 9, 1943—Etty's parents were gassed immediately. Mischa survived until March 1944. On November 30, 1943, the prisoner population at the Auschwitz complex consisted of 54,446 men and 33,846 women. Of that number 9,273 men and 8,487 women were reported as sick and unable to work. A Red Cross report lists November 30, 1943, as the date of Etty Hillesum's death.

Born in Middleburg, Holland, on January 15, 1914, Hillesum was a sensitive, intelligent, and gifted young woman. In 1932 she enrolled in the University of Amsterdam. She took a degree in law and then studied Slavonic languages, developing into an accomplished linguist. By the time World War II began, she had embarked on the study of psychology, working with Julius Spier, a Jewish refugee from Germany who had studied under C. G. Jung and who is credited with being the founder of psychochirology—the study and classification of palmprints. Hillesum became Spier's assistant, intellectual partner, and lover, experiences that deepened her intense emotional life.

Between 1941 and 1943, first in German-occupied Amsterdam and then in Westerbork, this young Jewish woman filled eight notebooks with her diary writings. As it recorded the plight of Dutch Jewry, Hillesum's diary reflected transformations that were taking place within her as well. Her notebooks, portions of which were published in 1983 under the title An Interrupted Life: The Diaries of Etty Hillesum, 1941–1943, *reveal that she possessed profound, if unconventional, spiritual sensitivity and deep, if unorthodox and nontraditional, religious faith.*

Etty Hillesum was also a prolific letter-writer. Many of her letters went to the same friends to whom she gave her notebooks for safekeeping when she was sent to Auschwitz. One of them—probably it was sent to her older intimate friend and landlord, Han Wegerif, whom she affectionately called Father Han—is reprinted here. When she wrote it, Etty had been working for the Jewish Council that had been formed under German orders, as in other countries occupied by the Third Reich, to "mediate" between the Nazis and the Jews. Although this job exempted her from Westerbork, Hillesum volunteered to go there as a Jewish Council "social worker." This status enabled her to leave her hospital work in Westerbork from time to time. From what we now know, Hillesum could have gone into hiding—she had offers from friends and from the Resistance—but she refused to do so, choosing instead to return to Westerbork to share the fate of her people. Although Hillesum did not know in detail what awaited them, their fate included Auschwitz, and Hillesum had her premonitions as she witnessed the weekly transports (usually Tuesday was departure day) that headed East. Her August 24, 1943, letter to Father Han details the agony she saw and felt just two weeks before her own time ran out.

In the letter from Westerbork that follows, Hillesum strives to fulfill the vow she took to be "the thinking heart of these barracks." Bearing witness against the hell created by Nazi Germany, and particularly against its targeting of women and children, she records the grievous harmdoing. In her letter we hear desperate mothers pleading for help: "Can't you hide my child for me? Go on, please, won't you hide him, he's got a high fever, how can I possibly take him along?" We glimpse the old, the sick, the pregnant, all caught in the Nazi net of death. In recording their voices—poignant, defiant, resigned, consoling—we hear Hillesum's, too, including questions like the one asked by a girl in a green silk kimono: "Surely God will be able to understand my doubts in a world like this, won't He?"

With unmitigated honesty, absence of posturing, and lack of embellishment, Etty Hillesum bore witness through her writing to all she observed and endured in the grotesque and dehumanizing world of Westerbork. Auschwitz silenced her voice, but testimony to the power of her words is found in the fact that the Dutch Resistance published this letter illegally in 1943 to help rally the determination that eventually brought the Third Reich to an end.

A Letter From Westerbork

[*Probably to Father Han and friends[1]*]

24 August 1943

There was a moment when I felt in all seriousness that after this night, it would be a sin ever to laugh again. But then I reminded myself that some of those who had gone away had been laughing, even if only a handful of them this time . . . There will be some who will laugh now and then in Poland too, though not many from this transport, I think.

When I think of the faces of that squad of armed, green-uniformed guards—my God, those faces! I looked at them, each in turn, from behind the safety of a window, and I have never been so frightened of anything in my life. I sank to my knees with the words that preside over human life: And God made man after His likeness. That passage spent a difficult morning with me.

I have told you often enough that no words and images are adequate to describe nights like these. But still I must try to convey something of it to you. One always has the feeling here of being the ears and eyes of a piece of Jewish history, but there is also the need sometimes to be a still, small voice. We must keep one another in touch with everything that happens in the various outposts of this world, each one contributing his own little piece of stone to the great mosaic that will take shape once the war is over.

After a night in the hospital barracks, I took an early-morning walk past the punishment barracks. And prisoners were being moved out. The deportees, mainly men, stood with their packs behind the barbed wire. So many of them looked tough and ready for anything. An old acquaintance—I didn't recognize him straightaway; a shaven head often changes people completely—called out to me with a smile, "If they don't manage to do me in, I'll be back."

But the babies, those tiny piercing screams of the babies, dragged from their cots in the middle of the night . . . I have to put it all down quickly, in a muddle, because if I leave it until later I probably won't be able to go on

From Etty Hillesum, *Letters from Westerbork*, trans. Arnold J. Pomerans. New York: Pantheon Books, 1986. English translation copyright © 1986 by Random House, Inc. Reprinted by permission of Pantheon Books, a division of Random House, Inc. Notes have been edited.

believing that it really happened. It is like a vision, and drifts further and further away. The babies were easily the worst.

And then there was that paralyzed young girl, who didn't want to take her dinner plate along and found it so hard to die. Or the terrified young boy: he had thought he was safe, that was his mistake, and when he realized he was going to have to go anyway, he panicked and ran off. His fellow Jews had to hunt him down. If they didn't find him, scores of others would be put on the transport in his place. He was caught soon enough, hiding in a tent, but "notwithstanding" . . . "notwithstanding," all those others had to go on transport anyway, as a deterrent, they said. And so, many good friends were dragged away by that boy. Fifty victims for one moment of insanity. Or rather: he didn't drag them away—our commandant did, someone of whom it is sometimes said that he is a gentleman. Even so, will the boy be able to live with himself, once it dawns on him exactly what he's been the cause of? And how will all the other Jews on board the train react to him? That boy is going to have a very hard time. The episode might have been overlooked, perhaps, if there hadn't been so much unnerving activity over our heads that night. The commandant must have been affected by that too. "*Donnerwetter*, some flying tonight!" I heard a guard say as he looked up at the stars.

People still harbor such childish hopes that the transport won't get through. Many of us were able from here to watch the bombardment of a nearby town, probably Emden. So why shouldn't it be possible for the railway line to be hit too, and for the train to be stopped from leaving? It's never been known to happen yet. But people keep hoping it will, with each new transport and with never-flagging hope . . .

The evening before, I had walked through the camp. People were grouped together between the barracks under a gray, cloudy sky. "Look, that's just how people behave after a disaster, standing about on street corners discussing what's happened," my companion said to me. "But that's what makes it so impossible to understand," I burst out. "This time, it's *before* the disaster!"

Whenever misfortune strikes, people have a natural instinct to lend a helping hand and to save what can be saved. Tonight I shall be helping to dress babies and to calm mothers—and that is all I can hope to do. I could almost curse myself for that. For we all know that we are yielding up our sick and defenseless brothers and sisters to hunger, heat, cold, exposure, and destruction, and yet we dress them and escort them to the bare cattle cars—and if they can't walk, we carry them on stretchers. What is going on, what mysteries are these, in what sort of fatal mechanism have we become enmeshed? The answer cannot simply be that we are all cowards. We're not that bad. We stand before a much deeper question . . .

In the afternoon I did a round of the hospital barracks one more time, going from bed to bed. Which beds would be empty the next day? The transport lists are never published until the very last moment, but some of us know well in advance that our names will be down. A young girl called me. She was sitting bolt upright in her bed, eyes wide open. This girl has thin wrists and a peaky little face. She is partly paralyzed, and has just been learning to walk again, between two nurses, one step at a time. "Have you heard? I have to go." We look at each other for a long moment. It is as if her face has disappeared; she is all eyes. Then she says in a level, gray little voice, "Such a pity, isn't it? That everything you have learned in life goes for nothing." And, "How hard it is to die." Suddenly the unnatural rigidity of her expression gives way and she sobs, "Oh, and the worst of it all is having to leave Holland!" And, "Oh, why wasn't I allowed to die before . . ." Later, during the night, I saw her again, for the last time.

There was a little woman in the washhouse, a basket of dripping clothes on her arm. She grabbed hold of me; she looked deranged. A flood of words poured over me: "That isn't right, how can that be right? I've got to go and I won't even be able to get my washing dry by tomorrow. And my child is sick, he's feverish, can't you fix things so that I don't have to go? And I don't have enough things for the child, the rompers they sent me are too small, I need the bigger size, oh, it's enough to drive you mad. And you're not even allowed to take a blanket along, we're going to freeze to death, you didn't think of that, did you? There's a cousin of mine here, he came here the same time I did, but he doesn't have to go, he's got the right papers. Couldn't you help me to get some too? Just say I don't have to go, do you think they'll leave the children with their mothers, that's right, you come back again tonight, you'll help me then, won't you, what do you think, would my cousin's papers . . .?"

If I were to say that I was in hell that night, what would I really be telling you? I caught myself saying it aloud in the night, aloud to myself and quite soberly, "So that's what hell is like." You really can't tell who is going and who isn't this time. Almost everyone is up, the sick help each other to get dressed. There are some who have no clothes at all, whose luggage has been lost or hasn't arrived yet. Ladies from the "Welfare" walk about doling out clothes, which may fit or not, it doesn't matter so long as you've covered yourself with something. Some old women look a ridiculous sight. Small bottles of milk are being prepared to take along with the babies, whose pitiful screams punctuate all the frantic activity in the barracks. A young mother says to me almost apologetically, "My baby doesn't usually cry; it's almost as if he can tell what's happening." She picks up the child, a lovely baby about eight months old, from a makeshift crib and smiles at it. "If you don't behave yourself, Mummy won't take you along with her!" She tells me about some friends. "When those men in green came to fetch them in Amsterdam, their children cried terribly. Then their father said, 'If you don't behave yourselves, you won't be allowed to go in that green car, this green gentleman won't take you.' And that helped—the children calmed down." She winks at me bravely, a trim, dark little woman with a lively, olive-skinned face. She is dressed in long gray trousers and a green woollen sweater. "I may be smiling," she says, "but I feel pretty awful." The little woman with the wet washing is on the point of hysterics. "Can't you hide my child for me? Go on, please, won't you hide him, he's got a high fever, how can I possibly take him along?" She points to a little bundle of misery with blond curls and a burning, bright-red little face. The child tosses about in his rough wooden cot. The nurse wants the mother to put on an extra woollen sweater, tries to pull it over her dress. She refuses. "I'm not going to take anything along, what use would it be? . . . my child." And she sobs, "They take the sick children away and you never get them back."

Then a woman comes up to her, a stout working-class woman with a kindly snub-nosed face, draws the desperate mother down with her on the edge of one of the iron bunks, and talks to her almost crooningly. "There now, you're just an ordinary Jew, aren't you? So you'll just have to go, won't you . . .?"

A few beds further along I suddenly catch sight of the ash-gray, freckled face of a colleague. She is squatting beside the bed of a dying woman who has swallowed some poison and who happens to be her mother . . .

"God Almighty, what are You doing to us?" The words just escape me. Over there is that affectionate little woman from Rotterdam. She is in her ninth month. Two nurses try to get her dressed. She just stands there, her swollen body leaning against her child's cot. Drops of sweat run down her face. She stares into the distance, a distance into which I cannot follow her, and says in a toneless, worn-out voice, "Two months ago I volunteered to go with my husband to Poland. And then I wasn't allowed to, because I always have such difficult pregnancies. And now I do have to go . . . just because someone tried to run away tonight." The wailing of the babies grows louder still, filling every nook and cranny of the barracks, now bathed in ghostly light. It is almost too much to bear. A name occurs to me: Herod.

On the stretcher on the way to the train, her labor pains begin, and we are allowed to carry the woman to the hospital instead of to the freight train— which, this night, seems a rare act of humanity . . .

I pass the bed of the paralyzed girl. The others have helped to dress her. I never saw such great big eyes in such a little face. "I can't take it all in," she whispers to me. A few steps away stands my little hunchbacked Russian woman; I told you about her before. She stands there as if spun in a web of sorrow. The paralyzed girl is a friend of hers. Later she said sadly to me, "She doesn't even have a plate, I wanted to give her mine, but she wouldn't take it. She said, 'I'll be dead in ten days anyway, and then those horrible Germans will get it.'"

She stands there in front of me, a green silk kimono wrapped around her small, misshapen figure. She has the very wise, bright eyes of a child. She looks at me for a long time in silence, searchingly, and then says, "I would like, oh, I really would like, to be able to swim away in my tears." And "I long so desperately for my dear mother." (Her mother died a few months ago from cancer, in the washroom near the WC. At least she was left alone there for a moment, left to die in peace.) She asks me with her strange accent in the voice of a child that begs for forgiveness, "Surely God will be able to understand my doubts in a world like this, won't He?" Then she turns away from me, in an almost loving gesture of infinite sadness, and throughout the night I see the misshapen, green, silk-clad figure moving between the beds, doing small services for those about to depart. She herself doesn't have to go, not this time, anyway . . .

I'm sitting here squeezing tomato juice for the babies. A young woman sits beside me. She appears ready and eager to leave, and is beautifully turned out. It is something like a cry of liberation when she exclaims, arms flung wide, "I'm embarking on a wonderful journey; I might find my husband." A woman opposite cuts her short bitterly. "I'm going as well, but I certainly don't think it's wonderful." I remembered admitting the young woman beside me. She has been here only a few days and she came from the punishment block. She seems so level-headed and independent, with a touch of defiance about her mouth. She has been ready to leave since the afternoon, dressed in a long pair of trousers and a woollen sweater and cardigan. Next to her on the floor stands a heavy rucksack and a blanket roll. She is trying to force down a few sandwiches. They are moldy. "I'll probably get quite a lot of moldy bread to eat," she laughs. "In prison I didn't eat anything at all for days." A bit of her history in her own words: "My time wasn't far off when they threw me into prison. And the taunts and the insults! I made the mistake of saying that I couldn't stand, so they made me stand for hours, but I managed it without making a sound." She looks defiant. "My husband was in the prison as well. I won't tell you what they did to him! But my God, he was tough! They sent him through last month. I was in my third day of labor and couldn't go with him. But how brave he was!" She is almost radiant.

"Perhaps I shall find him again." She laughs defiantly. "They may drag us through the dirt, but we'll come through all right in the end!" She looks at the crying babies all around and says, "I'll have good work to do on the train, I still have lots of milk."

"What, you here as well?" I suddenly call out in dismay. A woman turns and comes up between the tumbled beds of the poor wailing babies, her hands groping around her for support. She is dressed in a long, black, old-fashioned dress. She has a noble brow and white, wavy hair piled up high. Her husband died here a few weeks ago. She is well over eighty, but looks less than sixty. I always admired her for the aristocratic way in which she reclined on her shabby bunk. She answers in a hoarse voice, "Yes, I'm here as well. They wouldn't let me share my husband's grave."

"Ah, there she goes again!" It is the tough little ghetto woman, who is racked with hunger the whole time because she never gets any parcels. She has seven children here. She trips pluckily and busily about on her little short legs. "All I know is, I've got seven children and they need a proper mother, you can be sure of that!"

With nimble gestures she is busy stuffing a jute bag full of her belongings.

"I'm not leaving anything behind; my husband was sent through here a year ago, and my two oldest boys have been through as well." She beams. "My children are real treasures!" She bustles about, she packs, she's busy, she has a kind word for everyone who goes by. A plain, dumpy ghetto woman with greasy black hair and little short legs. She has a shabby, short-sleeved dress on, which I can imagine her wearing when she used to stand behind the washtub, back in Jodenbreestraat. And now she is off to Poland in the same old dress, a three days' journey with seven children. "That's right, seven children, and they need a proper mother, believe me!"

You can tell that the young woman over there is used to luxury and that she must have been very beautiful. She is a recent arrival. She had gone into hiding to save her baby. Now she is here, through treachery, like so many others. Her husband is in the punishment barracks. She looks quite pitiful now. Her bleached hair has black roots with a greenish tinge. She has put on many different sets of underwear and other clothing all on top of one another—you can't carry everything by hand, after all, particularly if you have a little child to carry as well. Now she looks lumpy and ridiculous. Her face is blotchy. She stares at everyone with a veiled, tentative gaze, like some defenseless and abandoned young animal.

What will this young woman, already in a state of collapse, look like after three days in an overcrowded freight car with men, women, children, and babies all thrown together, bags and baggage, a bucket in the middle their only convenience?

Presumably they will be sent on to another transit camp, and then on again from there.

We are being hunted to death all through Europe . . .

I wander in a daze through other barracks. I walk past scenes that loom up before my eyes in crystal-clear detail, and at the same time seem like blurred age-old visions. I see a dying old man being carried away, reciting the Sh'ma to himself[2] . . .

Slowly but surely six o'clock in the morning has arrived. The train is due to depart at eleven, and they are starting to load it with people and luggage. Paths to the train have been staked out by men of the *Ordedienst*, the Camp Service Corps. Anyone not involved with the transport has to keep to barracks. I slip into one just across from the siding. "There's always been a splendid view from here," I hear a cynical voice say. The camp has been cut in two halves since yesterday by the train: a depressing series of bare, unpainted freight cars in the front, and a proper coach for the guards at the back. Some of the cars have paper mattresses on the floor. These are for the sick. There is more and more movement now along the asphalt path beside the train.

Men from the "Flying Column" in brown overalls are bringing the luggage up on wheelbarrows. Among them I spot two of the commandant's court jesters: the first is a comedian and a songwriter. Some time ago his name was down, irrevocably, for transport, but for several nights in a row he sang his lungs out for a delighted audience, including the commandant and his retinue. He sang *"Ich kann es nicht verstehen, dass die Rosen blühen"* ("I know not why the roses bloom") and other topical songs. The commandant, a great lover of art, thought it all quite splendid. The singer got his exemption. He was even allocated a house, where he now lives behind red-checked curtains with his peroxide-blonde wife, who spends all her days at a mangle in the boiling-hot laundry. Now here he is, dressed in khaki overalls, pushing a wheelbarrow piled high with the luggage of his fellow Jews. He looks like death warmed over. And over there is another court jester: the commandant's favorite pianist. Legend has it that he is so accomplished that he can play Beethoven's Ninth as a jazz number, which is certainly saying something . . .

Suddenly there are a lot of green-uniformed men swarming over the asphalt. I can't imagine where they have sprung from. Knapsacks and guns over their shoulders. I study their faces. I try to look at them without prejudice.

I can see a father, ready to depart, blessing his wife and child and being himself blessed in turn by an old rabbi with a snow-white beard and the profile of a fiery prophet. I can see . . . ah, I can't begin to describe it all . . .

On earlier transports, some of the guards were simple, kindly types with puzzled expressions, who walked about the camp smoking their pipes and speaking in some incomprehensible dialect. One would have found their company not too objectionable on the journey. Now I am transfixed with terror. Oafish, jeering faces, in which one seeks in vain for even the slightest trace of human warmth. At what fronts did they learn their business? In what punishment camps were they trained? For after all, this is a punishment, isn't it? A few young women are already sitting in a freight car. They hold their babies on their laps, their legs dangling outside—they are determined to enjoy the fresh air as long as possible. Sick people are carried past on stretchers. I almost find myself laughing; the disparity between the guards and the guarded is too absurd. My companion at the window shudders. Months ago he was brought here from Amersfoort, in bits and pieces. "Oh, yes, that's what those fellows were like," he says. "That's what they looked like."

A couple of young children stand with their noses pressed to the windowpane. I listen in to their earnest conversation. "Why do those nasty, horrid men wear green; why don't they wear black? Bad people wear black, don't they?" "Look over there, that man is really sick!" A shock of gray hair above a rumpled blanket on a stretcher. "Look, there's another sick one . . ."

And, pointing at the green uniforms, "Look at them, now they're laughing!" "Look, look, one of them's already drunk!"

More and more people are filling up the spaces in the freight cars. A tall, lonely figure paces the asphalt, a briefcase under his arm. He is the head of the so-called *Antragstelle*, the camp Appeals Department. He strives right up to the last moment to get people out of the commandant's clutches. Horse trading here always continues until the train has actually pulled out. It's even been known for him to manage to free people from the moving train. The man with the briefcase has the brow of a scholar, and tired, very tired shoulders. A bent little old woman, with a black, old-fashioned hat on her gray, wispy hair, bars his way, gesticulating and brandishing a bundle of papers under his nose. He listens to her for a while, then shakes his head and turns away, his shoulders sagging just a little bit more. This time it won't be possible to get many people off the train in the nick of time. The commandant is annoyed. A young Jew has had the effrontery to run away. One can't really call it a serious attempt to escape—he absconded from the hospital in a moment of panic, a thin jacket over his blue pyjamas, and in a clumsy, childish way took refuge in a tent, where he was picked up quickly enough after a search of the camp. But if you are a Jew you may not run away, may not allow yourself to be stricken with panic. The commandant is remorseless. As a reprisal, and without warning, scores of others are being sent on the transport with the boy, including quite a few who had thought they were firmly at anchor here. This system happens to believe in collective punishment. And all those planes overhead couldn't have helped to improve the commandant's mood, though that is a subject on which he prefers to keep his own counsel.

The cars are now what you might call full. But that's what you think. God Almighty, does all this lot have to get in as well? A large new group has turned up. The children are still standing with their noses glued to the windowpane; they don't miss a thing. "Look over there, a lot of people are getting off, it must be too hot in the train." Suddenly one of them calls out, "Look, the commandant!"

He appears at the end of the asphalt path, like a famous star making his entrance during a grand finale. This near-legendary figure is said to be quite charming and so well disposed toward the Jews. For the commandant of a camp for Jews, he has some strange ideas. Recently he decided that we needed more variety in our diet, and we were promptly served marrowfat peas—just once—instead of cabbage. He could also be said to be our artistic patron here, and is a regular at all our cabaret nights. On one occasion he came three times in succession to see the same performance and roared with laughter at the same old jokes each time. Under his auspices a male choir has been formed that sang *"Bei mir bist du schön"* on his personal orders. It sounded very moving here on the heath, it must be said. Now and then he even invites some of the artistes to his house and talks and drinks with them into the early hours. One night not so long ago he escorted an actress back home, and when he took his leave of her he offered her his hand; just imagine, his hand! They also say that he specially loves children. Children must be looked after. In the hospital they even get a tomato each day. And yet many of them seem to die all the same . . . I could go on quite a bit longer about "our" commandant. Perhaps he sees himself as a prince dispensing largesse to his many humble subjects. God knows how he sees himself. A voice behind me says, "Once upon a time we had a commandant who used to kick people off to Poland. This one sees them off with a smile."

He now walks along the train with military precision, a relatively young man who has "arrived" early in his career, if one may call it that. He is absolute master over the life and death of Dutch and German Jews here on this remote heath in Drenthe Province. A year ago he probably had not the slightest idea that it so much as existed. I didn't know about it myself, to tell the truth. He walks along the train, his gray, immaculately brushed hair just showing beneath his flat, light-green cap. That gray hair, which makes such a romantic contrast with his fairly young face, sends many of the silly young girls here into raptures—although they dare not, of course, express their feelings openly. On this cruel morning his face is almost iron-gray. It is a face that I am quite unable to read. Sometimes it seems to me to be like a long thin scar in which grimness mingles with joylessness and hypocrisy. And there is something else about him, halfway between a dapper hairdresser's assistant and a stage-door Johnny. But the grimness and the rigidly forced bearing predominate. With military step he walks along the line of freight cars, bulging now with people. He is inspecting his troops: the sick, infants in arms, young mothers, and shaven-headed men. A few more ailing people are being brought up on stretchers. He makes an impatient gesture; they're taking too long about it. Behind him walks his Jewish secretary, smartly dressed in fawn riding breeches and brown sports jacket. He has the sporty demeanor yet vacuous expression of the English whisky drinker. Suddenly they are joined by a handsome brown gundog, where from, heaven knows. With studied gestures the fawn secretary plays with it, like something from a picture in an English society paper. The green squad stare at him goggle-eyed. They probably think—though *think* is a big word—that some of the Jews here look quite different from what their propaganda sheets have led them to believe. A few Jewish big shots from the camp now also walk along the train. "Trying to air their importance," mutters someone behind me. "Transport Boulevard," I say. "Could one ever hope to convey to the outside world what has happened here today?" I ask my companion. The outside world probably thinks of us as a gray, uniform, suffering mass of Jews, and knows nothing of the gulfs and abysses and subtle differences that exist between us. They could never hope to understand.

The commandant has now been joined by the *Oberdienstleiter*, the head of the Camp Service Corps. The *Oberdienstleiter* is a German Jew of massive build, and the commandant looks slight and insignificant by his side. Black top boots, black cap, black army coat with yellow star. He has a cruel mouth and a powerful neck. A few years ago he was still a digger in the outworkers' corps. When the story of his meteoric rise is written up later, it will be an important historical account of the mentality of our age. The light-green commandant with his military bearing, the fawn, impassive secretary, the black bully-boy figure of the *Oberdienstleiter* parade past the train. People fall back around them, but all eyes are on them.

My God, are the doors really being shut now? Yes, they are. Shut on the herded, densely packed mass of people inside. Through small openings at the top we can see heads and hands, hands that will wave to us later when the train leaves. The commandant takes a bicycle and rides once again along the entire length of the train. Then he makes a brief gesture, like royalty in an operetta. A little orderly comes flying up and deferentially relieves him of the bicycle. The train gives a piercing whistle. And 1,020 Jews leave Holland.

This time the quota was really quite small, all considered: a mere thousand Jews, the extra twenty being reserves. For it is always possible—indeed, quite certain this time—that a few will die or be crushed to death on the way. So many sick people and not a single nurse . . .

The tide of helpers gradually recedes; people go back to their sleeping quarters. So many exhausted, pale, and suffering faces. One more piece of our camp has been amputated. Next week yet another piece will follow. This is what has been happening now for over a year, week in, week out. We are left with just a few thousand. A hundred thousand Dutch members of our race are toiling away under an unknown sky or lie rotting in some unknown soil. We know nothing of their fate. It is only a short while, perhaps, before we find out, each one of us in his own time. For we are all marked down to share that fate, of that I have not a moment's doubt. But I must go now and lie down and sleep for a little while. I am a bit tired and dizzy. Then later I have to go to the laundry to track down the facecloth that got lost. But first I must sleep. As for the future, I am firmly resolved to return to you after my wanderings. In the meantime, my love once again, you dear people.

NOTES

1. This is the second of two letters (along with one dated December 18, 1942) published illegally by the Resistance in 1943.
2. *Sh'ma:* "Hear, O Israel: the Lord our God, the Lord is one." This is a line of the prayer said when death is approaching.

3

Charlotte Delbo

Women and children first, they are the most exhausted. After that
the men. They are also weary but relieved that their women and
children should go first. For women and children go first.

CHARLOTTE DELBO

She was not Jewish, but French: a novelist, dramatist, poet, and intellectual. When she died on March 1, 1985, her obituary drew attention to her literary achievements. Charlotte Delbo, however, was also an Auschwitz survivor, and that achievement marked her life even more. As literary critic Lawrence L. Langer says, Delbo made "atrocity the substance as well as the subject of her art." Reimagined rather than imagined, the reality she wrote about was something she could never forget.

On September 3, 1939, two days after Hitler's army invaded Poland, France declared war on Germany. Eight months of inaction followed: It was the time of la drôle guerre, "the funny war." Then, on May 12, 1940, Germany invaded France. Four days later, the aging hero of World War I, Marshal Henri-Philippe Pétain, took over as head of the French government. He quickly asked for an armistice, which was signed at Compiègne on June 22. French collaboration resulted in a two-zone division of the country. The northern two-thirds, including Paris, was occupied directly by the Nazis; southern France, with governmental headquarters at the resort town of Vichy, was left unoccupied until early November 1942. Under these arrangements, the Germans allowed a French government, led by Pétain and then by Pierre Laval, to remain in place in exchange for its cooperation, which included financial exploitation that benefited Germany, labor brigades sent to work in German industry, and punitive measures against Jews.

Delbo was in Brazil with the great French director Louis Jouvet's theater company when France fell to the Germans in June 1940. She returned to occupied France in 1941, joining her husband, Georges Dudach, a Communist leader in the French underground. She, too, became active in the Resistance. Both were arrested by the collaborationist French police in March 1942, turned over to the Gestapo, and thrown into prison. Dudach refused to go to a German labor camp. He was executed in May 1942. Delbo was deported to Auschwitz in January 1943. She survived, returned to France, but never remarried.

Delbo wrote None of Us Will Return, *the first part of a trilogy called* Auschwitz et après (Auschwitz and After), *immediately after her liberation and return to Paris at the end of the war. But she put her manuscript away, waiting twenty years before she was ready to publish it.* None of Us Will Return *is one woman's lament, but Delbo never intended to write only a personal memoir. As suggested by her friend Rosette C. Lamont, the translator of many of her works, including those found in this book, Delbo's companions "begged her to remember, to be their voices if she survived." Taking that mission as a sacred trust, Delbo succeeded in writing prose and poetry combined to speak for them all.*

"Arrivals, Departures" speaks about trains and people that go to Auschwitz— "the end of the track," as Delbo puts it. This place, she says, is one where the arrivals may "expect the worst," but "they do not expect the unthinkable." It is also a place where "women and children go first." Delbo's words evoke feelings about what she and so many others, Jews and non-Jews alike, endured at Auschwitz: thirst, hunger, exhaustion, fear, confusion, humiliation, terror, separation from loved ones.

"Useless knowledge," Delbo sometimes said, was what her experience in Auschwitz produced: "It would have been far better," she wrote, "never to have entered or found out." For what happened in Auschwitz did little to unify, edify, or dignify life; it divided, besieged, and diminished life instead. Charlotte Delbo loathed abstraction, rejected sentimentality, and despised dishonesty even more. So, "useless" though her knowledge might be, she used it to show how dangerous it would be to forget that there was a time when Auschwitz was "the largest station in the world."

Arrivals, Departures

People arrive. They look through the crowd of those who are waiting, those who await them. They kiss them and say the trip exhausted them.

People leave. They say good-bye to those who are not leaving and hug the children.

There is a street for people who arrive and a street for people who leave.

From Charlotte Delbo, *None of Us Will Return*, trans. Rosette C. Lamont, Vol. 1: *Auschwitz and After*. New Haven, Conn.: Yale University Press, 1992. Copyright © 1992 by Yale University Press. Reprinted by permission of Yale University Press.

There is a café called "Arrivals" and a café called "Departures."
There are people who arrive and people who leave.

But there is a station where those who arrive are those who are leaving, a station where those who arrive have never arrived, where those who have left never came back.
It is the largest station in the world.
This is the station they reach, from wherever they came.
They get here after days and nights
having crossed many countries
they reach it together with their children, even the little ones who were not to be included.
They took the children because for this kind of trip you do not leave without them.
Those who had it took gold because they believed gold might be useful.
All of them took what was most valuable because you must not leave what is valuable when you take a long trip.
All of them brought their life, because above all it is your life you must take with you.
And when they arrive
they believe they have arrived
in Hell
possibly. And yet they did not believe it.
They had no idea you could take a train to Hell but since they were there they got their courage up and got ready to face what was coming
together with their children, their wives and their old parents with their family memories, and family papers.

They did not know there is no arriving in this station.
They expect the worst—they do not expect the unthinkable.
And when the guards shout to line up five by five, the men on one side, women and children on the other, in a language they do not understand, the truncheon blows make them understand and so they line up by fives expecting anything.
Mothers keep a tight hold on their children—they tremble at the thought they might be taken away—because the children are hungry and thirsty and dishevelled by lack of sleep crossing so many countries. They have arrived at last, they will be able to take care of them.
And when the guards shout to leave their bundles, comforters and memories on the platform, they do so because they must be prepared for the worst, and do not want to be surprised by anything. They say: "We'll see." They have already seen so much and are weary from the trip.

The station is not a station. It is the end of the track. They look and are distressed by the desolation around them.

In the morning, the mist hides the marshes.

In the evening floodlights reveal the white barbed wire as distinctly as astrophotography. They believe that this is where they are being taken, and they are afraid.

At night they wait for the day with the children heavy in their mothers' arms. They wait and wonder.

With daylight there is no more waiting. The columns start out at once. Women and children first, they are the most exhausted. After that the men. They are also weary but relieved that their women and children should go first.

For women and children go first.

In the winter they are chilled to the bone. Particularly those who come from Candia, snow is new to them.

In the summer the sun blinds them when they step out of the cattle-cars locked tight on departure.

Departure from France the Ukraine Albania Belgium Slovakia Italy Hungary Peloponnesus Holland Macedonia Austria Herzegovina from the shores of the Black Sea the shores of the Baltic the shores of the Mediterranean the banks of the Vistula.

They would like to know where they are. They do not know that this is the center of Europe. They look for the name of the station. This is a station that has no name.

A station that will remain nameless for them.

Some of them are traveling for the first time in their lives.

Some of them have traveled in all the countries in the world, businessmen. They knew all the landscapes but did not recognize this one.

They look. They will be able to say later on how it was.

All want to remember the impression they had and how they felt they would never return.

This is a feeling one might have had already in one's life. They know you cannot trust feelings.

Some came from Warsaw with large shawls and tied-up bundles
   some from Zagreb the women their heads covered with scarves
   some from the Danube wearing multi-colored woolen sweaters knitted through long night hours
   some from Greece, they took with them black olives and loukoums
   some came from Monte-Carlo
   they were in the casino

they are still wearing tails and stiff shirt fronts mangled from the trip
paunchy and bald
fat bankers who played keep the bank
there are married couples who stepped out of the synagogue the bride all in
white veiled all wrinkled from having slept on the floor of the cattle-car
the bridegroom in black wearing a top-hat his gloves soiled
parents and guests, women holding pearl-embroidered handbags
all of them sorry they could not stop home to change into something less
delicate.

The rabbi holds himself straight, heading the line. He has always been a
model for the rest.

There are boarding-school girls wearing identical pleated skirts, their hats
trailing blue ribbons. They pull up their knee socks carefully as they clamber
down, and walk neatly five by five, as though on a regular Thursday outing,
holding hands, unaware. What can they do to little boarding-school girls
shepherded by their teacher? The teacher tells them: "Be good, children!"
They don't have the slightest desire not to be good.

There are old people who used to receive letters from their children in
America. Their idea of foreign lands comes from postcards. Nothing ever
looked like what they see here. Their children will never believe it.

There are intellectuals: doctors or architects, composers or poets. You can
tell them by the way they walk, by their glasses. They too have seen a great deal
in their lifetimes, studied much. Many made use of their imagination to write
books, yet nothing they imagined came close to what they see now.

All the furriers of large cities are gathered here, as well as the men's and
women's tailors, and the manufacturers of ready-to-wear who had moved to
western Europe. They do not recognize in this place the land of their fore-
bears.

There is the inexhaustible crowd of city dwellers where each one lives in his
own beehive cell. Looking at the endless lines you wonder how they ever fit
into the stacked-up cubicles of a metropolis.

A mother slaps her five-year-old because he won't hold her hand and she
wants him to walk quietly by her side. You run the risk of getting lost if you are
separated in a strange, crowded place. She hits her child, and we who know
cannot forgive her for it. Yet, were she to smother him with kisses, it would
not make a bit of difference.

There are those who having journeyed eighteen days lost their minds,
murdering one another inside the boxcars and
those who suffocated during the trip when they were tightly packed together
these will not step out.

There's a little girl who hugs her doll against her chest, dolls can be
smothered too.

There are two sisters wearing white coats. They went out for a walk and never got back for dinner. Their parents still await their return anxiously.

Five by five they walk down the street of arrivals. It is actually the street of departure but no one knows it. This is a one-way street.

They proceed in orderly fashion so as not to be faulted.

They reach a building and heave a sigh. They have reached their destination at last.

And when the soldiers bark their orders, shouting for the women to strip, they undress the children first, careful not to wake them completely. After days and nights of travel the little ones are edgy and cranky

then the women start to strip in front of their children, nothing to be done

and when each is handed a towel they worry whether the shower will be warm because the children could catch cold

and when the men enter the shower room through another door, stark naked, the women hide the children against their bodies.

Perhaps at that moment all of them understand.

But understanding doesn't do any good since they cannot tell it to those waiting on the railway platform

those riding in the dark boxcars across many countries only to get here

those held in detention camps who are afraid of leaving, wondering about the climate, the working conditions, or being parted from their few possessions

those hiding in the mountains and forest who have grown weary of concealment. Come what may they'll head home. After all why should anyone come looking for them since they harmed no one

those who imagined they found a safe place for their children in a Catholic convent school where the sisters are so kind.

A band will be dressed in the girls' pleated skirts. The camp commandant wishes Viennese waltzes played every Sunday morning.

A blockhova shall cut homey window curtains out of the holy vestments worn by the rabbi to celebrate the sabbath in whatever place, no matter what.

A kapo will masquerade herself by donning the bridegroom's morning coat and top hat, with her girlfriend wrapped in the bride's veil. They'll play "wedding" all night while the prisoners, dead tired, lie in their bunks. Kapos can have fun since they're not exhausted at the end of the day.

Black Calamata olives and Turkish delight cubes will be sent to ailing German women who don't like Calamata olives, nor olives of any kind.

All day all night
every day every night the chimneys smoke, fed by this fuel sent from every
part of Europe
standing at the mouth of the crematoria men sift through ashes to find gold
melted from gold teeth. All those Jews have mouths full of gold, and since
there are so many of them it all adds up to tons and tons.

In the spring, men and women sprinkle ashes on drained marshland plowed
for the first time. They fertilize the soil with human phosphate.
From bags tied round their bellies, they draw human bone meal which they
sow upon the furrows. By the end of the day their faces are covered with white
dust blown back up by the wind. Sweat trickling down over the white powder
traces their wrinkles.
They need not fear running short of fertilizer since train after train gets here
every day and every night, every hour of every day and every night.
This is the largest station in the world for arrivals and departures.

Only those who enter the camp find out what happened to the others. They
cry at the thought of having parted from them at the station the day an officer
ordered the young prisoners to line up separately
people are needed to drain the marshes and cover them with the others'
ashes.
They tell themselves it would have been far better never to have entered or
found out.

4

Isabella Leitner

Was it only a year ago? Or a century?

ISABELLA LEITNER

Fragments of Isabella, *the Holocaust memoir of a Hungarian Jewish woman named Isabella Leitner, was written immediately after she immigrated to the United States in 1945, but it was not published until 1978. Near the end of it, she says:*

> *The world ended in May. I was born in May. I died in May. We started the journey of ugliness on May 29th. We headed for Auschwitz. We arrived on May 31st.*
>
> *The scent of spring wasn't delicious. The earth didn't smile. It shrieked in pain. The air was filled with the stench of death. Unnatural death. The smoke was thick. The sun couldn't crack through. The scent was the smell of burning flesh. The burning flesh was your mother.*
>
> *I am condemned to walk the earth for all my days with the stench of burning flesh in my nostrils. My nostrils are damned. May is damned. May should be abolished. May hurts. There should be only eleven months in a year. May should be set aside for tears. For six million years, to cleanse the earth.*

Even in early 1944, Hungary seemed to be a haven of relative security for its 825,000 Jews, the last great Jewish community in Europe. Hungarian Jewish leaders had heard reports about the fate of other Jews in Nazi-occupied Europe, and they did live in a precarious situation, given Hungary's alliance with Hitler and Nazi Germany. But compared to the situation of other Jewish communities, what was left of them, their discomfort was minimal. Indeed, until March 19, 1944, when the Germans occupied the country of their faltering ally, the Jews of Hungary suffered from what Ida Fink calls "the poverty of imagination." They simply did not

65

think that what had happened to the Jews in Nazi-occupied Europe would happen to them. But on April 29–30, 1944, it began: two transports, carrying about 3,800 able-bodied men and women between the ages of 16–50 departed Hungary. They reached Auschwitz on May 2. The "selection" there spared 486 men and 616 women for labor. The remaining 2,698 were gassed. By July 15, 1944, 450,000 Jews had been deported to Auschwitz. More than 75 percent were killed on arrival.

Isabella Leitner's twentieth birthday was on Sunday, May 28, 1944. Her "celebration" included preparation for a journey that began the next day. This journey was deportation. It took Leitner, her four sisters, her brother, and her mother—along with hundreds of other Hungarian Jews—from the ghetto at Kisvarda to Auschwitz. Her mother and youngest sister were killed on arrival. Another sister perished in Bergen-Belsen, but Isabella and her other siblings managed to survive. Eventually Isabella was reunited with her father, too. In desperation he had gone to the United States in an effort to save his family by obtaining visas for them. He was spared the Nazi horrors but suffered the rest of his life from an irrational guilt that he had not done enough to save his family.

After her liberation and arrival in the United States, Leitner could hardly reconcile "real" time—"New York, May 1945"—with "that time." Fragmented, she went back and forth, attracted to an American life of Garbo films, stunning clothes, jewelry, stylish hair, dates with young men, and yet unable to leave behind that other life in the ghetto, on the train, in the camps—amenorrhea, shaved head, lice, diarrhea, rags that passed for clothing.

Like many Holocaust survivors, Isabella Leitner has given her oral history to the Fortunoff Video Archive for Holocaust Testimonies at Yale University. "You have one vision of life," she says during one of those interviews, "and I have two. . . . I lived on two planets." Speaking for many other former victims of the Holocaust, she adds "we have these . . . these double lives. We can't cancel out. It just won't go away. . . . It's very hard." Hearing her speak, we can hear her feel.

Fragments of Isabella

NEW YORK, MAY 1945

Yesterday, what happened yesterday? Did you go to the movies? Did you have a date? What did he say? That he loves you? Did you see the new Garbo film? She was wearing a stunning cape. Her hair, I thought, was completely different and very becoming. Have you seen it? No? I haven't. Yesterday . . . yesterday, May 29, 1944, we were deported . . .

From Isabella Leitner, *Fragments of Isabella: A Memoir of Auschwitz*, ed. and with an epilogue by Irving A. Leitner. New York: Thomas Y. Crowell, 1978. Copyright © 1978 by Isabella Leitner and Irving A. Leitner. Reprinted by permission of Isabella Leitner.

Are the American girls really going to the movies? Do they have dates? Men tell them they love them, true or not. Their hair is long and blonde, high in the front and low in the back, like this and like that, and they are beautiful and ugly. Their clothes are light in the summer and they wear fur in the winter—they mustn't catch cold. They wear stockings, ride in automobiles, wear wrist watches and necklaces, and they are colorful and perfumed. They are healthy. They are living. Incredible!

Was it only a year ago? Or a century? . . . Our heads are shaved. We look like neither boys nor girls. We haven't menstruated for a long time. We have diarrhea. No, not diarrhea—typhus. Summer and winter we have but one type of clothing. Its name is "rag." Not an inch of it without a hole. Our shoulders are exposed. The rain is pouring on our skeletal bodies. The lice are having an orgy in our armpits, their favorite spots. Their bloodsucking, the irritation, their busy scurrying give the illusion of warmth. We're hot at least under our armpits, while our bodies are shivering.

MAY 28, 1944—MORNING

It is Sunday, May 28th, my birthday, and I am celebrating, packing for the big journey, mumbling to myself with bitter laughter—tomorrow is deportation. The laughter is too bitter, the body too tired, the soul trying to still the infinite rage. My skull seems to be ripping apart, trying to organize, to comprehend what cannot be comprehended. Deportation? What is it like?

A youthful SS man, with the authority, might, and terror of the whole German army in his voice, has just informed us that we are to rise at 4 A.M. sharp for the journey. Anyone not up at 4 A.M. will get a *Kugel* (bullet).

A bullet simply for not getting up? What is happening here? The ghetto suddenly seems beautiful. I want to celebrate my birthday for all the days to come in this heaven. God, please let us stay here. Show us you are merciful. If my senses are accurate, this is the last paradise we will ever know. Please let us stay in this heavenly hell forever. Amen. We want nothing—nothing, just to stay in the ghetto. We are not crowded, we are not hungry, we are not miserable, we are happy. Dear ghetto, we love you; don't let us leave. We were wrong to complain, we never meant it.

We're tightly packed in the ghetto, but that must be a fine way to live in comparison to deportation. Did God take leave of his senses? Something terrible is coming. Or is it only me? Am I mad? There are seven of us in nine feet of space. Let them put fourteen together, twenty-eight. We will sleep on top of each other. We will get up at 3 A.M.—not 4—stand in line for ten hours. Anything. Anything. Just let our family stay together. Together we will endure death. Even life. . . .

A NEW MODE OF TRAVEL

We drag ourselves to the railroad station. The sun is mercilessly hot. People are fainting, babies screaming. We, the young and healthy teen-agers, are totally spent. What must the old, the sick, feel? Totally stripped of our dignity, leaving the town we were born in, grew up in—what happens after this long wait? Where are we off to?

I am ready to go. Away from my cradle of love. Away from where every pebble and every face are familiar. Those familiar faces now reflect gladness. I must be away before I learn to hate them. I shall not return.

You, my former neighbors, I cannot live with you again. You could have thrown a morsel of sadness our way while we were dragging ourselves down Main Street. But you didn't. Why?

Please take me away from here. I don't know these people. I don't ever want to know them. I can't detect the difference between them and the SS, so I'll go with the SS.

Soon we are packed into the cattle cars . . . cars with barred windows, with planks of wood on the bars, so that no air can enter or escape . . . 75 to a car . . . no toilets . . . no doctors . . . no medication.

I am menstruating. There is no way for me to change my napkin . . . no room to sit . . . no room to stand . . . no air to breathe. This is no way to die. It offends even death. Yet people are dying all around me.

We squeeze my mother into a sitting position on the backpacks. Her face has an otherworldly look. She knows she will not live. But she wants us to live, desperately. All these years I've carried with me her face of resignation and hope and love:

"Stay alive, my darlings—all six of you. Out there, when it's all over, a world is waiting for you to give it all I gave you. Despite what you see here— and you are all young and impressionable—believe me, there is humanity out there, there is dignity. I will not share it with you, but it's there. And when this is over, you must add to it, because sometimes it is a little short, a little skimpy. With your lives, you can create other lives and nourish them. You can nourish your children's souls and minds, and teach them that man is capable of infinite glory. You must believe me. I cannot leave you with what you see here. I must leave you with what I see. My body is nearly dead, but my vision is throbbing with life—even here. I want you to live for the very life that is yours. And wherever I'll be, in some mysterious way, my love will overcome my death and will keep you alive. I love you."

And that frail woman of love lived until Wednesday.

5

Olga Lengyel

How should I have known? I had spared them from hard work, but I had condemned Arvad and my mother to death in the gas chambers.

OLGA LENGYEL

Formerly a part of Romania, the city of Cluj in northern Transylvania had come under Hungarian control in 1940. Its residents included the family of a well-known Jewish physician named Miklos Lengyel. Assisted by his wife Olga, who was also trained in medicine, he directed a hospital in Cluj. The Lengyels had two sons, Thomas and Arvad. "No one," Olga Lengyel thought before war broke out, "could be happier than we were."

Even as the war years accumulated, the Lengyels "looked upon Germany as a nation which had given much culture to the world" and found it hard to believe the frightening stories of concentration camp atrocities that could be heard in Cluj. All too soon, however, seeing became believing. For according to statistics cited in Israel Gutman's Encyclopedia of the Holocaust, *more than 1.4 million Jews lived in Romania and Hungary in 1941. By the end of the Holocaust, half a million Hungarian Jews and more than 270,000 Romanian Jews were dead.*

In May 1944 the Lengyel family was deported to Auschwitz. Their journey in the stifling cattle cars took seven days. Upon arrival, the usual routine followed. Nearly five thousand men, women, and children from this Cluj transport "formed fives" in columns that stretched on and on. Men were separated from women and children. Miklos Lengyel and Olga Lengyel's father were in one column, Olga's mother and two sons stayed with her in the other. Then the "selection" started.

Isabella Leitner lost her mother at Auschwitz. So did Olga Lengyel, and her

69

intensely personal 1947 memoir, Five Chimneys, *describes the especially painful way in which she lost her children, too. It involved a version of what Lawrence Langer calls* choiceless choices. *As Langer understands them, choiceless choices do not "reflect options between life and death, but between one form of abnormal response and another, both imposed by a situation that [is] not of the victim's own choosing." For its victims, as Lengyel came to know, the Holocaust made choiceless choices commonplace.*

Olga Lengyel may have anticipated the worst but not what Charlotte Delbo calls "the unthinkable." She survived Auschwitz, but Nazi cruelty condemned her to live the rest of her life with the consequences of her choiceless choice. Her testimony drives home the point that no one should have to face such bleak options again.

The Arrival

Today, when I think about our arrival at the camp, the cars of our train appear to me as so many coffins. It was, indeed, a funeral train. The SS and Gestapo agents were our undertakers; the officers who later evaluated our "riches" were our greedy and impatient heirs.

We could feel nothing but a deep sense of relief. Anything would be better than this terrible uncertainty. In a prison on wheels, could there be anything more appalling than the oppressive gloom, reeking with foul odors, alive with heartbreaking groans and lamentations?

We hoped to be released from the car without delay. But this hope was soon blasted. We were to spend an eighth night in the train, the living piled on top of one another to avoid contact with the decaying corpses.

No one slept that night. Our sense of relief gave way to anxiety as though a sixth sense were warning us of impending disaster.

With difficulty, I ploughed through the compact mass of animal humanity to reach the little window. There I saw a weird spectacle. Outside was a veritable forest of barbed wire, which was illuminated at intervals by powerful searchlights.

An immense blanket of light covered everything within view. It was a chilling sight, yet reassuring, too. This lavish expenditure of electricity undoubtedly indicated that civilization was nearby and an end to the conditions we had endured.

Still, I was far from apprehending the true meaning of the display. Where were we and what fate awaited us? I conjectured wisely, yet my imagination could not supply a reasonable explanation.

Finally, I went back to my parents, for I felt a great need to talk to them. "Can you ever forgive me?" I murmured, as I kissed their hands.

From Olga Lengyel, *Five Chimneys*, trans. Clifford Coch and Paul P. Weiss. Chicago: Ziff-Davis Publishing Company, 1947.

"Forgive you?" asked my mother with her characteristic tenderness. "You have done nothing for which you need to be forgiven."

But her eyes dimmed with tears. What did she suspect in this hour?

"You have always been the best of daughters," added my father.

"Perhaps we shall die," my mother went on quietly, "but you are young. You have the strength to fight, and you will live. You can still do so much for yourself, and the others."

This was to be the last time that I embraced them.

At last the pale day broke. In a little while an official we learned was the camp commandant came to accept us into his custody. He was accompanied by an interpreter who, we later were told, spoke nine languages. The latter's duty was to transmit every instruction into the native tongues of the deportees. He warned us that we were to observe the strictest discipline and carry out every order without discussion. We listened. What reason had we to suspect worse treatment than we had already received?

On the platform, we saw a group in convict-striped uniforms. That sight made a painful impression. Would we become broken, emaciated like these wrecks? They had been brought to the station to take over our luggage, or rather, what remained of it after the guards had exacted their "taxes." Here we were completely dispossessed.

The order came, curt and demanding: "Get out!"

The women were lined up on one side, the men on the other, in ranks of five.

The doctors were to stand by in a separate row with their instrument bags. That was rather reassuring. If doctors were needed, it meant that the sick would receive medical attention. Four or five ambulances drove up. We were told that these would transport the ailing. Another good sign.

How could we know that all this was window-dressing to maintain order among the deportees with a minimum of armed force. We could not possibly have guessed that the ambulances would cart the sick directly to the gas chambers, whose existence I had doubted; and thence to the crematories!

Quieted by such cunning subterfuges, we allowed ourselves to be stripped of our belongings and marched docilely to the slaughter houses.

While we were assembled on the station platform, our luggage was taken down by the creatures in convict stripes. Then the bodies of those who had died on the journey were removed. The corpses that had been with us for days were bloated hideously and in various stages of decomposition. The odors were so nauseating that thousands of flies had been attracted. They fed on the dead and attacked the living, tormenting us incessantly.

As soon as we left the cattle cars, my mother, my sons and I were separated from my father and my husband. We now stood in columns that extended for hundreds of yards. The train had discharged from four to five thousand passengers, all as dazed and bewildered as we were.

More commands, and we were paraded before about thirty SS men, including the head of the camp and other officers. They began to choose, sending some of us to the right and some to the left. This was the first "selection," in the course of which, as we could not dream could be true, the initial sacrifices for the crematories were picked.

Children and old people were told off automatically, "to the left!" At the moment of parting came those shrieks of despair, those frantic cries, "Mama, Mama!" that will ring forever in my ears. But the SS guards demonstrated that they were moved by no sentiments. All those who tried to resist, old or young, they beat mercilessly; and quickly they re-formed our column into the two new groups, right and left, but always in ranks of five.

The only explanation came from an SS officer who assured us that the aged would remain in charge of the children. I believed him, assuming naturally that the able-bodied adults would have to work, but that the old and very young would be cared for.

Our turn came. My mother, my sons, and I stepped before the "selectors." Then I committed my . . . terrible error. The selector waved my mother and myself to the adult group. He classed my younger son Thomas with the children and aged, which was to mean immediate extermination. He hesitated before Arvad, my older son.

My heart thumped violently. This officer, a large dark man who wore glasses, seemed to be trying to act fairly. Later I learned that he was Dr. Fritz Klein, the "Chief Selector." "This boy must be more than twelve," he remarked to me.

"No," I protested.

The truth was that Arvad was not quite twelve, and I could have said so. He was big for his age, but I wanted to spare him from labors that might prove too arduous for him.

"Very well," Klein agreed amiably. "To the left!"

I had persuaded my mother that she should follow the children and take care of them. At her age she had a right to the treatment accorded to the elderly and there would be someone to look after Arvad and Thomas.

"My mother would like to remain with the children," I said.

"Very well," he again acquiesced. "You'll all be in the same camp."

"And in several weeks you'll all be reunited," another officer added, with a smile. "Next!"

How should I have known. I had spared them from hard work, but I had condemned Arvad and my mother to death in the gas chambers.

6

Livia E. Bitton Jackson

*We are lined up and several husky girls in gray cloaks begin
shaving our hair—on our heads, under the arms, and on the pubic
area.*

LIVIA E. BITTON JACKSON

*It is no coincidence that many memoirs by Holocaust survivors come from Hungarian
Jews such as Isabella Leitner, Olga Lengyel, and Livia E. Bitton Jackson, the next
selection's author. In Raul Hilberg's words, "Truly the Hungarian Jews were living
on an island." Comparatively unscathed until 1944, Hungarian Jews could have a
relatively better chance of survival than populations targeted earlier—if they were
spared for work when "selections" such as those at Auschwitz were made. That if was
a big one, especially for Hungarian Jewish women, and by no means did it ensure
survival. Nearly all the former Auschwitz victims—male and female—agree that
luck had more to do with their survival than any factor that was directly in their own
control. The choices people made—"choiceless" or not—did make a difference, but
factors such as the following probably mattered just as much, if not more: a person's
age and sex; when one was deported; whether he or she could ward off sickness;
whether one might draw a work assignment that would reduce energy output or
enable one to obtain better food; whether one could avoid the punishing whims of
guards or the caprice of periodic selections; whether there was help of any kind that
one could count on.*

*The Israeli novelist Amoz Oz points out that, for a long time, "we have been
teaching ourselves that the murder of European Jewry can be explained but not
understood."* Elli: Coming of Age in the Holocaust, *Livia E. Bitton Jackson's
autobiographical account, offers a different perspective. This account is about a girl*

who matured, aged, and changed so much in Auschwitz, Plaszow, and Dachau that, after she was liberated, German civilians thought she was an "old" man. For in the Nazi camps, "breasts began to sag . . . then became virtual hanging empty sacks. . . . Then the empty sacks became shorter. Eventually the skin, too, was absorbed and the breasts disappeared completely. We were all like men. Flat." Jackson does not offer theories that "explain," let alone ones that "understand." She concentrates on detail instead. The detail concentrates on the experience of women during the Holocaust. It shows what happened.

Elli grew up in a religiously observant Orthodox Jewish family that lived in Somorja, a small Hungarian town at the foot of the Carpathian Mountains. She had turned thirteen on February 28, 1944. Three months later she was in Auschwitz. Elli lived to tell about it. What she tells involves the particularity of "metal buttons" glistening on SS uniforms; babies' "diapers" left on an Auschwitz transport; a "spasm of nausea" hurling "a charge of vomit" up Elli's throat; hair sheared roughly from every part of a woman's body; descriptions of work on the "stone chain," the cleaning commando, and the digging and leveling commando ("To me," Elli laments, "this is the most difficult work. Sometimes you dig up small bones and skulls. The bones of children. Of infants.") And ever-present among the women were the effects of starvation:

We stopped menstruating because we are near starvation. We lost weight and our organs are too weak to function properly. . . . Even our stomachs slowed down in time. Hunger became less nagging, and the fullness of the stomach after the evening meal— less satisfying. The women stopped "cooking up" imaginary meals during work, and talk about food became less frequent.

Jackson's father perished in Bergen-Belsen two days before that camp was liberated. Elli's beloved Aunt Szeren lost her life in a gas chamber at Auschwitz. Her mother and brother, Bubi, survived. When Jackson decided to write her story, she reports, her mother and her husband did much to help her concentrate on "the agonizing task of remembering." That task brought back how much she loved her Schwinn bicycle. The thirteenth-birthday present her family had given her, "it was a bright-yellow girls' bike with bright red-and-yellow webbing on the back wheel. It had a dark-yellow leather seat and the shiny chrome handlebars were tucked into handles matching the seat. It was beautiful."

Before the Soviet Army liberated Auschwitz, the Germans evacuated most of their loot. But, among other things, the storehouses still contained nearly 350,000 suits of men's clothes, 840,000 women's dresses, and some seven tons of shorn human hair— the latter only a small part of the total collected at Auschwitz, the rest having been sold to German companies that turned it into felt and mattresses. The Germans expropriated every bit of personal property they could take from the Jews, including Elli's Schwinn bike. Humiliation, shame, degradation—these were her feelings as the Nazis took everything that was not theirs. Those details, and the intense feelings—outrage among them—that they continue to provoke, are also part of what it means to have "come of age in the Holocaust" and to be a woman who survived it.

Coming of Age

Sometime during the fourth night, the train comes to a halt. We are suddenly awakened by the noise of sliding doors thrown open and cold night air rushing into the wagon.

"Heraus! Alles heraus! Alovanti!"

A rough voice. A figure clad in a striped uniform. Standing in the wide open doorway, his back illuminated by an eerie, diffused light, the man looks like a creature from another planet.

"Schnell! Heraus! Alles heraus!"

Two or three other striped figures leap into the wagon and begin shoving the drowsy men, women, and children out into the cold night.

A huge sign catches my eye: AUSCHWITZ

The pain in my stomach sends a violent wave of nausea up my gullet.

The night is chilly and damp. An other-worldly glow lights up tall watch-towers, high wire fences, an endless row of cattle cars, SS men, their dogs, a mass of people pouring out of the wagons.

"Heraus! Heraus! Los! Heraus!"

Metal buttons glisten on SS uniforms.

"My things! I left everything in the wagon!"

"On line! Everyone stand on line! By fives! Men over there! Women and children over here!"

"The diapers! I forgot the diapers in the wagon!" Young Mrs. Lunger starts for the wagon at a run, a child in each hand. Little Frumet is crying but Yingele is fast asleep on her shoulder. The man in the striped suit holds her back. "You won't need any diapers."

"But I do. Both children are in diapers. I brought a large bundle of diapers along. Let me get them, please . . . please!"

"You are not allowed to go back to the wagon. Stay on line right here! Where you are going, you won't need any diapers."

Mrs. Lunger's beautiful brown eyes open wide with astonishment. Uncomprehending, she hesitantly joins the others on the line. I stand behind her and her mother-in-law and the two Lunger girls. Lunger *bácsi* is on the other side of the tracks. Mommy and Szerén *néni* and I make only three. Two more women are shoved alongside us to make it five. My brother is hustled farther,

From Livia E. Bitton Jackson, *Elli: Coming of Age in the Holocaust*. New York: Times Books, 1980. Copyright © 1980 by Livia E. Bitton Jackson. Reprinted by permission of the Gloria Stern Literary Agency.

on the other side of the tracks. He turns to say good-bye to us and trips on the wire flanking the tracks. Daddy's new gray hat rolls off his head. He reaches to pick it up. An SS man kicks him in the back sending him tumbling on the tracks. Mother gasps. Szerén *néni* gives a shriek and grasps Mommy's arm. I hold my mouth: A spasm of nausea hurls a charge of vomit up my throat.

"Marchieren! Los!"

The column of women, children, infants begins to move. Dogs snarl, SS men scream orders, children cry, women weep good-byes to departing men, and I struggle with my convulsing stomach. And I march on. Behind the lovely young Mrs. Lunger with her two little children on her arms and the oldest one hanging on to her skirt. Behind Mrs. Bonyhádi and her Tommi and Suzie docilely marching in the line before them. Next to me Mommy is silently supporting Aunt Szerén by the shoulder. I march and the sights and sounds of Auschwitz only dimly penetrate my consciousness. Daylight is slowly skirting the clouds, and it turns suddenly very cold. We left our coats in the wagons. We were ordered to leave our belongings behind. Everything. We will get them later, they told us. How will they find what belongs to whom? There was such wild confusion at the trains. Perhaps they will sort things out. The Germans must have a system. Leave it to them. The famous German order.

The marching column comes to a sudden halt.

An officer in gray SS uniform stands facing the lines of women and children. Dogs straining on short leashes held by SS soldiers flank him on both sides. He stops each line and regroups them. Some to his right and some to his left. Then he orders each group to march on. I tremble as I stand before him. He looks at me with a soft look in friendly eyes.

"Goldene Haar!" he exclaims as he takes one of my long braids into his hand. I am not certain I heard it right. Did he say "golden hair" about my braids?

"Bist du Jüdin?" Are you Jewish?

The question startles me. "Yes, I am Jewish."

"Wie alt bist du?" How old are you?

"I am thirteen."

"You are tall for your age. Is this your mother?" He touches Mommy lightly on the shoulder: "You go with your mother." With his riding stick he parts Szerén *néni* from my mother's embrace and gently shoves Mommy and me to the group moving to the right.

"Go, and remember, from now on you are sixteen."

Szerén *néni*'s eyes fill with terror. She runs to Mommy and grabs her arm. "Don't leave me, Lórika! Don't leave me!"

Mother embraces her fragile, older sister and turns to the SS officer, her voice a shrieking plea:

"This is my sister, *Herr Offizier*, let me go with her! She is not feeling well. She needs me."

"You go with your daughter. She needs you more. March on! *Los!*" With an impatient move of his right hand he shoves Mother toward me. Then he glares angrily at my aunt: "Move on! *Los!* You go that way!" His stick points menacingly to the left.

Aunt Szerén, a forlorn, slight figure against the marching multitude, the huge German shepherd dogs, the husky SS men. A savage certainty slashes my bruised insides. I will never again see my darling aunt! I give an insane shriek: "Szerén *néni!* Szerén *néni!* I'll never see you again!"

A wild fear floods her large hazel eyes. She stretches out her arms to reach me. An SS soldier gives her a brutal thrust, hurling her into the line marching to the left. She turns again, mute fear lending her added fragility. She moves on.

The road to the left leads to the gas chambers. . . .

Our march to the right slows to a halt. A tall, metal gate looms darkly ahead. Above it huge metal letters arch like a sinister crown:

ARBEIT MACHT FREI!

Work sets you free! Perhaps Mommy was right. We will work. And be treated like human beings. Fed and clothed. But *"frei"*? Free? What do they mean by that? Will they really let us move about freely if we work? Where?

The immense portals of the gate open and we march through them into an enclosure with tall wire fences. Several rows of wire. Plain wire fence flanked by barbed wire.

It's growing lighter rapidly. And colder. I wonder when we will get our things. I need my coat. The eerie light of the watchtowers grows dimmer. Rows of barracks, long, flat buildings, on both sides of the black pebble-strewn road enclosed in barbed wire. It's a road without an end. It stretches far into the fog. And we march.

Motorcycles. SS officers. Dogs. *"Marchieren. Los. Los!"*

It's cold. We march on.

Groups of people linger about the barracks on the other side of the fence. Are they men or women? Their heads are shorn but they wear gray, dresslike cloaks. They run to the fence as we pass. They stare at us. Blank stares. They must be insane. This must be an asylum for the mentally ill. Poor souls.

The road ends. Our silent, rapid march ends. By fives we file through the entrance of a long, flat gray building. A low-ceilinged room. Long and narrow. Noise. Shouts. Unintelligible.

"Ruhe!" Quiet!

A tall, husky blonde in SS uniform. *"Ruhe! Wer versteht deutsch? Deutsch? Austreten. Wer versteht deutsch!"* Who understands German? Step forward!

I step forward. A few other girls also step forward. We understand German.

"Tell them to keep quiet at once. If they won't listen they will be shot. Tell them."

I attempt to shout above the din and so do my fellow interpreters. To no avail. The low ceiling compresses the sounds. The noise like a tidal wave hurls back and forth.

"Ruhe!" The buxom SS woman begins to swing her whip above the heads, and the other SS soldiers in the room, as if on cue, begin cracking their whips, snapping into faces. A sharp pain slashes at my left cheekbone. I feel a firm welt rise across my face. Why? I am the interpreter. No one hears me. Quickly, I step back into the crowd. Perhaps it is safer there.

In seconds it becomes quiet.

"Sich auskleiden! Alles herunter!" Get undressed, everybody! Take off everything! *"Los!"*

The room is swarming with SS men. Get undressed, here? In front of the men? No one moves.

"Didn't you hear? Take off your clothes. All your clothes!"

I feel the slap of a whip on my shoulders and meet a young SS soldier's glaring eyes.

"Hurry! Strip fast. You will be shot. Those having any clothes on in five minutes will be shot!"

I look at Mommy. She nods. Let's get undressed. I stare directly ahead as I take off my clothes. I am afraid. By not looking at anyone I hope no one will see me. I have never seen my mother in the nude. How awful it must be for her. I hesitate before removing my bra. My breasts are two growing buds, taut and sensitive. I can't have anyone see them. I decide to leave my bra on.

Just then a shot rings out. The charge is ear-shattering. Some women begin to scream. Others weep. I quickly take my bra off.

It is chilly and frightening. Clothes lie in mounds on the cement floor. We are herded, over a thousand, shivering, humiliated nude bodies, into the next hall, even chillier. More foreboding. It is darker here. Barer.

"Los! Schneller, blöde Lumpen!" Faster. Move faster, idiotic whores.

We are lined up and several husky girls in gray cloaks begin shaving our hair—on our heads, under the arms, and on the pubic area. My long, thick braids remain braided and while the shaving machine shears my scalp, the hair remains hanging, tugging at the roots. The pain of the heavy braid tugging mercilessly at the yet unshaven roots brings tears to my eyes. I pray for the shaving to be done quickly. As my blonde tresses lie in a large heap on the ground, the indifferent hair butcher remarks: "A heap of gold." In a shudder I remember the scene at the selection—the SS officer's admiration of my "golden hair," the separation from Aunt Szerén. Where is she now? Is her hair shorn off and is she stripped of her clothes, too? Is she very frightened? Poor, darling, Szerén *néni*. If my hair were shorn before the selection, we would be together with her now. We would not have been separated. It's because of my blonde hair that Mommy and I were sent to the other side. Poor darling. If only we could have stayed together!

The haircut has a startling effect on every woman's appearance. Individuals become a mass of bodies. Height, stoutness, or slimness: There is no distinguishing factor—it is the absence of hair which transformed individual women into like bodies. Age and other personal differences melt away. Facial expressions disappear. Instead, a blank, senseless stare emerges on a thousand faces of one naked, unappealing body. In a matter of minutes even the physical aspect of our numbers seems reduced—there is less of a substance to our dimensions. We become a monolithic mass. Inconsequential.

From *blöde Lumpen,* "idiotic whores," we became *blöde Schweine,* "idiotic swine." Easier to despise. And the epithet changed only occasionally to *blöde Hunde,* "idiotic dogs." Easier to handle.

The shaving had a curious effect. A burden was lifted. The burden of individuality. Of associations. Of identity. Of the recent past. Girls who have continually wept at separation from parents, sisters and brothers now began to giggle at the strange appearance of their friends. Some shriek with laughter. Others begin calling out names of friends to see if they can recognize them shorn and stripped. When response to names comes forth from completely transformed bodies, recognition is loud, hysterical. Wild, noisy embraces. Shrieking, screaming disbelief. Some girls bury their faces in their palms and howl, rolling on the ground.

"Was ist los?" What's the matter? A few swings of the SS whip restores order.

I look for Mommy. I find her easily. The haircut has not changed her. I have been used to seeing her in kerchiefs, every bit of hair carefully tucked away. Avoiding a glance at her body, I marvel at the beauty of her face. With all accessories gone her perfect features are even more striking. Her high forehead, large blue eyes, classic nose, shapely lips and elegant cheekbones are more evident than ever.

She does not recognize me as I stand before her. Then a sudden smile of recognition: "Elli! It's you. You look just like Bubi. Strange, I have never seen the resemblance before. What a boyish face! They cut off your beautiful braids . . ."

"It's nothing. Hair can grow."

"With the will of God."

We are herded en masse into the next hall. Clutching a cake of claylike object handed to me at the door, the nude mass of bodies crushing about me, I shriek with sudden shock as a cold torrent gushes unexpectedly from openings in the ceiling. In a few minutes it is over, and once again we are rushed into another room. Gray dresses are handed to us and we are urged with shouts of *Los!* and *blöde Schweine* to pull them over wet, shivering bodies. Everyone has to pick a pair of shoes from an enormous shoe pile. *"Los! Los!"*

As we emerge, still wet, in gray sacks, with clean-shaven heads, from the other end of the building and line up, by now relatively quickly, in rows of five, the idea strikes me. The people we saw as we entered the camp, the shaved, gray-cloaked group which ran to stare at us through the barbed-wire fence, they were us! We look exactly like them. Same bodies, same dresses, same blank stares. We, too, look like an insane horde—soulless, misshapen figures. They, too, must have arrived from home quite recently: Their heads were freshly shaven. They were women just like us. They, too, were ripe mothers and young girls, bewildered and bruised. They, too, longed for dignity and compassion; and they, too, were transformed into figures of contempt instead.

The *Zehlappel* lasts almost three hours. This word, meaning "roll call," became the dread and the life style of Auschwitz. Twice daily we would be lined up with lightning speed by fives in order to be counted. Lined up at 3 A.M. We would stand three or four hours until the official SS staff showed up to count our heads. In the evening it lasted from five to nine. The lineup had to be accomplished in seconds in order to stand endless hours awaiting the roll call, *Zehlappel*.

It was inconceivable to me that the mad rush inside the showers would culminate in an endless wait outside. We bodies in a single loose cotton robe exposed to the chill morning, traumatized bodies hurled out to the cold wind to stand in a senseless, long wait.

The smartly stepping German staff appears briskly. With the tip of a stick lightly touching the head of the first girl in every row of five, we are counted and officially initiated into the camp. We become members of an exclusive club. Inmates of Auschwitz. . . .

Three weeks pass and I do not menstruate. Neither does anyone else. With amazement we all realize that menstruation ceased in the camps. The first week after our arrival there were many menstruant women, even in the wagon on our way to Plaszow there were several girls who bled profusely. Then, menstruation ceased abruptly. There is bromide in our food, we are told by old-timers. Bromide is supposed to sterilize women. The Germans are experimenting with mass sterilization.

The information causes panic among the inmates and at first many refuse to eat the cooked food, determined to survive on the bread ration alone. Soon hunger wins, and the food is consumed as before. The whole sterilization story may be just a rumor anyway.

I am secretly grateful for the bromide. Avoiding the fear, pain and embarrassment of menstruation is worth any sacrifice to me at the moment.

But the topic does not die. Married women keep wondering about the bromide in their food again and again. Will they bear children again? What will their husbands say when they find out? Perhaps less of the food will cause less of a damage. Some try to eat less and the conflict is painful. Rejection of a means of survival for the sake of a dubious gain.

No one can help. Rumors have no way of being checked. The old-timers, mostly Polish Jews who have been in the camps for over two years, bitterly resent us, Hungarian Jews. They are bitter about the fact that we arrived only recently. We lived in the security and comfort of our homes for the past two years while they were exposed to the torture of the camps. "You went to the theaters and resorts in Hungary, while our families were shot and burned, and we suffered in the camps," they would say to us. Then they would dramatize the dangers of the camp. They would tell us to forget our families, we will never see them again. Whoever was separated from us was promptly killed. They hinted darkly at the gas chambers and crematoriums. They told of torture of children. Of medical experiments. They told us we were fortunate our children were killed by gas and then burned. Their children were shot and often tortured or burned alive. Years ago there were no gas chambers, only crematoriums, and whole families were burned in them alive.

When I first heard some of these things I could not sleep. Everyone of us believed they were untrue and told to us by the Polish Jews in order to torture us, to avenge our "soft life." But I wondered. I sensed an ominous, horrible ring of truth to their words. Where would they get such cruel ideas? Where, indeed, are the little children? And the elderly? And the invalids? Where was any provision for them in Auschwitz? I saw our living conditions there, or here in Plaszow. No child, no infirm person can survive under these circumstances. This food, this exposure to cold and heat. The barracks, the facilities. Where are our families? Is it possible that they get "special treatment" as we were made to believe? Why would they get special treatment? Why would the Germans give us sub-animal treatment and to them . . . Is it possible that it is all true? My God, is it true? Is it? What kind of "special treatment" did they receive?

Every night I used to cry myself to sleep. In the morning Mommy would say it is all nonsense. Of course, they are all lies. Incredible, cruel lies. The Polish Jews knew we were ignorant about the camps and were trying to frighten us. Everyone knew the things they said were lies. So was the rumor about bromide in the food. We stopped menstruating because we are near starvation. We lost weight and our organs are too weak to function properly. Look what happened to our breasts.

Mommy was right in that. The breasts began to sag at first and then became virtual hanging sacks. Some very fat ladies had the most ridiculously hanging empty sacks, like long, narrow, stretched-out empty balloons weighed down by a single marble in each, reaching almost to the navel. Then the empty sacks became shorter. Eventually the skin, too, was absorbed and the breasts disappeared completely. We were all like men. Flat. In time the bones began to protrude and shrunken skin lay taut on every pointed bulge.

It is true. Even our stomachs slowed down in time. Hunger became less nagging, and the fullness of the stomach after the evening meal—less satisfying. The women stopped "cooking up" imaginary meals during work, and talk about food became less frequent.

Even talk about our families lessens. We think about them less frequently. We think less and talk less in general.

There remains only our daily routine—the *Zehlappel*, the work commandos, the evening meal. Dodging the more difficult commandos and making every effort to get into lighter ones.

In time we discover that there are less cruel *Kapos*, easier work, a longer lunch period. There are *Arbeitführers* who actually talk to you in polite tones, and get two cauldrons of food instead of one for their commando. There are ways to avoid the worst *Kapos* and to be picked by the nicer ones. In time we learn the game of the camp. This game is the stuff of our life. Beyond it things start to matter less and less.

The stone commando is the worst. We are lined up in a chain reaching the top of a steep hill. From the bottom of the hill large rocks have to be passed through the chain up to the top. The rocks are heavy and the *Kapo* of the stone commando, the most tyrannical. He murdered his father and would boast about it when administering some especially cruel punishment. He demands that the stones be passed quickly. If a stone is dropped, it hurtles against the women below. Work on the stone chain is the dread of the camp.

When Mother and I are picked up for the stone commando, she would order me to pass only the smaller stones, and the larger ones she would pass to the girl beyond me, skipping me. This would be dreadful. Mother would have to lean forward with the heavy rock, balancing it precariously, while the girl above me would have to lean down to receive it from her hand, causing additional burden to her. I would then insist on passing the large rocks and Mother would angrily ignore me. This caused me so much hurt and anxiety that my dread of the stone commando turned into perpetual nightmare. But Mother would not yield. She did not understand that it is easier to bear the heavy stones than her indulgence at the expense of her effort and that of another woman.

There are days when we managed to move a huge hill of rocks to the top of the mountain, and the following day we are ordered to move it down again to the foot of the mountain. With the same speed.

The next in line of hard work is the *Planierung*, the digging and leveling. This is a feared commando mostly because of the *Kapo*, Jacko, who makes it into a torture labor. There is no talking, no stopping for rest. And very little food.

One of the commandos is digging up graves in the nearby Krakow Jewish cemetery. It is being turned into a new concentration camp, an extension to the ground we are leveling for construction. Work in this commando is easier because the large monuments afford shade and hiding places for occasional rest. To me, however, this is the most difficult work. Sometimes you dig up small bones and skulls. The bones of children. Of infants. Despite lowered sensitivity, I am still pained by handling these bones. Despite a lack of contemplative powers, I think about the skeletons long after I am supposed to sleep.

Once I was picked for the cleaning commando, the favorite of commandos. It is a small commando in charge of cleaning the barracks of the Germans. We are given pails and washcloths and told to scrub the floors in about fifty barracks. At noon we are given scraps from the meals of the German soldiers. This makes it into a dream commando. But that day it was Tish'a B'Av, and I was fasting. With tears of regret I gave my lunch to another girl. This is my destiny. Two thousand years ago, the Romans picked the day when I was to taste real food to destroy the Temple in Jerusalem.

One hot day in July our lunch is interrupted by the arrival of large-covered trucks rolling into the square. We have been working in *Planierung* right above the camp and have our lunch on the shady slope directly opposite the center square of the camp. Men and women in civilian clothes descend from the trucks and are herded into the command barrack. They are well-dressed and have an air of independence about them. Like people. Not like camp inmates.

One of the men makes a defiant gesture as an SS man shoves him forward with the point of his gun. The civilian, a man in a light gray trench coat, turns and shoves the German soldier. A shot is heard and the civilian collapses. Then he stands up and begins to run. Another shot. He tumbles. A third shot levels him prone on the ground. He begins to crawl, drawing a line of red in the dust. The SS soldier goes wild. He discharges a barrage of bullets into the crawling figure, then starts kicking him uncontrollably. The others are herded into the barrack of the SS command and the single figure remains lying in the dust in the center of the square, a pool of blood ever widening about him.

We go on eating. There is no time to pause: This is Jacko's commando and the lunch hour is short.

7

Pelagia Lewinska

Nothing was accidental, all was consciously accomplished, all to a specific end. At long last I was grasping the true meaning of Auschwitz; it was created for systematically smashing and destroying people.

PELAGIA LEWINSKA

Although the reasons for her arrest by the Germans were unspecified, a Polish woman named Pelagia Lewinska found herself in Cracow Prison in the winter of 1942–1943. The prison was badly overcrowded, and so the prisoners suspected that one of three fates would be theirs. Of the first two, release seemed much less likely than death. But the third option—concentration camp—seemed even more menacing than death. That fate, which Lewinska called at first "a vertiginous plunge into unfathomable vagueness," began to be hers on January 23, 1943, the date she got her Crawcow Prison departure notice.

Cracow is not far from Auschwitz, only forty miles or so. But the train trip that took Lewinska and about 160 other women to that place was a journey into the unknown. What was unknown would become known—too soon, too well—and yet, Lewinska reports, it could still take time for a prisoner to figure out what was happening at Auschwitz. Twenty Months at Auschwitz, *Lewinska's book about her experience there, uses the detail of life and death in the camp to focus what she calls "the ultimate purpose of Auschwitz." Her observations, after liberation as well as during her captivity, convinced her that Auschwitz existed to smash, destroy, and exterminate people systematically. This purpose meant that, strictly speaking, nothing happened by accident at Auschwitz. Everything—the camp's mud, lice, lack of water, and capricious violence—advanced the intended goals of degradation and destruction.*

84

No Auschwitz memoir is silent about the camp's filth: the stench, the foulness, the squalor, the prisoners' soiling one another when they tried to relieve themselves. Lewinska writes about "the piles of excrement behind the blocks," and she concentrates particularly on the latrines. They were so crude, primitive, and disgusting that "unheard-of disorder reign[ed] there." But, she concluded, these horrible conditions were not a sign of administrative incompetence or uncontrolled chaos. To the contrary, the intention was that Auschwitz prisoners should "die in our own filth . . . drown in mud, in our own excrement." Excremental assault, to use the term that Lewinska helped Terrence Des Pres to coin, was a key part of the logic of destruction.

"The enemy's intention was for us to be devoured by filth," writes Lewinska. "Very well, then, it was necessary to keep clean." Doing so was virtually impossible in Auschwitz, but Lewinska describes her defiant determination to resist the Nazi effort to dehumanize her. Lewinska's struggle was to remain visibly human. Her voice echoes those of other survivors when she insists that "to abandon the struggle meant letting oneself be broken; capitulating meant losing and going under."

Were women, because of their socialization, more concerned than men about cleanliness, about personal hygiene and appearance, despite the lack of water and sanitary facilities in the camps? It is difficult to sustain that argument, although there are scholars who think it is correct. What we do know, based on Lewinska's memoir and those of other women and men, is that when conditions of filth are enforced, befoulment of the body can be experienced as befoulment of the spirit. When this most personal dimension of the human being is violated, when the human spirit is ruined beyond repair, a human being's will to live is destroyed. At Auschwitz, the Nazis knew what they were doing. Nothing, as Lewinska says, was accidental.

Twenty Months at Auschwitz

MUD

On first being seen, the camp impresses one with the extraordinary contrast between its external appearance of total order and the wretchedness that hits one as soon as one crosses its threshold. The tall cement pillars with their glittering lights, the barbed wire enclosure, the high watchtowers—all strike one with the neatness of their construction and maintenance and suggest to the spectator that all is well run.

Yet the camp's interior presents a picture of fearful distress. An alley, constituting the main thoroughfare and bearing the name of the *Lagerstrasse*, runs from the entrance across the entire camp. It is here that the work columns are formed and it is from here that they leave. This is where the main roll calls take place. It is the most dangerous part of the camp, for here pass the SS men and women. At any instant you are in danger of a cudgel blow to the head or a punch in the face for no reason you can determine. Inmates avoid it like the plague when they have to move about. *Lagerstrasse* is more or less paved, and feet do not sink into clay up to the ankles as in the rest of camp but a thick layer of mud covers it, splashing over the feet of those passing through.

Three rows of barracks sheds line each side of *Lagerstrasse*. Wretched, low-built places with roofs awry, doors askew and only tiny windows, they squat along the ground like gypsy huts of greatly expanded length and width. Brown and grey, they are all exactly alike in their forbidding appearance. The rows are twenty feet apart from each other. Narrow paths coming at right angles out of *Lagerstrasse* separate these vast shacks on their transverse side. Ditches have been dug the length of paths and roadways, and the earth thrown up from them forms long embankments. Of course, there are no footbridges. To get to a neighboring block you have to jump across at least one ditch.

At first glance that doesn't seem so terrible but, when you take into consideration the fact that the entire camp is a bottomless pit of clayish mud that constantly sticks to our heavy shoes and that it is hard to pull our feet out of the gluey stuff, you can begin to understand why each step taken, whether under orders or to satisfy our own needs, imposes a strain on our weakened bodies. When, after work, we go to the latrine or in search of water or merely to join a friend in another block, the effort often is too great for our exhausted bodies. The latrines are in the farthest row, and sometimes the struggle to get there is so painful that inmates relieve themselves anywhere en route.

. . . In the beginning such hard facts filled us with veritable horror. We felt within us some of the positive will to act that characterized our former free life. But later . . . later we understood. We were sick, unable to feed ourselves for weeks at a time while typhus epidemics raged, and our bladders were stiff with cold and our legs kept getting more bloated. When we returned from work like that, soaked and frozen, then I understood why the least added effort was literally an act of heroism for so many among us.

And those latrines!

At the outset the living places, the ditches, the mud, the piles of excrement behind the blocks, had appalled me with their horrible filth. The unheard-of disorder reigning there made me think that no real organization existed and that the camp command was totally incapable of carrying out its assignment.

It seemed to me that all was bound to change in time, that we would address the camp authorities with demands and suggestions of self-help so we could put things a bit in order. I recalled how in the Girl Scouts we successfully built forest camps with our own hands. Why not try the same thing here? There were so many women, so many hands to do the work!

I started asking around among the older inmates. With all my heart I wanted to avoid passive acceptance, a prospect which filled me with fear. I still did not understand the true purpose of a Nazi concentration camp. It was the latrines which finally pointed me toward the truth.

The latrines consisted of a large ditch bisected by a narrow board which served as a perch. Even now I do not see the use of this tiny perch which, naturally, was always covered with filth. It was endlessly occupied on both sides. . . . Our backs practically touched and it was not rare for us to soil each other.

And then I saw the light! I saw that it was not a question of disorder or lack of organization but that, on the contrary, a very thoroughly considered conscious idea was in back of the camp's existence. They had condemned us to die in our own filth, to drown in mud, in our own excrement. They wished to abase us, to destroy our human dignity, to efface every vestige of humanity, to return us to the level of wild animals, to fill us with horror and contempt toward ourselves and our fellows. Such was the PURPOSE, the IDEA behind it all!

The Germans made a perfect job of it; they knew we were incapable of looking at each other without disgust. They didn't have to kill a human being in that camp to subject her to suffering; they had only to give her a kick that sent her falling into the mud. Falling equaled perishing. What rose to its feet was no longer human but a ridiculous monster of mud. The SS, with their well-cultivated sense of humor, kicked a woman into the gluey morass of mud as soon as they saw her faltering or plodding along with difficulty. It was impossible to get up by oneself alone, and help was not forthcoming. So, every day when our columns parted for work, several of the weakest—sometimes even dozens of them—would remain behind, immersed in mud.

To pick oneself up, to wash and clean oneself—all that is the simplest thing in the world, isn't it? And yet it was not so. Everything in Auschwitz was so organized as to make these things impossible. There was nothing to lean on; there was no place for washing oneself. Nor was there time. One could only stay in the mud of *Lagerstrasse* where a special unit each day gathered up those who had fallen and threw them on a cadaver pile—whether or not they were still living.

I will never forget one thing I saw in the men's camp one day: some inmates were dragging a man by his legs, the rest of his body, covered with mud, tracing a great furrow in the black mire. If you had seen your child so, oh mother, or you, wife, if you had seen your love and joy in such a state, what would you be saying today to those who speak of pity and generosity toward the conquered master race?

One of my friends and I, as proof of our mutual devotion, exchanged oaths never to leave each other dying in the mud. It seems unbelievable that tendering a helping hand to a fellow human being who falls could be the ultimate proof of devotion, and yet that was so. To help someone rise from the mud meant to risk staying with her in the mud. Our SS lords and masters not only beat those who had fallen, setting their dogs against them, but the SS did the same with those who stayed behind to help if they did not immediately catch up with the work column.

Mud was the queazy foundation of our life; it constituted a purpose and meaning for Auschwitz. We dug ditches in muddy fields and marshlands in a twenty-five-mile radius of Auschwitz. Three thousand women lie in those fields and marshes.

They had already covered up with the mud of Auschwitz itself (and this is not a figure of speech) twelve thousand Soviet prisoners of war who had been kept there. These dead mouldered beneath our great barracks.

WATER

It is my fifth day at Auschwitz. I have been looking everywhere but can find neither a well nor a water tap where our women may wash up in the morning and evening. Nor is there anything like that in the block itself. I disgustedly regard my dirty hands which I have now been washing for several days with snow. Today I am incapable of doing even that because the snow is icier and chaps my hands. I have nothing to dry them on and I no longer have gloves to protect them after washing.

We are always busy, always immersed in that mass of women with whom we arrived. No more than I, can they adjust themselves to the camp's organization. And we have so many other needs tormenting us: we are hungry, cold, in need of sleep, fatigued past all human limits. So the need to maintain one's toilet becomes a secondary matter.

But I finally do stop a longtime inmate who seems to know what is going on around camp and ask her when we will be able to get cleaned up. She considers me, astonished by my naivete, then answers with a smile, "You'll find out by yourself. . . ."

. . . So I would have to make my own research. But when? It was still dark when we got up and by sunrise we were already at work. At night when we returned from work we had to wait in line an hour for food. I hoped Sunday would be the magic day when I could find out where water was available.

Finally, Sunday came and with it a moment of liberty between two rollcalls. I left our shed. Women were squatting in little groups, cleaning their soup bowls with snow. Others were washing hands and faces as well as plates in a ditch that ran the length of the barracks. The ditchwater was green and horribly foul but there was not much snow left and they ignored the foulness. The ditch was the camp's all-purpose sewer; nevertheless, they went right on washing their food utensils in it.

Icy snow revolted me less than that. I approached a small group of French-women who were digging into some snow to get to the cleaner layer beneath. I joined them and we fell into a conversation about the lesson the Germans were giving us in their legendary cleanliness. None knew where we could readily draw water and soon they had to leave, but I did pick up one precious piece of information. There was a built-up latrine area with a real water tap at its side from which water flowed into a ditch. That was all. This place also had some laundry tubs for German inmates to do their washing and was the only spot where one could obtain water for washing and cooking.

And that was in a camp of fourteen thousand women!

I found a crowd of women with pots, basins and pitchers shoving forward to get at that single water tap. I, too, fell in line. My attention was attracted to the way one inmate from time to time would launch a storm of abuse in German at some other prisoner and would chase her away with kicks and punches. It turned out this tub and the water were only for German women. Jewesses had *no* right to go there. As to other Aryans, they could only use it as long as no German women, who had a priority which permitted them to go ahead of the waiting line, were there.

Water was only destined for the superior race.

I didn't have much hope of getting to the tap before the next rollcall but, all the same, I patiently waited, determined to take advantage of this one day's opportunity to wash up a bit. Jewesses, chased from the tap area, begged for a few drops from those lucky ones who had succeeded in filling their receptacles. I wanted that luxury of cleaning myself and yet saw all around me thirst-stricken women with lips burned and chapped by fever and with the large, brilliant eyes of the sick. They hadn't the strength to stand and plead with the others, offering their bread in exchange for a cup of water.

Thirst tormented us all from the first moment, the first spoonful of soup tasting of saltpeter. The coffee or infusion granted us each evening was insufficient to desalt us. In many of the blocks, particularly those of the Jewesses, there was nothing at all to drink in the evening. The unfortunate women surrounded the other sheds and clung to us on the paths, pleading to buy a little to drink at no matter what price. They would give up all their food for that little water.

I did not reach my block with the water that I had obtained so painfully and after such a long wait. The thirsty women begged. I explained to them that one shouldn't drink this water; always before my eyes was the sign over the lone tap—*This water not for drinking purposes*. I remembered the twelve thousand corpses of Soviet prisoners buried in our soil. On top of that I saw myself, so dirty now, about to lose my sole chance to wash myself for the long week ahead. Despite all this, I could not refuse them the water.

Thirst was to be a constant torment for us all, even when we were not suffering from fever. The food, impregnated with saltpeter, burned our entrails and set our mouths afire.

Going and coming from work, it was always the same thought that assailed us and kept us thinking of those ditches and holes en route where we had seen water. Our guards stormed at us, beat us, sent their dogs against us—and in spite of all that, women held their containers always at the ready to make a dash for slop water. No one can render an accurate accounting of all the punishment meted out for such actions. And still it was the same story every time we passed a water area.

People were dying of artificially induced thirst. So what attention did the washing problem merit? We passed days and weeks in this mud, surrounded by all sorts of rot and filth. Our hands were grey, our faces without any color, our eyes bleary. Every bit of skin itched. The women scratched at their wounds and the smell of unwashed bodies suffocated us.

We were here by the thousands, and in my barracks alone there were hundreds jammed together. I had supposed that concentration camps meted out a solitary form of punishment through the deprivation of liberty, hard labor and periods of miserable isolation. Hadn't I seen what prison was like?

But the Nazi concentration camp was a very different thing, a place of slow and inevitable dying. What had at first looked like negligence was basic, deliberate perversion. What had struck me as disorder was thoroughly planned. What had seemed ignorance was the result of great subtlety. They had put into the organizing of these camps all the great German talent for precision, all the degenerated culture of the German spirit, all the absolute brutality of Hitlerism. Nothing was accidental, all was consciously accomplished, all to a specific end. At long last I was grasping the true meaning of Auschwitz; it was created for systematically smashing and destroying people.

Until that moment the blows which fell, one after the other, on us and the loss of those closest to us seemed to have prevented our grasping the true significance of our travail. It had been getting more and more difficult to keep our heads above water, to rise above the moment-to-moment situation, to look straight ahead. But from the instant when I grasped the motivating principle of these German bandits, it was as if I had been awakened from a dream. All right, to perish was to satisfy the enemy's intentions, to fulfill his plans. No! He would not have his way so easily!

I felt under orders to live. It was my duty toward those who were gone, to those who remained and those who awaited us in the free world. My duty toward a great and sacred cause.

I got a new grip on myself to sustain the heritage from my beloved friends and teachers. I had to keep living. I had to husband all my strength so as not to cave in despite all that was happening. And if I did die at Auschwitz, it would be as a human being, I would hold on to my dignity. I was not going to become the contemptible, disgusting brute my enemy wished me to be.

And a terrible struggle began which went on day and night. It lasted from that moment of revelation to the one when, having steeled my will, I threw myself into a stream to escape. To abandon the struggle meant letting oneself be broken; capitulating meant losing and going under.

The enemy's intention was for us to be devoured by filth. Very well then, it was necessary to keep oneself clean.

For us each day represented twelve miles of marching in heavy shoes, and twelve hours of toil with shovel in hand—altogether seventeen hours on our feet. After the return from work a band of us trooped to the single tap with our bowls to get water for making our toilet. Then we sought out a free corner by the latrines and, wetting an end of a rag, cleaned ourselves up.

That, too, was part of the battle.

LICE

There was no place in the camp where prisoners could wash their body linens. People simply did not wash their clothing (clothing originally removed from dead victims of Auschwitz who no longer needed it).

As I already pointed out, the chemise they gave me had seemed to be stitched with a special dark thread. A companion in my berth had shown me that it was neither threads nor knots in the material but lines of tiny insects. I had the great good fortune to share my berth with women who, like me, were steeling themselves to battle against dirt and lice. They helped me both in word and in deed. Unhappily, there were more opportunities for picking up lice from others than getting rid of those we already had. Each day we picked up some at rollcalls, during marches and waiting in the queue for food.

It is hard for people to imagine just how overwhelmed a person can be by the devious inroads of lice. Not only by their bites that carry typhus and death but also by the way, night and day, they irritate the skin and keep one, puffy-eyed, from sleep, and by the way they cover the body with sores and pus. Thousands of the women who died at Auschwitz were killed by lice. Typhus, borne by them, was something almost all the women suffered from at one time or another and it occupied second place among all epidemics in number of victims.

We were helpless in the face of such infestations. The shed was not illuminated. We had neither the time nor the place for freeing ourselves of the parasites which gnawed at us. That is why we looked forward to Sunday with its brief respite from call-ups. It was then that we hoped to clean ourselves up. We had to organize not to lose this unique opportunity.

The women would undress and spread their clothes out on their bunks or in front of the blocks. Those in passable health seized every chance to go through their clothing. We did not have a moment to ourselves during the course of the day, although we lost long hours twice a day in roll calls. Naturally, the roll calls were too "dignified" for us to be permitted even a furtive search in our clothing while they went on. Consequently, many women had to sacrifice their eating time to hunt down their lice.

We presented such a funny picture! After my escape I saw posters showing a detainee in a German camp. He was tranquilly seated on a bench behind barbed wire close to a barracks and . . . doing nothing else, he was looking straight ahead.

My artist friend, you do not know what they were actually trying to make of your brothers and sisters. The true picture of this mass of women devoting their free moments to delousing themselves invariably suggested their resemblance ... to monkeys! And yet these were mothers, wives, young girls, *human beings* struggling furiously to hold on to their dignity in the most monstrous conditions imaginable.

What, in these circumstances, was the fate of the ill, lying at least three or four in the same bed? The lice were everywhere, not only in their scalps which, fortunately, were tonsured, but even in their eyebrows. Our blankets, as one sick woman said, were woven by and with lice. It's difficult to grasp that, and yet it is the precise truth.

They never changed our body linens and never washed them. Instead they tried a delousing procedure. Every three months they took away the clothes of all the barracks inhabitants and along with these carried the blankets and mattresses to the gas chambers. During this time, the women took steam baths and then showers—if there was enough water. But their clothing came back even dirtier, foul with the odor of gas and warmed-over sweat. We sought, as much as possible, to escape this procedure, which often had a result precisely contrary to the ostensible intentions of those organizing the clean-up. The gas was too weak, did not always kill the lice and did no harm whatsoever to the nits.

On top of that, the inmates who had managed to clean away most of their parasites ended up reinfested. All this was accompanied by so many humiliations, hours passed naked in bitter cold, truncheon blows from those guardians of order, the SS men. No wonder we considered these delousing sessions as one more miserable torment in our miserable lives.

But you cannot say that the Germans gave *no* thought to body linens. Yes, they thought about them. Trucks, whole trains, filled with the most beautiful linens, rich vestments plundered from their victims, went to Germany. There they were placed on sale in shops where all was kept neat and clean.

The linens warehouses were inspected on the occasion of visits from superior authorities of the SS. It was difficult to know for whom these goods were destined—surely not directly for us. But indirectly, yes! Simply put, we stole them. We aptly called this theft process "organizing." The "Organization" was our savior. Obviously only those who worked in the appropriate service could do the stealing. It was these wonderful workers in warehouse stores who, despite prohibitions, seizures, beatings and the threat of the special penitents' column, the *strafkolonne*, "organized" and brought to others the stolen goods. These effects were passed around from friend to friend, and one could buy them with food or other provisions. Of course, we could not obtain enough clothing items to meet all our basic needs, but the few items we obtained were all that saved us from our tragic situation. From time to time people even had to throw relatively new, pretty things into the latrines because they were so filthy and there was no water to wash them.

I will never forget you, Jeanne, the schoolteacher, nor you, Salome, the laundress from Cracow; sometimes you came late in the evening, most often when it was very dark outside, bearing a warm slip for someone, stockings for other women and me. It is thanks to you, brave "organizers," that the Germans did not succeed in exterminating all of us.

In principle, it was forbidden for us to have any linens save what we had on us. It was not permitted for such items to be left behind on the bunks. And at the same time we were not supposed to carry anything extra on us. Special searches, beatings, punishments, confiscations, all these befell us endlessly.

We shunned encounters with the authorities whoever they were, always menaced by them, always uncertain from what direction the next blow would fall. As nothing could be left behind in the bunk, we carried all our "organized" wealth in a little sack and under other clothing—to roll call, to work, everywhere. Unfortunately, we never held on long to a towel or handkerchief because of seizures in those perpetual special inspections.

Undisciplined, not submitting, we would give up meals to make new efforts to procure other necessities. And things went on that way. I sometimes had the impression that the Germans felt themselves helpless in the face of our incorrigible "organization." As for us, we never had a moment of security, of tranquillity, neither at roll calls nor at work nor on the march. We were always under surveillance and living under the threat of the truncheon. After my flight from the transport, when I had come out of the water under a bridge which hid me, my first feeling was of astonishment at finding for a certainty that I was walking all by myself and that there was nobody behind me armed with a gun or cudgel.

At Auschwitz we were always asking ourselves whether we would ever succeed in freeing ourselves from this perpetual fear, if we would know how to find ourselves once more, to liberate the human being still deep within each of us! . . .

A DAY IN CAMP

The columns are returning from work. It is about six in the evening. Today the sun, hidden behind dense layers of clouds, cannot serve as our clock. It has been drizzling all day, a rain as fine as fog. The humid southwest wind has soaked our clothes through. Auschwitz is not only the land of mud but also that of windy weather.

Our spattered clogs are heavy and slow the rhythm of our march. The softened roadway, broken by deep ruts and puddles, stops us from keeping step. The front ranks move comparatively quickly but behind them several hundred women drag themselves along, no longer in neat rows of five across. Still pushed forward by threats and blows, they try to catch up. The weakest bring up the rear and suffer a double martyrdom, because under the rain of blows they must keep running. Being at the rear demands the most effort of all.

The column has stretched out a great deal today and, although the overseers keep screaming *"Auf gehen!"* (get going), and liberally distribute punches, many of the women are scattered far behind, trying to drag themselves along. The wind whips rain across body and face, knocking the breath from one's lungs. Wet clothes stick to the flesh, and water trickles down one's back. While the camp's pillars and towers are already visible on the horizon, it's still a long, hard way to go today. We raise our bent heads to estimate with a longing look the distance still separating us from the gate and how long it will take to get there.

The tiring road back has drained us all of strength and we mechanically place one foot ahead of the other like robots. Our yearning for the dark, stifling block gives the measure of our exhaustion. Finally the pestilential, rotten stench attacks our nostrils and heralds our approach. The fetid air of Auschwitz is already assailing us from a mile away, thickening with each step until the nose becomes deadened to it.

We are now at the entry gate. The guards spread out on both sides with their dogs who, wet and muddy, have lost even the desire to bark and stand sullenly apart from the column. The chief woman overseer, the *Oberaufseherin*, is counting us as we come in. The women already inside are lined up for roll call. We, too, take our places in the *Lagerstrasse* and stare at those still coming in. Each woman carried two bricks or a log. Our chiefs, faithful to the rules, have not forgotten that people returning from work ought not to march with empty hands. Free hands would make marching easier which, in turn, would give one the chance to do some thinking.

Now appear the SS ladies on their bicycles, in a hurry to finish the roll call. Although shod in high leather boots and protected by hooded capes, they also suffer from this bad weather and want to be done with their daily duties. Thanks to that, the roll call is briefer than usual.

Eight hundred women return to our block with but one thought in mind, to get out of their wet clothing and, sheltered from the rain which has been falling fifteen hours today, to spread out a blanket that, as always, is damp but at least is not soaked like their clothes. Where to put these things, though, so they can dry a little overnight? There is no place. One will have to put one's jacket over the blanket. As to the dress, matters will be more complicated. The only thing is to double over the blanket with the dress in between to keep it from whatever has dried. Of course, the question of completely or even half drying them out does not arise. If one puts them on again tomorrow and there's no rain, they will then dry out in the field, and if it rains, it will at least be a bit more difficult for water to seep through the material shrunken the night before.

As to our feet, the problem is worse. Our footwear is not dry day or night. And if you can't struggle along in wooden clogs for twelve miles day after day, your feet in leather shoes must *always* be soaked. The paper with which we wrap our feet will protect them a little as long as movement and humidity don't ruin it. Our feet hurt all night. Sometimes it takes hours for the iciness to disappear. Sometimes they do not warm up at all and one passes the night shivering with cold until morning.

The first moment when we put our rags back on is horrible; the whole body is seized with trembling. The wet clothes have been steaming all night, have been penetrated through and through with a repugnant odor, and our one hope lies in the sun coming out and drying them.

But now we have to get our evening meal of bread and coffee, for which the eight hundred women of this block must wait in line at least an hour. It will be eight o'clock by the time we have our food and get into our crowded bunks to eat it and then rest. There have been times when we were simply too tired to stand a whole hour more in these sopping garments. To sit down at any cost! Today we have been seventeen hours on our feet and now we will have no rest either while awaiting our food because there is no dry place to sit down.

Our poor feet are puffed up after all the effort and, ankles swollen, refuse to carry us further. We are also suffering from varicose veins; in Auschwitz it is one's legs that work hardest of all.

To have been subject to the forces of nature for twenty months and often this many hours at a stretch! Come rain, snow, ice or broiling sun, no matter, you must stay in the fields. Rocks, subject to erosion, wear away, but human strength is greater than that of rocks. It finds the hardness of diamonds in the will that *demands one survive . . .*

Field toil was considered the most terrible of all work assignments in camp because of the effort it demanded. Moreover, being away from camp the greater part of the day made it all the harder to organize one's personal life. And women who kept working in the fields were considered social pariahs by the other inmates. Almost every prisoner had to do such work for a time before, possibly, being passed on to something else. This was insisted upon by the German authorities.

I belonged to a very small group of intellectuals who had deliberately chosen permanent field toil. During twenty months of my imprisonment I only worked out there. Why? It's possible that my peasant beginnings, plus tourist and scouting experiences, contributed to the decision as much as my personal nature. Freed of the surrounding barbed wire, my thoughts could wander more uninhibitedly. And then out in the field there were trees and grass—nature. After three months in Cracow Prison and a few days in camp, the sight of a growing tree moved me deeply. Some beauty was accessible even to the inmates of a German concentration camp!

In camp it was very different. What tightened one's heart during long hours of roll calls was the picture our surroundings presented. Swarms of crows perched on the roofs of our shed-barracks, sharpening their beaks and waiting. I never saw a sparrow or any other kind of songbird at Auschwitz.

Then there were the hordes of mice, everywhere, hiding in our bunks, sharing the bread we kept at our side for morning, brushing past our faces, awakening us through the night. And finally, the camp was the rats' kingdom. Human cadavers were gnawed at each night. The rats lived in clover here.

Once, during a roll call, haunted by those crows, I suddenly saw an animal on the roof of one of the blocks. Joy shook me from my torpor; there was a cat here, man's friend, destroyer of mice! On closer observation, though, I noticed something strange about the animal, and when it turned its head toward me I no longer had any doubts: it was an enormous rat. In one bound it jumped into a chimney and disappeared. I shuddered. Was even nature turning away from us, condemned as we were to death? Only crows and rats and mice remained our companions. I raised my eyes, seeking support elsewhere, but the sky itself was barred from my view by the flames and smoke of the crematory oven.

Death! Everywhere death! Here was my biggest reason for preferring work in the fields.

The way back from work was hardest on rainy days. Fatigue became deadly and the thought of standing in the queue destroyed all desire to eat. But the urge to have a few swallows of hot coffee pushed us to a final effort and we usually decided to join the line. Reason told us, also, that the bread was absolutely essential as the basic part of our food for the following day.

Little candle flames gleamed here and there in the shed's darkness. Seated on their bunks, women remained silent, their faces closed, unhappy, even sinister. What were they considering? The fate that drove them into this abyss of misery, the mother who brought them into the world to suffer, the Germans who ripped them from their homes and reduced them to an animal existence? It was impossible to control one's reflexes in such suffering. Grief, compacted and aggravated, would explode and the resulting rage be turned on one's closest neighbor because she had jostled by, upset some coffee, or done something even more trivial.

When I used to look at our women's bitter faces I sensed, like a seismograph, the degree of their enervation and hunger. Of course, things were different when a common ideal united people. But it could not always be like that in such a motley mass of humanity as Auschwitz contained.

Ah, if we only had some little corner permitting one an instant of isolation with one's grief and the chance to ease nervous pressures! But here, too, the Germans gave proof of fiendish ingenuity. By forcing us to live *en masse* twenty-four hours a day, they were attempting to make hateful *all* collective living, to destroy all fraternal solidarity among us. The chance to live alone or with only a few people in a room, to have a corner of one's own, to have a separate existence—that chance was unthinkable and had become the most fantastic of dreams.

Black silhouettes stirred at all levels in the barracks darkness. Here is the over-all view that women on top bunks got: other inmates of top bunks, immobile, extended on their backs, still others sitting on their haunches staring at some invisible point, a few still holding bread on their knees and eating, others picking through their clothing for lice and (this more rarely) little groups conversing here and there in the block. The middle area of the bunks looked like a puppet show. Here people could only sit doubled up or they had to stretch out with their sticklike limbs restricted to minimal gesturing. As for those lowest down, you couldn't see them at all. They slipped into their bunks as if sliding into dank tombs.

Now was the time to try to clean up. Not many could make the effort, though. In truth, if it had been solely a matter of physical cleanliness, none of us would have had the necessary courage. But for some of us it was something more, an act of will to show ourselves we could defy Auschwitz. It was our part in an act of protest which said: We will not let ourselves be broken!

As for me, forcing myself to clean my footwear was one of the ways to reaffirm self-mastery. Most of the time the effort was useless; the next morning after taking a few steps the shoes were as dirty as the evening before. Nevertheless, it gave my morale a boost. So each evening, half-dead, I cleaned my footwear.

The nights which should have given us renewed strength were brief. During my first days in Auschwitz, the nightmarish reality of the place exceeded my capacity to comprehend, exceeded any human conception of monstrousness, and seemed a sick fantasy, some impossibly cruel dream. By way of contrast, night brought dreams which were the true reality: beloved friends, home, normal responsibilities with their joys and sorrows. The dream life was real. What I lived on awakening was only a nocturnal nightmare. Nights I lived my normal life, days my terrible dreams.

This reversal of things was not unique with me. Thanks to it, I was able to survive those first, most difficult days and weeks. When we newcomers met women who had already been at Auschwitz two or three months we viewed them with both skepticism and admiration. To live that way for two months, sixty days, when each day seemed like an unending century to us, that was impossible. And yet I, myself, came to survive over twenty months of it!

Night not only brought some relief to our bodies but, in permitting us another, dreamed reality, gave new strength to our spirits.

Unfortunately it is soon three in the morning and the whistles, accompanied by the command *"Aufstehen!"* (stand up), wrench us from our own world, plunging us back into Auschwitz. We have to get up quickly and cautiously go about our business so as not to lose our things or upset those of our berthmates. Every movement must be logically controlled so we won't lose any of those little things whose great importance can later become all too evident.

I never fully understood the importance of small details until sad camp experience taught me. All I had to do was lose some bit of string with which I tied a clog. The poorly attached clog would then stick in the mud and fall off my foot. Even if I got it back, my foot was filthy. If I didn't, I would have to return barefooted through miles of mud. As to later consequences, one can easily imagine them. It was the same with other details which at first looked so trivial and harmless—with consequences which could become so tragic and deadly.

We don't have time to dress before the block overseers start ordering people to go for the big coffee kettles. There are no volunteers for this job which everybody tries to dodge because it means a walk through many yards of deep mud across newly dug ditches and in total darkness, all the while lugging a kettle containing about twenty-five gallons.

Coffee is quickly distributed and we drink it standing up. This is our breakfast and must sustain us through work until noon when we will have our bowl of soup. It is soon four o'clock and we must group ourselves in columns for roll call.

> . . . The stars go out above us.
> Dawn is still a grey smudge . . .
> A baby cries in my home.
> Perhaps mother's remembering me?
> Will I ever see her again? . . .

Our wandering thoughts seek out the distant home which is ceasing to exist for us. The stars are going out above Auschwitz and the plume of flaming, red smoke over the crematory lights up the dark morning. It never goes out, night or day.

At five the overseers make the roll call. While we await its end, the sky keeps getting lighter but the sun has not yet risen when we start marching (it is about six o'clock by German time but five by the sun).

The overseers and *kapos* after roll call have taken over the column and will soon be joined by the chiefs and guards with their dogs. We are already outside the camp. The barking of the dogs and the cries of the overseers deafen us. But soon our thoughts are returning to our homes as we wonder whether any world still exists other than this one of prison garb and rifle-bearing guards moving along with their dogs.

Finally we arrive at the ditches, already tired but with shovel in hand. It will be impossible really to think until the soup break. It would be difficult to say which is most exhausting, the physical effort or the terrible sterility of long hours when the mind grasps nothing but the boring labor of ditch-digging. But hard work is preferable to easier forms of monotony because time that is passed unperceived wearies us less even if our limbs end up aching.

The afternoon goes a little more quickly and we impatiently wait for the whistle announcing the end of work. And then, once more, our column lines up in ranks of five. The sun is now far down the sky. It is six o'clock. Auschwitz's inmates are returning from work.

And thus pass our days, our weeks, our months.

8

Charlotte Delbo

No one believes she'll return when she's alone.

CHARLOTTE DELBO

What did it take to survive? Ingenuity? Cunning? Defiance? Were the claims of self-interest sounder, more logical, than concern for others? What made the difference between giving up and holding out?

As the preceding selection by Pelagia Lewinska shows, water was essential for survival in Auschwitz. Charlotte Delbo, whose writing has appeared earlier in this book, makes a similar point: There was morning thirst, afternoon thirst, evening thirst, and night thirst—each different, all the same. To drink was to be alive, but thirst was everywhere. Prisoners died from it, not least because any water to be found was likely to be polluted. The thirst that only water can quench was especially acute and agonizing; many Auschwitz memoirs say so. But not all thirst is the kind that water can quench. In None of Us Will Return, *Delbo had much to say about thirst of other kinds as well.*

After World War II, Delbo declared, "I must not be discussed as a woman writer. I am not a woman in my writing." She even told her friend Cynthia Haft that there was not "a distinctive female experience of the Holocaust," arguing that "the camp system grants complete equality to men and women." Her themes—for example, hunger, fear, nudity, death, memory, courage, and thirst—do transcend gender distinctions. Yet a play she wrote after the Holocaust, Who Will Carry the Word, *has an all-woman cast and "Lulu," the poignant vignette reprinted here, has distinctly feminine qualities.*

"As soon as you're alone, you think: What good does it do? What for? Why not give up . . . on the spot?" Delbo responds to herself by saying "Surrounded by the others, one

99

is able to hold out." Whether their memoirs do so more than men's is not the point, but the testimonies of Auschwitz women often stress the encouragement and comfort women gave one another in that place. "Lulu looks at me, smiling. Her hand grazes mine, to comfort me," Delbo recalls. In Auschwitz the two of them developed a bond of friendship that was nurturing, tender, and understanding. When Charlotte says "I can't take it anymore," Lulu, "a practical woman," intuitively senses that Charlotte needs to have "a good cry." She takes the risk of shielding her friend from sight. "Softly" she wipes Charlotte's tears. Lulu, "a practical woman," also makes her stop crying and get back to work when danger nears.

Being "a practical woman" could entail the attitude that Ella Lingens-Reiner reports in her Auschwitz memoir, Prisoners of Fear: *"How did I keep alive in Auschwitz?" she heard another survivor say. "My principle is: myself first, second and third. Then nothing. Then myself again—and then all the others." Auschwitz was deadly; survival required looking out for oneself. Yet in recalling a moment of intimacy and care between two women—"It's as though I had wept against my mother's breast"—Charlotte Delbo shows an example of simple human kindness that helped one woman hold out and not give up. We who never experienced the Nazi death camps will never know the depth or intensity of the suffering they caused. But because of women like Lulu, we can hear better what many women feel when they bear witness that not only self-interest but also kinship and friendship, bonding with other women, were the basis for their emotional, and often physical, coping and survival.*

Lulu

We were deep down in that ditch since early morning. The three of us. The commando was working further on. From time to time the kapos prodded us, just to see where we were at digging that ditch again. We were able to talk, had been talking since early morning.

To talk was to plan going home, because to believe we would return was a way of forcing luck's hand. Those who had stopped believing they were going back were dead. One had to believe it, against all odds, incredible as it might seem, one had to lend to this return certainty, reality and color, to prepare it by conjuring up each and every detail.

Occasionally, one of the women voicing a common thought interjected: "How do you envision getting out?" There we were. The question sank in silence.

To shake off silence and the anguish it covered, another would venture:

From Charlotte Delbo, *None of Us Will Return*, trans. Rosette C. Lamont, vol. 1: *Auschwitz and After*. New Haven, Conn.: Yale University Press, 1992. Copyright © 1992 by Yale University Press. Reprinted by permission of Yale University Press.

"Perhaps one day we'll no longer wake up for roll call. We'll sleep a long time. When we'll wake it'll be broad daylight, and the camp will be still. Those who'll step out first from the barracks will notice that the guard post is empty. All the SS will have fled. A couple of hours later, the Russian reconnaissance units will be here."

Another silence answered this anticipation.

She added: "First, we will have heard the cannons' report. Far off at first, then drawing closer. The battle of Cracow. With Cracow taken it'll be the end. You'll see, the SS will flee."

The more detailed her description, the less we believed it. By tacit agreement, we'd drop the subject and pick up again our impossible plans with that particular logic of all crazy talk.

We were talking since early morning, glad to be away from the rest of the commando, away from the kapos' shouts. We didn't have to bear the truncheon's blows punctuating these shouts. The ditch was getting deeper with every passing hour. Our heads no longer protruded over the top. As we reached the marl, we stood with our feet in water. The mud we cast over our heads was white. It wasn't cold—one of the first mild days. The sun warmed our shoulders. We were at peace.

A kapo came along, shouting. She signaled to my companions to get out, and marched them off. The ditch was deep enough, not sufficient work for three. My friends knew well the fear each and every one of us feels when we're separated from the rest, when we're left alone. To hearten me, they said: "Come on, hurry up. You'll join us."

I'm alone at the bottom of the ditch, desperate. The others' presence, their words made a return possible. They've left and I'm afraid. I can't believe I'll ever return when I'm alone. With them there, since they seem to believe in it so firmly, I believe in it also. As soon as they leave me, I'm seized with panic. No one believes she'll return when she's alone.

Here I am, at the bottom of the ditch, alone, and so disheartened that I wonder whether I'll reach the end of the day. How many hours are left before the blow of the whistle which marks the end of work, the moment we line up to go back to camp, in ranks of five, arm in arm, talking, talking to distraction?

Here I am all alone. I can't think of anything any longer, because all my thoughts collide with the anguish which dwells in all of us: How will we get out of here? When will we get out? I'd like to think of nothing. But if this lasts, no one will get out. Those who are still alive say to themselves each day that it's a miracle they held out for eight whole weeks. No one can see further than a week ahead.

I'm alone and frightened. I try to keep on digging. The work isn't moving. I attack a last bump at the bottom, evening it out. Perhaps the kapo will decide it's enough. I feel my bruised back, its curve paralyzed, my shoulders torn by the shovel, my arms unable to cast spadefuls of muddy marl over the top. I'm here, all alone. I feel like lying down in the mud to wait. To wait for the kapo to find me dead. It's not so easy to die. It takes a long time, hitting someone with a shovel, or a bludgeon, before he dies.

I continue digging a little longer, scooping up two or three spadefuls of earth. It's too hard. As soon as you're alone, you think: What good does it do? What for? Why not give up . . . Better now, on the spot. Surrounded by the others, one is able to hold out.

I'm all alone, alone with my haste to join my companions, and my temptation to give up. Why? Why must I keep on digging this ditch?

"Enough! That's it for now!" A voice shouts from above. "*Komm schnell!*" I pull myself out, leaning on the shovel. My arms are weary, the back of my neck aches. The kapo is running. She runs across the road by the side of the marsh. There's the fill. Women like ants. Some carry sand to those who pound it flat, levelling the terrain. A huge, flat space, stretching under the sun. Hundreds of women are standing, like a frieze of shadows profiled against the light.

I follow the kapo who hands me a pounder and a blow. She directs me towards a team of workers. I look for my friends. Lulu calls me: "Come next to me, there's a spot," and she makes room for me, in the line of women who are pounding the ground, holding the pounder with both hands as they raise it, and let it fall. "Come here, to pestle the rice!" How does Viva find the strength to joke like this? I can't move my lips, even to venture a smile. Lulu is worried: "What's the matter with you? Are you ill?"

"No, I'm not ill. I can't take it anymore. I'm all in today."

"That's nothing. You'll get over it."

"No, Lulu, I won't. I'm telling you I can't take it any more."

She didn't answer anything. It's the first time she heard me speak like this. A practical woman, she lifts my tool. "Your pounder is real heavy. Take mine. It's lighter and you're more tired than I am because of the ditch."

We exchange tools. I start pounding the sand, like the others. I look at all these women going through the same gestures, with their arms weaker and weaker as they raise the heavy mass. Armed with their bludgeons, the kapos move from one to the other. I am overwhelmed with despair. "How will we ever get out of here?"

Lulu looks at me, smiling. Her hand grazes mine, to comfort me. And I repeat, letting her know it's useless: "I'm telling you I can't take it any more today. This time it's true."

Lulu has a good look around us, and seeing there's no kapo nearby she takes hold of my wrist, saying: "Get behind me, so they won't see you. You'll be able to have a good cry." She speaks in a whispering, timid voice. Probably this is just what I needed since I obey her gentle shove. Dropping my tool upon the ground, but still leaning on its long handle, I cry my eyes out. I thought I did not want to cry, but my tears welled up, and they're running down my cheeks. I let them flow, and when one of them touches my lips, I taste the salt and go on weeping.

Lulu continues to work and stay on the lookout at the same time. Occasionally she turns back, and with her sleeve, softly, wipes my face. I keep on crying. I'm not thinking of anything. I just go on crying.

Now I no longer know why I am crying, when Lulu suddenly pulls me: "That's enough now! Back to work. Here she comes!" She says it so kindly that I'm not ashamed of having cried. It's as though I had wept against my mother's breast.

9

Gisella Perl

I had to remain alive. . . . It was up to me to save the life of the mothers, if there was no other way, then by destroying the life of their unborn children.

GISELLA PERL

For a woman in Auschwitz there were few, if any, "crimes" greater than pregnancy. Normally, as numerous survivors attest, only if the baby perished did the mother have a chance to prolong her life. In that place there was little respite from the inhuman: "No one will ever know what it meant to me to destroy those babies," Dr. Gisella Perl testifies in her memoir, I Was a Doctor in Auschwitz, which was first published in 1948. To destroy life to preserve life—that "choiceless choice" was among the monstrous cruelties forced uniquely on women during the Holocaust and at Auschwitz in particular.

A Hungarian Jew, Dr. Gisella Perl was an obstetrician and gynecologist who practiced medicine in her hometown of Sighet. Her husband was a surgeon; before the Germans arrived in 1944, they operated a small hospital. Except for her daughter Gabriella, who was hidden during the war with a non-Jewish family, Perl and her family were seized by the Gestapo and deported to Auschwitz–Birkenau. There the infamous Dr. Josef Mengele "selected" her to run a "hospital" ward within the confines of the death camp. Under the most primitive conditions—no beds, bandages, drugs, or instruments—she tended the tortured, starving, diseased, and dying with her only remedies: "words, encouragement, tenderness."

When the Red Army approached in January 1945, the Germans evacuated Perl to Berlin, then to a labor camp near Hamburg, and finally to Bergen-Belsen. Liberated by the British in April 1945, she never again saw her parents or her *husband and son. After the war, she immigrated to the United States, received American citizenship by a special act of Congress in 1948, and practiced medicine in New York City until she went to Israel in the 1970s. There she worked at the Shaare Zedek Medical Center in Jerusalem, often caring for the children of former prisoners she had assisted in Auschwitz and helping, in particular, women who had difficulty conceiving. Perl died in 1985.*

Different horrors, same hell—Gisella Perl's testimony makes Myrna Goldenberg's phrase ring true. Women and men did suffer the "same hell" at Auschwitz, but the horrors were often remarkably different. Perl illustrates both the hell and the horrors with vivid detail.

Hunger? "We waited for food with the same burning impatience, the same excited imagination with which a young girl waits for her lover." And when "it" finally arrived, these starving women ate the "horrible concoction" from containers that only a short time before had been used "for entirely different purposes": bodily waste.

Shoes? "Shoes were a question of life and death." After two months of being without any, Dr. Perl managed to exchange "two days' bread ration" for a pair, but they were too big. She needed a "piece of ordinary string" to keep them on her feet. Eventually she discovered that an old Polish prisoner—"a short, stocky, pock-marked man" deprived of "his last vestige of human dignity"—had the string she needed. Yes, he would trade it, not for her bread ration but for sex. "How high the price of a piece of string had soared," Perl recalls.

When there is nothing to trade, what does a woman have but her body? Women who in their former lives might never have dreamed of "prostitution," often had no alternative during the Holocaust. In Auschwitz everything—real food, shoes, clothing, pots, combs, even string—cost something. "Love" might have to be a woman's commodity of exchange. Particularly when a woman is starving to death, "joyless sexual intercourse" may be her only option.

Hitler's "new world order" excluded Jews. It followed that Jewish women and their newly born or unborn babies were doomed. When she realized the fate that awaited pregnant women, especially Jews, Gisella Perl became a clandestine Auschwitz abortionist. She was determined to save all the pregnant women she could. "If I had not done it," she says, "both mother and child would have been cruelly murdered." It was that simple, that difficult, to be a woman in Auschwitz—same hell, different horrors.

A Doctor in Auschwitz

DINNER AT AUSCHWITZ

We had always known that hunger existed. We had read Knut Hamsun's book *Hunger* and suffered together with his hero, and we had read Fink's *I am hungry*... But the great writer who could describe the hunger we had to endure at Auschwitz has yet to be born.

No one who has not experienced the unbearable pain of hunger during the intervals between Auschwitz dinners has any idea as to what hunger really means.

At night, lying on the cold boards of our cage, we tried to pacify our throbbing entrails with the promise of food. Tomorrow we'll get dinner—we said to ourselves. Tomorrow they'll distribute some warm food.

In the morning, when we had to stand roll call under the clouds tinged red by the flames of the crematory, we were trembling with expectancy, hardly able to stand the slow passing of time until dinner. Standing or kneeling, in scorching heat, or driving rain or snow, we had only one thought, one desire carried by our blood-stream into every part of our body: food... We were hungry. We wanted food. Warm food...

We waited for the food with the same burning impatience, the same excited imagination with which a young girl waits for her lover. Dinner was the most important moment of the day, the only moment worth living for.

The kitchen was far away from the barracks, at the end of the camp, and that was where they prepared our luxurious dinner: the turnip soup. When the soup was done, the prisoners working in the kitchen put out the tremendous pots on the street, thirty to fifty pots in a line. Then, under constant supervision by the SS women, these pots were carried to the barracks to be distributed among the inmates.

The block superintendent, the Blockova, chose ten to twelve prisoners to be sent for the soup. "Dinner distribution!" she yelled, and the poor, starved skeletons took their places in their cages to wait for the life-giving liquid. Our tortured stomachs hurt more and more at the thought of food, our salivary glands worked overtime and we could already feel the smell of food in our noses long before it arrived.

Finally it arrived. It was there. The superintendent stood in the middle of the floor beside the steaming pot and distributed the horrible concoction into three-quart containers, which were to serve six prisoners each. The containers

From Gisella Perl, *I Was a Doctor in Auschwitz*. Salem, N.H.: Ayer Company, Publishers, Inc., 1984. Copyright © 1988 by the American Committee for Shaare Zedek Hospital in Jerusalem, Inc. Reprinted by permission of the American Committee for Shaare Zedek Hospital in Jerusalem, Inc.

were dirty and smelly, having been used the night before for entirely different purposes, but their smell blended beautifully with the indescribable smell of the turnip soup. We didn't care. It was warm and it was food, even if there were pieces of wood, potato peeling and unrecognizable substances swimming in it.

The container went from hand to hand and we swallowed quickly, convulsively, so as to get some of it down before the next in line grabbed it from our hands. We counted each other's swallows, jealously, enviously, careful that none of us should get more than her share. Sometimes we agreed that everyone should get ten mouthfuls and waited patiently for our turn. Ten miserable mouthfuls and it was over. We were hungrier than before . . . If only once we could have kept the whole container to ourselves! If only once we could have eaten the whole three quarts of soup alone! How much strength, how much new hope we would have gained from having our hunger stilled, at least once.

Sometimes the can fell out of a weakened hand and the soup spilled over, leaving nothing for the sixth person whose mute tears were the most terrible punishment for the offender whose carelessness had deprived her of the miserable nourishment.

Dinner was over and the barracks were loud with the screams, the plaints of the prisoners who were begging for a little more, just a little more soup. But the pots were empty; two prisoners picked them up and carried them back to the kitchen to be filled again, tomorrow, with the same miserable amount of thin, unnourishing liquid, which would again leave us hungrier, more unhappy than before.

Quickly the strongest, most energetic among us jump down from their cages and run to the door, where they catch up with the prisoners carrying the empty pot. Screaming, pushing each other aside, fighting, they stick their arms into the pot to get another mouthful of turnips or potato peeling, which stuck to the side of the pot.

Sometimes they come face to face with the last transport of soup intended for the last of the barracks. Like wild animals they attack the carriers, unmindful of the blows and kicks showering down on them, and using their palms as spoons try to get a little more food into their unsatisfied stomachs. There must have been something in that turnip soup, I don't know what, that made us hungrier than we were before.

I always was busiest after dinner. There were bleeding heads to bandage, broken ribs to be taped, scratches to be cleaned, burn wounds to be soothed. I worked and worked, knowing only too well that it was hopeless, because tomorrow everything would begin again, even the patients would probably be the same.

Dinner distribution was over, and before we had swallowed the last mouthful we already began to wait for tomorrow, hoping that then, maybe, we would at last be able to satisfy our gnawing, desperate hunger.

And not far from us, at the other end of the camp at the SS kitchen, cooks dressed in white were preparing the most elaborate dishes, white bread, sweets, and real coffee with cream, for our jailers. . . .

THE VALUE OF A PIECE OF STRING . . .

One day followed another in a horrible, nerve-racking monotony and the third month of my stay in Auschwitz arrived without my even being aware of it. We had long ago lost track of time, holding on in our minds to the past, the only escape from insanity. We sank deeper and deeper into the sub-human existence where filth, pain, and crime were natural, and a decent impulse, a human gesture, something to be sneered at and disbelieved. I knew that I had died on that March 19, when the Germans overran Hungary and compelled us to give up everything that meant anything to us, pushing us into a ghetto first, then robbing us of possessions, freedom and finally even of human dignity, in this seething, crawling, burning inferno. Here I was only a shadow without identity, alive only by the power of suffering.

It took a piece of string to shake me out of my apathy and remind me that while there was one single breath in me I could not permit myself to be engulfed in this swamp of human depravity.

For two months I had stood on my bare feet during the two daily roll calls. I had no shoes. My feet swelled up and were covered with sores—which was not only painful but also dangerous. Sore feet were reason enough for our Dr. Mengele to send us to the crematory. I had to have shoes . . . shoes at any price . . . Then one of the women working near the crematory stole a pair of shoes for me in exchange for my two days' bread ration. Hunger was not new to me, in a way, I had become accustomed to it, and after only two months at Auschwitz my strength was still holding out—but shoes were a question of life and death.

I received a pair of men's shoes, about size ten, and I refused to listen when they tried to tell me the story of the man who had worn them, maybe not so long ago . . . I was happy. My aching feet were protected from the mud, the sharp gravel and the filth covering everything. They could rest in those shoes and heal in peace. But my happiness did not last long. The shoes were so big that I could not walk in them. I needed shoe strings. A piece of ordinary string. Anything to keep those shoes on my feet . . .

The thought of string filled my dreams and every minute of my waking hours. I wanted it so much, so desperately that nothing else seemed to matter anymore. A piece of string . . .

And then one of my acquaintances told me jubilantly that a few old prisoners, Polish men, were working around the latrines, and one of them had a piece of string . . . I snatched up my bread ration for the day and ran. The man with the string, my prospective savior, was a short, stocky, pockmarked man with wild eyes and a ferocious expression. The Inferno Auschwitz had succeeded in depriving him of his last vestige of human dignity.

I stopped beside him, held out my bread and asked him, begged him to give me a piece of string in exchange for it. He looked me over from head to foot, carefully, then grabbed me by the shoulder and hissed in my ear: "I don't want your bread . . . You can keep your bread . . . I will give you a piece of string but first I want you . . . you . . ."

For a second I didn't understand what he meant. I asked him again, smiling, gently, to give me a piece of string . . . My feet were killing me . . . The shoes were useless without string . . . It might save my life . . .

He wasn't listening to me. "Hurry up . . . hurry up . . ." he said hoarsely. His hand, filthy with the human excrement he was working in, reached out for my womanhood, rudely, insistently.

The next moment I was running, running away from that man, away from the indignity that had been inflicted on me, forgetting about the string, about the shoes, about everything but the sudden realization of how deeply I had sunk . . . How my values had changed . . . How high the price of a piece of string had soared . . .

I sank down on my bunk, dazed with suffering and fear . . . but a moment later I was on my feet again. No! I would not let this happen to me! I would come out of the apathy which had enveloped me for the last two months and show the Nazis, show my fellow prisoners that we could keep our human dignity in the face of every humiliation, every torture . . . Yes, I was going to remain a human being to the last minute of my life—whenever that would come.

The same evening, after retiring to our bunks, I began to put my plan into effect. Instead of going to sleep as usual, I began talking in a low voice to the women lying close to me. I told them about my old life in Maramaros Sziget, about my work, my husband, my son, the things we used to do, the books we used to read, the music we used to listen to . . . To my surprise they listened with rapt attention, which proved that their souls, their minds were just as hungry for conversation, for companionship, for self-expression as mine. One after the other, they opened up their hearts, and from then on half our nights were spent in conversation.

Later, as we came to know one another better, we invented games to keep our minds off the sordid present. We recited poetry, told stories of the books we had read and liked, and sang songs, in a low voice, with tears in our eyes, careful that the Blockova shouldn't hear us.

Other evenings we played another game, which spread from block to block until every woman in Auschwitz played it enthusiastically. We called the game "I am a lady . . ."

I am a lady—I said one night—a lady doctor in Hungary. It is morning, a beautiful, sunny morning and I feel too lazy to work. I ring for my assistant and tell her to send the patients away, for I am not going to my office today . . . What should I do with myself? Go shopping? Go to the hairdresser? Meet my friends at the café? Maybe I'll do some shopping. I haven't had a new dress, a new hat in weeks . . .

And I went shopping and lunching and walking, went to the theatre with my husband and son, had supper afterwards . . . And my fellow prisoners hung on my every word, following me around that little town they had never seen, and when my happy, lovely day was over, they fell asleep with a smile on their faces.

These evenings acted like a stimulant. They reminded us that although the odds were all against us, it was still our duty to fight. We had no longer homes to defend. All we had was our human dignity, which was our home, our pride, our only possession—and the moral strength to defend it with. . . .

BLOCK VII: THE LATRINE

Before we knew what went on in there, it was the ardent desire of all of us to be admitted to Block VII. This block was considerably cleaner, and better built than the others. Rain did not seep through the roof, the cages were more solid and even the air was cleaner. Block VII was the "Worker Block" and it housed fewer women than the others.

One morning a group of unknown SS officers and women appeared at the morning roll call. Their visit resulted in a new kind of "selection," in which the young, the pretty, the well-built were pulled out of the ranks, not the weak, the old and the sick-looking. Out of the thirty thousand inhabitants of Camp C about seven hundred young women were selected. The others watched in silence, not knowing whether to pity or envy the chosen ones. We followed them with our eyes and saw that they were being herded into Block VII, the Worker Block.

The camp was soon seething with rumors. We heard that somewhere, far away, there was a radio factory in the middle of a forest and that's where these women would go to work. We did not know that the story about the radio factory was carefully planted among us. We did not know that all these fairy tales about the privileges accorded to those who were taken away for work were only part of the ghastly joke played on us.

About four weeks later an SS physician came to Camp C and with a group of strong-armed SS men entered Block VII and locked the door from the inside. No one was permitted to go near the block. We still had no idea of what was happening, but waited with fear and curiosity in our hearts.

A few hours later the doctors of the hospital were sent for. The sight which greeted us when we entered Block VII is one never to be forgotten. From the cages along the walls about six hundred panic-stricken, trembling young women were looking at us with silent pleading in their eyes. The other hundred were lying on the ground, pale, faint, bleeding. Their pulse was almost inaudible, their breathing strained and deep rivers of blood were flowing around their bodies. Big, strong SS men were going from one to the other sticking tremendous needles into their veins and robbing their under-nourished, emaciated bodies of their last drop of blood. The German army needed blood plasma! The guinea pigs of Auschwitz were just the people to furnish that plasma. *Rassenschande* or contamination with "inferior Jewish blood" was forgotten. We were too "inferior" to live, but not too inferior to keep the German army alive with our blood. Besides, nobody would know. The blood donors, along with the other prisoners of Auschwitz would never live to tell their tale. By the end of the war fat wheat would grow out of their ashes and the soap made of their bodies would be used to wash the laundry of the returning German heroes . . .

We were ordered to put these women back on their feet before they returned to camp so as to make place for others. What could we do without disinfectants, medicines, liquids? How could we replace the brutally stolen blood? All we had were words, encouragement, tenderness. And yet, under our care, these unfortunate creatures slowly returned to life and they even smiled when saying: "This is still better than the crematory . . ."

Block VII was always full. Once it was the women with beautiful eyes who were told to come forward, once the women with beautiful hands . . . And the poor wretches always believed the stories they were told, came forward, and to the amusement of the SS henchmen gave their last drops of precious blood for the German soldiers who used the strength robbed from us to murder our friends, our relatives, our allies . . .

One of the basic Nazi aims was to demoralize, humiliate, ruin us, not only physically but also spiritually. They did everything in their power to push us into the bottomless depths of degradation. Their spies were constantly among us to keep them informed about every thought, every feeling, every reaction we had, and one never knew who was one of their agents.

There was only one law in Auschwitz—the law of the jungle—the law of self-preservation. Women who in their former lives were decent self-respecting human beings now stole, lied, spied, beat the others and—if necessary—killed them, in order to save their miserable lives. Stealing became an art, a virtue, something to be proud of. We called it "organization". Those who were working near the crematories had an opportunity to "organize" an occasional can of food, a pair of shoes, a dress, a cooking pot, a comb, which they then sold on the black market operating in the latrine for food, for special favors, and—if the buyers were men—for "love".

But among those who had no connections among the crematory workers there were many who "organized" the piece of bread of their neighbor, regardless of whether she might starve to death as a consequence, or "organized" their bedfellow's shoes, no matter if her bleeding feet would condemn her to be cremated. By stealing bread, shoes, water, you stole a life for yourself, even if it was at the expense of other lives. Only the strong, the cruel, the merciless survived. The SS were, of course, greatly amused by these practices and encouraged them by showing special favors to some, so as to awaken the jealousy, the hatred, the greed of the others.

A few privileged persons were tacitly permitted to own small aluminum drinking cups stolen from the crematory. Such a cup made it possible for them to get more water than the others who could only drink from their cupped hands. These cups were jealously guarded, their owners carried them on a piece of string tied around their waist. After they filled it with water, they would seek out a quiet corner where they could enjoy their long drink in peace. But more likely than not, they would not succeed. No sooner had they found a lonely spot than one of the strongest, most brutal fellow prisoners would sneak up behind them, hit them over the head to rob them of their water and their cup. Many survived these attacks, but others, who had a thin skull or had no resistance left, lost their lives for a drink of water and an aluminum cup . . .

The latrine—without water, of course—was one of the most important places in Camp C. It was our community hall, the center of our social activities and our news-room. In the second month of my stay in Auschwitz the tiny hut which served as a latrine was closed down and a whole block was consecrated to this worthy purpose. Ditches were dug along the walls and wooden planks thrown across the ditches. In the middle of the building ran a wide passage and this is where the latrine superintendents walked up and down with filthy clubs in their hands, hitting those who spent too much time satisfying their urges or talking to their friends.

The latrine was also our black market, our commodity exchange building. Here you could buy bread for your sausage, margarine for your bread, exchange food, shoes, a piece of cloth for "love" . . . It was here that we made plans for the future, gave expression to our despair, to our thirst for vengeance, our hatred. It was here that we heard all rumors, the good and the bad, and sometimes, miraculously, they proved to be true. Sometimes I feel that if it hadn't been for the latrine we would all have gone crazy in the deadly monotony of camp life.

Once in a while an SS woman came to inspect the latrine and chased us out with her whip and gun. Such an inspection had many victims, many casualties, but the next day our club life would continue, as if nothing had happened.

The latrine also served as a "love-nest." It was here that male and female prisoners met for a furtive moment of joyless sexual intercourse in which the body was used as a commodity with which to pay for the badly needed items the men were able to steal from the warehouses. The saltpeter mixed into our food was not strong enough to kill sexual desire. We did not menstruate, but that was more a consequence of psychic trauma caused by the circumstances we lived in than of saltpeter. Sexual desire was still one of the strongest instincts and there were many who lacked the moral stamina to discipline themselves.

Detachments of male workers came into Camp C almost daily, to clean the latrines, build streets, and patch up leaking roofs. These men were trusted old prisoners who knew everything there was to know about camp life, had connections in the crematories and were masters at "organizing". Their full pockets made them the Don Juans of Camp C. They chose their women among the youngest, the prettiest, the least emaciated prisoners and in a few seconds the deal was closed. Openly, shamelessly, the dirty, diseased bodies clung together for a minute or two in the fetid atmosphere of the latrine—and the piece of bread, the comb, the little knife wandered from the pocket of the man into the greedy hands of the woman.

At first I was deeply shocked at these practices. My pride, my integrity as a woman revolted against the very idea. I begged and preached and, when I had my first cases of venereal disease, I even threatened to refuse treatment if they didn't stop prostitution. But later, when I saw that the pieces of bread thus earned saved lives, when I met a young girl whom a pair of shoes, earned in a week of prostitution, saved from being thrown into the crematory, I began to understand—and to forgive.

Our SS guards knew very well what was going on in the latrine. They even knew who was whose "kochana" (lover), and were much amused by it all. They were always amused by what was insane, filthy, bestial, horrible . . . The man-eating furnaces were burning, their flames were licking the sky . . . Millions were dying on their feet eaten up alive by lice, hunger, disease—and in the latrines, lying in human excrement before the eyes of their fellow prisoners, men and women were writhing in sexual paroxysm. Hitler's dream of a New Order . . .

CHILDBIRTH IN CAMP C

The poor, young women who were brought to Auschwitz from the various ghettos of Hungary did not know that they would have to pay with their lives and the lives of their unborn children for that last, tender night spent in the arms of their husbands.

A few days after the arrival of a new transport, one of the SS chiefs would address the women, encouraging the pregnant ones to step forward, because they would be taken to another camp where living conditions were better. He also promised them double bread rations so as to be strong and healthy when the hour of delivery came. Group after group of pregnant women left Camp C. Even I was naive enough, at that time, to believe the Germans, until one day I happened to have an errand near the crematories and saw with my own eyes what was done to these women.

They were surrounded by a group of SS men and women, who amused themselves by giving these helpless creatures a taste of hell, after which death was a welcome friend. They were beaten with clubs and whips, torn by dogs, dragged around by the hair and kicked in the stomach with heavy German boots. Then, when they collapsed, they were thrown into the crematory—alive.

I stood, rooted to the ground, unable to move, to scream, to run away. But gradually the horror turned into revolt and this revolt shook me out of my lethargy and gave me a new incentive to live. I had to remain alive. It was up to me to save all the pregnant women in Camp C from this infernal fate. It was up to me to save the life of the mothers, if there was no other way, than by destroying the life of their unborn children. I ran back to camp and going from block to block told the women what I had seen. Never again was anyone to betray their condition. It was to be denied to our last breath, hidden from the SS, the guards and even the Blockova, on whose good will our life depended.

On dark nights, when everyone else was sleeping—in dark corners of the camp, in the toilet, on the floor, without a drop of water, I delivered their babies. First I took the ninth-month pregnancies, I accelerated the birth by the rupture of membranes, and usually within one or two days spontaneous birth took place without further intervention. Or I produced dilatation with my fingers, inverted the embryo and thus brought it to life. In the dark, always hurried, in the midst of filth and dirt. After the child had been delivered, I quickly bandaged the mother's abdomen and sent her back to work. When possible, I placed her in my hospital, which was in reality just a grim joke. She usually went there with the diagnosis of pneumonia, which was a safe diagnosis, not one that would send her to the crematory. I delivered women pregnant in the eighth, seventh, sixth, fifth month, always in a hurry, always with my five fingers, in the dark, under terrible conditions.

No one will ever know what it meant to me to destroy these babies. After years and years of medical practice, childbirth was still to me the most beautiful, the greatest miracle of nature. I loved those newborn babies not as a doctor but as a mother and it was again and again my own child whom I killed to save the life of a woman. Every time when kneeling down in the mud, dirt and human excrement which covered the floor of the barracks to perform a delivery without instruments, without water, without the most elementary requirements of hygiene, I prayed to God to help me save the mother or I would never touch a pregnant woman again. And if I had not done it, both mother and child would have been cruelly murdered. God was good to me. By a miracle, which to every doctor must sound like a fairy tale, every one of these women recovered and was able to work, which, at least for a while, saved her life.

My first such case was the delivery of a young woman called Yolanda. Yolanda came from my hometown. She was the child of an impoverished family and made a living by doing fine embroidery on expensive underwear, handkerchiefs—and baby clothes. To make beautiful baby clothes was the greatest pleasure in her life and, while working on them until late into the night, she would dream about the baby she, herself, would one day have. Then she got married. Month after month she waited and prayed, but Nature refused to grant her most ardent wish. This is when she began coming to me. I treated her for a long time until finally my treatment showed results and Yolanda became pregnant. She was radiant. "I shall give you the most beautiful present in the world when my baby arrives . . ." she would then tell me every time we met.

In the end it was I who gave her a present—the present of her life—by destroying her passionately desired little boy two days after his birth. Day after day I watched her condition develop, fearing the moment when it could be hidden no longer. I bandaged her abdomen, hid her with my body at roll call and hoped for a miracle which would save her and her baby.

The miracle never came, but one horribly dark, stormy night Yolanda began having birthpains. I was beside her, waiting for the moment when I could take a hand in the delivery, when I saw to my horror, that she fell into convulsive seizures. For two days and nights the spasms shook her poor, emaciated little body and I had to stand by, without drugs, without instruments to help her, listening to her moans, helpless. Around us, in the light of a few small candles I could see the thirteen-hundred women of her barracks look down upon us from their cages, thirteen-hundred death-masks with still enough life left in them to feel pity for Yolanda and to breathe the silent but ever-present question: Why?

The third day Yolanda's little boy was born. I put her into the hospital, saying that she had pneumonia—an illness not punishable by death—and hid her child for two days, unable to destroy him. Then I could hide him no longer. I knew that if he were discovered, it would mean death to Yolanda, to myself and to all these pregnant women whom my skill could still save. I took the warm little body in my hands, kissed the smooth face, caressed the long hair—then strangled him and buried his body under a mountain of corpses waiting to be cremated.

Then, one day, Dr. Mengele came to the hospital and gave a new order. From now on Jewish women could have their children. They were not going to be killed because of their pregnancy. The children, of course, had to be taken to the crematory by me, personally, but the women would be allowed to live. I was jubilant. Women, who delivered in our so-called hospital, on its clean floor, with the help of a few primitive instruments that had been given to me, had a better chance to come out of this death-camp not only alive but in a condition to have other children—later.

I had two hundred ninety-two expectant mothers in my ward when Dr. Mengele changed his mind. He came roaring into the hospital, whip and revolver in hand, and had all the two hundred ninety-two women loaded on a single truck and tossed—alive—into the flames of the crematory.

In September 1944, Camp C was liquidated to make place for new arrivals. I shall tell later, what this liquidation meant. All I want to say here is that out of thirty thousand women only ten thousand remained alive to be put into other blocks or taken to Germany to work.

As soon as we were installed in Camps F, K and L, a new order came from Berlin. From now on, not only could Jewish mothers have their children in the "maternity ward" of the hospital but the children were to be permitted to live.

Eva Benedek was eighteen years old. She was a violinist from Budapest, a beautiful, talented young woman who was separated from her husband only a few days after her wedding. Eva Benedek believed with an unconquerable faith that her life and the life of her child would be saved. The child, growing in her womb, was her only comfort, her only pleasure, her only concern. When the SS organized an orchestra among the prisoners Eva became the violinist of that orchestra. I bandaged her abdomen and in her formless rags, amidst women whose stomachs were constantly bloated with undernourishment, her condition went unnoticed.

Then came the "liquidation" of Camp C and Eva Benedek came with me to Camps F, K and L. When the order for the conservation of Jewish children came, nobody was happier than she. Her delivery was only a day or two off and we both believed that the miracle had happened, a miracle of God for the sake of Eva Benedek. She smiled all day and in the evening, in our barracks, she whistled Mozart concertos and Chopin waltzes for us to bring a little beauty into our terror-filled, hopeless lives.

Two days later she had her baby, a little boy, in the "maternity ward." But when the baby was born, she turned her back on it, wouldn't look at it, wouldn't hold it in her arms. Tears were streaming down her cheeks incessantly, terrible, silent tears, but she wouldn't speak to me. Finally I succeeded in making her tell what was on her mind.

"I dare not take my son in my arms, Doctor," she said. "I dare not look at him, I dare not kiss him, I dare not get attached to him. I feel it, I know it, that somehow they are going to take him away from me . . ."

And she was right. Twenty-four hours after Eva Benedek had her son, a new order came, depriving Jewish mothers of the additional food, a thin, milky soup mixed with flour, which swelled their breasts and enabled them to feed their babies. For eight days Eva Benedek had to look on while her son starved slowly to death.

His fine, white skin turned yellow and blotched, his smooth face got wrinkled and shrivelled and on the eighth day I had to take him out and throw him on a heap of rotting corpses. . . .

IRMA GRIESE

Irma Griese was sentenced by the British "to be hanged by the neck until dead." The sentence was executed, but this act of "justice" (real justice would have called for her dying again and again, for every life she had destroyed, or her being tortured and mutilated, for every victim she had tortured and mutilated) will not bring back the dead and neither will it restore to health those whom she had driven to insanity or maimed for life.

She was one of the most beautiful women I have ever seen. Her body was perfect in every line, her face clear and angelic and her blue eyes the gayest, the most innocent eyes one can imagine. And yet, Irma Griese was the most depraved, cruel, imaginative sexual pervert I ever came across. She was the highest ranking SS woman in Auschwitz and it was my bad luck to be under her eyes during my entire camp life.

One day she happened to visit the hospital while I was performing an operation on a young woman's breast, cut open by whipping and subsequently infected. I had no instruments whatsoever, except a knife which I had to sharpen on a stone. Breast operations are particularly painful, and, as there was not a drop of anesthetic in this mock hospital, my patient screamed with pain all through the operation.

Irma Griese put down her whip, the handle of which was inlaid with colored beads, sat down on the corner of the bench which served as an operating table and watched me plunge my knife into the infected breast which spurted blood and pus in every direction.

I happened to look up and encountered the most horrible sight I have ever seen, the memory of which will haunt me for the rest of my life. Irma Griese was enjoying the sight of this human suffering. Her tense body swung back and forth in a revealing, rhythmical motion. Her cheeks were flushed and her wide-open eyes had the rigid, staring look of complete sexual paroxysm.

From that day on she went around in camp, her bejewelled whip poised, picked out the most beautiful young women and slashed their breasts open with the braided wire end of her whip. Subsequently those breasts got infected by the lice and dirt which invaded every nook and corner of the camp. They had to be cut open, if the patient was to be saved. Irma Griese invariably arrived to watch the operation, kicking the victim if her screams interfered with her pleasure and giving herself completely to the orgiastic spasms which shook her entire body and made saliva run down from the corner of her mouth.

One day she ordered me to report to her in the afternoon at the so-called "maternity ward" of our hospital.

"I have watched you operate," she said, "and I have perfect confidence in you as a doctor. I want you to examine me. I think I may be pregnant . . ."

I knew that it was against the rules for a prisoner to touch a guard, and breaking that rule was punishable by death. At the same time, refusing an order was punishable by death, too. She lay down on the bench and I proceeded with the examination. She was, indeed, pregnant.

"Be here tomorrow afternoon," she ordered. "You are going to perform an abortion on me . . ."

"But I have absolutely no instruments," I replied, "and if someone finds out, that will mean death for me . . ."

"No arguments. Leave everything to me . . ."

Next afternoon, at the appointed hour, I was ready, waiting for her. When she arrived, she brought a case of instruments—and her gun.

"They are sterilized," she said handing me the instruments. Then she lay down on the bench and put the gun under her head.

I knelt down on the floor and began to operate. There was absolutely no doubt in my mind that this was going to be the last professional act of my life. We were both breaking the rules. Should anyone find out about it, it would mean the end of her career as an SS woman. I would be sent "left" . . . We were both equally guilty in the eyes of her superiors, yet she held all the cards.

No one besides me needed to know about it. She could easily kill me without even having to make an excuse or to give an explanation. I was sure that this was what she intended to do.

While my hands worked almost mechanically, my mind was busy with the thought of death. I had often wondered, while reading about a condemned man's last seconds before death, whether it was true that his whole life unfolds before his eyes in a flash. Yes, it is true. I finished the operation and sat back on my heels, too weary even to get up and face death standing. Suddenly I remembered the examination at the end of my first year of high school. I had to figure out how old I was by subtracting the date of my birth from the date of the current year. Then, one picture followed another, until I relived, if not every incident, at least the mood and color of my entire life. It had been a happy life. Happy, successful, filled with love and work which satisfied me completely. I had lost everything, and there was nothing more to live for.

Irma Griese got up from the bench, arranged her clothes, picked up her gun and smiled. I looked up into her smiling face and waited for the bullet which was to put an end to the Dr. Gisella Perl I had been before and to Prisoner No. 25,404 I was now. But she did not shoot.

"You are a good doctor," she said. "What a pity that you have to die. Germany needs good doctors . . ." I said nothing.

"I am going to give you a coat," she continued. "And I don't have to tell you to keep quiet about this. If you ever open your mouth, I'll find you, wherever you are, and kill you . . ."

With this she walked out of the shack and left me alone with my newly-won life. Now that I knew I wasn't going to die, at least not right then, I remembered my sick and wounded lying on the bare floor of the hospital . . . I remembered all the pregnant women in camp whose lives depended on my skill, courage and readiness to help . . . and suddenly I knew why I had been spared. I was responsible for those women . . . I had to remain alive so as to save them from death . . . I was their doctor . . .

By-the-way, I never got the coat Irma Griese promised me.

10

Olga Lengyel

Such was the polluted atmosphere of Birkenau, a hell unto itself. Here the Nazis trampled on the most private of all rights.

OLGA LENGYEL

This book's first excerpt from Olga Lengyel's Five Chimneys *described the loss that resulted when she arrived at Auschwitz with her family. Like Gisella Perl, however, Lengyel's medical training led to work in the camp's "hospitals." There she witnessed how "the Nazis trampled on the most private of all rights."*

The Germans had thousands of prisoners at their disposal. At any moment, women, men, and even children could be and were selected as human guinea pigs. Nazi doctors forcibly subjected these unfortunate people to so-called medical experiments. Often sadistic, usually bizarre, few, if any, of these experiments had any true scientific value. Many of them, however, did exemplify what the logic of Nazi racism and sexism entailed: control of reproduction.

Professor Dr. Carl Clauberg was one of the leaders of the sterilization experiments at Auschwitz. Repeatedly during its entries for 1944, Danuta Czech's Auschwitz Chronicle *indicates that Clauberg kept hundreds of women available for his work. Lengyel's position in the camp during much of that year made her "well informed on the sterilization experiments," because she tried her best to care for their victims. There was not much she could do to heal the abuse they had experienced. Lengyel stresses that men were targeted as well as women, but in that same hell the horrors differed. Their bodies subjected to X-ray and "short-wave ray" procedures, their genitals infused with caustic substances, their uteruses and ovaries surgically removed—in these experiments, and more, women had fundamental aspects of their womanhood stripped away. The brutal techniques of the Nazi doctors often killed*

119

their Auschwitz guinea pigs. If that result did not occur, these women usually had no further use as far as the Nazis were concerned, and thus their lives ended in the gas chambers.

When Lengyel states that the Nazis "trampled on the most private of all rights," she has more than their destructive medical experiments in mind. She also observes how German domination degraded the most intimate of human relationships. Lengyel is sometimes less than sympathetic toward the prisoners' moments of sexual respite from the horrible reality of camp life. That women attempted to cope by turning to other women for tenderness and solace should scarcely be surprising, but Lengyel is especially dismissive of the lesbian relationships she observed in Auschwitz. Nevertheless her greatest hostility aims at the Nazis, and it is not misplaced. Her overriding question—"Who can forgive [the Nazis] all the crimes they committed?"—testifies to that.

Scientific Experiments

While I was working at the hospitals in Camp F. K. L. and Camp E., I had to take care of many human guinea pigs, the victims of the "scientific" experiments carried out at Auschwitz-Birkenau. The German doctors had hundreds and thousands of slaves at their disposal. Since they were free to do whatever they wished, they decided to experiment with these people. It was a rich windfall which decent men and women would have scorned, but which the Nazi medical contingent gloried in.

Not only did they make experiments, but they compelled many of the deportee doctors, too, to labor under the supervision of the SS physicians. Horrible as these experiments were, the men who had to conduct them might have been able to excuse themselves could they have believed that they were at least serving science and that the sufferings of these unfortunate guinea pigs might, in the end, spare others from suffering.

But there was no scientific benefit. Human beings were sacrificed by the hundreds of thousands, and that was all. So the shackled deportee doctors, almost all of whom finally ended in the crematory ovens, sabotaged the "experiments" as far as they could. Besides, such disorder and lack of method was evident in these "scientific experiments" that they were cruel games rather than serious quests for truth. Everyone has heard of heartless children who amuse themselves by tearing off the legs and wings of insects. Here there was one difference: the insects were human beings.

One of the most common experiments, and also one of the most useless, was

From Olga Lengyel, *Five Chimneys*, trans. Clifford Coch and Paul P. Weiss. Chicago: Ziff-Davis Publishing Company, 1947.

the inoculation of a group of inmates with a disease germ. For, in the interim, the German doctors usually lost their interest in the project. As for the guinea pigs? When they were lucky, they were sent to the hospital; when they were not, they went to the gas chamber. Only in exceptional instances were they put under observation.

Often, the experiments were absolutely absurd. A German doctor conceived the idea of studying how long a human being could exist on nothing but salt water. Another submerged his human guinea pigs in ice water and claimed he could observe the effect of the bath on internal temperatures. After undergoing such experiments, the inmates needed no hospital, but were ready for the gas chamber. One day several nurses entered the infirmary and asked, "Who cannot sleep?" About twenty inmates accepted a dose of an unknown white powder, which might have had a morphine base. The next day ten were dead. The same experiments were conducted among the older women, and seventy more died the same night.

When the Germans sought new treatments for the wounds caused by American phosphorous bombs, they burned fifty Russians on the back with phosphorous. These "controls" received no medication. The men who survived were exterminated.

One of the favorite experiments was conducted on newly arrived women whose menstruation was still normal. During their periods, they were told roughly, "You will be shot in two days." The Germans wanted to know what effect such news would have on the menstrual flow. A professor of histology in Berlin even published an article in a German scientific periodical on his observation on hemorrhages provoked in women by such bad news.

Dr. Mengele, the chief physician, had two favorite studies; twins and dwarfs. From the first selections, the twins of each convoy were set apart, if possible with their mothers. Then they were sent to Camp F. K. L. No matter what their age or sex, twins interested Mengele deeply. They were favored and even allowed to keep their clothing and their hair. He went so far in his solicitude for twins that when they were exterminating the Czech Camp, he gave orders to spare a dozen sets of twins.

Upon arrival, twins were photographed from every possible angle. Then the experiments began, but these were disconcertingly juvenile in character. For example, one twin would be inoculated with certain chemical substances, and the doctor was to watch for the reaction, if he did not happen to forget about it. But even when the doctor followed through, there was no gain for science for the simple reason that the product injected offered no particular interest. Once they used a preparation that was supposed to cause a change in the pigmentation of the hair. Many days were lost in pondering over the hair and examining it under a microscope. The results showed nothing sensational, and the experiments were allowed to lapse.

Dwarfs were Dr. Mengele's greatest passion. He collected them zealously. The day he discovered a family of five dwarfs in a transport he was beside himself with joy. But his was the mania of a collector, not of a savant. His experiments and observations were carried out in an abnormal fashion. When he made transfusions, he purposely used incorrect blood types. Of course complications followed. But Mengele had no one to account to but himself. He did whatever pleased him and conducted his experiments like a mad amateur.

One experimental station which was installed some distance from the camp appeared to have a more scientific character. But only at first glance. There one could see that the "work" was only a criminal debauchery of human material and a total lack of scruples on the part of the inquirers. The experiments were theoretically intended to gather information for the Wehrmacht. Most of the time, they consisted of tests of human endurance, resistance to cold or to heat, or to high altitudes. Hundreds of internees died in the course of these experiments in the Auschwitz station, as well as in other camps. At the price of the lives of thousands of victims, German science finally concluded that a human being can subsist in ice water, at a predetermined temperature, for just so many hours. It had also been established with precision (!) how long it took for death to come after scaldings at different degrees of temperature.

I have mentioned experiments to determine the resistance of the human organism to hunger. Musulmans, especially the most emaciated specimens, were forced to drink unbelievable quantities of soup. These cramming experiments were often fatal. I heard of a few cases where the deportees, suffering horribly from hunger volunteered for this forced feeding. The son of Prime Minister M., was so famished that he offered himself as a guinea pig for malaria experiments. The subjects of this experiment received double bread rations for a few days.

Experiments were also made in diagnostics. Interesting cases were taken from the hospital and simply killed so that they could be dissected for the purpose of an autopsy! When several cases suffered from the same ailment, they might be given different treatments and, after a certain phase, be killed, so that conclusions might be drawn from the experiments. Most of the time a patient was killed, and no one dreamed of examining his body—there were too many dead in Auschwitz.

The German Bayer Company sent medicines in vials with no labels to indicate their contents. People suffering from tuberculosis were injected with this product. They were not sent to the gas chamber. Their overseers waited for them to die, and death came quickly. After that, parts of the lungs were taken to a laboratory chosen by Bayer.

Once the Bayer Company brought one hundred and fifty women from the camp administration and experimented on them with unknown medicaments, perhaps for hormone tests.

The Weigel Institute of Cracow sent vaccines to the camp. These, too, had to be experimented on and "improved." The victims were chosen from French political prisoners, especially members of the French underground whom the Germans wanted to be rid of.

About two thousand organic preparations had to be dispatched to the University of Innsbruck. According to instructions, these preparations had to be made from absolutely healthy bodies, which had been gassed, hanged, or shot *while in good health!*

One day a large number of women, mostly Polish, were used for vivisection experiments: grafting of the bones and muscles, and various others. German surgeons arrived from Berlin to make the experiments and watch the result. The vivisections were carried out under terrible conditions. The victim was bound to the operating table in a primitive barrack, and the operation was made *without aseptic care*. Even after the operations, the human guinea pigs suffered terribly. They were given nothing to alleviate their sufferings.

To enrich their racial science, the Germans regularly extracted blood. Apart from the scientific interest, the blood of the internees was used for transfusions to German wounded. Five hundred cc. of blood were taken from each "voluntary" donor and sent immediately to the army. To save the lives of the Wehrmacht soldiers, the Germans forgot that Jewish blood was "of inferior quality."

I have already mentioned the "injections in the heart," as the inmates called the intracardiac injections of phenol. Sometimes, these intracardiac injections were made with benzine or petroleum. This method was used in the hospitals to kill the sick or the feeble and the "superfluous."

I spoke to a Polish doctor who was forced to give these injections to his fellow inmates for two days.

"When the SS doctor called me to the hospital," he told me, "I did not know what it was all about. He ordered me to inject the patients in the cardiac cavity. He told me that I should inject the liquid as soon as I had proof that the needle was in the cardiac cavity."

The Polish doctor followed orders, and the patients then fell dead on the floor.

In another mad experiment they laid hundreds of sick out in the blazing sun. The Germans wanted to know how long it would take a sick person to die under the sun without water.

Twenty miles from our camp was an experimental station which specialized in artificial insemination. To this station were sent the most endowed of the doctor inmates and the most beautiful of the women. The Germans attached great importance to these experiments. Unfortunately, I could not see the work that went on there, for this station was the most jealously guarded of all. Some data, however, I did obtain.

The Germans practiced artificial insemination on a number of women, but the investigations offered no results. I knew women who had been subjected to artificial insemination and had happened to survive, but they were ashamed to admit the experiments.

Another group was injected with the sex hormones. It had not been possible to determine the nature of the substance injected or the results the Germans obtained. After these injections, many women had abscesses which were lanced in Barrack 10.

But I am well informed on the sterilization experiments. These took place in Auschwitz-Birkenau under the direction of a Polish doctor who was executed by the Germans a few days before the camp was evacuated.

These experiments attempted to compare the results of the surgical methods and X-ray treatments. At the hospital, we saw numerous sick women who had come from this experimental station. They showed serious burns caused by the clumsy application of these rays. Through them and the deportee doctors we learned about the experiments. The subject was placed under X-ray radiation, which was made more and more intense. From time to time the treatment was interrupted in order to see if the subject could still copulate. All this took place under the vigilant eyes of the SS in Barrack 21. When the physician verified that the X-rays had definitely destroyed the genital faculties, this subject was dispatched to the gas chamber. Occasionally, when the irradiation took too long to produce the desired effect, the victim was castrated surgically.

In August, 1944, the Germans sterilized about one thousand boys between the ages of thirteen and sixteen. Their names and the dates of sterilization were registered. After some weeks the boys were brought to Barrack 21. In the laboratory they were questioned about the result of the first "treatment," their desires, nocturnal pollutions, loss of memory, etc.

Then the Germans forced them to masturbate. They provoked the erection by massaging the prostate glands. When this work tired the "masseur," the German "scientists" used a metal instrument, which caused the patient great pain.

The sperm was examined by a bacteriologist who determined the vitality of the spermatozoa. In 1944, the Germans sent a phosphorescent microscope to the camp. This enabled them to see the difference between the living and the dead spermatozoa.

Sometimes the Germans made incomplete castrations: a quarter or a half of the testicle was removed. Sometimes the whole testicle was sent to Breslau in a tube sterilized with formalin (10 per cent) for an histophatological study of the tissues. These operations were made with intrarachidian injections of novocaine. The boys were separated from the others in Barrack 21 and were closely watched. When the experiments were finished, the reward was, as usual, the gas chamber.

I remember one case of a Polish boy named Gruenwald, who was about twenty years old. Professor Klauber ordered treatment with X-rays. After two months the X-rays had not produced the desired effect. So the boy was taken to Barrack 21 for a complete castration. But the X-rays had been given in such doses that he had been seriously burned. Cancer followed and the boy suffered terribly. In January, 1945, he was still alive in the hospital at Birkenau.

These methods were also applied to the women. Sometimes the Germans used short-wave rays which caused unbearable pains in the lower part of the abdomen. Then the belly of the sick woman was *opened* to observe the lesions. The surgeons usually removed the uterus and the ovaries.

Professor Schuman and Dr. Wiurd made many such experiments on young girls about sixteen or seventeen years old. Of the fifty girls used for this experiment, only two survived, Bella Schimski and Dora Buyenna, both from Salonika. They told us that they had been put under short-wave rays, one plate placed on the abdomen and the other on the back. The electricity was directed toward the ovaries. The dose was so great that the subjects were gravely burned. After two months of observation, the girls had to suffer a "control" operation.

A group of young women, mostly Dutch, were subjected to a series of experiments for which only the author, Clauberg, German gynecologist of Kattowitz, could have known the reason. With the aid of an electrical apparatus, a thick whitish liquid was infused into the genital organs of these women. It caused a terrible burning sensation. This infusion, repeated every four weeks, was each time followed by a radioscopy.

These same women were simultaneously subject to another series of experiments by another doctor. This time it was an injection in the chest. The physician injected five cc. of a serum, whose nature I do not know, at the rate of from two to nine injections each session. The reaction came in the form of a painful swelling the size of a fist. Certain women received more than a hundred of these inoculations. Some were also injected in the gums. After a number of such experiments the women were declared useless and sent away.

Once we asked an Aryan German inmate, a former social worker, for the basic reason for the sterilization and castration. Before his captivity he had been active in German politics and had known many eminent people. He told us that the Germans had a geopolitical reason for these experiments. If they could sterilize all non-German people still alive after their victorious war, there would be no danger of new generations of "inferior" peoples. At the same time, the living populations would be able to serve as laborers for about thirty years. After that time, the German surplus population would need all the space in these countries, and the "inferiors" would perish without descendants.

When I think of these experiments, I cannot help but recall the drama of the little French woman, Georgette, who died at the hospital on Christmas day, 1944. She had been used as a guinea pig in sterilization experiments, and when she returned to the hospital she was no longer a female.

Georgette had a Polish fianceé, who was to visit her on that day. But she was resolved never to see him again. Rather than admit her degradation, she chose to pass for dead.

The lover came, but Georgette hid under the blanket on the third tier of the koia as immobile as though dead. Because the sick woman desired it, we had told him the day before that she now was dead. But he had not come to see

Georgette. He went to the bed of another young girl, from Cracow, to whom he had brought his gifts.

From under her cover, Georgette saw everything. With her last remaining strength she raised herself and threw herself from the top of the koia. The fall was fatal.

Love in the Shadow of the Crematory

Nature dictates that wherever men and women are together there shall also be love. Even in the shadow of the crematory the emotions could not be entirely suppressed. Love, or what passed for it in the degraded atmosphere of the death camp, was but a distortion of what it is for normal people, for society in Birkenau was but a distortion of a normal human society.

The supermen in charge of our destinies sought to extinguish every desire in the inmates. Camp gossip had it that certain powders were mixed into our food to reduce or destroy sexual appetite. So that the SS might not become overly excited by the presence of many young and beautiful internees whom they saw naked and in every degree of exposure, there were brothels supplying German prostitutes for their use. Despite the Nazi theories on racial pollution, we heard that a number of attractive internees were drafted for these brothels. Similar privileges were available to inmates in the men's camps. Admission for the inmates was, naturally, to be regarded as an exceptional favor.

Furthermore, rules and artificial procedures counted for nothing. The constant nervous tension under which we lived did little to depress our desires. On the contrary, the mental anguish seemed to provide a peculiar stimulus.

The relations among the internees of both sexes were characterized by the absence of social conventions. Everyone addressed everyone else in the familiar "thou," and by the first name. Such familiarity did not imply solidarity, nor was it always entirely free from vulgarity.

The only men we met besides the SS guards and the Wehrmacht troops were male internees who did road repairs, ditch-digging, and similar tasks in our camp. As a rule the only time that we mixed was during lunch, either in the washroom or in the latrines where many of the men ate their food. They were usually surrounded by women of all ages and shapes who clamored piteously for crumbs.

The women stood around them in circles, three or four deep, their hands stretched forth like beggars. Pretty girls sang the latest songs to attract attention. Sometimes the men relented and gave away parts of their lunch. Only then could a woman enjoy a potato, that most luscious of camp luxuries which was ordinarily reserved only for the kitchen workers and the blocovas.

Yet it was rarely pity that made the men share their not-too-abundant food. For food was the coin that paid for sexual privileges.

It would be heartless to condemn women who had to sink so low for a half crust of bread. The responsibility for the degradation of the internees rested with the camp administration.

Be that as it may, prostitution with all its lamentable consequences: venereal diseases, pimps, etc., was an ordinary phenomenon at Birkenau. Many of the objects stolen in "Canada" were destined for the women of those men who were smartest in these exchanges.

However, all love here was not sordid. There were instances of sincere and touching affection and companionship. But even where tenderness was absent, a woman with a lover enjoyed real distinction, for there were very few men in the camp.

Most of the younger women achieved flirtations. The blocovas, who had private corners in the barracks, were at an advantage which they did not hesitate to use. Cronies of the blocova acted as sentinels while the chief entertained her guest. Of course, these rendezvous were strictly *verboten*. When an SS approached the block, the watchers sounded the alert. It often happened that a rendezvous was disturbed three or four times, but the couples were not easily discouraged.

Occasionally a blocova might, for a reasonable consideration, lease her quarters to a friend. The compensation was high, for the risk was great. If caught receiving a man, or even facilitating such a meeting, the blocova faced severe punishments. Her hair would be shaved again, she would be beaten unmercifully, and, worst of all, she would be demoted from her exalted rank.

Standards of beauty vary. In Birkenau, a world apart, the woman with the fullest figure and the most opulent charms was considered the ultimate in female pulchritude. The male inmates, themselves reduced to living skeletons, were repelled by bony bodies and hollow cheeks. Those women—few enough—who miraculously retained some flesh were envied by others who a year earlier, would have endured tortuous diets to reduce their weight.

As in all prisons, Birkenau had its perverts. Among the women there were three categories. Those who were lesbians by instinct formed the least interesting group. More troublesome was the second classification, which included women who, because of the abnormal conditions, suffered changes in their sexual viewpoint. Often they yielded under the pressure of necessity.

We had a Polish woman, about forty, who had once been a professor of physics. Her husband had been killed by the Germans and her children shipped off to some dread place, perhaps to death. One of the prisoners, a functionary, paid particular court to this lovely, delicate, and intelligent woman. The professor knew that if she responded she would at least be spared from hunger. She must have fought a great battle against the temptation, but in the end, she surrendered. Six weeks later she was referring to her "friend" with much enthusiasm. In another two months she declared that she could not live without her consort.

In the third category were those who, unlike my Polish acquaintance, discovered their lesbian predilections through an association with corruption. This was encouraged by the "dance soirées" that were sometimes organized in this Dantesque world of Birkenau. During the long winter nights of 1944, when the Germans were more preoccupied with the advancing Russians than with us, the inmates gave "parties" that parodied gruesomely the mundane affairs they had known in the old life. They gathered around a charcoal bin to sing and dance. A guitar and a harmonica from the camp orchestra helped these parties to continue until daybreak.

The heads of our barracks played a prominent role in these affairs. The Lageraelteste, the "uncrowned queen of the camp," who was an inmate at Camp E where I now lived, was always present. She was a young, fragile thing, a German girl of about thirty. She managed to exist for ten years, knocking about from one camp to another.

During these orgies the couples who danced together gradually became attached to each other. Some of the women assumed male attire to lend an air of reality to the proceedings.

One of the chief initiators of these soirées was a Polish countess whose name I don't recall. When I first saw her, she was sitting in the doorway of our hospital. I looked at her in surprise. "What is that man doing in this place?" I wondered. For she looked exactly like a male. She wore a black velvet artist's jacket, the kind that was familiar in the Parisian art quarter, and a flowing black bow tie. Even her hair was cut short in mannish fashion. She really seemed to be a handsome man of about thirty. When I questioned a fellow inmate, I was told, "This 'man' is not a man—'He' is a she!"

In her general behavior and mannerisms the countess acted like a man. Once when I had crawled up into the kioas because I was on "Lice Control Duty," I felt a courteous hand assisting my descent. I was indeed surprised. But it was the countess! With this gallant gesture, she opened a siege of courtship. I actually had to run to escape her.

While the others cavorted about during the dances, I was often asleep in my bunk. On many an occasion, I was awakened by kisses and other amorous gestures. The countess! It got so I feared to sleep during the dances. The others were amused by her ardent courtship, but I was not. They had expected the countess to seek a new attachment; her former "girl friend" had been removed in a transport.

I was sorry for this unhappy woman. German humor had placed her in our camp. When she had arrived she had been dressed in men's clothing, and the Germans had wanted to place her in the male camp. She argued desperately and tried to prove that she was a woman. They obliged her, for it was a three-ring circus for our captors to observe the antics of this "man-woman" amongst us. Of course, we dared not complain or protest. It amused the Germans.

The soirées always reminded me of the "Dance Macabre." When I thought of the common fate that waited these unfortunates, I could not repress a shiver of horror.

But perhaps my disgust was groundless under the circumstances. The horrible distractions provided a few hours of forgetfulness, and that in itself was worth almost anything in the camp. Besides these parties were better than many other things that took place there. The prisoners, men or women, were frequently abused by the German barrack leaders, among whom was a high percentage of homosexuals and other perverts.

I shall never forget the agony of one mother who told me that she was forced to undress her daughter and to look on while the girl was violated by dogs whom the Nazis had specially trained for this sport. That happened to other young girls. They were compelled to labor in the quarries for twelve or fourteen hours a day. When they dropped from exhaustion their guards' favorite form of amusement was to urge the dogs to attack them. Who can forgive them all the crimes they committed?

The heads of the camp were noted for their aberrations. The Griese woman was bisexual. My friend, who was her maid, informed me that Irma Griese frequently had homosexual relationships with inmates and then ordered the victims to the crematory. One of her favorites was a blocova, who survived as Irma's slave a long time before the camp chief tired of her.

Such was the polluted atmosphere of Birkenau, a hell unto itself. Here the Nazis trampled on the most private of all rights. Here love became corrupt excitement for the slaves and sadistic entertainment for the overseers. . . .

11

Anna Heilman and Rose Meth

*In March 1943 Estusia approached me. She told me that re-
sistance was being organized and we were in a position to help
because we were the only ones who had access to powder. Would I
be willing to risk the danger of being caught? Of course, I agreed
right away because it gave me a way to fight back.*

ROSE METH

*Gisi Fleischmann, Haika Grossman, Rozka Korczak-Marle, Zivia Lubetkin, Fran-
ceska Mann, Vladka Meed, Mala Zimetbaum. None of their names are as well
known as Anne Frank's. But they deserve to be well known because each of these
women, and many more, valiantly resisted the "Final Solution." Until she was
captured and gassed at Auschwitz, Fleischmann helped run an underground railroad that got Jews out of Poland. Grossman was a resistance fighter in Bialystok;
Korczak-Marle organized partisans in Vilna; Lubetkin and Meed were leaders in
the Warsaw ghetto uprising. Franceska Mann shot SS men in an Auschwitz–
Birkenau crematorium before she lost her life, and Mala Zimetbaum was the first
woman to escape from Auschwitz. She was caught at the Slovakian border, returned
to Auschwitz, and sentenced to be hanged. Her suicidal defiance at the gallows—it
prevented the Germans from carrying out the sentence—became legendary in the
camp.*

*Such acts of resistance did not crush the Third Reich. It took massive military
power to do that. But physical resistance was crucial nonetheless, for, as Rose Meth*

130

said, *"it gave me a way to fight back." There was profound meaning in such action—not only for the individuals directly involved but also symbolically for others in the ghettos and camps and for those who live after Auschwitz as well.*

Rose Meth and Anna Heilman became members of a Jewish resistance group in Auschwitz. Their work assignment involved making parts for bombs, a task that gave them access to explosives. Day after day for eight months, and at the risk of their lives, they worked to smuggle small amounts of gunpowder from the factory where they worked. "In a day," Meth recalls, "three of us could collect about two teaspoons full." This precious powder passed through many women's hands before it reached the Sonderkommando *that used it to sabotage Crematorium IV in Auschwitz–Birkenau on October 7, 1944. One of those women was Estusia Wajcblum, Anna Heilman's sister. Early on, she enlisted Anna and Rose Meth to help in the resistance effort. Along with Alla Gaertner, Roza Robota, and Regina Saperstein, Estusia Wajcblum was caught and hanged by the Germans on January 6, 1945. Anna Heilman and Rose Meth were never apprehended. In giving her oral history, Heilman says that she finds it difficult to speak about what happened in Auschwitz. But, she adds, "I want to bring about the commemoration of the four girls who were executed in Auschwitz." Thanks to her testimony and Rose Meth's, the names of these women of valor are better known; as they well deserve to be.*

Resistance

Anna Heilman was born in 1928 in Warsaw. During the Warsaw Ghetto Uprising she was living with her parents on the Aryan side, going back and forth from the ghetto as a courier for HaShomer HaTzair, *the Zionist organization active in resistance to the Nazis. Eventually, she was forced to choose between remaining permanently in the ghetto and participating in the uprising or remaining with her family on the Aryan side. She opted to remain with her family. In May 1942 she was arrested with her family and taken to Majdanek. From there, she was transferred to Auschwitz.*

We were first in *Lager* (Camp) A[1] which was called the quarantine camp.[2] There were all kinds of rumors flying; we heard it was good to say that you are a metallurgist. So we did. We were transferred to *Lager* B[3] and from *Lager* B we were assigned to the Union Werke, a German munitions factory.[4]

From "Women of Valor: Partisans and Resistance Fighters," *Center for Holocaust Studies Newsletter* 6 (1990): 35–41. The *Newsletter* is edited by Yaffa Eliach and Bonnie Gurewitsch. Reprinted by permission of Anna Heilman, Rose Meth, and the Museum of Jewish Heritage, New York, N.Y., with which the Center for Holocaust Studies merged in 1990.

At that time we did not know exactly what the factory produced. We knew that this was an ammunition factory. Now we know that V2 missiles were made there.

Two shifts worked in the factory, one night shift and one day shift. The day shift worked from very early in the morning till five and the night shift worked immediately after. My sister and I worked the day shift.

Alma was our *Kapo* (work supervisor). She was German, non-Jewish. There were German SS women who were *Aufseherin* (prisoner-trusty in concentration camp) and there were also four Jewish *Arbeiterin* (workers) who were responsible for the Jewish girls. This was the hierarchy.

My job was to inspect some of the manufactured pieces on the production line. They were round bakelite pieces very much in the shape and size of a checker. Each piece had a little indentation. My job was to check those indentations and move the pieces on to the second person on the line.

My sister[5] also worked in the *Union* factory, but she worked in the *Pulverraum* (gunpowder room) together with Ruzia Meth. The *Pulverraum* was the only place in the factory where they were handling gunpowder. Nine girls were involved in this small department.

We smuggled the gunpowder from the factory into the camp. It was smuggled in tiny little pieces of cloth, tied up with a string. Inside our dresses we had what we called a little *boit'l* (small sack), a pocket, and the *boit'l* was where everybody hid their little treasures, wrapped in pieces of cloth. Often there were searches. When they conducted searches we used to untie the string and spill the gunpowder behind us on the ground so it wouldn't be found.

My sister brought the gunpowder out. She gave it to me and to other girls, whose names I don't remember.[6] I gave it to another girl in the camp, and this girl gave it to another girl who was running between Auschwitz and Birkenau. The fourth girl,[7] who was executed, was the one who used to give it directly to the man who worked in the crematorium. I think we were involved in it for about eight months.

Very little contact was permitted between men and women but we managed somehow. None of the people in charge had any idea that gunpowder was being smuggled out. There was one man that I knew, a Belgian Jew whose name I don't remember, who was participating in the resistance in the men's *Lager*. He was my link with the men. He was blond, slight and had green eyes. He was about 30 or 35 years old. I had contact with him. When my sister was taken to the bunker,[8] which was a prison in the men's *Lager*, I approached him to ask for information. I needed to know what others were saying so that my explanation would coincide with theirs. But he pushed me away saying, "Don't ever come near me. I don't want anybody to see you with me." This was the end of my contact with him.

I'm not sure how many people were involved because there was such great secrecy. I only knew about myself, about Ruzia,[9] about Estusia,[10] and I think Alla.[11] I cannot remember anybody else. We only knew each other and we were very, very careful.

It began this way. A small group of girls were getting together after work in Auschwitz dreaming of Israel, singing Hebrew songs and talking about life outside, or in the future, if we survive.

I remembered my agonizing decision in Warsaw, whether to go with *HaShomer HaTzair*[12] into the ghetto or to stay with my parents. It left me terribly guilty. The last order of the day in *HaShomer HaTzair* was that we were not going to let ourselves be taken alive. We were all going to die, but were not giving our lives for nothing. I survived the Warsaw ghetto, and I felt guilty. Nobody in Auschwitz, unless they came from the Warsaw ghetto, knew about what happened there. We, too, decided that we were not going to let ourselves be taken without a struggle. We came from different countries, from different walks of life, from different organizations and some were not affiliated with any organizations. We were about seven or eight girls, no more.

Out of this friendship evolved the ideas of resistance. I can't tell you who initiated it . . . The idea was what could we do, each one of us, to resist? I thought, "You are working in the *Pulverraum*. How about taking gunpowder?" We started to talk about the idea. The gunpowder was within our reach. We thought, "We can use it!" Somebody in the group knew that the *Sonderkommando* (special work squad, usually workers in the crematoria) was preparing resistance. We said, "Let us give the gunpowder to them!" We gave it through Marta to Anitchka who was working in Birkenau. She ran between Auschwitz and Birkenau and gave it to Roza Robota. Roza Robota gave it to the men in the *Sonderkommando*. This is how it went.

Among a very select few there was talk about a plan for mass escape, but we didn't know who or when or where. We only knew that they would use the gunpowder for blowing up the crematorium. We knew that the *Sonderkommando* had decided to burn the crematorium because they knew that every *Sonderkommando* was going to be executed.[13] There was contact between the Resistance in the camp and the PPR,[14] the Resistance outside of camp. In our group there was a girl who had direct contact with PPR. We were waiting for word from the PPR to tell us when they would start from the outside.[15] We would then start to rebel from the inside, to break the camp down because the Russians were coming. But somebody from the *Sonderkommando* snitched on them and they were attacked by the Germans before they had a chance to carry out their planned revolt. A crematorium was blown up.[16] And then the time to die approached.

We went on the famous death march in January.[17] We walked on foot in snow piled so deep we felt we were walking on our knees. We didn't see our legs anymore. Marta took me bodily. She had to force me to come; I wanted to stay in Auschwitz. It was worse than a nightmare. We stayed in Ravensbrück[18] just a few days. Then we were transferred to Neustadt Glewe[19] by train in cattle cars.

After liberation I was in a hospital. I was operated on several times for gangrene and then I refused to be operated on again. Finally we were repatriated, but I decided that I didn't have anything to go back to Poland for. I convinced my camp sister, Marta, to come with me to Belgium because one of the nurses was telling us that the best ice cream in the world was in Belgium. I said, "We are going to Belgium." We were flown there by the Red Cross plane and I stayed in Belgium for a year before I went with Youth Aliyah to Israel. I married in Israel in 1950. We came to the States in 1958, and after two years we went to Canada.

I find it very difficult to speak about it; I find it very difficult to remember, but I understand that this is my responsibility and I want to bring about the commemoration of the four girls who were executed in Auschwitz. This is what I wanted to do; this is the essence of my talk.

My Auschwitz number was forty-eight, one hundred and fifty. (48150) The numbers add up to *Chai*.[20] The girl who tattooed my numbers told me: "You are going to come out alive because your number is *Chai*."

Interviewed by:
Bonnie Gurewitsch, 10/14/85

NOTES

1. *Lager* A in the main camp, Auschwitz I.
2. Prisoners stayed in the quarantine camp for a few weeks, where they were physically and psychologically "broken-in" to the inhuman routine and torture of the camp. (*Auschwitz 1940–1945, Guidebook Through the Museum*, pp. 45–46.)
3. *Lager* B, also in Auschwitz I.
4. The *Union Werke* munitions factory was located near the base camp. (*Amidst a Nightmare of Crime*, p. 155.) Its full name was *Weichsall-Metall Union Werke*.
5. Esther Wajcblum, born in 1924. She was eventually executed for her part in smuggling the gunpowder.
6. Explosives were brought from the *Union* factory by several women, including Esther Wajcblum, Alla Gaertner, and Regina Saperstein and given to Roza Robota, who worked sorting clothing and luggage in Birkenau BIIg, adjacent to crematorium IV.
7. Roza Robota. According to Israel Gutman, a woman named Hadassah transferred the explosives to him or to a fellow prisoner in the *Sonderkommando*. (Israel Gutman, *Smoke and Ashes: The Story of Auschwitz-Birkenau*. Israel: Sifriyat Poalim, 1957.) A footnote to the diary of Salmen Lewental says that it was Roza Robota who transferred the gunpowder to a Jewish prisoner named Wrobel. (*Amidst a Nightmare of Crime*, p. 155.)
8. Esther Wajcblum, along with other girls from the *Union* factory, was interrogated in Block 11, the punishment barrack of the men's camp. "The upper windows

were sealed off and the basement windows barred." Most survivors of interrogation in Block 11 were shot at the "Black Wall." (Konnilyn Feig, *Hitler's Death Camps: The Sanity of Madness,* New York: Holmes & Meier, 1979, p. 347.)

9. Rose Grunapfel Meth.
10. Anna's sister, Esther Wajcblum.
11. Alla Gaertner.
12. *HaShomer HaTzair*, a left-wing Zionist organization.
13. Salmen Lewental, a worker in the *Sonderkommando* wrote in his diary, which was hidden in Auschwitz and unearthed after the war, "We believed that the Germans would want at all costs to obliterate all traces of their crimes . . . by killing our entire *Kommando* . . ." (*Amidst a Nightmare of Crime,* pp. 154–155.)
14. *Polska Partja Robotnicza,* a resistance group formed by Polish communists who escaped and returned from territory initially held by Russia, together with the remnants of the Polish Communist Party. (Stefan Korbonski, *The Polish Underground State*, New York: Columbia University Press, 1978, p. 110.)
15. Additional assistance came from Soviet Prisoners of War who were brought to Auschwitz from Majdanek and assigned to the *Sonderkommando* on April 16, 1944. They helped organize plans for a mutiny and escape. However, it became clear that assistance from outside the camp would not be forthcoming. When 200 men of the *Sonderkommando* were taken and killed, it became obvious that "the date of the final liquidation was approaching." The *Sonderkommando* decided: "To act, to act, over." (*Amidst a Nightmare of Crime*, pp. 157–163.)
16. One crematorium was blown up on Oct. 7, 1944.
17. "Evacuation" of KL Auschwitz started on Jan. 18, 1945. Columns of prisoners left in groups of 500 all day and night, on foot, and were marched west for days. Those who could not keep up died where they fell or were shot. (*From the History of KL Auschwitz,* Vol. 1, Oswiecim: 1967, p. 215.)
18. Ravensbrück concentration camp, near Fürstenberg, Germany. They must have walked more than 150 miles.
19. Neustadt Glewe, Germany, near Ludwigslust.
20. Hebrew letters have numerical equivalents. The sum of the numbers on her arm equals 18, which is the same as the sum of the letters of the Hebrew word *chai*, meaning "life."

Rose Meth was born in 1925 into a prominent Hasidic family in Zator, Poland, a small town between Oswiecim and Cracow. She was the fourth of six children. In prewar years, Rose's father welcomed the President of Poland on a state visit to Zator, as representative of the Jewish community. When the Nazis occupied Poland in September 1939, the family tried to escape eastward, but the effort was futile. Rose and her sisters were taken to clean German army lodgings; her father was forced to scrub the German carriages. As a result of this his shoes were ruined. Rose was denounced by the Polish shopkeeper from whom she purchased new shoes for her father. For this "crime" she was imprisoned for six months.

From the Zator ghetto, where she lived after serving her sentence, Rose and other young people were sent to the Wadowice[1] ghetto to sew uniforms for the Wehrmacht.

*They were hoping that their labor would protect their families in Zator, when they
learned of the liquidation of the Zator ghetto and the deportation of the Jews to their
deaths in Belzec,[2] July 1942. In August 1943 the Wadowice ghetto was liquidated.
Rose and her three sisters were deported with the Wadowice Jews to Auschwitz.*

We arrived in Auschwitz late in the afternoon of August 10, 1943. It was
Tisha B'Av (the ninth day of the month of Av, a fast day to commemorate the
destruction of the Temple in Jerusalem). My sisters and I were fasting. There
was a selection on the platform by SS man Tauber.[3] He was in charge next to
Mengele.[4] We dressed up my little sisters to make them look older and we all
passed the selection. Then we were brought to Birkenau. I can't begin to
describe the shock and the humiliation. We were sheltered children. They
made us undress completely naked in front of the Nazi soldiers. We wanted to
die. They shaved our heads. They shaved all our hair, everywhere. We were
given numbers. Mine was *Vier und funfzig, drei sieben achtzig* (54387). I'm
alive because of confusion with these numbers, 54387. 3,8,7 adds up to 18.
You know what that is in "*gimatria*" (Hebrew numerology)? There was a
selection in October 1943. My number was taken down. As you read the
number in Polish it's 54387. In German, the seven is read before the eight. We
had to dictate our numbers to the *kapo* (prisoner-trusty in concentration
camp), and I translated from the Polish: 54387, but in German the kapo wrote
down the seven before the eight. When they were calling the numbers, I knew
my number was written down, and I wanted to step forward, but my friend
Estusia[5] grabbed me by my arm and said, "That's not your number." I asked,
"What if somebody else goes?" She said, "You'll have time to go then." The
correct number never came up.

First we were carrying rocks from one place to another and back. Just cruel,
busy work. Nothing constructive was being done with the rocks. I was in a
state of shock because my sisters were taken to the gas chambers in December
1943. I had typhus. I swelled up with what we called the "elephant sickness,"
and I also developed some sort of joint ailment but I continued to go to work.
Finally, I was taken on a litter to the *Revier* (infirmary). I was so very sick that I
couldn't walk.

In the *Revier* there was a lady, Mrs. Oleander, from Cracow. She said to me,
"Quickly, get off that bed and go back where you came from." I cried. I told
her, "I can't walk." She said, "I don't care what you say. You'd better go." She
chased me out of the *Revier* and I returned to the camp. The entire *Revier* was
sent to the gas chamber. I don't know why she did it. I don't know why she
picked me.

In the late fall of 1943, just before *Hanukkah*, I was taken to work in the
Union factory[6] and in the fall of 1944 I was transferred from Birkenau to
Auschwitz. In the *Union* factory I was working in the *Pulverraum* (gunpowder

room). It was an enclosed room about 10 ft. by 6 or 7. On one side were tables with six or seven press machines. We were making the part that ignited a bomb, called a *Verzögerung* (delayed action fuse for a rocket or bomb). The *Verzögerung* itself was a little smaller than a checker and there was a hole in it, $1/8''$ in diameter. This hole had to be filled with gunpowder. We used a certain measure, a tiny spoon, to pour the gunpowder into that hole and then press it down in the machine. That was our job. The *Meister* (foreman), Von Ende, brought us allotments of powder. Each girl got a certain allotment and she had to produce, I don't remember how many hundreds of *Verzögerungs* with her allotment. After we finished our allotment, it was put on a tray the size of a cookie sheet and it was tested to see whether the caps exploded. *Meister* Von Ende pulled out a few at random. We were not punished if there were five or ten that did not pass the test, but if there were more, then we had to do it all over or we had our rations taken away. Most of the time we were careful not to be caught with poor work. We were extremely careful.

Regina Saperstein[7] had to stand next to *Meister* Von Ende, and watch when he pulled caps out of the tray at random for testing. He had a habit of doing it in a certain pattern. Since we were allowed some defective pieces, Regina tried to put them on the tray in such a pattern that she more or less felt sure the defective caps would not be pulled out. When we pressed down the handle on the machine, some of the powder had to overflow because we had to put enough in the hole to pack it down. The overflow was a little mangled. It was not powerful enough. It was called *Abfall* (waste). We saved this *Abfall* and sometimes we mixed it with the good powder even though we were supposed to discard it. Von Ende collected the *Abfall* but we made sure that there was always enough so that they couldn't catch on that we were stealing some of it.

No one was permitted to enter except the *Meister*, who collected the finished product, and one other person. I don't remember who that was. We did not know where the part we made belonged, or how it was assembled. In the part of the *Union* factory that I could see, the prisoners were producing all sorts of metal pieces and tubes. We found out from people who worked in the plant that V2 rockets were made there.

We started working at daybreak. Sometimes it was dark. There was a *Zahlappell* (roll-call in concentration camp) at daybreak. We got our tea or coffee and a slice of bread and we marched to work in formation. We continued working till noon, when they blew a siren. We went into formation again and they dished out our bowl of soup and then we continued working until 5 o'clock or later. I think only one shift worked in the *Pulverraum* because I don't remember ever seeing any other. The other parts of the factory had two shifts, day and night. In the *Pulverraum* were eight or nine girls. There were Estusia, from Warsaw, Inge Frank and Ilse Michel from Germany, Genia Fischer, whom I approached to work with us, another girl, and myself. Regina Saperstein was a *Forarbeiterin* (work foreman). We were all more or less the same age. Not all of those girls were working in the Underground. Regina Saperstein was a lovely person, quiet and very nice, a Jewish girl, one of us. She helped us with the powder.

In March 1943, Estusia approached me. She told me that resistance was being organized and we were in a position to help because we were the only ones with access to powder. Would I be willing to risk the danger of being caught? Of course, I agreed right away because it gave me a way to fight back. I felt very good about it and I didn't care about the danger. None of us did. She taught me how to collect and save powder. She told me to try and mix the *Abfall* with the good powder and fill several of the *Verzögerungs* with the bad powder in order to accumulate good powder. The good powder we put in little pieces of cloth. We tied them up and we put them either in our bosom or into a pocket, if we had one. We tore off a piece of a shirt or you gave away a piece of bread for a kerchief and you cut it up. You could do many things when you force yourself to do them. We kept the powder on our bodies or in our pockets. Very often before we entered the camp, they stopped and searched us.

When we saw from afar that there was going to be a search, we sprinkled the powder on the ground and stepped on it, ground it into the ground so there was no way of catching us. The powder was charcoal grey. Very dark. Almost black. It wasn't powder-like, it was more like tiny grains. It couldn't get under the nails. In a day three of us could collect about two teaspoons full.

We were observing the other girls. We were talking to them. We were asking them: "What would you do if you had a chance to do something?" It was done very subtly.

One friend whom I approached refused. She didn't give me a reason. After the war, we met and she said her conscience bothered her. She had to get it off her chest. She told me, "I was afraid that I would not be strong enough under duress, if they would catch me, whether I could withstand pain." I gave her credit for being honest. She's a very good friend and I never held it against her, even though I didn't know the reason at the time.

When I accumulated this gunpowder, Estusia took it from me and she gave it to someone. We did not know many names for safety reasons, so I really don't know exactly but I knew that a girl who was a runner delivered the powder to other people who had connections with men and the men used it.[8] I knew that we were going to try a mass escape. The men would go first and maybe the women later. Whether anyone would survive, was doubtful, but at least we would try. That was our main goal.

Only later on I learned the names of two of the girls, Roza Robota and Alla Gaertner.[9] They did not work in the *Pulverraum*. I started the stealing sometime in March 1944 and continued until the crematorium was blown up, October 7, 1944. Regina Saperstein, Estusia, Genia Fischer and I participated. Three others did not. The *Sonderkommando* (special work squad, usually workers in the crematoria) was changed every few weeks.[10] They didn't want the same people. These 300 men knew that they were going to be gassed, so they blew up the crematorium and tried to escape, but they were caught.[11] From what I heard it was a gruesome story. They were caught and shot. Then they made a *Zahlappel* of shot bodies to make sure that no one escaped.[12] That's what I heard. I didn't see it but it was immediately repeated to us. It was the general talk in the *Pulverraum*, where we were immediately isolated. An SS woman was assigned especially to us. We called her "The Frog"; she was the ugliest thing in the world. She was a huge woman and she watched us. She listened to whatever we were talking about and whenever we went out, she searched us. It was bad before but it was miserable after the crematorium was blown up. They knew there was no other way of getting gunpowder but from this *Pulverraum*. Regina was taken because she was responsible for the room. With Estusia, there was a tragedy. One day she had sick leave. A Russian girl, Clara, saw Estusia on the block, talking to a man, and denounced her. I heard that right after the explosion they caught this Clara with something which she was not supposed to have and she made a deal with them that if they go easy on her, she'd tell about Estusia's connection with the men. About two weeks afterwards they took Estusia and Regina to Block 11,[13] into a bunker and they were beaten beyond description. Their bodies looked like pieces of raw liver.

Since I was always working next to Estusia, they took me too, for interrogation. Well, the beating that I got was not as severe as theirs. They showed me a drawing of a man and asked me whether I ever saw this man. They told me right away, "This is Estusia's friend. Did you see him often?" They started interrogating me. Of course I denied I had ever seen the man or been in contact with him, which was true. They threatened me with shooting and all sorts of things but they couldn't get anything out of me, so they sent me back. From their questioning, I thought that they suspected the whole world. All the Jews were their enemies. They couldn't even suspect Regina or Estusia of anything specific because they didn't have anything on them, except that Regina was responsible for the *Pulverraum*, and the *Pulverraum* was the only source of gunpowder. This much they could suspect but they couldn't know who gave it.

Two weeks later, Estusia and Regina were released. The SS didn't have any tangible evidence which they could tie to them.[14] So Estusia and Regina were released and sent back to work. They were in such agony after their beating. They were with us for a very short while. Before Christmas the Gestapo took them back to Block 11 and of course, January 6th was the hanging, the execution of the four girls.[15] All the women of the camp were outside and they called the *Pulverraum* to the front, right next to the gallows where the chairs were. This I remember. I marked it down in my notes. Hoessler,[16] the camp *Führer* called *"Pulverraum nach vorne,"* which means "Pulverraum to the front" and he read the verdict, "In the name of the German law you are sentenced to death."

What a paradox that was, "in the name of law." In Auschwitz, to read a verdict in the name of law! I passed out. I hardly remember anything afterwards. Complete numbness set in for me. I didn't care for anything. Nothing mattered to me. We were all silent. We couldn't talk for quite a while. Thirteen days later we were evacuated from Auschwitz.

I wrote down some notes in Auschwitz but when we were evacuated, I threw them away. I tore them up because I thought perhaps I'd be searched and there may be incriminating information in the notes. I traded bread for paper or I sewed little aprons for the *Blockaltester*. She gave me the needle and thread, and for the apron she gave me an extra piece of bread. My father always wanted us to remember what was happening, to be able to tell the world, so the world should know of the heinous crimes the Germans committed. He always told us, "Remember what is happening." It was my father's strong message to survive and tell the world.

Estusia and I were like sisters. People never knew that we were not really sisters. As soon as all my sisters were taken away from me and Estusia saw my condition, she helped me a lot morally. She told me I must be strong and survive. I had told her things that my father said. He prepared us for the hardship. He was a very unusual, a very unique person. Through *meshalim* (parables) he gave us courage and taught us how to live in spite of difficulties.

Just before we were separated from our parents, before we went to Wadowice, my father took us four girls aside. He told us a parable of two men. They were tired of life. They had difficulties and problems. They went to a river, stood on the bridge, and contemplated suicide. One of the men courageously jumped into the water and was gone. The other one shivered and went away. Which is the coward and which is the brave man? Of course, as children, we said it was the one who had the courage to jump into the river. My father said, "No, you're wrong. The one who took up the fight and continued to live and fight for what he wanted, this one is the brave man." I had told this to Estusia before, and she kept on repeating it to me. Other things my father told us made us have faith, to believe that some good will come of it. I feel that it was my father's blessing that helped me survive.

Rose Meth was evacuated from Auschwitz on January 18, 1945, on a death march to Wroclaw on the Polish–German border. From there she was transported to Ravensbrück and then to Neustadt-Glewe, where she was liberated by the American Army on May 3, 1945. In Neustadt-Glewe, Mrs. Meth again wrote notes about her experiences in Auschwitz. The original notes are in the archives at Yad Vashem. She arrived in the USA in May 1946.

Interviewed by:
Bonnie Gurewitsch, 10/28/85

NOTES

1. Wadowice, Poland, 23 miles WSW of Cracow. Pope John Paul II was born there, as Karol Wojtyla, on May 18, 1920.
2. Belzec extermination camp, located 120 km. southwest of Warsaw, built for the exclusive purpose of murdering the Jews of southeastern Poland. It was in operation between March 17, 1942 and June 1943, and claimed an estimated 600,000 Jewish lives in its six carbon monoxide chambers. (Konnilyn Feig. *Hitler's Death Camps, The Sanity of Madness,* New York: Holmes & Meier, 1979 pp. 276–277.)
3. SS *Rapportführer* Tauber is mentioned by Sara Nomberg-Przytyk in her memoir, *Auschwitz: True Tales from a Grotesque Land.* (Chapel Hill: University of North Carolina Press, p. 53.) He "was famous in Auschwitz for his ability to kill a person in two motions," knocking the prisoner unconscious with a blow to the head, then strangling the prisoner with pressure of his foot on the prisoner's throat.
4. Dr. Josef Mengele, highest ranking doctor of Auschwitz.
5. Estusia, Esther Wacjsblum, sister of Anna Heilman, referred to in other sources as Toszka. Testimony of Marta C., "New Testimonies: Women's Resistance in Auschwitz," *The Voice of Auschwitz Survivors in Israel* No. 34, April 1986, p. 11.
6. *Weichsel Union Werke* Factory in Auschwitz I produced rockets and munitions, among which were shell fuses. (*KL Auschwitz as Seen By the SS*;. State Museum at Oswiecim, p. 185.)
7. Regina is mentioned in *Amidst a Nightmare of Crime: Notes of Prisoners of Sonderkommando Found at Auschwitz.* State Museum at Oswiecim, 1973, p. 155, and in Marta C.'s testimony.
8. This was probably Roza Robota, who worked in the *Effektenlager* (warehouses where confiscated clothing and personal possessions of prisoners were sorted) at Birkenau (BIIg) sorting clothing, which adjoined the area of Crematorium IV. She transferred the gunpowder to the prisoner Wrobel, a member of the Resistance movement who worked in the Sonderkommando. ("Diary of Salmen Lewental," *Amidst a Nightmare of Crime,* p. 155.) Israel Gutman describes another girl, Hadassah, who he says was the courier who would bring the gunpowder to him or to a prisoner named Yehuda. (Israel Gutman, *Smoke and Ashes: The Story of Auschwitz-Birkenau,* Israel: Sifriyat Poalim, 1957, p. 151.)
9. Roza Robota was 23 years old, from Ciechanow, Poland, an active member of the Zionist Organization, *HaShomer HaTzair.* She was an early, active recruit to the Resistance organization in Auschwitz. (Gutman, p. 155.) Alla Gaertner was deported to Auschwitz from Sosnowiec, Poland, and was a work foreman in Auschwitz. (Conversation with Rose Meth, 5/15/90.)
10. "All our *Kommando* had always been of the opinion that we were in a much greater danger than all the other prisoners in the camp, much more even than the Jews in the camp. We believed that the Germans would want at all costs to obliterate all traces of their crimes committed till now. They would not be able to do this otherwise than by killing our entire *Kommando,* leaving not a single one alive . . ." ("Diary of Salmen Lewental," *Amidst a Nightmare of Crime,* pp. 154–155.)
11. In the revolt of the *Sonderkommando* on October 7, 1944, Crematorium II was exploded. (Gutman, pp. 153–154 and conversation with Tsippi Tichauer,

5/16/90.) Crematorium III was burned (testimony of Henry Fuchs, Center for Holocaust Studies, RG 1656 and original notes of Rose Meth, Center for Holocaust Studies, RG 1347, A 398). Professor Erwin Tichauer reports that a fire damaged the ceiling and roof of Crematorium IV (conversation 5/16/90). Damage in crematoriums II & IV is confirmed by the report of Henryk Tauber: "The revolt . . . also spread to Krematorium II . . . Before fleeing, we set Krematorium IV on fire . . ." (Jean Claude Pressac, *Auschwitz: Technique and Operation of the Gas Chambers.* New York: Beate Klarsfeld Foundation, 1989, p.498.) Gutman reports that the revolt of the *Sonderkommando* involved about 600 men, that one of the cruelest *Kapos* was thrown alive into the flames, four SS men were killed in hand to hand combat, and others were wounded. In the chaos, some prisoners broke down the fence and tried to escape, but most were killed by a force of 2000 Nazi guards who were alerted. Professor Tichauer stressed the lack of coordination and cooperation among the several resistance groups. The explosives experts worked at Crematorium II. When the noise of the explosion in Crematorium II was heard by the others, the fires were started in crematoriums III & IV.

12. This is confirmed by Gutman, p. 153.
13. Block 11 was the punishment block in Auschwitz I, where interrogations and torture took place. Gutman confirms the account of the interrogations of the girls (pp. 154–157).
14. Gutman points out that initially, the possibility that Jewish women could be involved in transferring explosives was inconceivable to the Gestapo, and after the initial investigation they tried other avenues of inquiry. According to Gutman, the Kapo Eugene Koch, who had befriended Alla Gaertner, informed to the Gestapo and told them what he knew of the Resistance and the role of the women. After Koch's testimony the Jewish women were arrested again and interrogated further. The women, in spite of severe torture, did not reveal any information. (Gutman, p. 155.)
15. Roza Robota, Regina Saperstein, Alla Gaertner and Esther Wajcblum. Roza Robota's last word, prior to her execution, was, "*Nekama!*" Revenge! (Gutman, p. 157.)
16. SS *Hauptsturmfuhrer* Franz Hoessler, appointed in June 1944 *Lagerführer* of the men's camp at Auschwitz. He was executed as a war criminal on December 13, 1945. (*Amidst a Nightmare of Crime*, p. 50.)

12

Sara Nomberg-Przytyk

*How is this possible? I pondered. On one side such bestiality, and
on the other unselfish love toward another creature.*

SARA NOMBERG-PRZYTYK

*Sara Nomberg-Przytyk was born in Lublin, Poland, in 1915. Growing up in
an Orthodox Jewish environment, she experienced Polish antisemitism early
on. She attended the University of Warsaw, spent several years in Polish jails because of her leftist political activities, and fled east to Bialystok when the Germans
invaded Poland in 1939. Caught in the Bialystok ghetto in 1943, she was sent to a
camp at Stutthof and then deported to Auschwitz. Danuta Czech's* Auschwitz
Chronicle *mentions a transport that reached Auschwitz from Stutthof on January
12, 1944. It contained nearly 1,000 prisoners—male and female. Only 120 men
and 134 women were spared from immediate death. Probably Nomberg-Przytyk
was among that "lucky" 134, because her* Auschwitz: True Tales from a Grotesque Land *notes that she became a* Zugang *(a new arrival) on January 13.
About a year later, along with hundreds of other women, she was force-marched to
Ravensbrück.*

*Returning to Poland to "build a socialist society" after her liberation in late April
1945, Nomberg-Przytyk married in 1946, started a family, and worked as a
journalist in Lublin. She also took time to write about her Holocaust experiences. In
fact,* Auschwitz: True Tales from a Grotesque Land *was accepted for publication
and was about to go to press when Poland's Communist government instigated an
outburst of antisemitism following Israel's victory in the 1967 Six-Day War.
Nomberg-Przytyk was told that her book would be published only if she eliminated all*

references to Jews. Protesting that "deal," she emigrated to Israel in 1968, smuggling her precious manuscript out of Poland and eventually depositing it in the archives at Yad Vashem, the Holocaust Martyrs' and Heroes' Remembrance Authority in Jerusalem. Her book was published in English in 1985.

Nomberg-Przytyk is a teller of tales that are true. Like Ida Fink, she draws on her own experience, but she turns history into vignette and story. The result is not fiction but imagination and creativity that reveal truth to be both stranger and more compelling than fiction. Nomberg-Przytyk's narratives are unique for the extraordinary gifts of observation and memory the author brings to them. These gifts appear in her writing's stark simplicity, which reflects the stance she assumed deliberately to protect herself: "From the moment I got to Auschwitz," she explains, "I was completely detached. I disconnected my heart and intellect in an act of self-defense, despair, and hopelessness." Throughout her book, the author's tone is neutral and understated—but as if a scream were stuck in her throat. Nomberg-Przytyk's style intensifies the horror it describes.

The setting for "The Camp Blanket," the vignette that follows, is a railroad flatcar—"the kind that you ship lumber in." This one, however, is loaded with women. Having trudged to it over miles of wintry terrain, they are squeezed in "so tightly that we could not even move an arm or a leg." This train will take them the rest of the way to Ravensbrück, if their miserable conditions allow them to live that long.

Nomberg-Przytyk finds a little space to herself in what she calls "a booth located between the cars." But the space gained also leaves her exposed to the cold that becomes more bitter and deadly once the transport begins to move. Wanting to sleep, she is probably freezing to death when she hears a woman's voice. It warns her to stay awake, and then she hears it say something even more remarkable: "Please stretch out your hand and take the blanket. Quick." Later the voice tells her to stretch out her hand again. Doing so, she receives a crust of bread. Nomberg-Przytyk asks, more than once, to learn the name that goes with the voice, with the warmth and the food. The voice never reveals its name, but neither has Nomberg-Przytyk forgotten how much it meant to her.

While a gray blanket is the subject, the real focus of this true story is a question that touches the core of human existence: How is it possible for "bestiality" and "unselfish love" to exist in such close physical proximity? The two orders of simultaneous experience are so different, so irreconcilable, that their coexistence is an unyielding paradox. And yet what Sara Nomberg-Przytyk clings to is that, in an inhuman situation, she encountered a human being whose simple gestures of unselfish love were anything but simple because of their overwhelming generosity. Her contact with that woman may have enabled Nomberg-Przytyk to reconnect her "heart and intellect." Her remembrance of that contact may have restored some fragment of hope—for, after all, hope is always joined to memory.

The Camp Blanket

We dragged ourselves along the highways for a few more days, until we reached a side station where flatcars were waiting for us, the kind that you ship lumber in. It is difficult for me to say how long the terrible walk lasted. I could no longer tell the difference between day and night. There was no food, and we quenched our thirst with snow, which was plentiful. At one point, someone in the escort brought the news that the Bolsheviks were getting closer. From that time on, the tempo of our wandering speeded up. Everybody mustered the last remaining ounce of strength; none of us wanted to fall behind just when freedom seemed so close.

As usually happens in situations of this kind, news traveled from mouth to mouth, which caused wings to grow on our shoulders.

"Listen," Zenia whispered into my ear while walking, "the Russian command sent out a special company of soldiers just to liberate the transport from Auschwitz. They will be here soon."

I believed what she was saying. I did not even ask where she heard the news. I listened for the echo of shots, and I waited for freedom.

Next to me two girls were talking about something very quietly. By their sad faces you could tell that the news was not very good.

"What happened?" I asked.

"Not far from here, on the side of the road," one of them explained, "is a little forest. The machine guns are already set up there. They will take care of us quickly."

"Don't babble nonsense," I said sharply. "There are too many of us. They wouldn't have time to cover their tracks. The escorts are afraid of the Russian army. They won't do it."

But anxiety remained. It was already dark when we found ourselves standing in front of the open railway cars. They started loading us onto the flatcars, which were slippery with ice. There was a chaos of squeezing, shrieking, beating, and shooting. I became separated from my friends. Someone pushed me from behind, and I found myself in the car. The first women to be herded into the car tried to sit down, but they had to get up quickly in order not to be trampled by the women who were being pushed in after them. We were squeezed into the car so tightly that we could not even move an arm or a leg. I thought to myself that if we had to travel this way for any distance nobody

From Sara Nomberg-Przytyk, *Auschwitz: True Tales from a Grotesque Land*, ed. Eli Pfefferkorn and David H. Hirsch and trans. Roslyn Hirsch. Chapel Hill: The University of North Carolina Press, 1985. Copyright © 1985 by The University of North Carolina Press. Reprinted by permission of The University of North Carolina Press.

would survive. Standing motionless we would all freeze. I even imagined that we would all become one stony mass with many heads.

Before the train left, two older soldiers got into the cars. They were our escort. They set a little bench in the back of the wagon, sat down, and did not even look at us. They spoke quietly to each other in Hungarian. The train pulled out and picked up speed quickly. The wind almost tore our heads off. Our legs were burning, as if exposed to real fire. No one spoke, because it would have been impossible to hear. The pervasive death-like silence was broken only by the roar of the wheels and the whistle of the wind.

Not far from me stood two young Polish girls.

"Zosiu," one said to the other, "I am going to jump off the train. What about you?"

"I will jump after you," answered the other.

Slowly they moved to the wall of the wagon. My heart stopped beating out of fear. I wished they would succeed. In fact, it was possible to try to escape. The car was open, and the escort consisted of two Hungarians who had their own problems. I did not turn my head in their direction. I just listened very carefully.

"Where are you crawling, you louse?" I heard the German *kapo* call out. There followed a terrible beating with a stick. The girl fell on the floor. That was the end of her. She was trampled to death by the German functionaries.

"Hey, there!" one of them yelled to the escorts. "A woman died here. Can we get rid of the body? There is no room for it in the wagon."

"Throw her out," one of them answered.

"Hey, hop, hey, hop." The body of the young girl went flying out of the car. None of us said anything. No one could be found who reacted like a human being to this monstrous crime. Why did we keep quiet? After all, it was not fear that closed our mouths. They numbered about ten to fifteen, and we were more than a hundred. It was all part of the routine. In camp they were the ones who did the hitting, while we were the ones who got the beatings and who did not even have the right to defend ourselves or shield ourselves from the blows. That is what the camp had done to us. It had stripped us of the capacity to make a human gesture or to react normally when confronted by an enemy.

Once again the thumping of the wheels made the time go by. We passed by large estates and small towns. Everything was so dark that it was difficult for us to orient ourselves and figure out where we were. A noise reached my ears, some sort of whining explanation. A woman had seated herself because she could no longer stand. The criminals pounced on her.

"Hey, there. Escort!" shouted one of the *kapos*. "A woman died. Can we throw her out?"

Once again there was the thump of a body cast out of the car. Now this sound started to repeat itself often. I came to the realization that the *kapos* were killing the women and getting rid of the bodies so that they would have more comfortable accommodations. Maybe, I thought, they will kill us all. They would be by themselves, and then they would be able to lie down comfortably on the floor. I was standing far enough from the German *kapos*, separated from them by a crowd of women. My legs hurt terribly, and I dreamt of only one thing, to sit down. I wanted to sit just for a moment, a short moment. But to sit in this car was impossible.

My attention was drawn to a booth located between the cars; inside the booth was a bench. I was seized with a desire to get to the booth. I thought that I would sit down and leave behind this car where the criminals were killing women before our very eyes, instead of standing here silent and scared. This nagging idea even killed my fear; the soldier escorting us might think that I was trying to run away and he might gun me down. Slowly I moved to the back of the car, and without thinking I put one leg over and then the other. I was in the booth. I sat down. I was sweating like a church mouse. I had succeeded! I sat down on the bench. I stretched my legs out in front of me. No one told me to return; I could travel here quietly. I felt so good, so comfortable. I dozed off. The cold awakened me. Now I felt cold. I had nothing to cover myself with. The wind and frost were tearing my head off. I was freezing. In the car the bodies were packed tightly together and were warming each other. Here I was alone and there was no place to move. I was afraid that the Hungarian soldiers or the German *kapos* might notice me.

I blew into my hands. I rubbed my feet together, but that did not help much. Sleep, which I could not shake off, overcame me. I fell asleep. Then a knocking on the wall of the booth woke me up, and I heard a feeble whisper:

"Please, ma'am, don't sleep! It's dangerous. You will freeze."

At first I was sure that I must be dreaming, that I must be talking to myself. With all my might I tried to open my eyes and lift my wobbly head. But I could not. It was beyond my strength. I fell asleep again.

"Please, ma'am," a loud whisper and a knocking on the wall reached me as if through a fog. "Please stretch out your hand and take the blanket. Quick," the urging voice insisted from the other world. "Please don't think about it. Just stretch out your hand."

I stretched out my arm and someone from the car really handed me a gray blanket from the camp. It was not a dream after all. "There is somebody in the car," I thought, "who wants to help me. Somebody wants me to live." I threw the blanket over my head. I wrapped my back and chest and hid my hands.

Now I knocked on the wall of the booth. "Please, ma'am, you saved my life. I feel warm now. Do you need the blanket?"

"No," a whisper came back. "We had two blankets, my daughter and I. We covered ourselves with one, and we are warm."

How is this possible? I pondered. On one side such bestiality, and on the other unselfish love toward another creature. Then I realized that I did not even know my savior's name and that I would never be able to repay her for the gray blanket that, for me, meant the difference between life and death.

"Ma'am." I knocked again. "Please give me your name. I really must know your name." Silence. "Can you hear me?" I called out loud. "Please. Your name." "Your name, your name, your name," was repeated in the echo of the wheels.

"Stretch out your hand." I heard a whisper from behind the wall. I stretched out my hand. In my hand I found a dry crust of bread from the camp. I chewed it up and then let the dry crumbs dissolve in my mouth. "Your name, your name," I insisted.

"Your name, your name, name." The wind was blowing in my ears.

Suggestions for Further Reading

Appleman-Jurman, Alicia. *Alicia: My Story*. New York: Bantam, 1988.

Begley, Louis. *Wartime Lies*. New York: Knopf, 1991.

Berg, Mary. *Warsaw Ghetto: A Diary*. Edited by S. L. Shneiderman. Translated by Norbert and Sylvia Glass. New York: L. B. Fischer, 1945.

Blatter, Janet, and Sybil Milton, eds. *The Art of the Holocaust*. New York: W. H. Smith, 1981.

Birnbaum, Halina. *Hope Is the Last to Die*. Translated by David Welsh. New York: Twayne, 1971.

Borowski, Tadeusz. *This Way for the Gas, Ladies and Gentlemen; and Other Stories*. Translated by Barbara Vedder. New York: Penguin, 1967.

Dafni, Reuven, and Yehudit Kleiman, eds. *Final Letters: From Victims of the Holocaust*. New York: Paragon House, 1991.

Dawidowicz, Lucy S. *From That Place and Time: A Memoir 1938–1947*. New York: Norton, 1989.

Dribben, Judith. *A Girl Called Judith Strick*. New York: Cowles, 1970.

Duras, Marguerite. *The War: A Memoir*. New York: Pantheon, 1986.

Dufurnier, Denise. *Ravensbrück, the Women's Camp of Death*. London: George Allen & Unwin, 1948.

Eliach, Yaffa, and Bonnie Gurewitsch, eds. "Women of Valor: Partisans and Resistance Fighters." *Center for Holocaust Studies Newsletter* 6 (Spring 1990).

Fénelon, Fania. *Playing for Time*. Translated by Marcelle Routier. New York: Berkley, 1979.

Ferderber-Salz, Bertha. *And the Sun Kept Shining*. New York: Holocaust Library, 1980.

Frank, Anne. *The Diary of Anne Frank: The Critical Edition*. Edited by David Barnouw and Gerrold van der Stroom. Translated by Arnold J. Pomerans and B. M. Mooyaart-Doubleday. New York: Doubleday, 1989.

Gluck, Gemma La Guardia. *My Story*. New York: David McKay, 1961.

Gurdus, Luba Krugman. *The Death Train*. New York: Holocaust Library, 1979.

Hart, Kitty. *I Am Alive*. London: Abelard-Schuman, 1962.

————. *Return to Auschwitz: The Remarkable Story of a Girl Who Survived the Holocaust*. New York: Atheneum, 1982.

Hillesum, Etty. *An Interrupted Life: The Diaries of Etty Hillesum 1941–43*. New York: Pantheon, 1982.

Hoess, Rudolf. *Commandant of Auschwitz: The Autobiography of Rudolf Hoess*. Translated by Constance FitzGibbon. London: Pan Books, 1974.

Hoffman, Eva. *Lost in Translation: A Life in a New Language*. New York: Penguin, 1989.

Isaacson, Judith Magyar. *Seed of Sarah: Memoirs of a Survivor*. Urbana: University of Illinois Press, 1990.

Karmel, Ilona. *An Estate of Memory*. New York: Feminist Press at the City University of New York, 1986.

Kielar, Wieslaw. *Anus Mundi*. New York: Times Books, 1980.

Klee, Ernst, Willi Dressen, and Volker Reiss, eds., *Those Were the Days: The Holocaust Through the Eyes of Perpetrators and Bystanders*. Translated by Deborah Burnstone. London: Hamish Hamilton, 1991.

Klein, Cecilie. *Sentenced to Live*. New York: Holocaust Library, 1988.

Klein, Gerda Weissman. *All But My Life*. New York: Noonday Press, 1990.

Latour, Anny. *The Jewish Resistance in France*. New York: Schocken, 1981.

Leitner, Isabella, with Irving A. Leitner. *Saving the Fragments: From Auschwitz to New York*. New York: New American Library, 1986.

Levy-Haas, Hanna. *Inside Belsen*. Translated by Ronald Taylor. Totowa, N.J.: Barnes & Noble, 1982.

Lewin, Rhoda G., ed. *Witnesses to the Holocaust: An Oral History*. Boston: Twayne, 1990.

Lingens-Reiner, Ella. *Prisoners of Fear*. London: Gollancz, 1948.

Lixl-Purcell, Andreas, ed. *Women of Exile: German Jewish Autobiographies Since 1933*. Westport, Conn.: Greenwood Press, 1988.

Lubetkin, Zivia. *In the Days of Destruction and Revolt*. Tel Aviv: Hakibbutz Hameuchad, 1981.

Maurel, Micheline. *An Ordinary Camp*. Translated by Margaret S. Summers. New York: Simon & Schuster, 1958.

Meed, Vladka. *On Both Sides of the Wall*. New York: Holocaust Library, 1979.

Millu, Liana. *Smoke Over Birkenau*. Translated by Lynne Sharon Schwartz. Philadelphia: The Jewish Publication Society, 1991.

Morhange-Begue, Claude. *Chamberet: Recollections from an Ordinary Childhood*. Translated by Austryn Wainhouse. Marlboro, Vt.: The Marlboro Press, 1987.

Penny, Frances. *I Was There*. New York: Shengold, 1988.

Senesh, Hannah. *Hannah Senesh: Her Life and Diary*. Translated by Marta Cohn. New York: Schocken, 1972.

Shelley, Lore, ed. and trans. *Secretaries of Death: Accounts by Former Prisoners Who Worked in the Gestapo of Auschwitz*. New York: Shengold, 1986.

———, ed. and trans. *Auschwitz—the Nazi Civilization: Twenty-three Women Prisoners' Accounts*. Lanham, Md.: University Press of America, 1992.

Szmaglewska, Seweryna. *Smoke Over Birkenau*. Translated by Jadwiga Rynas. New York: Holt, 1947.

———. *United in Wrath*. Warsaw: "Polonia" Foreign Languages Publishing House, 1955.

Tedeschi, Giuliana. *There Is a Place on Earth: A Woman in Birkenau*. New York: Pantheon, 1992.

Ten Boom, Corrie. *The Hiding Place*. New York: Bantam, 1975.

Vinke, Herman. *The Short Life of Sophie Scholl*. New York: Harper, 1984.

Weiss, Reska. *Journey Through Hell: A Woman's Account*. London: Valentine, Mitchell, 1961.

"Women Who Fought the Nazis." *Lilith* 16 (Spring 1987).

Zuker-Bujanowska, Liliana. *Liliana's Journal, Warsaw, 1939–1945*. New York: Dial, 1980.

Zyskind, Sara. *Stolen Years*. Translated by Marganit Inbar. New York: New American Library, 1983.

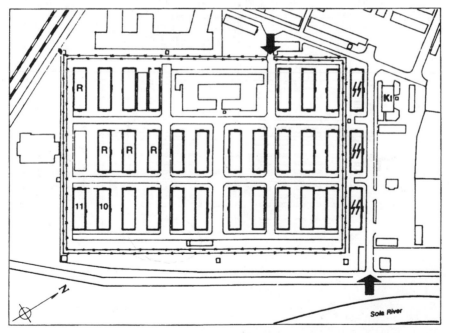

Plan of Auschwitz I.
K: Crematory I; R: camp hospital barracks; 10: barracks where pseudo-medical experiments were conducted; 11: "death barracks." The rest of the barracks inside the barbed wire were prisoners' residences.

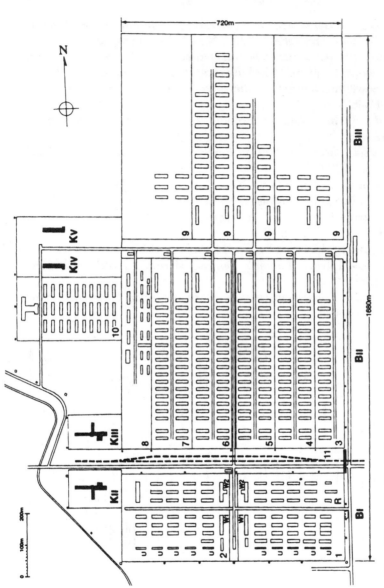

Plan of Auschwitz II—Birkenau.

1 and 2: The women's camp. 3: Men's camp. 4: Family camp for Czech Jews. 5 and 6: The men's camp. 7: Family camp for Gypsies. 8: Hospital in men's camp. 9: Under construction; known as "Mexico." 10: Storehouses of plundered effects; known as "Canada." K: Crematories and gas chambers. 11: Rail platform; site of "selections" for gas chamber. R: Hospital barracks in women's camp. W1: Kitchens. W2: Bathhouses; place to get water in women's camp. U: Washrooms and toilets without running water.

Continuous lines around sections = electrically charged barbed wire.

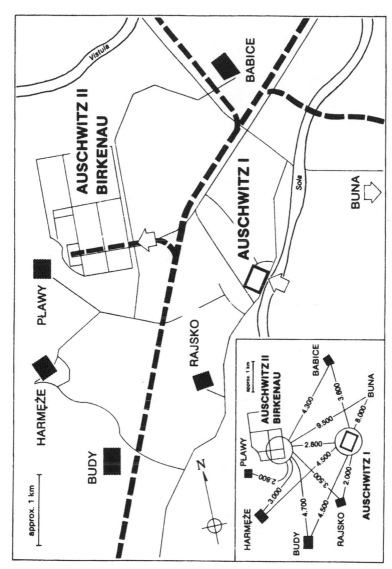

Distances to work sites outside camp (in km.).

Part Two

VOICES OF
INTERPRETATION

And when your throat is gagged, your bleeding cry suppressed,
When brutal shackles bind your trembling arms,
Oh let me be the voice that echoes down the shaft of all eternity,
The hand stretched high to touch God's towering heaven.

GERTRUD KOLMAR

If Auschwitz was *anus mundi*, Berlin was where that "asshole of the world" began. During the summer of 1941, SS officer Rudolf Höss, who at the age of forty had been officially named commandant of Auschwitz on May 4, 1940, was summoned there to meet Heinrich Himmler, the SS commander in chief. Höss did not keep a daily Auschwitz diary, but while he was under investigation for war crimes in 1946–1947, he wrote an autobiography. Höss is vague about the exact time of his meeting with Himmler, but one probable date is July 29, 1941, two days before Hermann Göring officially ordered Reinhard Heydrich to lay plans for the "Final Solution."

Höss precisely recollects Himmler's directives to make Auschwitz a major extermination center to carry out the "Final Solution." Instructed to keep Himmler's orders "absolutely secret," he learned that Himmler expected him to take the steps necessary for the camp's expansion.[1] Immediately after their meeting, Höss returned to Auschwitz and got to work. Later that summer, Adolf Eichmann, the SS leader responsible for organizing Jewish transports to Auschwitz and other killing centers, met with him at the camp. "We discussed the ways and means of effecting the extermination," Höss recalls.[2] Gassing, they agreed, was the only feasible way, but questions remained about the best implementation of that procedure.

Historian Raul Hilberg underscores that the Nazi order to proceed with the "Final Solution" was "an authorization to invent. . . . In every aspect of this operation invention was necessary . . . because every problem was unprecedented."[3] Höss became one of the inventors. Before 1941 was over, he had discovered the deadly virtues of a pesticide manufactured by a subsidiary of I. G. Farben. Zyklon B, as it was called, would obliterate the Jews and other people whom Nazi ideology regarded as vermin.

Höss's inventiveness cost well over a million lives. It led to his own execution by hanging in Auschwitz on April 16, 1947. The site of that sentence was close to the villa that Höss had occupied with his wife and children while he administered the camp's affairs. The Hösses had five children between 1930 and 1943, two sons and three daughters. The last child was born during Höss's leadership of the camp. "My family," he wrote, "were well provided for in Auschwitz. Every wish that my wife or children expressed was granted them. The children could live a free and untrammeled life. My wife's garden was a paradise of flowers."[4] Auschwitz was home.

Hedwig Hensel Höss left no autobiography, but her husband says they were well suited to each other. Their values apparently were the same, although Höss reports that his wife chided him for working too hard at Auschwitz and not spending enough time with his family. The two of them did not talk much, Höss admits, and his autobiography notes that he never told his wife about "all that lay so heavily on my mind."[5] Camp rumors had it that his home life might have been less satisfactory than his autobiography said. There is some evidence, for example, that Höss had a sordid love affair with a woman prisoner named Eleonore Hodys.[6] In any case, his was a high-stress job. Seeing that thousands of people went to forced labor or to the gas chamber each day were responsibilities not to be taken lightly. Höss's autobiography reveals that this bureaucrat took them with the utmost seriousness.

Although he often lamented the difficulty of his work, Höss appears never to have questioned whether it should be done. His concern was to get it done efficiently, but on this score he did not always succeed to Himmler's liking. In a late-autumn administrative shakeup in 1943, Höss was relieved of his duties as commandant and reassigned to Berlin. Several months later, however, he reappeared at Auschwitz to preside over the destruction of the Hungarian Jews.

Meanwhile the worries that plagued Höss's earlier administration included the mediocre quality of the female personnel sent from Ravensbrück to administer the women's camp when it opened at Auschwitz. To no avail he tried to persuade Himmler to give up the idea that the women's camp should be commanded by a woman. Which of his SS men, he questioned, "would be willing to take his orders from a woman?"[7] But then, apparently taking the convenient path of forgetting that he was the one in charge, Höss not only states that "the most wretched conditions prevailed in the women's camp" but also places the blame on the "the inadequacy of the chief supervisor and of the female supervisors in general."[8]

"I have always had a great respect," Höss claimed, "for women in general. In Auschwitz, however, I learned that I would have to modify my views, and that even a woman must be carefully examined before she is entitled to enjoy a full measure of respect."[9] No doubt Hedwig Höss passed her husband's test, at least for the most part. But what happened when Höss went home at the end of his working day? What did Frau Höss say? What did she know? What did she feel? What did she want? Since our subject is women and the Holocaust, Hedwig Höss certainly belongs, but who was she, this woman who helped make Auschwitz home for its commandant?

Two testimonies by people who knew her in Auschwitz are worth considering.[10] First, on August 7, 1946, Stanislaw Dubiel, a Polish Roman Catholic, testified that he had been a political prisoner in Auschwitz from November 6, 1940, until January 18, 1945. He worked as a gardener at the Höss villa from April 6, 1942, until the Höss family left Auschwitz for good in the autumn of 1944.

Dubiel indicates that the Hösses entertained numerous guests and did so with some elegance. With the assistance of prisoners who worked for her, Frau Höss kept a well-stocked kitchen and set a good table. Food was always abundant at their house because it was available in Auschwitz and cost them very little. With Dubiel's aid, for example, she could either help herself to the loot that accumulated as the hapless transports arrived or she could take liberties at the camp's commissaries. As Höss's spouse, her perks meant that she could get almost anything she wanted. Clothes, shoes, furniture, valuables of one kind or another—all of these found their way into the Höss household from the camp's workshops and storehouses.

Dubiel was not the only prisoner who served the Höss family. For instance, once women prisoners were on the scene, Hedwig Höss used two of them steadily as dressmakers. Dubiel sums up his impressions by indicating that the Hösses had "such a well-appointed and magnificent home [in Auschwitz] that his wife remarked '*hier will Ich leben und sterben*' [I want to live here till I die]."[11] As it concludes, Dubiel's deposition remarks on Frau Höss's deep anti-Polish and anti-Jewish feelings. They exist to work until they perish, Dubiel remembers her saying of Poles. As for Jews, Frau Höss apparently believed in the "Final Solution," because Dubiel claims that she thought they should disappear from the earth. Last but not least, the Dubiel deposition states that four train cars were needed to move the Höss's accumulated possessions when they departed Auschwitz.

Janina Szczurek was not an Auschwitz prisoner, but she lived nearby. Her sewing skills must have been well known, because, prior to the arrival of female prisoners at the camp, Hedwig Höss approached her with an offer of employment at the Höss villa. At the time, Szczurek adds, she did not know that Frau Höss was the wife of the commandant of Auschwitz. But soon enough she did know, and Szczurek also learned that Frau Höss paid low wages and offered little food. "I could earn more working at home," she reports, but Hedwig Höss urged her back with a raise. Szczurek's employment ended, however, when Jewish seamstresses became available. Frau Höss got their work for free.

Hedwig Höss had a hand in the Holocaust. So did many, many other German women. On the whole, their hands were by no means as dirty as those of Nazi men, but they were part of the Third Reich's destruction process nonetheless. For that process to unfold as smoothly and thoroughly as it did, in fact, there had to be women like Frau Höss, women who fit what Nazi ideology expected. Frau Höss suited that profile quite well. She was loyal and subservient to her husband. She had a large family. She held politically correct views about Jews and Poles. She knew how to run a household that could provide a haven from the rigors of men's work, thus enabling them to keep at the tasks that Nazi duty required. If she was not the perfect wife for the commandant of Auschwitz, Hedwig Höss was more than adequate.

Frau Höss's status was not high-profile. However pious its pleadings about the virtues of womanhood, Nazi ideology aimed at lowering the profile and status of women in society. Respectability and dedication to national purpose were the hallmarks of the Nazi woman. Nazi ideology, imbued with the concept of racial supremacy, dictated that every effort should be made to increase the right segments of the population. Nazi women were to be attractive and bear children, give attention to the spiritual and physical health of their families, and be guardians of the home, but they were not to be much involved in public life and politics. Hitler himself summed up the Nazi position as follows:

> We do not consider it correct for the woman to interfere in the world of the man, in his main sphere. We consider it natural if these two worlds remain distinct. To the one belongs the strength of feeling, the strength of soul. To the other belongs the strength of vision, of toughness, of decision, and of the willingness to act. In the one case this strength demands the willingness of the woman to risk her life to preserve this important cell and to multiply it, and in the other case it demands from the man the readiness to safeguard life.
>
> The sacrifices which the man makes in the struggle of his nation, the woman makes in the preservation of that nation in individual cases. What the man gives in courage on the battlefield, the woman gives in eternal self-sacrifice, in eternal pain and suffering. Every child that a woman brings into the world is a battle, a battle waged for the existence of her people. And both must therefore mutually value and respect each other when they see that each performs the task that Nature and Providence have ordained. And this mutual respect will necessarily result from this separation of the functions of each.[12]

A racist ideology fueled the Nazi genocide, complemented by the central role sexism played in Nazi thought and action. But if the status of German women in the Third Reich was distinctly second-class no matter what the official pronouncements said about mutual respect, that fact entailed that the status of "non-Aryan" women, and even of some "degenerate" German women, was much lower still. Though not at first perhaps, Jewish women in particular would eventually find themselves lowest on the Nazi scale of values.

Although they suffered oppression early on from the anti-Jewish legislation that the Nazis passed, German Jewish women were largely spared the worst brutalities until World War II broke out. Once the war was under way, the Nazis escalated their oppression, sparing no one, neither women nor children. As the Nazis targeted their victims—Jewish and non-Jewish, non-German and German—how did women respond? What choices did they have? What power was theirs? How did they cope?

Already the voices of experience in this book's first part have addressed aspects of those questions. That beginning is supplemented now by seven voices of interpretation who take the inquiry further. Five of them—Gisela Bock, Marion A. Kaplan, Sybil Milton, Vera Laska, and Claudia Koonz—reckon with the larger sociopolitical picture as only good historians can. Two others—Gitta Sereny and Magda Trocmé—focus on the experiences of individuals. As all of these writers explore how Nazi racism and sexism conspired to take both a Hedwig Höss and a Gertrud Kolmar to the *anus mundi* that was Auschwitz, they also shed light on steps that still need to be taken to remove people from harm's way.

In her poem "We Jews," Kolmar yearned for voices that could speak for those whose throats are gagged, their bleeding cries suppressed. She wanted those voices to echo "down the shaft of all eternity." On first hearing, her poetic hope might seem to call for different voices than those that emphasize historical analysis and concern for detail. But if one listens twice, the dissonance recedes, for the accumulation of small detail creates the fullest picture, and the clear, even cool, statement of fact best reveals the immensity of the "Final Solution." Gertrud Kolmar's yearning receives the care it deserves, if not the fulfillment it seeks, in the hands that have written what comes next about women and the Holocaust.

NOTES

1. See "Autobiography of Rudolf Höss," *KL Auschwitz Seen by the SS: Höss, Broad, Kremer*, ed. Jadwiga Bezwinska and Danuta Czech and trans. Constantine FitzGibbon (New York: Howard Fertig, 1984), 109–141.
2. Ibid., 110.
3. See Claude Lanzmann, *Shoah: An Oral History of the Holocaust* (New York: Pantheon, 1985), 72–73.

4. "Autobiography of Rudolf Höss," *KL Auschwitz Seen by the SS*, 106–107.
5. Ibid., 108.
6. For more information on this matter see Jerzy Rawicz's foreword to *KL Auschwitz Seen by the SS*, 21. According to Rawicz, several SS men alleged that Höss had an affair with Hodys, who worked in the Höss household for several months. Apparently she was condemned to death by starvation in an Auschwitz prison cell when her pregnancy became known.
7. Ibid., 81.
8. Ibid., 81.
9. Ibid., 83.
10. See "Deposition of Stanislaw Dubiel" and "Report of Janina Szczurek," *KL Auschwitz Seen by the SS*, 287–294.
11. Ibid., 291.
12. Cited in Konnilyn G. Feig, *Hitler's Death Camps: The Sanity of Madness* (New York: Holmes & Meier, 1981), 159.

13

Gisela Bock

Both Nazi racism and sexism concerned all women, the inferior as
well as the superior.

GISELA BOCK

*The Holocaust happened, but people still wonder how and why. Such questions
require more answers than anyone can give, but, as far as the fate of women during
the Shoah is concerned, some of the most telling are provided by Gisela Bock. Long
associated with work on women's history, she has been for many years a scholar at the
Historical Institute of the Technical University in Berlin. As shown by her essay on
racism and sexism in Nazi Germany, the roads that led to Auschwitz were as long as
they were full of twists and turns. But specifically, she argues, there would have been
no need for Olga Lengyel, Gisela Perl, and Charlotte Delbo to talk about Auschwitz
unless a tradition of "scientific racism," as Bock calls it, helped to make the Holocaust
happen.*

*Outlining significant background, Bock documents how pre-Nazi eugenic theories
paved the way for Hitler and his followers to act on the lethal conclusion that there
are "lives unworthy of life"* (lebensunwertes Leben). *Race-hygiene principles
espoused by Nazi ideology decreed that inferior breeds had to be eliminated while the
superior German one had to be strengthened and improved. So the Third Reich
embraced a principle that had been articulated in 1909, some years before the Nazi
party even existed: "If we want to practice race hygiene seriously, we must make
women the target of our social work."*

*One of the first to focus on the interrelationships between racism and sexism in
Nazi policy, Bock's essay concentrates particularly on the Third Reich's determination to control reproduction. It might be argued that making the issue of motherhood*

and compulsory sterilization the center of discussion shifts the focus too far away from the anti-Jewish nature of Nazi racism and its "war against the Jews." To the contrary, however, Bock reveals that there is significant documentary evidence— legislation, documents, public statements—to support the idea that "the Nazis were by no means simply interested in raising the number of [superior] childbearing women. They were just as bent on excluding many [inferior] women from bearing and raising children—and men from begetting them. . . ." While Jews were not the only ones the Nazis considered unworthy of life, they topped that list. The surest method of birth control, moreover, is death, and Jewish women were targeted accordingly.

Nazi racism and sexism, propagated by men and supported actively or passively by German women, were major instruments of social control during the Third Reich. More than that, Bock reveals, Nazi race hygiene and the "Final Solution" were inextricably bound together.

Racism and Sexism in Nazi Germany: Motherhood, Compulsory Sterilization, and the State

"ALIEN RACES" AND THE "OTHER SEX"

By presenting some largely unexplored features of women's lives under National Socialism in Germany, this essay considers larger questions about the complex connections between racism and sexism. It does not presume to exhaust the issue, or even touch on all its aspects. Instead, it approaches it through the perspective of one part of women's lives affected by state policy: reproduction or, as I prefer to call it, the reproductive aspect of women's unwaged housework. It can be no more than a contribution for two reasons. First, dealing with racism in Germany during this period involves considering an unparalleled mass murder of millions of women and men, an undertaking beyond the scope of any single essay. Second, this analysis is a first approach, for neither race nor gender, racism nor sexism—and even less their connection—has been a central theme in German social historiography.[1] When historians deal with women in modern Germany, they generally do not consider racism or racial discrimination against women,[2] while the literature dealing with anti-Jewish racism and the Holocaust generally does not consider either women's specific situation or the added factor of sexism.

From Renate Bridenthal, Atina Grossman, and Marion Kaplan, eds., *When Biology Became Destiny: Women in Weimar and Nazi Germany.* New York: Monthly Review Press, 1984. Copyright © 1984 by Renate Bridenthal, Atina Grossman, and Marion Kaplan. Reprinted by permission of the Monthly Review Foundation.

The extent to which the racist tradition was concerned with those activities that then and now are considered "women's sphere"—that is, bearing and rearing children—has also not been recognized. Perhaps we might argue even further that a large part of this racist tradition remained invisible precisely because the history of women and of their work in the family was not an issue for (mostly male) historians and theoreticians.[3]

To make the issue of motherhood and compulsory sterilization the center of discussion places the focus not so much on anti-Jewish racism, on which we have an extended literature, as on another form of racism: eugenics, or, as it was called before and during the Nazi regime and sometimes also in Anglo-Saxon literature, race hygiene.[4] It comprises a vast field of more or less popular, more or less scientific, traditions, which became the core of population policies throughout the Nazi regime.

Beyond the plain yet unexplored fact that at least half of those persecuted on racial grounds were women, there are more subtle reasons for women's historians' interest in the "scientific" or eugenic form of racism. The race hygiene discourse since the end of the nineteenth century deals with women much more than do most other social or political theories, since women have been hailed as "mothers of the race," or, in stark contrast, vilified as the ones guilty of "racial degeneration." Then, too, definitions of race hygiene made at the time show some conscious links between this field and women's history, describing it, for instance, as "procreation hygiene" (*Fortpflanzungshygiene*).[5] In fact, we might consider that most of the scientific and pseudoscientific superstructure of eugenic racism, especially its mythology of hereditary character traits, is concerned with the supposedly "natural" or "biological" domains in which women are prominent—body, sexuality, procreation, education—the heretofore "private" sphere.[6]

For a third reason, eugenics and racism in general are significant to women's history. After a long hiatus, the result in part of Nazism, interest in the history of women in Germany has seen a revival during the past half decade or more. However, this interest has focused almost exclusively on the historical reconstruction and critique of those norms and traditions that underlined women's "natural" destiny as wives, mothers, and homemakers whose work was not paid. Those with this perspective see National Socialism as either a culmination of, or a reactionary return to, belief in women's "traditional" roleas mothers and housewives; motherhood and housework become essential factors in a backward, premodern, or precapitalist "role" assigned to women.[7]

Thus most historians seem to agree that under the Nazi regime women counted merely as mothers who should bear and rear as many children as possible, and that Nazi antifeminism tended to promote, protect, and even finance women as childbearers, housewives, and mothers. It seems necessary to challenge various aspects of this widely held opinion, but particularly its neglect of racism.[8] Printed and archival sources on Nazi policies, passages from Hitler's writings, other often-quoted sources like the Minister of Agriculture Walter Darré's breeding concepts, and documents from the lower echelons of the state and party hierarchy[9] show quite clearly that the Nazis were by no means simply interested in raising the number of childbearing women. They were just as bent on excluding many women from bearing and rearing children—and men from begetting them—with sterilization as their principal deterrent. It is true that the available literature does not altogether lose sight of these latter women. However, they are at best briefly hinted at, between quotation marks and parentheses, as mere negations of the "Aryan," the "racially and hereditarily pure"; the general conclusions on "women in Nazi society" usually neglect them further.[10]

Although the desirability of a new perspective seems clear, the historical singularity of the Holocaust and the need for more research before models can be constructed qualify the extent to which we may compare the interaction of racism and sexism under Nazism and under other historical conditions.[11] Yet specific comparative approaches seem possible and necessary: first, to compare the eugenics movements internationally in the first half of this century both with international population policy today and with the new sociobiological "biocrats";[12] and second, in accord with new approaches in the United States, stimulated largely by women of color, to conceptualize the connection between racism and sexism not as the mere addition of two forms of exploitation—as a double oppression—but as a manifold and complex relationship.[13]

VALUE AND WORTHLESSNESS: WOMEN IN THE RACE HYGIENE TRADITION

In the late nineteenth century, a theory of the possibility, even necessity, of eugenic, race hygienic, or social hygienic sterilization emerged, which argued that those considered transmitters of hereditary forms of "inferiority" (*erbliche Minderwertigkeit*) should be prevented from having children. Presumably lacking in social value and usefulness, they and their offspring were seen as not serving the interest of the folk or the "racial body."[14] By the end of World War I, when German aggrandizement and stability seemed at its lowest, such sterilization was widely and passionately recommended as a solution to urgent social problems: shiftlessness, ignorance, and laziness in the workforce; deviant sexual behavior such as prostitution and illegitimate births; the increasing number of ill and insane; poverty; and the rising costs of social services.[15] Recommendations for sterilization came from elements of the right and of the left, from men and women, from those leaning toward theories of heredity and from those with a more environmental orientation.[16] Criteria of what constituted inferiority were elaborated not only by political ideologists, but also by anthropologists, medical doctors, psychiatrists.

This type of reasoning, with all its subtle appeal to naïve belief in modern science, social rationality, and planning, has been called *scientific racism*, which transcends the more traditional and more overt *gut racism*.[17] Based on a polarity between "progress" and "degeneration," its criteria of inferiority had at their center concepts of "value" and "worthlessness" (*Wert* and *Unwert*, *Minderwertigkeit* and *Höherwertigkeit*) that were related to the social or racial "body" and its productivity. The use of eugenic sterilization was intended both to control procreation and, by defining and proscribing what was unacceptable, to impose a specific acceptable character on women and men: the hard-working male breadwinner, his hard-working but unpaid housewife, and children who were a financial burden to no one but their parents. This was the "valuable life": a gender-specific work and productivity, described in social, medical, and psychiatric terms. Or, in the more flowery language of gut racists: "German-blooded, Nordic-raced beings: right-angled in body and soul."[18]

What were the social motives behind these policies and their wide acceptance? The principal and most haunting spectre for the race was seen not only in the women's movement and in the lower-class uprisings between the turn of the century and the 1920s, but in a phenomenon that seemed to encompass both: the unequal propagation of the "talented" and the "untalented," the "fit" and the "unfit," the rich and the poor, the deserving and the undeserving poor, those of social value and the "social problem group."[19] The better-off, the fit, those thinking rationally, the upwardly mobile, those pursuing or competing for hard and honest work, and women seeking emancipation all limited the number of their children. The decline of the birthrate after the 1870s, reaching an international low point in 1932 and perceived as a "birth-strike" after about 1912, was attributed mainly to women.[20] On the other hand, the mentally and financially poor and the restless were seen as copulating and propagating indiscriminately, as in a "witches' sabbath,"[21] transmitting to their offspring, by the mechanism called heredity, their poverty and restlessness and their search for income from public welfare funds.[22]

Whatever the historical reality of this differential birthrate may have been,[23] its social interpretation came to be the double-edged essence of what was defined as "racial degeneration" or "race suicide." It was charged that the problem stemmed from women, possibly associated with the women's movement, who preferred to have fewer children than their mothers, and from women or couples who raised their children against prevailing norms and at the expense of community and state.[24] The proposed remedy was to reverse both trends: to impel the "superior" to have more children and the "inferior" to have fewer or none. The first aim was to be achieved through a heightened public concern as well as financial and social incentives; the latter through sterilization or, more generally, the eugenic use of just those means by which certain women or couples had limited their fertility.[25] This policy was sexist in its demand for state control of procreation, and racist in its differential treatment of superior and inferior procreation. It can therefore be seen as a dual attack against the birth-strike of the desirable people and against the social maladjustment of those not trained to orderliness and to the work ethic, the natural task of valuable mothers. Thus special concern was given to women. "If we want to practice race hygiene seriously, we must make women the target of our social work—woman as mother and not as sexual parasite," urged the main race hygiene review in 1909. In 1929, a widely known book, *Sterilization on Social and Race Hygienic Grounds*, suggested that "the number of degenerate individuals born depends mainly on the number of degenerate women capable of procreation. Thus the sterilization of degenerate women is, for reasons of racial hygiene, more important than the sterilization of men."[26]

"KAISERSCHNITT" AND "HITLERSCHNITT": NAZI BODY POLITICS

Along with discrimination and segregation of Jewish women and men, Nazi sterilization policies were the main strategy of "gene and race care," as eugenics or race hygiene was now called, from 1933 to 1939. Sterilization policy was one form of comprehensive Nazi racism. Jews, those eligible for sterilization, were defined as inferior. Along with the Jews, National Socialism had a second scapegoat held responsible for the degeneration of the race: millions of non-Jewish, inferior women and men, who supposedly were a "burden" to the state. Like Jews, they were seen as "ballast" and "parasites" to the "body" of *Volk* and race, though Jews were seen as threatening this body from the outside, and other inferior beings were seen as threatening it from the inside. For Jewish as for non-Jewish inferior people, one decree or law followed the other from 1933 on. Among other things, they served to identify them. Thus, having a Jewish grandmother defined a Jew or a Jew of "mixed blood," and a schizophrenic episode—one's own or that of one's grandmother—served to define a sterilization candidate. The identification of human beings as valuable, worthless, or of inferior value in supposedly hereditary terms was the common denominator of all forms of Nazi racism. Birth strategy was one of these forms.

Nazi pronatalism for desirable births and its antinatalism for undesirable ones were tightly connected. On May 26, 1933, two pieces of penal legislation preceding the 1926 reforms were reintroduced, prohibiting the availability of abortion facilities and services. More important was the stricter handling of the old antiabortion law, resulting in a 65 percent increase in yearly convictions between 1932 and 1938, when their number reached almost 7,000.[27] From 1935 on, doctors and midwives were obliged to notify the regional State Health Office of every miscarriage. Women's names and addresses were then handed over to the police, who investigated the cases suspected of actually being abortions.[28] In 1936 Heinrich Himmler, head of all police forces and the SS, established the Reich's Central Agency for the Struggle

Against Homosexuality and Abortion, and in 1943, after three years of prepa-ration by the Ministries of the Interior and of Justice, the law entitled Protec-tion of Marriage, Family, and Motherhood called for the death penalty in "extreme cases."[29]

The corollary measure was race hygiene sterilization. Along with the new antiabortion legislation, a law was introduced on May 26, 1933, to legalize eugenic sterilization and prohibit voluntary sterilization.[30] Beyond this, the Cabinet, headed by Hitler, passed a law on July 14, 1933, against propagation of "lives unworthy of life" (*lebensunwertes Leben*), called the Law for the Prevention of Hereditarily Diseased Offspring. It ordered sterilization for certain categories of people, its notorious Paragraph 12 allowing the use of force against those who did not submit freely.[31] Earlier, on June 28, the Minister of the Interior Wilhelm Frick had announced: "We must have the courage again to grade our people according to its genetic values."[32]

Before we turn to the outcome of such value-grading, it is important to understand some laws that aggravated this policy, enabled its realization, and linked it closely both to antiabortion policy and to future race hygienic extermination. Beginning in January 1934, on the initiative of the "Reich's Medical Doctors' Leader" Gerhard Wagner, abortion of "defective" pregnan-cies on the grounds of race hygiene was secretly practiced with Hitler's approval; it was introduced by law on June 26, 1935.[33] It was legal only with the consent of the woman, but after being declared of inferior value, she was sterilized, too, even against her will, and after 1938 she could not even decide to revoke her initial consent.

In 1933, the government passed a law against "habitual delinquents" that provided for castration (i.e., took sterilization one step further to the destruc-tion of the gonads) in specified cases.[34] While this law concerned men only (2,006 up to 1940), castration of women by destruction of the gonads (beyond tubal ligation: ovarectomy) was introduced in 1936, when steriliza-tion by X-rays was included in the sterilization law.[35] Later, officials favored this procedure as an easy method for mass sterilization of camp inmates without their knowledge.[36]

The law that provided for the enactment of all these policies was passed in July 1934. It created a centralized system of State Health Offices with Depart-ments for Gene and Race Care. Numbering 1,100 and staffed by 1943 with 12,000 State Medical Officials, they became, from 1934 on, the main agents of sterilization proposals and marriage approvals.[37] They also were the pillars of another huge enterprise: a centralized index of the hereditary value of all inhabitants of Germany (*Erbkartei*) to become the basis for all state decisions on the professional and family life of its subjects.[38]

Popular vernacular expressed the situation pungently. Eugenic sterilization was called *Hitlerschnitt* (Hitler's cut), thereby linking it to an antiabortion policy that refused abortions even to women who had gone through two previous *Kaiserschnitte* (caesarean operations). Only after three caesareans did a woman have the right to an abortion, and then only on the condition that she also accept the sterilization.[39] Transcending older political partnerships, prohibition of abortion and compulsory sterilization, compulsory motherhood and prohibition of motherhood—far from contradicting each other—had now become two sides of a coherent policy combining sexism and racism. Only for descriptive purposes do the following sections deal with them separately.

FORCED LABOR FOR MOTHERS OR CHILDREN OF CONFIDENCE?

Nazi population planners liked to register the gradual rise of the extremely low birthrate after 1933 (the birthrate of the years 1934–1939 was, on average, a third above the level of 1933, thus reaching again the level of the mid-twenties) as "a completely voluntary and spontaneous proof of [the] confidence of the German people in its Reich, its Führer, its future, a confession which could not be more beautiful" than in the form of "children of confidence."[40] Sometimes (and not only in the past) this increase has been considered a proof of the suspicion that women favored rather than rejected the regime and that they redirected themselves toward *Kinder, Küche, Kirche* (children, kitchen, church) after their emancipation in the 1920s.[41] Such an argument, however, confusing as it does childlessness and liberation, motherhood and backwardness, does not seem an adequate instrument for the historical analysis of women's lives. What was the real effect of the pronatalist aspect of Nazi population policy on women specifically as well as on the whole society?

Nazi and non-Nazi demographers agree on the limited extent of the rise in the birthrate.[42] More importantly, from the limited evidence we have on women's motives for contributing to its rise, none seems to be the result of Nazi policies and goals. Voluntary births clearly increased as economic conditions improved. Wives of party officials and SS men, who may have been close participators in Nazi goals (but who, as part of the upper class, had easier access to voluntary birth control), had extremely few children.[43] From the outbreak of war in 1939 when, mainly under the command of Fritz Sauckel, unemployed (mostly middle-class) women were encouraged or forced to join the war effort in the munitions industries and employed (mostly lower-class) women were forbidden to quit their jobs, hundreds of thousands of women used the only alternative to forced employment open to them: pregnancy. Popular wit called these women *Sauckelfrauen* and their children *Sauckelkinder*, while Nazi leaders accused them of "lack of comprehension of the necessity of war."[44]

However, while women's positive response to pro-natalism seems limited, we must also try to relate the rise of the birthrate to the one directly coercive measure of pro-natalism: forced labor for mothers through the prohibition of abortion for "valuable," "German-blooded" women. Antiabortion policies are sometimes considered the main reason for the rise in births. In fact, there is some evidence, though locally limited, that after 1932 the rise in births nearly equalled the decline in abortions.[45] This argument could be decisive, if it were measurable. Fortunately for those women who resorted to abortion it is not; the relationship between known and unknown abortions and that between spontaneous and induced miscarriages is controversial, not only in democratic societies, but even under the tight control and supervision of the Nazi regime.

While abortions are estimated at one-half to 1 million per year between 1930 and 1932, a gynecologist in 1939 counted 220,000 miscarriages in hospitals, of which he estimated 120,000 to be abortions. Criminal police experts estimated that the number of unknown abortions equalled the number that came to their attention.[46] In the 1930s, very much as in the 1920s, various documents tell of regional "abortion epidemics" in which abortions were performed by pregnant women themselves or by "old shrews."[47] In 1937 Himmler gave various estimates in secret documents ranging from 400,000 to 800,000 abortions per year.[48]

These numbers seem high, particularly if measured against the rising number of trials and convictions for abortion. Taken together, they permit conclusions that may well question women's easy compliance with Nazi pro-natalism. Nonetheless, those who were denied abortion or who did not want to risk prosecution, even if they did not want children or were endangered by childbirth, had to accept motherhood as forced labor: the labor of childbirth in its modern misogynist form and the labor of additional unpaid housework.[49]

A last consideration helps to answer our initial question. The qualitatively neutral birthrate does not tell us about the proportion of undesirable children to the desirable ones so dear to Nazi population politicians. Although it makes little sense to try through numerical count to match one against the other and thus as a women's historian to repeat the favorite eugenics game called "differential birthrate of the inferior and superior," we should definitely not assume that all children were welcome to the state.[50] While on the one hand, around 1937, the Nazis became worried about something they called *Erbangst*—people's fear of having children because there was so much talk about unworthy genes[51]—on the other hand there were German (though not "German-blooded") women who succeeded in conceiving during the time lag between their sentence of sterilization and its actual enforcement.[52] Most important, Nazi pro-natalism excluded from the ranks of honor and allowances every large family found to be undesirable because it was "hereditarily defective or racially mixed or asocial, alcoholic, lacking an orderly family life, and one in which children [are] a burden."[53]

"LIVES UNWORTHY OF LIFE"

The sterilization law, meant to prevent "lives unworthy of life," came into force on January 1, 1934. It listed nine diagnostic causes whereby a person could be sentenced by a specific genetic health court to sterilization; five categories were related to psychiatric "invalidity," three to physical "invalidity," the last to alcoholism. Authorities gave differing estimates of how many should be sterilized, somewhere between 5 and 30 percent of the population; the minister of the interior recommended 20 percent in his speech of June 1933.[54] During the nearly five and one-half years preceding the outbreak of World War II, about 320,000 persons (nearly 0.5 percent of the population) were sterilized under the terms of this law. This figure included some 5,000 eugenic abortions with subsequent sterilizations (under comparable laws in thirty states of the United States, 11,000 persons were sterilized between 1907 and 1930, and 53,000 more by 1964). While men alone determined sterilization cases in court, the victims were divided evenly between women and men. Three-quarters were sterilized under the law's first two categories: 53 percent (with a somewhat higher share among women) for "feeblemindedness," 20 percent (with a somewhat higher share among men) for "schizophrenia."[55] Between 1934 and 1937, about 80 men and 400 women died in the course of the operation.

One of the reasons why men also became subject to eugenic sterilization, in contrast to the period preceding the legislation when it had been practiced only in birth clinics frequented by poor women, was the new and efficient bureaucracy established for this purpose. Between 1933 and 1936, about 250 special sterilization courts were established as parts of the judiciary, and race hygiene experts along with judges decided on the desirability of sterilizations. Directors of institutions such as hospitals, schools, prisons, workhouses, and concentration camps, as well as welfare authorities, were responsible for selecting candidates for sterilization from among their charges. But the bulk of applications to the courts came from the newly established State Medical Officers, who got their information from the above-mentioned institutions, from mayors and private doctors, and, more rarely, from employers and neighbors of the candidates, as well as through the medical and eugenic examination of all recipients of state funds. Hardly anybody applied to be sterilized him- or herself.

The reactions of the victims were bitter and complex, as can be seen from their letters to the courts and from contemporary investigations. A medical student, checking up on sterilized women in 1936, observed that some of them

> were morally so inferior, that they welcomed sterilization. . . . Other women saw sterilization as a relief, because they were in such financial straits. In these cases, moral indifference and economic need are so great that they dominate their

thoughts and attitudes toward children and toward the sterilization law. . . . On leaving, I often heard behind me scornful and mocking laughter at the idea that childlessness was a sacrifice. Many said bitterly "that children only cost money; only the rich can afford them." . . . Others viewed the loss of motherhood as a loss of purpose in life and, moreover, as a devaluation of their humanity, a source of shame and disgrace. . . . For them, the only solace could be the conviction that their sacrifice had not been in vain, but had been made to the German people.[56]

The actual criteria for sterilization can be deduced from the meticulous records kept by the courts. These criteria include mentally and physically defective kin—a broad spectrum of deficiencies ranged from quarrelsome aunts, alcoholic grandparents, and spendthrifts to sexual deviancy, particularly alleged promiscuity of women and the resulting illegitimate births. Intelligence tests examined for the ability to read, write, and do arithmetic, as well as for a knowledge of geography, history, and the names of Nazi leaders. The category "general ethical concepts" asked:

> Why does one study? Why and for whom does one save money? Why should one not burn even one's own house? If you won the lottery, what would you do with the money? How do you plan your future? What is the meaning of fidelity, piety, honor, modesty? What is the opposite of bravery?[57]

A ghastly crowd of people who did not live up to the social expectations voiced by these questions populated the voluminous official commentary to the sterilization law. They included currently ill and recovered schizophrenics, backward students, so-called promiscuous women, "asocials," and prostitutes.

Resistance came early and took various forms. Examination questions and answers were passed on, rendering the standardized intelligence tests useless. Poorly educated Nazi supporters were hauled into sterilization courts. Some victims, mostly men, hired lawyers and sometimes succeeded in protracting their cases for years. The combined resistance led to renewed debate over the criteria of inferiority in 1936–1937 and to modification of the intelligence test and its use. The individual's proof of social worth (*Lebensbewährung*) was now officially established as the decisive criterion, thus bringing into the open the contents of the medical rhetoric of eugenic psychiatry. A 1936 government decree to the sterilization courts described such "proof":

> If a person has a profession demanding achievement based on independent judgment, we can assume there is no feeble-mindedness. However, if a person performs only steady and repetitive mechanical work, shows no inclination to change or to become more efficient, and also seems unintelligent, we will be close to a diagnosis of "feeble-mindedness." . . . We almost certainly find it in people unable to earn a steady livelihood or otherwise unable to adapt socially. Such feeble-minded persons are morally underdeveloped and unable correctly to understand the order of human society.[58]

An attempt to identify the actual victims of race hygienic sterilization may help to illuminate not only their lives and social situations, but also the forms and functions of reproductive racism and some links with racism's better-known historical "solutions." The majority of those sterilized under the law were not (as in the United States) asylum inmates, or ethnic minorities, but noninstitutionalized persons of German ethnicity. The poorer strata of the population had the highest share (unskilled workers, particularly agricultural laborers), and three categories of women were far overrepresented: servants, unskilled factory or farm workers, and jobless housewives, especially those married to unskilled workers. Many prostitutes and unmarried mothers were among them.[59] "Deviancy from the norm," from "the average," was the crucial criterion in the courts. The norm itself was elaborated even more clearly as demonstrable through adherence to the work ethic, self-sacrifice, parsimony, and through the resulting upward mobility: the "German work character." For women, this ideal was represented by the worker who performed ungrudging housework and efficient labor in outside employment; her antithesis was the slut, the prostitute.

The other sterilization victims between 1934 and 1939 were inmates or ex-inmates (searched out in the old files) of institutions, mainly of psychiatric clinics and of psychiatric departments of regular hospitals. More precisely, they were all those discharged from the clinics as recovered, but whose recovery did not, according to race hygienic thought, involve their "genes," which they might pass on to posterity. It is well known that most inmates of psychiatric institutions came from a background of poverty. Patients in specified, sexually segregated "closed institutions" were not sterilized if they stayed there at their own expense.[60] A considerable number of people used this loophole and entered such an institution if they could afford one. However this option was closed by the "euthanasia" project "T 4," in which from 1939 to 1941 up to 100,000 inmates of these institutions were killed outright as "useless eaters"; after August 1941 many more were killed through plain starvation. In another way, race hygienic sterilization was a direct prelude to mass murder: the prohibition against bearing "unworthy" children was expanded into the mass murder of about 5,000 such children, sixteen years and under, between 1939 and 1944. In order to get control over these children, the government would often force their mothers into the war industry so that home child care was impossible.[61] For both sorts of mass murder, a secret and elaborate machinery was set up, resembling in its procedures the publicly acknowledged sterilization bureaucracy.

The transition to still another form of mass murder is clearly visible. T 4 was meant to be kept secret, but the news spread rapidly, arousing fear and the suspicion that sterilization of the "useless" was just a first step. Public opinion and pressure—which was, in 1941, largely led by women, children, and old people—in fact forced Hitler and his SS doctors to stop T 4 and the planned murder of three million "invalids." But the gas chambers, used for the first time in this enterprise, were transported with their entire staff to occupied Poland, where they were installed for the "final solution."[62] The terror that had met resistance within Germany was exported beyond its frontiers to work more smoothly.

These links between race hygiene inside and outside the death-and-work and death-by-work camps suggest that only the merger of gut racism with the more scientific, bureaucratic, and planned approach of eugenic racism was able to bring to reality a bureaucratic, scientific, and faultlessly efficient genocide on the scale of the Holocaust.

Connections between these two expressions of racism are evident not only in their methods but also in their victims: along with the "deviant" groups already mentioned, ethnic minorities such as Gypsies and the few Germans of black color were targets for sterilization. In 1935, people of the Polish minority of Upper Silesia protested against sterilization of members of their group. German Jews, defined out of the German *Volk* from 1933 on, were not defined out of it through "negative race hygiene," that is, sterilization. While sterilizations of Jewish women and men were common in areas with a substantial proportion of Jews, and especially of poor, often eastern Jews, such as in Berlin, and while in 1938 abortions were "permitted" to Jewish women, by 1942 it was declared that "no more applications for sterilization of Jews need to be made."[63] The reason was that at this time Jews were being killed in concentration camps. The division between those who were and were not eligible for race hygienic sterilization according to the 1933 law coincided to a large degree with a prior division within the lower classes: between the subproletarian strata including part of the ethnic minorities on the one side and, on the other, the proper and orderly German workers hailed by many Nazis as the hard and hard-working core of racial superiority. Predominantly unskilled, the former were not integrated into the stable norm of waged work for men and unwaged housework for women; the official labor movement, which had largely excluded them, had during the 1920s taken a position toward the unskilled and toward ethnic minorities very much like that of the American Federation of Labor.

However, we should not disregard the number, though limited, of middle- and upper-class victims of racist psychiatry and sterilization.[64] To some extent, race hygiene crosses class lines, as do, to a larger degree, sexist and gut racism (most visibly in the case of anti-Semitism). To the extent that it does, it can be seen as a policy directed against those who deviate not just from general social norms but from the norms and expectations of their specific class. Its purpose is to "select" against those who do not fit into the class or the class-specific sex role to which they supposedly belong. In this way, race hygiene contributes to a confirmation of the class structure not just at its lower level, but at all its levels. Thus race hygiene carries over the attitudes and implementation of racism from the social conflicts between ethnicities into social conflicts within an ethnicity. From the perspective of its victims, the terms *ethnic racism* and *social racism*[65] might denote the connection as well as the difference between both expressions of racism.

Moreover, scientific (and gut) racism had a decisive function in the spread and confirmation of two sexual double standards: assignment of typically modern, sexually differentiated roles and labors to women and men,[66] and assignment of different roles and labors to superior and inferior women. According to theoreticians of race and race hygiene, the difference and polarity between the sexes (reason/emotion, activity/passivity, paid work/housework) is fully developed only in the superior, and Nordic, races; among inferior races, including those of low hereditary value, the sexes are less differentiated—and thus heavy and cheap labor is good for both.[67] These assignments might both appropriately be called aspects of *sexist racism*.

"VALUE" OF RACE AND OF SEX: NAZI MONEY POLITICS

Financial population policy was another form of racism and sexism practiced by the Nazi regime. Historians have usually examined it as an instrument of population increase, by which, it has been argued, women were bribed back into the home, became grateful adherents of the regime, and were bought off in order to reconcile them to Nazi antifeminism.[68] However, while demographic evidence (referring to the number of births in families receiving state support) remains inconclusive at best, it suggests that the rise in births was not due to such incentives. The economic aspect of Nazi population policy is more significant to questions of racism and sexism. It can be shown by comparing the intentions and effects of state investments in births, their racist and sexist distribution, and some of the social struggles around them.

All family subventions were given to husbands, and only under strong eugenic restrictions to unwed mothers. Mothers themselves received only the nonmonetary Mother Cross, introduced in 1939. Equally important, both financial and honorary entitlements were tied to race hygienic qualifications. This was most visible in the case of marriage loans and child allowances.[69]

The June 1, 1933, Law to Reduce Unemployment, in its section "Promotion of Marriages," provided for marriage loans up to one thousand marks for those men whose wives gave up their jobs (there were similar loans in France, Italy, Spain, and Sweden); in fact, only half of this sum was paid. Three weeks after the law was passed, a new provision forgave one-fourth of the debt with each childbirth, popularly seen as "paying off in children" (*abkindern*). It was argued that the marriage loans would reduce female pressure on the labor market and give jobs to male heads of households. It did not have this result, since men rarely took up "women's work," and the condition of female nonemployment was soon abrogated, when the employment of both sexes increased. The real aim of the marriage loan was to allow men to marry at an earlier age by helping them to establish a household, and to increase the number of births. However, the loan recipients practiced family planning despite reduced access to birth control: between 1933 and 1943, two million husbands "paid off" their loans with an average of just 1.1 children each.[70]

The distribution of financial family subventions was not only sexist, since it privileged men, but also racist, since people with "defects" considered hereditary were excluded: people eligible for sterilization (even if the sterilization tribunal had absolved them) included Jews, Gypsies, and other "alien races" as well as asocials whose "aggregate hereditary value" was considered to be below average. The latter category included "those with police records, shirkers, those with behavior problems, uneconomical persons or those on welfare, and those unable to conduct an orderly household or to raise their children to be useful citizens."[71] Ultimately, about two-thirds of all couples marrying did not apply for the loan in the first place, largely because of the eugenic restrictions, and it was denied to about 3 percent of the applicants.[72] Thus, while most loans went to working-class heads of households, they failed to reach many couples who really needed help. The main purpose of the loans was met: discrimination between the hereditarily pure and those with no or low race or hereditary value.

Child allowances, introduced in 1936, were similarly used. They consisted of a one-time benefit of 65 marks for each child and 10 marks monthly thereafter for children after the fifth, and later after the third, child; unlike in contemporary Sweden, they were given not to mothers, but to fathers. Moreover, race hygienists distinguished between "full families rich in children" and "asocial large families," between those with desirable and those with undesirable children. The latter were denied allowances, along with those of alien races and of unwed mothers with more than one child, especially if the father was not known.[73] In 1940, when these restrictions were sharpened, crowds of women and children harassed city officials demanding what they thought was rightfully theirs.[74] What had been hailed by hopeful race hygienists as the "quiet struggle of mothers for Germandom"[75] became instead a vocal resistance of mothers against discrimination against inferior women.

"BIRTH-WAR" IN THE WORLD WAR

With the declaration of war in 1939, another stage of the "birth-war"[76] was inaugurated, exacerbating previous trends. Only a few of its features can be presented here. A decree of August 31, 1939, ruled that the sterilization law was to be applied only in those cases "where a particularly great danger of propagation is imminent."[77] While this change in policy may give some insight into the earlier handling of this "danger," its principal rationale lay in the war. Sterilization candidates could not be counted on to be compliant war workers, and the old race hygiene personnel were needed for other purposes.[78] In fact, the number of sterilization trials was drastically reduced.

Simultaneously, however, sterilization policy was extended and radicalized in three dimensions beyond the 1933 law. First, mass sterilizations were executed in concentration camps, mostly on Jewish women and Gypsy women and men. Gypsy women and men were sterilized outside the camps also, sometimes with a "choice" between camp and sterilization. Future mass sterilizations were planned for those Jews who, defined as of mixed blood (*Mischlinge*), were not transported to the camps. Sterilizations of Jewish and Gypsy people in and outside the camps were done both for the sake of medical experiments and for population control, that is, in order to prevent inferior offspring.[79] Second, many women from the conquered and occupied territories in the east—about 2 million women had been deported as forced labor into Germany—were subjected to compulsory abortion and sterilization for the sake, again, of population control and in order to maintain an efficient workforce unhampered by the care of children. Little as yet is known about their lives. It is clear, however, that abortion was "allowed" to them, and that from 1942 on, an eastern working-woman's pregnancy was reported—via management and regional labor offices—to a special regional SS officer who tested her racially and decided about the outcome of her pregnancy.[80]

Less is known about the third dimension of the new policy, the birth-war against the asocials. Asociality had been an important criterion in the sterilization courts; many persons had been sterilized and asocials, including prostitutes, had been proportionately high among those deported to concentration camps during the second great wave of imprisonment from 1936 to 1941.[81] However, this criterion still had smacked too much of the "social" instead of the "biological," and it had not always been easy to classify such persons under one of the four psychiatric categories of the 1933 law.[82] Meanwhile, race hygiene theory had established the hereditary character of the disease "asociality" with such efficiency that it had become a central category of racism. After 1940, when many asocials were released from the camps to answer an urgent shortage of labor, a new law was being elaborated that provided for their sterilization. In terms of contemporary psychology, the definition of asocial was extended from the psychotic to the psychopathic and the neurotic, while the bill called them simply "parasites," "failures," "itinerant," "good-for-nothing." The legislation was to be enforced right after the war, and many high and low government and party agencies continued to discuss it throughout the war.[83]

Among women, the good housewife and industrious mother could be sure to evade sterilization. Unwed and poor mothers with "too many" children, women on welfare, and prostitutes could not be so sure. Ever more obviously, the birth-war applied typically racist measures that violated the bodily integrity of those considered socially deviant and linked ever more closely the various forms and victims of racism. In an official, though secret, decree of September 1940, the "Reich's Health Leader" Leonardo Conti granted the

State Health Offices permission to perform eugenic sterilization and abortion on prostitutes, on women of inferior character, and on those of alien race.[84] The sterilization law planned for the future was anticipated in practice.

CONCLUSION: SEXISM AND RACISM

One should not assume, as is often done, that Nazi sexism concerned only superior women and Nazi racism concerned only inferior women. Both Nazi racism and sexism concerned all women, the inferior as well as the superior. The "birth achievement" demanded of acceptable women was calculated carefully according to the numbers of those who were not to give birth.[85] And the strongest pressure on such acceptable women to procreate, to create an orderly household for husband and children, and to accept dependency on the breadwinner perhaps came not so much from the continuous positive propaganda about "valuable motherhood," but precisely from its opposite: the negative propaganda and policy that barred unwelcome, poor, and deviant women from procreation and marriage and labeled either disorderly women or single women with too many children inferior. Thus, racism could be used, and was used, to impose sexism in the form of increased unwaged housework on superior women.

On the other hand, women who became or were to become targets of negative race hygiene tended also to be those who did not accept, could not accept, or were not supposed to accept the Nazi view of female housework, whose main features can be traced back to the late eighteenth century. Sexism, which imposed economic dependency on superior married women, could be used, and was used, to implement racism by excluding many women from the relative benefits granted to desirable mothers and children and forcing them to accept the lowest jobs in the labor-market hierarchy in order to survive. In fact, modern sexism has established, below the ideological surface of theories on "women's nature" and the "cult of true womanhood," two different though connected norms for women. The demand was made of some women to administer orderly households and produce well-educated children, the whole enterprise supported by their husbands' money; others, overburdened and without support, were obliged to adopt menial jobs that paid little or nothing, while their children, like themselves, were treated as ballast. Racist-sexist discourses of various kinds have portrayed socially, sexually, or ethnically alien women as non-women, and thus as threatening to the norms for all other women: thus a racist view of Jewish or Gypsy women as prostitutes, the eugenic sexologists' view of lesbians as pseudo-men, the race hygienic view of prostitutes as asocial and infectious to the "racial body,"[86] the fantasy of Polish or feeble-minded women "breeding like animals." But of course, much more is involved here than (predominantly male) images and symbols,[87] influential though they may be in determining women's very real treatment and self-image. Women's history needs to concentrate on the lives of those "non"-women without marginalizing them as (male) history has done.

Precisely because of the complex links between sexism and racism and, therefore, because of the relevance of reproductive racism to all women, we should be careful not to term simply "sexism" the demand placed on ethnically or socially superior women to have children they may not want, and not to term simply "racism" the ban against ethnically or socially inferior women having children, even though they may want them. More strictly speaking, we might call the imposition on the first group of women *racist sexism*, since their procreation is urged not just because they are women, but because they are women *of a specific ethnicity or social position declared superior*. Accordingly, we might call the imposition on the second group of women *sexist racism*, since their procreation is prohibited not just on grounds of their genes and race, but on grounds of their real or supposed deviation, *as women, from social or ethnic standards for superior women*. Establishing in such terms the dual connection between racism and sexism does not (as may be evident from the context) give different weights to the experiences of racism and sexism, or suggest that racism is primary in one case and sexism primary in the other. Precisely the opposite is true: where sexism and racism exist, particularly with Nazi features, all women are equally involved in both, but with different experiences. They are subjected to one coherent and double-edged policy of *sexist racism* or *racist sexism* (a nuance only of perspective), but they are segregated as they live through the dual sides of this policy, a division that also works to segregate their forms of resistance to sexism as well as to racism.

Attempting to look at the situation of all women from the perspective of "non"-women may help to analyze and break down the boundaries of such segregation. As far as the struggle for our reproductive rights—for our sexuality, our children, and the money we want and need—is concerned, the Nazi experience may teach us that a successful struggle must aim at achieving both the rights and the economic means to allow women to choose between having or not having children without becoming economically dependent on other people or on unwanted second and third jobs. Cutbacks in welfare for single mothers, sterilization abuse, and the attacks on free abortion are just different sides of an attack that serves to divide women. Present population and family policy in the United States and the Third World make the German experience under National Socialism particularly relevant. In Germany, new attacks on free abortion, the establishment of a university department of "population science," sterilization experiments on women and sterilization of welfare mothers without their knowledge, pressure on Gypsy women (especially those on welfare) not to have children, xenophobic outcries against immigrants "breeding like animals" and sometimes asking for their castration or sterilization, all-too-easy abortions and sterilization on Turkish women, the reduction of state money connected to human reproduction, both private and public, have all occurred during the last two years.[88] It is an open question what will follow from these—still seemingly unconnected—events in the course of the present economic crisis.

NOTES

This is a revised version of the essay that appeared in *Signs: Journal of Women in Culture and Society* 8, no. 3 (1983).

1. The more progressive new generation of social historians in Germany since the 1960s has tended to present racism as a mere ideology, its application as more or less economically/politically "rational" or "irrational," often as merely instrumental, and mostly as an appendage to more important developments, "political" or "economic." See, for example, Peter M. Kaiser, "Monopolprofit und Massenmord im Faschismus: Zur ökonomischen Funktion der Konzentrationslager im faschistischen Deutschland," *Blätter für deutsche und internationale Politik* 5 (1975): 552–77.

2. A rare exception is Marion A. Kaplan, *The Jewish Feminist Movement in Germany: The Campaigns of the Jüdischer Frauenbund, 1904–1938* (Westport, Conn.: Greenwood Press, 1979).

3. However, three conferences of women historians on women's history have taken place: "Women in the Weimar Republic and under National Socialism," Berlin, 1979; "Muttersein und Mutterideologie in der bürgerlichen Gesellschaft," Bremen, 1980; and "Frauengeschichte," Bielefeld, 1981. Some of the workshops of the latter are documented in *Beiträge zur feministischen Theorie und Praxis* 5 (April 1981). Thus, women's history has been exploring this and similar themes in recent years, but much work still needs to be done, and many questions cannot yet be answered in a consistent way.

4. A good overview of the American and international eugenics movement is Allan Chase, *The Legacy of Malthus: The Social Costs of the New Scientific Racism* (New York: Knopf, 1977). Although there had been, at the beginning of this century, a debate among experts on distinctions between "eugenics" and "race hygiene," I use these terms interchangeably, as does Chase, for I believe the issue dealt with in this article requires my doing so. On this debate see Georg Lilienthal, "Rassenhygiene im Dritten Reich: Krise und Wende," *Medizinhistorisches Journal* 14 (1979): 114–34.

5. See Alfred Grotjahn, *Geburten-Rückgang und Geburten-Regelung im Lichte der individuellen und der sozialen Hygiene* (Berlin and Coblenz, 1914; 2d ed., 1921), p. 153, and the chapter "Birth Regulation Serving Eugenics and Race Hygiene"; and Agnes Bluhm, *Die rassenhygienischen Aufgaben des weiblichen Arztes: Schriften zur Erblehre und Rassenhygiene* (Berlin: Metzner, 1936), esp. the chapter "Woman's Role in the Racial Process in Its Largest Sense."

6. Good examples are the classic and influential books by Grotjahn, *Geburten-Rückgang* (1914) and *Die Hygiene der menschlichen Fortpflanzung* (Berlin and Vienna: Urban and Schwarzenburg, 1926); Erwin Baur, Eugen Fischer, and Fritz Lenz, *Grundriss der menschlichen Erblichkeitslehre und Rassenhygiene*, Vol. 2, *Menschliche Auslese und Rassenhygiene* (Munich: Lehmann, 1921). These volumes had many interestingly divergent editions. I have used Vol. 1 (1936) and Vol. 2

(1931). For a scientific critique of the pseudoscientific theory of character traits see, e.g., Chase, chap. 8.

7. For a preliminary critique of this view, analyzing housework as no less modern and no less capitalist than employment outside the house, see Gisela Bock and Barbara Duden, "Arbeit aus Liebe—Liebe als Arbeit: Zur Entstehung der Hausarbeit im Kapitalismus," in *Frauen und Wissenschaft: Beiträge zur Berliner Sommeruniversität für Frauen, Juli 1976* (Berlin: Courage Verlag, 1977), pp. 118–99. Parts of it have been translated as "Labor of Love—Love as Labor," in *From Feminism to Liberation*, ed. Edith Hoshino Altbach, 2d ed. (Cambridge, Mass.: Schenkman, 1980), 153–92.

8. Dörte Winkler, *Frauenarbeit im "Dritten Reich"* (Hamburg, Hoffmann und Campe, 1977), esp. pp. 42–65, revised this picture by showing that under Nazism, employment of lower- and middle-class women was not reduced. This is confirmed by various authors in the anthology edited by Frauengruppe Faschismusforschung, *Mutterkreuz und Arbeitsbuch: Zur Geschichte der Frauen in der Weimarer Republik und im Nationalsozialismus* (Frankfurt a.M.: Fischer, 1981). Leila J. Rupp, *Mobilizing Women for War: German and American Propaganda, 1939–1945* (Princeton: Princeton University Press, 1978), esp. pp. 11–50, revised the current view of the Nazi image of women. It was more diversified than usually assumed and did not simply stress home and housework, but any "woman's sacrifice" for the state and "the race," including employment. See also Leila J. Rupp, "Mothers of the *Volk*: The Image of Women in Nazi Ideology," *Signs: Journal of Women in Culture and Society* 3, No. 2 (Winter 1977): 362–79. In relation to racism, I have tried to revise the picture in "Frauen und ihre Arbeit im Nationalsozialismus," in *Frauen in der Geschichte*, ed. Annette Kuhn and Gerhard Schneider (Düsseldorf: Schwann Verlag, 1979), pp. 113–49; and " 'Zum Wohle des Volkskörpers': Abtreibung und Sterilisation unterm Nationalsozialismus," *Journal für Geschichte* 2 (November 1980): 58–65.

9. Clifford R. Lovin, *"Blut und Boden*: The Ideological Basis of the Nazi Agricultural Program," *Journal of the History of Ideas* 28 (1967): 279–88, esp. 286.

10. Cf. Hans Peter Bleuel, *Das saubere Reich: Theorie und Praxis des sittlichen Lebens im Dritten Reich* (Bern-Munich-Vienna: Scherz, 1972), p. 273; Jill Stephenson, *Women in Nazi Society* (London: Croom Helm, 1975), pp. 64, 69, 197.

11. Obviously, approaches exclusively or mainly based on ethnic women's labor-force participation are not useful to the issue of reproduction: e.g., Diane K. Lewis, "A Response to Inequality: Black Women, Racism and Sexism," *Signs* 3, No. 2 (Winter 1977): 339–61.

12. For a critique of the new sociobiology, see Ruth Hubbard, Mary Sue Henifin, and Barbara Fried, eds., *Women Look at Biology Looking at Women: A Collection of Feminist Critiques* (Cambridge, Mass.: Schenkman, 1979); Chandler Davis, "La sociobiologie et son explication de l'humanité," *Annales*, E.S.C. 36 (July-August 1981): 531–71. For the international dimension of older eugenics, see Chase, *Legacy of Malthus*; Loren R. Graham, "Science and Values: The Eugenics Movement in Germany and Russia in the 1920's," *American Historical Review* 82 (1977): 1133–64; G. R. Searle, *Eugenics and Politics in Britain, 1900–1914* (Leyden: Nordhoff International, 1976); and Anna Davin, "Imperialism and Motherhood," *History Workshop* (1978): 10–65. It is important to note that in fascist Italy, race hygiene did not take hold. Of course, present policies in the

United States and women's campaigns for reproductive rights are immediately relevant to the issue and approach of this essay: Committee for Abortion Rights and Against Sterilization Abuse, *Women under Attack: Abortion, Sterilization Abuse, and Reproductive Freedom* (New York: CARASA, 1979).

13. Such new approaches have been presented at the Third National Women's Studies Association Conference, "Women Respond to Racism," Storrs, Connecticut, May 31–June 6, 1981. Of particular significance seemed to me the presentations by Vicky Spelman, Arlene Aviakin, and Mary Ruth Warner on "Feminist Theory and the Invisibility of Black Culture." See also Bonnie Thornton Dill, "The Dialectics of Black Womanhood," *Signs* 4, Vol. 3 (Spring 1979): 543–55, and Cherríe Moraga and Gloria Anzaldúa, eds., *This Bridge Called My Back: Writings of Radical Women of Color* (Watertown, Mass.: Persephone Press, 1981). For a different version of the double-oppression approach, see Gerda Lerner, "Black Women in the United States: A Problem in Historiography and Interpretation" (1973), in *The Majority Finds Its Past: Placing Women in History* (New York and Oxford: Oxford University Press, 1979), pp. 63–82; and *Teaching Women's History* (Washington, D.C.: American Historical Association, 1981), pp. 60–65.

14. For early sterilization practice and theory, see Otto Krankeleit, *Die Unfruchtbarmachung aus rassenhygienischen und sozialen Gründen* (Munich: Lehmann, 1929), pp. 41–45; Hans Harmsen, *Praktische Bevölkerungspolitik* (Berlin: Junker & Dünnhaupt, 1931), p. 84; Baur, Fischer, and Lenz, *Grundriss*, p. 270.

15. There was extensive writing on this subject in the 1920s, and Chase (*Legacy of Malthus*, p. 349) seems to underestimate the German roots of the movement. Compare, as examples, note 6 above.

16. Marielouise Janssen-Jurreit, "Sexualreform und Geburtenrückgang," in Kuhn and Schneider, eds., *Frauen in der Geschichte*, pp. 56–81.

17. Chase, *Legacy of Malthus*, pp. xv–xxii and chap. 1.

18. *Die Sonne: Monatsschrift für nordische Weltanschauung und Lebensgestaltung* 10, No. 2 (1933):111.

19. The latter term is taken from the address of the president of the British Eugenics Society at the Third International Congress of Eugenics, New York, 1932, cited in Chase, *Legacy of Malthus*, p. 20.

20. In 1913, 4,000 working-class women assembled in Berlin to hear about the "birthstrike" and attracted huge attention. See Anneliese Bergmann, "Geburtenrückgang—Gebärstreik: Zur Gebärstreikdebatte in Berlin," *Archiv für die Geschichte des Widerstands und der Arbeit* 4 (1980); 7–55. Cf. G. Ardersleben, *Der Gebärstreik der Frauen und seine Folgen* (Lorch: Rohm, 1913); and Ernst Kahn, *Der internationale Gebärstreik* (Frankfurt: Societäts-Verlag, 1930).

21. Gustav Boeters, "Die Unfruchtbarmachung geistig Minderwertiger," *Wissenschaftliche Beilage zur Leipziger Lehrenzeitung* 28 (August 1928): 217.

22. *Von der Verhütung unwerten Lebens-Ein Zyklus in 5 Vorträgen* (Bremen: Bremer Beiträge zur Naturwissenschaft, 1933), pp. 15, 52, 61.

23. The differential birthrate is a main issue in all books on eugenics. On social differences in fertility, see John Knodel, *The Decline of Fertility in Germany, 1871–1939* (Princeton: Princeton University Press, 1974), pp. 223–45; Chase, *Legacy of Malthus*, pp. 403–05.

24. E.g., Roderich von Ungern-Sternberg, *Die Ursachen des Geburtenrückganges im*

europäischen Kulturkreis (Berlin: Schoetz, 1932), esp. pp. 63–75, 174, 203; Grotjahn, *Geburten-Rückgang*, pp. 316–17.

25. E.g., Grotjahn, *Geburten-Rückgang*, p. 187: "Indeed, we should not underestimate the danger, that the methods of birth prevention, which . . . are necessary for a future rational eugenic regulation of the process of the human species, are presently abused for limiting the number of children independently of their value." Therefore he wants "to turn the technique of birth control into the point of departure for an essential control of human reproduction" (p. 43).

26. Josef Grassl, "Weiteres zur Frage der Mutterschaft," *Archiv für Rassen- und Gesellschaftsbiologie* 6 (1909): 351–66, esp. 366; Krankeleit, *Die Unfruchtbarmachung*, p. 95. These and all other translations from the German are my own.

27. *Reichsgesetzblatt* 1933/I, p. 296 (hereafter RGB); *Wirtschaft und Statistik* 15 (1935): 737, and 19 (1939): 534.

28. RGB, 1935/I, p. 1035; Stephenson, *Women in Nazi Society*, p. 68.

29. Bundesarchiv Koblenz, R 18/5517, pp. 251–52 (hereafter BAK); RGB, 1943/I, p. 140.

30. RGB, 1933/I, p. 296; Eberhardt Schmidt, "Das Sterilisationsproblem nach dem in der Bundesrepublik geltenden Strafrecht," *Juristenzeitung* 3 (February 5, 1951): 65–70.

31. RGB, 1933/I, p. 529; Martin Broszat, *Der Staat Hitlers* (Munich: Deutscher Taschenbuch Verlag, 1969), p. 356; Kurt Nowak, *"Euthanasie" und Sterilisierung im "Dritten Reich": Die Konfrontation der evangelischen und katholischen Kirche mit dem "Gesetz zur Verhütung erbkranken Nachwuchses" und der "Euthanasie"-Aktion* (Göttingen: Vanderhoeck & Ruprecht, 1980), esp. pp. 64–65.

32. Wilhelm Frick, *Ansprache auf der ersten Sitzung des Sachverständigenbeirates für Bevölkerungs- und Rassenpolitik* (Berlin: Schriftenreihe des Reichsausschusses für Volksgesundheitsdienst 1, 1933), p. 8.

33. Broszat, *Der Staat Hitlers*, pp. 356–57; Nowak, *"Euthanasie,"* p. 65.

34. Law of November 24, 1933, RGB, 1933/I, p. 995.

35. RGB, 1936/I, pp. 119, 122; BAK, R 22/943, p. 234.

36. Léon Poliakov and Josef Wulf, eds., *Das Dritte Reich und die Juden* (Berlin: Arani, 1955), p. 385; Alexander Mitscherlich and Fred Mielke, *Medizin ohne Menschlichkeit* (Frankfurt: Fischer, 1978), pp. 240–48; BAK, R 18/5519.

37. Law of July 3, 1934, RGB, 1934/I, p. 531; BAK, NSD 50/626, p. 10; Arthur Gütt, Herbert Linden, and Franz Massfeller, *Blutschutz- und Ehegesundheitsgesetz* (Munich: Lehmann, 1937). By the two laws described in the latter official commentary, marriage was prohibited with "alien races" as well as with the "defective" among the "German-blooded." In the "Blutschutz" (= Nuremberg) law, marriage prohibition concerned, besides Jews, "Negroes, gypsies, and bastards" (p. 16).

38. Gütt, Linden, and Massfeller, *Blutschutz*, pp. 9–10, 283–87.

39. Richard Grunberger, *The 12 Year Reich: A Social History of Nazi Germany, 1933–1945* (New York: Holt, Rinehart & Winston, 1972), p. 365; see also my article on sterilization and abortion, " 'Zum Wohle.' "

40. Friedrich Burgdörfer, *Geburtenschwund: Die Kulturkrankheit Europas und ihre Überwindung in Deutschland* (Heidelberg-Berlin-Magedeburg: Vowinckel, 1942), p. 80, and *Kinder des Vertrauens* (Berlin: Eher, 1942).

41. Bleuel, *Das saubere Reich*, pp. 21, 45; Grunberger, *12 Year Reich*, chaps. 16, 17;

Tim Mason, "Women in Germany, 1925–1940: Family, Welfare, and Work," *History Workshop* 1 (1976): 74–113, esp. 87.

42. For demographic debate see David V. Glass, *Population: Policies and Movements in Europe* (1940; reprint ed., London: Frank Cass, 1967), pp. 269–313 on Germany and *passim* for other European countries; Knodel, *Decline of Fertility*; Bergdörfer, *Geburtenschwund*; Stephenson, *Women in Nazi Society*; Mason, "Women in Germany," *History Workshop* 1 (1976): 74–113, esp. 95–105, and 2 (1976): 5–32, esp. 12–14; Wolfgang Köllman, "Bevölkerungsentwicklung in der Weimarer Republik," in *Industrielles System und politische Entwicklung in der Weimarer Republik*, eds. Hans Mommsen, Dietmar Petzina, and Bernd Weisbrod (Düsseldorf: Athenäum-Droste, 1977), Vol. 1, pp. 76–84.

43. K. Astel and E. Weber, *Die Kinderzahl der 29,000 politischen Leiter des Gaues Thüringen der NSDAP* (Berlin: Metzner, 1943); Heinrich Himmler, *Geheimreden 1933–1945*, ed. Bradley F. Smith and Agnes F. Peterson (Frankfurt-Berlin-Vienna: Ullstein, 1974), p. 91.

44. Leila J. Rupp, "I Don't Call That *Volksgemeinschaft*: Women, Class, and War in Nazi Germany," in *Women, War and Revolution*, ed. Carol R. Berkin and Clara M. Lovett (New York and London: Holmes and Meier, 1980), p. 43; Bleuel, *Das saubere Reich*, p. 81; Winkler, *Frauenarbeit*, pp. 72–73. The quotation is from a high government official: Gitte Schefer, "Wo Unterdrückung ist, da ist auch Widerstand: Frauen gegen Faschismus und Krieg," in Frauengruppe, Faschismusforschung, ed., *Mutterkreuz*, p. 289.

45. Glass, *Population*, pp. 311–13.

46. BAK, R 18/2957; Atina Grossmann, "Abortion and Economic Crisis: The 1931 Campaign Against Paragraph 218 in Germany," *New German Critique* 14 (Spring 1978): 119–37.

47. BAK, R 18/2957.

48. Himmler, *Geheimreden*, p. 91.

49. Adrienne Rich, *Of Woman Born: Motherhood as Experience and Institution* (New York: Norton, 1976), chap. 7.

50. Mason, "Women in History," p. 101; Bleuel, *Das saubere Reich*, p. 43.

51. Alexander Paul, "Ist Erbangst berechtigt?" *Volk und Rasse* 16 (1941): 130–35.

52. This is evident from the documents of the sterilization courts on which I am working. See also Theresia Seible (a sterilized German Gypsy woman), "Aber ich wollte vorher noch ein Kind," *Courage* 6 (May 1981): 21–24.

53. *Vom Sieg der Waffen zum Sieg der Wiegen* (Berlin: Reichsbund der Kinderreichen, 1942), p. 23. Space does not permit me to deal with an important financial corollary to the race-hygienic body policies: "incentives" such as marriage loans and child allowances given only to the "desirables" and only to husbands, not to wives.

54. Frick, *Ansprache*, p. 3.

55. For the social and historical significance of the first category see Chase, *Legacy of Malthus*, esp. chap. 7; of the second, see Thomas S. Szasz, *Schizophrenia* (New York: Basic Books, 1976). The precise number of sterilizations is unknown. Compare Nowak, *"Euthanasie,"* pp. 65, 118 n. 6. In 1967, an interstate commission of the Federal Republic of Germany investigated the number of "those unjustly sterilized under Nazism." While the number estimated (300,000 to 320,000) seems justified, this is certainly not true for the number of "unjust"

sterilizations (83,000); the document has not been published. The other information is taken from BAK, R 18/5585, pp. 329–31. See Arthur Gütt, Ernst Rüdin, and Falk Ruttke, *Gesetz zur Verhütung erbkranken Nachwuchses vom 14. Juli 1933* (Munich: Lehmann, 1936). For the United States, see Chase, *Legacy of Malthus*, p. 350; Baur, Fischer, and Lenz, *Grundriss*, Vol. 2, p. 271.

56. Elisabeth Hofmann, *Körperliches Befinden und Einstellung von Frauen, die nach dem Erbgesundheitsgesetz sterilisiert wurden* (Heidelberg: 1937), pp. 14–17.

57. Gütt, Rüdin, Ruttke, *Gesetz zur Verhütung*, 1934 ed., pp. 73–78, and *passim*.

58. BAK: R 18/5585, p. 337. This official ruling corresponds to Gütt, Rüdin, Ruttke, *Gesetz zur Verhütung*, p. 125.

59. This is a preliminary evaluation of the records of the sterilization courts in three German cities; it agrees, generally, with the results of Gisela Dieterle (Freiburg), who is working on the records of another city, and with Wilfent Dalicho, "Sterilisation in Köln auf Grund des Gesetzes zur Verhütung erbkranken Nachwuchses, . . . 1934–1943" (Medical diss., Cologne, 1971), esp. pp. 160–65. There has been no research on the sterilization of male homosexuals, mostly performed outside the court procedure of sterilization law. Lesbian women are hardly ever mentioned in the court records (and very rarely in other archival documents from 1933 to 1945). We must assume, however, that they were strongly represented among the women in the asylums, and from reports given by women who were inmates of concentration camps, we know that many lesbians were among those incarcerated. See, e.g., Fania Fenelon, *Das Mädchenorchester in Auschwitz* (Frankfurt: Röderberg, 1980), chap. 21.

60. According to an addition to the law of December 5, 1933: Gütt, Rüdin, and Ruttke, *Gesetz zur Verhütung*, p. 84. For the general poverty of asylum inmates, see Klaus Dörner, *Bürger und Irre* (Frankfurt: Europäische Verlagsanstalt, 1969).

61. Klaus Dörner, "Nationalsozialismus und Lebensvernichtung," *Vierteljahreshefte für Zeitgeschichte* 15 (1967): 121–52, reprinted in Dörner, *Diagnosen der Psychiatrie* (Frankfurt and New York: Campus, 1975), pp. 59–95, esp. pp. 76–82; Dörner et al., eds., *Der Krieg gegen die psychisch Kranken* (Rehburg and Loccum: Psychiatrie-Verlag, 1980); Nowak, *"Euthanasie,"* pp. 77–85.

62. Mitscherlich and Mielke, *Medizin*, pp. 197–205. For the merger between gut and scientific racism in Germany, see esp. Chase, *Legacy of Malthus*, chap. 15. For the continuity of methods and means, see Gerald Reitlinger, *The Final Solution: The Attempt to Exterminate the Jews of Europe, 1939–1945* (London: Vallentine, Mitchell & Co., 1953), chaps. 6 and 7; Raul Hilberg, *The Destruction of the European Jews* (Chicago: Quadrangle, 1961), pp. 268–77, and chap. 9.1, esp. pp. 562–63, n. 21.

63. Decree of March 19, 1942, quoted in Werner Feldscher, *Rassen-und Erbpflege im deutschen Recht* (Berlin-Leipzig-Vienna: Deutscher Rechtsverlag, 1943), p. 123; BAK:R 43 II/720, p. 92; Stephenson, *Women in Nazi Society*, pp. 62–63; *Vom Sieg der Waffen*; Reiner Pommerin, "The Fate of Mixed Blood Children in Germany," *German Studies* Review 5/3 (1982): 315–23.

64. Dalicho, "Sterilisation," pp. 157–60 (12 to 20 percent).

65. These terms are, as might be obvious, not meant to mark the "ethnic" as "nonsocial" and therefore as "biological." Clearly what is meant by "biological" in the racist tradition is plainly "social" and often enough described in plainly social concepts. The above terms are meant to call attention to the links between

different historical forms of racism. Moreover, "social racism" seems to me more accurate than "social Darwinism," as it is usually called, since Darwin certainly did not start it. Even though social history is more complicated than "Malthus started it all" (Chase, *Legacy of Malthus*, p. 12), it is true that the issues in question have older and/or different roots than Darwinism.

66. An illuminating example is the race hygiene classic by Baur, Fischer, and Lenz, *Grundriss*, esp. Vol. 2, and Bluhm, *Die rassenhygienischen Aufgaben*.
67. E.g., Paul Schultze-Naumburg, "Das Eheproblem in der Nordischen Rasse," *Die Sonne* 9 (1932), esp. pp. 20–25. Compare Karin Hausen, "Family and Role Division: The Polarization of Sexual Stereotypes in the 19th Century," in *The German Family*, ed. Richard J. Evans and W. R. Lee (London: Croom Helm, 1981), pp. 51–83; Barbara Duden, "Das schöne Eigentum: Zur Herausbildung des bürgerlichen Frauenbildes an der Wende vom 18. zum 19. Jahrhundert," *Kursbuch* 47 (March 1977): 125–41.
68. Bleuel, *Das saubere Reich*, p. 178; Stephenson, *Women in Nazi Society*, p. 46; Winkler, *Frauenarbeit*, p. 49; Grunberger, *12 Year Reich*, chap. 16; Mason, "Women in History," pp. 87, 94–96, 100–02.
69. A list of further pertinent measures: Burgdörfer, *Geburtenschwund*, pp. 202–14.
70. *Monatsberichte über die deutsche Sozialordnung* 10 (1943), p. 6. These were, of course, not all children born in these families but just the ones that might be, if at all, linked to the "incentive." For the others, the general tendency is very similar to that described by Kälvemark for Sweden.
71. BAK: R: 18/3768; Gütt, Linden, Massfeller, *Blutschutz*, pp. 301–304. BAK: NS 19/1838; Uwe Adam, *Judenpolitik im Dritten Reich* (Droste Verlag: Düsseldorf, 1972), p. 169.
72. *Neues Volk* 1, no. 9 (1935): 30.
73. Burgdörfer, *Geburtenschwund*, p. 187. *Verfügungen, Anordnungen, Bekanntgaben*, ed. Parteikanzlei (Munich, 1942). Vol. 2, pp. 85–86, 93–103, 105–107 (decrees of the Minister of Finance from January 30, March 3, July 26, 1941); *Der Gemeindetag* 5/6 (1942).
74. Documents on this recurring event are scattered through the files of various large cities.
75. Burgdörfer, *Geburtenschwund*, p. 39.
76. Paul Danzer, *Geburtenkrieg* (Munich: Politische Biologie 3, 1939).
77. RGB, 1939/I, p. 1560.
78. Manfred Höck, *Die Hilfsschule im Dritten Reich* (Berlin: Marhold, 1979), p. 75.
79. See note 37 above, and Jan Sehn, "Carl Clausbergs verbrecherische Unfruchtbarmachungsversuche an Häftlings-Frauen in den Nazi-Konzentrationslagern," *Hefte von Auschwitz* 2 (Oswiecim, 1959), pp. 2–32.
80. On foreign women mainly from the east, see Ingrid Schupetta, " 'Jeder das Ihre': Frauenerwerbstätigkeit und Einsatz von Fremdarbeitern und -arbeiterinnen im Zweiten Weltkrieg," in Frauengruppe Faschismusforschung, ed., *Mutterkreuz*, pp. 292–318; Franciszek Polomski, *Aspekty Rasowe w postepowanin z r robotnikami przymnsowymi i jeucami wojennymi III rzeszsy, 1939–45* [Racial Aspects in the Treatment of Forced Laborers and War Prisoners of the Third Reich] (Wroclaw: Ossolinskich, 1976); *Documenta Occupationis*, Vols. 9 and 10 (Poznan: Instytut Zachodni, 1975, 1976).

81. Frank Pingel, *Häftlinge unter SS-Herrschaft* (Hamburg: Hoffmann & Campe, 1978), pp. 69–80; Dalicho, "Sterilisation," pp. 54, 58, 60, 61, 63, 66.

82. Karl Ludwig Lechler, "Erkennung und Ausmerze der Gemeinschaftsunfähigen," *Deutsches Ärtzeblatt* 70 (1940): 293–97.

83. The documents are scattered in many files of such agencies.

84. The pertinent documents are scattered in various archives.

85. E.g., Burgdörfer, *Geburtenschwund*, pp. 136–47; G. Pfotenhauer, "Fortpflanzungspflicht—die andere Seite des Gesetzes zur Verhütung erbkranken Nachwuchses," *Der öffentliche Gesundheitsdienst* 2 (1937): 604–08.

86. For lesbian women and their presentation as "pseudo-men" by male psychiatrists since the last third of the nineteenth century, see Esther Newton and Carroll Smith-Rosenberg, "Male Mythologies and their Internalization of Deviance from Krafft-Ebing to Radclyffe Hall," and Gudrun Schwartz, "The Creation of the *Mannweib*, 1860–1900" (papers presented at the Fifth Berkshire Conference on the History of Women, Vassar College, June 16, 1981). For male views of prostitutes, see my article "Prostituierte im Nazi-Staat" in *Wir sind Frauen wie andere auch*, ed. Pieke Biermann (Reinbek: Rowohlt, 1980), pp. 70–106; Judith Walkowitz, *Prostitution and Victorian Society: Women, Class and the State* (New York: Cambridge University Press, 1980), esp. chap. 10.

87. For an approach focusing on such symbols, see Elizabeth Janeway, "Who is Sylvia? On the Loss of Sexual Paradigms," *Signs* 5, No. 4 (Summer 1980): 573–89.

88. "Population Science" has been established in Hamburg and Bielefeld, while women have been, in vain, trying to get women's studies recognized and financed: *Beiträge zur feministischen Theorie und Praxis* 5 (April 1981): 119–27. For other information on immigrant women, sterilization, welfare, and state benefits, see the following issues of *Courage:* (March 1977): 16–29; 3 (April 1978): 14–29; 3 (September 1978): 11; 3 (October 1978): 44–47; 4 (June 1979): 39–40; 4 (September 1979): 27–29; 4 (October 1979): 12–17; 5 (April 1980): 12–13; 5 (May 1980): 12–13; 6 (March 1981): 5–8, 52; 6 (May 1981): 16–33; 6 (December 1981): 22–33; 7 (January 1982): 8–11. See also *Zu Hause in der Fremde*, ed. Christian Schaffernicht (Fischerhude: Verlag Atelier, 1981), pp. 74–75.

14

Marion A. Kaplan

Racism and persecution as well as survival meant something different for women than men—in practical and psychological terms.

MARION A. KAPLAN

Responding to the history of her Jewish people, Gertrud Kolmar wanted to be "the voice that echoes down the shaft of all eternity." The voice of that Jewish woman in Nazi Germany, though not its poetry, was silenced at Auschwitz. Others, many of them historians, have used their voices of interpretation to carry on the responsibility that Kolmar stressed. One of them is Marion A. Kaplan. In 1984 she made a lasting contribution to the study of women and the Holocaust by co-editing a book entitled When Biology Became Destiny: Women in Weimar and Nazi Germany. *Previously she published* The Jewish Feminist Movement in Germany: The Campaigns of the Jüdischer Frauenbund, 1904–1938, *and since 1984 she has written much more in these fields, including the essay reprinted here.*

A study of what happened to Jewish women in Nazi Germany between 1933 and 1939, the prewar era of the Third Reich, Kaplan's essay is packed with detail. Concentrating on "the increasingly difficult daily lives of Jewish middle-class women," Kaplan sharpens her focus even more by paying particular attention to "housewives and mothers." In addition to forming a large percentage of German Jewry's prewar female population, these women in their twenties, thirties, and forties also wrote the most memoirs. They are crucial sources for a historian with Kaplan's concerns.

Kaplan shows that, even as the Nazi vise tightened around them, German Jewish women continued to manage the responsibilities of employment (especially as

187

their husbands and fathers were squeezed out of the marketplace), housework, and child care. In addition, they did volunteer work with Jewish women's organizations and increasingly assumed the "escalating emotional caretaking" of family and friends that became the inevitable result of Nazi Germany's antisemitic racism and sexism.

Gertrud Kolmar was neither a housewife nor a mother. Nor is she named in Kaplan's essay. But glimpses of her can also be found in the wealth of data that Kaplan shares. Although they may have sensed the danger more deeply than men, "fewer women," Kaplan observes, "left Germany," and one reason was that daughters typically "remained as the sole caretakers for elderly parents." Segregated from opportunities they had enjoyed before 1933, Jewish women's organizations in Germany "resisted their exclusion from German cultural life by creating their own." Jewish education was promoted, and perhaps Gertrud Kolmar began her study of Hebrew in that way. It is possible, too, that her writing was read and enjoyed in those circles.

Kaplan's descriptions should not be mistaken for silver linings in the clouds of destruction that formed from 1933 to 1939. "Needless to say," she concludes, "neither organizations nor individuals were able to withstand the force of state persecution and terror or to prevent the annihilation of the Jewish community in Germany and the rest of Europe." Kaplan's task is a somber one. As she describes German policy that eventually produced the Holocaust, her voice of historical interpretation also helps uncover how much Nazi Germany took from Jewish women.

Jewish Women in Nazi Germany: Daily Life, Daily Struggles, 1933–1939

"We were so German," "we were so assimilated," "we were so middle-class"— these are the refrains one reads over and over in the memoirs of German Jews who try to explain to us (and to themselves) what their lives were like before Nazi barbarism overpowered them. They stress how normal their lives were, how bourgeois their habits and attitudes. German Jews—a predominantly middle-class group comprising less than 1 percent of the German population—had welcomed their legal emancipation in the second half of the nineteenth century and lived in a relatively comfortable, secure environment until 1933. Between 1933 and 1939, however, they saw their economic livelihoods imperiled and their social integration destroyed. Inexorably, they

From *Feminist Studies* 16 (1990): 579–606. Reprinted by permission of *Feminist Studies*, Inc., c/o Women's Studies Program, University of Maryland, College Park, MD 20742.

were engulfed in the maelstrom that led to the Holocaust: impoverishment and ostracism for most; emigration for many; hiding for a handful; and ghettoization, forced labor, and extermination for the rest.[1]

The calamity that hit German Jews affected them as Jews first. But Jewish women had gender-specific experiences as well. In addition to suffering the persecution that afflicted all Jews, Jewish women also had the burden of keeping their households and communities together. Racism and persecution as well as survival meant something different for women than men—in practical and psychological terms.

This essay explores the increasingly difficult daily lives of Jewish middle-class women and the work of their main organization, the League of Jewish Women, *Juedischer Frauenbund* (JFB), in prewar Nazi Germany. By focusing on the 1930s, we can locate the intensification of persecution and its effects on women and their families in a time when few dreamed that developments would end in anything like Auschwitz. In fact, this period is often neglected for either the earlier, more hopeful era of the Weimar Republic (1918–33) or the later shocking years of genocide. But the intermediate era—the nazification of daily life, when the victims had to learn to cope, and when even relationships among ordinary Germans were coarsened—is often far more instructive politically. Moreover, exploring the lives of Jews as they interacted daily with Gentiles challenges the myth of political innocence with which so many Germans today surround their accounts of "daily life in Nazi Germany."[2] Most importantly for our purpose, gender differences in the experience of being a persecuted Jew can be illustrated more clearly for these years than for later ones. Finally, a brief look at Jewish women's organizations shows how women responded collectively to increasing persecution.

The focus will be on housewives and mothers, largely because they are the ones who left the most memoirs. Still, they also made up a large portion of the female community. In their twenties, thirties, and forties, these women had embarked upon marriage, created families, and, sometimes, started careers. Like the vast majority of Jews, they experienced the impending catastrophe from their situation as ethnically or religiously Jewish and politically liberal citizens, increasingly shocked by the abrogation of the rights and liberties they once had taken for granted. Other Jewish women will receive less attention here: rarely did those who intermarried, who remained in Germany after the war broke out, or who died, leave memoirs behind, at least ones that are accessible today. Of those who managed to escape, single women and the elderly are underrepresented in memoir collections.[3] Finally, memoir collections are often found in Jewish libraries and archives. Hence, writers who were more self-consciously Jewish might have deposited them, possibly creating a sample of Jews who were slightly less integrated into German society than the actual range of women's situations.[4]

OVERVIEW OF JEWISH WOMEN AND
THEIR COMMUNITY

In 1933, 500,000 people were registered as Jews in Germany (excluding those who had officially left Judaism), or about 0.77 percent of the population. Seventy percent lived in large cities with populations of over 100,000 (one-half of non-Jews lived in places with under 10,000 inhabitants), and one-third (over 160,000) lived in Berlin, where they made up close to 4 percent of the population. Like every minority, the Jewish minority had a career profile that differed significantly from that of the general population. Historically prohibited from a variety of economic endeavors, almost 62 percent of Jews (compared with 18 percent of non-Jews) worked in business and commerce. They were underrepresented in agricultural careers, where less than 2 percent of Jews (but 29 percent of other Germans) were employed. The employment of Jewish women had gradually increased to 27 percent by 1933, but it was still less than that of non-Jewish women (34 percent). Of those who worked, over one-third were salaried employees; about one-fifth were assistants in family enterprises (*mithelfende Familienangehoerige*). Another one-fifth were self-employed (this could include a large business or a tiny one), and about one-tenth were workers (mostly in industry, but often in the offices rather than on the factory floor).[5]

The socioeconomic position of Jews was overwhelmingly middle class, although the inflation of the early 1920s and the Great Depression had definitely set them back. More women had to assist or support their families—a trend that intensified in the Nazi period—and more Jews had to rely on financial aid from Jewish welfare organizations.[6] In addition, almost one in five Jews in Germany was a refugee from Eastern Europe. Most of these *Ostjuden*, as they were called, eked out humble existences as industrial workers, minor artisans, or peddlers.

In comparison with non-Jewish women, Jewish women generally had smaller families and more education. They were less likely to work outside the home and more likely to have household help. Although married Jewish women devoted themselves to their families, parents expected their unmarried daughters to prepare for a career. Many—seven times as many proportionally as Christian women—went to the university.[7] As we shall see, after 1933, career development was increasingly obstructed just as wage earning became more urgent.

During the Weimar Republic, strictly religious education and practices were on the decline and mixed marriages on the rise.[8] In the large cities, marriage to Christians was becoming so common—especially among Jewish men—that some Jewish leaders actually feared the complete fusion of their community into German society by the end of the twentieth century.[9] Jews eagerly joined non-sectarian organizations. For example, the Jewish feminist movement (League of Jewish Women) belonged to the German bourgeois feminist movement from 1908 until 1933, and individual Jewish women were prominent members of other German women's organizations. Jews felt a deep allegiance to the ideals of German civilization as they understood them—the Enlightenment values of tolerance, humanism, and reason. They enjoyed general acceptance in the worlds of art and culture, participated in center and moderate Left politics, and excelled in the "free" professions of medicine and law. Possibly as many as one-third of all women physicians in the Weimar Republic were Jewish.[10]

Although Jews adapted to the social, political, or cultural styles of their surroundings, "quoting Goethe at every meal,"[11] they also preserved a sense of ethnic solidarity and religious cohesion. They did so through organizing religious or secular Jewish groups and through maintaining traditional family holiday celebrations. Women's organizations, in particular, fostered a sense of Jewish identity—including religious identity—throughout the Weimar years. Thus, as we shall see, the interest by women's organizations in their Jewish heritage during the Nazi period was not a sudden shift; it was an intensification of a trend already well under way. Finally, a small Zionist movement, while failing to make significant inroads into the assimilationist commitments of most German Jews, sharpened Jewish self-consciousness.[12]

Jewish cohesion was also a response to a pervasive anti-Semitism with roots in Imperial Germany (1871–1918). Virtually all Jews knew of anti-Semites or of an anti-Semitic incident directed against someone in their immediate circle of friends or relatives. The mission of one of the largest Jewish organizations in Germany, the Central Union of German Citizens of the Jewish Faith, founded in 1893, was to fight anti-Semitism politically and judicially and to strengthen Jewish and German consciousness within the Jewish communities. Germany's defeat in World War I and postwar political and economic instability magnified anti-Jewish passions. To the radical Right and its diverse followers, Jews became the scapegoats for all social and economic ills. Even more common and widespread was what Donald Niewyk has called "moderate anti-Semitism, that vague sense of unease about Jews that stopped far short of wanting to harm them but that may have helped to neutralize whatever aversion Germans might otherwise have felt for the Nazis."[13] This atmosphere could be found in churches, universities, political parties, and the government as well as in relationships between Jews and other Germans.

Even those Jewish women who worked closely with other German women commented on the distance between Jew and Christian: "We lived among each other, sat together in the same school room, attended university together, met each other at social events—and were complete strangers."[14] There were exceptions, close and lasting friendships that extended until deportation or even until today, but for the vast majority of Jews, their tenuous friendships with other Germans dissolved as the Nazi terror grew.

OSTRACISM AND ECONOMIC STRANGULATION: THE LIVES OF JEWISH WOMEN IN PUBLIC AND PRIVATE

With the Nazi seizure of power in January 1933, Jews as individuals had to struggle for daily survival and Jewish organizations had to begin providing unprecedented and massive economic, social, and cultural aid. Jews were forced into an era of "dissimilation"—a process of separation and then segregation—that took about six years, gradually gathering speed and thoroughness. A brief outline of this interim, before the deportations and genocide, provides necessary background for understanding the variety of Jewish responses.

Soon after taking power, the Nazis scheduled an official boycott of Jewish businesses and professional establishments for 1 April 1933. On that day, storm troopers stood in front of Jewish stores, threatening and exhorting shoppers to "buy German." As *un*official boycotts continued, the Nazis enacted discriminatory legislation. The "April Laws" of 1933 provided for the expulsion of Jews from the civil service, the legal and medical professions, and postprimary schools and universities. This "legal" attack reached its peak in late 1935 with the "Law for the Protection of German Blood and Honor," or Nuremberg Laws, which forbade sexual intercourse or intermarriage between Jews and "Aryans" (perceived as "pure" Germans) and made it unlawful for a Jew to employ an "Aryan" domestic servant under the age of forty-five. The "laws" were followed by over 400 pieces of anti-Jewish legislation promulgated by the Nazis between 1933 and 1939.[15] The last stage before outright and organized violence was "aryanization," the attempt to drive Jews from the economy. Proceeding fitfully throughout 1936 and 1937, aryanization speeded up in 1938 and 1939 to the point where the economy could be considered *judenrein* (free of Jews). In 1938, persecutions reached a new level of intensity culminating in the November pogrom, commonly called Crystal Night. This milestone claimed the lives of at least 100 Jews and destroyed over a thousand synagogues and countless homes and shops. Over 30,000 Jewish men were incarcerated in concentration camps.

Despite what appears in hindsight to be the increasing speed and clarity of persecution, Nazi policy followed what one historian described as a "twisted road to Auschwitz." Contradictory pronouncements, regional variations, conflicting satrapies, lack of coordination at the top, and the attempt to appear moderate to other nations gave contemporaries profoundly mixed signals. It was only after the November pogrom that most Jews were finally convinced of their peril. At every stage, some Jews thought, and others hoped, that the government would cease its persecutions. As the Jewish community moved from a relatively porous relationship with the surrounding society to a severely encapsulated one, many believed they could make peace with the new circumstances. Even after the Nuremberg Laws, for example, the central organization of Jews was willing to see them as a "tolerable arrangement" and to work for a *modus vivendi* with the Nazi state.[16]

As dissimilation intensified, the concept of "normal" became increasingly elastic. This was a complicated process. For some, there was the longing to make life "normal" within the ever-narrowing boundaries drawn by the Nazis; for others, there was a denial of what they saw happening; for many, there was a combination of both at the same time: the desire and need to believe that they and their families could remain in their homeland, even under new and trying conditions. Today, historians of daily life in Nazi Germany are attempting to capture the double character of normality and terror, the effects of both a normal bureaucratic state and an exceptional state on its citizens. This double character is all the more pronounced—and more complicated—for its victims, whose perceptions of the conflicting signals were colored not only by their anxieties but also by their hopes.[17]

Life for German-Jewish women changed dramatically with the beginning of the Nazi regime. One of the first signs of a "new era" (even before one lost a job or one's husband, father, or brother did) was the loss of former friends. One woman reported that she had enjoyed getting together with friends from her hometown in a cafe once a month:

> Since the Nazis came to power, I hadn't taken part in these gatherings. I didn't want to cause difficulties for my friends as a result of my [Jewish] presence.

One day she met one of her friends:

> She tried to convince me that they were all still my friends, so I decided to go to the next meeting. . . . I couldn't sleep at all the night before the gathering. I was worried about my Christian friends, but I was also worried about myself. . . . I knew I would observe them very carefully. I would notice even a shadow of their discomfort at my entry. . . . But I didn't have to read their eyes or note a change in their tone. The empty table in the booth where we had always met spoke loudly and clearly. . . . But I couldn't blame them. Why should they have risked the loss of their jobs only to prove to me that Jews could still have friends in Germany?[18]

Of course, not all Germans abandoned their Jewish friends. In fact, it was often precisely an experience of loyalty—the friend who came by ostentatiously, the former classmate who went out of her way to shake hands with a Jewish woman in a crowded store,[19] or the "sympathy purchases" after the April boycott[20]—that gave Jews mixed messages, letting some deceive themselves into staying. Furthermore, in the early years, Jews experienced only isolated local ostracism or attacks, often based on economic rivalries and resentments rather than on purely racial grounds.[21]

But the government intended to completely isolate Jews and could count on grass roots enthusiasm. Well before the Nazis prohibited friendly contacts with Jews, gossip and denunciations discouraged such associations. Basing his research on Gestapo (Secret State Police) files, Robert Gellately has observed "an extraordinary degree and variety of accommodation . . . to the regime's doctrines on race. Friendships and business relationships going back many years were broken off."[22] Of interest here is not only the fear of terror, but also the often zealous autosurveillance by the Germans themselves. This had an effect on the Jews too. For example, in a small Rhineland town, in late 1933, a Christian woman went to visit her Jewish friend. When she arrived at the door, her friend looked at her in horror: "For God's sake, Frieda, leave, don't come in, we are already being watched." With tears in their eyes, they turned away from each other.[23] Thus, companionship with non-Jews became the rare exception. Jews felt as if they were becoming society's lepers.

Loss of friends was accompanied by general social ostracism. The Gestapo and the courts used charges of friendship and, more seriously, "race defilement," "to discipline [or 'educate'] society at large about the importance of the race issue . . . but beyond that . . . to adjust all opinions to bring them into line with Nazi teachings."[24] By 1936, the Nazis had "brought off a deepening of the gap" between Jews and other Germans.[25] Officials, neighbors, even the postal carrier looked past or through Jews as they crossed paths at the local market or in the corridors. I suspect that the loss of friends and the decline of sociability in the neighborhood affected Jewish women more than men, because women were more integrated into and dependent upon the community and neighborhood. They were more accustomed to neighborly exchanges and courtesies. Their lives straddled the interface between family and community. Highly organized and active in communal, volunteer, or women's organizations, women suffered acutely when they were ostracized. Moreover, women probably had more frequent contacts with the state than men. They had more meetings with such state agents as post office and railroad clerks; social workers; and, for mothers in particular, teachers. Men saw less of neighbors to begin with and had less time to engage in communal or volunteer activities. Also, although men now suffered the loss of even a modicum of courtesy at work, they were more used to competition and a certain degree of conflict in their everyday work life.[26]

The pain of being the object of a general, hateful taboo affected most Jews long before the actual violence began. One woman recalled that when she traveled on the tram, on the day of the April 1933 boycott, she felt self-conscious about being Jewish and feared that the people next to her might move away from her if they guessed her true identity.[27] Another woman wrote that anxiety accompanied her wherever she went.

> If I had to talk to shop attendants I'd be afraid they would be hostile to me as soon as they discovered I was Jewish; when I waited for the tram, I always thought the conductor wouldn't stop for me if he knew I was Jewish. . . . I waited for such

events all the time and this anxiety tormented me unceasingly. Long before the Nazis forbade it, I had stopped going to movies or the theater, because I simply couldn't stand being around people who hated us.[28]

Rapidly, more concrete dislocations began to affect women. The loss of jobs—their own, their husbands', and fathers'—threatened economic well-being. In early April 1933, a teacher reported:

> Briefly before 8:00 A.M., when I arrived at the school building . . . the principal, saying "Good Morning" in his customary, friendly way, stopped me, and asked me to come to his room. . . . When we were seated, he said, in a serious, embarrassed tone of voice, he had orders to ask me not to go into my classroom. I probably knew, he said, that I was not permitted to teach anymore at a German school. I did know, but was it to happen so abruptly? . . . Mr. B. was extremely sorry, he assured me. . . . I collected myself. . . . I also collected my belongings. . . . There was nobody . . . to say goodbye to, because everybody else had gone to the classroom. . . .
>
> I rode home. . . . In the afternoon . . . colleagues, pupils, their mothers came, some in a sad mood, others angry with their country, lovely bouquets of flowers, large and small, in their arms. In the evening, the little house was full of fragrance and colors, like for a funeral, I thought; and indeed, this was the funeral of my time teaching at a German public school.[29]

Immediately after the "April Laws," about one-half of Jewish judges and prosecutors and almost one-third of Jewish lawyers lost their jobs. One-fourth of Jewish physicians lost their German National Health Insurance (*Krankenkasse*) affiliation.[30] In September, the Nazis excluded Jews from the Chambers of Culture, and from the worlds of art, film, music, literature, and journalism, areas in which they had been disproportionately active. Restrictions, official and unofficial harassment, and economic boycotts all increased in their frequency and fervor. As a result, many Jewish businesses, particularly small ones, were forced to shut down or sell out.

Unemployment began to plague the Jewish community. In 1933, about two-thirds of Jewish salaried employees worked in Jewish businesses and firms. With the disappearance of many Jewish firms, joblessness among Jewish employees became rampant. By the spring of 1933, nearly one-third of Jewish clerks—compared with one-fifth of the non-Jewish ones—were looking for jobs.[31] Because over one-half (53 percent) of employed Jewish women worked in business and commerce, largely as family assistants (22 percent) and salaried employees (40 percent), they lost their jobs as family businesses and Jewish shops closed down. Furthermore, Jewish sources estimated that three-quarters of Jewish women in business and trade were affected by the discriminatory laws and the early anti-Jewish boycotts.[32] By April 1938, more than 60 percent of all Jewish businesses did not exist, and Jewish social workers were trying to help 60,000 unemployed people. Furthermore, those businesses that lingered on tended to be either at the very top (a few banks and financial institutions) or at the bottom (independent artisans).[33] Women rarely worked in either.

Women's economic future looked bleak. The exclusion of Jews from German universities and institutions of higher learning restricted employment possibilities. Even new admissions in trade and vocational schools were limited to 1.5 percent "non-Aryans." By mid-1935, the apprenticeship office for Jewish girls reported that every second young woman now aimed to be a seamstress. Before 1933, these same young women would have looked forward to business or professional careers. By 1937, when young women had shifted their focus to jobs useful in countries of emigration, 24 percent of high school seniors planned to learn a craft, largely preferring tailoring (20 percent). Sixteen percent trained for domestic service, 13 percent for commerce, and 12 percent for social work.[34] Moreover, the choices available to girls were more limited—if one excludes housework—than those open to boys. Welfare organizations suggested sewing-related jobs for women, such as knitting, tailoring, or making clothing decorations, whereas men could consider many more options, including becoming painters, billboard designers, upholsterers, shoemakers, dyers, tailors, or skilled industrial workers.[35]

To make matters worse, it seems that parents preferred to keep girls home, either to shelter them from unpleasant work or to help out around the house. The old-fashioned idea that girls would not need a career because they would marry continued even as that fantasy became more inconsistent with reality. As late as July 1936, the emigration preparatory career training school at Gross-Breesen could not fill its girls' section but had to turn down 400 boys.[36] Also, Jewish community welfare organizations often gave preferential treatment to boys seeking career training. The newsletter of the Jewish feminist movement announced that one provincial welfare office had given subsidies to seventy-two boys and only ten girls.[37]

As the situation for Jews in Germany worsened, an internal migration took place. Economic strangulation occurred most quickly in small towns, where often more than 80 percent of the Jewish population was left destitute.[38] Furthermore, Jews attempted to escape from the personal hostility of villages and smaller towns by seeking the anonymity and, hence, relative safety, of large cities. Thus, the Jewish population was in constant flux. Women who moved their families had to adjust their households to a new urban environment and deteriorating political circumstances and still try to maintain a relatively stable family life. Women who stayed in big cities participated as never before in social welfare work within Jewish communities and Jewish women's organizations to integrate the steady stream of newcomers. Often women did this while preparing their own families for emigration.

To meet new and mounting economic hardships, Jewish housewives tried, where possible, to prepare less expensive meals, to make home and clothing repairs themselves, and to make do with less help around the house. The

Nuremberg Laws (which severely restricted "Aryan" household help in Jewish homes) left Jewish women to their own devices in running a household with greater problems, in shopping for food in increasingly hostile stores and in doing these tasks with ever-shrinking resources.

The pain of their children—who often faced anti-Semitism more immediately than their parents from classmates and teachers in German public schools—disturbed both women and men profoundly as parents, but women learned of and dealt with the children's distress more directly than men. When children came home from school, their mothers heard the stories first and had to respond. Mothers also supervised their children's homework. Imagine the contradictory emotions of a Jewish mother who was *reassured* to learn that her son had sung patriotic songs, said "Heil Hitler" to the teacher, and received praise for his laudatory essay about Hitler: his "gross political miseducation at school would keep [him] out of trouble." About a year later the same child, now enrolled in a Jewish school, wrote a story about Jewish resistance as a Mother's Day gift for his mother. Upon reading it, she was frightened, for his "political awakening . . . could lead to trouble for the whole family."[39] Principals summoned mothers to pick up their children when they were expelled from school, and these mothers then sought new schools for their children.[40] Mothers were usually the ones whom teachers phoned when children were to be excluded from class events. One mother reported that her children were not allowed to participate in any special event:

> My daughter cried, not because she couldn't go to the theater . . . she cried, because she was ostracized from the group, as though she wasn't good enough for her classmates. . . . I believe that the Nazi teacher was ashamed of herself now and then, when she looked into the sad eyes of my little daughter, because she phoned me several times and asked that I not send the child to school on the days when something enjoyable had been planned for the children.

On Mother's Day, Jewish children had to take part in the school festivities but were not allowed to sing along. When the Jewish children protested, their teacher responded: "I know that you have a mother too, but she is only a Jewish mother."[41]

This kind of harassment provoked many families to enroll their children in Jewish schools. Still, about one-half of Jewish children between the ages of six and fourteen remained in the public elementary schools, subject to torment by teachers and other children, until November 1938 when the Nazis barred their attendance.

Between 1934 and 1939, about 18,000 Jewish children left Nazi Germany for safer havens on what were called "children's transports" (*Kindertransporte*). Immediately after the November pogrom, with husbands in concentration camps, many mothers had to make the excruciating decision to send their children abroad.[42] About 8,000 children went to England, 3,400 to

Palestine,[43] and the rest to other European countries and the United States.[44] There they received foster care (or in the case of Palestine, lived on *kibbutzim* or in children's homes) until their parents could join them. Many parents never made it.

"Children turn into letters" was a phrase expressing the despair of parents who remained behind. The loss of daily intimacy with their children affected parents, but again, mothers most immediately. And, for those increasingly nervous and frightened children who stayed on—the children's transports, like other exits, never were sufficient—parents watched their opportunities dwindle. By the early war years, Jewish children found it difficult to play freely in the fresh air. The Nazis banned Jews from the parks and forests, and even small groups of children were no longer allowed to play in outdoor yards. They were permitted to play only in Jewish cemeteries.[45]

Women's organizations urged women to preserve the "moral strength to survive" and looked to biblical heroines for role models. In the face of progressively worsening living conditions, it was women who were supposed to "make things work." For example, as families moved into smaller apartments, or as others took in boarders in order to make ends meet, tighter living quarters caused strains. The League of Jewish Women noted:

> It is the duty . . . of the Jewish woman to regulate the schedule and the organization of the household so that everyone is satisfied. She has to give her husband, the head of the household, the necessary time to be alone to relax. . . . She has to adjust without being subordinate. This is more necessary than ever, given today's living arrangements. Then, living together, even with many people in tight circumstances, will bring about that kind of communal feeling that will bring peace to the household.[46]

The women's organization, nevertheless, acknowledged that, because women felt called upon to do more for their families and more often became the sole support of families, men should begin to do housework too. Timidly they reminded their readers:

> It won't always be avoidable, that our men will have to take part of the household duties, as is customary in North American homes. It is necessary to get together and talk about our resistance to this—a resistance found more in women than in men . . . in order to overcome it.[47]

Women frequently made tough demands on themselves, taking responsibility for the psychological work necessary to raise the spirits of their children and husbands and to tide the family over until better times. These expectations even affected Jewish women whose husbands were "Aryan" and, therefore, safe. One woman who lived in constant dread of what could happen to her mother (before she admitted to herself that she, too, was in danger) restrained herself from sharing her worries with her husband. She confided to her diary: "I can't burden my husband . . . with my family problems. . . ."[48] This heightened sense of familial obligation—fostered by community and friends—was certainly an extra burden but also, perhaps, a source of solace and strength. Suffering a nervous breakdown around the time of the November pogrom, one woman wrote:

> No doctor could help me. . . . I also was struck by a dangerous case of asthma, the attacks came ever more frequently and seriously. . . . Everyone tried to convince me that I alone had to be able to overcome my fear and desperation in order to help my family in these terrible times instead of lying there so helpless. They insisted on the urgency of this to such an extent that I finally gathered all my strength in the hopes of finding a way out of Germany.[49]

WOMEN AND EMIGRATION: PERCEPTION AND REALITIES

It was most often women who saw the danger signals first and urged their husbands to emigrate from the terrors of Germany. One woman's memoir noted that, in a discussion among friends about a physician who had just fled in the spring of 1935, most of the men in the room condemned him.

> The women protested strongly: they found that it took more courage to go than to stay. . . . "Why should we stay here and wait for our eventual ruin? Isn't it better to go and to build up a new existence somewhere else, before our strength is exhausted by the constant physical and psychic pressure? Isn't the future of our children more important than a completely senseless holding out. . . ." All the women, without exception, shared this opinion. . . , while the men, more or less passionately, spoke against it. Also, on the way home, I discussed this with my husband. Like all other men, he simply couldn't imagine how one could leave one's beloved homeland and the duties that fill a man's life. "Could you really give that all up . . . ?" The tone of his voice told me how upset he was at the mere thought of this. "I could," I said, without hesitating a second.[50]

The different attitudes of women and men described here seem to reflect a gender-specific reaction remarked upon by sociologists and psychologists: in dangerous situations, men tend to "stand their ground," whereas women avoid conflict, preferring flight as a strategy.

A more important reason why women were more amenable to emigration than their husbands is that women were less tied to the public worlds of jobs or businesses. Women were—as Claudia Koonz has pointed out—less assimilated than men into the economy and culture.[51] The daughter of a wealthy businessman commented, "When the Nazis appeared on the scene, he was too reluctant to consolidate everything and leave Germany. He may have been a bit too attached to his status, as well as his possessions."[52] Although their decision to leave Germany was as fraught with practical consequences as their husbands', because they, too, would face the uncertainties and poverty associated with emigration, wives did not have to tear themselves away from their life work—whether a business or professional practice—or from patients, clients, or colleagues. Women had far less to leave behind. But, even business or career women were apparently less reluctant than their spouses to leave. One wife, a wealthy manufacturer whose husband had married into and managed *her* business, wanted to pack their bags and flee immediately in 1933. He, on the other hand, refused to leave the business. Although the wife could not convince her husband that they should flee, she insisted that they both learn a trade that would be useful abroad. After his arrest and release from a concentration camp in November 1938, they managed to escape to Shanghai, where their new skills helped them survive.[53] In short, in light of men's primary identity with their work, they often felt trapped into staying. Women, whose identity was more family-oriented, struggled to preserve what was central to them by fleeing with it.

Women and men led relatively distinct lives, and they often interpreted daily events differently. Although less integrated than men into work and culture, women were more integrated into their community. As noted earlier, there were the daily pleasantries with neighbors, regular exchanges with the grocer and baker, occasional visits to the school, attendance at concerts or local lectures, and, often, participation in local women's organizations. Raised to be sensitive to interpersonal behavior and social situations, women's social antennae were more finely tuned than their husbands'. They registered the increasing hostility of their immediate surroundings, unmitigated by a promising business prospect, a deep feeling for German culture (as experienced by their more educated husbands), or the patriotism of husbands who had fought in World War I. Women's constant contacts with their own and other people's children and the community probably alerted them to the warning signals that come through interpersonal relations—and they took those signals very seriously. Men, on the other hand, scrutinized and analyzed the confusing legal and economic decrees and the often contradictory public utterances of the Nazis. Men mediated their experiences through newspapers and broadcasts. Politics may have remained more abstract to them, whereas women's "business"—their neighbors, direct everyday contacts, the minutiae (and significance) of ordinary details—brought politics home.

That women and men often assessed the dangers differently reflected their different contacts and frames of reference. But, *decisions* seem to have been made by husbands—or circumstances.[54] The widespread assumption that women lacked political acumen gave their warnings less credibility in the eyes of their husbands. Thus, one woman's prophecies of doom met with her husband's amusement: "He laughed at me and argued that such an insane dictatorship could not last long . . . he was so certain that there would be a positive outcome. . . ." Even after their seven-year-old son was beaten up at school, her husband was still optimistic.[55]

Some of the men who did not take their wives' warnings seriously were those who had received reprieves from the exclusionary decrees of April 1933 (although the reprieves proved to be temporary). In 1933, President Hindenburg interceded to protect those Jewish civil servants, lawyers, physicians, or teachers who had fought in World War I; whose fathers or sons had served; or who had been hired for their posts before 1918. The wives of these men typically could not convince their husbands that they were in danger. For example, Hindenburg's move restored one severely wounded veteran's faith in Germany. He would keep his job as a jurist, so he could not take seriously the idea of emigrating with four small children.[56] One woman, who argued in vain with her husband to leave Germany, noted that she was "powerless against his optimism . . . he constantly fell back on the argument that he had been at the front in World War I."[57] Carol Gilligan's psychological theories may apply here: men tended to view their situation in terms of rights, women in terms of affiliations and relationships.[58]

Not only were men inclined to trust their own political perceptions more than those of their wives, but their role and status as breadwinner and head of household also often contributed to their hesitancy to emigrate. One housewife described her attempt to convince her husband to flee: "A woman sometimes has a sixth feeling. . . . I said to my husband, 'You know, I think we will have to leave.' He said, 'No, you won't have a six-room apartment and two servants if we do that.' But I said, 'OK, then I'll have a one-room flat with you: but I want to be safe.' " Despite his reluctance to leave, she studied English and learned practical trades for emigration, including sewing furs, making chocolate, and doing industrial ironing. After his arrest by and release from the Gestapo, the couple left Germany and she supported the family in Australia.[59]

Women's subordinate status in the public world and their focus on the household may have made them more amenable to the kinds of work they would have to perform in places of refuge. In England and the United States, for example, refugee wives frequently "made do" for the duration, working as domestic servants, while husbands attempted to reestablish their businesses or professional careers. In couples where husbands became butlers and wives maids, the husband often experienced a loss of status more intensely. A daughter described how her mother, formerly a housewife and pianist, cheerfully and successfully took on the role of maid, whereas her father, formerly a chief accountant in a bank, failed as a butler and barely passed as a gardener.[60] Even when both sexes fulfilled their refugee roles well, women seemed less status conscious than men. Perhaps women did not experience the descent from employing a servant to becoming one to the same degree as men because their public status had always been derivative of their fathers' or husbands' anyway.

A combination of events usually led to the final decision to leave. For one woman, who wrote that every Jewish person "knew a decent German" and recalled that many Jews thought "the radical Nazi laws would never be carried out because they did not match the moderate character of the German people," the decision was induced by the abuse her husband and children faced and by the difficulties of running a household after the Nuremberg Laws.[61] For those who had not yet made a decision, the violence of the November pogrom definitively tipped the balance toward emigration. The pogrom provided another example of the contradictory behavior of Germans toward Jews—the mixture of rampant viciousness with occasional kindness. As mobs attacked and burned Jewish homes, businesses, and synagogues, one woman recalled the events as follows:

> While I was sweeping up some of the debris, I noticed another mob of hoodlums, among them women. They were armed with axes as they approached . . . [and] proceeded to ransack the entire house. . . . Everyone who could have given us shelter was in a similar situation. Then I thought of Anna K., the former parlor maid. . . . Soon we were on our way in hope that there would be some straw bed in her barn. . . . She had two such beds, but we would have to leave early the next day, . . . because her brother had become a member of the SA.[62]

Whereas up to this point the number of Jewish emigrants per year had fluctuated between 21,000 (1935) and 40,000 (1938), it became a mass flight reaching 78,000 in 1939.[63]

This is not to imply that the handwriting was always clearly on the wall. That conclusion emerges largely with the advantages of hindsight. In the 1930s, Nazi "deception and cynical dishonesty served the purpose of tranquilizing the Jewish community."[64] More significantly, perceptions by Jews of their predicament were not the only factors affecting emigration. A major obstacle to mass Jewish emigration lay in the occupational and age structure of the Jewish community—middle-aged and elderly businesspeople who would face grave difficulties resettling. Most importantly, the restrictions of foreign countries against immigrants prevented escape. In July 1938, the thirty-two nations assembled at the Evian Conference "regretted" that they could not take in more Jews. The *New York Herald Tribune* concluded: "Powers Slam Doors against German Jews."[65] A final obstacle to emigration was simple lack of luck, for most would-be emigrants were not fortunate enough to have relatives or friends abroad who could sponsor their admission into a country of refuge.

The above analysis of the *desire* to emigrate highlights women's different expectations, priorities, and perceptions. It does not follow, however, that more women than men *actually* left. In fact, the opposite seems to be the case. Fewer women than men left Germany. Why was this so?

There were still compelling reasons to stay, although life became increasingly difficult. First, women, especially young women, could still find jobs in the Jewish sector of the German economy more easily than men.[66] As Jews were expelled from German social welfare programs, the social service sector within the Jewish communities grew. This Jewish sector hired young women for domestic, welfare, or educational jobs such as social workers, nurses, administrators in hospitals or homes, and teachers or administrators in home economics schools.[67]

Although the employment situation of Jewish women helped keep them in Germany, that of men helped get them out. Some husbands or sons had business connections abroad, facilitating their immediate flight, and others emigrated alone in order to establish themselves and then send for their families. Women's organizations agreed that wives should not "hinder" husbands from emigrating alone if there was no alternative. They argued, however, that it was often no cheaper for men to emigrate without their wives. A single man still had to pay nearly as much for rent, meal, and laundry service as when a wife ran the household for both. Besides, women could earn the extra income necessary to establish the family or act as breadwinners "at first." Most importantly, they stressed that women were necessary because they gave men support and advice.[68]

Another compelling reason why more women remained behind was the fact that, before the war, men faced more immediate, physical danger than women and were forced to flee promptly. In a strange twist of fortune, the men interred in concentration camps during the November pogrom were released only upon showing proof of their ability to leave Germany immediately. Families—mostly wives and mothers—strained every resource to provide the documentation to free these men and send them on their way. Further, as more sons left, daughters remained as the sole caretakers for elderly parents. One female commentator noted that she knew of "a whole slew of young women who can't think of emigration because they don't know who might care for their elderly mother in the interim, before they could start sending her money. In the same families, the sons went their way without any thought."[69] By 1936, the League of Jewish Women saw cause for serious concern regarding the "special problem of the emigration of women which is often partly overlooked and not correctly understood."[70] Not only did it seem to the League of Jewish Women that far fewer women than men were leaving, but also that, if the trend continued, Jewish men of marriageable age would live abroad and would intermarry, but Jewish women would stay behind in Germany with no chance at all of marrying. The League of Jewish Women reminded parents of their "responsibility to free their daughters too . . . [even if daughters] feel stronger psychological ties to their families than sons do, [which] probably lies in the female psyche."[71]

The growing disproportion of Jewish women in the German Jewish population also resulted from the fact that there were more Jewish women than men in Germany to begin with. Thus, in order to stay even, a greater absolute number of women would have had to emigrate. In 1933, 52.3 percent of Jews were women, resulting from such factors as male casualties during World War I and greater exogamy among Jewish men. The slow rate of female emigration meant that the female proportion of the Jewish population had risen to 57.5 percent by 1939.[72] Because many of the young had emigrated by 1935, the percentage of elderly Jews—among them a large number of widows—also increased proportionately. In 1933, there had already been 1,400 women to 1,000 men over the age of sixty-five.[73] By October 1938, 11,000 elderly Jewish women were in need of Winter Relief (*Winterhilfe*).[74] In short, in slightly less than eight years, two-thirds of German Jews emigrated (many to European countries where they were later caught up in the Nazi net), leaving a disproportionate number of the elderly and women.[75] The statistics, memoirs, and interviews all give the impression that the Nazis, whose propaganda trumpeted the threat of Jewish men as rapists, thieves, and crooks, murdered a high percentage of elderly Jewish women.[76]

WOMEN'S ORGANIZATIONS

Jewish women's organizations, and the League of Jewish Women in particular, tried to alleviate the worsening conditions of all Jews, with special attention to the plight of women. Whereas from its inception in 1904, the league had focused on feminist issues of concern to Jewish women, between 1933 and its demise in 1938, the league took part in a battle for survival along with other Jewish organizations. This endeavor aimed to keep communal organizations intact and to maintain Jewish customs and traditions, to help needy Jews, and to prepare people for emigration.

With the Nazi seizure of power, the league began to work closely with the Central Organization of German Jews (*Reichsvertretung der deutschen Juden*)[77] and its welfare bureau (*Zentralausschuss fuer Hilfe and Aufbau*). As the Jewish community continued to draw closer together under the pressure from outside, the league also strengthened its ties to other Jewish women's organizations and to the Jewish youth movement. Furthermore, it founded new chapters and welcomed new members. When, for example, professional women's organizations were nazified in the process called *Gleichschaltung* and Jewish women were thrown out, the league set up its own groups for Jewish career women. In Berlin, the league's Professional Women's Group grew so large that it consisted of nine subgroups, including welfare workers, technical assistants, kindergarten teachers, nursery school teachers, youth group leaders, physicians, gym teachers, arts and crafts instructors, and groups interested in pedagogy.[78] A letter written by one of these new members noted that

as everything crumbled around us, as our professional groups were dissolved, as we lost our jobs, the league invited all professional women. Soon, various groups were formed to give everyone the opportunity to meet with professional colleagues and to attend professionally interesting lectures.

Typically, the women's organization also looked after members' morale. It instituted neighborhood evenings "so that women of different professions living in one neighborhood could meet . . . to come together both intellectually and spiritually in a small circle." One woman reported: "The first evening was unforgettable. Everyone introduced themselves by name and profession, skimmed over their education, hiring and job, and—the disintegration. . . . Then we spoke of our adjustment to our current lives."[79]

Unwilling to accept complete cultural deprivation, Jews resisted their exclusion from German cultural life by creating their own. German Jews continued to appreciate German music and the Enlightenment classics in their own theaters and auditoriums. This included holding concerts and public lectures on secular topics in the synagogues.[80] They also promoted Jewish education, opening two Jewish continuing education institutions in 1934.[81] The League of Jewish Women sponsored cultural activities, such as reading circles, lectures, and a newsletter, which were primarily concerned with Jewish custom, history, and religion. For example, in Bochum, women studied *Mishna*.[82] In Gelsenkirchen, forty-five to fifty participants formed a study group called "A Path through the Jewish Year."[83] In Munich, they studied the weekly Torah section, attended a Bible course, and heard guest lectures on the era of Jewish Emancipation. Koenigsberg women participated in a lecture series on the Bible. And in Cologne, a study group met to discuss Jewish newspapers and the philosophy of Martin Buber.[84] Local league groups also organized traveling libraries like those in Dortmund, concerts, and exhibits of Jewish women artists.[85]

Local sections of the league also, but more rarely, discussed general topics relating to cultural issues and women. As late as January 1935, the Berlin local discussed "Recent Literature on the Woman Question." In these early years of Nazism, Jewish women, like Jewish men, refused to give up their dual identities as Germans and Jews. As they turned more to Jewish learning and culture, they upheld their version of German culture—enlightened and liberal—against the barbarism around them. The leaders of the League of Jewish Women reaffirmed their allegiance to the women's movement, seeing themselves as "trustees of the German women's movement in its purest, most spiritual, social-ethical, unpolitical form." Bertha Pappenheim, the founder of the league, refused to yield her German heritage, insisting that "being a German, a woman and a Jew are three duties that can strain an individual to the utmost, but also three sources of . . . vitality. They do not extinguish each other, in fact they strengthen and enrich each other."[86]

The league knew that people whose social and economic conditions had declined so rapidly needed psychological and material support. One creative way to resist demoralization was to publish a cookbook, which helped solve a nutritional dilemma for Jews who had difficulty buying kosher meat after Hitler forbade ritual slaughtering. It went through four editions in its first year (1935). When the Nuremberg Laws of 1935 excluded Jews from the German Winter Relief, the league participated in a Jewish winter relief program. In numerous cities, its members helped collect money, clothing, and fuel. In Berlin, eighteen collecting depots sent about 30,000 care packages to needy families every month.[87]

As more Jews lost their jobs or businesses—at the end of 1936, about 20 percent were on welfare and another 20 to 25 percent were living off the capital they had received for the sale of their businesses[88]—the league tried to help Jewish women and their families adjust to lower living standards. Its local chapters offered courses in cooking, darning, ironing, knitting, tailoring, sewing, first-aid instruction, and household repairs. In Bochum, for example, one branch organized four evenings with the theme of "Self-Help."[89] In various cities, the league set up communal kitchens, small play groups for children whose mothers needed to do part-time work, and discussion sessions where women could talk about their problems and receive practical and moral support. In Munich, 130 women regularly attended such *Hausfrau* afternoons.[90]

The league also expanded its childcare facilities (which included a lunch program and a home and rest home for children), its rest home for working women, and its support of the retired women and widows' groups. Furthermore, it increased its subsidies for needy women who had to take recuperative vacations or visit a health spa. In October 1938, the league's newsletter recommended setting up communal apartments as a way of stemming the housing shortage and caring for the Jewish elderly. Aware of a growing need among men as well, the league instituted home economics courses for boys, opened one of its homes for the aged to "older gentlemen," and offered places in its Berlin dormitory (formerly a dorm for women students) for "possibly also young men."[91]

Repeatedly, the league's newsletter underlined the essential role of women in providing persecuted families with a peaceful home environment. The league took for granted the notion that women were the ones who preserved the family's equilibrium. It assumed that women would persevere in their usual role of providing optimism and sustenance. In turn, it helped women with practical, spiritual, and intellectual advice when they could no longer face the misery around them.[92]

The last important effort of the League of Jewish Women involved preparing women for emigration. At first, the organization did not support emigration. However, after the Nuremberg Laws, it intensified its efforts to train girls for agriculture, domestic service, and crafts—careers in demand in Palestine and other countries of destination.[93] By 1936, the league's newsletter and counseling centers focused extensively on the question of emigration, discussing practical problems, cultural differences, and the legal status of women in such faraway places as Paraguay, Shanghai, or New York. Furthermore, the league intended to organize its members abroad so that they could extend aid to newly arrived refugees. Yet, as already mentioned, the league remained dissatisfied with the slow rate at which women emigrated.[94]

After the November pogrom, the league was ordered dissolved. Its treasury and institutions were absorbed into the Central Organization of German Jews, and its leaders joined the staff of that organization. Although many of these women had opportunities to emigrate (many had accompanied children out of the country only to return), they chose to continue their work for the Jewish community. Their duties became more difficult and depressing. In July 1942, Hannah Karminski, former executive secretary of the League of Jewish Women, wrote a friend: "This work can no longer give any satisfaction. It hardly has anything to do with what we understood 'social work' to mean . . . but, because one continues to work with people, once in a while there are moments in which being here seems to make sense."[95] Most of these women were deported in 1942 and became victims of Hitler's war against the Jews.

German Jewish women had lived in familiar, comfortable surroundings until these had turned hostile and murderous, like a grotesque dream. Their roles as housewives and mothers sharpened their alertness to danger, helping some plan for the future. Others, confronted with the increasing dreadfulness of daily life, uncomprehending children, escalating deprivation and anxiety, and the loss of friends tried to manage as best they could. They were able to resist complete despondency through family and social networks. They had to manage the proverbial double burden of employment and housework, and, indeed, a triple burden when one adds escalating emotional caretaking. In addition, many volunteered to work with women's organizations, which attempted to alleviate some of the practical and psychological stress within a community suddenly impoverished, ostracized, and torn apart by the emigration of its loved ones. In the limited time and space allotted them and with the restricted means at their disposal, women's organizations encouraged job retraining, emigration, and self-help and attempted to boost morale and a positive Jewish consciousness. Needless to say, neither organizations nor individuals were able to withstand the force of state persecution and terror or to prevent the annihilation of the Jewish community in Germany and the rest of Europe.

NOTES

I would like to thank the following groups for their careful reading of earlier versions of this essay: the German Women's History Study Group, the Rockefeller Foundation Bellagio Center Conference on "Women in Dark Times," and the Columbia University Seminar on Women and Society. I would also like to thank Renate Bridenthal, Douglas Morris, Monika Richarz, and Sydney Weinberg for their scrupulous reading and supportive criticisms.

1. About 270,000 out of the approximately 500,000 Jews in Germany managed to emigrate. Not all of these people, however, escaped; many were caught up in the Nazi net in Europe.

2. See Mary Nolan, "The Historikerstreit and Social History," *New German Critique*, no. 44 (Spring/Summer 1988): 51–80.

3. Single women may not have had the motivation to write memoirs because memoirs are often intended as family histories for future generations, and age may have impinged on the desire or ability of the elderly to write their stories.

4. People who were, or who considered themselves, on the edges of the Jewish community—such as women who intermarried or whose ethnic/religious identities were superseded by political loyalties—were less likely to donate their materials to Jewish organizations.

5. The employment breakdown is for Prussia in 1925, but it is representative of Germany as a whole as well. See *Israelitisches Familienblatt*, no. 8, (23 Feb. 1933): 9.

6. Monika Richarz, ed., Introduction, *Juedisches Leben in Deutschland: Selbstzeugnisse zur Sozialgeschichte*, 1918–1945 (Stuttgart: Deutsche Verlags-Anstalt, 1982). See also Erich Rosenthal, "Trends of the Jewish Population in Germany, 1910–39," *Jewish Social Studies* 6 (1944): 233–73.

7. Marion Kaplan, *The Jewish Feminist Movement in Germany: The Campaigns of the Juedischer Frauenbund*, 1904–1938 (Westport, Conn: Greenwood, 1979), 193, n. 31.

8. See Richarz, 15. Twenty out of 100 marriages were mixed in 1930, but conversions were down in comparison with the Imperial era.

9. Karl Schleunes, *The Twisted Road to Auschwitz: Nazi Policy toward German Jews, 1933–39* (Urbana: University of Illinois Press, 1970), 7. For gender-specific intermarriage statistics, see Usiel O. Schmelz, "Die demographische Entwicklung der Juden in Deutschland von der Mitte des 19. Jahrhunderts bis 1933," in *Zeitschrift fuer Bevoelkerungswissenschaft* 8 (January 1982): 42, 52–53.

10. This is my estimate based on the number of Jewish female medical students before the war. Jews had only received the right to become judges, diplomats, and civil servants in 1918.

11. George L. Mosse, *German Jews beyond Judaism* (Bloomington: Indiana University Press, 1985), 14.

12. Donald Niewyk, *The Jews in Weimar Germany* (Baton Rouge: Louisiana State University Press, 1980), 164.

13. Ibid., 80.

14. Ibid., 93–94.

15. Joseph Walk, *Das Sonderrecht fuer Juden im Ns Staat* (Heidelberg: D.F. Mueller, 1981); Schleunes, 109.

16. Schleunes, 109, 126.

17. See Nolan.

18. Quoted in Richarz, 233. I have translated all quotations from the Richarz volume.

19. Liselotte Kahn, Memoirs, Leo Baeck Institute, New York (hereafter cited as LBI), 16. About her classmate's behavior, Kahn noted: "This I considered already a heroic deed in 1933."

20. Hans Mommsen and Dieter Obst, "Die Reaktion der deutschen Bevoelkerung auf

die Verfolgung der Juden, 1933–1943," in *Herrschaftsalltag im Dritten Reich*, ed. Hans Mommsen (Dusseldorf: Schwann, 1988), 374, 378.

21. Michael H. Kater, "Everyday Anti-Semitism in Prewar Nazi Germany: The Popular Bases," *Yad Vashem Studies* 16 (1984): 129–59.

22. In April 1935, Nazi party members were forbidden from having personal relationships with Jews, unless in the line of duty. Still, even Nazi party members kept business ties to Jews through 1935 and some until even as late as 1938. Friendships with Jews were not officially a crime for nonparty members until November 1941, but local laws frequently forced Germans to break all relations with Jews much earlier. (See Mommsen and Obst, 387, 428–31.) For more on denunciations, the "key link between the police and the people in Nazi Germany [which made] the terror system work," see Robert Gellately, "The Gestapo and German Society: Political Denunciation in the Gestapo Case Files," *Journal of Modern History* 60 (December 1988): 664, 669, 673–74, 677. Gellately pointed out the centrality of gossip to the functioning of the Nazi terror system in "Terror System, Racial Persecution, and Resistance in Nazi Germany: Remarks on the Historiography," presented to the GDR-USA Symposium on Nazi Terror and Resistance, Princeton, N.J., 4–6 May 1989.

23. Francis Henry, *Victims and Neighbors: A Small Town in Nazi Germany Remembered* (S. Hadley, Mass.: Bergin and Garvey, 1984), 92.

24. Gellately, "The Gestapo and German Society," 677.

25. Sopade report (of the Social Democratic party in exile), quoted by Peter Pulzer in a lecture on the Anniversaries of the Annexation of Austria and Crystal Night, Harvard Center for European Studies, 14 Apr. 1989.

26. Thanks to Peter Pulzer for this insight.

27. Hanna Bergas, Memoirs, LBI, 1.

28. Quoted in Richarz, 232.

29. Hanna Bergas, Memoirs, 2.

30. Schleunes, 109.

31. Rosenthal, 262.

32. *Blaetter des Juedischen Frauenbundes* (hereafter *BJFB*), January 1934, p. 7; *Israelitisches Familienblatt*, no. 8 (23 Feb. 1933): 9; *Juedische Wohlfahrtspflege und Sozial Politik*, Berlin (hereafter *JWS*), 1931, Heft 2, pp. 77–78; *BJFB*, March 1935, p. 2. By 1936, many areas of small business, particularly those associated with agriculture, were declared *judenrein*, "free of Jews" (Schleunes, 145).

33. Avraham Barkai, "Der wirtschaftliche Existenzkampf der Juden im Dritten Reich, 1933–38," in *The Jews in Nazi Germany, 1933–38*, ed. Arnold Paucker (Tuebingen: 1986), 156–57.

34. *BJFB*, March 1935, p. 4; May 1935, p. 5; February 1937, pp. 2–3.

35. *JWS*, 1937, pp. 140–43.

36. Werner T. Angress, "Juedische Jugend zwischen nationalsozialistischer Verfolgung und juedischer Wiedergeburt," in *The Jews in Nazi Germany*, 219. It may be that Eastern European Jewish women took greater advantage of these career programs than German Jewish women, a function of the more precarious economic situation of the former. See Trude Maurer, "Auslaendische Juden in Deutschland, 1933–39," in *The Jews in Nazi Germany*, 205.

37. *BJBF*, March 1938, p. 3.

38. David Kramer, "Jewish Welfare Work under the Impact of Pauperisation," in *The Jews in Nazi Germany*, 183.

39. Steve J. Heims, ed., *Passages from Berlin* (South Berwick, Maine: Atlantic Printing, 1987), 73, 76.

40. Erna Segal, Memoirs, LBI, 78–79.

41. Quoted in Richarz, 234.

42. Rita R. Thalmann, "Juedische Frauen nach dem Pogrom 1938," in *The Jews in Nazi Germany*, 297.

43. Jehuda Reinharz, "Hashomer Hazair in Nazi Germany," in *The Jews in Nazi Germany*, 334.

44. Herbert Strauss, "Jewish Emigration from Germany: Nazi Policies and Jewish Responses," *Leo Baeck Institute Yearbook*, 1980, 328.

45. Richarz, 378.

46. *BJFB*, February 1935, p. 12; July 1938, p. 13.

47. Ibid., October 1938, pp. 4, 14.

48. Erna Becker-Kohen, Diary, Memoir collection, LBI, 4.

49. Erna Segal, Memoirs, LBI, 93–94. Segal and her husband and two children were unable to escape, but they survived underground in Berlin.

50. Richarz, 237.

51. Claudia Koonz, "Courage and Choice Among German Jewish Women and Men," in *The Jews in Nazi Germany*, 285. Also, see Koonz's *Mothers in the Fatherland: Women, the Family, and Nazi Politics* (New York: St. Martin's Press, 1987), chap. 10.

52. Marianne Berel, "Family Fragments," Memoirs, LBI, 16.

53. Lecture by Evelyn Rubin, her daughter, at Queens College, December 1988. See also *The Long Island Jewish Week* 188 (19 Nov. 1978). This points in a different direction from Koonz who suggested that women with strong business ties judged the situation much as men did (p. 364).

54. This does not mean that wives took no initiatives, but the ultimate decision seems to have rested with the husband. In early 1938, for example, Ilse Strauss's mother "applied to the American authorities for a quota number without my Father's knowledge; the hopeless number of 33,243 was allocated. It was a last desperate act and Papa did not even choke with anger anymore." Her parents and young brother were deported and killed. See Memoirs, LBI, B32/54, chap. 8, p. 44.

55. Erna Segal, Memoirs, LBI, 45–47, 61.

56. Charlotte Hamburger, Memoirs, LBI, 40–41.

57. Erna Segal, Memoirs, 45–46, 61.

58. Carol Gilligan, *In a Different Voice: Psychological Theory and Women's Development* (Cambridge: Harvard University Press, 1982).

59. John Foster, ed., *Community of Fate: Memoirs of German Jews in Melbourne* (Sydney, London, Boston: Allen & Unwin, 1986), 28–30.

60. Lore Siegal, *Other People's Houses* (New York: Fawcett Crest, 1958).

61. Charlotte Hamburger, Memoirs, 41, 46.

62. *LBI News*, no. 56 (Summer/Fall 1988): 4–5.

63. Statistics are from Richarz, 53.

64. Herbert Strauss, "Jewish Autonomy within the Limits of National Socialist Policy: The Communities and the Reichsvertretung," in *The Jews in Nazi Germany*, 126. See also Schleunes for the confusing plethora of decrees and exceptions.

65. Cited in Rita Thalmann and Emmanuel Feinermann, *Crystal Night* (London and New York: Holocaust Library, 1974), 22.

66. *JWS*, 1937, pp. 7–13; 27.

67. Home care assistants (*Pflegerinnen*) were recruited among women who were previously sales personnel, independent businesspeople, nurses' aides, artists, kindergarten teachers, and housewives (*JWS*, 1937, pp. 78–81). Avraham Barkai has discovered that some Jews protested against Jewish women who worked in the social service sector of the Jewish communities as "double earners" (women whose husbands also had jobs). Also, he has found letters to the editor of the *CV Zeitung*—the newsletter of the Central Union of German Citizens of the Jewish Faith—proposing that these women should become domestics in order to let older and more experienced men who needed jobs take their places (Barkai, "Der wirtschaftliche Existenzkampf der Juden im Dritten Reich," 163).

68. *BJFB*, December 1936, p. 5.

69. Ibid., April 1937, p. 5. A daughter recalled urging her parents to leave Germany after she experienced anti-Semitism in school: "Uppermost in my mother's mind was that she would not leave her mother behind alone. . . ." (Ruth Glaser, Memoirs, LBI, 18.) See also Erika Guetermann, "Das Photographien Album," Memoirs, LBI, for another example of a woman who would not leave her parents and was later killed by the Nazis.

70. *BJFB*, December 1936, p. 1. Also, among Eastern European Jews who returned east between 1934 and 1937, the majority were male even though almost one-half of them were married (Maurer, 204).

71. *BJFB*, April 1937, p. 10; December 1936, p. 1.

72. Richarz, 43.

73. Rosenthal, 248.

74. *BJFB*, October 1938, p. 4.

75. Richarz, 61.

76. Of the German-speaking Jews deported to the Lodz Ghetto in 1941, 81 percent were over the age of fifty and 60 percent were women. Of the 4,000 Berlin Jews in that transport, 94 percent were over sixty. See Avraham Barkai, "Between East and West: Jews from Germany in the Lodz Ghetto," *Yad Vashem Studies* 16 (1984): 282–83, 288. See *JWS*, 1937, pp. 96–97 for statistics on the German Reich; *JWS*, 1937, pp. 161–63 (for Hessen-Nassau); and *JWS*, 1937, pp. 200–01 (for Koenigsberg). See also M. Gruenewald Collection, LBI, memoirs of "Tante Emma." When the last Jews of her small town were deported, it was "almost only elderly women" (p. 31).

77. Rita Thalmann notes that the male-led Reichsvertretung never acknowledged the important work of the league, agreeing only in April 1938 to have one woman recommended by the league on its board. However, unlike the representatives from other major Jewish organizations on the board, this woman would not represent the league but only herself. See "Juedische Frauen," p. 296.

78. *BJFB*, January 1935, p. 10.

79. Ibid., December 1935, p. 13.

80. Jonathan J. Helfand, "*Halakhah* and the Holocaust: Historical Perspectives," in *Perspectives on the Holocaust*, ed. Randolph Braham (Boston: Kluwer-Nijhoff, 1983).

81. See Herbert Freeden, "Kultur 'nur fuer Juden': 'Kulturkampf' in der juedischen Pressen in Nazideutschland," in *The Jews in Nazi Germany*.
82. *BJFB*, May 1935, p. 10.
83. Ibid., February 1935, p. 5.
84. Ibid., p. 12; *Juedische Rundschau*, no. 11 (14 Mar. 1935): 18.
85. *BJFB*, January 1935, p. 10; February 1935, p. 5; May 1935, p. 10.
86. "Aus der Welt der Frau," *Juedische Rundschau*, 14 Feb. 1935, p. 18.
87. *BJFB*, February 1935, p. 11; November 1935, p. 6; January 1936, p. 6.
88. Barkai, "Der wirtschaftliche Existenzkampf der Juden im Dritten Reich," 164; Kramer, 1983.
89. These were divided into classes on the care of linens and clothing, the home tool chest, thrifty and practical cooking, the home first-aid and pharmacy kit. See *BJFB*, February 1935, pp. 4, 11; May 1935, p. 10.
90. *BJFB*, December 1935, p. 6; February 1935, p. 12.
91. Ibid., October 1938, p. 4; January 1935, p. 9; February 1935, p. 11; October 1937, p. 13.
92. Ella Werner Collection, LBI, no. 3079 (22).
93. Affiliates provided a variety of training: crafts were taught in the home economics schools in Breslau, Frankfurt/Main and Hamburg; tailoring was taught in Hamburg and Cologne; infant nursing was taught at Neu Isenburg and in Frankfurt/Main; teacher's aide training was available in Frankfurt/Main; courses for governesses took place in Cologne; technical teachers' training was provided in the Jewish Home Economics School, Frankfurt/Main. The main Home Economics School of the League of Jewish Women at Wolfratshausen expanded all its courses (see *BJFB*, March 1938, p. 3).
94. Ibid., June 1936; December 1936.
95. Cited in "Letters from Berlin," *Leo Baeck Institute Year Book*, vol. 1 (1957), 312.

15

Sybil Milton

The study of women and the Holocaust has barely begun, and the complexities and contours of the subject . . . will keep historians and other analysts occupied for many years.

SYBIL MILTON

In any field of research there are pioneers, scholars who are willing to take the risks of exploring unmapped territory. The historians in this part of Different Voices *all fit that description, none more so than Sybil Milton. Reprinted here, Milton's 1984 essay on "Women and the Holocaust: The Case of German and German-Jewish Women" is a case in point. The overview she provides in this article is detailed and carefully nuanced. It also points the way toward many areas where more research is needed. Other scholars who write about women and the Holocaust refer to this article again and again. It sets a high standard for study about women and the Holocaust.*

The resident historian at the United States Holocaust Memorial Council in Washington, D.C., Milton has published many important articles and books about the Holocaust. These works often discuss neglected areas of study—art during the Holocaust, for example; the plight of Gypsies; the Nazis' use of computers and other technologies; or what happened to women in the Third Reich. Uncovering what has been hidden or obscured by inattention, Milton's scholarship stays on—indeed helps to form—the cutting edge.

Earlier in this book, Gisela Bock focused on the impact of eugenic theory and race hygiene on German women. Marion Kaplan concentrated on the ways in which German-Jewish "housewives and mothers" coped with adversity prior to the outbreak of World War II. Now Milton broadens the scope to include an even larger array of factors and practices that persecuted German and German-Jewish women for "racial, religious, or political reasons." To anticipate just a few of her themes, she discusses the origins of concentration camps for women, analyzes what happened at Ravensbrück in particular, and appraises how women may have had "significantly different survival skills and techniques than did men."

Milton wrote this essay hoping that her study of "the gender-specific experiences of German and German Jewish women" would improve "understanding of the Holocaust in its entirety." Her work stands up well when measured by that demanding criterion.

Women and the Holocaust:
The Case of German and German-Jewish Women

The general subject of women and the Holocaust has received no systematic coverage in the growing literature on Nazi Germany and the Jewish catastrophe. Apart from memoirs, partisan literature, television productions, and token references, women have been largely invisible in the current historiography on the subject.[1] The classic secondary literature on the Holocaust is not sex-specific in language, referring to prisoners, victims, survivors, and perpetrators. This limits any analysis of gender-specific experiences and conditions. Recent literature, based mostly on the experiences of male perpetrators, male victims, and male survivors, has provided incomplete—and sometimes even biased and misleading—accounts of women's experiences under Nazi persecution. Although both men and women were victims of the organized state system of terror, the experiences that separated women from male prisoners have remained unexplored.

At the outset, two general premises must be stated explicitly. First, although Nazi Germany was in theory and practice a male-dominated society, this essay will not deal with the general victimization of women in that society, but only with women persecuted for racial, religious, or political reasons. Second, it is difficult and probably impossible to conceptualize these persecuted women as a unified group, since there are enormous and complex variations in their backgrounds. Thus this essay examines aspects of women's tragic odyssey between 1933 and 1945. It focuses, in particular, on German and German-Jewish women . . . because Nazi policies were developed and tested in their own homeland, Germany, before being exported throughout Nazi-occupied Europe. The subject of women and the Holocaust is moreover a field in its

From Renate Bridenthal, Atina Grossman, and Marion Kaplan, eds., *When Biology Became Destiny: Women in Weimar and Nazi Germany.* New York: Monthly Review Press, 1984. Copyright © 1984 by Renate Bridenthal, Atina Grossman, and Marion Kaplan. Reprinted by permission of the Monthly Review Foundation.

infancy, and it is too early to begin to understand the contours of this subject on a pan-European basis. Thus, we ought to explore the gender-specific experiences of German and German-Jewish women in German concentration camps and in hiding, flight, and resistance outside the camps. Their experiences should contribute to our understanding of the Holocaust in its entirety.

THE VICTIMS OF VIOLENCE: GERMAN AND GERMAN-JEWISH WOMEN

Nazi coercion and violence against female political opponents began immediately after Hitler assumed power. Women socialist, communist, and moderate liberal parliamentary deputies on the national, state, and municipal levels were among the first targets. They were harassed by the Gestapo and the SA, who repeatedly searched their homes and offices; they were also often brutally interrogated and beaten. Many were held hostage for politically active male relatives in flight or in hiding. The women were arrested and confined in correctional and penal institutions; many were subsequently remanded to indefinite detention in concentration camps. A few were murdered.

Some examples will suffice to show the arbitrary brutality and calculated violence that the Nazis used equally against men and women to exact political revenge and enforce social control. Minna Cammens, former Socialist Reichstag deputy from Breslau, was arrested in March 1933 for distributing anti-Nazi leaflets and was murdered by the Gestapo during detention in protective custody.[2] Leni Rosenthal, Socialist ex-deputy in the Prussian State Legislature, was murdered by the Gestapo in October 1936.[3] The Communist Reichstag deputies Franziska Kessel and Helene Fleischer were also killed; Kessel was found hanged, probably murdered, in her jail cell in April 1934, and Fleischer died in the Moringen concentration camp for women in 1940, the result of seven years of brutal maltreatment while incarcerated.[4]

Vigilante SA thugs severely beat the Berlin Socialist municipal councilor Marie Jankowski in March 1933. This incident led to a formal protest to Reichstag President Goering by Jankowski's socialist friend and colleague Clara Bohm-Schuch. As a result, Bohm-Schuch was subjected to repeated house searches by the Gestapo and arrested for fifteen days in April 1934. Her death in May 1936 was attributed to the abuses she suffered.[5] The Communist Helene Overlach became severely ill after five years of mistreatment in the women's prisons of Aichach, Ziegenhain, and Gotteszell.[6] Even moderates, like the Democratic Party deputy Marie-Elisabeth Lüders and the Center Party's Christine Teusch, spent many months in Gestapo jails.[7]

The politics of intimidation and reprisal led to the arrest of wives, sisters, and daughters for the political activities of their absentee male relatives. The use of female hostages continued after the initial Nazi seizure of power in Germany, eventually extending to all of occupied Europe after 1940. When

Gerhart Seger published his account in Czech exile in 1934 about his experiences and flight from the Oranienburg concentration camp, his wife and daughter were arrested in reprisal and released only after international protest.[8] Senta Beimler and her sister-in-law, Maria Dengler, were sentenced to indefinite protective custody in the Moringen women's concentration camp after her husband, Bavarian Communist deputy Hans Beimler, escaped from Dachau in 1933.[9] Similarly, Rudolf Meissner, a Jehovah's Witness, learned after emigrating in 1935 that his sister was arrested as a hostage for his behavior abroad.[10] Although the Socialist Franz Müller was safe across the Czech border, his wife was vulnerable. She was arrested in Chemnitz in June 1935 and held for over eleven months, despite the fact that their four children, aged six to twelve, were left bereft of parental support.[11] Else Steinfurth received a one-year jail term, soon extended for an indeterminate period, after her husband, an official of the Communist welfare organization Red Help (*Rote Hilfe*), was shot in 1934 "while trying to escape." The official rationale for her continued detention was that her husband's death might cause "atrocity propaganda abroad" were she released.[12] At the end of 1935, 75 percent of the women in the Hohenstein jail—thirty-three out of forty-five women—were hostages for their male relatives.[13] Persecuted for either their own politics or as symbolic targets for their dissident male relatives, these women were vilified as traitors and blacklisted from public and professional employment in Nazi Germany.

Comparatively little historical attention has been focused on German prisons during the Nazi years, although they were the initial and primary place of detention for women until 1939. Precise statistics of the inmate population and its component groups are not easily available. It is estimated that 1,500 to 2,000 German women political opponents and hostages were confined in Nazi jails before 1939; this figure represented about 15 to 20 percent of all protective custody prisoners (*Schutzhäftlinge*) detained in prewar Nazi Germany. After 1935, this category for domestic subversives also included female Jehovah's Witnesses and Gypsies. The number of Jewish women detained in jails under protective custody cannot be established for these early years, although they probably represented less than 25 percent of the women held in *Schutzhaft*. The total female inmate population of the Nazi prisons between 1933 and 1939 was between 6,000 and 8,000 women, a majority arrested as so-called asocials (a category covering prostitutes, lesbians, vagrants, shirkers, and any person the police thought unfit for civilian society) and criminals (murderers, thieves, and violators of laws prohibiting sexual intercourse between Aryans and Jews).[14] Jewish women were incarcerated in the jails and concentration camps of Nazi Germany before 1939, *only if* they belonged to one of the other affected categories.

Jewish women were targets as Jews and not as women in the sporadic violence that accompanied the April 1933 boycott, the Nuremberg legislation in September 1935, the expulsion of Polish Jews in late October 1938, and the

"Crystal Night" (*Kristallnacht*) pogrom in early November 1938. Vignettes from daily life before 1938 reveal that Jewish women were more vulnerable to verbal assaults than to physical violence in early encounters with Nazi vigilantes.[15] Normal social inhibitions still operative before 1939 prevented street violence against even Jewish women, despite their position as social pariahs.

After 1933, Jewish women were vulnerable to an unending barrage of insults and propaganda, including pressure exerted on their Christian husbands to divorce them. They were also subject to an "insidious creeping persecution" that legally excluded them from professional employment and inexorably banished them from the social, cultural, intellectual, and economic life of Germany.[16] Occasionally, they were also the targets of physical violence and sporadically of sexual assaults.[17]

Before "Crystal Night," ideological hostility was not immediately transformed into physical violence. Capricious and random acts of courtesy provided a small measure of protection even for Jewish women, who were otherwise ostracized and intimidated. Occasional acts of kindness did not prevent their ultimate deportation or murder, but it did show the limits of Nazi ideology and power during the early years. Neither racist propaganda nor government pressure could modify traditional behavior patterns towards "weaker" members of society (women, the elderly, and children of both sexes), nor could it always sever close social and personal ties between individuals. In the early years, this occasionally subverted or even ameliorated the excesses of Nazi behavior. Thus, for example, during the April 1933 boycott, local bus drivers in Pömbsen, Westphalia, were officially prohibited from carrying Jewish passengers between the railroad depot and the town business district. They nevertheless continued to transport vacationing Jewish school children and old women.[18]

During the expulsion of Polish Jews from Germany in late October 1938, 483 Polish Jews residing in Chemnitz were interned overnight in a local dance hall. The sudden expulsion meant that Jews left clothing, luggage, food, and other possessions behind. The interned Jewish women were treated with greater consideration and allowed to return to their homes under police guard in order to pack necessities for the trip to Poland.[19] Perhaps the police considered this concession to the incarcerated women a necessary expedient in order to pacify the frightened mass of prisoners, thereby ensuring an easier job of guarding the convoy on the journey to Poland. Packing household goods for the family was considered a woman's job, and women, intimidated by police presence, were less likely to smuggle valuables or escape custody. In Baden, women and minor children were left unmolested in their homes and only the men were expelled.

During the pogrom of November 9–10, 1938, 30,000 German-Jewish men were arrested and sent to concentration camps, but no women were arrested or deported to camps. Examples of correct behavior and practical assistance did occur,[20] but were probably exceptional, since vandalism, looting, theft, and rapes occurred during the excesses of "Crystal Night."[21]

Between 1933 and 1939 a large increase occurred in the ratio of Jewish women to men residing in Germany. In 1933, there were 1,093 Jewish women to 1,000 Jewish men; by 1939, this increased to 1,366 Jewish women to 1,000 Jewish men.[22] This relatively large increase in the number of Jewish women can be attributed to several factors: the excess number of German-Jewish women (including war widows) in the post-World War I population; the higher male mortality rate, since women usually outlived men and men were more vulnerable to confinement and maltreatment in Nazi concentration camps; and the substantial rise in international emigration by Jewish young and middle-aged single men after 1933. Thus the census of April 1939 recorded respectively 123,104 female Jews and 90,826 male Jews in Germany.[23] The comparatively large number of Jewish women meant that more German-Jewish women than men were deported and murdered after October 1941.[24]

As already mentioned, German-Jewish women found in concentration camps before October 1938 had been arrested as *individuals*. However, from October 1938 to October 1940, German and foreign Jewish women were treated as a *group* in a series of three experimental mass deportations. The first event was the expulsion of male Polish Jews and their family dependents (parents, wives, and minor children) on October 28 and 29, 1938. The expulsion pattern varied locally. In Bochum, Leipzig, and Dresden, whole families were deported together on "a freezing October day" in sealed trains guarded by the SS and police. "Most of the women and children herded into third class waiting rooms had been dragged out of bed without being allowed to pack."[25] In Frankfurt/Main and Nuremberg, women and children were expelled one day later than their spouses and were refused entry into Poland. Their return train fare was paid by local Jewish communities, who also negotiated the release of their sealed and sequestered homes and property. In Baden, only healthy male Jews above the age of eighteen were expelled, leaving wives and children impoverished, bewildered, and distraught. About 4,000 to 5,000 women and children from these last two groups were issued exit visas to Poland in June 1939, when some families were reunited.[26] About 6,000 of the 17,000 Polish Jews expelled in October 1938 were trapped in a primitive refugee camp near the Polish border at Zbaszyn, unable to return to Germany or to enter the interior of Poland.[27]

Two further trial deportations involving Jewish women occurred after the German occupation of Poland and northern France during 1940. The first occurred in February 1940, when 6,000 Jewish residents from Stettin, Vienna, Prague, and Moravian Ostrava were removed to Lublin in the General Government (the official name for Nazi-occupied Poland).[28] The last experimental deportation, in October 1940, dumped 7,000 German Jews from Baden and the Palatinate into internment camps in unoccupied southern

France. Approximately 3,800 German Jewish women were among the Baden deportees sent to Gurs; they constituted 88 percent of the 5,000 German and Austrian women (predominantly Jewish) interned as enemy aliens in Gurs and other French camps after 1939. These women became vulnerable after 1941 to further deportations to the east.[29] After 1941, the deportations increased in size and frequency and systematically involved German-Jewish women as well as native Jews from every nation of occupied Europe.

CAMPS FOR WOMEN, 1933–1945

After arrest, administrative commitment, or judicial trial, women were sent to prisons, penitentiaries, converted workhouses, and concentration camps, where they were vulnerable to Gestapo whims and the arbitrary abuses of police power. Despite the presence of courts, the Gestapo had broad powers of interference in German jails. A pattern of indeterminate and indefinite sentences first in prisons and later in concentration camps became the norm. Women political prisoners were not sent to the early well-known concentration camps like Oranienburg, Dachau, or Esterwegen. They were instead interned in six centralized protective-custody centers located after the spring of 1933 in penal and correctional institutions. These were: (1) Gotteszell prison near Schwäbisch-Gmünd in Württemberg; (2) Stadelheim prison in Munich; (3) the Barnim Street women's prison in Berlin; (4) Fuhlsbüttel prison near Hamburg; (5) the Brauweiler penitentiary in Westphalia; and (6) Hohenstein castle near Schandau in Saxony.[30] Women were also held in other local jails and improvised detention centers throughout Germany, such as the Aichach penitentiary in Upper Bavaria and the Moringen workhouse, located near Hanover in Lower Saxony.

Gotteszell was opened in March 1933 in a vacant convent. It initially held fifty-four women political inmates, who shared two small overcrowded cells. The first warden at Gotteszell was a lenient and proper administrator, schooled in the Weimar penal system.[31] The inmates were allowed material for knitting and sewing; they could also play chess and read books from the prison library. They even held an illegal May Day demonstration in 1933, improvising a flag from strips of red cloth torn from their clothing. Conditions at Gotteszell were atypical because of the absence of physical intimidation.[32]

The prison at Stadelheim was more typical, characterized by notoriously long detentions in solitary confinement for women politicals and miserably inadequate prison food.[33] Another typical jail was the penitentiary at Aichach in Upper Bavaria, which housed about 1,000 women; the majority were convicted criminals (thieves and prostitutes), who were involuntarily subjected to illegal sterilizations. A few of the prisoners at Aichach were political detainees.[34]

The jail facility at Hohenstein, located among the forests and isolated mountain peaks of Saxon Switzerland, was once a notorious sixteenth-century dungeon converted into a large and attractive youth hostel during the Weimar Republic. The Nazi commandant, his deputy, and the all male staff were exceedingly brutal. The facility housed between 25 and 40 women politicals in the same building with nearly 600 male prisoners.

New prisoners were greeted by taunts and humiliating dirty tricks on arrival. SA men tripped the marching women with night sticks and extended legs, threw water at their skirts and then teased them for "urinating," and insulted them as "slovenly sluts." The women lived in a single overcrowded cell, containing double-tiered bunk beds covered with thin straw mattresses. They sometimes spent both days and nights in this single cell, unable to sit or move about if even half of them were present.

The women were assigned labor inside the castle in the prison laundry, where they washed both guard and prisoner uniforms, linen, and towels, without the aid of washing and drying machines. Hanging huge lines of wet laundry in the cold damp air resulted in severe illness for many of the older and frailer women; inadequate prison clothing made even younger healthier prisoners vulnerable to the combined toll of undernourishment, forced labor, and exposure. The laundry faced the SA offices and women often inadvertently witnessed the interrogation of other inmates. Unlike the male prisoners, employed outside the castle on road construction crews affording them limited possibilities for escape and inside the castle in the prison kitchen, where they could secure better rations, the women's work assignments offered no possibilities for flight or improved conditions. The results of overcrowding, filth, and vermin were compounded by the lack of adequate medical care; the prison physician, a member of the SA, visited the facility only once a week for two hours. The women were also vulnerable to heterosexual rape by guards and criminal inmates.[35]

The regime at Hohenstein was capricious, brutal, corrupt, and incompetent; these conditions were duplicated in many other women's prisons throughout Nazi Germany. Before 1935 women's prisons resembled conditions in the "wild camps" for men (improvised places of detention run by individual local Nazis without rules for the settling of old scores and private vendettas; these temporary detention pens were dissolved after the first year of Nazi rule).[36]

The repressive apparatus of the state extended to the family life and childcare arrangements of arrested dissident women and Jehovah's Witnesses. As spouses were often already in flight, hiding, or emigration, children were involuntarily abandoned when the mother was arrested. Occasionally, the children could be sent to safety abroad or given to relatives and friends, who assumed temporary guardianship over them. Often, however, the children became wards of the Nazi state and were placed in Nazi foster homes, orphanages, and schools. This loss further eroded the morale of interned women, even more than the imprisonment itself.

A few women were released when their jail terms expired, none were paroled early, and many were subsequently detained indefinitely in concentration camps. The first centralized women's concentration camp was created during the winter of 1933; it was followed by a series of similar camps that co-existed alongside the Nazi prison system until 1945. The first camp was located in the former workhouse at Moringen, between Göttingen and Hanover. It remained in operation from October 1933 to March 1938. The second women's camp was Lichtenburg in Saxony, which opened in March 1938 and closed in May 1939. On May 15, 1939, a permanent installation for women was founded at Ravensbrück, located near the town of Fürstenberg in Mecklenburg.[37]

Very little is known about Moringen. Initially, from March to June 1933, the workhouse was used for the administrative incarceration of 300–400 male political enemies.[38] However, by the end of November 1933, Moringen held only a handful of women prisoners; the few Jewish women among them were nevertheless segregated in separate residential quarters. After the Prussian Ministry of Interior designated Moringen a women's concentration camp (*Frauenkonzentrationslager*; FKL) for women arrested in protective custody in all of Germany (order of October 28, 1933), the inmate population stayed between 26 and 70, except during the spring and autumn of 1935 when more women were paroled than detained. The categories of female prisoners did change: in 1933 most were political opponents (communists, socialists, and hostages) or Jehovah's Witnesses; after 1935, the inmate population included an increasing number of Aryan and Jewish women arrested for violations of the racial laws.[39]

New inmates at Moringen could not receive or send mail; after the first month censored mail was permitted once every two weeks. The combination of isolation from their families and the outside world plus constantly over-crowded surroundings resulted in many nervous breakdowns. Women worked inside the camp washing, sorting, and refashioning old clothing collected by the Winter Welfare (*Winterhilfe*); outside labor assignments for women involved physical labor in limestone quarries in all types of weather.

At first, Moringen did not operate according to the concentration camp model established at Dachau: inmates wore neither concentration camp uniforms nor triangular insignia denoting their arrest category. The director of Moringen, Hugo Krack, was a civil servant in the provincial penal and rehabilitation system. The SA and SS were not used as guards or administrators during the first years. The staff of women guards worked under male supervision and was recruited from the Nazi Women's Group (NS Frauenschaft). Two Nazi women physicians were assigned medical duty at Moringen. Nothing is known about the previous employment or training of women guards at Moringen or about personnel changes between 1933 and 1938. After several years, Krack was replaced as director by an SS-man, Cordes.[40] Moringen was dissolved as a women's camp in March 1938; it continued as a juvenile penal institution until the end of the war. The last twenty-five women imprisoned there on March 21, 1938, were transferred to the new women's concentration camp at Lichtenburg.

The second women's concentration camp, Lichtenburg, was located in Saxony near Prettin on the Elbe River. It was a dilapidated sixteenth-century fortress, still in use as a penitentiary in 1928. After June 1933, it became a men's concentration camp until the summer of 1937, when both the inmates and the SS guard units were transferred to Buchenwald. After a brief hiatus when the camp was closed in 1937–1938, it reopened as a women's camp from March 1938 to May 1939. It is not clear whether it was intended as an interim accommodation for housing the growing number of female prisoners arrested in 1937 and 1938, or whether it was to be a permanent FKL. The female inmate population consisted of 1,415 prisoners. This figure included a large number of politicals in protective custody and about 260 Jehovah's Witnesses; there were also large numbers of professional criminals, asocials, and violators of the race-defilement laws. Many prisoner categories included German-Jewish women. Lichtenburg was clearly larger and harsher than Moringen. Punishment for inmate infractions of the camp rules consisted of denial of food, being forced to stand at military attention for hours, and solitary confinement in unlighted cells. Unlike Moringen, the camp commandant and guards were members of the SS.[41]

The first two directors of Lichtenburg were trained at Dachau, the prototype of all later concentration camps.[42] The second, SS Captain Max Koegel, had served in Dachau from 1934 to 1937, assumed command in Lichtenburg on September 1, 1938, and was promoted to the rank of SS Lieutenant-Colonel as the first head of Ravensbrück from May 1939 to August 1942.[43] Although the women's camps were smaller in size and fewer in number than the men's camps before 1939, it is clear that many male and female SS made their professional careers within the camp system and—like the prisoners— were transferred between camps.

Koegel viewed his Lichtenburg inmates as "hysterical females" requiring strict discipline. In a letter of March 14, 1939, Koegel wrote to the Inspector of the Concentration Camps requesting the construction of thirty to forty detention cells at the new Ravensbrück facility. The letter shows his concept of order and authority.

> We will soon move into the new women's camp at Ravensbrück, where I have established the fact that detention cells have neither been built nor planned. Women have been placed in solitary confinement by Gestapo orders in the Lichtenburg camp. It is impossible to maintain order if the defiance and stubbornness of these hysterical females cannot be broken by strict confinement, since no more severe punishment can be used in a women's camp. Denial of food does not suffice for discipline and order in a women's camp.[44]

The solitary confinement cells were built, Koegel was promoted, and 860 German and 7 Austrian female prisoners were transferred to the new camp at

Ravensbrück on May 18, 1939.[45] Koegel's letter is important for two reasons: it reveals first, that the worst punishment allowed for German female inmates was solitary confinement and *not* corporal punishment; and second, that the Nazis recognized the importance of camp friendships and bonding in women's resistance and survival. These bonds could be physical, occupational, intellectual, religious, or political, and were often effective in combating the depersonalization and disorientation caused by the camp regimen.[46] Corporal punishment for women inmates was introduced at Ravensbrück only in January 1940 after an inspection by Himmler, although it had existed in the men's concentration camps almost from the first.[47]

Ravensbrück, ostensibly a model camp, was constructed on reclaimed swamp land by male inmates from Sachsenhausen during the winter of 1938–1939. Designed to hold 15,000 prisoners, it eventually housed over 42,000 women from 23 nations. Over 130,000 women passed through Ravensbrück between 1939 and 1945. During the first two years, German and Austrian women inmates dominated the camp population; after 1941, they were out-numbered by new arrivals and categories of prisoners from every country of Nazi-occupied Europe. The average camp population by nationality during the war consisted of: 25 percent Polish women; 20 percent German; 19 percent Russian and Ukrainian; 15 percent Jews from all over Europe; and 21 percent representing several other groups (i.e., 7.3 percent French, 5.4 percent Gypsies, 2.9 percent Belgian, 1.9 percent Czech, 1.2 percent Yugoslavian, and 2.2 percent in other categories).[48] These groups included two barracks of prominent internees like Gemma LaGuardia Gluck, Geneviève de Gaulle, and Rosa Thälmann.[49]

Housing was initially allotted by prisoner category (identified by the color-coded triangles sewn on the inmates' uniforms) rather than by nationality, although this broke down during the massive overcrowding of 1944. Only Gypsy and Jewish women were segregated from the first. The inmate hierarchy placed the earliest arrestees—the politicals, professional criminals, and Jehovah's Witnesses—in a marginally better position for assignments to clerical jobs inside camp offices; Jews, Gypsies, and Soviet women prisoners of war were generally more exploited by the SS guards and rival inmate groups.[50] Ravensbrück was "like a circus, but one without clowns; a circus where crying was heard and no laughter."[51]

Ravensbrück had a similar administrative structure to the men's camps.[52] Until 1942, the inmate mortality among Ravensbrück women was the lowest among all concentration camp prisoners (ca. 84 deaths among 4,000 prisoners in 1941). Even in August 1943, the women's camp at Ravensbrück had a lower mortality than the male camp at Ravensbrück: .27 percent per month for women and .84 percent per month for men.[53] The low mortality rate among women until 1941 was attributed to the relatively uncrowded housing and somewhat better conditions during the early years at Ravensbrück. Later, women showed "greater ingenuity in many things touching directly on the simple preservation of life,"[54] such as nursing sick inmates, refashioning clothing from discarded items, and stretching limited food supplies. Traditional homemaking skills taught to women effectively lowered their vulnerability to death and disease, despite the obviously inadequate lavatory and sanitary facilities.[55]

Ravensbrück later included a separate men's camp, a children's camp at Uckermark, and an extermination installation for women that operated from January to April 1945, when the camp was liberated by the Soviet Army. Before early 1945, women prisoners were retransported to Auschwitz, Lublin-Maidanek, and Bernberg, where they were murdered. Women assigned to labor crews outside the camp worked in nearby factories sewing SS uniforms; manufacturing shoes, furs, airplane parts; and also working an old salt mine. Inside the camp, the labor details were assigned to the SS or to the prisoner laundries and kitchens, to the manufacturing of clothing, and to skilled labor, such as plumbing, carpentry, and masonry.

Ravensbrück was the site of notorious medical experiments on Polish women in 1942 and 1943. The victims of sterilization experiments were called "rabbits" by their SS medical experimenters. Some Ravensbrück inmates, generally referred to as *Schmuckstücke* (literally translated as pieces of jewelry), were the female counterparts to the male inmate *Muselmänner* (the emaciated walking corpses of Auschwitz and other camps). The Nazis used the term ironically and pejoratively, transmuting objective language into terms of contempt to describe the victims that their own policies and deeds had created. It seems probable that gender-specific usage was not peculiar to Ravensbrück, although since it was the largest and earliest major women's concentration camp, the usage probably began there.[56]

Although there has been no systematic study of the uniformed SS women guards (*Aufseherinnen*) assigned to the concentration camp system, some data are available. More than 3,000 women served as uniformed and supervisory guards (*Oberaufseherinnen*) in the network of main and auxiliary camps between 1939 and 1945. A few were volunteers; most were labor conscripts assigned to camp duty. They worked in many camps: 550 at Ravensbrück, 490 at Gross-Rosen, 150 at Neuengamme, 140 at Oranienburg, and 60 at Auschwitz.[57] The majority of these women supervised inmates in the subsidiary camps and labor details allotted to various industrial enterprises. A few worked as nurses and physicians in camp medical facilities. Their activities often included pseudomedical experiments.[58]

The camp at Ravensbrück was staffed by 500–550 uniformed SS women; 300 were assigned to the main camp and 200–250 supervised outside labor details. Just as Dachau served as a training center for men in the Death Head's units serving in the camps, Ravensbrück was a school for training women guards needed in the vastly expanded network of camps and labor centers where women were interned after 1940. Irma Griese and Maria Mandel, both infamous at Auschwitz, were trained in 1941 and 1942 at Ravensbrück.[59]

Several women were notorious for their cruelty; they seemed to engage in a bizarre rivalry emulating the excesses and brutalities of their male superiors.[60] Other women guards tried to mitigate the worst extremes. For example, Johanna Langefeld, trained in the social welfare and penal institutions of the 1920s, served initially as a guard at Moringen and Lichtenburg during the 1930s. She was promoted to the post of chief warden at Ravensbrück in May 1939, a position she retained until April 1942. Her ambivalence toward her job was noticed by both inmates and superiors. It brought her into conflict with Camp Commandant Koegel, resulting in her forced reassignment to Auschwitz from April to October 1942.[61] Commandant Höss considered her "incapable of commanding and organizing the women's camp."[62] She was transferred back to Ravensbrück in October 1942. Langefeld was subsequently dismissed, arrested for dereliction of duty, and tried by an SS tribunal in the spring of 1943.[63] She was clearly an exception among the SS women assigned to Ravensbrück. Margarete Buber-Neumann, for example, described Langefeld in relatively complimentary terms, although she portrayed the other women guards as brutal, stocky, obese women in knee-high leather boots, with frizzy, overpermanented hair and too much makeup.[64]

Ironically, the SS women suffered sex discrimination on the job. Höss held the women guards in very low esteem:

> I must emphasize that the women I was sent from Ravensbrück were not the best. These supervisors had been thoroughly spoiled at Ravensbrück. Everything had been done to persuade them to remain in the women's concentration camp. . . . They were given the best accommodations, and were paid salaries they could never have earned elsewhere. . . . These supervisors were now posted to Auschwitz; none came voluntarily . . . From the very beginning most of them wanted to run away and return to the quiet comfort and easy life at Ravensbrück.[65]

Höss's contempt toward the women SS guards trained in crash courses at Ravensbrück and "let loose on the prisoners" appears to reflect the actual conditions that prevailed at Ravensbrück and Auschwitz.[66]

The camps created for Austrian and German women before 1939 became the models for the vastly expanded network of concentration and labor camps created after 1940 throughout occupied Europe. The size and number of camps grew with the increasing number of incarcerated women, now including new groups such as resistance fighters from western Europe, Poles caught in the "General Pacification" roundups, and Soviet women prisoners of war.[67]

After 1941, women were no longer restricted to Ravensbrück, but were found in fenced-off enclosures separated from men's camps in places like Gross-Rosen and Auschwitz-Birkenau. With increasing labor shortages as the war expanded, women were also assigned to labor details in satellite camps in larger numbers. A survey of the women interned at Mauthausen shows that apart from a small number of prostitutes, women were registered as transients until the autumn of 1944, when they were recorded in substantial numbers in Mauthausen and its satellites. In April 1942, four Yugoslav women were shot at Mauthausen and in June 1942, 10 prostitutes were selected from Ravensbrück for a minimum of six months' service in the Mauthausen and Gusen camp bordellos. Although promised release after six months, most of the women were returned to Ravensbrück. In October 1942, 130 Czech women were executed in Mauthausen and 189 Soviet women prisoners of war were shipped to Auschwitz via Mauthausen. SS statistics show that a permanent population of women internees existed from September 1944 until liberation in May 1945. In April 1945, approximately 3,077 women were found in the main camp and an additional 1,514 were incarcerated in the auxiliary camps.[68] In the last eight months of the war, women from Ravensbrück, Auschwitz, and Flossenbürg were evacuated to Mauthausen. They were employed as clerks; in agricultural labor, gardening, sewing, and laundry; in the armaments industry; and also as servants. Their heads were shaven on arrival and they faced the same brutal camp regime that the male prisoners did.[69]

By late 1944, as the fronts contracted from both east and west, large numbers of women were also recorded in other previously all-male camps.[70] During these closing chaotic months of the war, when forced marches and evacuations led to the dumping of exhausted prisoners of both sexes into the older German camps and their satellites, the rigid sex segregation of the earlier camps broke down completely. There is no complete statistical tally on the total number of women prisoners, nor are there any lists that establish all the places where they were detained.

Women were also sent to special police camps (*Polizeihaftlager*) and work camps (*Arbeitserziehungslager*). The women's work "training" camps had mandatory minimum sentences of six weeks at hard labor. The camp at Rudersberg in Württemberg created in 1942 was typical. Although the total number of women interned there between 1942 and 1945 is not known, it appears that the camp initially held 200 women and girls transported from the Soviet Union, Poland, and France. About 80 women were assigned as woodcutters in the nearby Welzheim forest; 40 were rented to the Bauknecht Corporation in Welzheim; and others were assigned to local peasants as farm laborers. Political detainees were not permitted on outside work crews, and were assigned jobs in the camp laundry, kitchen, and tailor shops. Severe overcrowding, heavy labor, and inadequate food rations were common. The daily ration in 1944 consisted of 400 grams of bread, ersatz coffee in the morning, watery turnip mixed with acorn soup at noon, and small quantities of cottage cheese, margarine, and jam at night. Selections for transports to Ravensbrück and Auschwitz occurred once a week. After the prisons in Stuttgart were destroyed in Allied bombing raids in late 1944, many of the prisoners from there were transferred to Rudersburg.[71] Other women's labor camps existed at Radeberg in Saxony, Cologne-Deutz, and Hägerwelle in Pomerania.[72]

From August 1944 until the end of the war, a number of new satellite camps were created specifically for women evacuees from other already liberated eastern and western camps. Very little is known about these last transitory detention centers except for their names.[73]

SURVIVAL PATTERNS INSIDE THE CAMPS AFTER 1939

The fate of the deported women depended less on nationality and the reason for arrest than on a variety of other factors: date of arrest, place of incarceration, and conditions of deportation. Survival also depended on luck, special skills, physical strength, and membership in a supportive group.[74] Women had significantly different survival skills and techniques than did men. Although there were neither killing centers nor ghettos in western Europe, German-Jewish women and those of other nationalities frequently used similar strategies for coping with unprecedented terror. Women's specific forms of survival included doing housework as a kind of practical therapy and of gaining control over one's space, bonding and networks, religious or political convictions, the use of inconspicuousness, and possibly even sex.

Women appear to have been more resilient than men, both physically and psychologically, to malnutrition and starvation. Clinical research by Jewish physicians in the Warsaw Ghetto confirmed the impressionistic accounts of contemporaries and brought proof to the assertion that women were less vulnerable to the effects of short-term starvation and famine.[75] Women in Gurs, Theresienstadt, and Bergen-Belsen reported that men "were selfish and undisciplined egoists, unable to control their hungry stomachs, and revealed a painful lack of courage."[76] Women also shared and pooled their limited resources better than did men. In Berlin, the Gestapo allowed small groups of Jewish women to provide food for the deportees at the railroad station. The women, experienced in trading for scarce and rationed food, performed this job until the end of 1942.[77] In the camps, women swapped recipes and ways of extending limited quantities of food. Men could be overheard discussing their favorite banquets and restaurants.[78] Since women had been primarily responsible for their families as housewives and cooks, there was some direct correlation between their own survival and previously acquired skills.

After the initial trauma of deportation in freight trains and cattle cars, women were separated from their husbands and children when they entered the camps. Entire groups were automatically sent to the gas chambers at Auschwitz on arrival: the old, the young, and the weak. Usually, mothers were not separated from their small children and, thus, perished immediately with them. Fathers were not linked to children in this way. Instead of the protection normally extended to these weaker individuals, women were more vulnerable and their chances of survival decreased if they were pregnant or accompanied by small children.[79]

Those who survived the deportations and selections faced great depriva-
tions. Stripped naked, shorn of hair, and with all possessions confiscated, the
women were shocked and numbed. At Auschwitz and Ravensbrück this scene
was repeatedly enacted. France Audoul, deported from France to Ravensbrück in 1943, described being "skinned and shorn":

> One day the order came to go to the showers and there all illusions soon ended.
> Baggage, clothes, jewelry, letters, souvenirs, and even our hair disappeared under
> the hands of expert prisoners, hardened by this kind of work. Cries and tears only
> brought beatings. A hot shower was soothing, but only for a brief moment, for
> the distribution of shoes and bathrobes was made without any thought of size and
> height, and this horrible leveling, this ugliness was completed at the political
> office by the loss of all identity. Names were replaced by triangles with numbers
> on them. The concentration camp system closed over the terrified women.[80]

Religious Jewish women, who, once married, kept their hair covered in public
under either a wig or scarf, felt both a physical and a spiritual nakedness, thus
unprotected and exposed to the whims of their Nazi tormentors.[81] The initial
trauma of loss and separation was compounded by isolation in quarantine
followed by claustrophobically cramped living conditions in noisy overcrowded barracks, where sometimes as many as seven women shared one bunk
or straw mattress.[82] The brutal separation of husbands from wives and parents
from children only increased the sense of shock and despair. Even in the milder
conditions of the Theresienstadt ghetto and transit camp, lack of space led to
mass dormitory housing in separate men's, women's, and children's barracks.
Many of the German-Jewish women were of middle-class origin; others came
from small, close-knit rural communities; all were stunned by the noise of the
overcrowded ghettos and camps.[83]

Epidemics also spread more quickly in the confined quarters, exacerbated by
constant hunger and thirst. Inadequate sanitary facilities, latrines, and even
water for drinking and washing reached unusual extremes in the women's
camp at Auschwitz-Birkenau. In January 1943, one faucet served 12,000
women for drinking and washing. Charlotte Delbo mentioned being unable to
wash for sixty-seven days, unless it snowed or rained.[84] Even Camp Commandant Höss remarked that "general living conditions in the women's camp were
incomparably worse [than in the men's camp]. They were far more tightly
packed-in and the sanitary and hygienic conditions were notably inferior."[85]

Vignettes and diaries by women interned in Gurs, Ravensbrück,
Auschwitz-Birkenau, and Bergen-Belsen revealed that women's traditionally
domestic roles as wives, daughters, and mothers aided them under conditions
of extreme duress. In Gurs, during the winter of 1940–1941, despite the
increased overcrowding caused by the dumping of the Baden Jews, women
fought against the primitive conditions. "They fought the dirt and lassitude
with cleaning, scrubbing, and orderliness."[86] This cleaning apparently low-

ered the spread of disease and consequently decreased mortality in the women's barracks. Comparative mortality statistics by gender in Ravensbrück for August 1943 reveal a similarly lower death rate in the women's barracks. Survivors of other camps in western and eastern Europe reported similar experiences. In Bergen-Belsen, it was reported that "women revealed signs of a more practical and community-minded attitude, chiefly for the sake of the children. They steel themselves to find ways of remedying the situation and show real courage, even prepared, if necessary, to make sacrifices."[87] Cleaning not only prevented the spread of disease; it also functioned as did other familiar "housework" routines as a form of therapy enabling women to gain control over their own space.

Small groups of women in the same barracks or work crews formed "little families" and bonded together for mutual help.[88] Hanna Schramm reported that in Gurs "at first, the women were an undifferentiated mass; one did not recognize individual faces and personalities. Gradually, tentative friendships began."[89] These small families, usually not biologically related, increased protection for individual internees and created networks to "organize" food, clothing, and beds, and to help cope with the privations and primitive camp conditions. At the French jail at Rieucros, 360 refugee women pooled their pennies to buy a second-hand kettle, since the prison food was inedible and the water unsanitary to drink.[90]

Mutual support also came from membership in a religious, political, national, or family unit. Clandestine channels of communication existed in every concentration camp. Lone individuals, men as well as women, had a smaller chance for survival. Kitty Hart attributed her survival to the fact that her mother, deported along with her, was always in close contact.[91] Homogeneous religious groups like Jehovah's Witnesses retained a cohesiveness and comradeship that increased the emotional and physical will to survive. Depending on the situation, this could be either life-saving or very dangerous. Contemptuously nicknamed "Bifos, Bible-Bees, and Bible-Worms" by their SS tormentors, the Witnesses earned a reluctant and secret respect, which occasionally resulted in lighter work assignments as domestic servants in SS homes. But their religious scrupulousness sometimes proved dangerous; a small group of fundamentalists in Ravensbrück refused to eat blood sausage because of biblical injunctions and thus increased their risk of malnutrition and starvation as well as corporal punishment. [This refusal to eat prohibited foods also applied to some Orthodox Jews.] The Witnesses' pacifism led to their refusal to tend rabbits, whose fur was used in military clothing, resulting in the execution of several women for treason.[92]

Similar group cohesion existed among Orthodox Jewish women from Hungary and Subcarpathian Ruthenia. When Sabbath candles were unavailable they blessed electric light bulbs; their colleagues assigned to the Canada barracks at Auschwitz (the barracks where food, clothing, jewelry, and other goods taken from prisoners were stored) filched supplies for them to make

Sabbath candles improvised from hollowed-out potato peels filled with margarine and rag wicks. During Channukah, *dreidels* (tops) were clandestinely carved from small pieces of wood.[93] Christmas was celebrated among the arrested French and Spanish women members of the resistance at the French camp of Les Tourelles "crouched on our straw mattresses, heads hidden under the covers, each sang whatever song she knew . . . through the night."[94] If caught violating camp prohibitions against religious observance, the women were punished by whippings or detention in dark, cagelike solitary confinement cells, and often "selected" for the gas chambers. Similar episodes of religious observant behavior also occurred in men's camps and barracks. Bonding because of religious or political convictions may not have been specific to women, but the degree of group cohesion and noncompetitive support available to women seems markedly greater than among men.

Survival frequently depended on a prisoner's ability to remain inconspicuous; reading a Bible or prayer book during roll call was a conscious risk. Religious Jewish women interned in Gurs during 1940 and 1941 sometimes refused to take advantage of Saturday releases from the internment camps, because of the traditional prohibitions against travel on the Sabbath. By staying, they were sometimes trapped and later deported to Auschwitz, where they perished.[95] Religious group cohesiveness among Orthodox Jews and fundamentalist Christians had both positive and negative implications for survival. During 1944 and 1945 it was tolerated, even in Auschwitz, whereas earlier in the war it often marked a prisoner for more rapid death.

Ability to withstand the extremes of winter made survival more likely. Almost all the memoirs refer to the miserable climate and swampy or clay soils that turned into seas of mud in Gurs, Birkenau, and Ravensbrück.[96] In freezing winter rains, this mud became as slippery as ice. Fetching food in Gurs during the winter was an acrobatic balancing act; prisoners sank up to their thighs in mud with arms filled with cauldrons of hot soup or ersatz coffee. Those women who were deported from the warmer and milder Mediterranean climates of Greece and Italy could not adjust to the harsh winters of eastern Poland; this increased their vulnerability to disease and death. Inadequate thin prisoner clothing and clogs were unsuitable for standing in rain, ice, and snow during roll calls, many of which lasted up to ten hours. Some of the women repaired their ragged garments and groomed themselves carefully despite the lack of water for washing; this imitation of normal behavior was a conscious and rational attempt at survival. A few prisoners with special skills, like the Communist plumber Charlotte Müller in Ravensbrück, enjoyed somewhat better living conditions. Favored labor brigades were plumbers, masons, and electricians; they received better barracks and rations, which increased their odds of survival.

A popular postwar myth, sometimes exploited and sensationalized, held that Jewish women were forced to serve as prostitutes in the SS bordellos and were frequently raped. Although such cases did undoubtedly occur, it was not the norm and reflects a macabre postwar misuse of the Holocaust for popular titillation. Kitty Hart calls these sexual fantasies of postwar literature and television "ridiculous misconceptions."[97] Sexuality, either heterosexual or lesbian, was most likely practiced by prisoners who were camp functionaries and therefore better fed.[98]

Still, clandestine heterosexual liaisons did occur, even in Auschwitz, where men were assigned to labor details in women's camps. Brief stolen moments were arranged in potato storage sheds, clothing depots, warehouses, laundry vans, the bakery, the canteen, and even in chicken coops. Despite the risks if caught, the border zone between the men's and women's subcamps in Ravensbrück and Auschwitz became a place for reassuring visual contact, signals, and covert messages. In Gurs, a limited number of passes were allotted to each barracks so that women could visit their interned husbands in the men's enclosure. Although privacy was hard to find, in Theresienstadt, for example, lovers met hurriedly in the barracks' coal bunker at night. Weddings also took place in Theresienstadt and other ghettos and transit camps where milder conditions prevailed; and if both spouses survived, these symbolic marriages were often legalized in postwar civil ceremonies.[99] There were also deep friendships between women that may have become lesbian relationships.[100] These have been difficult to document given the inhibitions of survivors and historians. Occasionally, flirtation and sex were used to buy food or a better work situation; even sex could have served as a strategy for survival.[101] Traditional anxieties and guilt about sex were not applicable in the world of total subservience reinforced by terror in the camps.

Every camp had an active resistance movement linked to the outside world. Women were observed to be more resourceful and skillful than men at passing messages between jail cells and barracks, on work details, and during roll calls. They were also more skilled at trading cigarettes and food to obtain essentials for their friends and prison families.[102] Inmate physicians in Ravensbrück saved many prisoners from selections; for example, the Yugoslav doctor Najda Persic wrote false diagnoses and the Polish doctor Maria Grabska tried to remove or change the tattoos on Austrian women slated for death.[103]

There were even open revolts in which women participated at Sobibor, Treblinka, Auschwitz, and possibly even Bergen-Belsen.[104] It is believed that French-Jewish women inmates revolted during October 1942 at the satellite camp of Budy near Auschwitz and were consequently massacred by those arrested as asocials and prostitutes together with SS officers. The only surviving evidence is from the memoirs of Pery Broad, an SS man in the Political Department at Auschwitz.[105] This event, if accurately reported in documents by the perpetrators, is unique, since there is no other instance of one category of prisoners massacring fellow prisoners on the same work detail.

Flight, escape, subversion of the rules, noncompliance, and sabotage on work details were common forms of resistance in every camp and ghetto of occupied Europe. Every camp had an active clandestine cultural life with concerts, theater performances, puppet shows, reading circles, music, and art.[106] Schools for children were also secretly organized. The care, supervision, and teaching of children were tasks that were frequently allotted to the interned women. Child care and education in the home were traditionally women's work and, after deportation, those children who survived were usually housed with the women. Hanna Lévy-Hass recorded in her Bergen-Belsen diary that she tried to teach 110 children of various ages ranging from three to fifteen.[107]

WOMEN OUTSIDE THE CAMPS: RESISTANCE, HIDING, AND FLIGHT

Very little systematic research has been done about women's resources for survival in resistance, hiding, and flight (including emigration). It is clear that there were two basic types of resistance: (1) organized networks linked by a common ideology; and (2) autonomous personal acts of noncompliance. It is important to remember that all classes of German women participated in the resistance movement between 1933 and 1945. Resistance meant opposing Hitler in the name of socialism, communism, monarchism, Christianity, or democracy, but not necessarily helping persecuted Jews in the name of humanitarianism. Women were statistically overrepresented in many resistance groups because of the severe demographic imbalance of the sexes due to the huge demands of the war for males in the army and war industries. Furthermore, many politically vulnerable men were already in flight, hiding, or incarcerated in jails and camps, leaving women as the mainstay of many anti-Nazi political groups. Women previously employed in subordinate and ornamental positions in many male-dominated political organizations suddenly assumed responsibility for directing and devising clandestine political strategies. They also continued their traditional domestic chores. German women were actively involved in the White Rose movement in Hamburg and Munich, the Lechleiter group in Mannheim, the Schulze-Boysen-Harnack group, and the Red Orchestra.[108]

Although there were genuine limitations on what could be done to thwart the Nazi aim of mass murder, many ordinary women and men showed decency and compassion in helping Jewish and other victims of Nazi terror. One form of resistance involved the clandestine publication and distribution of anti-Nazi literature. These pamphlets and fliers, written and printed secretly in Germany and abroad, often contained eyewitness accounts of tortures and conditions in the men's and women's concentration camps. This literature was distributed widely in Germany and before 1939 was often smuggled across the borders. There are no clear statistics of the number of German Jews or the number of German-Jewish women among the organized anti-Nazi groups (Communists, Zionists, Socialists, or dissident Christians). A substantial number of the dissidents arrested for producing or distributing such clandestine political literature were German-Jewish women and *Mischlinge* (persons of mixed blood defined as non-Aryans under the Nuremberg Laws).[109] Public support for Nazi policies increased hostility and the risk of exposure, but anti-Nazi resistance groups proliferated and slowly developed effective strategies to combat the network of Nazi informers, collaborators, and police spies. These political dissidents were never able to dent the general passivity and indifference to the Nazi regime, nor could they develop effective strategies that combated mass deportations of Jews and rapid population transfers across Nazi-occupied Europe.

The fragmentary information currently available reveals that German-Jewish women used two distinctive types of resistance behavior: (1) open protest, exemplified by the female members of the Herbert Baum group; and (2) escape by evasion and improvisation, exemplified by the adolescent women in the Chug Chaluzzi (an underground Zionist Pioneer group).[110] The absence of data does not allow us to distinguish gender-specific behavior. It is possible that conditions in resistance and hiding were not different for men and women. Despite the obvious risks of capture and their isolated situation as Jewish compulsory laborers in the Berlin Siemens factories, the young women who worked with the Herbert Baum group openly distributed Zionist and Communist leaflets after 1939. They were captured because of their participation in burning down an anti-Soviet exhibition in Berlin in May 1942. After torture, interrogation, and trial, five women were executed in August 1942. Two surviving women, awaiting their execution in Berlin prisons, communicated secretly and sought to raise their respective morale: "In spite of everything, I always pull myself together and I am not giving in."[111] The male and female adolescents recruited by the Chug Chaluzzi continued training for an eventual emigration and survived despite their lack of identity papers and ration coupons. They improvised temporary shelters and slept on the subways and night buses of the Berlin transit system; they also received food and warm clothing from their Aryan protectors, whom they nicknamed *Aufbewarier* (a combination of the two German words *aufbewahren* and *Arier*, meaning an Aryan who protected them).[112] Despite their lack of contingency plans, many survived the war with such help.

Often other autonomous individuals and groups provided temporary asylum, forged papers, and rations for Jews in hiding. Dr. Gertrud Luckner, head of the Catholic Charities (*Deutscher Caritas Verband*) extended financial help to Jews and non-Aryan Christians (converts and offspring of mixed marriages) in Germany; she was arrested and subsequently deported to Ravensbrück. Often members of the Confessing Church and their families and Jews in privileged mixed marriages helped others to safety after 1943. Their rescue work has been relatively well documented in memoirs and oral histories, although the story of the Jews who survived in hiding has received less systematic attention. There have been no histories of German-Jewish women surviving underground, and the limited and incomplete nature of the available sources does not yet allow analysis by gender.[113]

There were also unique and spectacular gestures of mass popular resistance inside Germany. In one instance, 200 to 300 Christian wives living in privileged mixed marriages demonstrated for a week outside several Berlin assembly centers after their Jewish husbands had been rounded up without warning at their workplaces during the so-called Factory Operation of late February 1943. The men had not been permitted to return home to pack their belongings and could not notify their wives and families. Despite police efforts to disperse the growing crowds of women, rumors spread and more women demonstrated each day in front of the assembly centers and police stations. They demanded the release of their husbands and attempted to ameliorate their situation by passing them packages with food and clothing. In a rare conciliatory gesture, possibly fearing the reactions of Christian relatives of the internees, the Gestapo released those men married to German non-Jews.[114] Jewish women with Christian husbands were also trapped in this raid:

> The loading of people onto SS trucks was carried out with such speed that most of the women, who were wont to sit at work in colored overalls, were taken as they were, without overcoats and without their breakfasts, which remained at their factory wardrobes.[115]

Jewish women in privileged mixed marriages were probably also released, although there is no evidence indicating that their Christian husbands joined in the demonstrations of late February 1943. Smaller similar protests occurred at a Jewish old-age home on March 6, 1943, resulting in a temporary cessation of the deportation of the residents.[116] These were the only demonstrations against deportations of Jews that ever took place in Germany.

Another demonstration, similar to a food riot, occurred when 300 women and children evacuated from heavily bombed mining towns in the Ruhr and Rhineland demonstrated in November 1943 in the town of Witten. The women protested about their new housing and the lack of ration cards for food, and expressed fears that their families would be split apart by the relocation. These German women, predominantly Catholic, also feared anti-Christian Nazi propaganda in the schools their children would attend. In Witten, the police called to disperse the demonstration refused to intervene, since they felt the women's protest was justified because the bureaucracy had withheld ration cards for the relocated women and children. Similar demonstrations occurred in Hamm, Lünen, and Bochum.[117] It is probable that these public demonstrations expressing discontent with the war were not unique, but there has been little systematic investigation of the forms of and participants in public protests in Nazi Germany.[118] Empathy, war weariness, and police hesitancy to arrest German women must be explored as possible explanations for the success of these two larger female demonstrations in February and November 1943.

More common than public protest and group resistance were private, often unrewarded, gestures by many individuals, whose decency and compassion helped Jews evade the increasing restrictions placed on their daily lives after November 1938. Restricted hours for food shopping (in Berlin from 4:00 to 5:00 P.M.; in Leipzig at three designated stores from noon to 12:30 P.M.) made buying essentials exceedingly difficult, especially when most Jews had to perform compulsory conscript labor for ten hours every day. After January 1940, Jews did not receive ration cards for textiles, shoes, and leather goods; and in September 1940, the range of prohibited items increased. Jews could not purchase fish, coffee, alcoholic beverages, sweets, tobacco, meat, eggs, fresh milk, ice cream, or cut flowers. Many of the essentials of daily life were confiscated: radios were seized on September 29, 1939 (the day of Yom Kippur); telephones, except for physicians', on September 30, 1940; and, in June 1942, German Jews had to surrender all privately held electrical appliances, phonograph equipment, records, typewriters, bicycles, and optical goods (cameras and microscopes). Many neighbors, friends, acquaintances, employers, and even strangers occasionally provided necessities for German-Jewish survival. Inge Deutschkron, a young Jewish journalist, reported that stores where she once regularly shopped held food until she could pick it up, blatantly disregarding the rules.[119] Another Berlin Jewish woman reported that her governess shared coffee and other rationed food when life in hiding without papers had left her impoverished and near starvation.[120] German-Jewish women in hiding or living discreetly on forged Aryan papers lost access to the accoutrements of respectability, such as hair-dressers and laundromats. More significant was their loss of education and any professional life. These women had few support systems available to them and no outlet for amusement or resentment. Daily existence became a constant battle with fear of deportation and certain death if their deception was discovered. The price of nerve-wracking isolation was high, since before 1933 the majority of German-Jewish women lived in a relatively secure middle-class milieu.

Despite the risks of denunciation, many Germans aided Jews in finding underground escape routes and hiding places. In order to evade detection, the artist Valerie Wolffenstein moved eighteen times in two years.[121] In another case, a woman and her physician husband fled Berlin for southern Germany in 1943. Armed with two sets of bogus identity papers with the surnames of Günther and Perger, he assumed the identity and profession of a traveling salesman, his wife the traditional domestic jobs of cook and mother's helper. They were led to safe houses on an underground railway made up of ten pastors of the Confessing Church, including four women curates.[122] Warned of the intention of a Gestapo raid by fellow employees at a Berlin bakery, another couple went into hiding in Berlin from late 1942 until liberation. They survived without identity papers or ration coupons, sometimes sleeping with friends, but often living as homeless transients who slept in stairwells, railroad stations, and parks.[123]

Many German Jews who emigrated before 1938 found asylum in their adopted homelands.[124] Others, like Paula Littauer, fled from Berlin to Brussels in 1942 and survived with frequent changes of residence and constant identity changes, "so that I almost forgot my real name."[125] Fugitives lived a sub-rosa existence, successful if they could pass as local inhabitants in language, manner, and appearance—if luck was with them and their hosts. After 1941, they were colloquially called *camouflés* in France, *onderduikers* in Holland, and *U-Boote* (submarines) in Germany and Austria.

Despite the overwhelming odds, about 3,000 Jewish fugitives survived the war in Berlin, about 1,500 in other parts of Germany, and about 1,000 German Jews in other European countries. The Jews who survived in hiding were about 25 percent of the surviving 12,500 German Jews alive in May 1945 (out of the May 1939 population of approximately 240,000 Jews). There are no precise statistics available about the percentage of women among the Jews in hiding.[126] Systematic literature by region, class, or nationality, or about the background of the survivors and rescuers has not appeared. It is not yet clear whether women's experiences in hiding differed from men's in any substantial way.[127]

Many German-Jewish women sought to escape Nazi Germany after 1933 by emigrating to adjacent European nations or more exotic locations overseas. Although a substantial body of literature has already appeared about the odyssey of prominent political, literary, academic, and scientific professionals who fled abroad, there has been no systematic study of average emigrants nor has there been any focus on women forced to rebuild their lives.[128]

Although there are no conclusive statistics for the German and German-Jewish emigration of 1933–1941, it is believed that 270,000 to 300,000 Jews fled Germany; this figure was 80 percent of all emigrés from Germany.[129] The precise number of German and German-Jewish women is not known. However, it is clear that women formed approximately half of all refugees to the United States during these years. German-Jewish demographic trends were visible in the occupational profile of female emigrants; in the first period, until 1938, a majority of women were young or early middle-aged professionals and semiskilled workers. In the second phase, after 1938, the number of older women without job-related skills increased dramatically, as did the number of minor children. The number of single and married women was about equal between 1933 and 1941; there were few widows or divorcées.[130] Predominantly urban and middle class in pre-1933 Germany, these women already had certain distinctive career patterns before emigration.[131] In Nazi society, women's work outside the home was considered unnecessary and inappropriate; flight did not increase female status nor did it improve professional opportunities. The 1930s were the nadir of women's rights and the complex cultural and political forces of the Depression strengthened hostility to all alien job competitors. With few exceptions, this was reinforced for emigrant women by an ambiguous lack of support from male refugee colleagues and even within their own families, despite the dictates of economic necessity. Thus, the number of women domestics, cooks, and clerical workers increased dramatically among German-Jewish female refugees during the 1930s.[132] In one instance, Käte Frankenthal, a former doctor, supported herself as an itinerant peddler of ice cream during her periodic bouts of unemployment after arriving in New York.[133]

It is generally believed that although women and men faced similar difficulties in learning new languages and adapting to new milieus, women were faster and more proficient in acquiring new languages because they needed to communicate for shopping and child care. Female writers like Vicki Baum and Martha Albrand became widely known popular novelists in the United States, Helen Wolff a fixture in American publishing, and Lotte Lenya and Lili Palmer starred in English-language film and theater.[134]

The study of women and the Holocaust has barely begun, and the complexities and contours of the subject must be explored in future historical research. . . . This essay has focused on German and German-Jewish women. Future work must include horizontal pan-European studies, focusing on different female prisoner categories and camps across occupied Europe and integrating the literature on western and eastern Europe. There will also have to be new vertical studies on women in German jails, on their underground experiences and their odysseys as refugees forced to rebuild new lives abroad. I hope this essay clears away some misunderstandings and opens the way for future investigations by scholars from many disciplines. The complexity of the subject will keep historians and other analysts occupied for many years.

NOTES

The author would like to thank Werner T. Angress, Henry Friedlander, Atina Grossmann, Marion Kaplan, Walter Peterson, and Joan Ringelheim for their advice and constructive suggestions in revising this essay, which was first presented at Southeastern Massachusetts University in June 1982 and again at the Stern College, Yeshiva University, Conference on Women and the Holocaust in March 1983.

1. For the general literature, see Raul Hilberg, *The Destruction of the European Jews* (Chicago, 1961); Martin Broszat, "Nationalsozialistische Konzentrationslager, 1933–1945," in *Anatomie des SS-Staates*, ed. Helmut Krausnick et al., 2 vols. (Munich, 1967), Vol. 2, pp. 11–133; Adalbert Rückerl, ed., *NS-Vernichtungslager* (Munich, 1977); and Falk Pingel, *Häftlinge unter SS-Herrschaft* (Hamburg, 1978). Two useful recent bibliographical surveys are conspicuous for their respective lacunae: a survey of Holocaust historiography fails to mention women's history, and a recent survey article on women's history omits all

references to the Holocaust. See Konrad Kwiet, "Zur historiographischen Behandlung der Judenverfolgung im Dritten Reich," *Militärgeschichtliche Mitteilungen* 27, no. 1 (1980): 149–92; and Richard J. Evans, "Feminism and Female Emancipation in Germany, 1870–1945," *Central European History* 9, no. 4 (1976): 323–51. Two recent volumes are disappointing and occasionally misleading: Konnilyn G. Feig, *Hitler's Death Camps* (New York, 1979), pp. 133–90; and Hanna Elling, *Frauen im deutschen Widerstand, 1933–1945* (Frankfurt, 1978). Of greater value for the discussion of women in Nazi Germany and women as perpetrators are Dorothee Klinksiek, *Die Frau im NS-Staat* (Stuttgart, 1982); Maruta Schmidt and Gabi Dietz, eds., *Frauen unterm Hakenkreuz* (Berlin, 1983); Frauengruppe Faschismusforschung, eds., *Mutterkreuz und Arbeitsbuch: Zur Geschichte der Frauen in der Weimarer Republik und im Nationalsozialismus* (Frankfurt, 1981); Claudia Koonz, "Mothers in the Fatherland: Women in Nazi Germany," in *Becoming Visible: Women in European History*, ed. Renate Bridenthal and Claudia Koonz (Boston, 1977), pp. 445–73; and Michael H. Kater, "Frauen in der NS-Bewegung," *Vierteljahrshefte für Zeitgeschichte* 31, no. 2 (1983): 202–41. Several capsule biographies of Nazi women perpetrators are found in the valuable essay by Henry Friedlander, "The Nazi Concentration Camps," in *Human Responses to the Holocaust*, ed. Michael D. Ryan (New York and Toronto, 1981), pp. 33–69.

2. Bundesarchiv Koblenz [hereafter BA], Akte NS 10/66. See also Leo Baeck Institute, New York [hereafter LBI, NY], Wiener Library Press clippings microfilms, AR 7187/Reel 95 (Nazis and Women, 1933–1939), and 7187/Reel 109 (Nazis and Women, 1939–1945).

3. Elling, *Frauen im deutschen Widerstand*, p. 198; and Wolf Hammer, *Hohes Haus in Henkers Hand* (Frankfurt, 1956), p. 77.

4. For Kessel, see Elling, *Frauen im deutschen Widerstand*, pp. 57, 89; Hammer, *Hohes Haus*, p. 57. For Fleischer, see Max Schwarz, *MdR: Biographisches Handbuch der Reichstage* (Hanover, 1965), p. 648.

5. For the Marie Jankowski incident, see the emigré exposé *Braunbuch über Reichstagsbrand und Hitlerterror* (Basel, 1933), pp. 210–11; LBI, NY: 7187/Reel 95; and Käte Frankenthal, *Der dreifache Fluch: Jüdin, Intellektuelle, Sozialistin*, ed. Kathleen Pearle and Stephan Leibfried (Frankfurt and New York, 1981), pp. 126, 292. For Bohm-Schuch, see Marie Juchacz, *Sie lebten für eine bessere Welt* (Hanover, 1971), pp. 93–98; Franz Osterroth, *Biographisches Lexikon des Sozialismus*, Vol. I: *Verstorbene Persönlichkeiten* (Hanover, 1960), p. 32; and Hammer, *Hohes Haus*, p. 30.

6. For Overlach, see "Women Politicals in German Goals," *Manchester Guardian*, 29 January 1937 (also found in LBI, NY: E. J. Gumbel Papers).

7. For Lüders, see Hammer, *Hohes Haus*, p. 65. Hammer mentions that Lüders also hid Berlin Jews in her home between 1938 and 1942. For Teusch, see ibid., p. 93.

8. *Biographisches Handbuch der deutschsprachigen Emigration nach 1933* (Munich and New York, 1980), Vol. 1, pp. 685–86. See also Gerhart Seger, *Oranienburg* (reprint; Berlin, 1979).

9. LBI, NY: E. J. Gumbel Papers, "Frauen als Geisel," *Sonderdienst der deutschen Informationen. Das Martyrium der Frauen in deutschen Konzentrationslagern*, No. 41 (11 June 1936).

10. Ibid.

11. Ibid.

12. Ibid.

13. Ibid.

14. There is almost no systematic literature on German jails and prisons in the twentieth century and in Nazi Germany. Some useful information on the prison conditions of Nazi women political opponents is found in two anthologies of memoirs: Gisela Dischner, ed., *Eine stumme Generation berichtet: Frauen der dreissiger und vierziger Jahre* (Frankfurt, 1982); and Gerda Szepansky, ed., *Frauen leisten Widerstand: 1933–1945; Lebensgeschichten nach Interviews und Dokumenten* (Frankfurt, 1983). Estimates of German women political prisoners are discussed in Schmidt and Dietz, *Frauen unterm Hakenkreuz*, pp. 158–67; and *Braunbuch über Reichstagsbrand und Hitlerterror*, pp. 274–76. For information on Jehovah's Witnesses, see Michael H. Kater, "Die Ernsten Bibelforscher im Dritten Reich," *Vierteljahrshefte für Zeitgeschichte* 5, No. 2 (1969): 181–218; and Christine E. King, "Strategies for Survival: An Examination of the History of Five Christian Sects in Germany, 1933–1945," *Journal of Contemporary History* 14 (1979): 211–33. See also LBI, NY: E. J. Gumbel Papers, "Die Zeugin Jehovas," *Beilage der Deutschen Information*, No. 6 (6 June 1936). For information on homosexuals, see Frank Rector, *The Nazi Extermination of Homosexuals* (New York, 1981); James D. Steakley, *The Homosexual Emancipation Movement in Germany* (New York, 1975); Hans-Georg Stümke and Rudi Finkler, *Rosa Winkel, Rosa Listen* (Reinbek bei Hamburg, 1981); and Rüdiger Lautmann, "Das Leben homosexueller Männer unter dem Nationalsozialismus," in *Terror und Hoffnung in Deutschland, 1933–1945*, ed. Johannes Beck et al. (Reinbek bei Hamburg, 1980), pp. 366–90. The literature on homosexuals contains only token references to lesbians. No literature about female asocials and criminals in Nazi prisons has been located.

15. See the memoirs of Marta Appel in Dortmund published in Monika Richarz, ed., *Jüdisches Leben in Deutschland: Selbstzeugnisse zur Sozialgeschichte, 1918–1945* (Stuttgart, 1982), pp. 231–33. Appel also tells of the growing social isolation of Jewish women, who met former Aryan women friends only infrequently even in public places (ibid., p. 233). German women guilty of racial misconduct under the Nuremberg Laws were photographed and their names and addresses published in *Stürmer* and displayed in the advertisement cases known as *Stürmerkästen*. Similar photos and lists of names and addresses appeared for Jewish men and women living in mixed marriages (see *Stürmer*, Nos. 37 and 40, 1935, reproduced in *Der gelbe Fleck* [Paris, 1936], pp. 197–218). This propaganda could misfire, producing sympathy for the victim and resulting in demonstratively friendly behavior to Jewish neighbors. See Ian Kershaw, "The Persecution of the Jews and German Popular Opinion in the Third Reich," *Leo Baeck Institute Yearbook 26* (1981): 264–74.

16. The phrase "insidious creeping persecution" (*schleichende Judenverfolgung*) comes from Helmut Genschel, *Die Verdrängung der Juden aus der Wirtschaft im Dritten Reich* (Göttingen, 1966), p. 139. The persecution of Jews in Nazi Germany is documented in Uwe Dietrich Adam, *Judenpolitik im Dritten Reich* (Düsseldorf, 1972); and Helmut Eschwege, ed., *Kennzeichen J* (Frankfurt, 1979).

17. Hilberg, *Destruction*, pp. 28–29; and Christine E. King, "Strategies for Survival," pp. 216–19.

18. LBI, NY: Max Gruenewald Papers, Box 1, file 7: Simon Gruenewald, "Tante Emma," unpubl. ms., pp. 24–28.
19. LBI, NY: Celia Rosenzweig collection, AR 7128/1. This document is translated and annotated in Sybil Milton, "The Expulsion of Polish Jews from Germany, October 1938 to July 1939: A Documentation," *Leo Baeck Institute Yearbook* 29 (in press).
20. LBI, NY: Max Gruenewald Papers, "Tante Emma," pp. 26–28.
21. Three instances where mob violence was directed against German-Jewish women in rural small towns during the November 1938 pogrom are documented in Heinz Lauber, *Judenpogrom: Reichskristallnacht November 1938 in Grossdeutschland* (Gerlingen, 1981), pp. 110–14 and 221–33. Comparative statistics of violence against Jewish men and women during November 1938 are not available.
22. The 1939 statistics are based on Nazi racial definitions, regardless of actual religion, and thus include converts and *Mischlinge*. Furthermore, the figures include Jewish residents of annexed Austria and the Sudetenland. See Erich Rosenthal, "Trends of the Jewish Population in Germany, 1910–39," *Jewish Social Studies* 6, No. 1 (1944): 247–51; and Monika Richarz, *Jüdisches Leben in Deutschland, 1918–1945*, p. 61.
23. Fewer Jewish women were interned in the camps before 1938. They were also unable to emigrate and obtain visas in the same numbers as single Jewish men. See LBI, NY: Bruno Blau, "Die Entwicklung der jüdischen Bevölkerung in Deutschland von 1800 bis 1945," unpubl. ms. (New York, 1950), pp. 335–44; and Bruno Blau, "The Jewish Population in Germany, 1939–45," *Jewish Social Studies* 12 (1950): 161–72.
24. Complete statistics by gender and age for the deportation of German Jews between October 1941 and the last transport in April 1945 are not available. The problem of establishing statistics is discussed in Henry Friedlander, "The Deportation of German Jews: Postwar German Trials of Nazi Criminals," *Leo Baeck Institute Yearbook* 29 (in press). The Erich Rosenthal essay (see note 22) speculates that male Jews also participated more in internal migration to industrial and urban centers in Germany between 1910 and 1939. This may have had significant ramifications on survival by gender after 1941, since large urban centers like Berlin offered Jews more opportunities for survival in hiding than did small rural towns.
25. The quote is from Ottilie Schönewald's description of the expulsion in Bochum; see Martin Gilbert, *Final Journey* (New York, 1979), pp. 18–21.
26. H. G. Adler, *Der verwaltete Mensch: Studien zur Deportation der Juden aus Deutschland* (Tübingen, 1974), pp. 91–105.
27. For further information on Zbaszyn, see: LBI, NY: Wilhelm Graetz Collection, AR 4121/VI 15.
28. Adler, *Der verwaltete Mensch*, pp. 140–54.
29. Ibid., pp. 155–67; Michael R. Marrus and Robert O. Paxton, "The Nazis and the Jews in Occupied Western Europe, 1940–1944," *Journal of Modern History* 54, No. 4 (December 1982): 687–714; and Adam Rutkowski, "Le camp d'internement de Gurs," *Le Monde Juif* 36, No. 100 (October–December 1980): 131–33. The population of Gurs in November 1940 was 13,000 individuals, mostly German and Austrian Jews. Families were split up with men, wives, and children housed separately. There were 5,000 women and 450 children held in the camp, including many elderly Jews (2,500 people were older than sixty). Conditions in Gurs and women's strategies for survival will be discussed in a later part of this essay.

30. Elling, *Frauen im deutschen Widerstand*, pp. 23–37; and LBI, NY: E. J. Gumbel Papers, press clippings file, 1933–1936.

31. The first director at Gotteszell was Government Councillor Henning, who had previously served as director of the Moringen workhouse.

32. Julius Schätzle, *Stationen zur Hölle: Konzentrationslager in Baden und Württemberg, 1933–1945* (Frankfurt, 1974), pp. 25–27.

33. LBI, NY: E. J. Gumbel Papers, "Die werktätige Frau unter der faschistischen Knute: Sechs Frauen als Geiseln in Stadelheim," *Die Neue Welt*, 31 October 1934; and *Deutsche Information*, No. 41 (11 June 1936).

34. Elling, *Frauen im deutschen Widerstand*, p. 90 (interview with Maria Deeg). These appear to be the earliest illegal sterilizations in the Nazi period.

35. "Frauen im Konzentrationslager," *Deutsche Freiheit*, 5 October 1934, containing an excerpt of the subsequently published refugee anthology about concentration camps issued by the Socialist Graphia Verlag in Czechoslovakia. See Otto Urban, "Burg Hohenstein," *Konzentrationslager: Ein Appell an das Gewissen der Welt* (Karlsbad, 1934), pp. 217–38.

36. Friedlander, "The Nazi Concentration Camps," p. 34.

37. For information about these three women's camps, including substantial data about Moringen, see Ino Arndt, "Das Frauenkonzentrationslager Ravensbrück," in *Studien zur Geschichte der Konzentrationslager*, ed. Martin Broszat (Stuttgart, 1970), pp. 93–129; Schmidt and Dietz, eds., *Frauen unterm Hakenkreuz*, pp. 140–48; Elling, *Frauen im deutschen Widerstand*, pp. 23–24; *Konzentrationslager* (Karlsbad, 1934), pp. 213–16; Hannah Vogt, ed., *KZ Moringen, Männerlager, Frauenlager, Jugendschutzlager: Eine Dokumentation* (Göttingen, 1983); Wolf-Dieter Haardt, "Was denn, hier—in Moringen?" in *Die vergessenen KZs: Gedenkstätten für die Opfer des NS-Terrors in der Bundesrepublik*, ed. Detlef Garbe (Bornheim-Merten, 1983), pp. 97–108; and Internationaler Suchdienst, *Vorläufiges Verzeichnis der Haftstätten unter dem Reichsführer-SS, 1933–1945* (Arolsen, 1969), p. 5.

38. Vogt, *KZ Moringen*, p. 15. The two women, Marie Peix and Hanna Vogt, were arrested for their Communist activities.

39. Arndt, "Das Frauenkonzentrationslager Ravensbrück," pp. 94–99.

40. For more data on Moringen, see ibid.; Elling, *Frauen im deutschen Widerstand*, pp. 23–24; and *Konzentrationslager* (Karlsbad, 1934), pp. 213–16. An explanation of the Dachau model is found in Friedlander, "The Nazi Concentration Camps," pp. 35–39.

41. Arndt, "Das Frauenkonzentrationslager Ravensbrück," pp. 99–101.

42. The heads of female camps were called *director;* those in the male camps carried the title of *commandant*. It is unclear whether this change in title implied any substantive difference in administrative organization or authority, or whether posting to women's camps had less prestige.

43. Berlin Document Center (BDC): Personnel Dossier of Max Koegel, SS no. 37,644. Koegel's predecessor at Lichtenburg, SS Colonel Günther Tamaschke, SS No. 851, was also trained at Dachau. Excerpts from both personnel dossiers at the BDC are used as facsimile reproductions in Elling, *Frauen im deutschen Widerstand*, pp. 33–36.

44. Facsimile of Koegel's March 14, 1939, letter is reproduced in the memoir by Charlotte Müller, *Die Klempnerkolonne in Ravensbrück: Erinnerungen des Häftlings*

Nr. 10787 (Berlin, 1981), illustration facing p. 48; my translation. For the pattern of corporal punishment against male and female prisoners, see *Trial of the Major War Criminals before the International Military Tribunal*, 42 vols. (Nuremberg, 1947–1949), Vol. 4, p. 201, and Vol. 29, pp. 315–16 (Nuremberg Document PS 2189). See also excerpt from Himmler's regulations for permitted punishments in the camps, 1941, ibid., Vol. 39, pp. 262–64 (Nuremberg Document USSR 011).

45. BA: R58/1027, Gestapo circular of 2 May 1939. The inmate registration numbers at Ravensbrück continued with 1,415, showing a complete congruity and continuity with the registration numbers assigned prisoners at Lichtenburg.

46. I would like to thank Marion Kaplan and Joan Ringelheim for suggesting this connection. See G. Zörner, ed., *Frauen-KZ Ravensbrück* (Berlin, 1982).

47. Zörner, *Ravensbrück*, pp. 93–95; and Arndt, "Das Frauenkonzentrationslager Ravensbrück," pp. 112–13. Tuesdays and Fridays were designated for flogging, and a maximum of 25 blows with a leather whip were permitted, once Himmler and the camp physician certified an inmate "fit" to receive punishment. In 1942, the rules changed, allowing whipping on women's bare buttocks, and also permitting designated prisoner trusties to whip other prisoners. The latter rule was qualified so that German women could not be beaten by foreigners. This rule was designed to weaken any sympathy or solidarity between prisoners. It is believed that the formal rules were often violated with impunity.

48. Arndt, "Das Frauenkonzentrationslager Ravensbrück," pp. 119–20.

49. See Gemma LaGuardia Gluck, "LaGuardia's Sister: Eichmann's Hostage," *Midstream* 7, No. 1 (1961): 3–19. Geneviève de Gaulle was the general's niece and Rosa Thälmann was the wife of the imprisoned leader of the German Communist Party. No research has been done about the special barracks and somewhat preferential treatment accorded to the privileged prisoners and *Prominenten* in Ravensbrück, Auschwitz, Theresienstadt, or other camps.

50. The composition of barracks (called *Blocks*) with inmate housing is described in several memoirs: Margarete Buber-Neumann, *Als Gefangene bei Stalin und Hitler: Eine Welt im Dunkel* (Stuttgart, 1958); Germaine Tillion, *Ravensbrück*, trans. Gerald Satterwhite (Garden City, N.Y., 1975); Isa Vermehren, *Reise durch den letzten Akt: Ravensbrück, Buchenwald, Dachau* (Reinbek bei Hamburg, 1979); and the anthology edited by the Amicale de Ravensbrück, *Les Françaises à Ravensbrück* (Bordeaux, 1971). See also Arndt, "Das Frauenkonzentrationslager Ravensbrück," pp. 112–19.

51. LaGuardia Gluck, "LaGuardia's Sister," p. 5.

52. Arndt, "Das Frauenkonzentrationslager Ravensbrück," pp. 101–04; Tillion, *Ravensbrück*, pp. 67–71; and Friedlander, "The Nazi Concentration Camps," pp. 33–69.

53. Arndt, "Das Frauenkonzentrationslager Ravensbrück," p. 121.

54. Tillion, *Ravensbrück*, p. 39.

55. Ibid.; all memoirs report similar stories about women's experiences in Ravensbrück and other camps.

56. There have been no studies of the Nazi manipulation of language as applied to women, and the whole subject of gender-specific usage requires further analysis, as does the appropriation of that language by the prisoners themselves. This type of research is needed especially in light of Nazi sexual ideology stressing masculine

superiority. An excellent introduction to this subject is found in Henry Friedlander, "The Manipulation of Language," in *The Holocaust: Ideology, Bureaucracy, and Genocide; the San Jose Papers*, ed. Henry Friedlander and Sybil Milton (Millwood, N.Y., 1980), pp. 103–13.

57. Statistics on women SS guards are found in Tillion, *Ravensbrück*, pp. 68ff., and Zörner, *Ravensbrück*, pp. 27ff.

58. Personnel dossiers of these SS women are available in the files of the BDC; the BA; the Ravensbrück Museum in Fürstenberg, German Democratic Republic; and the pretrial investigations and interrogations of the Nuremberg, U.S. Army war crimes trials, and British trials (see National Archives, Washington, D.C.: Record Groups 153 and 238). See BDC, typescript inventory of holdings, December 1970, 6 pages; also Robert Wolfe, ed., *Captured German and Related Records: A National Archives Conference* (Athens, Ohio, 1974), pp. 131–43. See also Gerhard Granier, Josef Henke, and Klaus Oldenhage, eds., *Das Bundesarchiv und seine Bestände*. 3d expanded ed. (Boppard am Rhein, 1977). The Association of Those Persecuted under Nazi Rule (Vereinigung der Verfolgten des Naziregimes; VVN) and their regional offices have archives on various camps and data revealed by trials; their national newsletter is extremely useful in reconstructing the careers of SS women guards and other perpetrators. Similar relevant holdings exist with the Amicale de Ravensbrück and other survivors' umbrella organizations existing in every country once occupied during World War II. See also George O. Kent, "Research Opportunities in West and East German Archives for the Weimar Period and the Third Reich," *Central European History* 3, No. 1 (1979): 38–67.

59. Hermann Langbein, *Menschen in Auschwitz* (Frankfurt and Vienna, 1972), pp. 444, 447–49.

60. Conversations with Raul Hilberg and Joan Ringelheim.

61. Tillion, *Ravensbrück*, pp. 68ff.; Zörner, *Ravensbrück*, pp. 21–31. See also Buber-Neumann, *Gefangene bei Stalin und Hitler*, pp. 301–31; and idem, *Die erloschene Flamme: Schicksale meiner Zeit* (Munich and Vienna, 1976), pp. 30–42.

62. Jadwiga Bezwinska and Danuta Czech, eds., *KL Auschwitz seen by the SS: Höss, Broad, Kremer* (Auschwitz, 1972), p. 81 (Höss autobiography).

63. Bezwinska and Czech, *Auschwitz Seen by the SS*, pp. 79–82 (Höss); Buber-Neumann, *Gefangene bei Stalin und Hitler*, pp. 301–31; and idem, *Die erloschene Flamme*, pp. 30–42.

64. Buber-Neumann, *Gefangene bei Stalin und Hitler*, pp. 318–22, 325–32, 335–37; also Erika Buchmann, ed., *Die Frauen von Ravensbrück* (Berlin, 1960), pp. 7–22.

65. Bezwinska and Czech, *Auschwitz Seen by the SS*, p. 80 (Höss).

66. Ibid., p. 82.

67. Henry Friedlander, "Concentration Camps," in Janet Blatter and Sybil Milton, *Art of the Holocaust* (New York, 1981), pp. 136–37. The Soviet women POWs arrived in late February 1943, captured at the battle of Sebastopol.

68. The number of women in Mauthausen's satellites in April 1945 were: Lenzing—600; Amstetten—500; Hirtenberg—400; St. Lambrecht—20; Mittersill—15; and Gusen—14. See Hans Marsalek, *Die Geschichte des Konzentrationslagers Mauthausen* (Vienna, 1980), pp. 115–18.

69. In March 1945, several German prostitutes were drafted into a unit of women guards at Mauthausen, similar to the German and Austrian male criminal prisoners given arms during the Auschwitz' evacuation march or those drafted into military

formations from Sachsenhausen. See Marsalek, *Mauthausen*, pp. 115–18; Kazimierz Smolen et al., *Auschwitz: Geschichte und Wirklichkeit des Vernichtungslagers* (Reinbek bei Hamburg, 1980), pp. 169–80; and Hilberg, *Destruction*, p. 623. The women who survived in Mauthausen and its subsidiaries consisted in April 1945 of the following subgroups: 1,453 protective custody prisoners; 608 Jewish women; 79 Gypsies; 62 "asocials"; 43 Jehovah's Witnesses; and 5 Spanish Communist women. More than half the surviving women were between 20 and 40 years old (Marsalek, *Mauthausen*, pp. 16, 137–39).

70. At the end of 1944, there were 5,000 women at Dachau; 14,600 at Flossenbürg; and 13,500 at Neuengamme. See Ernst Antoni, *Von Dachau bis Auschwitz: Faschistische Konzentrationslager, 1933–1945* (Frankfurt, 1979), pp. 30–38, 50–56; Fritz Bringmann, *Neuengamme: Berichte, Erinnerungen, Dokumente* (Frankfurt, 1981); Werner Johe, *Neuengamme: Zur Geschichte der Konzentrationslager in Hamburg* (Hamburg, 1981); and Barbara Distel and Ruth Jakusch, eds., *Concentration Camp Dachau, 1933–1945* (Brussels, n.d.).

71. Schätzle, *Stationen zur Hölle*, pp. 45–48.

72. The whole phenomenon of special labor camps in Germany for women, Jews, and other prisoner categories has not been adequately explored in the current literature. For treatment of forced labor camps for Jews, see Friedlander, "The Nazi Concentration Camps," pp. 43–50. See also Internationaler Suchdienst, *Vorläufiges Verzeichnis*, pp. VI–XLI.

73. A list of the last women's camps is found in Internationaler Suchdienst, *Vorläufiges Verzeichnis*, p. XIII.

74. Henry Friedlander and Sybil Milton, "Surviving," in *Genocide: Critical Issues of the Holocaust*, ed. Alex Grobman, Daniel Landes, and Sybil Milton (Los Angeles and Chappaqua, N.Y., 1983), pp. 233–35.

75. Leonard Tushnet, *The Uses of Adversity: Studies of Starvation in the Warsaw Ghetto* (London and New York, 1966).

76. Hanna Lévy-Hass, *Vielleicht war das alles erst der Anfang: Tagebuch aus dem KZ Bergen-Belsen, 1944–1945*, ed. Eike Geisel (Berlin, 1979), pp. 10–11. Also, LBI, NY: Eva Noack-Mosse, "Theresienstädter Tagebuch, January–July 1945," unpubl. ms. (1945); and Hanna Schramm, *Menschen in Gurs: Erinnerungen an ein französisches Internierungslager, 1940–1941* (Worms, 1977), p. 88.

77. Richarz, *Jüdisches Leben in Deutschland, 1918–1945*, pp. 429–31.

78. LBI, NY: Eva Noack-Mosse, "Theresienstädter Tagebuch," p. 85; and Hanna Lévy-Hass, *Inside Belsen*, trans. Ronald Taylor (Great Britain and New Jersey, 1982), pp. 6–7, 46–49.

79. Langbein, *Menschen in Auschwitz*, pp. 121–22.

80. France Audoul, *Ravensbrück: 150,000 femmes en enfer* (Paris, 1968), unpag.

81. Daniel Landes, "Modesty and Self-Dignity in Holocaust Films," in Grobman, Landes, Milton, eds., *Genocide*, pp. 11–13.

82. H. G. Adler, Hermann Langbein, Ella Lingens-Reiner, eds., *Auschwitz: Zeugnisse und Berichte* (Frankfurt, 1962); and Olga Lengyel, *Five Chimneys* (London, 1981).

83. Lévy-Hass, *Inside Belsen*, pp. 14–15; Adler, Langbein, and Lingens-Reiner, *Auschwitz*, pp. 111–62; and LBI, NY: Eva Noack-Mosse, "Theresienstädter Tagebuch," pp. 74–75.

84. Charlotte Delbo, *None of Us Will Return*, trans. John Githens (Boston, 1978).

85. Bezwinska and Czech, *Auschwitz Seen by the SS*, p. 75 (Höss).

86. Schramm, *Menschen in Gurs*, p. 88; Lévy-Hass, *Inside Belsen*, pp. 28–35 (entry for 22 October 1944); and Vermehren, *Reise durch den letzten Akt*, p. 26. Although this particular quote is from Schramm, almost identically worded descriptions are found in other memoirs; see also Buber-Neumann and Tillion.

87. Lévy-Hass, *Inside Belsen*, p. 8.

88. Joan Mariam Ringelheim, "The Unethical and the Unspeakable: Women and the Holocaust," *Simon Wiesenthal Center Annual 1* (1984): 69–87; and *Proceedings of the Conference Women Surviving the Holocaust*, ed. Esther Katz and Joan Ringelheim (New York, 1983), pp. 22–26.

89. Schramm, *Menschen in Gurs*, pp. 14–16; see also Kitty Hart, *Return to Auschwitz* (New York, 1982), and Anna Pawelczynska, *Values and Violence in Auschwitz: A Sociological Analysis*, trans. Catherine S. Leach (Berkeley and Los Angeles, 1979).

90. American Jewish Joint Distribution Committee Archives, New York: "Germans in France," *Friday* 1, No. 10 (17 May 1940), clipping in the 1940 files on French Refugees.

91. Hart, *Return to Auschwitz*, pp. 76–80, 104–09.

92. Buber-Neumann, *Gefangene bei Stalin und Hitler*, p. 227; and Bezwinska and Czech, *Auschwitz Seen by the SS*, p. 77 (Höss).

93. Naomi Winkler Munkacsi, "Jewish Religious Observances in Women's Death Camps in Germany," *Yad Vashem Bulletin 20* (April 1967): 35–8.

94. France Hamelin, unpublished diary, Christmas 1943 (unpag.), by permission of France Hamelin, Paris; see Blatter and Milton, *Art of the Holocaust*, p. 251.

95. Schramm, *Menschen in Gurs;* and LBI, NY: archival collections on Gurs and the French internment camps.

96. Schramm, *Menschen in Gurs;* Blatter and Milton, *Art of the Holocaust*, interviews of prisoner-artists interned in Gurs, Birkenau, and Ravensbrück; the memoirs of Tillion and Buber-Neumann; and the archives of the LBI, NY and the American Jewish Joint Distribution Committee, New York.

97. Hart, *Return to Auschwitz*, p. 122; also Langbein, *Menschen in Auschwitz*, pp. 450–63.

98. Langbein, *Menschen in Auschwitz*, pp. 457–58; and Bezwinska and Czech, *Auschwitz Seen by the SS*, p. 83 (Höss).

99. H. G. Adler, *Theresienstadt, 1941–1945* (Tübingen, 1960); and Buber-Neumann, *Gefangene bei Stalin und Hitler*, pp. 260ff. Also LBI, NY: Noack-Mosse, "Theresienstädter Tagebuch," pp. 74–75.

100. Lesbian relationships are mentioned in very few memoirs; see Lengyel, *Five Chimneys*, pp. 191–93 for a detailed analysis of lesbian relationships in Birkenau. The excerpts from Erna Nelki's memoir, "Eingesperrt im englischen Frauenlager," reprinted in Walter Zadek, ed., *Sie flohen vor dem Hakenkreuz: Selbstzeugnisse der Emigranten; Ein Lesebuch für Deutsche* (Reinbek bei Hamburg, 1981), pp. 120–26, describes life without men among 3,000 mostly German-Jewish women interned on the Isle of Man. The whole subject of sexuality, love, and friendships in prisons and camps requires further systematic investigation. The taboos of historical literature have limited discussion and investigation of these subjects in the past.

101. The swapping of sex for food is described in the memoirs of Lengyel, *Five Chimneys*, pp. 189–90; and Fania Fénelon, *Playing for Time*, trans. Judith Landry (New York, 1979).

102. Vermehren, *Reise durch den letzten Akt*, pp. 25–27; and Hermann Langbein, *Nicht wie die Schafe zur Schlachtbank: Widerstand in den nationalsozialistischen Konzentrationslagern* (Frankfurt, 1980).

103. Langbein, *Widerstand*, pp. 178, 336–39.

104. Blatter and Milton, *Art of the Holocaust*, pp. 136–37; and Lévy-Hass, *Inside Belsen*, pp. 25–26.

105. Bezwinska and Czech, *Auschwitz Seen by the SS*, pp. 163–68 (Broad). The Budy revolt is unconfirmed by prisoner sources and requires further research to fill the gaps. See Langbein, *Menschen in Auschwitz*, pp. 135–38, for skepticism about the existing source literature on Budy.

106. Blatter and Milton, *Art of the Holocaust*; and Adler, *Theresienstadt*.

107. Lévy-Hass, *Inside Belsen*, p. 7; LBI, NY: Noack-Mosse, "Theresienstädter Tagebuch," pp. 75–76.

108. Peter Altmann et al., *Der deutsche antifaschistische Widerstand 1933–1945 in Bildern und Dokumenten* (Frankfurt, 1977); and Günther Weisenborn, *Der lautlose Aufstand: Bericht über die Widerstandsbewegung des deutschen Volkes, 1933–1945*; 4th rev. exp. ed. (Frankfurt, 1974).

109. Helmut Eschwege, "Resistance of German Jews against the Nazi Regime," *Leo Baeck Institute Yearbook* 15 (1970): 143–80; idem, *Kennzeichen J*, pp. 299–322; and Konrad Kwiet, "Problems of Jewish Resistance Historiography," *Leo Baeck Institute Yearbook* 24 (1979): 35–57.

110. See footnote 109. Also Margot Pikarski, *Jugend im Berliner Widerstand: Herbert Baum und Kampfgefährten* (Berlin, 1978); Lucien Steinberg, *Jews against Hitler*, trans. Marion Hunter (London and New York, 1974), pp. 19–53; and Wolfgang Wippermann, *Die Berliner Gruppe Baum und der jüdische Widerstand*, Brochure 19 of the Informationszentrum Berlin Gedenk- und Bildungsstätte Stauffenbergstrasse (Berlin, 1981). For the *Chug Chaluzzi*, see Jizchak Schwersenz and Edith Wolff, "Jüdische Jugend im Untergrund: Eine zionistische Gruppe in Deutschland während des Zweiten Weltkrieges," *Bulletin des Leo Baeck Instituts* 12 (1969): 5–100. See also the 1968 conference proceedings on Jewish resistance published as *Jewish Resistance during the Holocaust* (Jerusalem, 1971).

111. Eschwege, "Resistance of German Jews against the Nazi Regime," pp. 176–77.

112. Schwersenz and Wolff, "Jüdische Jugend im Untergrund," pp. 51–58.

113. Information on Gertrud Luckner is in Adler, *Der verwaltete Mensch*, pp. 825–28. See also Sybil Milton, "The Righteous Who Helped Jews," in Grobman, Landes, and Milton, eds., *Genocide*, pp. 282–87; Philip Friedman, "Righteous Gentiles in the Nazi Era," in his *Roads to Extinction: Essays on the Holocaust* (New York and Philadelphia, 1980), pp. 209–21; and idem, *Their Brothers' Keepers* (New York, 1978). Case studies are found in the interviews reproduced in Jochen Köhler, *Klettern in der Grossstadt: Volkstümliche Geschichten vom Überleben in Berlin, 1933–1945* (Berlin, 1979); Gerda Szepansky, ed., *Frauen leisten Widerstand: 1933–45*; Ilse Rewald, *Berliner, die uns halfen, die Hitlerdiktatur zu überleben*, Brochure 6 of the Informationszentrum Berlin Gedenk; und Bildungsstätte Stauffenbergstrasse (Berlin, 1982); Inge Deutschkron, *Berliner Juden im Untergrund*, Brochure 15 of the Informationszentrum Berlin pamphlet series (Berlin, 1982); and Charles Whiting, ed., *The Home Front: Germany* (Time-Life Books, 1982), pp. 96–109.

114. Blatter and Milton, *Art of the Holocaust*, pp. 255, 258–9, 1980 interview with Mieke Monjau about the arrest and deportation of Julo Levin in the February 1943 "Factory Operation." Single Jewish males and females and spouses in all-Jewish marriages were not released in February 1943. See also Monika Richarz, *Jüdisches Leben in Deutschland, 1918–1945*, pp. 64, 414; Kurt Ball-Kaduri, "Berlin wird judenfrei," *Jahrbuch für die Geschichte Mittel-und Ostdeutschlands* 22 (Berlin, 1973), pp. 196–241; and Wolfgang Wippermann, ed., *Steinerne Zeugen: Stätten der Judenverfolgung in Berlin* (Berlin, 1982), pp. 59–70; and LBI, NY: Microfilm Reel 239: Anklageschrift in der Strafsache gegen Otto Bovensiepen et al. (1969) [the indictment of the Berlin Gestapo for the deportation of the Jews of Berlin].

115. Quote from the memoirs of Hildegard Henschel, wife of the last head of the Berlin Jewish community, Moritz Henschel, in K. J. Ball-Kaduri, "Berlin is 'Purged' of Jews: The Jews in Berlin in 1943," *Yad Vashem Studies* 5 (1963): 274–75; also Hildegard Henschel, "Aus der Arbeit der jüdischen Gemeinde Berlin während 1941–1943," *Zeitschrift für die Geschichte der Juden* (Tel Aviv) 9, Nos. 1–2 (1972): 33–52; see also LBI, NY: Wiener Library microfilms containing eyewitness statements and a list of women participants in the February demonstrations (AR 7187/Reel 600).

116. Goebbels reported in his diary entry for March 6, 1943: "Unfortunately there have been a number of regrettable scenes at a Jewish home for the aged, where a large number of people gathered and in part even took sides with the Jews. I ordered the SD not to continue Jewish evacuation at so critical a moment. We want to save that up for a couple of weeks. We can then go after it all the more thoroughly" (Louis P. Lochner, ed. and trans., *The Goebbels Diaries, 1942–1943* [Garden City, N.Y., 1948], p. 276). There is no information about the composition of the crowd that demonstrated in this incident.

117. Heinz Boberach, ed., *Meldungen aus dem Reich: Auswahl aus den geheimen Lageberichten des Sicherheitsdienstes der SS, 1939–44* (Neuwied and Berlin, 1965), pp. 445–55 (report of 13 November 1943).

118. Kwiet, "Problems of Jewish Resistance Historiography," pp. 37–57.

119. H. D. Leuner, *When Compassion Was a Crime: Germany's Silent Heroes, 1933–1945* (London, 1973); Kurt R. Grossmann, *Die unbesungenen Helden: Menschen in Deutschlands dunklen Tagen* (Berlin-Grünewald, 1957); Bruno Blau, "The Jewish Population of Germany, 1939–45," *Jewish Social Studies* 12, No. 2 (April 1950): 161–72; Deutschkron, *Berliner Juden im Untergrund*, p. 6.

120. Rewald, *Berliner, die uns halfen*, p. 10.

121. Whiting, *The Home Front*, p. 102.

122. Richarz, *Jüdisches Leben in Deutschland*, 1918–1945, pp. 429–42; and LBI, NY: Pineas Collection, AR 94/1–52, containing the bogus identity and ration cards of the Pineas family between 1943 and 1945. See also Grossmann, *Unbesungene Helden*, pp. 159–61.

123. LBI, NY: Berthold Freundlich family collection, AR 3774/1–4.

124. LBI, NY: Hermann Haymann family collection, AR 3216/1–4.

125. LBI, NY: Max Kreutzberger Research Papers, AR 7183, Box 8, folder 1, Paula Littauer, "My Experiences during the Persecution of the Jews in Berlin and Brussels, 1939–1944," unpubl. ms. (mimeographed by the Jewish Central Information Office, London, October 1945).

126. Further, the subject of suicides needs more investigation. See Kwiet, "Jewish Resistance Historiography," p. 57; and Richarz, *Jüdisches Leben in Deutschland, 1918–1945*, pp. 65, 394–400.

127. See the recent popular survey of underground life in Berlin by Leonard Gross, *The Last Jews in Berlin* (New York, 1982); and Sybil Milton, "In Hiding," in Blatter and Milton, *Art of the Holocaust*, p. 124 (and the interviews and biographies of Leo Mayer-Maillet and Toni Simon-Wolfskehl).

128. Two systematic archival guides provide data about sources for emigrant institutions and prominent refugee personalities: Steven W. Siegel, comp., and Herbert A. Strauss, ed., *Jewish Immigrants of the Nazi Period in the USA: Archival Resources*, vol. 1 (New York and Munich, 1978); and John M. Spalek with Sandra H. Hawrylchak and Adrienne Ash, *Guide to the Archival Materials of the German-speaking Emigration to the United States after 1933* (Charlottesville, 1978). See also Herbert A. Strauss, "Jewish Emigration from Germany: Nazi Policies and Jewish Responses," *Leo Baeck Institute Yearbook 25* (1980): 313–61; and ibid., 26 (1981): 343–409; and see Werner Röder and Herbert A. Strauss, eds., *Biographisches Handbuch der deutschsprachigen Emigration*, Vol. 1.

129. Herbert A. Strauss, "Jewish Emigration from Germany," *Leo Baeck Institute Yearbooks* 25 and 26. See footnote 128.

130. Sophia M. Robinson, *Refugees at Work* (New York, 1942), pp. 28–31. Only in the year from 1938 to 1939 did fewer women arrive in the United States. From 1933 to 1938, 89,553 female immigrants and 85,686 male immigrants were registered. Statistics of marital status between 1933 and 1938 show that 52 percent of all refugees were single, 42.6 percent married, 4.3 percent widowed, and 1.1 percent divorced. During the two subsequent periods of 1938–39 and 1939–40, the percentage of married immigrants increased respectively to 49.2 and 54.6 percent of all immigrants to the United States.

131. Marion A. Kaplan, "Tradition and Transition: The Acculturation, Assimilation and Integration of Jews in Imperial Germany; A Gender Analysis," *Leo Baeck Institute Yearbook 27* (1982): 3–35.

132. See A. J. P. Taylor, *From Sarajevo to Potsdam* (London, 1965); and Renate Bridenthal, "Something Old, Something New: Women between the Two World Wars," in Bridenthal and Koonz, eds., *Becoming Visible*, pp. 422–44.

133. Frankenthal, *Der dreifache Fluch*, pp. 242–43.

134. Aggregate data for the study of German and German-Jewish refugee women is available for research, for example, the case files of the American Jewish Joint Distribution Committee held at the archives of the LBI, NY (AR 7196; 13½ linear ft. of case records); the HIAS, ORT, and OSE immigration records at the Yivo Institute for Jewish Research in New York; and the records of agencies like Self-Help and the American Federation of Jews from Central Europe or the Association of Jewish Refugees in Great Britain still held by the agencies themselves. Papers of prominent female refugees are readily available. The archives of the LBI, NY holds the literary estates or substantial fragments for Alice Salomon, Else Lasker-Schüler, and Gertrude Urzidil.

The story of German and German-Jewish women who fled to adjacent European nations after 1933 has received some attention in conferences and anthologies, like Jarrell C. Jackmann and Carla M. Borden, eds., *The Muses Flee Hitler: Cultural Transfer and Adaptation, 1930–1945* (Washington, D.C., 1983).

The story of women who fled to the Soviet Union and ended up serving time in the Siberian Gulag is told in memoirs like Buber-Neumann, *Gefangene bei Stalin und Hitler*; Susanne Leonhard, *Gestohlenes Leben: Schicksal einer politischen Emigrantin in der Sowjetunion* (Frankfurt, 1956); and in archival sources about Zenzl Mühsam in the LBI, NY: Erich Mühsam papers, AR 1806/IV and V. The story of double migrations is revealed mostly through biographical works. Systematic emigration investigation is still in its infancy where refugee women are concerned.

16

Vera Laska

*I am not an interpreter, or a psychologist, or a philosopher. I am a
gatherer of memories.*

VERA LASKA

In The Triumph of Memory, *a documentary film about non-Jewish survivors of
Nazi concentration and death camps, historian Vera Laska tells why she and other
young people joined the resistance in her native Czechoslovakia. "We were really
idealistic," she explains, "and we believed that truth must prevail. We believed in
democracy. We simply hated the Nazis and everything they stood for." Laska claims
she was only "a small cog in the wheel of the Czech resistance." Until she was captured
by the Gestapo, however, Laska and her friends helped Jews and rescued Allied pilots.
They forged papers and carried messages for the underground. They did whatever
they could to help defeat the Nazis.*

Women in the Resistance and in the Holocaust: The Voices of Eyewitnesses
*is a fine book that Laska edited and introduced in 1983. She concludes it with an
epilogue in which she writes:*

I see not much use philosophizing, interpreting or engaging in metaphysical speculations
over the Holocaust. Such exercises limit the scope of communication to a select few. (That
is also the reason why I switched from studying philosophy to the study of history.) What
IS needed is the propagation of the stark truth, for facts are the clearest and most
comprehensible carriers of the message, understood by all.

*Among the facts that she most wants to be "understood by all" are those that make
clear how "women from many walks of life laid their lives on the line for freedom."*

250

In the essay reprinted here—part of Laska's introduction to Women in the Resistance and the Holocaust—*she makes the case that women were extensively involved in anti-Nazi resistance activities everywhere in Europe. "It was to the advantage of women," she points out, "that most of their adversaries were male, and women were less suspected of illegal activities by them—the old male underestimation of the power of a woman." The essay that follows also speaks about Gypsies and about sexual realities in the camps. As a "keeper of memories," Laska casts her net widely and carefully. In the process, despite her disclaimer, her voice proves to be full of insightful, wisely tested interpretation as well. "Praying at times and places prescribed by custom to the God of your choice does not make you your brothers' and sisters' keeper," her epilogue to* Women in the Resistance and in the Holocaust *concludes. "Only by reaching out a helping hand and by actively opposing wrongdoing do we earn the right to be called human."*

Women in the Resistance and in the Holocaust

When I met the American liberators face to face on that glorious April day in 1945 near my last concentration camp in Germany, they were surprised to hear that women had also been in concentration camps, and equally incredulous to find out that women were also in the resistance, facing the same dangers, torture, execution or gas chambers as the men.

I vowed then that one day I shall bring the role of women in the cataclysm of World War II to the attention of the public. Mine is the story of but one woman. It was repeated in countless variations by others. That is the reason why I collected the memoirs of many women who all speak for themselves.

I am not an interpreter, or a psychologist, or a philosopher.

I am a gatherer of memories.

RESISTANCE

Stories of invasions are not new to history. In 416 B.C. " 'the glory that was Athens' attacked and devastated the island of Melos, massacred the men, and sent into slavery the women and children," as Euripides tells us in his *Trojan Women*.[1]

In the conflagration of World War II, in which over fifty million people perished, the Nazi occupation often followed that pattern. Lidice in

From Vera Laska, ed., *Women in the Resistance and in the Holocaust: The Voices of Eyewitnesses.* Westport, Conn.: Greenwood Press, 1983. Copyright © 1983 by Vera Laska. Reprinted by permission of Greenwood Publishing Group, Inc., Westport, Conn. Notes have been edited and renumbered.

Czechoslovakia was but one village that was razed to the ground, the men shot and the women taken to concentration camps;[2] in Oradour-sur-Glane in France the women and children were also killed. Only Madame Marguerite Roufflance survived to bear witness. In both cases this outrage was perpetrated in retaliation for actions of the resistance.

This opposition to the totalitarianism of National Socialism started in 1933, the moment the Nazis came to power. One must remember that concentration camps were originally set up for political dissenters in Germany, the resisters who from the start opposed the regime. Dachau, Osthofen and Moringen for women were all established in 1933, long before perverted minds came upon the idea of exterminating Jews or Gypsies.

Resistance or underground activities covered a wide range of actions, from passive resistance in not viewing a German film, to outright guerrilla warfare by partisans against the invaders. Americans should be familiar with partisan warfare; they had learned it so well from the Indians that they used it successfully against the British in the American Revolution (but forgot the "art" by the 1960s in Southeast Asia). There was considerable partisan fighting in World War II, with women participating in it, mostly in the Soviet Union and Yugoslavia, and corresponding maquis actions in France. Partisan statistics are usually inflated by both sides; still, partisans performed a valuable service for the Allies. The Soviet partisans claimed 500,000 operations against the invading German armies, who admitted less than half that number.[3] Most activities were directed against railroads and bridges to disrupt troop movements.

In Yugoslavia the partisans under Tito actually liberated the country, the women fighting alongside the men. Greek partisans twice blew up the Athens-Saloniki railroad viaducts, slowing down German troops at critical moments.[4] The Warsaw uprising of August 1944 (not to be confused with the Warsaw ghetto uprising in 1943), was doomed from the start because it was turned into a pawn on the chess board of the East-West power struggle. The Poles lost at least 150,000 people, every tenth of them a partisan man or woman; German casualties went over 10,000.[5] No wonder that the use of the word "partisan" was banned by the Germans for psychological reasons.[6] They usually substituted "bandits." The Slovak uprising of August 1944 was ill-timed and also had political overtones; the revolution in Prague in May 1945 was an urban rather than a strictly partisan uprising,[7] with the Allies *ante portas*. The former uprising failed, the latter succeeded.

The heroic French maquis struggle on the Vercours plateau near Grenoble was also premature, and hopes for Allied help did not materialize in time.[8] In general, partisan groups were underarmed and often suffered for reasons of political rivalry.[9] Many men joined their ranks to escape forced labor in Germany. Although we shall encounter women among the partisans on the following pages, traditionally there were fewer women than men among them. The lines cannot be drawn precisely; many resisters, including women, at times placed explosives under German tanks or carried out violent sabotage against the German war machine, without being partisans.

The activities of the resistance were infinite. Planning and carrying them out involved thousands of women, men and even children. Resisters came from all walks of life, from princes to paupers, and they served as messengers, couriers, typists, writers, editors, guides, chauffeurs, pilots, nurses, doctors, radio operators, cipher clerks, artists, photographers, saboteurs, experts on explosives, forgers of documents and ration coupons. Women on an equal footing with men collected military and economic information, and prepared films, photographs and microfilms to be sent to the Allies. They printed and disseminated information from the BBC, also from WRUL in Boston and WCBX in New York. They wrote, printed and distributed news releases, speeches, pamphlets and jokes about the occupiers, and instructions for sabotage of all degrees. Secretly, they put flowers on patriots' monuments, in defiance of German rules. They placed German leaflets with anti-Nazi propaganda into German newspapers, cars and mailboxes. They arranged classes when the universities were forcefully closed. They displayed at public places posters of bombed cities and crying children, of the burning of books or bombings of synagogues, all under the heading "German Culture."

They purloined German equipment, including arms. They sabotaged railways, blew up fuel depots, mined bridges and tunnels, cut telephone and telegraph wires. They placed explosives into barracks and under vehicles. They slashed tires. They dropped lice on German personnel. They blackmailed or talked the Germans into selling their insignia, belts, identification cards and even their guns.

Some resisters worked alone, others in small groups or in networks. One of the most spectacular networks was that of the French "Alliance," nicknamed by the Gestapo "Noah's Ark." Its chief was Marie-Madeleine Fourcade, known as "Hedgehog"; it cooperated with the Allies and consisted of about 3,000 agents, all under code names of animals. . . . Another example of what a resistance network could accomplish is illustrated by the Czechs whose resistance groups maintained a connection with their central organ. ÚVOD (Ústřední vedení odboje domácího, or Central Leadership of Home Resistance). Between 1940 and 1942, they sent 20,000 telegrams over clandestine radio transmitters to the Allies. They supplied information about "Sea Lyon," the planned German invasion of Great Britain, about the date of the invasion of the USSR (which Stalin allegedly did not believe), and about the developments of the V-1 and V-2 rockets at Pennemünde.[10]

Humor was not lacking in these undertakings. An Italian priest's group transported Jews to safety in German army trucks, with a German driver, as "pilgrims."[11] All over occupied Europe it became the custom to turn around the arrows at highway crossings or switch street signs, creating utter confusion among the supermen of the German armies. Cooks placed laxatives into their food. The "Only for Germans" signs were removed from certain places of entertainment and hung from lampposts. The Danes invaded movie houses and replaced German films with the likes of "In Which We Serve," the British war film.[12] They also distributed Danish cookbooks, but the last pages contained anti-Nazi recipes, urging German soldiers to desert (with one "s").

A most serious side of the resistance was the smuggling of people across closely watched borders to safety. Politicians, officers and young men intending to join the Allied armies, Jews, prisoners of war, or people who simply needed to escape the clutches of the totalitarian regime, were spirited away often under circumstances that put the best of sleuths to shame. This was a dangerous undertaking as smuggling people and aiding members of enemy armed forces carried the death penalty after December 7, 1941. Just like the underground railroad of the American Civil War era, these lines crossed several states, but in this case the frontiers were heavily guarded. One well-traveled line led from the Netherlands through Belgium, France, across the Pyrenees to Spain; another from Bohemia or Poland through Slovakia, Hungary, Yugoslavia and Greece to Lebanon. . . . The organization of these lines was complex, involving messengers, guides and people at each safe-house or meeting point. Some of the best safe-houses were brothels and convents. There were countless women who risked their lives repeatedly to help others escape, and they went back to do it over and over again. Many were caught and perished in concentration camps.

In Denmark women and men, young and old, rich and poor were simply outraged when the Nazis wanted to deport the Jews. They spontaneously organized a network of boats and managed to get most Danish Jews across the sea to Sweden. . . . In some cases resistance continued even in concentration camps and in the factories where camp prisoners were detailed. The extent of this resistance depended on the circumstances of time and place. There were political resistance cells in most camps, the strongest in Buchenwald. They usually aided the few attempts at escape. Only once did resistance succeed in sabotaging a crematorium in Auschwitz, and the members of the Sonderkommando (Special Detail) paid for it with their lives. Less spectacular sabotage went on in most places of work, slowing down production or causing damage. From my own experience I recall weakening hemp threads in the spinning factory of the Gross-Rosen concentration camp complex, or mismeasuring with a micrometer—as I did—the rings that went into the V-2 buzz-bombs, which were manufactured in the infamous tunnel at Nordhausen, next to the concentration camp Dora. It was gratifying after the war to hear Churchill acknowledge the value of our sabotage. Where there was a will, there always was a way to leave a window open overnight so pipes would freeze, or drop a wire among the ball-bearings. We were also alert, collecting evidence for future reference, observing the SS men and women in their treatment or mistreatment of prisoners.

It has been attested by no lesser authority than M.R.D. Foot that "women given the opportunity, were quite as good at sabotage as men." In the underground, "in the secret war against the Nazis, women without number played an invaluable part, participating on terms of perfect equality with men." He acknowledged that "in this field at least the cry for women's liberation was just." He pointed out that some of the most daring women were prostitutes in the service of the resistance, who could easily rifle the pockets of their German customers.[13]

Another well-known resistance leader, the Polish Jan Karski, paid tribute to women who according to him were better suited for undercover or conspiratorial work because they were quicker to perceive danger, more optimistic of the outcome, and could make themselves less conspicuous; they were more cautious and discreet, had more common sense and were less inclined to risky bluffing. He singled out for praise the "liaison women" or couriers, whose lot was the hardest, yet whose contributions were least rewarded. They were more exposed than the organizers, planners, or executors; they often carried incriminating materials or anti-Nazi literature for distribution. One of his couriers visited 240 places a week. She yearned for a sedentary job after the war, even if it meant being a matron in a ladies room![14]

As their fathers and brothers, husbands or lovers were being persecuted, arrested, tortured or executed, as their countries were totally exploited, the women did not lack tangible reasons to be motivated to enter the ranks of the resistance. Others joined to remain true to their beliefs in the principles of human decency, justice and democracy. Teenagers matured into women, mild-mannered women turned into Amazons, and many a time personal jealousies were cast aside in the interest of the cause.

Women, as well as men, in the resistance had to have courage and daring, nerves of steel and a quick wit; they had to possess endurance, a good memory and the rare gift of knowing how to remain silent. Speaking the native language in the place of operation always meant a multiple insurance for a successful mission. It was to the advantage of women that most of their adversaries were male, and women were less suspected of illegal activities by them—the old male underestimation of the power of a woman. This was especially true in feudalistic regions such as Hungary or the less progressive parts of Slovakia. A smile could often accomplish more than a bribe or a gun.

Women proved as inventive as men and often more imaginative. They played the roles of deception more convincingly. Only a woman could have talked her way out of the infamous Star prison of Szeged in Hungary, after having been arrested with two dozen or so foreign men whom she had been guiding toward the Yugoslav border. . . . Only a woman could have had the nerve to slip into a German prison, contact her resistance chief, then convince his captors to release him for money and a promise of immunity after the war, as Christine Granville (the Countess Skarbek) did.[15]

At times girls or women were assigned by the underground to date Germans in order to pry information out of them. This carried an additional burden, for such females were ostracized by their friends in whom they could not confide. Unfortunately, some of them were "taught a lesson" by having their heads shaven the same way as the ones who truly fraternized with the occupiers.

One group of women has to be singled out here for special mention. They were volunteers for the British Special Operations Executive (SOE) in London. About one-third of the 10,000 people in SOE were women. They engaged in sabotage, subversion and escape operations in Belgium, Poland, Yugoslavia and elsewhere. Fifty of them were flown or parachuted into France. Of the fifty, fifteen fell into German hands. Ten were executed by shooting or injections of poison: four in Dachau, three in Natzweiler and three in Ravensbrück, the women's concentration camp. One each died in Ravensbrück and Bergen-Belsen; three survived Ravensbrück.[16] Among those shot at Dachau was Noor Inayat Khan, the wireless operator of the PHONO circuit of SOE, born in the Kremlin to an Indian prince and a cousin of Mary Baker Eddy. She had been betrayed for £500, and was kept in chains after she tried twice to escape. After having successfully organized escape routes between Budapest and Poland, Christine Granville also joined SOE in France. She lived through the maquis disaster at Vercours and caused the desertions of scores of soldiers from the German ranks. "She was certainly the bravest woman I have ever known," Major Peter J. F. Storr of SOE said of her.[17]

They were all heroes, these women of SOE, whether they were princesses, seamstresses or students, daring to do resistance work under false identities, using their minicameras, radio transmitters and compasses hidden in buttons, all under the noses of the Germans.

Women from many walks of life laid their lives on the line for freedom: Jana Feierabend spent three years in Ravensbrück for supporting her husband, a Czech cabinet member in exile. Dr. Milada Horáková, the fearless adversary of all totalitarianism, survived Ravensbrück only to be executed by the Communists. Young Electra Apostolou, involved in student resistance, was defenestrated from the Security Police headquarters in Athens; it was called a suicide. Barbara and Danuta Kolodziejska, the twin nurses with the Polish Home Army (AK)—whatever happened to them and to the thousands of their sisters whose names history no longer recalls?

Then there was Mary Lindell, Countesse de Milleville, "Marie-Claire" in the resistance, her World War I medals dangling from her old Red Cross uniform, majestically ordering about even the German police on her errands on behalf of her boys, the escaped Allied airmen and soldiers. She was determined to outrace death in Ravensbrück—and so she did, but she lost a son to the war.[18]

Beautiful, witty and multilingual Amy Thorpe of Minneapolis, "Cynthia" to the resistance in several countries, a magnetic personality with feline instincts, charmed the Vichy and the Italian naval codes out of the enemy, claiming that there was no rule of thumb for patriotism. "Ashamed? Not in the least," she commented, "my superiors told me that the results of my work saved thousands of British and American lives. Even one would have made it worthwhile."[19]

In most countries, the lines were not always clearly drawn between political resisters and Jews. The rape of their country and hatred toward the same Nazi foe created a common cause. There were Jews in the resistance movements from France to the USSR, from Denmark to Yugoslavia. They ran a double risk if caught. There were gentiles aiding Jews to hide and escape.

There were also separate Jewish resistance and partisan groups.[20] Agents from Palestine infiltrated enemy-occupied territories. In each of these cases women were participating, as did Hannah Senesh, the brave radio-operator parachuted into Hungary. . . .

It is generally believed that the Jews did not fight back. It seems as if there had been a blackout on Jewish resistance since the time of Masada in A.D. 73 to the Warsaw ghetto uprising between April 19 and May 16, 1943. On that Passover morning in April, the fighting leadership of the 60,000 Jews left in the ghetto (over 300,000 had already been shipped out to the east and annihilation at Treblinka) launched an energetic revolt. According to at least one source, a fifteen-year-old girl hurled the first grenade from a balcony. The men and women fought valiantly, with primitive and insufficient arms, against the flame-throwers, machine guns, tanks and planes. The ghetto kept calling for help, but the cry was not answered.

Already in 1942 "Veronika," the writer Sophia Kossak-Szczucka, and "Alina," wife of the former Polish ambassador to the United States Filipowicz, together with other women in the Polish Catholic resistance, had urged organized support for the Jewish Fighters' Organization (ZOB) in the Warsaw ghetto; food, arms, money and false documents were needed. At the time of the ghetto uprising, the AK had hundreds of machine guns, thousands of rifles and pistols, and 30,000 grenades, much of this in Warsaw, according to the report of the Polish Military Attaché in Washington to the Allied High Command.[21] The little and late support coming from the Polish resistance is one of the saddest chapters of the Holocaust, and is outside the scope of the women's participation in it. Among the leaders of the uprising were many women, and several survived to bear testimony of the fierce, desperate fighting and of the merciless heartlessness of man to man. Zivia Lubetkin, Wanda Rothenberg, Masha Glytman, Hela Schipper and Feigele Peltel (who writes under the name of Vladka Meed) were among the eyewitnesses and participants of one of the greatest tragedies within the cataclysm of the Holocaust.

One gets the taste of Nazi behavior from the case of a young girl found in the rubble months after the fighting was over. She was burned and barely alive. The Gestapo was so surprised that they nursed her and gave her decent clothes. After a few weeks of this charity they took her back to the ruins and shot her.[22]

"Little Wanda with the Braids," Niuta Teitelboim, was a self-appointed executioner. She walked into the Gestapo office, shot an officer and walked out with a smile. She repeated it in another Gestapo officer's house, shooting him in bed. In the ghetto she organized the women, teaching them how to use weapons. She smuggled hand grenades and people in and out of the ghetto. She joined the Polish underground, participating in bank robberies and bombings of German coffee houses. She was eventually captured and killed.[23]

It is a myth that the Jews gave in to slaughter without protest or fight. They revolted in five extermination camps, including Treblinka and Auschwitz. It was a Jewish girl, Rosa Robota, who smuggled in the explosives that blew up the Auschwitz crematorium.[24] In Sobibor, where as many as 15,000 Jewish bodies were burned a day at the height of the "production" in 1943, Soviet officer Alexander Pechersky led 600 prisoners in a breakout that put an end to that camp.[25] There were revolts in the ghettos of Czestochowa, Vilno, Bialystok, Minsk, Lachwa and several others. Considerable smuggling of people, food, medicines and arms went on in the ghettos. Babies were drugged with sleeping pills and carried out in coffins. Inventiveness to outsmart the Nazis and death was almost limitless, but unfortunately could not be applied on a large scale.

In Berlin the Jewish Baum Group of men and women operated from 1937 to 1942; they once blew up one of Goebbels' propaganda exhibits. Jewish resistance groups also functioned in Paris and other European cities. "Jews held leadership positions in over 200 partisan detachments" in the Soviet Union.[26] There is no lack of evidence that the Jews fought back.

The Jews also organized their own underground railroad that tried to rescue Jews and take them to Palestine. Ruth Klüger was the only female of a ten-member underground cell that operated the line in Rumania. She was fearless and resourceful; she had to be, dealing with corrupt ship owners, drunk captains and crew, and often unruly passengers on the one hand, and with shifting political intrigue and informers on the other. She sacrificed her marriage and her love, and years of her life for the cause.[27] Another illegal line under William Perl performed similar services in Central Europe. The gentile Lore Rolling married him secretly in order to share his fate and ended up in Ravensbrück. Lola Bernstein, a British subject, joined them as messenger. They defied Nazis and Britons, and while some of their boats sank with great loss of lives, they managed to get 40,000 people out of the Holocaust and to Palestine.[28] These rescues in often leaky boats were among the most traumatic and tragic ones of the war. The main trouble was that they could not accomplish more without massive assistance from abroad.

The least is known about the resistance activities of the other racial group persecuted by the Nazis. Perhaps because so many of them were illiterate at the time, the Gypsies, properly called Romanies, have hardly any chroniclers. We know from a Belgian co-opted into a Gypsy family that both Gypsy men and women took part in the Western European resistance movement, successfully hiding and transporting resistance fighters and fugitives from German justice. One of their safe-houses was a Catholic convent in Paris, where the Mother Superior and the nuns supported the resistance.[29]

Last but not least a few words about resistance among German women, who were, after all, the first victims of the "night and fog" that was descending over Europe. Antifeminism was a subspecies of racism. If a German judge in 1930 said that Jews were not human beings,[30] that could be explained by the lunacy of Nazism. But it seems that Goebbels also placed women outside the human race, when he proclaimed that "the female bird pretties herself for her mate and hatches the eggs for him."[31] The women of Germany in the 1930s were between the devil and the deep blue sea. Hitler was pointing them back to the three k-s, Küche, Kirche, Kinder (kitchen, church, children). If they joined the opposition, much of which was leftist, they encountered the Marxist creed, which placed class liberation above women's liberation. That symbiosis was like the old English legal view of marriage: man and wife were one, and the man was the one; in this case it was Marxism.[32] Still, many resisters joined the Socialist or Communist resistance, and women started filling the jails and the Moringen concentration camp from 1933 on. . . .

Let it be said in summary here that German women inaugurated the march of women up the calvary of resistance against Nazism. Their numbers were relatively small because, politically speaking, both the temptations of rewards for conforming and the threats of punishments for opposing the regime were great. In later years, if a German woman was caught with a Pole, of an inferior race, she could not only have her head shaven bald for shame but also be sent off to Ravensbrück and a twenty-five lash welcome for *Rassenschande* (defiling the race). Even Himmler's own sister Olga did time in Ravensbrück for that very reason.[33] This crime was referred to as "Bett-Politik," bed politics.

It took exceptional moral backbone to stand up to that kind of pressure. Few equaled educator Elisabeth von Thadden, whose school was closed because she would not follow the party line; she was executed on trumped-up charges of treason in 1944, at the time of the mass executions after the coup against Hitler.[34]

The sporadic resistance activities, like that of the White Rose of Sophie and Hans Scholl in 1943 at the University of Munich, were the exception rather than the rule; they were "sucked up like grains of dust in a vacuum cleaner." Without counting Jews, 302,000 Germans were imprisoned in concentration camps for political reasons before the war.[35] It is not known what percentage of them were women. . . .

GYPSIES

Like the Jews, Gypsies were singled out by the Nazis for racial persecution and annihilation. They were "nonpersons," of "foreign blood," "labor-shy," and as such were termed asocials. To a degree, they shared the fate of the Jews in their ghettos, in the extermination camps, before firing squads, as medical guinea pigs, and being injected with lethal substances.

Ironically, the German writer Johann Christof Wagenseil claimed in 1697 that Gypsies stemmed from German Jews. A more contemporary Nazi theorist believed that "the Gypsy cannot, by reason of his inner and outer makeup (Konstruktion), be a useful member of the human community."[36]

The Nuremberg Laws of 1935 aimed at the Jews were soon amended to include the Gypsies. In 1937, they were classified as asocials, second-class citizens, subject to concentration camp imprisonment.[37] As early as 1936, some had been sent to camps. After 1939, Gypsies from Germany and from the German-occupied territories were shipped by the thousands first to Jewish ghettos in Poland at Warsaw, Lublin, Kielce, Rabka, Zary, Siedlce and others.[38] It is not known how many were killed by the Einsatzgruppen charged with speedy extermination by shooting. For the sake of efficiency Gypsies were also shot naked, facing their pre-dug graves. According to the Nazi experts, shooting Jews was easier, they stood still, "while the Gypsies cry out, howl, and move constantly, even when they are already standing on the shooting ground. Some of them even jumped into the ditch before the volley and pretended to be dead."[39] The first to go were the German Gypsies; 30,000 were deported East in three waves in 1939, 1941 and 1943. Those married to Germans were exempted but were sterilized, as were their children after the age of twelve.[40]

Just how were the Gypsies of Europe "expedited"? Adolf Eichmann, chief strategist of these diabolical logistics, supplied the answer in a telegram from Vienna to the Gestapo:

> Regarding transport of Gypsies be informed that on Friday, October 20, 1939, the first transport of Jews will depart Vienna. To this transport 3–4 cars of Gypsies are to be attached. Subsequent trains will depart from Vienna, Mährisch-Ostrau and Katowice [Poland]. The simplest method is to attach some carloads of Gypsies to each transport. Because these transports must follow schedule, a smooth execution of this matter is expected. Concerning a start in the Altreich [Germany proper] be informed that this will be coming in 3–4 weeks. Eichmann.[41]

Open season was declared on the Gypsies, too. For a while Himmler wished to exempt two tribes and "only" sterilize them, but by 1942 he signed the decree for all Gypsies to be shipped to Auschwitz.[42] There they were subjected to all that Auschwitz meant, including the medical experiments, before they were exterminated.

Gypsies perished in Dachau, Mauthausen, Ravensbrück and other camps. At Sachsenhausen they were subjected to special experiments that were to prove scientifically that their blood was different from that of the Germans. The doctors in charge of this "research" were the same ones who had practiced previously on black prisoners of war. Yet, for "racial reasons" they were found unsuitable for sea water experiments.[43] Gypsies were often accused of atrocities committed by others; they were blamed, for instance, for the looting of gold teeth from a hundred dead Jews abandoned on a Rumanian road.[44]

Gypsy women were forced to become guinea pigs in the hands of Nazi physicians. Among others they were sterilized as "unworthy of human reproduction" (*fortpflanzungsunwürdig*), only to be ultimately annihilated as not worthy of living. . . . Gypsies and Jews could have joined in the Polish resistance song: "When a German puts his foot down, the soil bleeds a hundred years."[45] At that, the Gypsies were the luckier ones; in Bulgaria, Greece, Denmark and Finland they were spared.[46]

For a while there was a Gypsy Family Camp in Auschwitz, but on August 6, 1944, it was liquidated. Some men and women were shipped to German factories as slave labor; the rest, about 3,000 women, children and old people, were gassed.[47]

No precise statistics exist about the extermination of European Gypsies. Some estimates place the number between 500,000 and 600,000, most of them gassed in Auschwitz.[48] Others indicate a more conservative 200,000 Gypsy victims of the Holocaust.[49]

SEX

A few remarks are in order about the various sex relationships in concentration camps. I start out with the homosexuals since they were accorded a special category among the inmates and "merited" a separate, pink triangle. The following color-coding was established for the triangles worn below the prisoners' numbers:

yellow—Jews   purple—religious offenders
red—political   pink—homosexual
black—asocials   green—professional criminals

Very little has been written about the tens of thousands of homosexuals who were the damnedest of the damned, the outcasts among the outcasts in the concentration camps. There are really only estimates of figures. During the twelve years of Nazi rule, nearly 50,000 were convicted of the crime of homosexuality. The majority ended up in concentration camps, and virtually all of them perished.[50] According to a recent study, "at least 500,000 gays died in the Holocaust."[51] As Stefan Lorant observed in 1935, the homosexuals "lived in a dream," hoping that the heyday of gays in Germany of the 1920s would last forever. Their awakening was terrible.[52] Yet, the few survivors among them did not qualify for postwar restitution as the Jews or the politicals, because as homosexuals they were outside the law. By German law homosexuality was a crime. After prison sentences most homosexuals were automatically shipped to concentration camps. In 1935, a new law legalized the "compulsory sterilization (often in fact castration) of homosexuals."[53] A special section of the Gestapo dealt with them. Along with epileptics, schizophrenics and other "degenerates," they were being eliminated. Yet homosexuality was still so widespread that in 1942 the death penalty was imposed for it in the army and the SS.

In concentration camps, some pink triangles became concubines of male kapos or other men in supervisory positions among the inmates. They were known as doll boys;[54] this brought them certain protection while the love affair lasted. The pink triangles were constantly abused by the SS, camp officials and fellow prisoners. They were seldom called other names than arseholes, shitty queers or bum-fuckers. They were allowed to talk only to each other, they had to sleep with the lights on and with hands above their blankets. These people were not child molesters; those were considered professional criminals, green triangles.

While men with pink triangles were given the hardest jobs and were being constantly abused for their admitted sexual preference, considerable numbers of "normal" men engaged in homosexual acts with impunity—that was an emergency outlet. This double standard was an additional psychological burden for the pink triangles.

The SS considered it great sport to taunt and torture the homosexuals. The camp commander at Flossenburg often ordered them flogged; as the victims were screaming, he "was panting with excitement, and masturbated wildly in his trousers until he came," unperturbed by the hundreds of onlookers.[55] A sixty-year-old gay priest was beaten over his sexual organs by the SS and told: "You randy old rat-bag, you can piss with your arse-hole in the future." He could not, for he died the next day.[56] Eyewitnesses tell of homosexuals being tortured to death by tickling, by having their testicles immersed alternately into hot and icy water, by having a broomstick pushed into their anus.[57]

Himmler, who wanted to eradicate homosexuals "root and branch," had the idea to "cure" them by mandatory visits to the camp brothel at Flossenburg. Ten Ravensbrück women provided the services with little success. The women here also were told that they would go free after six months, but instead they were shipped to Auschwitz.[58]

The pink triangles worked in the clay pits of Sachsenhausen, the quarries of Buchenwald, Flossenburg and Mauthausen; they shoveled snow with their bare hands in Auschwitz and elsewhere; they were used as living targets at the firing range; they had the dirtiest jobs in all camps. Towards the end of the war, they were told that they would be released if they let themselves be castrated. The ones who agreed were shipped to the infamous Dirlewanger penal division on the Russian front.[59]

While homosexuals were treated in a manner that even within the concentration camp framework was ghastly, their female counterparts, the Lesbians, were seldom hunted down for special treatment. Lesbianism was not on the books as illegal. The Nazis were confident that they could handle females properly to keep them to their "kitchen, church, children." After all, the Führer told women that "emancipation of women is only an invention of the Jewish intellect."[60]

If there is hardly any documentation on male homosexuals in the camps, there is even less available on Lesbians. This will not change until a former inmate who was a Lesbian comes out of the closet and writes her memoirs. There were without doubt hundreds of Lesbian relationships in the camps, but they were difficult to identify and to distinguish from the numerous close friendships that developed among the women in each camp and block.

Stripped almost totally of male companionship by the division of sexes, women formed warm relationships with one another. Occasionally, these relationships developed into Lesbianism, especially if one partner was a bona fide Lesbian. If a woman had a position of eminence in the camp hierarchy, such as a block senior or kapo, with separate quarters, chances were better for such friendships to evolve into a sexual relationship. Endless months or years of living without psychological or physical love, in the constant shadow of death where the slightest move could land one in the gas chamber, compelled many women to the only sexual outlet available to them, that is, an erotic tie with a person of their own sex. As in many prisons, in concentration camps women who would otherwise regard Lesbianism with abhorrence would gradually slide into the acceptance of such liaisons. This was again mostly true in the cases of couples where one of the lovers was in a privileged position, either as a camp trustee disposing with private quarters or working at a place like Canada in Auschwitz, where she was at the source of endless trading in goods—food, clothing, cigarettes or medicine, which served as an irresistible incentive for gaining a sexual partner. While such relationships were dangerous, they could provide a submissive partner with the means for survival and an influential protective arm that could place her in a better job, or exempt her from a death transport.

Survivors are often asked how they could exist without sex. The answer is simple. The instinct for survival, the primary concern for maintaining one's body alive by supplying it with food, took precedence over any other instinct, including the sexual one. The chemical added to the "soup" caused the cessation of menstruation in women and also dulled the senses. The only constantly present yearning was for food, a piece of bread, a potato peel, a rotten piece of vegetable, anything to fuel the body. The will to live manifested itself "in a total devaluation of anything that did not serve this exclusive interest."[61] Viktor E. Frankl, the psychiatrist-survivor, confirms what most former inmates will say, namely, that "everything that was not connected with the immediate task of keeping oneself and one's closest friends alive lost its value."[62] Moral values from the "outside" and conscience were shoved aside by pangs of hunger. An aristocratic and cultured British woman admitted after her liberation: "Nothing else counted but that I wanted to live. I could have stolen from husband, child, parent" just to get some food.[63] While I personally would not have gone that far, I know that hunger took absolute precedence over sex. "Sexual energies . . . were withdrawn in order to rescue the ego from an overpowering excitation. The ego, frustrated by the outer world to an almost unbearable extent, abandoned its genital claims."[64] In simpler language, women in concentration camps had one priority: eat to keep alive.

This also helps explain the fact that sexual relations were carried on almost exclusively among the camp elite, those who were in a position to "organize" food at their place of work, in the kitchens, in the Canada detail where the belongings of new arrivals were sorted, or in the field, wherever they could get their hands directly or indirectly on food. The ever-present fear of punishment and the lack of privacy for physical love making also dampened sexual desire.

Even individual masturbation or fleeting touches of bed partners inviting to sexual play were made difficult by the cramped conditions most prisoners encountered, sleeping as they did five or six on a double cot. The fear of being discovered, ridiculed or beaten up by bed partners prevented many attempts at Lesbian relations.

Because of the hushed up and often hypocritical attitude of society outside and inside the concentration camps at the time and until recently, very little is known about the sexual relations between persons of the same sex in concentration camps. Since the male homosexuals were branded with the pink triangles and were visible, there are at least references to their treatment in the camps. Women's memoirs say little on the subject, either because they considered the subject indelicate or because they chose to remain in the closet. The women who were Lesbians when they entered the camps or became so afterward are hidden behind a double veil of hypocrisy and silence.

Normal sexual relations among female and male inmates were also rare. The keepers of the camps made sure that there was no mingling of the sexes. In some camps female and male working details when passing had to look the other way. On the few occasions when male prisoners entered the women's camp for repairs, they came under guard. They could establish platonic relationships with a girl, even pass her a piece of bread or a note, but they were strictly forbidden to talk to her. Here and there at work in factories or in the field, sex could be possible but was highly dangerous, and given the nature of the sexual act, few women were willing to run the risk and get nothing out of it. Long-time inmates, toughened to camp life and in privileged positions, resorted to sex with their own gender or with members of the opposite sex usually of equally prominent status.

Occasional prostitution, paid in goods or favors, also existed among inmates of the opposite sex, and the "erotic availability became a coin of incommensurate worth, in return for which the chance of biological survival could be won."[65] But such situations were exceptional.

In a place like Auschwitz, a much talked about love affair might consist of two or three fleeting glances over the fence; in a factory it might consist of a piece of bread or a turnip passed stealthily to the "lover" of choice. While postwar marriages between survivors of similar traumatic experiences were not uncommon, few if any germinated inside a concentration camp.

It would take a highly trained and specialized psychiatrist to analyze Hitler's attitudes toward women and their treatment in concentration camps. If it is true that he was a masochist in his own sexual practices, allegedly gratified by young women urinating and defecating on his head,[66] and given the fact that the Reich encouraged the impregnation of unmarried females by the SS in specially provided homes for unwed mothers, then it is contradictory[67] that the SS in the camps—thank God—were so strictly forbidden to have intercourse with female inmates of any nationality. If the Führer feared the thinning of true German blood through Jewish or Slavic mothers, proverbial German efficiency could have certainly found ways of limiting the production of babies to the non-Jewish, non-Slavic women, even though the large proportion of the inmates were Jewish and Polish women. Was it an indication of little faith in the future of the thousand-year Reich that the Nazis did not plan ahead for more babies by potential German fathers serving in the concentration camps?

Considering the tens of thousands of women incarcerated in the camps, rape by the SS was relatively rare. While it is a fact that the SS could—and did—do as they pleased with any female inmate, raping them was not their preference. First of all, most of these women looked unattractive, without hair, dirty, smelly. Second, if caught in intercourse with an inmate, the SS were punished, usually by being shipped to the Russian front, and most SS cherished their camp job which was a sinecure with power. If caught in the act with a Jewess, they could be shot for defaming or defiling the master race. When the affair of SS doctor Rolf Rosenthal and the inmate nurse Gerda Quernheim was discovered in Ravensbrück, they were both confined to the punishment bunker.[68]

In some concentration camps the SS had brothels available, as did a few selected privileged male inmates. Most of all, however, the SS guards had a better selection of sexual partners among their own kind, the female SS guards, who were only too eager to oblige with sexual encounters, under conditions that were much more leisurely and less fraught with danger.

Some of the meanest female guards with bizarre sadism liked to use sex as a means of further tormenting the women in their charge. They paraded in front of the women lined up for rollcall with their boyfriends. They encouraged the men to fondle and paw them.[69] These were not so much cases of voyeurism in reverse, as acts of taunting helpless women whose loved ones were far away or had been murdered. At Ravensbrück chief SS supervisor Dorothea Binz, a former maid, a pretty blond of nineteen with a whip and a dog constantly with her, would come accompanied by Captain Edmund Bräuning to watch the floggings. They would stand arm in arm enjoying the show and "were often seen in a passionate embrace during or after this type of 'ceremony.' "[70] Anthropologist Germaine Tillion, who observed this in Ravensbrück, concluded—and so did others with similar experiences—that there was a close relationship between cruelty and debauchery among the SS of both sexes.[71]

It was also a primitive and perverted instinct that often brought the SS men to the women's showers. On the rare occasions that the women were marched to the real showers (rather than to the ones in the gas chambers), the grapevine somehow always reached the lewdest of the SS, who came to jeer, tease and taunt the defenseless women. Stripping the women naked was also practiced at times of camp selections, or on long and boring Sunday afternoons, when the SS had nothing better to do than to order a roll call and expose the powerless women to a cruel parade.

The situation was worst when Jewish transports arrived in Auschwitz. In that first phantasmagorical hour, the women were in utter shock. They had just been separated from their men; their children had been brutally torn from their arms (they could not know then that it saved their own lives). They were hit by a Babel of voices screaming at them. They smelled burning flesh and singed hair. They were pushed and shoved into the shower rooms, ordered to strip naked and line up to have all their hair shaved from their heads, underarms and pubic regions. In this pandemonium, as they stood quivering and huddling to hide their nakedness, their modesty was further violated by the SS men, who arrived for their bonus show. They made lewd remarks, pointed at them, commented on their shapes, made obscene suggestions, poked into their breasts with their riding crops and sicked their dogs on them. It was the most shocking of all the shocks, a deep blow to their very womanhood. They were petrified with panic, not knowing what to expect next. The depravity of the men, indulging themselves in this cheapest, basest and most disgusting of games, as much for the pleasure of seeing naked females as for the sport of frightening them out of their minds, was one of the cruelest tortures to which women were subjected in the concentration camps. Jaded old-timers stood up to their tormentors by ignoring them. But those newly arrived to these jaws of hell were crushed under the deluge of foul language, obscene gestures and the fact that they were paraded like cattle on the market in front of men. To many women it meant an unforgivable and never to be forgotten humiliation.

NOTES

1. Jacob Glatstein, et al., eds., *Anthology of Holocaust Literature* (New York: Atheneum, 1973), p. xviii.
2. It was this atrocity at Lidice that provided the Allies with the impetus to set up the International Military Tribunals for the war crime trials after the war. Cordell Hull, *Memoirs*, 2 vols. (New York: Macmillan, 1948), II, p. 1185.
3. Walter Laqueur, *Guerrilla: A Historical and Critical Study* (Boston: Little, Brown, 1976), p. 203.
4. M.R.D. Foot, *Resistance: European Resistance to Nazism, 1940–45* (New York: McGraw-Hill, 1977), pp. 180–81.
5. Laqueur, *Guerrilla*, pp. 222–23.
6. Ibid., p. 426.
7. Ibid., p. 205.
8. Michael Pearson, *Tears of Glory: The Betrayal of Vercours, 1944* (London: Macmillan, 1978).
9. Laqueur, *Guerrilla*, p. 230.
10. Henri Bernard, *Histoire de la résistance européenne* (Verviers, France: Gérard, 1968), p. 98.
11. Alexander Ramati, *The Assisi Underground* (London: Sphere Books, 1981), pp. 72–86.
12. Ronald Seth, *Noble Saboteurs* (New York: Hawthorne Books, 1966), p. 62.
13. Foot, *Resistance*, pp. 48, 13–14.
14. Jan Karski, *Story of a Secret State* (Boston: Houghton Mifflin, 1944), pp. 277, 281, 285.
15. Madeleine Masson, *Christine—A Search for Christine Granville* (London: Hamish-Hamilton, 1975), pp. 206–7.
16. M.R.D. Foot, *SOE in France* (London: HMSO, 1966), pp. 465–69.
17. Masson, *Christine*, pp. 213–14.
18. Barry Wynne, *The Story of Mary Lindell, Wartime Secret Agent* (Milton Keynes, England: Robin Clark, 1980).
19. H. Montgomery Hyde, *Cynthia, the Story of the Spy Who Changed the Course of the War* (New York: Farrar, Straus & Giroux, 1965).
20. Jack N. Porter, ed., *Jewish Partisans*, 2 vols. (Washington, D.C.: University Press of America, 1982).
21. Dan Kurzman, *The Bravest Battle, The Twenty-Eight Days of the Warsaw Ghetto Uprising* (New York: G. P. Putnam's Sons, 1976), p. 54.
22. Ibid., p. 336.
23. Yuri Suhl, ed., *They Fought Back* (New York: Crown, 1967), pp. 51–54.
24. Ibid., p. 2. See also Martin Gilbert, *The Holocaust, Maps and Photographs* (New York: Hill and Wang, 1978), pp. 42, 44.
25. Ibid., pp. 7–9.
26. Ibid., pp. 55–68, 3.
27. Ruth Klüger and Peggy Mann, *The Last Escape* (New York: Doubleday, 1973).

28. William R. Perl, *The Four-Front War, From the Holocaust to the Promised Land* (New York: Crown, 1979).

29. Jan Yoors, *Crossing, A Journal of Survival and Resistance in World War II* (New York: Simon & Schuster, 1971), pp. 33–35.

30. George L. Mosse, ed., *Nazi Culture, Intellectual, Cultural and Social Life in the Third Reich* (New York: Grosset & Dunlap, 1966), p. 336.

31. Ibid., p. 41.

32. Lydia Sargent, ed., *Women and Revolution* (Boston: South End Press, 1981), p. 2.

33. Gemma La Guardia Gluck, *My Story* (New York: David McKay, 1961), p. 53.

34. Irmgard von der Lühe, *Elisabeth von Thadden und das Dritte Reich* (Freiburg, Germany: Herder Verlag, 1980).

35. Henry Bernard, *L'Autre Allemagne* (Paris: La Renaissance du livre, 1976), p. 206.

36. Raul Hilberg, *The Destruction of the European Jews* (Chicago: Quadrangle Books, 1961), p. 641; quotation by Staatsrat Turner, chief of the civil administration in Serbia, October 26, 1941, in ibid., p. 438.

37. Donald Kenrick and Grattan Puxon, *Destiny of Europe's Gypsies* (New York: Basic Books, 1972), p. 72.

38. Yoors, *Crossing*, pp. 33–34.

39. Hilberg, *Destruction*, p. 439.

40. Růžena Bubeníčková, et al., *Tábory utrpení a smrti* [Camps of Martyrdom and Death] (Prague: Svoboda, 1969), pp. 189–90.

41. Simon Wiesenthal, *The Murderers Among Us* (New York: Bantam, 1967), pp. 237–38.

42. Kenrick, *Destiny*, pp. 88–90.

43. Hilberg, *Destruction*, pp. 608, 602; the doctors were Hornbeck and Werner Fischer.

44. Ibid., p. 489.

45. Julian E. Kulski, *Dying We Live* (New York: Holt, Rinehart & Winston, 1979), p. 106.

46. Kenrick, *Destiny*, p. 100.

47. Ota Kraus and Erich Kulka, *Továrna na smrt* [*Death Factory*] (Prague: Naše vojsko, 1957), p. 200.

48. Yoors, *Crossing*, p. 34; Bubeníčková, *Tábory*, p. 190.

49. Gilbert, *Holocaust*, p. 22; Kenrick, *Destiny*, p. 184.

50. Eugen Kogon, *The Theory and Practice of Hell* (New York: Farrar, Straus & Co., 1950), p. 38.

51. Frank Rector, *The Nazi Extermination of Homosexuals* (New York: Stein and Day, 1981), p. 116.

52. Stefan Lorant, *I Was Hitler's Prisoner* (New York: G. P. Putnam's Sons, 1935), p. 8.

53. Heinz Heger, *The Men with the Pink Triangle* (Boston: Alyson, 1980), p. 12. This is a unique memoir of an Austrian who spent six years in Sachsenhausen and Flossenburg, surviving as a lover of camp kapos, and ultimately as one of the very few kapos with a pink triangle.

54. Rector, *Nazi Extermination*, p. 144.

55. Heger, *Men*, p. 56.

56. Ibid., p. 42.

57. Ibid., p. 82–83.

58. Ibid., p. 96.

59. Ibid., p. 98.

60. *The Speeches of Adolf Hitler, April 1922–August 1939*, 2 vols. (London: Oxford University Press, 1942), II, p. 731.

61. Elie A. Cohen, *Human Behavior in the Concentration Camp* (New York: Grosset & Dunlap, 1953), p. 139.

62. Viktor E. Frankl, *From Death Camp to Existentialism* (Boston: Beacon Press, 1959), p. 49.

63. Cohen, *Human Behavior*, p. 136.

64. H. O. Blum, "How Did They Survive?" *American Journal of Psychotherapy* 2, No. 1 (1948): 12, quoted in Cohen, *Human Behavior*, p. 140.

65. Anna Pawelczynska, *Values and Violence in Auschwitz* (Berkeley, Calif.: University of California Press, 1979), p. 99.

66. Robert G. L. Waite, *The Psychopathic God, Adolf Hitler* (New York: NAL, 1977), p. 63.

67. Another contradiction was that Hitler never fully mobilized German women for his war machine, yet had no scruples about employing women of other nationalities, mostly Slavs, by the hundreds of thousands in the German factories.

68. Germaine Tillion, *Ravensbrück* (Garden City, N.Y.: Doubleday, 1975), p. 73.

69. Ibid., pp. 62–63.

70. Ibid., pp. 58–59.

71. Ibid., p. 62.

17

Gitta Sereny

. . . The truth can be a terrible thing, sometimes too terrible to live with.

GITTA SERENY

Conservative calculations indicate that more than 800,000 people—mostly Jews but also Gypsies and other non-Jews—were gassed at Treblinka. Another 250,000 victims were murdered at Sobibor. Franz Stangl was sentenced to life imprisonment by a West German court on December 22, 1970, because he had served as commandant at both of those Nazi death camps on Polish soil.

At the end of World War II, Stangl had fled from Europe with the help of Bishop Alois Hudal, one of a number of highly placed Roman Catholic clergymen who enabled ex-Nazis to elude justice. Stangl went to Syria, then to Brazil. There he worked at a Volkswagen plant and reestablished his family life until he was arrested in 1967 and extradited to Germany for trial.

A journalist and Holocaust scholar, Gitta Sereny reported Stangl's trial. Judging him to be "an individual of some intelligence," she wanted to speak with him personally, too. Sereny met Stangl for the first time on April 2, 1971. The result was a memorable series of interviews not only with Stangl but also with his wife, family, and many of his associates. These ingredients formed the basis for Sereny's 1974 book Into That Darkness: An Examination of Conscience. *It remains among the most instructive studies about the Holocaust.*

In the excerpt that follows, the emphasis is not so much on Franz Stangl as it is on his wife, Theresa. So unlike the resisting women discussed by Vera Laska, Frau Stangl mirrors what the Nazis expected of their women and their wives in particular: loyalty, submissiveness, and comfort. True, she did confront her husband: "I

270

know what you are doing in Sobibor. My God, how can they? What are you doing in this? What is your part in it?" For several days, she withheld her sexual favors from him. But in the end she submitted: Though not without its strain, their marriage remained a haven. Thus it helped Stangl to continue his work at Sobibor and Treblinka and to resume a "normal" life after that work was done.

Sereny's disturbing montage of human frailty, self-deception, and blindness shows how memory and justice both can be manipulated, blocked, and denied. Theresa Stangl commanded no death camps, but Sereny probes the responsibility that was hers because she knew so intimately a man who did. Into That Darkness *emerged from the hope that it might reveal, as Sereny put it, "some new truth which would contribute to the understanding of things that had never yet been understood." Reflecting on her findings, she draws the following conclusions: Individuals remain responsible for their action and its consequences, but persons are and must be responsible for each other, too. What we do as individuals, Sereny contends, "is deeply vulnerable and profoundly dependent on a climate of life" that reflects "the fatal interdependence of all human actions."*

Into That Darkness

PREFACE

My dialogues with Franz Stangl, Kommandant of Sobibor and Treblinka, which were published in an abbreviated version in October 1971 in the *Daily Telegraph Magazine* in England (and subsequently in magazines throughout the world), represent the framework upon which this book is constructed: its focus. But they are finally only a small part of it.

I originally conceived the idea of talking with Stangl when, attending his trial in Germany in 1970 (as, in the course of journalistic work, I had attended other Nazi crime trials), I realized that whatever else he might have been, he was, unlike many others I had observed under similar circumstances, an individual of some intelligence.

He was the only Kommandant of an *extermination* camp who had been brought to trial. There were, extraordinarily enough, only four men who specifically filled that function: one is dead, and two have managed to disappear from sight. I had felt for many years that, despite the great number of books and films on the Nazi era, there was a whole dimension of reactions and behaviour we had never yet understood and which yet is deeply relevant to the pressures and perils which beset us now and may threaten us in the future.

I thought it essential, before it became too late, to try at least once, as far as possible unemotionally and with an open mind, to penetrate the personality of a man who had been intimately involved with the most total evil our age has produced. It was important, I thought, to assess the circumstances which led up to his involvement, for once not from our point of view, but from *his*. It was a chance, I felt, to evaluate, through examining his motivations and reactions as he described them rather than as we wished or prejudged them to be, whether evil is created by circumstances or by birth, and to what extent it is determined by the individual himself, or by his environment. Stangl was the last and ultimately the only man of that particular calibre with whom such an experiment could be attempted.

The seventy hours I talked with him—in German—provided a beginning of the answers I sought. But others were needed to complete the picture; not only because his words—those of a profoundly troubled man who frequently revealed extraordinary manifestations of a dual personality—needed to be evaluated against the historical records and the memory of others who had known him, but also because—I came to recognize—no man's actions can be judged in isolation from the external elements that shape and influence his life.

I spent another eighteen months studying records, and seeking out men and women in several corners of the world who were involved in one way or another with the story Stangl told.

Some were intimately involved, like his family in Brazil who continue to love him; some appallingly, like the SS personnel who worked under him and who are now back in society after serving prison sentences, and like high Nazi officials, at one time his administrative superiors; some tragically, like the camp survivors who, after miraculously escaping, have now remade their lives in different countries; some marginally, as diplomatic observers, or as innocent witnesses to the catastrophes in German-occupied Poland. And lastly there were the priests who helped people like Stangl escape from Europe after the Third Reich ceased to exist.

My talks with such priests, and others who were bent on justifying the actions of Pope Pius XII and his advisors, faced me with a disconcerting moral conflict, for I am very conscious of the value to society of the continuity—the stability—which the churches provide, and of their present vulnerability. In the final analysis, however, despite my reluctance to add to the polemics about the record of the Vatican and Pope Pius XII during the Nazi period, the sombre facts, previously unpublished, which emerged during my research could not be ignored. It seemed essential to pinpoint responsibility, if for no other reason than to demonstrate how many men of the Church did *not* share the Vatican's attitude.

As far as it is possible for any thinking individual who was intensely involved, like most young people in Europe at the time, in the events of World

War II, I approached the research for this book with a minimum of prejudice and with determination to question but not to hurt.

The truth is however, that most of the men and women who agreed to relate and examine, with extraordinary honesty and at considerable sacrifice to their peace of mind, the most intense experiences of their lives, ended by revealing themselves deeply, not really for this book but out of their own need to explore the past. I have deleted a few things which appeared likely either to distress them, or cause damage to third persons. None the less, the journey between self-discovery at this level of intensity, and seeing one's thoughts and anguish reproduced in print is a long one, and unfamiliar to most people. I can only hope that the book will contribute to the understanding of all those who helped it come into being, and not cause them embarrassment or pain.

It is through all of them that the theme of this book evolved and crystallized. It is not intended to be primarily an account of horror, though horror is unavoidable, nor is it only an effort to understand one man who was uniquely implicated in the greatest tragedy of our time. It is a demonstration of the fatal interdependence of all human actions, and an affirmation of man's responsibility for his own acts and their consequences. . . .

1

"Did you want your family to come to visit you in Poland?" I asked Stangl.

"I wanted to see them, of course. But don't you see what the fact that they were allowed to come meant? Globocnik had said to me, months before, that I needed leave. But they weren't going to let me go home, like other people. I was in danger, it was quite obvious. And they were making damn sure I knew about it."

Stangl's wife and two little girls, six and four, arrived very soon after his wife had written to tell him of the forms she had filled out, and they all went to stay with the surveyor, Baurath Moser, in Chelm, twenty miles or so from the camp.

"Were you officially on leave then, or did you have to go to Sobibor during that time?"

"While we were in Colm, I was on leave."

"Did your wife ask you what you were doing in Sobibor? What sort of camp it was?"

"Very little then: as I told you she was used to my not being able to speak to her of service matters. And we were so glad just to be together. The funny thing was, though, that I heard nothing from Lublin, or from Wirth. I didn't have any official instructions how long my leave was to be, how long the family would be allowed to stay, or anything. After about three weeks I went to see Höfle and asked him. He said, 'Why make waves? If nobody's said anything to you, why not just keep them here for a while? Find a place to stay nearby, and don't worry.' "

"What did you think that meant?"

"I was so glad to have them there, you know; it was such a relief, I just decided not to think, just to enjoy it. I found rooms for us on an estate just a few kilometres from Sobibor camp, near the village. It was a fish-hatchery belonging to Count Chelmicki [he said 'Karminsky', but Frau Stangl corrected this later]."

"How far exactly was that from the camp?"

"Five kilometres."

Pan Gerung, the custodian of Sobibor, remembered the fish-hatchery well thirty years later; it had been demolished a year before I visited Poland. But he and his wife were dubious about the Stangl family having stayed there. "You are probably confusing it with a big white house the Germans built as a kind of country club for their officers, on the other side of the lake. They used to go there for weekends, for the fishing—and other days too, in the evenings. An enormous amount of drinking went on there, and other things. Poles weren't allowed in."

I replied that I was sure it was the fish-hatchery the Stangls had stayed at— no doubt they had requisitioned rooms there because the other place was unsuitable for small children.

"But the fish-hatchery was four kilometres from the camp, through the woods," said Pan Gerung. "If he really rode through these woods, on his own—why, anyone could have shot him, any time." This Polish inhabitant of a different Sobibor, in a different age, sounded honestly puzzled, even amazed. And what he said was true: everyone in those parts knew what Sobibor was; everyone knew Stangl was the camp's Kommandant; anyone— if for no other reason than a gesture—could have shot him on those almost daily rides through the woods. But no one did.

"The Chelmickis," I said to Stangl, *"must have known or guessed what was going on at Sobibor. However secret an operation it was, there must have been rumours. Did your wife still not know?"*

"The Chelmickis were very nice. But I don't think they would have dared to talk about it even if they had heard rumours." ("... The Jews who worked in the fish-hatchery," Frau Stangl was to write to me later, "were all treated very well. And so was I. . . .")

"But my wife *did* find out, though not from them," Stangl said. "One of the non-coms, Unterscharführer Ludwig, came by once while I was out. He had been drinking and he told her about Sobibor. When I got back she was waiting for me. She was terribly upset. She said, 'Ludwig has been here. He told me. My God, what are you doing in that place?' I said, 'Now, child, this is a service matter and you know I can't discuss it. All I can tell you, and you must believe me: whatever is wrong—*I* have nothing to do with it.' "

"Did she believe this, without further questions or arguments?"

He shrugged. "She spoke of it sometimes. But what else could I say to her?

It did make me feel, though, that I wanted her away from there. I wanted them to go home. The school term was about to start for the older of the girls anyway. . . ." the sentence trailed off.

"It was too difficult having them there now that she knew. Wasn't that it?"

He shrugged his shoulders again and for a moment buried his face in his hands. "Just about then I had a message that I was to come to Warsaw to see Globocnik—by this time he had two offices, one in Warsaw, the other in Lublin. Now it seemed even more urgent to me to get the family home. I got hold of Michel and said that I entrusted my family to him; for him to get them out as quickly as possible. Then I said goodbye to my wife and children and went to Warsaw."

"When did they leave?"

"Later I found that Michel got them out in four days. But I only found that out after they had gone. And I didn't know what awaited me in Warsaw. I thought that this was probably it—that I was finally for it. But when I got to Globocnik's office, he was nearly as friendly as he'd been the first time we met. I couldn't understand it. He said, almost as soon as I came in, 'I have a job for you; it is strictly a police assignment.' I knew right away there was something wrong with it, but I didn't know what. He said, 'You are going to Treblinka. We've already sent a hundred thousand Jews up there and nothing has arrived here in money or materials. I want you to find out what's happening to the stuff; where it is disappearing to.' "

"But this time you knew where you were being sent; you knew all about Treblinka and that it was the biggest extermination camp. Here was your chance, here you were, face to face with him at last. Why didn't you say right there and then that you couldn't go on with this work?"

"Don't you see? He had me just where he wanted me; I had no idea where my family was. Had Michel got them out? Or had they perhaps stopped them? Were they holding them as hostages? And even if they were out, the alternative was still the same: Prohaska was still in Linz. Can you imagine what would have happened to me if I had returned there under these circumstances? No, he had me flat: I was a prisoner."

"But even so—even admitting there was danger. Wasn't anything preferable by now to going on with this work in Poland?"

"Yes, that's what we know now, what we can say now. But then?"

"Well, in point of fact, we know now, don't we, that they did not *automatically kill men who asked to be relieved from this type of job. You knew this yourself, didn't you, at the time?"*

"I knew it *could* happen that they wouldn't shoot someone. But I also knew that more often they *did* shoot them, or send them to concentration camps. How could I know which would apply to me?"

This argument, of course, runs through all of Stangl's story; it is the most essential question at which, over and over, I found myself stopped when talking with him. I didn't know when I spoke with him and I don't know now at which point one human being can make the moral decision for another that he should have the courage to risk death.

However, my reactions to some of the things Stangl said in this part of his account changed slightly subsequently, as a result of my conversations with his wife. These demonstrated very clearly that—if nothing else—he had manipulated events, or his memory of events, to suit his need to rationalize his guilt, his awareness of his guilt or (at that point in our talks) his need to avoid facing it.

"He had written to me soon after he got to Poland saying he was 'constructing'," said Frau Stangl, "but he didn't say what. And all I could think of was how glad I was he wasn't at the front. And then, when he'd been there for a long time without leave [it was interesting that she considered two months 'a long time'], he wrote to say that they were going to let us come to visit him as he was not going to be allowed on leave away from the East at all. And shortly afterwards a Wehrmacht officer arrived with travel papers for us.

"The two children and I travelled out in June. I remember we missed the connection in Cracow; you can imagine what it was like travelling with two small girls in the middle of the war.

"No, I knew nothing—nothing whatever. He met us off the train, and, of course, we hadn't seen him in months, it was just wonderful to see him again. Once again, that was all I could think of. We went to stay in Chelm in the house of the chief surveyor, Baurath Moser. In a way I suppose that was the first time I came into contact with anything to do with Jews [in Poland] because he had two young Jewish girls there, as domestic servants. They were called the two *Zäuseln**—I don't really know why. They were nice girls, helped me with the children and all that. Although I hadn't any notion of the true situation, there were things that made me wonder: you see, the walls of the house were very thin and I would hear Baurath Moser in the room next to ours when I was in bed. He had both the girls—the *Zäuseln*—in there and . . . well . . . he did things to them, you know. It would start every night with his telling them what to take off first and then what next and what to do and so on . . . it . . . it was very embarrassing. And I didn't like what he did to the girls; but, you know, I mainly asked myself, 'Why do they do it? Why don't they just give notice?' That's how little I knew." (Later, in a letter, Frau Stangl mentioned these girls again—and this time slightly differently: "The two *Zäuseln* in Chelm," she wrote, "were always merry, had good food, and were very neat.")

"But I was very glad when Paul told me he had arranged for us to move to the fish-hatchery—it would be better for all of us, and I was glad to get the

---

* Probably best translated as "tousle-heads."

children away from that house. No, while we were in Chelm, Paul was on leave; it was when we moved to the fish-hatchery that he had to go back to work.

"And one day while he was at work—I still thought constructing, or working at an army supply base—Ludwig came with several other men, to buy fish or something. They brought schnapps, and sat in the garden drinking. Ludwig came up to me—I was in the garden too, with the children—and started to tell me about his wife and kids; he went on and on. I was pretty fed up, especially as he stank of alcohol and became more and more maudlin. But I thought, here he is, so lonely—I must at least listen. And then he suddenly said, *Fürchterlich*—dreadful, it is just dreadful, you have no idea how dreadful it is.' I asked him 'What is dreadful?'—'Don't you know?' he asked. 'Don't you know what is being done out there?'—'No,' I said, 'What?'—'The Jews,' he answered. 'The Jews are being done away with.'—'Done away with?' I asked. 'How? What do you mean?'—'With gas,' he said. 'Fantastic numbers of them [*Unheimliche Mengen*].'

"He went on about how awful it was and then he said, in that same maudlin way he had, 'But we are doing it for our Führer. For him we sacrifice ourselves to do this—we obey his orders.' And then he said, too, 'Can you imagine what would happen if the Jews ever got hold of *us*?'

"Then I told him to go away. I could hardly think. I was already crying. I took the children into the house. I sat there, staring, staring into an abyss— that's what I saw; *my* husband, my man, my good man, how could he be in this? Was it possible that he actually saw these things being done? I knew about Wirth—Paul had talked about him from the moment I arrived, even at the station—but that wasn't what I was thinking of then. . . . My thoughts were in a whirl; what I needed above all was to confront him, to talk to him, to see what he had to say, how he could explain. . . ."

She left the children playing in their room and went out along the path in the forest she knew he would have to take to ride home. "I walked for a long time and sat down on a tree-trunk to wait for him. When he rode up and saw me from afar, his face lit up—I could see it. It always did—his face always showed his joy the moment he saw me. He jumped off his horse and stepped over—I suppose to put his arm around me. But then he saw at once how distraught I was. 'What's happened?' he asked. 'The children?'

"I said, 'I know what you are doing in Sobibor. My God, how can they? What are *you* doing in this? What is your part in it?' First he asked me how I'd found out, but I just cried and cried; and then he said, 'Look, little one, please calm down, please. You must believe me, I have nothing to do with any of this.' I said, 'How can you *be* there and have nothing to do with it?' And he answered, 'My work is purely administrative and I am there to build—to supervise construction, that's all.'—'You mean you don't see it happen?' I asked. 'Oh yes,' he answered. 'I see it. But I don't *do* anything to anybody.'

"Of course, I didn't know he was the Kommandant: I never knew that. He told me he was the *Höchste Charge*. I asked him what that meant and he said again he was in charge of construction and that he enjoyed the work. I thought, 'My God.'

"We walked back to the house, me crying and arguing and begging him over and over to tell me how he could be in such a place, how he could have allowed himself to get into such a situation. I am sure I made no sense—I hardly knew any more what I was saying. All he did, over and over, was reassure me—or try. That night, I couldn't bear him to touch me—it was like that day in 1938 when I had kept away from him for weeks . . . weeks and weeks, until I finally felt sorry for him . . . but that night in Sobibor-Salovoce he seemed to understand. He just kept stroking me softly and trying to quiet me. Even so, it was several days before I . . . let him again. And that was only just before he was called to Lublin to see Globocnik. I finally allowed myself to be convinced that his role in this camp was purely administrative—of course I *wanted* to be convinced, didn't I? But anyway—I can't quite remember the sequence of events, but I know I wouldn't have parted from him in anger.

"We were rowing on the lake with the children that day when Michel arrived on the shore. This was the only time I saw him. No, *he* never did anything for us after Paul left. I don't know what Paul meant when he told you it was Michel who 'got us out'. Michel called to us across the lake and said that a message had come through to say that Paul was to report to Globocnik. We rowed back to the shore and Michel said, 'They mean now, at once; you have to come with me right away.'

"We went back to the house and I remember, I helped him get changed and then he left.

"After he had gone that day I got terribly depressed: you see, although I had allowed him to convince me that he wasn't really part of what was happening, I couldn't forget it; how could I have? That night Countess Chelmicki found me crying. In my terrible need to talk to somebody I told her what I had found out.

" 'Don't you think we know?' she asked. 'We've known about it since the beginning. But you must calm yourself; it is dreadful, but there is nothing to be done. We are convinced that your husband is a decent man.' She really cared. She spoke to me—you know—like a friend, intimately and warmly. I was very comforted by her kindness.

"The next day Paul came back, just for a day, or even less. He said he was being transferred, to Treblinka—a place, he said, that was in a terrible mess, where the worst *Schweinereien* were being done, and where it was necessary to make a clean sweep with an iron broom. I said, 'My God, I hope not another place like this one here,' and he said no, he didn't think so—for me not to worry. I said I wanted to go home."

I asked Frau Stangl whether it had not been her husband who told *her* he wanted them to go home.

"No, I told *him*. And, well . . . then he left. I'd told him I wanted to leave as quickly as possible—I didn't want to impose on the Chelmickis a moment longer than necessary. Anyway, the next day Reichleitner came to the fish-hatchery."

Franz Reichleitner, who had been with Stangl at Hartheim, took over as Kommandant of Sobibor after Stangl left. "He said he wanted to have a look around the fish-hatchery," Frau Stangl continued. "Well, of course I knew him, you know, because he had married my friend Anna Baumgartner from Steyr and so I felt I had something in common with him; I trusted him you know, so I said, 'You know, if I thought that my Paul had anything to do with the awful things which are being done at Sobibor, I wouldn't stay with him another day.'

"He answered quite spontaneously, you know, not thinking it over at all. He said right away, 'My God, Frau Stangl,' he said, 'but your husband has absolutely *nothing* to do with that. That's all Wirth. You don't think, do you, that he would allow anyone to rob him of the pleasure of doing away with the Jews? You know how he hates them. Your husband's part in this is purely administrative.' " (Before Frau Stangl told me this, she had already testified at the trial, that after the war, in Brazil, Gustav Wagner had also told her that her husband had had nothing to do with the extermination of the Jews in Sobibor.) "Well," she went on, "to be truthful, that really did relieve my mind and lighten my spirits. After all, unless Paul and Reichleitner had carefully planned it together—and to tell the truth, the possibility did occur to me—the fact that they told me exactly the same thing, in the same words, had to mean it was true. Why otherwise should Reichleitner have bothered to tell me?"

It didn't occur to Frau Stangl then or now that Reichleitner, who had just taken the job over from Stangl, could have found this conversation with his friend's wife awkward on his own account, and might conceivably have been indirectly stating, or justifying, his own case.

"I left a very few days after that," she said. "I think it was Reichleitner who brought me the travel documents signed by Globocnik—it may have been just two or three days after Paul left. I think Reichleitner also drove us to the train in Chelm. And so I went home. I had a letter from Paul soon after, but it said nothing about Treblinka; he had told me I must *never* mention Treblinka nor anything about it, or make any of my 'remarks' in my letters—he knew me so well—as all letters were censored. . . . I didn't see him after that for months. . . ."

"Resl and the two girls came to stay with me overnight on their way back from Poland," said Helene Eidenböck in Vienna. "I went to meet them at the East Station. No, she didn't seem very depressed, not that I remember. She said they'd been staying at a fish-hatchery and I saw all their photographs . . . was it then or later, I am not sure—of him too, yes, in that white jacket, with the children, and a big dog too I remember. . . . Later, of course, when we read what he was—I thought of that photo and thought, 'It only needed the riding crop and there he was, just as they described him at the trial. . . .' " . . .

2

"On the night it happened, February 28, 1967," said Frau Stangl, "I had seen a lot of cars around. Our street was full of them. But it was only in retrospect I realized that I had noticed this. At the time I thought nothing of it. Renate was already home. Isolde came with Paul—they had stopped on the way for a beer in a bar. I heard a commotion outside and went to the window. Police cars were drawn across the street, blocking it off on each side; our car was surrounded by crowds of police. Paul was pulled out of the car—handcuffed—Isi fell to the ground shouting for us; that's what I had heard, and rushed to the window; but the police car with Paul in it, followed by a string of others, was off before I could even get out of the door. Isi was almost incoherent with shock. She said Paul's face went yellow when it happened.

"We phoned Gitta and then we went from police station to police station to look for him, but nobody knew anything. Until finally we got to the DOPS. And they said we should be glad they had taken him—if they hadn't, the Israelis would have picked him up. After that, all we knew was what we read in the papers.

"In May or so we read that he had been moved to Brasilia, so we went up there. He was in a military prison. He looked—oh, just terrible, very very bad. And he said it was dreadful. He cried. I asked him about Treblinka; by this time, you know, we had read so much. 'I don't know what pictures you saw,' he said, 'perhaps you saw pictures of other camps. . . .' He was so distraught, all I could think of was to console him. All I wanted then was to be for him someone he could be sure of, someone he could lean on.

"The children had come up with me, each driving part of the way. He was so wonderful with them, never gave way, never cried while they were in the room, smiled at them, walked them to the gate and waved goodbye to them. But of course, this was the first time it became real to them; seeing him like this, in prison, was a traumatic experience for them. It was after that Brigitte became ill.

"After that I went up there two or three more times. And on June 22 he was extradited.

"The two years at our Brooklin house had been our happiest in Brazil. We had had friends—mostly the children's friends from Volkswagen, but they were friends for us too: Hungarian, Dutch, Brazilians. No, I don't remember any Germans we were friends with. I don't think Dr. Schulz-Wenk even knew we existed then," she said. [Dr. Schulz-Wenk, then Director of Volkswagen, SA, was one of the people about whom it was said that he helped former Nazis.]

"After Paul was taken to Germany, we moved back to São Bernardo. It was the only sensible thing to do; we had only the money the two girls were earning, and my small pension—200 cruzeiros. We knew we were going to need a great deal of money, for Paul's defence. If we sublet the Brooklin house and went back to live modestly in São Bernardo, there was a chance of being able to manage. We moved back in October 1967.

"Everybody drew away from us after this; everybody we knew at Volkswagen and everybody else. Thank God, the girls were allowed to keep their jobs—we were grateful for that. Dr. Schulz-Wenk is supposed to have said, 'The girls have nothing to do with it'; that's when he knew about us, you know, but not before."

It was about then that Frau Stangl had a visit from the Austrian Gustav Wagner, who had been at Hartheim and Sobibor with Stangl, and had fled with him from Austria. Suchomel had told me that the two men were "close friends". When Stangl had told me of his distress at Stanislav Szmajzner's "forty-page" attack on him, I had pointed out that in fact only about two pages of the book were devoted to him, whereas Szmajzner wrote with far greater bitterness and horror about Wagner. "Really?" said Stangl. "And yet they live cheek by jowl in Brazil." At first Frau Stangl said that she couldn't understand what he had meant by this remark. Later she said: "Oh, it's because Wagner went for a while with a girl who later married in Goiania [where Stan Szmajzner lives]." But it would appear that Wagner in fact never lived in Goiania, whereas he did live for a long time thirty kilometres away from the Stangls, in São Paulo.

Frau Stangl was somewhat reluctant to discuss Wagner. This, I think (although I felt differently at first) was primarily because she disliked him and didn't want to be associated in my mind with such a person—he is by all accounts a particularly nasty piece of work. Finally, however, she admitted that they knew him quite well and that he "dropped in" on them.

"But I didn't like Paul to associate with him," she said. "He is a vulgar man—we have nothing in common with him."

Gustav Wagner evidently felt otherwise. "He came to see me after Paul had been deported," said Frau Stangl. "He wanted money; he said he was down and out and would I lend him money to bury his wife who had just died. I said I didn't have any to lend him. He said, 'Why don't you and I set up house together? I haven't got anybody any longer and as for Franz—they are going to do him in anyway over there, and you'll be alone too.'" Frau Stangl said she was outraged and threw him out, and never saw him afterwards—but she did in fact lend him money which, she wrote later, he had never returned.

At Stangl's trial she was asked about Gustav Wagner and said that she heard he had gone to Uruguay. Later she wrote to me putting it slightly differently. "He informed me of his intention to emigrate to Uruguay," she wrote. She also told me that she heard, not long before I came to São Paulo in the autumn of 1971, that a woman had seen Wagner in São Bernardo, "looking like a beggar, with torn clothes and shoes."

"I didn't see Paul for three years," said Frau Stangl. "He wrote me once a week. All we did—all we could do—was hope. I still didn't believe he had been Kommandant; he denied it to me to the end. I know he admitted it to you—but never to me. To me he always spoke of the gold, the construction work, and Wirth—he did that every time, every single time—in Brasilia too.

"On May 8, 1968, I received a summons to testify at his trial and I flew to Germany on the 12th; I had been ready because I knew it was going to happen.

"I went to see Paul at the prison in Duisburg, where he was then; I went with his lawyer, Herr Enders. I found him enormously changed, depressed, terribly controlled.

"I testified on May 22. I didn't attend the trial because Paul didn't want me to; he was afraid, he said, I'd be attacked or that people—the public you know—would be rude to me. I was only in the court three times: when I testified; when Szmajzner testified; and the day of the sentencing. But even though I didn't attend any other day, I went to the building every day and sat outside, just to be near him. I told him, so that he would know while it was going on, that I was there, just outside the door, and thinking of him. I went there, or I went to church.

"When I first arrived in Düsseldorf they had arranged for me to stay at a kind of hostel, but it was horribly depressing—no, not that anyone was unkind to me, it wasn't that: nobody ever was. It was just that it was a kind of institution and I couldn't stand it. But then I went to stay with a wonderfully kind woman in her house and it saved my sanity. In the evenings we talked and she became a friend." Frau Stangl also said, in another conversation, that she went to museums and theatres.

Frau Stangl's sister Heli commented on this period too. "Resl," she said. "Yes, I've seen her, she stayed with me when she came over last [in 1970]. She went to see all the others in the family. We got closer this time than we had ever been. Still, I never could understand how she could bear to go back to Steyr where everybody knew her." She shrugged. "Well, she felt she could—it is her business. Last time she was here she was quite gay, chipper. . . .

"Do I think she could have stopped him?" She shrugged again. "I think she was ambitious too. You see, my life was good too, even though I was alone for so long. But it was so different—so very, very different—it's difficult for me to understand. But Resl always wanted to get to the top. Well, I suppose in a way she did get there. . . ."

"My own testimony took two hours," Frau Stangl said about the trial. "I had never been in a court before and I was horribly nervous. Of course I didn't tell them that I hadn't believed Paul's story about the illegal Party membership and how disappointed I was. How could I have told them? If Paul hadn't told you about this himself, perhaps I wouldn't have told you either. They didn't believe that I hadn't known about Hartheim, and yet it was true. Yes, they asked me whether I knew what Sobibor was when I was there. I told them that a drunken *SS* man told me about it. . . .

"When I first arrived," she said, "they only allowed me to see Paul twice a week, for fifteen minutes with a guard. Later—although the guards were always there—they became much nicer; I could stay longer and sometimes they even allowed me to bring him some beer. What was strange," she said, "was that often he would hardly talk to me. He'd sit opposite me at the table in that little interview cell, but he'd chat with the guards, not with me; he'd talk to them about their leaves, their excursions, places he knew, had been to. It hurt me, and sometimes I'd say, 'Don't you want to talk to *me*?' "

There was good reason for this: Stangl knew that by this time she had read everything about the trial and him. He desperately wanted her there—she was allowed to kiss and hug him—but he dreaded her questions and, by this nervous chatter with the guards, was avoiding them at all cost. In my conversations with him it emerged very clearly that in the end the only thing that mattered to him was her and his children's continued loyalty and love; and equally, how aware he was of his wife's profound aversion to what he had done. He was not sufficiently perceptive to realize how thin the line was—for her too—between rationalization of what he had done and accepting it, and living up to her own fundamental principles—and condemning him. He could only think, with real dread, of the possibility—or, as by that time, he probably knew, the probability—of her rejecting him.

Basically, it was when he came to terms with the realization that she knew—that after what had happened, even if he ever got out of prison, life with his family would be impossible—that he decided to talk to me. I came to understand this in the course of the conversations with him; and he, in a way, confirmed it in letters he wrote to his wife until shortly before he died, about his feelings about these talks.

3

The last time I saw Frau Stangl we talked about causes and effects, reasons beyond reasons.

"The day he was sentenced," she said, "I know you won't agree with me about this, as you haven't agreed about other things, but I must go on being honest with you: those other Germans who sat in judgment over him, what do you think they would have done in his place? One of the jury-men came up to me later and said, 'I don't want you to think that it was unanimous—it wasn't.' "

"You see, I can't help thinking that there has to be a reason for everything, even this terrible thing that happened. The universe isn't without reason—nothing is. My sister goes to Israel every year, to a kibbutz—she has told me so much about it. I really ask myself, these people who died—they were heroes, martyrs, wasn't there a reason, a sense in their sacrifice? Could that extraordinary country have been built if it hadn't been for this catastrophe?"

I could not help but suspect that she and her husband had come to this consoling conclusion together, for he had said something very similar to me. *"In retrospect,"* I had asked him, *"do you think there was any conceivable sense to this horror?"*

"Yes, I am sure there was," he replied. "Perhaps the Jews were meant to have this enormous jolt to pull them together, to create a people, to identify themselves with each other."

It is impossible not to feel a sense of outrage at hearing either of these two people, so horrifyingly involved, say this. And yet, the way they both said it, they were, if not honourable, certainly trying—and meaning—to search for honesty.

At the very end of our conversations I told Frau Stangl that I needed to ask her an extremely difficult question which I wanted her to think about deeply before attempting to answer. "It is the most important question as far as my talks with you are concerned," I said, "and to me, the reply you give me will determine your own position; the degree, if you like, of your own guilt." I suggested that, before replying, she should leave me for a while, lie down, think about it.

"Would you tell me," I asked, "what you think would have happened if at any time you had faced your husband with an absolute choice; if you had said to him: 'Here it is; I know it's terribly dangerous, but either you get out of this terrible thing, or else the children and I will leave you.' What I would like to know," I said, "is: if you had confronted him with these alternatives, which do you think he would have chosen?"

She went to her room and lay down; I could hear the bedsprings creak as she lowered herself on to the bed. The little house was silent. It was very hot outside and the sun shone into the living room where I sat waiting, for more than an hour. When she came back she was very pale; she had been crying, had then washed her face and combed her hair and, I think, put on some powder. She was composed; she had made a decision—the same decision her husband had made six months earlier in the prison in Düsseldorf; to speak the truth.

"I have thought very hard," she said. "I know what you want to know. I know what I am doing when I answer your question. I am answering it because I think I owe it to you, to others, to myself; I believe that if I had ever confronted Paul with the alternatives: Treblinka—or me; he would . . . yes, he would in the final analysis have chosen me."

I felt strongly that this was the truth. I believe that Stangl's love for his wife was greater than his ambition, and greater than his fear. If she had commanded the courage and the moral conviction to force him to make a choice, it is true they might all have perished, but in the most fundamental sense, she would have saved him.

This was not, however, the last word to be spoken between Frau Stangl and me on this trip to Brazil. The next morning I had to leave my hotel at 6 A.M. to fly to the interior, and only returned late in the evening. At the desk they handed me a letter. "A lady brought it," the clerk said, "early this morning."

"Dear Doña Gitta, I want to beg to correct an answer to a question you asked me where I had, at the time of our talk, too little time to ponder my reply.

"The question was whether my husband, in the end, would have found the courage to get away from Treblinka had I put before him the alternative 'me, or Treblinka'. I answered your question—hesitatingly—with, 'He would have chosen me.'

"This is not so, because as I know him—so well—he would never have destroyed himself or the family. And that is what I learned to understand in the critical month of July 1943.

"I can therefore in all truthfulness say that, from the beginning of my life to now, I have always lived honourably.

"I wish you, dear Doña Gitta, once more all the best,

your

Thea Stangl"

I telephoned Frau Stangl late that night.

"When did you write this letter?" I asked her. "It sounds like something written in the middle of the night. This isn't really what you want to say, is it?"

She cried. "I thought and thought . . ." she said. "I didn't know what to do. So finally I wrote it at 3 o'clock in the morning and brought it in on the first bus."

"What would you like me to do?" I asked.

"I don't know. I just don't know."

I told Frau Stangl that I would put in my book what she had said to me the previous day—which I thought was the truth. But that I would also add the letter, which only showed what we all know, which is that the truth can be a terrible thing, sometimes too terrible to live with. . . .

EPILOGUE

I do not believe that all men are equal, for what we are above all other things, is individual and different. But individuality and difference are not only due to the talents we happen to be born with. They depend as much on the extent to which we are allowed to expand in freedom.

There is an as yet ill-defined, little-understood essential core to our being which, given this freedom, comes into its own, almost like birth, and which separates or even liberates us from intrinsic influences, and thereafter determines our moral conduct and growth. A moral monster, I believe, is not born, but is produced by interference with this growth. I do not know what this core is: mind, spirit, or perhaps a moral force as yet unnamed. But I think that, in the most fundamental sense, the individual personality only exists, is only valid from the moment when it emerges; when, at whatever age (in infancy, if we are lucky), we begin to be in charge of and increasingly responsible for our actions.

Social morality is contingent upon the individual's capacity to make responsible decisions, to make the fundamental choice between right and wrong; this capacity derives from this mysterious core—the very essence of the human person.

This essence, however, cannot come into being or exist in a vacuum. It is deeply vulnerable and profoundly dependent on a climate of life; on freedom in the deepest sense: not license, but freedom to grow: within family, within community, within nations, and within human society as a whole. The fact of its existence therefore—the very fact of our existence as valid individuals—is evidence of our interdependence and of our responsibility for each other.

18

Claudia Koonz

Nazi wives did not offer a beacon of strength for a moral cause, but rather created a buffer zone from their husbands' jobs.

CLAUDIA KOONZ

Some time after Gitta Sereny interviewed Franz and Theresa Stangl, historian Claudia Koonz met a woman whose life also led "into that darkness." The subject of Koonz's interview was Gertrud Scholtz-Klink. Although she never had anything like the political clout of a Himmler, Göring, or Goebbels—no woman in the Third Reich could have expected to exert such influence—Scholtz-Klink did have an impressive title. She was Reichsfrauenführerin, *which meant that she had the dubious distinction of being the top women's leader in the Nazis' antifeminist regime. Her responsibilities were to tout the joys of childbearing, the importance of Nazi "family values," and all the ways in which the German woman could glorify the Third Reich.*

Koonz's encounter with Scholtz-Klink is the point of departure for her pathbreaking Mothers in the Fatherland: Women, the Family, and Nazi Politics. *It is one of the most extensive studies of women in Nazi Germany, a population whose importance has been underplayed, if not ignored, by too many historical studies. Compiling data for her book, Koonz studied not only Scholtz-Klink and the women who followed her but many others as well, including women who resisted Hitler and women who survived the Nazi camps.*

While the Nazi state gave women little political power, they did have their special spheres of influence: Kinder, Kirche, Küche (*children, church, and kitchen*). *Relatively few German women participated directly in the "Final Solution." Nevertheless, Koonz stresses, by holding their expected places in Nazi society German women sustained the Third Reich's racism and genocide, including the ways in which those policies targeted women in particular.*

Koonz details how that support was engendered by a split between private *and* public *life that Nazism encouraged. Specifically, with the help of Scholtz-Klink and her associates, the Nazi system urged women to create home environments that kept the private, feminine world of the family cocooned from the public, masculine sphere of political duty. The latter often required "brutality, coercion, corruption, and power"—the unpleasant work that somebody had to do if the Third Reich's "glory" was to be maintained. Thus Nazi wives, for example, "gave the individual men who confronted daily murder a safe place where they could be respected for who they were, not what they did."*

In a bureaucratized world like Hitler's Third Reich, it was possible for Nazi men to separate themselves from their public deeds because, at the end of the day, they could go home—or at least think of home—where their women awaited them, as Koonz says, "ready to still [their] nightmares and restore [their] humanity." In turn, most Nazi women, far from wanting to know the details of their men's public lives, cultivated instead their own ignorance of public life and thereby further helped their men avoid facing responsibility for participation in the Holocaust.

Koonz's study makes a key point painfully clear. Her examination of gender responses to the evil perpetrated by the Third Reich shows that German men and women often responded in a similar manner: poorly.

Consequences: Women, Nazis, and Moral Choice

. . . National Socialist policy produced chaos, while promising order. The organized female world of civic, religious, community, and ultimately Nazi organizations had been fragmented by 1939. [Frau Gertrud] Scholtz-Klink [the Third Reich's leader (*Reichsfrauenführerin*) for women's activities] presided over the Frauenwerk and Frauenschaft that had been reduced to the auxiliary status she had sworn to prevent when taking office. Thus, because of the virtual disappearance of Nazi women's organizations, Scholtz-Klink's women did not directly participate in the "final solution" (a term she still uses). But this ought not blind us to the fact that individual women—as officials and as wives and as guards—not only understood that genocide existed as a policy, but themselves sustained it. Gertrud Scholtz-Klink had been one of those women. Three years after speaking with Scholtz-Klink, I discovered in the Leo Baeck Institute Archives the memoirs of a woman who had lived in Berlin on the eve of the war. Erna Segal recalled how "one Klink-Scholtz—or maybe I have it backwards" sent a special "buyer" (a nurse) who removed the Segal family's valuables, then drew up a contract promising payment in full within four weeks. Since they were dealing with the Reichs-frauenführerin, they did not worry. Besides, the family desperately needed the money to pay a recently levied "tax" on all Jews. When no payment arrived, they hired a lawyer to collect the bill. Scholtz-Klink's representative agreed to pay a tiny fraction of the price written into the contract. "How can you reconcile yourself with this . . . blackmail?" Frau Segal asked the Reichsfrauen-führerin. To no avail. The Segals accepted the sum of money and used it to escape from Germany.[1]

When employees of government programs wanted new furniture, meeting space, clothing, and equipment, they appropriated the property of Jews who had been deported. On one occasion, [Frau Dr. Auguste] Reber-Gruber [the highest woman official in the Nazi Teachers' Union] resisted the temptation to profit from this custom, but not for moral reasons. When she was offered the chance to acquire the castle owned by the Bleichröder family (whose ancestor had achieved prominence as banker to Bismarck), she declined. It would not set the correct mood for her teachers because "although Frau von Bleichröder was not Jewish, her husband was."[2] Four decades later, Scholtz-Klink expressed indignation about Jewish ingratitude. Willful ignorance dominated her hindsight as totally as it had determined her vision before 1945.

A few wives of government officials shared their husbands' interests. The wife of Hans Frank (the governor-general of occupied Poland) helped build the family fortune. While Frank reduced the ghetto populations to starvation levels, his wife profiteered by exchanging small quantities of food for large quantities of furs, jewelry, furniture, and art.[3] Emmy Göring insists that her husband never understood the full implications of the "final solution," but witnesses remember that she helped out in her husband's deceitful "business" dealings with Jews who "sold" him magnificent art collections for scandalously low prices.[4] One wife acted not only out of greed but also from genuine commitment to racial ideology. Gerda Bormann (whom Speer described as "browbeaten") wrote to her husband in 1944,

My dearest Heart,

Every single child must realize that the Jew is the Absolute Evil in this world, and that he must be fought by every means, wherever he appears [Bormann scribbled "quite true" in the margin]. . . . As long as there exists somewhere in the world Germanic *Volk* who want to work hard, cleanly and faithfully and to live according to their own laws, in a State befitting their breed, the Eternal Jew will try to prevent it and to annihilate all positive life.[5]

Frau Bormann, with her intense anti-Semitism and her commitment to her husband's career, stands out, however, as an exception to the behavior of most wives, who were not above greed, but generally remained uninterested in their husbands' jobs and Nazi doctrine generally.

At the opposite extreme of the Nazi hierarchy, a few women worked as matrons or guards in concentration camps. Although they were statistically insignificant, descriptions of them fairly leap from the pages of survivors' memoirs. Susan Cernyak-Spatz recalled: "In my experience the matrons were cruel, more vicious (sadistically vicious) than any SS man. These women who, as I read later, ranged from baronesses and countesses to prostitutes, were the most vicious. You rarely found SS men who played games with their dogs in which the point was for the dog to get the prisoners' derrieres, but the matrons did." Maria Kaufmann-Krasowski testified at a trial in Düsseldorf about Hildegard Lächert, who assigned her to wash floors and beat her mercilessly with a whip until she was only "scraps of a human being," and then barked the order, "Get this piece of filth out of here!"[6] Margarete Armbruster, who was deported to Ravensbrück, reports that besides the SS men, 2,000 women assistants made their lives wretched. "Only one NS sister treated me decently. And she was transferred as punishment."[7] Nearly every concentration camp had its women's section—guarded by its Ilse Kochs—and small brigades of booted, uniformed women guards. Irma Griese at Auschwitz brought horror to her victims with her sadomasochistic sexual exploits.[8] For a woman to become a guard required so major a departure from the normal values and experiences of women, perhaps the few who ended up on camp assignments were more apt to be depraved or deranged than the men. Or perhaps women guards *seemed* more cruel because their behavior deviated farther from our conceptions of "feminine" models than men guards' behavior departed from stereotypes about men.

Jolana Roth told me she had seen very few women SS guards at Auschwitz. "But the ones you did see—they were worse than the men. I will never forget the one who would stand at the peephole of the gas chamber just because she wanted to." Was the woman guard at the peephole "worse" than the SS men, described by Jolana Roth in a different context, who used live babies for target practice? Such comparisons lose their meaning. Greedy, bigoted wives and heartless matrons remained exceptional. However deeply their acts repel us, they did not affect the workings of the Nazi state.

Far more important than these exceptional cases was the system that pre- scribed polarized gender identities for males and females. After 1939, wher- ever Nazi power held sway, men and women, "Aryans" and Jews, occupied separate spaces—and that was as true among the dying as among the living. "MEN TO THE LEFT! WOMEN TO THE RIGHT."

This phrase haunts concentration-camp memoirs. "An SS noncommis- sioned officer came to meet us, a truncheon in his hand. He gave the order: "Men to the left! Women to the right!" Those were the first words Elie Wiesel heard when he arrived at Auschwitz.[9] Victor Frankl remembered: "We were told to leave our luggage in the train and to fall into two lines—women on one side and men on the other—in order to file past a senior SS officer."[10] "There were loud announcements, but it was all fairly restrained: nobody did anything to us. . . . I followed the crowd: 'Men to the left, women and children to the right,' we had been told."[11] The phrase is ubiquitous. Miklos Nyiszli's account hints at a possible motivation for this practice. "To start, the SS quickly divided us according to sex, leaving all children under fourteen with their mothers. So our once united group was straightaway split in two."[12] Ilse Blumenthal-Weiss reported that at a camp for converted Jews in Holland (a privileged category), relatives could meet together during the day, but when they arrived in Theresienstadt, "families were torn apart."[13] Vladka Meed, one of the very few survivors of the Warsaw ghetto, recalled: "For me the final solution is the final isolation of women, men, and children, of both sexes, of young and old. . . ."[14]

Before the stripping, beatings, delousing, searching, and even the selection for work crew or crematorium came the separation of women and men. Camp life was planned to obliterate all signs of individuality: tattooed numbers replaced names; identical "uniforms" and shoes, shaved heads, and starvation reduced external differences to a minimum. From the prisoners' first minutes in a camp, however, gender remained as one of the few social markers. The other distinction (and this only for those "selected" to survive a few weeks or months longer in work camps) was a colored triangle: yellow for Jews, pink for homosexuals, blue for stateless, green for black marketeers (*Berufsverbrecher*), black for "asocials," red for politicals, and violet for Jehovah's Witnesses. Inmates with triangles of all colors shared common barracks and work assignments. Men and women were not allowed to mingle.

Nazi orders routinely linked genocide and gender. When Heydrich explained the "final solution" at the Wannsee Conference on January 20, 1942, he included as a matter of course both separation according to sex and then extermination based on race.

> In pursuance of the final solution, special measures will apply to conscript Jews for the labor service in the east. In large labor groups, with the sexes separated . . . while constructing roads [they will be] directed to these areas, whereby undoubtedly a large number will drop out through natural elimination. . . . The possible remainders, and they undoubtedly will be the toughest among them, will be treated accordingly, for [history teaches us that] they, being a natural selection, would if released become the germ cell of a new Jewish reconstruction.[15]

In procedures that defy belief, even when the "deportees" at extermination camps were to be murdered within a few minutes, camp officials scrupulously followed the ritual: men to the left and women to the right.[16] This did not result in favored treatment for women, as the following remarks about women in Treblinka illustrate:

[Menstruation] only afforded the Ukrainians and the SS one more opportunity for sadistic humor. There were, of course, no sanitary napkins, or even newspapers, and the girls used large leaves—burdock leaves if they could find them—to protect themselves. But any blood showing on a dress meant death; it was unaesthetic, and the SS were very keen on aesthetics.[17]

At Auschwitz, where able-bodied victims could at least hope to work and survive for a few weeks, or months or years, the same segregation prevailed—also without any special consideration for the "weaker" sex.

The SS-men showed no consideration for women in the camp. From the initial humiliation, when they were ordered to strip in the presence of soldiers and were shaved on the head and body by men, they went through every form of ill-treatment. They were put to work at making roads, leveling the ground, cleaning out ponds [and] had to live in the crowded barracks with the three-tiered bunks. . . . They died of hunger and fell beneath the blows of the SS-men's sticks, just as did the men.[18]

The SS brutalized women and men separately and equally.

To some extent, the separation of men and women resulted merely from conventional ideas about sex-appropriate work. For example, where victims served as Kapos (prisoners assigned to help the guards and granted special privileges), a traditional division of labor prevailed. At Treblinka, the "upper" camp included "gas chambers, the installations for the disposal of the corpses . . . and the barracks for the *Totenjuden*, the Jewish work groups. One of the barracks was for males, another, later, for females. The men carried and burned the bodies; the twelve girls cooked and washed."[19] But conventional notions about women's and men's work could have played only a small role in the basic decision to separate the sexes. More fundamentally, Nazi orders aimed at the destruction of family ties.

Separation of men and women meant more than preventing sexual activity, it meant eroding emotional bonds—leaving individuals bereft in a horrifying world. Survivors' memoirs testify eloquently to the truth of Nazi leaders' fears. Splitting women from men did stun the victims, but only temporarily. Nazi planners failed to realize that the separation from biological siblings or spouses did not prevent victims from restoring lost loved ones in new relationships. In a few cases, inmates found ways of clandestinely maintaining proscribed contact with family in other barracks. When this proved impossible (as it usually did), prisoners reconstructed lost bonds, for they carried with them the family as memory and model on which to build new ties. Eugene Weinstock recalled: "survival . . . could only be a social achievement, not an individual accident."[20] Kitty Hart made the same observation. "I soon realized that alone one could not possibly survive. It was necessary therefore to form little families of two or three."[21] These new "families" may not have looked like families. Usually they included only members of the same sex. But they felt like families. How many memoirs of concentration-camp life contain phrases like "She became my new sister" or "We were like brothers." These newly formed connections represented the first stage of resistance—the refusal to submit to the dehumanization of gender separation. And after the first stage, inmates formed emotional bonds by performing small acts of kindness that cost precious energy and food, thus preserving their own emotional world within the barbed wire and beyond the control of guards.

In society outside Nazi surveillance—among victims as among resisters—individuals unified behind a common goal. The family (sometimes in its biological sense, but more often as a myth or a model) formed the basis for secret preserves of decency, love, and trust. Victims and opponents of Nazism, searching for a vocabulary with which to describe the deep ties they formed to their fellows, adapted the familiar vocabulary that carried reassurances of steadfastness and shared devotion in the midst of a lethal environment. To them, as to us, the very word "family" brings reassuring visions of strength. But usually life underground or in the camps dissolved the patriarchal assumptions people brought with them. Memoirs written about that life suggest that often victims and opponents played out stereotypical roles for pragmatic reasons as well as because of unconscious assumptions. But memoirs also abound in stories about how men learned the skills that most women learn as children—nurturing, caring, cleansing, and sharing; and women discovered unknown strengths when they had to run dangerous missions in places where any man of draftable age would have been arrested on the spot.

In the camps as in the underground outside, women brought special skills to the errand, and the public-private split worked to their advantage. From childhood, they had learned to live in a bicultural world that severed the public persona from private feelings; as resisters, they "instinctively" knew how to appear harmless and even obsequious to their enemies while maintaining their inner integrity. Concentration-camp prisoners learned to avoid calling attention to themselves while preserving an internal set of values. Those who resisted Nazi rule knew that sporadic acts of defiance produced only martyrs. Resistance meant long-term, collaborative deviousness—pitting wit, not physical power, against the enemy. This quintessentially "feminine" strategy became universal in situations where resisters and prisoners commanded few of the superficial attributes of normal life and dignity.

Paradoxically but not accidentally, Nazi policy aimed at eroding family ties among victims and also among its own "Aryan" followers. In both cases, the goal was the same: to break down individual identity and to render people susceptible to whatever plans Hitler announced: eugenic breeding schemes for the chosen "Aryans" and genocide for the selected. Nazi guards sent "men to the left" and "women to the right" for the same reasons that they sent girls to the BDM and "Aryan" boys to the Hitler Youth. They divided up German society into peer-group associations, not only because each gender was to perform different tasks, but (contrary to rhetoric praising the "strong family") to weaken family bonding and enhance total loyalty to the Führer.

Given this strategic Nazi antipathy to family ties, however, it comes as a surprise to discover that the architects of death viewed the family in very different terms when it came to their own lives. While fostering a gender-separated social world for millions of ordinary people, the men around Hitler, who carried out his order for genocide, allowed for and even encouraged an older concept of womanhood. Eva Braun, dull, passive, and decorative, not zealous Gerda Bormann or opportunistic Scholtz-Klink, remained the proto-typical wife. The reasons for this apparent paradox become clear only after reflecting upon the masculine roles and tasks assigned to this elite by Hitler's orders for genocide. This reflection begins at the end—with the trials in Nuremberg—and centers on men, not women.

When we wonder about those men who issued and carried out genocidal orders, we ask with the judges at Nuremberg, "How was it possible that all you honorable generals could continue to serve a murderer with such unques-tioning loyalty?" How, they asked themselves, could the elite placed in charge of killing operations remain human with such acts on their consciences? Hitler's deputies, for all the unspeakable crimes they ordered, were not hard-ened sadists or pathological killers. When the defendants at the Nuremberg Trials watched films depicting the brutality of extermination and forced labor, William Shirer recorded their reactions.

GÖRING: Shielded his face with his right arm, and seemed especially upset as tortures were mentioned.

HESS: Showed sustained interest, glaring at the screen.

DÖNITZ: . . . Was quite upset, clenching his fists, and covering his eyes with his hands.

SCHACHT: Refused to look at the picture at all, turning his back on the screen. Showed no evidence of emotion.

FUNK: Broke down and cried.

FRANK: (the butcher of Poland . . .): Quite overcome. He bit his nails, clenched his hands, and showed evidence of great emotion.

The whole courtroom was as silent as a sepulcher. Justice Lawrence, hitherto equal to every occasion in his dry, matter-of-fact judicial way, even forgot to adjourn the court. The judges silently rose from their chairs and slowly strode out without saying a word.[22]

Just a few years earlier in Berlin, when Party leaders had translated the "final solution" from the Führer's wish into deadly reality, they had imagined the impact on the men who actually did the killing. Novels by Remarque, Jünger, and a generation of veterans vividly depicted the massive transformations wrought by four years of trench warfare. What would become of elite soldiers who slaughtered helpless men, women, and children? Nazi leaders devised several solutions, the most obvious of which was to employ non-German soldiers from conquered nations (like the Ukraine and Poland) to carry on most of the guard work; and to offer a few prisoners special treatment in exchange for performing the most horrifying jobs. Secrecy, too, helped. Members of the task forces (*Sonderkommando*) did not realize the exact nature of their job until the last minute.[23] Still, the camps required German administrators. The *Einsatzkommando* in the field were largely Germans, and eventually soldiers found out.

Raul Hilberg summarized the ways in which SS and Nazi leaders managed to remain sane while committing subhuman jobs. While Hilberg does not use the term, he describes traits that Western culture praises as especially masculine. First came patriotic duty. As Wilhelm Frick declared at Nuremberg, "I have a clear conscience . . . I am convinced that no patriotic American citizen . . . would have acted any differently in my place." . . .[24] This echoed Himmler's speech to the SS in 1940.

> In many cases it is considerably easier to lead a company into battle than to command a company responsible for some area where it has to hold down a hostile population, probably one with a long history, to carry out executions, to deport people, to remove shrieking, weeping women . . . to do this unseen duty—to maintain this silent activity . . . to be always consistent, always uncompromising—that is in many cases far, far harder.[25]

In the name of obedience to a higher law (the Führer, in this case), officers were admonished to abolish from their hearts "feminine" traits such as sentimentality or squeamishness. They were to think of the long-term gain for all "Aryans," which vindicated the evil they wrought in the short term.

Equally important, leaders encouraged their men to feel proud of their brotherhood—a tough, elite force. To perform well in a concentration camp or *Einsatzkommando* meant to be a "real man," to be ruthless, obedient, loyal, without moral scruples toward subhumans, and scrupulously honorable to equals. Himmler told his officers on October 4, 1943:

> The SS man is to be guided by one principle alone: honesty, decency, loyalty, and friendship toward those of our blood, and to no one else. . . . Whether other peoples live in plenty or starve to death interests me only insofar as we need them as slaves for our culture; for the rest it does not interest me. Whether 10,000 Russian women keel over from exhaustion in the construction of an antitank ditch interests me only insofar as the ditch for Germany gets finished. We will never be savage or heartless where we don't have to be; that is obvious. Germans are after all the only people in the world who treat animals decently, . . . but it is a crime against our own blood to worry about [human animals] and instill ideals

into them, only to create problems for our sons and grandsons. If someone comes to me and tells me, "I cannot dig these antitank ditches with children or with women, it is inhuman, they will die on the job," I must say to him, "You are a murderer of your own blood, because if the antitank ditch is not dug, German soldiers will die, and they are sons of German mothers. They are our blood."[26]

This extraordinary order commanded men to defend their own manhood, even though it involved killing women.

Although she was not speaking of this example specifically, American writer Susan Griffin describes the message conveyed by Nazi criminals at Nuremberg. "Implicitly, he tells his judges that he is not him*self*. He *is* only an empty shell of a man, a receptacle for the orders given him by the Nazi Party and by Hitler . . . he had acted only as a puppet."[27] SS men emptied themselves of their own autonomy and filled the void with a mythical vision of their own manliness to stiffen their resolve and still their consciences. Yet this picture of characterless automatons does not adequately convey the complexity of the men's personalities who ordered and carried out mass murder. On the one hand, Griffin describes a man who, contemporary sociologists would say, felt overidentified with his role. Like the careerist or workaholic, these men saw themselves as *totally* loyal, obedient, and rigorous. They saw themselves as paradigms of masculine virtue. In following orders, they cast aside the last vestiges of their humanity, but clung to a prefabricated and socially acceptable vision of masculinity.

But this portrait is too monolithic. To have totally internalized their tasks as the core of their identity would have completely brutalized them. This could (and occasionally did) produce men who identified with their jobs so enthusiastically that they began to find pleasure in them. Such a commandant or guard might then forget his overriding responsibilities to the SS and begin to enjoy his job. Nazi leaders wanted dedicated, cold administrators of death, not killers among their elite. Nor did they want madmen. Conventional ideas about "masculine" and "feminine" played a role in two very different aspects of genocide. First, male guards had been socialized to a code of behavior that prescribed gentleness toward defenseless people, especially women and children. Secondly, camp personnel brought with them deep emotional needs for contact with their own wives, children, and families, which enabled them to maintain their tenuous ties to the world beyond, to a sphere of private happiness and sanity. Even as a guard identified with his role as murderer, he kept his sanity by cultivating what sociologists call "role distance" from his actions. Paradoxically, he overidentified with his career and simultaneously withdrew from it as a source of his identity. He was aided in this psychological feat by specific policies.

In addition to extolling the virtues of the SS, propaganda vilified and dehumanized the most helpless victims. Camp personnel continued the process. Journalist Gitta Sereny asked Franz Stangl, the commandant of

Treblinka, why, if they were going to kill them anyway, what was the point of all the humiliation, why the cruelty? "To condition those who actually had to carry out the policies," he told her, "to make it possible for them to do what they did."[28] One inmate who survived asked the same question of a camp guard who had been "an absolute monster" when she had been in a camp. "You know," he said, "when you look at people . . . without any identity and that aren't human anymore, you feel so guilty you overcome the guilt with anger."[29] Saying "These are not humans," they could conclude, "I am not a murderer." By brutalizing their victims, they avoided brutalizing their own souls.

These shallow psychic tricks did not always work. Sometimes, like Amon Goeth (portrayed vividly in *Schindler's List* by Thomas Keneally) or Irma Griese (depicted by Olga Lengyel in *Five Chimneys*), guards began to enjoy their work—erratically and violently indulging their sadism. More commonly, the reverse reaction occurred. Despite psychological conditioning, horror at their actions seeped into administrators' and guards' consciousness. Stangl admitted that the undressing barracks were the most dreadful place in the camp. "I avoided it from my innermost being; I couldn't confront them; I couldn't lie to them; I avoided at any price talking to those who were about to die: I couldn't stand it."[30]

In Israel, Eichmann confessed he had been so sensitive that he could not bear the sight of blood and had become sick at the sight of Jews stripped in a large room. Mobile gas vans drove up to the door and sent carbon monoxide into the room. Eichmann had to watch. "I cannot tell . . . I hardly looked. I could not; I could not; I had had enough. The shrieking, and, I was too upset, much too upset. . . . I saw the most horrible sight I had thus far seen in my life. The doors of the truck were opened, near a ditch, and the corpses were thrown out, as though they were still alive, so smooth were their limbs. . . . I can still see the civilian extracting the gold teeth with the pliers. A physician in white overalls told me to look. I could not." Eichmann protested to an SS general in Lvov: "It is horrible what is being done around here. Young people are being made into sadists. Simply bang away at women and children. That is impossible. Our people will go mad, or become insane, our own people." The general shrugged. One of Himmler's officers reported after his men had witnessed the execution of "only" one hundred Jews: "Look at the eyes of the men in this *Kommando*, how deeply shaken they are! These men are finished [*fertig*] for the rest of their lives. What kind of followers are we training here? Either neurotics or savages!"[31]

More extreme measures had to be devised. This process began in Berlin and shrouded genocide at every level in euphemism, beginning with the benign-sounding code names devised by the "desk murderers" and ending with elaborate deception at the killing sites. Similarly, a series of schemes kept relatives outside the camps ignorant of the truth. The mother of a Dachau prisoner, who did not know of her son's death, received a packet with his clothes and a note: "Enclosed are the articles which the prisoner does not require on his discharge."[32] Stangl had a fake train station constructed (complete with painted clock with hands that never moved and signs TO BIALYSTOK), so that prisoners about to be murdered would not realize they were on their way to the "sorting house." And the anterooms to the gas chambers had carefully lettered signs telling prisoners to remember the numbers of the hooks on which they had hung their clothes. Each camp had its specialty—a greenhouse, a zoo, or park. Auschwitz had its orchestra, to keep *Kultur* alive. Fania Fénelon described the directors of the orchestra, Maria Mandel and Joseph Kramer, who both loved music passionately. "Kramer cried when we played *"Träumerei"* by Schumann. Kramer, who gassed 24,000 humans. When he was tired of his work he came to us and listened to music. That's what's so incomprehensible about the Nazis. They could shoot, murder, and gas—and afterward be so sensitive. We were not even humans in their eyes. We were lice. They wanted to exterminate us."[33] Fénelon's description itself suggests how such killers could love music. Kramer's and Mandel's ability to escape into music was not paradoxical but essential because it enabled them to identify with how they felt, not with what they did. As they divided the players from the music, so too did they split their own workaday reality from their deep attachment to culture.

Commandants and guards imposed on themselves a split reality, telling themselves that the fake world they had constructed matched their "real" inner selves. They relegated "obeying orders" to their public responsibilities, and created a private fantasy within which they deceived themselves into thinking they were not so bad after all. Speer, in his cell, wrote, "Today it seems to me that I was trying to compartmentalize my mind. On the one hand was the vulgar business of carrying out a policy proclaimed in the anti-Semitic slogans. . . . On the other hand there was my idealized picture of Hitler. I wanted to keep these two apart."[34]

Franz Stangl . . . made a similar remark. "That's what I am trying to explain to you; the only way I could live was compartmentalizing my thinking."[35] Later Stangl declared, "I had to do [my job] as well as I could. That is how I am." "My professional ethos was that if something wrong was going on [in the camp] then it had to be found out. That was my profession; I enjoyed it. It fulfilled me. And yes, I was ambitious about that; I won't deny that." Sereny asked Stangl, "Would it be true to say that you got used to the liquidations?"

He replied, "To tell the truth . . . one did become used to it."

"In days? Weeks? Months?"

"Months. It was months before I could look one of them in the eye. I repressed it all by trying to create a special place; gardens, new barracks, new kitchens, new everything; barbers, tailors, shoemakers, carpenters . . . and I drank."[36]

One central deception formed the core of all these pretexts: the ideal of womanhood. Paradoxically, the Nazi state, which sedulously undercut all forms of privacy and attempted to destroy parental influence over children, actually encouraged traditional notions of the family when selecting SS commanders who would oversee genocide. For all the emphasis on breeding programs and unwed motherhood, the Nazi leaders and SS chiefs remained as petty bourgeois as they accused their enemies of being. They relied on the sheltering family (or on its myth) to keep alive an ersatz sense of decency in the men who would work most closely with mass murder. Nazi policy for commandants and guards encouraged a vision of womanhood and the family that they had deeply opposed in social policy aimed at masses of ordinary Germans. They recreated the ideal of a family as refuge, as a place to renew contact with a private and more humane self. The SS man who excised "feminine" traits from his personality depended on a woman to salvage his sanity.

When Sartre and de Beauvoir analyzed anti-Semites and misogynists, they described the process by which the member of the dominant category objectifies the inferior social category. In Nazi Germany, the Nazi "subject" converted women and Jews into "objects" of both social policy and of their own fantasies. For Jews, there was no difference between the two processes. The propaganda that dehumanized the Jew prepared the way for the deportation and extermination. But for women the matter was more complex. Nazi men needed the women they subdued. On the simplest level, they viewed their wives as their property and did not want their possessions confiscated.[37] In addition, while designing vast programs to erode the family and the privacy it protected, Nazi leaders themselves realized they needed the haven they destroyed. Except for a few fanatics like Gerda Bormann, wives had little to do with husbands' careers; and records of Hitler's dinnertime conversations with women present testify to the apolitical mindlessness that predominated during those gatherings. Scholtz-Klink recalled when I spoke with her that Nazi husbands did not want fanatically loyal wives who might "talk shop" at the end of a hard day. Not even Nazi "shop." And leaders continually sent out memos warning their men against discussing their jobs with wives. When wives knew, the barrier between a "sane" and "decent" home life lowered. At a Party rally, Rudolf Hess reminded the elite, "In conversation with your wives, speak only of those matters which have been expressly marked for public distribution." Six months later, Nazi leaders in Prussia were told, "One does not chatter with women about politics; women must take care of their looks, politics is our business." Frau Hoess, wife of the Auschwitz commandant, eventually did begin to ask questions, and her husband told her reluctantly that he "bore the responsibility for hundreds of thousands of inmates."[38]

After choosing four hundred men to carry out euthanasia, one hundred were singled out as psychologically able to apply their skills to mass extermination. On the whole, good family men were chosen, and generous leave time was granted so husbands and fathers could rehumanize their psyches in the company of their families. When one of his physicians seemed to be on the verge of a nervous breakdown, Dr. Mengele sent for the man's wife to come to live in Auschwitz.[39]

After all the propaganda about totally loyal women who would select racially fit mates, carry out sterilization programs, direct a separate women's world, and indoctrinate their communities, most wives of the concentration-camp "elite" conformed to rather traditional expectations. Even Nazi memoirs keep the image of virtuous womanhood alive. Speer (who unstintingly criticized his male comrades), says of their wives:

> In general the wives of the regime's bigwigs resisted the temptation of power far more than their husbands. They did not lose themselves in the latter's fantasy world. They looked on at the often grotesque antics of their husbands with inner reservations and were not caught up in the political whirlwind in which their men were carried steeply upward. Frau Bormann remained a modest, somewhat browbeaten housewife, although blindly devoted both to her husband and the party ideology. I had the impression that Frau Göring was inclined to smile at her husband's mania for pomp. And in the final analysis Eva Braun, too, proved her inner superiority. At any rate she never used for personal ends the power which lay within her grasp.[40]

Scholtz-Klink, Reber-Gruber, and other women leaders directed their offices and shaped policy before 1939, but wives remained far from any public sphere, even a "womanly" one.

One of the central fantasies to which commandants and guards clung emerged from their love of their families. In the case of the Hoess family, the commandant and his wife lived together with their many children on the grounds of Auschwitz. In the memoirs he wrote while awaiting execution, Hoess reflected on his life.

> I had to go on with this process of extermination. I had to continue this mass murder and coldly to watch it, without regard for the doubts that were seething deep within me. . . . In Auschwitz I had no reason to complain that I was bored. If I was deeply affected by some incident, I found it impossible to go back to my home. . . . I would mount my horse and ride, until I had chased the terrible picture away. Often, at night, I would walk through the stables and seek relief among my beloved animals.
>
> When I saw my children happily playing or observed my wife's delight over our youngest, the thought would often come to me: how long will our happiness last? My wife could never understand these gloomy moods of mine, and ascribed them to some annoyance connected with my work.
>
> I was no longer happy in Auschwitz once the mass exterminations had begun. I had become dissatisfied with myself. . . . My wife's greatest pleasure would have been to give a present to every prisoner who was in any way connected with our household.[41]

Emotional stability, no less and probably more than false train stations, euphemistic terms, and dehumanized victims, provided the murderers with an ersatz sanity.

The reminiscences by men waiting to be hanged, however, ought not lead us into believing that commandants' home lives really conformed to such a loving and "humane" description. We know that often men with unrealistically high and rigid expectations about family abuse their wives and children. In Hoess's case, rumor reported that he had a lover-inmate at Auschwitz who at one point attempted to murder him. Myths about a happy home, like the fake train station and the symphony orchestra, did not provide a permanent refuge from reality.

Among the thousands of normal people who participated in genocide about whom Hilberg wrote, we have no evidence of any participant taking a stand against mass murder—nor did any SS man go insane in ways that hampered the efficient operation of the camps.[42] No man asked for a transfer. After 1945, ex-commandants and guards seem to have returned to domestic tranquillity and, although tormented by nightmares and fear of arrest, carried on with their lives unless they were apprehended. Their postwar readjustment was, in all probability, smoother than their victims' reentry into society.

The SS leadership, which in every other respect inculcated an entirely masculine élan among its corps, placed men who cared about their wives and children in charge of routine killing operations. This family connection played a vital role in maintaining "culture" among the murderers when they returned from "out there." Governor-General Frank told a group of SS men at a Christmas celebration in Cracow in 1940:

> Some of you have mothers, others parents, and still others your wives, your brides, your brothers, and your children at home. They will all be thinking of you during these weeks. And they will worry, "My god, there he sits over there in Poland with so many Jews and lice . . ." It would be very nice of you if we would take photographs to send back to the loved ones at home.[43]

Jacob, whose full name we do not know, became a police chief in occupied Poland, and wrote to a friend, "I have a nice apartment in a former kindergarten, with everything. . . . Nothing is lacking, except naturally my wife and children. They would understand me best of all. My Dieter and the little Lene write very often in their way. It could sometimes drive you to tears. It is not good if one loves children as much as I used to."[44] He asked his friend back home to write. "One is so lonely and abandoned here that every piece of news from home does so much good."

Sereny asked Stangl, "In the midst of all the horror that surrounded you, . . . what was there for you to hold on to?"

"I don't know. Perhaps my wife. My love for my wife?" At first, in 1941, he had successfully concealed the nature of his work from her. "The little time we had together, we usually talked about the children and ordinary everyday

things. But it is true [after she suspected], there . . . was tension." Among the
concentration and killing camp personnel, caring was confined to the deepest
emotional unit, the family, and excised from the routine activities of everyday
duty. Sereny asked Frau Stangl what would have happened if she had forced
her husband to choose between his profession and her.

"I have thought very hard . . . I believe that if I had ever confronted Paul
with the alternatives: Treblinka or me; he would . . . yes, he would in the final
analysis have chosen me."[45] Eventually, Frau Stangl realized the full extent of
her husband's participation in mass murder. She told Sereny, "I began to see
the terrible change in him. . . . I saw only glimpses." She urged him, " 'I am
afraid for your soul, . . . you *must* leave.' " He refused. She "couldn't stand it
any longer" and confessed to the Austrian priest. " 'I know you won't believe it
but there is this terrible place in Poland and they are killing people—they are
killing the Jews there. And my Paul . . . is working there. What shall I do?
Please tell me. Please help us. Please advise us.' " Then she told Sereny, "He
gave me such a terrible shock. . . . 'We are living through terrible times, my
child. Before God and my conscience, if I had been in Paul's place, I would
have done the same. I absolve him from all guilt.' I walked away like a zombie,
in a dream, in a nightmare."[46] Stangl, aided by his vision of a family guarded
by his virtuous and innocent wife, continued at his job, believing that one day
he would return to the full-time role that matched his inner feelings. In the
meantime, he removed his daily work from moral judgments altogether and
reserved his ethical considerations for private life.[47]

What you do is public, how you feel is private. This is the essence of a
system that severs masculine from feminine. Stangl, Hoess, and untold thousands of men felt their very sanity depended upon preserving an island of
serenity where love, tenderness, and devotion reigned. A place to "touch
base" and reaffirm one's humanity in the face of brutal criminality. A young
SS man, writing to a comrade, ricocheted back and forth between descriptions of "the horrifying figures of the Jews . . . with big bulging veins, crip-
pled, and stunned . . . not people, but ape-beings,"[48] to "sweet thoughts" of
his "sweet girlfriend," the pharmacist's assistant, in Hamburg. Felix Landau
(adopted son of a Jewish father in Vienna) worked with the Security Police
and fell in love with a woman who deceived him. In suicidal grief, he volunteered to join the *Einsatzkommando*. On June 30, 1941, he was shipped to the
front.

Wonderful music, "Oh, Do You Hear My Secret Call?" How soft a heart can
become. Strong are my thoughts about the person for whose sake I landed here
voluntarily. What I wouldn't give if I could see her for only ten minutes. Hundreds of Jews with blood streaming down their faces, holes in their skulls, broken
hands, and eyes hanging out, all running down the streets. A few Jews with blood
streaming over them carried others who had totally collapsed. We traveled to a
stronghold and there we saw things that certainly no one else has ever seen. At the

entry stood soldiers with cudgels as thick as a fist and beat everyone in all directions.[49]

But the young soldier continued writing on July 12, 1941, "It is really so strange. You love battle, and yet you have to shoot unarmed humans (*Menschen*). We got orders to shoot twenty-three, two of whom were women. They astonished us when they refused even to accept a glass of water from us. I was designated as a marksman and will have to shoot those who try to escape."[50] He confessed, "Evenings when I lie in bed, I get this desperate longing, this longing for peace, quiet and love."

As the Nazi state destroyed morality in the public sphere, wives and relatives were supposed to guard an emotional "space" for the men who oversaw the killing operations. "Each partner performed the function prescribed for it by nature," as Hitler put it. These wives did not directly participate in evil, but, on the contrary, fulfilled "nature's role" by normalizing a masculine world gone amok. While Nazi men expanded their German territorial *Lebensraum* and made the nation *judenrein* (literally "purified of Jews"), women chose between ignoring or recognizing their husbands' work. Meanwhile ordinary women decided whether to look away or offer an act of kindness when they knew a friend or neighbor was in danger.

Wives, when they remained in their "proper place," kept their family world apart from the masculine sphere of brutality, coercion, corruption, and power. As with so many other aspects of Nazi ideology, this vision of womanhood embodied a traditional ideal carried to extremes. Over a century before, Johann Wolfgang von Goethe, in *Wilhelm Meister*, described the ideal couple. "Man tortures himself with public affairs. . . . Meanwhile a sensible housewife truly governs her domain." By remaining outside politics, history, and change, women preserved an important part of what the Germans mean by *Kultur*, or the commitment to lofty ideals of humanity and creativity. At the turn of the century, sociologist Max Weber explained how *Kultur* functions in a highly developed nation such as Germany: "A people accustomed to refined *Kultur*, *and yet* capable of withstanding the horrors of war out there . . . and a *Volk* who then return *despite all that* as basically decent as the vast majority of our people, that is true humanity; this no one should ever forget. . . ."[51] When the man returned from "out there," woman would be waiting, like the "intended" in *Heart of Darkness*, ready to still his nightmares and restore his humanity. Kurtz decides that "we must help [women] to stay in that beautiful world of their own, lest ours gets worse," and Marlow agrees.[52]

In Hitler's Germany, women provided in a separate sphere of their own creation the image of humane values that lent the healthy gloss of motherhood to the "Aryan" world of the chosen. In addition, wives gave the individual men who confronted daily murder a safe place where they could be respected for who they were, not what they did. Stangl's daughter, after her father's arrest, said, "All I can say . . . is that I have read what has been written about my father. But nothing—nothing on earth—will make me believe that he has ever done anything wrong. I know it is illogical; I know about the trial and the witnesses. . . . I love him—I will always love him.[53] In a bureaucratized society in which men separate themselves from their public deeds, the home takes on special meaning. Although in many ways Nazi social policy invaded domestic life (with its racial fetishism, spies, and media control), the family continued to offer a haven from public horror for the men who arrested, deported, tortured, and killed those they defined as enemies of the *Volk*.

The private sphere, a "place" apart from the brutal world, offered respite to people at both extremes of the moral spectrum. Guards and commandants, victims and resisters—at the outer flanks of the Nazi world, all needed the psychological "space" offered by a home (or at least the myth of one) to gather strength with which to face the deformed world outside. In the Nazi world, man and woman operated in radically separated spheres. Leaders designed programs to drain the home of its emotional meaning for average people, but for the elite who actually oversaw the concentration camps and death camps, an older ideal prevailed. When the SS man returned home, he entered a doll's house of ersatz goodness in which he could escape from his own evil actions. He, in contemporary psychological terminology, "split" his identity as public man from his warm and loving feelings for his family. Nazi wives did not offer a beacon of strength for a moral cause, but rather created a buffer zone from their husbands' jobs. Far from wanting to share their husbands' concerns, they actively cultivated their own ignorance and facilitated his escape.

Victims and resisters, by contrast, did their best to integrate their private morality into their public acts—even as they learned to dissemble in public to avoid detection. Both men and women adapted, often learning new roles and attitudes from each other. Women as well as men operated in the public world they found repugnant and found solace in carefully guarded private spheres. Their personal lives remained clandestine, genuinely "private," and their underground communities genuinely moral. When they needed a vocabulary to express the concern, trust, and idealism they shared, words like "sister," "brother," and "family" came readily to mind.

Guards and commandants rationalized their participation in Nazi schemes for genocide and repression by divorcing what they did from who they were. Victims and resisters, in contrast knew that sanity and survival depended upon preserving private integrity against Nazi power.

NOTES

1. Erna Segal, "You Shall Never Forget," unpublished manuscript, Leo Baeck Institute, New York, Box No. 59, 99–100.
2. H. G. Adler, *Der verwaltete Mensch. Studien zur Deportation der Juden aus Deutschland* (Tübingen: J. C. B. Mohr, 1974), 594. Reber-Gruber to Frau von Hutten, June 28, 1940. Hauptstaatsarchiv/NSDAP/Munich/1007.

3. Eugene Davidson, *The Trial of the Germans* (New York: Collier, 1966), 434.
4. Ibid., 91–92. Emmy Göring, *An der Seite meines Mannes* (Göttingen: Schueltz, 1967), 64, 67, 70, 78.
5. Davidson, *Trial*, 102. Bormann had played a decisive role in the euthanasia program. *The Bormann Letters, January 1943–April 1945.* Intro. H. Trevor-Roper (London: Weidenfeld and Nicolson, 1954).
6. Cernyak-Spatz's remarks in Esther Katz and Joan Ringelheim, eds., *Proceedings of the Conference Women Surviving the Holocaust* (New York: Institute for Research on History, 1983), 147. Kaufmann-Krasowksi's comments in the biography of an SS woman guard, *Die Frauen von Majdanek. Vom zerstörten Leben der Opfer und der Mörderinnen*, ed. Ingrid Müller-Münch (Hamburg: Rowohlt, 1982), 115.
7. "Bericht Margarete Armbruster," in Hannah Elling, *Frauen im deutschen Widerstand, 1933-1945* (Frankfurt: Röderberg, 1981), 75.
8. Olga Lengyel, *Five Chimneys: The Story of Auschwitz*, trans. Paul P. Weiss (London: Mayflower, 1972). Fania Fénelon, *Playing for Time*, trans. J. Landry (New York: Berkley, 1979), 147, 194–212, 244–250.
9. Elie Wiesel, *Night* (New York: Avon, 1969), 39.
10. Viktor Frankl, *Man's Search for Meaning*, trans. Ilse Lasch, preface by Gordon W. Allport (New York: Simon and Schuster, 1962), first published in 1946, 9.
11. Gitta Sereny, *Into That Darkness. An Examination of Conscience* (New York: Viking, 1983). First printed 1974, 176.
12. Miklos Nyiszli, *Auschwitz: A Doctor's Eyewitness Account*, trans. T. Kremer and R. Seaver, foreword Bruno Bettelheim (Greenwich, Connecticut: Fawcett Crest, 1960), 23. This division seemed so natural that orders rarely even mention it. On occasion, however, an official would comment, "It goes without saying that the men are to be separated from the women." Order from the Reich Minister for the Occupied Eastern territories, 1941, quoted in Helmut Krausnick and Martin Broszat, *Anatomy of the SS State*, trans. Dorothy Long and Marian Jackson (London, Toronto, Sydney, New York: Granada, 1982), 115.
13. Blumenthal-Weiss memoirs, 42 and 76, at the Leo Baeck Institute, New York.
14. In Esther Katz and Joan M. Ringelheim, eds., *Proceedings*, 79. She added, "Men were separated and we did not know what to do." Vladka Meed, *On Both Sides of the Wall: Memoirs from the Warsaw Ghetto* (Ghetto Fighters, 1972).
15. Lothar Gall, ed., *Fragen an die deutsche Geschichte*, 9th ed. (Stuttgart: Bundestag, 1983), 317.
16. The stages in every camp proceeded according to the following plan: "The killings were organized systematically to achieve the maximum humiliation and dehumanization of the victims before they died. This pattern was dictated by a distinct and careful purpose, not by 'mere' cruelty or indifference: the crammed airless freightcars without sanitary provisions, food or drink, far worse than any cattle-transport; the whipped-up (literally so) hysteria of arrival; the immediate and always violent separation of men, women and children; the public undressing; the incredibly crude internal physical examinations for hidden valuables; and hair-cutting and shaving of the women; and finally the naked run to the gas chamber, under the lash of whips." Sereny, *Darkness*, 100–101. Since prisoners reported the immediate loss of sexual desire soon after arriving in the camps, it seems unlikely that Nazis separated men from women only to prevent sexual encounters.
17. Ibid., 237–238.

18. Jozef Garlinski, *Fighting Auschwitz* (New York: Fawcett, 1975), 150–151.

19. Sereny, *Darkness*, 164–165.

20. Eugene Weinstock, *Beyond the Last Path*, trans. C. Ryan (New York: Boni and Gaer, 1947), 74.

21. Kitty Hart, *I Am Alive* (London and New York: Abelard-Schumann, 1962), 63. Fénelon told new arrivals they depended on cooperation, otherwise "You may get out of here alive, but inwardly you'll be deader than any of those poor things they burn every day." *Playing*, 142. Camp policy fostered rivalry, 172.

22. William L. Shirer, *End of a Berlin Diary* (New York: Knopf, 1947), 317.

23. Former SS man Victor Brack at Nuremberg testified that he had "no idea" he would be ordered to direct mass killing operations. When he found out, he protested that men who worked on *"such an inconceivable assignment"* would "no longer be fit to be employed subsequently in mercy-killing." Sereny, *Darkness*, 105.

24. Nuremberg Doc. vol. 32, 385. Hilberg counts this as the first of five rationalizations. *The Destruction of the European Jews* (New York: New Viewpoints, 1973). Hannah Arendt, *Eichmann in Jerusalem. A Report on the Banality of Evil* (New York: Viking, 1964), 120–122, notes distinction between an order (limited in time and space) and a law (Hitler's wish, which had no temporal or spatial limitation at all). This demanded total loyalty to the *spirit* of the law, not the letter of the order. Eichmann says he felt like Pontius Pilate, but he did his *duty* and did not merely "obey orders." Göring often said, "I have no conscience. My conscience is Adolf Hitler," Hermann Rauschning, *Voice of Destruction* (New York: Putnam's, 1940), 78.

25. Helmut Krausnick and Martin Broszat, *Anatomie des SS-Staats* (Freiburg i. Br.: Walters, 1965), 265–266.

26. This often-quoted speech appears in Joachim Fest, *The Face of the Third Reich: Portraits of the Nazi Leadership*, trans. Michael Bullock (New York: Pantheon, 1970), 115. Karl Dietrich Bracher, *Die deutsche Diktatur, Enstehung, Struktur, Folgen des Nationalsozialismus* (Cologne: Kiepenheuer Witsch, 1969), 422. *Trials of War Criminals before the Nuremberg Military Tribunals*, Nuremberg. United States Government Printing Office, 1946–1949, Vol. 29, PS-1919, 122. Roger Manvell and Heinrich Fränkel, *Himmler* (Frankfurt: Ullstein, 1965), 131. "These animals . . . must not be treated as decent people," Himmler told his men. Bradley F. Smith and Agnes F. Peterson, eds., *Heinrich Himmler: Geheimreden, 1933 bis 1945* (Frankfurt: Propyläen, 1974), 185. Cf. Goebbels, *Diary*, February 14, 1942.

27. Susan Griffin, *Pornography and Silence* (New York: Pantheon, 1980), 195.

28. Sereny, *Darkness*, 101. By making victims look pathetic, euthanasia could seem ethical. In German, those who suffered could have "help in dying."

29. Quoted in Katz and Ringelheim, *Proceedings*, 140.

30. Sereny, *Darkness*, 203.

31. Quoted in Hilberg, *Destruction*, 218; Arendt, *Eichmann*, 83–84. Himmler behaved no differently on the one occasion when he witnessed a model execution. "At the first salvo . . . he almost fainted, and he screamed when the execution squad failed to kill two women outright." Fest, *The Face of the Third Reich*, 121.

32. Irmgard Litten, *A Mother Fights Hitler* (London: Allen and Unwin, 1940), 250.

33. Fania Fénelon, "Ensemble der Hölle," *Die Zeit*, no. 41 (October 3, 1980), 64. Idem., *Playing*, 194–212, 132–142.

34. Albert Speer, *Inside the Third Reich: Memoirs*, trans. Richard and Clara Winston (New York: Macmillan, 1970), 112. Fénelon said of Mandel, the woman commandant who took the baby she had adopted to the gas chambers, her brain was "compartmentalized like a submarine, made of watertight sections." *Playing*, 248.

35. Sereny, *Darkness*, 162, 229.

36. Ibid., 200.

37. Although Himmler supported divorce, especially for childless couples, he insisted that husbands (and not the SS or the state) must control their own wives. "Even the wife belongs to the SS. She is the part of the SS that shows we are not only a soldierly union but a community, an order. The wife, too, must obey. . . . For her, you are the highest Führer." Smith and Peterson, eds., *Himmler*, 84.

38. Memo, Führerhauptquartier, February 4, 1944, Anordnung 22/44. Reprinted in Ursula von Gersdorff, ed. *Frauen im Kriegsdienst* (Stuttgart: Deutsche, 1969), Doc. 213, 435. Michael Kater, *The Nazi Party* (Cambridge, Mass: Harvard, 1983), 148, from Göttingen, SF 6815. GA/6. Davidson, *Trial*, 317. Thus, policy toward women resembled the directives to Germans, which urged them to treat foreign workers kindly, but not to befriend them.

39. Hermann Langbein, H. A. Adler, and Ella Lingens-Reiner, eds., *Menschen in Auschwitz* (Vienna: Europa Verlag, 1972). My thanks to Amy Hackett for bringing this example to my attention. Robert Jay Lifton, *The Nazi Doctors: Medical Killing and the Psychology of Genocide* (New York: Basic Books, 1986). Hermann Langbein and Ella Lingens-Reiner, eds., *Auschwitz: Zeugnisse und Berichte*, 2nd ed. (Cologne: Europäische, 1979).

40. Speer, *Inside*, 147. Eva Braun, he reports, was the only person in the bunker who remained calm during the last days and hours. " 'Why do so many more people have to be killed? And it's all for nothing.' " 484–485. Cf. Erich Ebermayer, *Gefährtin des Teufels* (Hamburg: Hoffmann & Campe, 1952); Henriette von Schirach, *Frauen um Hitler* (Berlin: Herbig, 1983).

41. Rudolf Höss, *Commandant at Auschwitz. Autobiography of Rudolf Höss* (New York: Popular Library, 1964), 34.

42. Joel Dimsdale, *Survivors and Perpetrators* (Washington and New York: Hemisphere, 1980), Part III, which analyzes Rorschach data.

43. Hermann Langbein, *Liquidiert Sie Selber! . . . Wir haben es getan. Selbstporträts 1939–1945* (Vienna and Cologne: Europa, 1961), 49, 51.

44. Ibid., 51.

45. Sereny, *Darkness*, 361. Fénelon, *Playing*, describes Kramer's happy home life at Auschwitz, 196–198.

46. Ibid., 235. The one woman with whom Theresa Stangl spoke assured Frau Stangl that her husband must be innocent, and helped her to deny reality. Although Stangl's first name was Franz, his wife called him Paul.

47. Sociologists have examined the ways in which "amoral familialism" skews people's ethical thinking in other national settings. Edward C. Banfield, *The Moral Basis of a Backward Society* (Glencoe: Free Press, 1958). Renate Mayntz, "Role Distance Role Identification, and Amoral Role Behavior," *European Journal of Sociology* II, 2:368–378, also *Social Research* 37:3 (Autumn) 428–446.

48. Langbein, *Liquidiert*, 53, 57–65. The author describes with great sensitivity how nervous his dog has become.

49. 5.7.41, "Wunderbare Musik," ibid., 61.

50. Ibid., 62–63.
51. Emphasis in the original. Max Weber to his mother, quoted by Wolfgang J. Mommsen, *Max Weber und die deutsche Politik* (Tübingen: Mohr, 1974), 207.
52. Joseph Conrad, *Heart of Darkness* (London: Penguin, 1973), 69.
53. Sereny, *Darkness*, 350. In her conclusion, the author discusses the relationship between one's identity and his or her perception of guilt.

19

Magda Trocmé

. . . A poor woman came to my house one night, and she asked to come in. She said immediately that she was a German Jew, that she was running away, that she was hiding, that she wanted to have shelter. . . . And I said, "Come in."

MAGDA TROCMÉ

With winters that are long and harsh, Le Chambon is a mountain village in south-central France. Since the sixteenth century, it has been predominantly Protestant, an anomaly in Catholic France. Many of the villagers are descendants of Huguenots who fled to this high plateau so they could practice their Protestant Christianity without fear of punishment. But persecution persisted. Some people and pastors of Le Chambon were hanged or burned at the stake for fidelity to the biblical principles that gave meaning to their lives.

Far from weakening their faith, such persecution—and the memory of it—produced a strength that gave the hardy folk of Le Chambon a close-knit solidarity. That solidarity manifested itself when France was occupied by Nazi Germany. Le Chambon became "a haven from public horror," but not in the way that Claudia Koonz used those words to describe the "ersatz goodness" of Nazi homes. In Le Chambon, the goodness was real. It sheltered Jews—some five thousand of them—and other refugees who were fleeing, to use Koonz's words again, "the masculine sphere of brutality, coercion, corruption, and power" of Nazi Germany.

In "The Courage to Care," Magda Trocmé describes her late husband, André, the Protestant minister and spiritual leader of Le Chambon during World War II. André Trocmé was "a very impressive man," she says, "interesting and genuine, original." The words Madame Trocmé uses to describe her husband fit her as well.

According to those who knew them both, Magda was at least her husband's match in energy, devotion, and intelligence. Her life has not been without sorrow, but this vibrant, charming, and outspoken woman consistently embodied the principles she believed so deeply: "to give hope, to give love, to give help to those who are in need, whatever the need is."

Le Chambon did not become a Holocaust haven overnight. For years André Trocmé had preached the simple lessons of the Christian gospels: peace, understanding, love. His was a message of nonviolence, but a nonviolence that rejected inaction and deplored complicity with injustice. The Trocmés' way meant learning "to read the signs of the times" so that ways could be found to get people out of harm's way. It meant actively resisting evil when confronted by evil; it meant remaining human in inhuman times. When the time came for the people of Le Chambon to resist the Nazi death machine, to act in solidarity and on behalf of others, the villagers—Protestant and Catholic alike—backed André Trocmé. Unlike so many other "Christians" during the Holocaust, they made their village an ark of hope in a sea of flames and ashes.

Le Chambon's resistance to the Holocaust started with small gestures—with Magda Trocmé opening her door and welcoming a German Jewish woman into her home. She and everyone else in Le Chambon were well aware of the danger, but that did not deter them. They regarded their acts of rescue as natural, as just the right thing to do. As Madame Trocmé said, "None of us thought that we were heroes. We were just people trying to do our best." Women and the Holocaust: Theresa Stangl, Gertrud Scholtz-Klink, and Magda Trocmé, to name but three. Their different voices make one wonder.

The Courage to Care

My husband, André Trocmé, was a Protestant minister. During the war, we lived with our four children in the small village of Le Chambon-sur-Lignon in central France. People were content to be there, and we were happy to be able to take care of them, although it was the first time that we lived among peasants. Previously, we had lived in a city, but we appreciated this change, because it is always interesting to get to know different people.

The village of Le Chambon was a Protestant one, with a big church. On Sundays the sermon was something very important, because at that time there were no movies, no special lectures. The sermon was something that everyone wanted to hear. My husband's preaching was different because he was a

From Carol Rittner and Sondra Myers, eds., *The Courage to Care: Rescuers of Jews during the Holocaust.* New York: New York University Press, 1986. Copyright © 1986 by New York University Press. Reprinted by permission of New York University Press.

conscientious objector. The Protestant Church was not happy about it, because at that time conscientious objectors were not admitted as ministers. But the parish wanted a man like my husband, not only because of his ideas about war and peace but on account of his general ideas about truth and justice.

My husband was a very impressive man. He was interesting and genuine, original. He always thought that he had to preach for peace, for better love and understanding. The parish asked for him because the people wanted him. So later, when the danger came, how could they not back him?

My husband's mother was German and his father French. My father was Italian and my mother was Russian; we were a good combination. We tried to encourage the parish to be more broad-minded than they perhaps would have been if they had not been living with international people.

We had the opportunity to go to see our families, sometimes in Italy, sometimes in Germany, and we saw what was going on there, especially in Germany. Even before the war, we already knew the truth about what was happening to Jews and others. It was not that we were more clever than the others, but we had more experience and could guess what would happen if the Germans invaded France. Little by little, André tried to prepare the population, preaching to them, preparing them to stand fast. When the dangers came, we were not surprised.

The people in our village knew already what persecutions were because their ancestors were the old Huguenots who, when they accepted the Reformation, were persecuted by the Catholic kings of France. They talked often about their ancestors. Many years went by and they forgot, but when the Germans came, they remembered and were able to understand the persecution of the Jews better perhaps than people in other villages, for they had already had a kind of preparation.

When *la drôle guerre*, the "funny war," was declared in 1939, nothing happened. We knew, of course, that the Germans were coming always nearer to us. We also realized that our government was changing, that Marshal Pétain, who was a very old man, had become the head of the government and that many people believed in him and thought he was like the flag—a symbol—because he was a national hero from World War I. But what many people did not realize was that World War I was very different from World War II.

After the fall of France, André went on preaching as he always did. He spoke against the war. Little by little the Germans, having crossed the border and being in Paris, arrived in our region. The danger was there. They started to persecute the Jews, but we never imagined what would happen to the Jews in France.

Even before the Germans crossed the Vichy line, some Jews managed to get into our part of France, and they tried to come to where we were. It started with the French Jews who often came to our village for the summer. Our peasants were so poor that they took paying guests in the summer. Some of the French Jews were in Le Chambon before the real danger came because they were afraid to stay in the city. They were afraid of the Germans because they knew something about what was happening in Germany. Then the German Jews came. At first, they were paying guests in the hotels and at the farms. Later they became refugees.

Why did they come to us? Because we were in the mountains, because it was a Protestant place, because someone had spoken, perhaps, of a minister who at that time had funny ideas, who was a conscientious objector. You could not know how people knew that they might have a good place in our town. I can tell you what happened in our house, but I cannot tell you what happened in other houses, although I know that little by little there were Jews all over the place.

When the "funny war" started to be a real one, a poor woman came to my house one night, and she asked to come in. She said immediately that she was a German Jew, that she was running away, that she was hiding, that she wanted to have shelter. She thought that at the minister's house she would perhaps find someone who could understand her. And I said, "Come in." And so it started. I did not know that it would be dangerous. Nobody thought of that.

But all at once, many people were in the village. When you hear that there are nice people who will receive you in their homes in a certain place, and you think you are in danger—and later when you really are in danger—you will do anything to get there. But there was no advertisement. They just came.

Those of us who received the first Jews did what we thought had to be done—nothing more complicated. It was not decided from one day to the next what we would have to do. There were many people in the village who needed help. How could we refuse them? A person doesn't sit down and say I'm going to do this and this and that. We had no time to think. When a problem came, we had to solve it immediately. Sometimes people ask me, "How did you make a decision?" There was no decision to make. The issue was: Do you think we are all brothers or not? Do you think it is unjust to turn in the Jews or not? Then let us try to help!"

It was not something extraordinary. Now that the years have gone by, perhaps we exaggerate things a little, although I can tell you that things did get complicated later. But in the beginning, when the first Jew came to my house, I just opened the door and took her in without knowing what would happen later. It was even simpler than one might suppose.

In the beginning, we did not realize the danger was so big. Later, we became accustomed to it, but you must remember that the danger was all over. The people who were in the cities had bombs coming down and houses coming in on their heads, and they were killed. Others were dying in the war, in battles. Other people were being persecuted, like those in Germany. It was a general danger, and we did not feel we were in much more danger than the others. And, you see, the danger was not what you might imagine.

You might imagine that the people were fighting with weapons in the middle of the square, that you would have had to run away, that you would have had to go into a little street and hide. The danger was not that kind at all. The danger was in having a government that, little by little, came into the hands of the Germans, with their laws, and the French people were supposed to obey those laws.

The police were no longer "French" police; they were police that acted for the Vichy government that was under the Germans. At that time, we were more afraid of the police and the Vichy government than we were of the Germans, who were not yet really in our country.

We started to disobey in very little ways. For example, in our school it was suggested that we put a picture of Marshal Pétain on the wall. We decided not to do it. It was a small disobedience, but then we started to be more disobedient. In the mornings, to give another example, the flag had to be put up in front of the school and the children were supposed to salute it. We decided not to do it. Ours was a private school, a school founded by the Protestants, not the school of the state. The state school did as the marshal said, but we disobeyed.

Because the director of the public school was one of our friends, he said, "You don't want a flag. I understand. If they want to salute the flag, they can come to my school." At that time, we were just across the street. For a while, some teachers and students went to the flag at the public school. Little by little, it was forgotten and it stopped.

It is true that we had Jewish children in our village. Once when my husband was in Marseilles, he spoke to Burns Chalmers, who was responsible for many of the Quakers' activities on behalf of the inmates of the concentration camps in the south of France. André told him that he wanted to volunteer to go to one of the French camps where there were Jewish children and help take care of them. Chalmers said to him, "But Monsieur Trocmé, we have volunteers for the camps. We have lots of volunteers for the camps. What we do not have is a place, a village, a house, a place to put people who are hiding, people that we can save. We get people out of the camps, but nobody wants them. It is dangerous to take them. Is your village prepared to do such a thing?"

My husband came back to the village and he spoke to the council of the church, and they said, "OK, go ahead." Within minutes, they were willing to help. They did not always agree one hundred percent with all that my husband said, but they agreed in general with him, and so they helped.

Yes, there were dangers, but up until then, nothing had happened. More and more we would disobey. We had a habit of doing it. One day, finally, the governor—the prefect of the Department of the Haute-Loire—Monsieur Bach, came and said to my husband, "Now you must give the names of all the Jews that are here." It was at the time that the Jews had to put on the sign, the yellow star.

My husband said, "No, I cannot. First, I do not know their names"—they often changed their names—"and I don't know who they are. And second, these Jews, they are my brothers."

"No," Monsieur Bach said, "they are not your brothers. They are not of your religion. They are not of your country."

"No, you are wrong," André responded. "Here, they are under my protection."

"You must give me their names," said the prefect, "or who knows? Maybe you will be taken to prison, if you don't tell me who they are."

Immediately I prepared a suitcase. I put into it everything that I thought would be necessary in prison, something warm, a change, and so on. We called that suitcase "the prison suitcase." Then the prefect left, and it was put aside.

Some months later, it was February 13, 1943, around seven o'clock in the evening, two *gendarmes* knocked at the door of the old parsonage in Le Chambon-sur-Lignon. I was cooking and my husband was not home. They asked to see Pastor Trocmé, and I told them that he was at a meeting, and that he was coming back later, but that I could answer all their questions because I knew all about my husband's work. They said that it was something very personal and that they wanted to wait. So I put them in his office, and I went on cooking, doing whatever I had to do, and I forgot about them. When my husband came back, it was about eight o'clock or eight-thirty, he rushed into the house, with his Bible under his arm, with his papers, and went into his office. After awhile he came out and said, "I've been arrested." Why arrested? At that time, nobody even dared to ask why such things happened.

And I said, "Oh my goodness, what about the suitcase?" It was now February and the suitcase was empty, because it had been put together the past August.

And then the *gendarme* said, "What is this suitcase business?" So I told him and he said I could have all the time I needed to prepare André's things, but that no friends or neighbors could be aware of what was happening. These *gendarmes*, you know, were French people, and they were very much worried about doing what they were doing. It was a dirty job, but what could they do? If you are a *gendarme*, you arrest people. There we were, and it was time to eat, so I said to the *gendarmes*, "Sit down and eat."

People now, when they write a book, or when they write a newspaper article, or a magazine article, or when they speak of these things, they say, "Oh, what a wonderful woman. The *gendarmes* came to arrest her husband, and she invited them to sit down and eat with them." It was nothing at all. We always said, "Sit down" when somebody came. Why not say it to the *gendarmes*? And besides, I had to hunt around for the suitcase so that I could pack it. They could just as well sit down and get out of the way.

Before my husband left, you cannot imagine what happened. A young girl, Suzanne Gilbert, rang the doorbell. Her father was a church counsellor, and we had been invited to their home because it was her father's birthday. Of course, we had forgotten because of all the excitement. She came, saw the police, ran away, told everyone what was happening in the parsonage, and a few minutes later, the people of the village started a sort of "procession" coming to say goodbye and to bring presents—queer presents, things that we had not seen in years began to appear. A box of sardines, which is nothing now, but at that time a box of sardines was put aside for the worst time, for the future. A candle. We had no candles for light. At the end, we discovered that matches were missing, and the *gendarme* captain gave his own. Someone else brought a piece of soap—we had soap but it was like stone—but somebody brought my husband real soap. And someone brought toilet paper—not a roll, but loose, flat papers. There it was, wonderful toilet paper.

It was only later, when I was able to visit my husband in the camp—it was not a concentration camp, but a Vichy detention camp—that he said to me, "Do you know what was on that paper? With a pencil, very carefully, the person who gave this toilet paper had written on it verses of the Bible, of encouragement, of love and understanding. I had a message, but I don't know from whom."

My husband was a prisoner, and yet someone took the time to write him messages of love and understanding. It was a compensation. People would forget that there was some danger, because they were involved in the work.

I remember once toward the end of June 1943, my husband was not home, and I was called by a girl, Suzanne Heim, early in the morning. She told me that the Gestapo was taking away young people from the student home, "La Maison des Roches." Most of the students there were of military age and foreigners. The Gestapo had gone to the children's home where Daniel Trocmé, my cousin, lived, and had taken him with them to the student home. I went there immediately from my kitchen. I had an apron on, so when I arrived the Gestapo thought I was a maid of the house. They let me in, and I sat in the kitchen. I tried to go into the dining room where all the Jewish students were in a line. My cousin Daniel who was responsible for the students was with them. The Gestapo screamed at me and kicked me out, but they let me go into the kitchen, which meant that they thought I was a maid, that I was someone belonging to the house. After a while I had to go to the village.

When I returned, my young son Jean-Pierre, who was 13, came to be with me for the moment when the students were taken, because he did not want me to be alone. I saw all those boys passing to go into a little room where there was a man with a booklet with many names. He was interrogating them, interviewing them one by one. Most of those who went through had a little bit of paper and said to me, "Send this to my mother. Here's the address of my father. This is for my fiancée. I have some money in my room." They did not know that all the rooms had already been searched and that there was no longer any money, no jewels in the rooms. But it did not matter. We would help them anyhow if possible. My son was so upset when he saw those Gestapo beating those Jews as they were in line coming down the stairs, going into the trucks. They were beating some of those young boys and screaming, *"Schweine Juden! Schweine Juden!"*

We saw all those young people get into the trucks, and my cousin Daniel said to me. "Do not worry. Tell my parents that I was very happy here. It was the best time of my life. Tell them that I like traveling, that I go with my friends."

When they left, my son was green, I would say, like a sick boy. And he said, "Mother, I am going to get revenge later. Such things cannot happen again. I am going to do something when I am grown up." And I said to him, "But you know what your father says: "If you do such a thing, someone else is going to take revenge against you. And that is why we are never finished. We go on and on and on. We must forgive, we must forget, we must do better.'" He was silent, and we left. And Daniel never came back.

During the war things were very difficult. When my husband after a few weeks did return safely from the Vichy camp, we continued our work taking care of people. After the war, I traveled in America for the Fellowship of Reconciliation. I spoke English at that time much better. I was asked lots of times to speak about these things, to say what the lesson was that we must learn from all this.

The lesson is very simple, I think. The first thing is that we must not think that we were the only ones who helped during those times. Little by little, now that we speak of these things, we realize that other people did lots of things too. Also, we must not be afraid to be discussed in books or in articles and reviews, because it may help people in the future to try to do something, even if it is dangerous. Perhaps there is also a message for young people and for children, a message of hope, of love, of understanding, a message that could give them the courage to go against all that they believe is wrong, all that they believe is unjust.

Maybe later on in their lives, young people will be able to go through experiences of this kind—seeing people murdered, killed, or accused improperly; racial problems; the problem of the elimination of people, of destroying perhaps not their bodies but their energy, their existence. They will be able to think that there always have been some people in the world who tried—who will try—to give hope, to give love, to give help to those who are in need, whatever the need is.

It is important, too, to know that we were a bunch of people together. This is not a handicap, but a help. If you have to fight it alone, it is more difficult. But we had the support of people we knew, of people who understood without knowing precisely all that they were doing or would be called to do. None of us thought that we were heroes. We were just people trying to do our best.

When people read this story, I want them to know that I tried to open my door. I tried to tell people, "Come in, come in." In the end, I would like to say to people, "Remember that in your life there will be lots of circumstances that will need a kind of courage, a kind of decision of your own, not about other people but about yourself." I would not say more.

Suggestions for Further Reading

Baxter, Richard. *Women of the Gestapo*. London: Quality, 1943.

Bock, Gisela, and Pat Thane, eds. *Maternity and Gender Policies: Women and the Rise of the European Welfare States*. New York: Routledge, 1991.

Bridenthal, Renate, and Claudia Koonz, eds. *Becoming Visible: Women and European History*. Boston: Houghton Mifflin, 1977.

Evans, Richard. "German Women and the Triumph of Hitler." *Journal of Modern History*, March 1976.

Fein, Helen. *Accounting for Genocide: National Responses and Jewish Victims during the Holocaust*. New York: Free Press, 1979.

Gordon, Sarah. *Hitler, Germans and the "Jewish Question."* Princeton, N.J.: Princeton University Press, 1984.

Grunberger, Richard. *The 12 Year Reich: A Social History of Nazi Germany, 1933–1945*. New York: Holt, Rinehart and Winston, 1972.

Hallie, Philip. *Lest Innocent Blood Be Shed: The Story of the Village of Le Chambon and How Goodness Happened There*. New York: Harper, 1979.

Heller, Celia S. *On the Edge of Destruction: Jews of Poland between the Two World Wars*. New York: Columbia University Press, 1977.

Kaplan, Marion A. *The Jewish Feminist Movement in Germany: The Campaigns of the Jüdischer Frauenbund, 1904–1938*. Westport, Conn.: Greenwood Press, 1979.

Katz, Esther, and Joan Miriam Ringelheim, eds. *Proceedings of the Conference on Women Surviving the Holocaust*. New York: The Institute for Research in History, 1983.

Kopecky, Lilli. *In the Shadow of the Flames: Six Lectures on the Holocaust*. Atlanta: Emory University Center for Research in Social Change, 1982.

Le Chene, Evelyn. *Mauthausen: The History of a Death Camp*. London: Metheun, 1971.

Lifton, Robert Jay. *The Nazi Doctors: Medical Killing and the Psychology of Genocide.* New York: Basic Books, 1986.

Mason, Tim. "Women in Nazi Germany," Parts I and II. *History Workshop* (Spring and Autumn 1976).

Munckacsi, Naomi W. "Jewish Religious Observance in Women's Death Camps in Germany." *Yad Vashem Bulletin* 20 (1967).

Pauwels, Jacques R. *Women, Nazis and Universities: Female University Students in the Third Reich, 1933–1945.* Westport, Conn.: Greenwood Press, 1984.

Pawelczynska, Anna. *Values and Violence in Auschwitz: A Sociological Analysis.* Translated by Catherine S. Leach. Berkeley: University of California Press, 1979.

Phayer, Michael. *Protestant and Catholic Women in Nazi Germany.* Detroit: Wayne State University Press, 1990.

Proctor, Robert. *Racial Hygiene: Medicine under the Nazis.* Cambridge, Mass.: Harvard University Press, 1988.

Rabinowitz, Dorothy. *New Lives: Survivors of the Holocaust Living in America.* New York: Knopf, 1976.

Rittner, Carol, and Sondra Myers, eds. *The Courage to Care.* New York: New York University Press, 1986.

Rossiter, Margaret L. *Women in the Resistance.* New York: Praeger Publishers, 1986.

Rupp, Leila J. *Mobilizing for War: German and American Propaganda, 1939–1945.* Princeton, N.J.: Princeton University Press, 1978.

Sauvage, Pierre. *Weapons of the Spirit.* New York: First Run Features, 1988.

Schwertfeger, Ruth. *Women of Theresienstadt: Voices from a Concentration Camp.* New York: Berg, 1989.

Stephenson, Jill. *The Nazi Organization of Women.* London: Croom Helm, 1981.

———. *Women in Nazi Society.* New York: Barnes & Noble, 1975.

Syrkin, Marie. *Blessed Is the Match: The Story of Jewish Resistance.* Philadelphia: The Jewish Publication Society, 1976.

Tec, Nechama. *When Light Pierced the Darkness: Christian Rescue of Jews in Nazi-occupied Poland.* New York: Oxford University Press, 1986.

Tillion, Germaine. *Ravensbrück.* Translated by Gerald Satterwhite. Garden City, N.Y.: Anchor Books, 1975.

Showing Auschwitz–Birkenau in late May 1944, these photographs were taken by two SS men: Bernard Walter, head of the camp's Identification Office, and his assistant, Ernst Hoffmann. A special permit must have been issued. Ordinarily photography in Auschwitz–Birkenau was strictly forbidden.

Arrival Ramp at Auschwitz.   Taken from the roof of a railway car, this photograph of the notorious ramp at Auschwitz II (Birkenau) shows the inside of the camp. On this ramp, which became operational in the spring of 1944, Nazi doctors such as the infamous Dr. Josef Mengele, the "Angel of Death," decided on the spot who would live and who would die. In the background can be seen the arched railroad entrance to the camp, prison barracks, and trucks often used to transport prisoners directly to the gas chambers.

Women and Children Beside the Tracks.   Holding the hand of a small child, the woman in the flowered skirt appears to be pregnant. Pregnant women and children under fourteen were usually considered useless. Probably everyone in this photograph was murdered by the Nazis. In the background can be seen the windowless prefabricated huts originally designed as horse stables. Each one served as shelter for hundreds of human beings.

Women Wearing Babushkas.   These women have been "selected" for slave labor. Not all pregnant women were detected on arrival at Auschwitz–Birkenau. The woman third from the right may be an example. Perhaps she will be one of those Dr. Gisella Perl "saves" by drowning her baby at birth.

Women and Children in Front of Building. Perhaps the women in this photograph thought the building on the other side of the tracks, beyond the fence, was an administrative building. In fact, it was one of Birkenau's killing centers, housing fifteen high-speed ovens vented through a massive central chimney. These women expect the worst, but, as Charlotte Delbo wrote, "they do not expect the unthinkable."

Men Staring at Women. Still looking reasonably healthy, the women in this photograph will be processed for slave labor. Their faces reflect a range of emotion: anxiety, puzzlement, humiliation, fear. If they do not suspect what awaits them, the men staring behind the electrified fence could tell more than the women want to know.

On the Road of No Return.   This photograph shows no faces, nor does it give any names. But we do know who these people are: Hungarian Jews, an older woman with little children, including perhaps an infant cradled under her arm, human beings walking to their anonymous deaths.

Empty Baby Carriages.   Former prisoners such as Seweryna Szmaglewska and Giuliana Tedeschi emphasize that the German loot at Birkenau included baby carriages. A poignant reminder of what happened especially to Jewish mothers and children who were deported to that place, this photograph shows some of those empty carriages near the pole at the center.

Part Three

VOICES OF REFLECTION

I will not kiss the arm that wields the weighty scepter,
Nor the brazen knee, the earthen feet of demigods in desperate
*   hours;*
If only I could raise my voice to be a blazing torch
Amidst the darkened desert of the world, and thunder:
JUSTICE! JUSTICE! JUSTICE!

GERTRUD KOLMAR

The Holocaust did not result from random violence carried out by hooligans. It was instead a state-sponsored program of population elimination made possible by modern technological capabilities and political structures. The Nazi destruction process required and received cooperation from virtually every sector of German society. For the most part, those who permitted or carried out the orders were ordinary, decent folk, but many of them did extraordinary things. Teachers and writers helped to till the soil where Hitler's virulent antisemitism took root; their students reaped the wasteful harvest. Lawyers helped to draft and enforce the laws that isolated Jews and set them up for the kill. Artists polished the propaganda that made Hitler's policies persuasive to so many. Driven by their eugenic imperatives and biomedical visions, physicians implemented sterilization programs and experimented with the gassing of *lebensunwertes Leben*, "life unworthy of life." Scientists performed research and tested their racist and sexist theories on those branded sub- or nonhuman by German science. Some business executives found that Nazi concentration camps could provide cheap labor. Turning the Nazi slogan *Arbeit macht frei* (Work makes one free) into a

319

sardonic truth, they supplemented the toll taken in the gas chambers by extermination through work. Others made profits by supplying Zyklon B to gas people or by building crematoriums to burn the corpses. Meanwhile engineers drove trains of deportation and death, factory workers modified trucks so that they became deadly gas vans, city policemen became members of squadrons that made murder of Jews their speciality. At every point, these measures affected women and children as well as men.

The list above could go on and on. At Auschwitz it did, although probably none of the camp's administrative personnel originally had career plans leading in that direction. Those people, mostly men, had trained to be weavers or cooks, doctors or scholars, business managers or military officers of a more conventional kind before they swore allegiance to the Third Reich and began their journeys on the twisted road to Auschwitz. For a time, Commandant Rudolf Höss thought about a career in farming. Dr. Johann Paul Kremer might have spent his life as an obscure professor. As for a man named Pery Broad, he was almost too young to have been part of Auschwitz, but *anus mundi* became his home nonetheless.

For understandable reasons, Auschwitz survivors have had more to say about that place than the perpetrators who ran it. The latter have had no desire for Auschwitz memories to implicate them and inconvenience their lives. Höss's autobiography and Kremer's diary break some of the perpetrators' silence. So do the reminiscences of Pery Broad. Born in Rio de Janeiro in 1921, his father was a Brazilian merchant, but his mother was German, and she brought her son to Berlin when he was five. A schoolboy as the Third Reich began, Broad joined the Hitler Youth and then the SS in 1941. Assigned to Auschwitz, he worked initially as a guard, but in June 1942 this SS Private's request was granted: He was transferred to the Political Department, the camp's Gestapo office. This department processed admissions to the camp, kept records, handled investigations and interrogations, and carried out punishments and executions. Broad worked with the interrogation units. Torture was commonplace in extracting the confessions they wanted.

Remaining at Auschwitz until it closed in January 1945, Broad was well positioned to know a great deal about what happened there. After his capture by the British in May 1945, he voluntarily wrote a report about his Auschwitz experiences.[1] Broad's report ranges widely over the atrocities of Auschwitz. His detailed descriptions are quite accurate when checked against other reliable sources, but Broad's tone suggests—incredibly—that he was never directly involved in what went on. Eventually a German court convicted him of supervising selections, torturing prisoners, and executing them as well.

Not only does Broad discuss medical experiments that were performed on women by Dr. Carl Clauberg and others, his report is an important source of information about what happened to women as they were selected for work or sent to the gas chambers. In addition, his testimony is a chief source of information about a grisly massacre that happened on the night of October 5,

1942, at an evacuated village in the Auschwitz "Interest Zone."[2] Located about three miles from Auschwitz I and II, its name was Budy.

On June 25, 1942, a penal company for women was established there. Consignment to a penal company like the one at Budy was punishment tantamount to a death sentence. Included among the several hundred prisoners in the Budy penal company initially were Poles and French and Slovakian Jews. Isolated, those prisoners experienced especially harsh conditions—much poorer food and harder work than usual. In addition to the SS woman who served as overall supervisor and the SS men and dogs who guarded the area, Budy had its prisoner functionaries, German women—criminals and prostitutes—who added to the inmates' misery.

According to Broad, a detachment of the Political Department was sent to Budy on the morning of October 6, 1942. On entering the camp, Broad writes, "they heard a singular buzzing and humming in the air. Then they saw a sight so horrible that some minutes were gone before they could take it in properly."[3] The buzzing and humming sound, the Political Department personnel soon learned, came from swarms of flies attracted to "dozens of female corpses, mutilated and blood-encrusted."[4] About ninety women had been beaten to death, but others, even though badly wounded, remained alive.

As well as the evidence about the gruesome scene could eventually be pieced together, Jewish women in the penal company, most of them French, had been attacked by the SS and German women who had authority over them. Shots were fired, and using other available weapons—clubs, rifle butts, even an axe wielded by a woman identified as Elfriede Schmidt—the German women and SS did their worst. In trying to escape the onslaught, some of the hapless women had become entangled in the camp's barbed wire—it was not electrified at Budy—and had been beaten to death.

Broad reports that early on the German women had abused the Jewish women repeatedly. He adds that the German women's maltreatment of the Jewish women was often agitated by the SS guards, who threatened their German "sisters" with the fate of being shot while "trying to escape" if they did not cause the Jews sufficient misery. In any case, on this occasion the pretext for the hideous violence had been the necessity to thwart an alleged revolt and escape—presumably planned if not actually carried out—by the French Jewish prisoners.[5] As Broad tells the story, one of the German women, fearing reprisals from the French Jews, called to her SS lover for help, and the slaughter was under way. One death led to another as the SS and German women prisoners sought to kill everyone who might bear witness against them.

Commandant Rudolf Höss was informed of the alleged prisoner revolt at about 5:00 A.M. on October 6. He went to Budy, made a quick inspection, and directed the Political Department to handle the situation. Arriving later in the day, they proceeded by finishing any killing the SS and German women had left undone. With syringes that injected phenol into the women's hearts, they dispatched the wounded and dying, although not before hearing at least some of their side of the story.

Six of the German women prisoners who had led the massacre, including Elfriede Schmidt, were taken to the notorious Block 11 in Auschwitz I and promised a transfer in exchange for truthful statements. The Political Department, however, could not afford to leave these women alive. Their liability was not so much that they had murdered Jews in an unwarranted manner but that their knowledge could implicate the SS in unseemly ways. That possibility could not be tolerated; it would not be good for the SS's reputation and morale. Nor would it reflect well on Commandant Höss. Thus, a few days later, on October 24, 1942, these women received phenol injections in their hearts, too. The date of their execution is known not because Pery Broad recorded it but because their deaths were "properly" supervised by two SS medical officers. One of them, Josef Klehr, administered the injections. The other, witnessing the execution, was Dr. Paul Johann Kremer, whose diary entry for that day states matter-of-factly: "6 women from the Budy mutiny got injections (Klehr)."[6] Later Kremer would add that "all of these women were healthy, of German origin, I think. They were killed by Klehr in a sitting position."[7]

The families of the six German women were sent official notifications indicating that each had died of natural causes. As for the Budy SS personnel, Höss was loath to find them guilty of misconduct in such a messy case. He settled for admonishments, transfers, and a ruling that SS guards should not enter the Budy camp's interior in the future. With those measures, the case was closed.

At Budy one group of women wreaked havoc on another. But that, of course, is only a small part of the story and certainly not the most fundamental aspect, either. Budy was not a women's creation. Neither was Auschwitz nor the Holocaust. The fact is that those realities existed because there were men like Hitler and Himmler, Heydrich and Höss, Kremer and Broad. Not least because of the Nazi men's willingness to kill all the women who could sully their reputations and thwart their ambitions, the Budy massacre helps to make those points about the Holocaust abundantly clear.

At issue here is not a facile and unsupportable thesis about the moral superiority of all women. The violence at Budy is only an extreme example of the fact that during the Holocaust it was not only men who did massive harm to women. By direct or indirect means, women could do so to each other as well. Yet the Holocaust was fundamentally a male-made flood of catastrophe. Of course, men were also its victims; they died in huge numbers to stop the disaster. So neither is the issue here a facile and unsupportable thesis about the viciousness of all men. Instead the point here is to see more clearly how racism and sexism combined and conspired to unleash a "Final Solution" that included Budy. The task is to understand better how and why women— especially Jewish but also non-Jewish women—were central targets *as women* during the Holocaust. Both of those perspectives have much to do with feeling what is heard in Gertrud Kolmar's desire to raise her voice like "a blazing torch amidst the darkened desert of the world, and thunder: JUSTICE! JUSTICE! JUSTICE!"

After Auschwitz justice may be harder to come by than it was before, for in *anus mundi* anything was possible and nothing was sacred. Where that situation prevails, justice can hardly be done. The episode at Budy proves it. But Budy is no longer filled with the screams of bludgeoned Jewish women, though their voices may still echo in the silence. Block 11's cruel punishment cells are empty, though their space is still full of interrogating questions. Perhaps time should have stopped before Auschwitz, but it did not, and after Auschwitz is where time is now. What can be done with post-Holocaust time? What should be made of it?

Such questions invite and insist upon reflection. When that reflection happens, well, it will grapple with issues about memory, responsibility, faith, hope, and the questions that inevitably remain whenever such grappling occurs. When that reflection happens well, it will also see that the particularity of thought and feeling gets its due. Movement in those directions will be found in the women's voices of reflection that speak in this book's third and final part. Autobiographical, dramatic, historical, poetic, spiritual, philosophical, even statistical—their approaches reflect different perspectives and traditions. Yet, in their diversity as women, they look, each and all, for ways to face the void created by the Holocaust. They seek to mend together the fragments of a broken past, and to revitalize the courage to care that can make women and men alike more just and thereby more truly human.

NOTES

1. See "Reminiscences of Pery Broad," *KL Auschwitz Seen by the SS: Höss, Broad, Kremer*, ed. Jadwiga Bezwinska and Danuta Czech and trans. Krystyna Michalik (New York: Howard Fertig, 1984), 139–198.
2. Ibid., 163–168. For Sybil Milton's commentary on the Budy massacre, see "Women and the Holocaust: The Case of German and German-Jewish Women," *When Biology Became Destiny: Women in Weimar and Nazi Germany*, ed. Renate Bridenthal, Atina Grossman, and Marion Kaplan (New York: Monthly Review Press, 1984), 316. Milton's essay is reprinted in this book. See 231, 246, n.105.
3. Ibid., 165.
4. Ibid., 165.
5. Broad's description discounts the likelihood of an actual revolt by the French Jewish women. Sybil Milton gives more credence to the possibility that a revolt did occur or at least was being planned. See "Women and the Holocaust: The Case of German and German-Jewish Women," *When Biology Became Destiny*, 316.
6. "Diary of Johann Paul Kremer," trans. Krystyna Michalik, *KL Auschwitz Seen by the SS*, 226.
7. Ibid., 226.

20

Irena Klepfisz

These words are dedicated to those who died . . .
These words are dedicated to those who survived . . .

IRENA KLEPFISZ

Poet, feminist, lesbian, Jew, child survivor of the Holocaust—all of those descriptions fit Irena Klepfisz, who was born in Warsaw, Poland, in 1941. Her father escaped deportation to Treblinka, found his way back to the Warsaw ghetto, and lost his life heroically in the spring uprising of 1943. Her mother managed to survive and was reunited with her daughter after Irena had been hidden by Catholic nuns. In 1949 they emigrated to the United States. Klepfisz attended public schools in New York City, graduated from the City College of New York, and took her Ph.D. in English literature at the University of Chicago.

For years Klepfisz has taught English, creative writing, Yiddish, and women's studies as well as leading workshops on feminism, homophobia, Yiddish culture, antisemitism, and problems in the Middle East. She has not shied away from controversial issues. Active in both the Jewish and lesbian/feminist communities, she continues to raise serious questions related to Jewish identity, the Holocaust, and feminism. In addition to being a founder of Conditions, *a feminist periodical emphasizing the writing of lesbians, her literary credits include* Dreams of an Insomniac: Jewish Feminist Essays, Speeches and Diatribes *and* A Few Words in the Mother Tongue: Poems Selected and New (1971–1990).

One of Klepfisz's best-known works is a poem called "Bashert." Its title, a Yiddish word, evokes senses of inevitability and fate. Divided into two parts, the poem grieves, protests, and teaches all at once. Although never mentioned directly, the Holocaust shadows every line: "These words are dedicated to those who died. . . . These words are dedicated to those who survived." Like each contribution from the voices of reflection in this book's third part, Klepfisz's writing echoes those dedications. Three examples are provided by "during the war," "herr captain," and "death camp," the poems chosen for inclusion here. They display Klepfisz's immense artistic skill and moral integrity, the extraordinary power she gives to simple words.

The first of these poems is an autobiography, but it consists of scarcely more than thirty words divided into ten brief lines. Including so much that is not said, Klepfisz's brevity speaks volumes. The lines of the second poem, "herr captain," contain the terror-filled but often desperately silent screams of sexually exploited Jewish women. In "death camp" Klepfisz dares to let poetry enter the gas chambers and ovens themselves. In less sensitive hands, that attempt could be obscene, but Klepfisz's hard-won voices of experience and reflection combine to have an awesome effect. They make one feel what she means by saying "These words are dedicated to those who died. . . . These words are dedicated to those who survived."

A Few Words In the Mother Tongue

DURING THE WAR

during the war
germans were known
to pick up infants
by their feet
swing them through the air
and smash their heads
against plaster walls.

somehow
i managed
to escape that fate.

From Irena Klepfisz, *A Few Words in the Mother Tongue: Poems Selected and New (1971–1990)*. Portland, Ore.: The Eighth Mountain Press, 1990. Copyright © 1974, 1977, 1980, 1982, 1985, 1990 by Irena Klepfisz. Reprinted by permission of The Eighth Mountain Press.

HERR CAPTAIN

i whispered as he came   through the gate
captain   i am clean   i've been trained
well   i said   captain   i'm not over
used

he was hard   so hard   forcing bending me
till i could not breathe   slamming against me
my mouth filled with terror   i was pierced
in two   when he suddenly pulled out
my head back   he murmured   what a light rider
my grandmother   too   rode her cossack lover
in pain he moaned   harder quicker   ride me now
fearful   i ran   jumping the gate   with the guards
laughing   grimacing   through the window   nervous
biting their nails   the dogs barked   my legs spread   slapped
around his waist   i whipped him further   deeper   till
i felt the blood flooding the field   filling the drowning well
lapping over me   drinking in the smell of his hair
his stomach swollen against me   he collapsed
but i held on   pushing my heels into his back
my teeth clenched   i hissed for my grandmother   her crooked wig
her gold teeth   and her cossack lover   crawling from the well she
pushed up her buttocks   as she came over the wall   fell to the ground
head   first her wig cocked over one eye a butcher knife under her
skirt my mother floats in well water zeide in mourning tears his red
hair hears them again on the kitchen floor slipping in so smoothly she
was wet from the beginning the horse neighing outside and bobbe her ears
pierced at the age of three weeks pulls out the butcher knife begins
slashing till his hands severed he falls back

he brings me soap
his boots are shiny
not like the others   who arrive from the fields
crusted over

In my early teens I read *House of Dolls*, a novel written by a man under the pseudonym Katzetnik 134633 and based on a diary of an anonymous Jewish woman who did not survive the Holocaust. When I rediscovered it, I immediately recognized it as the main unconscious source for "herr captain." Although today, I see sexuality and violence from a different perspective than I did in the early 1970s when I wrote it, "herr captain" is to me still an important poem about Jewish women's experience and survival.

DEATH CAMP

when they took us   to the shower   i saw
the rebbitzin   her sagging breasts   sparse
pubic hairs   i knew   and remembered
the old rebbe   and turned   my eyes away
i could still hear   her advice   a woman
with a husband   a scholar

when they turned   on the gas   i smelled
it   first   coming at me   pressed myself
hard to the wall   crying   rebbitzin   rebbitzin
i am here with you   and the advice you gave me
i screamed   into the wall   as the blood burst from
my lungs   cracking   her nails in women's flesh   i watched
her capsize   beneath me   my blood in her mouth   i screamed

when they dragged my body   into the oven   i burned
slowly at first   i could smell my own flesh   and could
hear   them grunt   with the weight of the rebbitzin
and they flung   her on top   of me   and i could smell
her hair burning   against my stomach

when i pressed through   the chimney
it was sunny   and clear   my smoke
was distinct   i rose quiet   left her
beneath

21

Charlotte Delbo

Auschwitz is so deeply etched in my memory that I cannot forget one moment of it.

CHARLOTTE DELBO

Charlotte Delbo has been heard in these pages twice before. Her voice of experience spoke about arrivals and departures at Auschwitz. She remembered Lulu, too, that "practical woman" who found ways to help people when they lacked the strength to go on by themselves. Those recollections came from None of Us Will Return, *Delbo's first book, which was written shortly after her liberation. Translated by Rosette Lamont as* Days and Memory, La memoire et les jours, *the last of Delbo's books, is the source of the reflection that follows. Its theme is not a specific happening at Auschwitz. Instead, this essay meditates on what it means to remember Auschwitz. Because of Delbo's experience there, her voice reflects on how her past, present, and future fit together, if they do.*

Here Delbo ponders the challenge that will not leave her: "explaining the inexplicable." As she uses those words, they do not mystify. Nor are they a philosopher's abstract rendering of some cosmic puzzle. Her dilemma is personal and concrete. It involves coming to grips with awareness of time and place, with simple realities that turn out to be anything but simple—then and now, for instance, or there and here, before and after. Ordinarily such dimensions of experience cause few problems. Life's continuity makes it possible to feel without much difficulty the connections and relations they entail. But what if disjunction is more real than continuity in one's life? What if there is a devastating gap between then and now, there and here, before and after? What if the gap is Auschwitz? What if memory, far from closing that gap, keeps it open, deep, and terrifying?

328

As a defense against total self-destruction, Delbo tried for years to move beyond Auschwitz and her memory of it, to leave that horror behind the way a snake wiggles out of its skin when molting. Such escape proved impossible. Auschwitz was no skin to be shed. It remained with her always, imprinted in her very being. True, in the months and years after, she relearned what she had forgotten from before. Here she could do what was never possible there—things like using a toothbrush. Now she could do what was unthinkable then—things like eating calmly with a knife and fork. And yet, as she apparently became once more the person she had been before Auschwitz intervened—charming, cultivated, civilized—she could hardly experience the smell of rain, for example, without recalling that "in Birkenau, rain heightened the odor of diarrhea."

None of us will return, Delbo had thought, and after she did it seemed incredible. So at times she felt that "the one who was in the camp is not me, is not the person who is here, facing you." Confronting the question "So, you are living with Auschwitz?" Delbo's answer had to be "No, I live next to it." But that answer did not work completely, because she did not only live "next to it." Rather it also lived in her, a fact that dreams kept showing: "And in those dreams I see myself, yes, my own self such as I know I was . . . and I feel death fasten on me."

Delbo could speak and write about all of the disjointed experience that one life contained. But that fact gave her scant consolation. What she was able to put into words was not the same as what her feeling contained. "Deep memory," she wrote, "preserves sensations, physical imprints," but words do not come from that source. They are too intellectual, too external, for that.

"You hear me speak. But do you hear me feel?": Delbo also raises Gertrud Kolmar's question. Calling herself "a twofold being," she probably doubted that the response could ever be a simple yes, even for herself. How does one integrate the experience of Auschwitz into one's life? One never does, and, Charlotte Delbo might add, that is no answer.

Days and Memory

Explaining the inexplicable. There comes to mind the image of a snake shedding its old skin, emerging from beneath it in a fresh, glistening one. In Auschwitz I took leave of my skin—it had a bad smell, that skin—worn from all the blows it had received, and found myself in another, beautiful and clean, although with me the molting was not as rapid as the snake's. Along with the old skin went the visible traces of Auschwitz: the leaden stare out of sunken eyes, the tottering gait, the frightened gestures. With the new skin returned the gestures belonging to an earlier life: the using of a toothbrush, of toilet paper, of a handkerchief, of a knife and fork, eating food calmly, saying hello to people upon entering a room, closing the door, standing up straight, speaking, later on smiling with my lips and, still later, smiling both at once with my lips and my eyes. Rediscovering odors, flavors, the smell of rain. In Birkenau, rain heightened the odor of diarrhea. It is the most fetid odor I know. In Birkenau, the rain came down upon the camp, upon us, laden with soot from the crematoriums, and with the odor of burning flesh. We were steeped in it.

It took a few years for the new skin to fully form, to consolidate.

Rid of its old skin, it's still the same snake. I'm the same too, apparently. However . . .

How does one rid oneself of something buried far within: memory and the skin of memory. It clings to me yet. Memory's skin has hardened, it allows nothing to filter out of what it retains, and I have no control over it. I don't feel it anymore.

In the camp one could never pretend, never take refuge in the imagination. I remember Yvonne Picart, a morning when we were carrying bricks from a wrecker's depot. We carried two bricks at a time, from one pile to another pile. We were walking side by side, our bricks hugged to our chests, bricks we had pried from a pile covered with ice, scraping our hands. Those bricks were heavy, and got heavier as the day wore on. Our hands were blue from cold, our lips cracked. Yvonne said to me: "Why can't I imagine I'm on the Boulevard Saint-Michel, walking to class with an armful of books?" and she propped the two bricks inside her forearm, holding them as students do books. "It's impossible. One can't imagine either being somebody else or being somewhere else."

I too, I often tried to imagine I was somewhere else. I tried to visualize myself as someone else, as when in a theatrical role you become another person. It didn't work.

In Auschwitz reality was so overwhelming, the suffering, the fatigue, the cold so extreme, that we had no energy left for this type of pretending. When I would recite a poem, when I would tell the comrades beside me what a novel or a play was about while we went on digging in the muck of the swamp, it was to keep myself alive, to preserve my memory, to remain me, to make sure of it. Never did that succeed in nullifying the moment I was living through, not for an instant. To think, to remember was a great victory over the horror, but it never lessened it. Reality was right there, killing. There was no possible getting away from it.

How did I manage to extricate myself from it when I returned? What did I do so as to be alive today? People often ask me that question, to which I continue to look for an answer, and still find none.

Auschwitz is so deeply etched in my memory that I cannot forget one moment of it.—So you are living with Auschwitz?—No, I live next to it.

Auschwitz is there, unalterable, precise, but enveloped in the skin of memory, an impermeable skin that isolates it from my present self. Unlike the snake's skin, the skin of memory does not renew itself. Oh, it may harden further . . . Alas, I often fear lest it grow thin, crack, and the camp get hold of me again. Thinking about it makes me tremble with apprehension. They claim the dying see their whole life pass before their eyes . . .

In this underlying memory sensations remain intact. No doubt, I am very fortunate in not recognizing myself in the self that was in Auschwitz. To return from there was so improbable that it seems to me I was never there at all. Unlike those whose life came to a halt as they crossed the threshold of return, who since that time survive as ghosts, I feel that the one who was in the camp is not me, is not the person who is here, facing you. No, it is all too incredible. And everything that happened to that other, the Auschwitz one, now has no bearing upon me, does not concern me, so separate from one another are this deep-lying memory and ordinary memory. I live within a twofold being. The Auschwitz double doesn't bother me, doesn't interfere with my life. As though it weren't I at all. Without this split I would not have been able to revive.

The skin enfolding the memory of Auschwitz is tough. Even so it gives way at times, revealing all it contains. Over dreams the conscious will has no power. And in those dreams I see myself, yes, my own self such as I know I was: hardly able to stand on my feet, my throat tight, my heart beating wildly, frozen to the marrow, filthy, skin and bones; the suffering I feel is so unbearable, so identical to the pain endured there, that I feel it physically, I feel it throughout my whole body which becomes a mass of suffering; and I feel death fasten on me, I feel that I am dying. Luckily, in my agony I cry out. My cry wakes me and I emerge from the nightmare, drained. It takes days for everything to get back to normal, for everything to get shoved back inside memory, and for the skin of memory to mend again. I become myself again, the person you know, who can talk to you about Auschwitz without exhibiting or registering any anxiety or emotion.

Because when I talk to you about Auschwitz, it is not from deep memory my words issue. They come from external memory, if I may put it that way, from intellectual memory, the memory connected with thinking processes. Deep memory preserves sensations, physical imprints. It is the memory of the senses. For it isn't words that are swollen with emotional charge. Otherwise, someone who has been tortured by thirst for weeks on end could never again say "I'm thirsty. How about a cup of tea." This word has also split in two. *Thirst* has turned back into a word for commonplace use. But if I dream of the thirst I suffered in Birkenau, I once again see the person I was, haggard, halfway crazed, near to collapse; I physically feel that real thirst and it is an atrocious nightmare. If, however, you'd like me to talk to you about it . . .

This is why I say today that while knowing perfectly well that it corresponds to the facts, I no longer know if it is real.

22

Ida Fink

So you remember precisely . . .

IDA FINK

In her poem "We Jews," which provides the epigraph for this third part of Different Voices, *Gertrud Kolmar cried out:*

> *If only I could raise my voice to be a blazing torch*
> *Amidst the darkening desert of the world, and thunder:*
> *JUSTICE! JUSTICE! JUSTICE!*

She wrote those words before the Holocaust happened. After Auschwitz the intensity of their yearning escalates. It does so because the immensity of the "Final Solution" mocked justice and still does. The dead cannot return; the survivors must cope with the ruins of memory. The perpetrators have overwhelmed the resources and determination needed to bring them to judgment. Even the credibility of God to do so has been impugned, for, as Vera Laska once put it, "In Auschwitz God, finding it impossible to cope, went on an extended vacation, as if replaced by a sign: 'For the duration, this office is closed.' "

At the end of World War II there were courtroom efforts to keep the "Final Solution" from mocking justice completely. Sporadically those judicial proceedings have continued into the 1990s. Among the most famous of the war crimes trials were those held by the International Military Tribunal in the German city of Nuremberg from October 18, 1945, until October 1, 1946. Twenty-two of Nazi Germany's top leaders stood trial there. Three of the defendants were acquitted of the charges brought against them. The sentences of the nineteen found guilty ranged from ten-

year prison terms to death by hanging. There were no Nazi women among that first group of Nuremberg defendants, but they were more conspicuous in the Bergen– Belsen trial that a British military tribunal conducted from September 17 to November 17, 1945. This trial judged personnel from Auschwitz as well as from Bergen–Belsen. Of the forty-five defendants, twenty-one were women. Among those sentenced to hang for torturing and assaulting prisoners were Irma Griese and Elisabeth Volkenrath. A death sentence was also pronounced on Fritz Klein, the Nazi doctor whom Olga Lengyel encountered during her fateful Auschwitz arrival.

Whether they occurred in 1945 or nearly a half-century later, the trials of Holocaust perpetrators have involved memory, especially memories of the victims. Memory is not perfect. It can be powerful and penetrating; it can also be fallible and fragmented. Because it can err, memory can also be called into question; it can even be used against itself, especially by interrogators who are experts at detecting and exploiting inconsistencies and lapses. Even when memory fundamentally tells the truth, doubt shadows it—often because some detail has been forgotten or reported differently than someone else remembers.

Such dilemmas have much to do with justice. Ida Fink, whose voice of experience we have heard before, reflects on them in another of her scraps of time. This one is a play called The Table. *It begins in the middle of an interrogation. "Where did we stop?" the Prosecutor asks. "Oh, yes. So you remember precisely that there was a table there."*

Twenty-five years is a long time to remember details about a table, but much rides on the accuracy of memory, because this interrogation is about Germans who sentenced Jews to death during the Holocaust. Or is it? The Prosecutor's questioning of the two women and two men who testify against the SS and Gestapo seems to prosecute them as much as anyone else: "I am terribly sorry that I have to provoke you with such questions," the Prosecutor insists. "But you see, we can only convict people if we can prove that they committed murder. . . . The law requires proof. And I, as the prosecuting attorney, am asking you for proof."

Proof? What constitutes proof where the Holocaust, justice, and memory are concerned? The tension in Fink's play is skillfully orchestrated by the dramatic counterpointing of four witnesses who remember a terrible event (the murder of Polish Jews by members of the SS and Gestapo) and the Prosecutor who presses them relentlessly for exact details: "A small table? How small? . . . Are you certain that Kiper was striking his boots with a riding crop? . . . Were they all sitting at the table? . . . How were they seated, one beside the other?"

A misplaced and distorted insistence on detail, The Table *insists, assaults truth itself. That outcome can compound injustice. It can lead not only to acquittal of the guilty but also to denial that the Holocaust ever happened at all. Resisting such results, Fink's play echoes themes in the brilliant writings of Primo Levi, another survivor of the Holocaust. Calling human memory "a marvelous but fallacious instrument," he recognizes that "almost never do two eyewitnesses of the same event describe it in the same way and with the same words." Nevertheless, his ruling would be the just verdict that* The Table's *scrap of time reveals: "the concordances are abundant, the discordances negligible."*

The Table

A Play For Four Voices and Basso Ostinato

CHARACTERS:

FIRST MAN, 50 years old
FIRST WOMAN, 45 years old
SECOND MAN, 60 years old
SECOND WOMAN, 38 years old
PROSECUTOR, 35–40 years old

The stage is empty and dark. Spotlights only on the witness, seated in a chair, and the prosecutor, seated at a desk.

PROSECUTOR: Have you recovered, Mr. Grumbach? Can we go on? Where did we stop? . . . Oh, yes. So you remember precisely that there was a table there.

FIRST MAN: Yes. A small table.

PROSECUTOR: A *small* table? How small? How many people could sit at a table that size?

FIRST MAN: Do I know? It's hard for me to say now.

PROSECUTOR: How long was it? A meter? Eighty centimeters? Fifty centimeters?

FIRST MAN: A table. A regular table—not too small, not too big. It's been so many years . . . And at a time like that, who was thinking about a table?

PROSECUTOR: Yes, of course, I understand. But you have to understand me, too, Mr. Grumbach: every detail is crucial. You must understand that it's for a good purpose that I'm tormenting you with such details.

FIRST MAN: *(resigned)* All right, let it be eighty centimeters. Maybe ninety.

PROSECUTOR: Where did that table—that small table—stand? On the right side or the left side of the marketplace as you face the town hall?

FIRST MAN: On the left. Yes.

PROSECUTOR: Are you certain?

FIRST MAN: Yes . . . I saw them carry it out.

PROSECUTOR: That means that at the moment you arrived at the marketplace the table was not there yet.

FIRST MAN: No . . . Or maybe it was. You know, I don't remember. Maybe I

From Ida Fink, *A Scrap of Time and Other Stories*, trans. Madeline Levine and Francine Prose. New York: Schocken Books, 1989. Copyright © 1987 by Random House, Inc. Reprinted by permission of Pantheon Books, a division of Random House, Inc.

saw them carrying it from one place to another. But is it so important if they were bringing it out or just moving it?

PROSECUTOR: Please concentrate.

FIRST MAN: How many years has it been? Twenty-five? And you want me to remember such details? I haven't thought about that table once in twenty-five years.

PROSECUTOR: And yet today, while you were telling your story, on your own, without prompting, you said, "He was sitting at a table." Please concentrate and tell me what you saw as you entered the square.

FIRST MAN: What did I see? I was coming from Rozana Street, from the opposite direction, because Rozana is on the other side of the market. I was struck by the silence. That was my first thought: so many people, and so quiet. I noticed a group of people I knew; among them was the druggist, Mr. Weidel, and I asked Weidel, "What do you think, Doctor, what will they do with us?" And he answered me, "My dear Mr. Grumbach . . ."

PROSECUTOR: You already mentioned that, please stick to the point. What did you see in the square?

FIRST MAN: The square was black with people.

PROSECUTOR: Earlier you said that the people assembled in the marketplace were standing at the rear of the square, facing the town hall, and that there was an empty space between the people and the town hall.

FIRST MAN: That's right.

PROSECUTOR: In other words, to say, "The square was black with people," is not completely accurate. That empty space was, shall we say, white—especially since, as you've mentioned, fresh snow had fallen during the night.

FIRST MAN: Yes, that's right.

PROSECUTOR: Now please think, Mr. Grumbach. Did you notice anything or anyone in that empty white space?

FIRST MAN: Kiper was sitting in a chair and striking his boots with a riding crop.

PROSECUTOR: I would like to call your attention to the fact that none of the witnesses until now has mentioned that Kiper was walking around with a riding crop. Are you certain that Kiper was striking his boots with a riding crop?

FIRST MAN: Maybe it was a stick or a branch. In any case, he was striking his boots—*that* I remember. Sometimes you remember such tiny details. Hamke and Bondke were standing next to him, smoking cigarettes. There were policemen and Ukrainians standing all around the square—a lot of them, one next to the other.

PROSECUTOR: Yes, we know that already. So, you remember that Kiper was sitting in a chair.

FIRST MAN: Absolutely.

PROSECUTOR: So if there was a chair in the marketplace, wouldn't there have been a table as well?

FIRST MAN: A table . . . just a minute . . . a table . . . no. Because that chair seemed so . . . wait a minute . . . No, there wasn't any table there. But they carried out a small table later. Now I remember exactly. Two policemen brought a small table out from the town hall.

PROSECUTOR: (*relieved*) Well, something concrete at last. What time would that have been?

FIRST MAN: (*reproachfully*) Really, I . . .

PROSECUTOR: Please, think about it.

FIRST MAN: The time? . . . God knows. I have no idea. I left the house at 6:15, that I know. I stopped in at my aunt's on Poprzeczna Street, that took ten minutes, then I walked down Miodna, Krotka, Okolna, and Mickiewicza streets. On Mickiewicza I hid for a few minutes inside the gate of one of the houses because I heard shots. It must have taken me about half an hour to walk there.

PROSECUTOR: How much time elapsed from the moment you arrived in the square to the moment when you noticed the policemen carrying the table out from the town hall?

FIRST MAN: Not a long time. Let's say half an hour.

PROSECUTOR: In other words, the policemen carried a table into the marketplace around 7:15. A small table.

FIRST MAN: That's right. Now I recall that Kiper pointed with his riding crop to the place where they were supposed to set the table down.

PROSECUTOR: Please indicate on the map you drew for us the exact place where the policemen set the table down. With a cross or a circle. Thank you. (*satisfied*) Excellent. Kiper is sitting in a chair, the policemen carry in the table, the length of the table is about eighty centimeters. How was the table placed? I mean, in front of Kiper? Next to him?

FIRST MAN: I don't know. That I couldn't see.

PROSECUTOR: If you could see them carrying in the table you could see that, too—perhaps you just don't remember. But maybe you can remember where Kiper sat? At the table? Beside it? In front of it?

FIRST MAN: Obviously, at the table. When someone waits for a table, it's so he can sit at it. He was sitting at the table. Of course. That's what people do.

PROSECUTOR: Alone?

FIRST MAN: In the beginning? I don't know. I wasn't looking that way the whole time. But later—this I know—they were all there: Kiper, Hamke, Bondke, Rossel, Kuntz, and Wittelmann.

PROSECUTOR: (*slowly*) Kiper, Hamke, Bondke, Rossel, Kuntz, and Wittelmann. When you testified a year ago you didn't mention either Rossel or Wittelmann.

FIRST MAN: I must have forgotten about them then. Now I remember that they were there, too.

PROSECUTOR: Were they all sitting at the table?

FIRST MAN: No. Not all of them. Some of them were standing next to it.

PROSECUTOR: Who was sitting?

FIRST MAN: What I saw was that Kiper, Hamke, Bondke, and Kuntz were sitting. The rest were standing. There were more than a dozen of them, I don't remember all the names.

PROSECUTOR: How were they seated, one beside the other?

FIRST MAN: Yes.

PROSECUTOR: Is it possible that four grown men could sit one beside the other at a table that is eighty centimeters long?

FIRST MAN: I don't know. Maybe the table was longer than that; or maybe it wasn't big enough for all of them. In any event, they were sitting in a row.

PROSECUTOR: Who read the names from the list?

FIRST MAN: Hamke or Bondke.

PROSECUTOR: How did they do it?

FIRST MAN: People walked up to the table, showed their *Arbeitskarten*, and Kiper looked them over and pointed either to the right or to the left. The people who had good *Arbeitskarten* went to the right, and those whose work wasn't considered important, or who didn't have any *Arbeitskarten*, they went to the left.

PROSECUTOR: Was Kiper the one who conducted the selection?

FIRST MAN: Yes. I'm positive about that.

PROSECUTOR: Did Kiper stay in that spot during the whole time the names were read? Or did he get up from the table?

FIRST MAN: I don't know. Maybe he got up. I wasn't looking at him every minute. It took a very long time. And anyway, is it that important?

PROSECUTOR: I'm sorry to be tormenting you with these seemingly unimportant details . . . In other words, is it possible that Kiper got up and walked away from the table, or even left the square?

FIRST MAN: I can't give a definite answer. I wasn't watching Kiper every minute. It's possible that he did get up from the table. That's not out of the question. Still, he was the one in charge at the marketplace. Kiper—and no one else. And he was the one who shot the mother and child.

PROSECUTOR: Did you see this with your own eyes?

FIRST MAN: Yes.

PROSECUTOR: Please describe the incident.

FIRST MAN: The woman wasn't from our town, so I don't know her name. She was young, she worked in the brickworks. She had a ten-year-old daughter, Mala. I remember the child's name; she was a pretty little girl. When this woman's name was called she walked up to the table with her daughter. She was holding the child by the hand. Kiper gave her back her

Arbeitskarte and ordered her to go to the right. But he ordered the child to go to the left. The mother started begging him to leave the child with her, but he wouldn't agree. Then she placed her *Arbeitskarte* on the table and walked to the left side with the child. Kiper called her back and asked her if she knew the penalty for disobeying an order, and then he shot them—first the girl, and then the mother.

PROSECUTOR: Did you actually see Kiper shoot?

FIRST MAN: I saw the woman approach the table with the child. I saw them standing in front of Kiper. A moment later I heard two shots.

PROSECUTOR: Where were you standing at that moment? Please mark it on the map. With a cross or a circle. Thank you. So, you were standing near the pharmacy. How far was it from the table to the pharmacy?

FIRST MAN: Thirty meters, maybe fifty.

PROSECUTOR: Then you couldn't have heard the conversation between Kiper and the mother.

FIRST MAN: No, obviously. I didn't hear what they said, but I saw that the mother exchanged several sentences with Kiper. It was perfectly clear what they were talking about. Everyone understood what the mother was asking. Then I saw the mother place her *Arbeitskarte* on the table and go to the left with the child. I heard Kiper call her back. They went back.

PROSECUTOR: They went back and stood in front of the table, correct?

FIRST MAN: That's correct.

PROSECUTOR: In other words, they were blocking your view of the men who were sitting at the table, or at least of some of the men sitting at the table.

FIRST MAN: It's possible. I don't remember exactly. In any case, I saw them come back to the table, and a moment later there were two shots, and then I saw them lying on the ground. People who stood closer to them clearly heard Kiper ask her if she knew the penalty for disobeying an order.

PROSECUTOR: Was Kiper standing or sitting at that moment?

FIRST MAN: I don't remember.

PROSECUTOR: So, you didn't see him at the exact moment you heard the shots. Did you see a gun in his hand? What kind of gun? A pistol? A machine gun?

FIRST MAN: He must have shot them with a pistol. Those were pistol shots.

PROSECUTOR: Did you see a pistol in Kiper's hand?

FIRST MAN: No . . . perhaps the mother and child were blocking my view; or maybe I was looking at the victims and not at the murderer. I don't know. But in any case, I did see something that told me it was Kiper who shot them, and no one else.

PROSECUTOR: Namely?

FIRST MAN: Namely . . . immediately after the shots, when the mother and child were lying on the ground, I saw with my own eyes how Kiper rubbed his hands together with a disgusted gesture, as if to cleanse them of filth. I won't forget that gesture.

PROSECUTOR: (*summarizing*) And so, Mr. Grumbach, you saw Kiper sitting at a table in the company of Hamke, Bondke, Rossel, and Kuntz. Then you saw Kiper carrying out the selection and Kiper brushing off his hands immediately after you heard the shots that killed the mother and child. But you didn't see a gun in Kiper's hand nor the shooting itself. Is that correct?

FIRST MAN: Still, I assert with absolute confidence that the murderer of the mother and child was Kiper.

PROSECUTOR: Was Kiper sitting behind the table when your name was called?

FIRST MAN: (*hesitating*) I was one of the last to be called. My *Arbeitskarte* was taken and returned by Bondke. I don't remember if Kiper was present or not. By then I was already half dead.

PROSECUTOR: Of course. What time would it have been when your name was called?

FIRST MAN: What time? My God, I don't know, it was already past noon.

PROSECUTOR: Did you witness any other murders committed that day?

FIRST MAN: That day more than four hundred people were shot in the town. Another eight hundred at the cemetery.

PROSECUTOR: Did you see any member of the Gestapo shoot someone?

FIRST MAN: No.

PROSECUTOR: Were you one of the group that buried the victims in the cemetery?

FIRST MAN: No.

PROSECUTOR: Is there anything else that you would like to say in connection with that day?

FIRST MAN: Yes.

PROSECUTOR: Please, go ahead.

FIRST MAN: It was a sunny, cold day. There was snow in the streets. The snow was red.

FIRST WOMAN: It was a Sunday. I remember it perfectly. As I was walking to the square, the church bells were ringing. It was a Sunday. Black Sunday.

PROSECUTOR: Is that what the day was called afterwards?

FIRST WOMAN: Yes.

PROSECUTOR: Some of the witnesses have testified that the day was called Bloody Sunday.

FIRST WOMAN: (*dryly*) I should think the name would be unimportant. It was certainly bloody. Four hundred corpses on the streets of the town.

PROSECUTOR: How do you know the exact figure?

FIRST WOMAN: From those who buried the victims. The *Ordnungsdienst* did that. Later they told us, four hundred murdered in the town alone. A hard, packed snow lay on the streets; it was red with blood. The worst one was Kiper.

PROSECUTOR: Slow down. Please describe the events in the square as they occurred.

FIRST WOMAN: At six they ordered us to leave our houses and go to the marketplace. First I decided not to go, and I ran up to the attic. There was a window there, so I looked out. I saw people pouring down Rozana, Kwiatowa, Piekna, and Mickiewicza streets towards the square. Suddenly I noticed two SS entering the house next door. They stayed inside for a moment, then came out leading an elderly couple, the Weintals. Mrs. Weintal was crying. I saw that. They were elderly people. They owned a paper goods store. The SS-men ordered them to stand facing the wall of the house, and then they shot them.

PROSECUTOR: Do you know the names of the two SS-men?

FIRST WOMAN: No. One was tall and thin. He had a terrifying face. I might be able to recognize him in a photograph. You don't forget such a face. But they were local SS, because there were no outside SS in town that day. *They* did it, the locals. Four hundred murdered on the spot, twice that number in the cemetery.

PROSECUTOR: Let's take it slowly now. So, you saw two SS leading the Weintal couple out of the building and putting them against the wall. You lived on Kwiatowa Street. Was their house also located on Kwiatowa?

FIRST WOMAN: I lived on Kwiatowa at number I; it was the corner building. The Weintals lived in a building on Rozana.

PROSECUTOR: What number?

FIRST WOMAN: I don't know, I don't remember . . .

PROSECUTOR: Did you see which of the two SS shot them? The tall one or the other one?

FIRST WOMAN: That I didn't see, because when they ordered them to stand facing the wall, I knew what would happen next and I couldn't watch. I was afraid. I moved away from the window. I was terribly afraid.

PROSECUTOR: Afterwards, did you see the Weintal couple lying on the ground dead?

FIRST WOMAN: They shot them from a distance of two meters; I assume they knew how to aim.

PROSECUTOR: Did you see the bodies afterwards?

FIRST WOMAN: No. I ran downstairs from the attic, I was afraid—with good reason—I was afraid that they would search the houses for people who were trying to hide, but I didn't go out into the street, I took the back exit to the garden and made my way to the marketplace by a round-about route.

PROSECUTOR: Would you recognize those two SS in photos?

FIRST WOMAN: Perhaps. I'm fairly certain I could recognize the tall thin one. You don't forget such a face.

PROSECUTOR: Please look through this album. It contains photographs of members of the Gestapo who were in your town; but there are also photographs here of people who were never there.

FIRST WOMAN: (*she turns the pages; a pause*) Oh, that's him.

PROSECUTOR: Is that one of the men you saw from the window?

FIRST WOMAN: No, it's that awful murderer. It's Kiper. Yes, I remember, it's definitely him.

PROSECUTOR: Please look through all the photographs.

FIRST WOMAN: (*a pause*) No, I can't find that face. Unfortunately.

PROSECUTOR: You said "awful murderer". Did you ever witness a murder committed by Kiper?

FIRST WOMAN: (*laughs*) Witness? You're joking. The witnesses to his murders aren't alive.

PROSECUTOR: But there are people who saw him shoot.

FIRST WOMAN: I did, too. Sure—in the square, he fired into the crowd. Just like that.

PROSECUTOR: Do you know who he killed then?

FIRST WOMAN: I don't know. There were fifteen hundred of us in the square. But I saw him rushing around like a wild man and shooting. Not just him, others, too. Bendke, for example.

PROSECUTOR: When was that?

FIRST WOMAN: In the morning. Before the selection. But it's possible it also went on during the selection. I don't remember. I know that they fired into the crowd. Just like that.

PROSECUTOR: Who read the names from the list?

FIRST WOMAN: An SS-man. I don't know his name.

PROSECUTOR: How did they do it?

FIRST WOMAN: Very simply. Names were called out, some people went to the right and others to the left. The left meant death.

PROSECUTOR: Who conducted the selection?

FIRST WOMAN: They were all there: Kiper, Bendke, Hamm, Rosse.

PROSECUTOR: Which one of them reviewed the *Arbeitskarten*?

FIRST WOMAN: I don't remember.

PROSECUTOR: Who ordered you to go to the right? Kiper? Bendke? Hamm? Rosse?

FIRST WOMAN: I don't remember. At such a time, you know . . . at such a time, when you don't know . . . life or death . . . I didn't look at their faces. To me, they all had the same face. All of them! What difference does it make whether it was Kiper or Bendke or Hamm or Rosse? They were all there. There were ten or maybe fifteen of those murderers. They stood in a semicircle, with their machine guns across their chests. What difference does it make which one? They all gave orders, they all shot! All of them!

PROSECUTOR: Please calm yourself. I am terribly sorry that I have to provoke you with such questions. But you see, we can only convict people if we can *prove* that they committed murder. You say that all the members of the local

Gestapo were there. But it could be that one of them was on leave, or possibly on duty in the *Dienststelle*. And didn't shoot.

FIRST WOMAN: Every one of them shot. If not that day, then another. During the second or third action, during the liquidation.

PROSECUTOR: The law requires proof. And I, as the prosecuting attorney, am asking you for proof. I am asking for the names of the murderers, the names of the victims, the circumstances in which they were murdered. Otherwise, I can do nothing.

FIRST WOMAN: (*quietly*) My God . . .

PROSECUTOR: Excuse me?

FIRST WOMAN: Nothing, nothing.

PROSECUTOR: Please think: which one of them was in charge of the selection in the square?

FIRST WOMAN: They all participated in the selection. Kiper, Bendke, Hamm, Rosse. They were standing in a semicircle.

PROSECUTOR: Standing? Were all of them standing? Or perhaps some of them were seated?

FIRST WOMAN: No, they were standing. Is it that important?

PROSECUTOR: It's very important. Do you remember seeing a table in the marketplace at which several Gestapo men were seated? The others were standing near the table.

FIRST WOMAN: A table? I don't remember. There was no table there.

SECOND MAN: Here's the map. The marketplace was shaped like a trapezoid. At the top was the town hall, a beautiful old building that had been built by a Polish nobleman in the seventeenth century. The jewel of the town. The square sloped down towards the actual market where the stores were, as if the town hall reigned over the place. On the left, by the ruins of the old ramparts, stood those whose *Arbeitskarten* were taken away and also those who did not have *Arbeitskarten*. Note that the streets radiate out like a star. Here's Rozana, then Sienkiewicza, then Piekna, then Male Targi, then Nadrzeczna. There was no river in the town, but maybe once upon a time there was one, and that's why it was called Nadrzeczna—Riverside. Then came Zamkowa Street. All the streets I've named were later included in the ghetto, with the exception of Piekna. Beyond Male Targi there was a cemetery. Yes. That's where they were shot. Nadrzeczna was adjacent to the cemetery. Most of the people who lived on Nadrzeczna were Poles, but it was incorporated into the ghetto nonetheless, because of the cemetery. Because the cemetery played a major role in our life then. Between Rozana and Sienkiewicza there were shops. First, Weidel's pharmacy—he was killed in the camp; then Rosenzweig's iron shop—he was shot during the second action. Then Kreitz's dry goods store, the Haubers' restaurant and hotel—they were the wealthiest people among us, their daughter lives in

Canada—and then two groceries, one beside the other, Blumenthal's and Hochwald's. They were rivals all their lives, and now they're lying in the same grave. Oh yes, I can draw every single stone for you, describe every single person. Do you know how many of us survived?

PROSECUTOR: Forty.

SECOND MAN: How do you know?

PROSECUTOR: They are my witnesses.

SECOND MAN: And have you found all of them? And taken their testimony?

PROSECUTOR: I have found almost all of them, but I still haven't taken testimony from everyone. Several witnesses live in America; they will be questioned by our consular officials, and if necessary, subpoenaed for the trial. Two live in Australia, one in Venezuela. Now I would like to ask you about the details of the selection that took place during the first action. When was it, do you remember?

SECOND MAN: Of course. It was a Sunday, in December, towards the end of the month. It was a sunny, cold day. Nature, you see, was also against us. She was mocking us. Yes, indeed. If it had rained, or if there had been a storm, who knows, perhaps they wouldn't have kept shooting from morning till night. Darkness was already falling when they led those people to the cemetery. Oh, you want proof, don't you? The snow on the town's streets was red. Red! Does that satisfy you?

PROSECUTOR: Unfortunately, Mr. Zachwacki, snow doesn't constitute proof for judges, especially snow that melted twenty-five years ago.

SECOND MAN: The snow was red. Bloody Sunday. Four hundred fifty corpses on the streets. That's not proof? Then go there and dig up the mass graves.

PROSECUTOR: I'm interested in the selection. Who was in charge of it?

SECOND MAN: Kiper. A thug, a murderer. The worst sort. I can't talk about this calmly. No. Do you mind if I smoke? These are things . . . I'm sixty, my blood pressure shoots right up. A cutthroat like that . . .

PROSECUTOR: How do you know that Kiper was in charge of the selection?

SECOND MAN: What do you mean, how? I gave him my *Arbeitskarte* myself. He peered at me from under his brows and snarled, "*Rechts!*" I went to the right. Saved. Saved until the next time.

PROSECUTOR: Please describe the scene in more detail.

SECOND MAN: I was standing some distance away. We all tried to stand as far away from them as possible, as if that could have helped. I was standing near the Haubers' hotel. It was one in the afternoon. The church bell struck one, and since it was quiet in the square, you could hear the bell clearly even though the church was in a different part of town, near Waly Ksiazece. By then they had been calling out names for about an hour. Suddenly I hear, "Zachwacki!"

PROSECUTOR: Who called your name?

SECOND MAN: One of the Gestapo, but I don't know which one.

PROSECUTOR: Didn't you notice which of them was holding the list?

SECOND MAN: No, you're asking too much. There was a list, because they read the names from a list, but I didn't see it. If a person saw a scene like that in the theater, maybe he could describe it in detail. This here, that there, and so on. But when a tragedy like this is being played in real life? You expect me to look at a list when my life is hanging by a thread? I was standing there with my wife. She had an *Arbeitskarte* from the sawmill—that was a good place to work—and I had one from the cement works. Also a good place. When they called my name, my wife grabbed my arm. "Let's stay together!" she cried. Dr. Gluck was standing nearby, a kind old doctor. He told my wife, "Mrs. Zachwacki, calm down, your husband has a good *Arbeitskarte*, you have a good *Arbeitskarte*, get a grip on yourself." But she kept saying, "I want to stay together, if we don't we won't see each other ever again. Albert," she said, "I'm afraid." I literally had to tear myself away, she was holding on to me so tight. There, you see, so much for instinct, intuition . . . I never saw her again. All the women who worked in the sawmill were sent to the left. (*he clears his throat*)

PROSECUTOR: (*a short pause*) Then what happened?

SECOND MAN: I dashed through the crowd. There was an empty space between us and them, you had to walk about thirty meters to cross the empty square. First—I remember this—someone kicked me, who I don't know. I took a deep breath and ran as hard as I could to get to the town hall as fast as possible. When I handed them my *Arbeitskarte* my hand was trembling like an aspen leaf, although I'm not a coward. Not at all!

PROSECUTOR: To whom did you hand your *Arbeitskarte*?

SECOND MAN: I already told you, to Kiper. He opened it, read it, handed it back to me and snarled, "*Rechts!*" I was young, tall, strong. He gave me a reprieve.

PROSECUTOR: At the moment that you handed him your *Arbeitskarte*, was Kiper standing or sitting?

SECOND MAN: He was standing with his legs apart, his machine gun across his chest. His face was swollen, red.

PROSECUTOR: And the rest of the Gestapo?

SECOND MAN: I didn't see. I don't remember if any of them were standing next to Kiper.

PROSECUTOR: Did you see a table?

SECOND MAN: Yes, there was a table, but it was further to the right, as if it had nothing to do with what was happening there.

PROSECUTOR: A small table?

SECOND MAN: No, not at all. It was a big, long oak table, like one of those trestle tables you see in monasteries. It was probably one of those antique tables from the old town hall.

PROSECUTOR: Long, you say. What were its dimensions, more or less?

SECOND MAN: How should I know? Two, three meters. The Gestapo sat in a row on one side of the table; and there was quite a large group of them sitting there. Bondke was sitting, Rossel was sitting—them I remember. And there were at least six others.

PROSECUTOR: Did you by any chance notice whether Kiper was sitting at the table earlier and whether the reviewing of the *Arbeitskarten* took place at the table?

SECOND MAN: I didn't notice. When I was called, Kiper was standing several meters from the table.

PROSECUTOR: Who do you think was in charge of the action?

SECOND MAN: Kuntze. He had the highest rank.

PROSECUTOR: Did you see him in the square?

SECOND MAN: I don't remember if I saw Kuntze. Presumably he was sitting at the table. But I only remember Bondke and Rossel.

PROSECUTOR: Was the table already there when you got to the square?

SECOND MAN: Yes.

PROSECUTOR: Who was seated at it?

SECOND MAN: No one.

PROSECUTOR: Some people claim that Kiper was sitting in a chair even before the table was brought out and that afterwards he sat at the head of the table. That he took the *Arbeitskarten* while he was sitting.

SECOND MAN: It's possible. Everything is possible. When I was called, Kiper was standing.

PROSECUTOR: Mr. Zachwacki, do you recall an incident with a mother and child who were shot in the square?

SECOND MAN: Yes, I do. It was Rosa Rubinstein and her daughter Ala. They were from another town and had lived in our town only since the beginning of the war. I knew them.

PROSECUTOR: Who shot them, and under what circumstances?

SECOND MAN: I was standing in the group of workers on the right side of the square, beside the well.

PROSECUTOR: Please indicate the place on the map. With a circle or a cross. Thank you. There was a well there, you say. No one has yet mentioned that well.

SECOND MAN: It was an old well, wooden, with a wooden fence around it. All around it, in a semicircle, there were trees, poplars. At one moment I heard a shot, and people who were standing somewhat closer said that Rosa Rubinstein and her daughter had been shot. It seems that both of them had been sent to the left, but they went to the right. People said that Kiper ran after them and shot them.

PROSECUTOR: You said, "I heard a shot." Do you mean you heard a single shot?

SECOND MAN: Those were my words, but it's hard for me to say if I heard one shot, or two, or three. No doubt he fired at least twice.

PROSECUTOR: Did you see the shooting with your own eyes?

SECOND MAN: No. I saw the bodies lying on the ground. They were lying next to each other. Then the *Ordnungsdienst* picked them up. A red stain was left on the snow.

PROSECUTOR: You were part of the group that helped to bury the victims afterwards?

SECOND MAN: That's correct. There were so many victims that the *Ordnungsdienst* had to take twenty men to help. Four hundred and fifty people were killed in the town—in the square and in the house searches—and eight hundred and forty were shot in the cemetery. My wife was one of them.

PROSECUTOR: (*pause*) But you didn't see any murders with your own eyes? Can you say, "I saw with my own eyes that this one or that one shot so-and-so or so-and-so?"

SECOND MAN: I saw thirteen hundred victims. The mass grave was thirty meters long, three meters wide, five meters deep.

SECOND WOMAN: No, I wasn't in the square. Because I worked as a cleaning woman for the Gestapo, and in the morning, when everyone was going to the marketplace, Mama said to me, "See if they'll let you stay at work." I took my pail and a rag and a brush and said goodbye to my parents on the corner of Mickiewicza and Rozana. We lived on Mickiewicza Street. My parents kept going straight, and I turned onto Rozana. I had gone a few steps when suddenly I caught sight of Rossel and Hamke; they were walking towards me and I got terribly frightened, so I ran into the first gate, and they passed by, they didn't notice me. Later I saw them entering the building at number 13. I kept going.

PROSECUTOR: Who lived in the house?

SECOND WOMAN: I don't know, I was young, I was thirteen years old, but I said I was sixteen because children, you know, were killed. I was well developed, so I said I was sixteen and they let me work for them. That was good luck. That day the Gestapo were going around to all the houses looking for people who hadn't gone to the square, and if they found someone, they shot him either in his apartment or on the street.

PROSECUTOR: Was there a family named Weintal in the house at number 13?

SECOND WOMAN: Weintal? No, I never heard of anyone with that name. I stayed at the Gestapo all day long, hiding. I knew the building, I knew where I could hide. Well, I must say, I certainly was lucky.

PROSECUTOR: Which Gestapo members were in the building that day?

SECOND WOMAN: I don't know. I was hiding in an alcove next to the stairway to the cellar, at the very end of the corridor. Once I thought I heard Wittelmann's voice; he seemed to be on the telephone and was yelling something awful.

PROSECUTOR: Did you ever witness an execution while you worked there?

SECOND WOMAN: I know that they took place, and I know where. But I never saw them shoot anyone. I was afraid, and as soon as they brought someone in, I would hide, get out of their way. I was afraid that they might shoot me, too. They killed them against the fence.

PROSECUTOR: Which fence?

SECOND WOMAN: There was a courtyard at the back surrounded by a fence, and behind the fence there was a trench. That's where they were shot. I know, because afterwards the *Ordnungsdienst* would come and collect the bodies. Once I saw them carrying a doctor whom they had killed. His name was Gluck. But that was after the first action, in the spring. Another time I saw a group of Gestapo men walk out into the courtyard and immediately afterwards I heard a burst of machine-gun fire.

PROSECUTOR: Who did you see then?

SECOND WOMAN: Bondke, Rossel, Hamke, and Wittelmann.

PROSECUTOR: All together?

SECOND WOMAN: Yes. All together. I was washing the stairs to the cellar then.

PROSECUTOR: Were they all armed? Did each of them have a weapon?

SECOND WOMAN: Yes.

PROSECUTOR: Those shots you heard then, were they from a single machine gun or from several?

SECOND WOMAN: I don't know. I didn't pay attention. I wasn't thinking that someday someone would ask me about that. Maybe one of them shot, maybe two. Maybe they took turns. How should I know?

PROSECUTOR: When was that?

SECOND WOMAN: That was even before the first action, probably in the fall.

PROSECUTOR: Do you know how many people were shot then? Do you know their names?

SECOND WOMAN: I don't. I didn't see their bodies being taken away. I saw them collect the dead only once or twice. I don't know who was killed then.

PROSECUTOR: And you never saw a Gestapo man fire a gun?

SECOND WOMAN: No. I only worked there until the second action. I couldn't stand it any longer, I preferred to go to a camp. In general they were nice to me and never did anything bad. Once Bondke gave me cigarettes. The best-mannered was Kiper. He was an educated man, like Kuntze. But the others, no. Kiper had a lot of books in his room. He wanted fresh flowers in a vase every day. Once, when I didn't bring flowers, he yelled at me. Once he broke the vase because the flowers were wilted. On the desk in his room was a photograph of an elegant woman with a dog. But it was Hamke who had a dog. I used to prepare food for the dog. His name was Roosevelt. A wolfhound, very well trained. He tore the druggist Weidel's child to pieces. I heard Hamke boasting about him: *"Roosevelt hat heute ein Jüdlein zum Frühstück bekommen"*—Roosevelt had a little Jew for breakfast today. He said that to Kiper, and Kiper screwed up his face in disgust. Kiper couldn't stand Hamke and used to quarrel with Bondke. In general, he kept to himself. He didn't drink. That Sunday he was the first to come back from the marketplace.

PROSECUTOR: How do you know it was Kiper? Did you see him?

SECOND WOMAN: I heard his voice.

PROSECUTOR: Who was he talking to?

SECOND WOMAN: He was talking to himself. I thought he was reciting a poem. Anyway, that's what it sounded like. Then he went to his room and played his violin—I forgot to say that he was a trained musician. Bondke used to make fun of him and call him *Gestapogeiger*—Gestapo-fiddler. I don't know much about music, but I think he played very well. I heard him play several times. Always the same thing. I don't know what melody it was, I don't know much about music.

PROSECUTOR: Did you see him that day?

SECOND WOMAN: No, I only heard him playing.

PROSECUTOR: What time would that have been?

SECOND WOMAN: I don't know. It was growing dark.

PROSECUTOR: Could you hear the shots from the cemetery inside the Gestapo building?

SECOND WOMAN: I don't know. Maybe not. The cemetery is on Male Targi, and the Gestapo headquarters was on St. Jerzy Square. That's quite a distance. But maybe in the silence, in the clear air . . .

PROSECUTOR: Did you hear any shots when Kiper returned?

SECOND WOMAN: I can't say. Because the way I felt that Sunday and for several days afterwards, I was hearing shots all the time, and my parents thought I had lost my mind. I kept saying, "Listen, they're shooting . . . ," and I'd run and hide. Mama took me to Gluck, who gave me a powder, but it didn't help. I kept on hearing shots for a week. It was my nerves.

PROSECUTOR: When did the other Gestapo men come back?

SECOND WOMAN: I don't know. When it got dark, I sneaked out through the courtyard and returned home. The city was empty, as if no one was left alive. I was astonished: the snow was black. That was the blood. The most blood was on Sienkiewicza Street, and on Rozana. I didn't meet anyone in the marketplace either. It was empty. In the center of the square, lying on its back with its legs in the air, was a small, broken table.

23

Deborah E. Lipstadt

Toleh Eretz Al B'limah (*God suspends the earth over a void*). . . .
*How can we continue to believe when we know that not too long
ago millions of people were allowed to fall into that void, never to
emerge?*

DEBORAH E. LIPSTADT

*While it cannot compare with the anguish of surviving the Holocaust, studying it is
difficult and depressing work, for there is more darkness than any scholarship can
penetrate, let alone dispel. The discouragement can become especially acute when the
subject is not only the Holocaust itself but also denial that the Holocaust ever happened.
Inaccurately dubbed "Holocaust revisionists," there are people who make that claim.
Echoing all-too-familiar themes of antisemitism and adding newer anti-Israeli sentiments of their own, these "scholars" contend that there was no "Final Solution." Those
who say otherwise, they insist, are party to Jewish/Zionist plots that exploit others.*

*It would be tempting not to take such denials seriously, but historian Deborah E.
Lipstadt knows better. History belongs to those who interpret it. While it is discourag-
ing to think anyone would deny that the "Final Solution" occurred, Lipstadt believes
that it would be even worse to let these charges stand without contesting them
directly. Her book* Denying the Holocaust: The Growing Assault on Truth *takes
on that task successfully.*

One reason Lipstadt fears Holocaust denial so much involves Beyond Belief,
*another of her important books. Focusing on the American press's failure in the
thirties and forties to treat the destruction of European Jewry as urgent news, it shows
how high the costs turn out to be when truth is downplayed, ignored, denied, taken in
any way less than with the utmost seriousness.*

Discouragement, truth, belief—all of these themes, and more, resound in Lipstadt's meditation on "Facing the Void." In this essay, historical understanding informs a Jewish woman's spiritual quest. As bold in her religious thought as she is in her historical research, Lipstadt does not shy away from the demanding questions facing believers and nonbelievers in a post-Holocaust world. How can people continue to believe in God after the Holocaust? How can we preserve in ourselves, and encourage in others, a basic faith in humankind in the face of such inhumanity?

Lipstadt does not deny the Holocaust's enormity by excusing humankind or justifying God. The Holocaust is a void that is beyond excuse and justification. That void is not, however, beyond our caring. Turning to the resources of her Jewish tradition, Lipstadt advocates facing "the challenge of the looming void" in ways that create "a life worth living, a life that is a model for others, a life that brings goodness into the orbit in which it moves, a life of tenderness and gentleness, a life that is forgiving of those who have wronged us, a life that seeks forgiveness from those we have wronged, a life of loving kindness." As she says, this task is not easy, but is there any other more worthy of our striving in the face of the void that remains?

Facing the Void

There are certain prayers each of us identifies as representing the Days of Awe. When we hear them, we know that once again it is *that* time of the year. We are particularly familiar with some prayers because they are central or pivotal points in the service, e.g., the *Kol Nidre*, the haunting chant which marks the opening of the Day of Atonement; the *Ashamnu*, the Confessional, when we symbolically beat our breasts acknowledging the way in which we have transgressed. Other parts of the service demand our attention because they are so different from what we do the rest of the year, e.g., blowing the *shofar* or falling prostrate.

Then there are those moments in the service which are neither central nor pivotal but which, for no ostensible reason, may speak to us in a particular and personal way. For each person it is a different verse or prayer. Maybe we heard a parent or a rabbi or a friend discuss one of them. Maybe we like the imagery. Often there is no logical or metaphysical reason why that point is important to us; it just is. So it was with me and the phrase *Toleh Eretz Al B'limah* (God suspends the earth over a void), which is recited during the morning service of Rosh Hashanah and Yom Kippur as part of a poem describing the power of God.

Though I knew it resonated for me, I never thought about this phrase in a systematic fashion. In fact, though the verse had long appealed to me, until recently I was not sure exactly where it appeared in the service or what its precise origin was. Did it resonate for me because of its suggestion of the precariousness of our lives? Was it the idea of an unseen mover who had the ultimate power over us that caught my attention? Was it because so much of my professional work concerns the Holocaust, a time when for Jews in Europe life was suspended over the bleakest of voids? Was it a poetic rendition of the terrible reality of the horrors Jews faced during World War II? In its simple four words it seemed to contain the theological challenge facing every believer in a post-Auschwitz world. How can we continue to believe when we know that not too long ago millions of people were allowed to fall into that void, never to emerge?

The fact was that despite these compelling questions I did not seriously ponder why the phrase had made such an impression on me. But then something happened that made me realize I had to explore this verse in greater depth. A short while ago I was visiting a cousin with whom I had had little previous contact. A few minutes before I was supposed to leave her home, she told me that she had inherited our grandfather's Yom Kippur prayerbook. I never knew my grandfather and was anxious to hold in my hands something that had been his. I asked to see it. I opened to the flyleaf and there he had written two things: his name, Netanel Peiman, and one short verse from the liturgy: *Toleh Eretz Al B'limah* (God suspends the earth over a void).

A relatively obscure phrase of four words that is repeated but twice in over five hundred pages of liturgy linked me with another generation. I tend to be a skeptic. My professional training has only enhanced a pre-existing inclination towards skepticism and rationalism. And yet even I had to acknowledge that I had been the object of an intergenerational message.

When I first discovered the verse, I thought—allowing my skepticism to surface—that my mother might have learned it from her father. When I told my mother the story, she asked me to tell her exactly where the phrase was so that she would be sure not to miss it during services.

What does this phrase, "God suspends the earth over a void," which I now know comes from the latter chapters of Job—not an inconsequential fact— say to us? Sometimes when I read it, I envisioned the world dangling on a string. God just had to give it a nudge and we all stood a chance of falling into the void. Maybe it reflected what life is about: the stability and security we seek juxtaposed against the immediacy of the unknown. We like to think of ourselves as strong and solid. Yet we know that a great unknown is always in front of us. It reminds us, as Jews during the Holocaust learned in the most bitter ways, that despite the illusion of control, much of our future is suspended over a void. It seems to challenge us, almost to taunt us, to believe *despite* the void—despite the knowledge that in the recent past so many people were dropped into that void even though they had done nothing to deserve it.

Jewish theology in general and Yom Kippur in particular are full of reminders that there are limits to what we can control. This verse from Job is just
one such reminder. There are a myriad of others. In the prayer *Avenu Malkanu*
(Our Father, Our Monarch), we turn to God in a role that clearly indicates the
limits of our power. We ask rhetorically who will live and who will die; who in
their time and who before their time; who will have strength and who will be
afflicted with illness; who will face harm or even perish in floods, in fire, in
earthquakes. We cannot control any of that completely.

"Like the shepherd separating his flock, so too we are separated, so too our
fate is decreed."* But sometimes the shepherd's decisions seem arbitrary. On
Yom Kippur we read about the ancient ritual, practiced during the time of the
Temple in Jerusalem, of a goat for *azazel*. It was sent to the wilderness as
symbolic expiation for Israel's sins. Some commentators say that the goat is
chosen by lot in order to remind us how much of our lives are controlled by
chance and fate.

As I explored this idea in the liturgy of the Days of Awe, I realized that it
seemed to stand in dramatic opposition to the way I generally approached
these days. My personal understanding of the theology of this period and, for
that matter, the theology of much of Judaism, is rooted in a notion that
Teshuvah, repentance, is an ontological experience that changes our very sense
of being. *We* are the ones who are changed. *Repentance* primarily affects *us*.
Consequently during the Days of Awe we are in a state of transition. We bring
the awesome quality to this day. I even see *Yizkor*, the memorial prayer for the
dead, with its invocation of those who have come before us, as fitting into this
pattern. *Yizkor* is not a means of invoking the merit of our forebearers to speak
on our behalf, but a way of reminding ourselves that *our* actions today become
the memories of the next generation. Consequently, it is crucial for *us* to live
our lives in a way that makes us worthy of being remembered for good.

In these and in so many other ways, I saw and see this period of the Days of
Awe as one of genuine self-empowerment. This theology is exquisitely expressed in Maimonides' interpretation in *The Laws of Repentance* of the verse
from Genesis: "*Heyn ha'Adam haya k'eched memnu la'da'at tov me'rah*," which,
instead of reading in the traditional form "Now man is like one of us knowing
the difference between right and wrong," Rambam reads as "*Heyn ha'Adam
haya k'echad*." ("Now man is *echad*, singular and unique.") *Memenu*, from
within himself, he knows the difference between right and wrong.

But how does this image of "God suspending the earth" fit into a day in
which we are supposedly self-empowered? Is the real message of not only Yom
Kippur but of Jewish history, the Holocaust in particular, that we do not have
any control over that void, over our destiny? Certainly one of the possible
interpretations of the Holocaust is that all one's beliefs in the justice of an all-

---

* This sentence is from the *Netaneh Tokef* (Let Us Proclaim How Awesome Is This Day).

powerful deity are for naught. Jewish history and theology seem to be pulling us in two directions at one time: self-empowered and suspended over a void. Each seems mutually exclusive. In the wake of the knowledge of the void, even though we have not personally experienced it, how do we proceed? How do we reconcile it with our faith?

If we have so little control over matters of great significance, what then can we do? This, in great measure, is the question that emerges from the Holocaust. We could raise our hands in resignation and say: What does it matter? It's all the luck of the draw anyway. Why pray, why fast, why beat our chests when ultimately life is really a matter of chance. But the liturgy, the tradition, and the entire composition of this day come to fight against these approaches. It is a difficult fight given the reality of our own historical experience. But everything in our tradition mitigates against saying either life is all chance or that we play no role.

In the prayer *Netaneh Tokef*, after acknowledging what faces us, after listing the things which we do not control, after enumerating those fearful things we see hovering in the void, then we proclaim: *"Teshuvah, Tefilah, Zedakah ma'averim et roah ha'gezarah"* ("Repentance, Prayer and acts of Charity avert the severity of the decree"). This is the role we play. Long before the *Netaneh Tokef* was composed, the *Torah* taught us the lesson of *Teshuvah, Tefilah* and *Zedakah*. In the Book of Deuteronomy, which we read every year on the Sabbath before Rosh Hashanah, we are told *"lo ba'shamayim hee"* ("This Torah, this Covenant is not in the Heavens or on the other side of the sea. It is not too far for you to reach it. It is not too difficult for you to live it."). *"Kee b'pecha, u'belevavcha l'asot"* ("It is in your mouth, and in your heart to do it."). Your mouth—*Teshuvah*, repentance; your heart—*Tefilah*, prayer, which the rabbis describe as *"avodah sh'ba'lev,"* service of the heart; and to do—*Zedakah*.

There are things that we do not control, but there is much that we do. We do not control life and death but we do control the kind of life we lead. We know, *memenu*, from within ourselves, the difference between right and wrong. That is why on Yom Kippur, when it is life that we are praying for, life that we implore God to grant us, the unique symbols of the day are symbols of mourning: many of us wear no leather, the *Shaliach Tzibur*, the Cantor, wears a white *kittel* which is reminiscent of the burial shroud. Our personal behavior in relation to personal hygiene and sexual relations approximates those of mourners. These symbols remind us of the fleeting nature of life.

And here is the crux of what I believe these days come to teach us and how they can serve as a prototype for facing that void. How we control the things that *are* in our hands, how we live our lives, how we relate to one another, the good deeds we do, how we practice repentance, prayer, and charity in their broadest manifestation help determine how we face that which is out of our control. There remains the unknown, the mystery and the void. But that notion of mystery reminds us that our material possessions and professional achievements are not the sum total of our spiritual possibilities. In fact, the more we attain, the more we achieve, the more we possess, the more we need to know and remember how human we are, what frailties we have, how much guidance we need. There will be things in that void which will frighten us and cause us pain. There will be moments of loneliness. There will be moments of doubt. Consequently we must do two things.

We must try to turn to the *Toleh*, to the one who has suspended us, and reach out—not for an answer but for a moment of communion, of connection. This will only happen if we open ourselves up to it. One of the oft-cited theological responses to the Holocaust is the notion of *hester panim*, that God hid his face from those who suffered. But that notion can work in two directions: God may hide his face from us but sometimes we hide our face from God. Rabbi Menachem Mendel of Kotzk taught: Where is God? Wherever human beings let God in. We must let God in even as Job did in the depths of his bewilderment.

But there are those who find it hard, if not impossible, to turn to an unseen mover. They still can respond to the challenge of the looming void. Knowledge of that void reminds us that our life is a gift; it is precious but it is also tenuous and transitory. As good as it may be, as filled with wonderful things as it may be, it will not last. And this brings me to the second thing we must do. While our life does last, we should make it a life worth living, a life that is a model for others, a life that brings goodness into the orbit in which it moves, a life of tenderness and gentleness, a life that is forgiving of those who have wronged us, a life that seeks forgiveness from those we have wronged, a life of loving kindness.

Jewish tradition offers us a myriad of role models. In truth we know we cannot measure up to them. We do not have the fortitude of a Job who even in the depth of his pain was able to acknowledge God nor the faith of an Abraham who was willing to bind his son on the altar. Our prayers do not have the fervor of a Hannah, the mother of Samuel, nor do our tears have the power and pathos of Rachel who, the Book of Jeremiah says, wept as she watched her children being scattered from their homes. But that is not what we are asked to have. It is here that we need to remember the famous story of Rabbi Zusha. He wept on his deathbed because he feared being asked on his ultimate day of judgment not were you like Abraham, Moses, or David, but were you like Zusha? Did you do all that Zusha was capable of doing? That is the question each of us must ask ourselves.

The void remains. But even as we face it or contemplate how it must have been to face it, we must craft our lives to make them worthy of being remembered by those who follow us. We must try to find within ourselves our own faith, our own fortitude, our own way of reaching up to the *Toleh*, who, as Abraham Joshua Heschel said, is the One who gives ultimate meaning and purpose to the mystery. Neither task is an easy one. Neither task is ever fully completed. The struggle is ongoing, as is the void.

24

Mary Jo Leddy

It is my conviction that the "different voices" of women in the Holocaust call us, summon us, to exercise a different kind of power today.

MARY JO LEDDY

Several times this book has referred to Danuta Czech's Auschwitz Chronicle. *Day by dreary day, its more than eight hundred pages record what went on in that camp of death. If you open the book at random, there are likely to be entries akin to these for February 3–4, 1943: "Nos. 99792–99865 are assigned to 74 prisoners.... The corpses of 43 prisoners are delivered to the morgue of the main camp.... 1,000 Jewish men, women, and children arrive.... Following the selection, 181 men, given Nos. 99915–100095, and 106 women, given Nos. 34183–34288, are admitted to the camp. The other 713 people are killed in the gas chambers."*

Czech's Chronicle *makes a crucial fact abundantly clear. It is something that Hedwig Höss, Theresa Stangl, Gertrud Scholtz-Klink, and other Nazi women knew. So did Ida Fink, Etty Hillesum, Charlotte Delbo, Gertrud Kolmar, and countless other voices of experience. So does Mary Jo Leddy. The Holocaust was about power and powerlessness. It demonstrated what can happen when sufficient power gets placed in the hands of those who are hell-bent on dominating and destroying those who are essentially defenseless.*

Humanitarian, philosopher, theologian, Mary Jo Leddy is a Roman Catholic, a member of a religious order called the Sisters of Our Lady of Sion. She is an accomplished writer and editor, but often her work with words gets interrupted because of her work with refugees whom she helps, with powerless people whom she strives to empower. Her speaking voice is gentle, and no one would mistake it for a man's. There is urgency and firmness in it, too, because she worries about power, about those who have too much of it and use it coercively and about those who have too little of it and thus are vulnerable. She wants to "move beyond the forced extremes of a coercive form of power and the ideology of powerlessness." It is her conviction that the " 'different voices' of women in the Holocaust call us, summon us, to exercise a different kind of power today."

Coercion and control do not define the "different power" Leddy seeks. Instead she emphasizes relationships that spark creativity, that give birth to new beginnings and to life itself. "If we search for grounds for such a faith in a creative form of power," she concludes, "we need only remember that some Jewish women continued to give birth in the long and dark night of the Holocaust."

In the essay that precedes Mary Jo Leddy's, Deborah Lipstadt drew on her Jewish spirituality to face the Holocaust's void in ways that reflect the power of caring. Here a Catholic sister draws on her tradition to do the same; for, "after the Holocaust," she rightly insists, "it is imperative to discover and create new forms of human solidarity."

A Different Power

There are those who dare, sometimes in spite of themselves, to look into the furnaces of Auschwitz. Looking into those flames, their vision becomes at once sharper and more blurred.

One can see clearly, if one wants to, that this event has made a distinction forever between Jews and non-Jews. As Elie Wiesel has said so pointedly: "While not all the victims of the Nazis were Jews, all Jews were victims." Such a distinction, deadly in its consequences, offers for us now either the description of a permanent divide or the invitation to build a new, however fragile, bridge. My own belief is that there is no longer any human solidarity worth the effort which does not begin by acknowledging the chasms created in the course of history.

I

There are, perhaps, some historical situations in which the chasm of horror can be explored to the point of revealing one seismic fault that cracked open in the course of time. One is tempted to search for the "deepest" cause, the "real" cause of the historic gaps in human justice and mercy. Philosophically, this has been called the search for a single unifying cause theory in history. Such a search has fueled ideologies as diverse as scientific forms of Marxism (in which economics is viewed as both the root of all evil and the potential source of liberation) or those types of religious world views that have interpreted every event in terms of some demonic or divine intervention.

The desire to locate the one, deepest, most real or pervasive cause of evil is indicative more of the human need for clarity than of the human capacity to seek comprehension or to bear with incomprehension.

As we attempt to face the Holocaust (Shoah), the human temptation to settle for an easy clarity is always present. Volumes have been written in the attempt to identify the ultimate cause of this massive fault line in human history. The cause is alternately identified as racism, as antisemitism, as the dynamic of authoritarianism, as the cult of the leader figure, as nationalism run amok, as the economic dynamic or the class structure of the time, as the inevitable result of the enlightenment, as the consequence of Christianity's anti-Jewish teaching of contempt, as the stinking flower of a romantic mentality, as the upshot of a patriarchal militaristic mentality—the list could go on and on.

In all of these sincere efforts to plumb the depths of the evil of the Holocaust, there is a partial truth that soon becomes false if pushed beyond its limits to comprehend what really happened.

My own sense is that the Holocaust happened because of a complex of causes that configured at a certain time and place. While some of the causes are comprehensible, the configuration of causes did not make sense then and does not make sense now. We cannot comprehend why all the subterranean fissures of our human world simultaneously cracked open and left millions of innocent people without any ground to stand upon. They were pushed into a fire fueled by human weakness, self-interest, prejudice, indifference, ignorance, and more.

If we are honest, we cannot add it all up, we cannot subtract it down to some point zero, we cannot divide the responsibility neatly, cannot imagine its multiplication of horror in terms of human lives.

This is the formless shape of evil that we have caught a glimpse of in the twentieth century. It is the configuration of evil—but the various causes simply do not cumulatively yield an explanation. As Emil Fackenheim has written, the Holocaust exemplifies radical evil—evil done for the sake of evil. It defies causal analysis—either a single cause analysis or any attempt to understand why a configuration of causes resulted in hell on earth.

None of this denies the necessity of trying to comprehend what happened during the Holocaust. There are lessons to be learned, precedents that now serve as warnings about the consequence of action or inaction, stories of goodness beyond compare and survival without reason which must always be retold. Nevertheless, the more we comprehend, the more we are led into incomprehension—into the ultimate mystery of the power of evil and goodness.

II

All of these considerations lead me to read the stories of women in the Holocaust as they are recounted in this significant book and elsewhere. I have no doubt that sexual discrimination and oppression were a factor in the conflagration that was the Holocaust. Other writers in this collection of essays will give voice to the experiences of those women who endured the hell of the Holocaust in a particularly horrifying way.

We must read such stories again and again and forever. In doing so we must resist any attempt to reduce the singularity of human suffering. It is always incomparable, unique in quality, and beyond quantification. We must not reduce the infinite dignity of each life to some collective category of oppression and suffering. To do so would be to hand a posthumous victory to those who designated such deadly categories of discrimination and persecution in the first place.

Nevertheless, such an affirmation of the infinite value of each human person cannot and should not lead us to some abstract denial of a suffering that is held in common. Indeed, there are those who will say that, after the Holocaust, there can be no reclaiming of personal dignity apart from the redemptive process in a community of suffering. After Auschwitz, no Jew can be personally liberated until the whole Jewish community is freed from the threat of oppression. It is futile for a Jew to engage in some process of self-affirmation as long as Jewishness is a category of denial. After Auschwitz, being Jewish is a choice. It implies choosing to resist the categories of the oppressor by affirming one's community of hope.

Elsewhere, I have written extensively on the importance of Christians' recognizing that the very existence of the Jewish community after the Holocaust is an act of hope that we Christians have too long denied. Within the context of this book, I want to focus briefly on whether and how the stories of the suffering of women in the Holocaust speak to us today, Jews and non-Jews. I am convinced that memories serve us well when they make it difficult for us to deny either the realities of the past or the imperatives of the future.

It is my conviction that the "different voices" of women in the Holocaust call us, summon us, to exercise a different kind of power today.

III

The evil of the Holocaust was realized through the exercise of a certain kind of power—coercive power. It was a power that sought to dominate and control. It was a power legitimated through law, buttressed by propaganda, augmented by terror, and effected through all the institutions of society. It was a form of power with its own inner logic. To the victims, the bystanders, and perpetrators of such a power, it seemed invincible.

This coercive form of power is not new in human history. Grim records of humanity's inhumanity to humanity serve as reminders of its terrifying predictability. Yet never has such power seemed so omnipotent—or so unpredictable.

The fact is that this coercive form of power has, more often than not, been exercised by men. Whether this is an accident of history, an attribute of culture, or something inherently male is arguable. My own sense is that we will need centuries of experience to determine whether, given the opportunity, women would have a penchant for such a form of power, too.

In the meantime, we must reflect on the reality that this coercive form of power has generated, for centuries, an idealization of powerlessness among people of good conscience and good will. If power is seen as fundamentally coercive, then powerlessness becomes the only position of innocence.

One of the most impressive contemporary proponents of a spirituality of powerlessness is Jean Vanier. A professor of philosophy and the son of a famous Canadian diplomat, Vanier chose to live with and learn from those who were mentally retarded. He speaks of these people as the ones who taught him that the weak and vulnerable had more to say about love than those who were intelligent and in control—the powerful.

I once asked him, gently, whether he could honestly advocate such a spirituality to those who had been born powerless or to those who had been reduced to a state of powerlessness. I noted that his was a chosen powerlessness whereas many suffered from a humanly imposed sense of powerlessness. He replied, quite simply, that one could only choose powerlessness as a way of life if one did so from a position of power. If I understood him correctly, he was speaking about the power of domination and control.

After the Holocaust, an increasing number of Jewish thinkers have disavowed powerlessness as an ethical and spiritual option. Never again, they say, should a sense of powerlessness deal a hand to the power players. Writers such as Irving Greenberg, David Hartmann, and Michael Lerner have urged not the abdication of power but rather the assumption of power—in an ethically responsible manner. Such an assumption of power lies at the heart of the dilemmas of the State of Israel today.

This Jewish recognition of the deadly effects of an ideology of powerlessness runs parallel to the concerns of an increasing number of women today. I share the concern that, while powerlessness may appear morally innocent, it runs the risk of enforced complicity with the designs of the dominant powers in this world. Not as a Jew but as a woman, I am also aware that it is sometimes easier to remain powerless than to assume the ethical burden of exercising the power that is possible. Not as a Jew but as a woman, I have become conscious that a sense of powerlessness is sometimes a self-fulfilling process—if I feel I am powerless, then I will act and speak in ways which will ensure that I will remain powerless.

One feels caught between a rock and a hard place, between exercising a dominant form of power (however ethically) or remaining with a sense of powerlessness. The dilemma endures—unless or until one begins to sense that there may be a different form of power.

After more than twenty years of trying to confront the reality of the Holocaust, as a Christian and as a woman, I desire to move beyond the forced extremes of a coercive form of power and the ideology of powerlessness. I want to engage not in the struggle of responsibly exercising a dominant form of power but rather in the effort to actualize a more creative form of power. To move toward that goal, there are several historical assumptions I must reject.

First, I must reject the view (both widely popular and historically prevalent) that power is a thing, a substance that is quantifiable. To accept such a world view is to admit that power exists in a limited quantity, that it is something which a few have a lot of and many have a little of. To accept this definition of power has multiple political and spiritual implications: It implies a struggle in which there will be a few winners and many losers; it tends to emphasize power as an individual possession or the attribute of a position; it means that one cannot attain the privilege of power without denying the needs of the many; it means that the exercise of power will always be morally ambiguous and that the reality of powerlessness will remain not only innocent but also unrelenting.

Drawing on my Catholic tradition's teaching on grace, I believe that power is not a thing but rather an energy. Power is that which exists in the "in-between" of the divine and/or human life. It exists in-between people, in-between a person and God, in-between persons and God. As such, power is never a prerogative. It is that which arises, irrupts, in however a hidden way, whenever there is a genuine relationship between persons, between God and a person, or between God and two or three or more persons.

After the Holocaust, it is imperative to discover and create new forms of human solidarity. There are numerous historical examples of small groups of people, interacting with one another, who were able to exercise enormous spiritual or political influence. On many occasions those groups enhanced goodness out of all proportion to their numbers. It must also be said that the reality of power as interactive has enabled small groups to effect an evil intent out of all proportion to their numbers. A view of power as interactive does not dismiss but rather deepens the mystery of action both for good and for evil.

Second, I must reject the definition of power as control. Such a definition effectively reduces the possibility of anything new happening within the world, within human experience. If we only act upon that which we can know and can predict, then we will inevitably perpetuate the past—with minor variations. There is always a gap between the past and the future. We human beings will usually attempt to bridge it with something, some words, some ideology or theology, some prescribed position or someone familiar. In the process, we draw the future back into the past, rather than inviting the familiar into the new and the unknown.

If power is intrinsically associated with control, then we can easily back ourselves into an all-or-nothing situation: either we have control or we don't. If a sense of control becomes the condition for action, then most people will feel powerless to effect change in a situation. It is ironic and tragic that in the most powerful nations on earth the majority of people feel quite powerless to effect change in their personal and political lives. If the dominant cultural ethos reflects the view that having power means being in control, then most people will feel radically paralyzed, incapable of making any significant difference in the world. Simultaneously, such people may be very busy and active and yet paralyzed in the core of their being.

Such an all-or-nothing perception of power negates the possibility of partial but significant changes and limited but real gains. If we are faced with the forced option of changing everything or nothing, then we will probably seek to justify our ineffectiveness in the world with what feminist Susan Welch calls "the ideology of cultured despair."

There are some who cannot afford such despair. Among the poor, the desperate, and the dispossessed, there are those who cannot but seek any possibility for change—however fragile and partial it may seem. Never having been in control or having lost whatever control they had, these people stand as witnesses to a different kind of power. A more humble form of power, it is effective and real nonetheless.

Let me briefly suggest that there is not only a political and social price to be paid for accepting the dominant ideology of power. It has also resulted in a certain theological paralysis when faced with the reality of evil, with the reality of the Holocaust. If the omnipotence of God is associated with the possession of power and control, then we must seek to understand God's responsibility for evil in the world. After Auschwitz, some theologians have abandoned such an omnipotent God and prefer to speak about the powerlessness of God—in an effort to render God innocent once again.

My own view is that such a theological position ultimately reinforces the coercive power of evil in the world. If we proclaim a powerless God, then we are preaching a self-fulfilling prophecy. In the late twentieth century, our theological challenge is to bear witness to a God whose power is real but different from the powers that be in this world. We are summoned to bear witness to a God who is both powerful and vulnerable.

Thus, my reflections after the Holocaust have led me to reject a political and theological notion of power as a thing to be possessed or an activity of control. Such a rejection also implies an affirmation of a different kind of power— power that arises in relationship, interactively, power that acts even in the absence of clarity and control. It implies a faith in a more creative form of power.

The biblical book of Genesis opens with stunning words: "In the beginning." It affirms the creative power of God to begin something radically new. To believe in such a God is to believe in our own power to create something humanly new in history. To believe in God's absolute initiative is to believe in our own power to initiate something new in history. Women who give birth know in their flesh the possibility of such new, albeit small, human beginnings. The process of birth involves relationship, interaction. It is not a process involving clarity or control.

After the Holocaust, such faith in the power of human and divine creation has become imperative. Those of us who have chosen to speak about the radical evil of the Holocaust always run the risk that in doing so we are reinforcing the power of evil and the powerlessness of the good. Even as we acknowledge the coercive power of evil, we must affirm the creative power of goodness and life. To do otherwise would be to extend the victimization and sense of powerlessness generated during the Nazi regime.

The Holocaust was a terrifyingly new event in human history. Although there were precedents for such evil, the Shoah was nevertheless unprecedented in its radicality. The challenge now is to prevent the Holocaust from becoming the historical precedent that inspires destruction or legitimates the wasting of life. We need to believe that, together with God, we can make some new beginnings in history, that we can initiate healing alternatives to the Holocaust. We must hope that history will not automatically repeat itself. We must refuse to accept that we are merely the powerless victims and bystanders of the inexorable roll of the twentieth century.

Even as we admit the shocking reality of the power of destruction, we must acknowledge the surprising reality of the power of creation.

If we search for grounds for such a faith in a creative form of power, we need only remember that some Jewish women continued to give birth in the long and dark night of the Holocaust. Such a commitment to human beginnings was not merely an incident in an inevitable biological process—it was an act of faith that summons us now to hope.

25

Rachel Altman

. . . As a child I yearned to know my grandmothers. As an adult, I still yearn to know them, seeking connection in continuity and context. Like an archeologist, I dig through the past, unearthing fragments, putting together the pieces in an attempt to envision what once was whole.

RACHEL ALTMAN

She came of age not in the thirties or forties but in the sixties. Jewish, born in America—Vietnam and Watergate are part of her history. A freelance writer, she is married and the mother of a daughter. Balancing the responsibilities of home and profession, she is like so many American women. But not completely, for, unlike so many American women, Rachel Federman Altman is the daughter of Polish Jews who survived the Holocaust and emigrated to the United States after their liberation. Raised in freedom and security but with the Holocaust as her legacy, she is part of the "Second Generation," as the children of Holocaust survivors are often called. Thus she can identify with the comment that another child of survivors makes in Helen Epstein's book Children of the Holocaust: *"Our parents were not like other parents, and we children were not like other children."*

   Naming a child after a deceased relative is an ancient Jewish custom. It is a concrete way to ensure a sense of continuity from generation to generation. As the firstborn, Altman was named after her two grandmothers—"Ruchel . . . my father's mother, who died in the gas chambers, and Miryam . . . my mother's mother, who died before the war began." Wistfully, but not surprisingly, her life is intertwined with theirs. For example, she looks like her Grandmother Ruchel, but the resemblance runs deeper than that. It includes, her father says, Ruchel's "independent spirit, her rebellious

363

nature, her 'modern' ways and her insistence on standing alone." Hearing these things, Altman writes, "I felt a shiver of love and gratitude, then a deep sorrow at my not having known this woman. How is it possible," she wonders, "to be so like someone you never knew?"

Like so many children of Holocaust survivors, Altman longs to know—*about her relatives who were murdered by the Nazis, her connection to the life that was, and what her post-Holocaust Jewish identity means today. "The Eastern European* shtetl," *she acknowledges, "is not a world in which I would choose to live." But she does long to be part of that world. Specifically, she wants to know the women of her family, "the mothers and grandmothers and aunts and daughters." She wants to be part of that long line "reaching back in time and forward from this moment." She wants to welcome their spirit into her life and into her daughter's as well. But she wants to do all of this as the educated Jewish woman she is today, conscious of her traditions and the responsibilities she feels for the future.*

Knowing about the Holocaust, Altman underscores, is not enough. One must also know the questions it raises. Echoing in her own distinctive voice concerns shared by Deborah Lipstadt and Mary Jo Leddy, Rachel Altman asks specifically about her "obligations as a daughter of victims of oppression . . . as a woman and as a Jew, to others of the disadvantaged and oppressed." The Holocaust, she concludes, must be a shield, a protection "to make us more able to choose to rise above hatred, violence, fear."

In one of this book's earlier excerpts, Claudia Koonz portrayed Nazi women who wanted to know neither the Holocaust's facts nor its questions. Far from taking responsibility for the Holocaust and its legacy, they shirked it. Compared to theirs, Rachel Altman's second-generation voice is a different one indeed.

Fragments of a Broken Past

My mother, Ann Federman, and I are buying food for lunch in Wolbrom, a small town in Southern Poland that was my father's hometown. This is my parents' first trip back to their native Poland since leaving in 1945, after being liberated from concentration camps. For years my father swore he would never set foot on Polish or German soil again; now he has relented, seeing this journey as the consummate answer to the many questions that my brother, sister, and I ask about life in Poland. The cheese store where we shop—once owned by a Jewish family, as were all the shops on the town square—has a cross and a picture of the Virgin Mary on the wall. I watch my mother deal with the shopkeeper, asking prices and choosing cheeses in fluent Polish, her gestures and her language foreign to me, though she obviously feels at home. This is a woman who has shopped for forty-five years in a Midwestern suburban supermarket where everything comes prepackaged, wrapped in cellophane; where you don't bargain with the shopkeeper and question the quality or the freshness, or ask after her children. This is my mother—the shy woman who treads lightly in her new life, whose accent and misuse of the English language often embarrassed me as I was growing up. As a child, she rarely left the confines of the Jewish ghetto in her hometown of Bendzin; on one rare occasion when she did, she was chided by a Gentile girl: "You just wait! Hitler will come, and he will bury you!"

The Nazis came to Bendzin in September 1939. They marched into town on a Friday night, locked the doors of the wooden synagogue, and set it on fire with 500 men, women, and children inside, praying. They then took most of the town's able-bodied men, my mother's brothers included, to labor camps. In September 1942 they announced that the remaining Jews in Bendzin should all gather in the town square at 8:00 in the morning.

> I don't remember the date but it was a beautiful September day, the holiday season, you know—cool but pleasant. The trees were just beginning to turn, the sun was shining. It was crisp, and just cool enough to wear a sweater. And we went and picked up my brother's wife—my sister-in-law—and his two kids. We had decided to go together with her, to help her with the children, because we thought we were coming back home. . . . See, at that point nobody knew where we were going to be sent . . . they put my sister and me on a freight train, and they took us into the Czechoslovakian mountains.
>
> Ann Federman, from a taped interview, July 1976[1]

My mother tells of how she and the other girls (she was fourteen at the time) acted as if they were on holiday, singing songs as the train moved through the beautiful countryside. They eventually arrived at the labor camp of Parschnitz-Bei-Treitenau, in Sudentenland, near Prague. The women worked from six in the morning to six at night in the textile factory that had been taken over by the Nazis, their duties ranging from operating machinery to digging ditches. Their food supply for an entire day often consisted of a cup of coffee and a hunk of bread, which they sometimes supplemented with potatoes stolen from the kitchen at the risk of suffering a beating or, if they were to be used as an example, death.

Because my mother and her sister demonstrated themselves to be able workers, they managed to persuade the supervisor of the camp to allow their younger sister Leah, thirteen, to join them there. After a short time Leah fell ill with a cold and was taken to the infirmary; late that night a transport came through en route to Auschwitz. They never saw Leah again.

My mother and her sister were in the labor camp for almost three years, until being liberated by Russian troops in 1945.

This is the spot, right here, where they picked me up. I had gone out to get some groceries for my mom, some sugar and a piece of butter. Six SS forced me, at gunpoint, onto a truck and took me to [the labor camp at] Miechow. It was September 1939. I was seventeen years old.

> Isak Federman, September 1990, in Wolbrom, Poland

Miechow was the first of eighteen camps my father was in, including brief stays in Bergen–Belsen and Auschwitz. He bears the scars of bullet wounds on his head and wrist from an attempted escape. According to my father, he survived because he was aggressive and worked hard (he volunteered to do anything and everything, which often involved moving to a new camp) and because he was lucky. On May 5, 1945, having contracted typhus in the camp in Sand Posten, Germany, and debilitated from fever, he crawled to a spigot for water. Just as he began to drink he lost consciousness, and as he passed out he saw a British tank drive into the compound. He woke up three days later in a British army hospital and though he barely survived this illness, he was alive and free, and the war was over.

My father was the sole survivor of his family of five; it is probable that his family perished in the extermination camps of Belzec and Chelmno, but we are not certain of this.

Of my mother's eight brothers and sisters, three survived. When they left Parshnitz my mother and her sister, who by then was ill with tuberculosis, walked for ten days, hitching rides when they could, to return to Bendzin, where they found that their apartment building had been burned and looted. Eventually they were reunited with their two surviving brothers, Aron and Chaim, who had befriended my father. Through Chaim, my father and my mother met and fell in love. In 1945, my mother and her two brothers and sister, along with my father, were among the thousands of displaced European refugees to immigrate to America.

> When we got off the boat—we came in at night and we saw the lights, you know that big city, the flashing lights in New York. We were just overwhelmed, really, and we didn't know how we were going to start our lives, how we're going to adjust—what are we going to do here?
>
> Ann Federman, from a taped interview, July 1976[2]

In their early days in America, my parents have told me, they were dazzled by everything: their love for each other, their new life, automobiles, freedom. Here, in America, a Jew could walk the streets without fear. In America, a Jew could be anything!

I was their first child and was named after my grandmothers: Ruchel, for my father's mother, who died in the gas chambers, and Miryam, for my mother's mother, who died before the war began. We lived the life of an extended family (my surviving aunts and uncles all settled, with my parents, in Kansas City and we saw a great deal of each other); even so, as a child I yearned to know my grandmothers. As an adult, I still yearn to know them, seeking connection in continuity and context. Like an archaeologist, I dig through the past, unearthing fragments, putting together the pieces in an attempt to envision what once was whole.

This is what I know about my grandmother Miryam: She bore thirteen children, four of whom died in an influenza epidemic during World War I. Her husband Avram—a pious man, busy with his religious studies—earned a meager living and the family was poor; it fell to Miryam to make ends meet. She was ill for most of her adult life—an illness about which little was known (I've been told at times that she had "heart trouble," at others that she had diabetes)—and died in her early fifties, when my mother was nine.

This is what I know about my grandmother Ruchel: She went against custom and married a man she loved, rather than having an arranged marriage. When her first husband died of pneumonia, leaving her with three children, she took over his shirtmaking business, refusing many suitors, for fear that her new husband would not treat her children, his stepchildren, well. She ran the business with competence and acumen and expanded it, hiring three seamstresses who worked at the kitchen table of her small apartment. She eventually married again and bore another child with her second husband. Well-educated, unlike many women in the old country, and not religious, she was known as a rebel.

In Poland with my parents, I seek out these details and ask question after question, hungry for knowledge about them—these women from a shadowy past, always part of me, though absent. I try to picture my grandmother Miryam at the sanatorium in the forest, near Szewierz, where she was sent by her doctor for a rest cure; I try to imagine her feelings at this separation from her children. I try to put myself inside the mind of my grandmother Ruchel the day my father was taken to the camps—a mother whose son went out on an errand and never returned. Is she frantic, does she search the streets, how long does she wait, what does she feel, when does she find out, and then what does she do?

I've been told that I bear an uncanny resemblance to my grandmother and namesake Ruchel who, like me, was small with dark eyes and dark curly hair. I spend hours gazing at a photograph of her daughter, the one that resembles her: We have the same nose and chin and though she wore her hair parted in the middle and pulled back in a severe bun, I can see that it is the same thick, wiry hair. But it wasn't until recently—in fact, during the trip to Poland—that my father told me how like her I am in other ways—her independent spirit, her rebellious nature, her "modern" ways and her insistence on standing alone—and when he told me, I felt a shiver of love and gratitude, then a deep sorrow at my not having known this woman. How is it possible to be so like someone you never knew?

In Jewish life women are the guardians of tradition—family, values, morality. In the old country, men sat for hours discoursing and arguing the Talmud, the book in which the law is encoded. But it fell to the women to insist that people behave as they should—as a *mensch*, a human being, should. The rituals of Jewish life and religious practice are not reserved for the synagogue; built into the liturgy are prayers to be spoken on awakening, prayers to be said when washing the hands, when seeing a rainbow, when eating a meal— prayers to be recited in the midst of life. In its purest form, Judaism brings us into an atmosphere of appreciation and awareness of every moment of life as sacred. At the center of Jewish life is the home, and at the center of the home is the woman.

At the same time, Judaism has discriminated against women: in Jewish mythology and tradition, women are given a clearly second-rate status and until recently, we have been excluded from the study of Talmud and the rabbinate.

In thinking about the women in my family—in allowing myself to feel a longing to be part of their world—I recognize a certain irony. I bemoan the loss of my family, of the Jewish world that existed in Eastern Europe before the war, with a grief that will never be assuaged. However, as a modern woman, I acknowledge that the Eastern European *shtetl* is not a world in which I would choose to live.

How different my grandmothers' lives were from mine! How can I—a woman who is educated and has explored options; a woman whose marriage was not arranged; a woman with rights, living in a time when a woman can choose to actively confront discrimination, can even become a rabbi—pretend to know them, these women who sat separate from men in the *shul*, who walked down narrow streets and bargained with shopkeepers, who raced home to complete the preparations for the Sabbath before the sun went down, who kept the children quiet so their husbands' studies would not be dis- turbed? How can I pretend to know my grandmother Miryam, who was pregnant for thirteen years of her life, who lived at the mercy of an illness that could not be named (though today it could probably easily be treated), whose life revolved around stretching a tiny piece of meat to provide food for fifteen people, while her husband sat at the kitchen table and prayed?

> Late. I'm late again. I know that when I walk in the door my father and mother will be sitting in the living room, in their nightclothes, waiting for me—the white couch encased in plastic to protect it, plastic runners on the white rug marking your path, my father pacing and angry and my mother nervous, clutching her hands and turning her wedding ring around on her finger—watching for the car's lights in the driveway. They question me extensively about every boy I go out with: who is he, who are his parents, what does his father do, is he Jewish?

Throughout my teenage years, my parents and I raged at each other. It was complicated: I came of age during the sixties, a time when we sought open- ness and freedom, a time of tearing down the old—and the old was all my parents knew. Picture where they had come from: the small Jewish community, with its boundaries and modes of behavior clear and fixed; a society in which sexuality was controlled through early, arranged marriages, through religious strictures and convention; a patriarchy in which the home was ruled by the iron hand of the father.

I was their eldest child, a product of America, and even the most innocent, widely accepted behavior of American adolescents came as a shock to them. At the same time, their restrictions, their unceasing questions and worry, their inability to trust, confused and alienated me.

The fact of my femaleness was a further complication. In the old country, my mother often told me, the bride and groom first met "under the *chuppa*," the bridal canopy, the daughter protected in innocence until that moment. My adolescence could not have been more different.

I remember sitting at the kitchen table and arguing with my father: I am appalled the year he decides to vote Republican. We argue about the Vietnam War, about how to deal with our nation's racism and poverty. In these arguments I cannot win: Who am I to tell my father—who survived Europe's great crime against humanity, whose life began anew when he was transplanted to the United States—that this government's policies and way of life are inhuman? My father tells me time and again, fist pounding the table: "America is the greatest country that ever was. God bless America." The history of their suffering, their enormous loss—the scale of it—rules these conversations, making my questions and problems look petty and, whether spoken of or not, brings many a conversation to a screeching halt.

Eventually we stop talking about politics. Like many of my generation, I grow alienated from my family, rejecting what I see as their outmoded values. I flee the confines of Midwestern Jewry and embark on a search for my identity.

At dinner that night in Krakow, Mom tells a story I've never heard, about her brother Yitzhak's wife Chava. The day the Nazis came to take the rest of them away (Yitzhak and the older boys had all been taken to labor camps before this), a Polish neighbor woman, a friend, offered to keep Chava's two kids for her, "just for a little while, just until you return from the square"—but Chava couldn't agree to this. She insisted on taking her kids with her to the square, from where they were taken to the camps. The kids did not survive, though Chava did. Mom always insists that they didn't know where they were going, that they thought they would return home from the square. I wonder if Chava knew; in any case, she must have thought it best to keep her children with her, that whatever happened, only she could protect her children.

Excerpt from my diary, Poland, September 1990

When I visited Israel in 1971, Chava invited me for Shabbat dinner. She made a point of telling me she was not an observant Jew, that the dinner would be a secular celebration. At sundown, as is traditional, she lit the candles, her head covered with a shawl, her hands covering her face as she recited the prayer. Afterward, she turned to me sheepishly and said, "Since the war, I no longer believe in God. Every Friday night I light the candles and say the blessing over them, but I do not do it for God. I do it for the memory of my mother."

Like Chava, I am not an observant Jew, but I light candles on Friday night to usher in the Sabbath. I enjoy the peace that the ritual brings to my household, and I appreciate this weekly reminder to be grateful for the beauty of the creation. Also, it is a way of knowing them—the women of my family, the mothers and grandmothers and aunts and daughters who, in the midst of hunger, illness, war, persecution, brought light to the darkness. I visualize a procession of them, a line reaching back in time and forward from this moment. Covering my head with a scarf, circling my hands over the flames three times and reciting the blessing, I join this procession of women, welcoming their spirit into my life, into my daughter's life.

I am speaking to a neighbor across the street, in the small town where I live in California. She says, "You're a writer? What do you write about?" I take a deep breath. This is a question that I'm never sure how to answer; usually I try to gauge the sensitivity of the questioner, wondering how she will hear it. I consult my mood at the moment, whether or not I want to talk about *that* right now. It is a difficult subject: For some it evokes immediate feelings of shame and guilt, feelings that catch them off guard, flickering over their eyes and face; for some, I become an object of pity. The subject is big, filled with confusion of the most basic kind, raising the question that none of us wants to look at: How can we call ourselves human?

I tell my neighbor: My parents were victims of the Holocaust. They were in concentration camps. I am writing about my family's history.

Her eyes glaze over. "Oh," she says, "that must be interesting."

"Yes," I say, hurrying to fill the gap, the words pouring out of me before I can stop them, "interesting and important. The Holocaust is an example of how far things can go, that we cannot allow racism and prejudice to rule our lives, that we must be tolerant, we must behave as human beings."

She sniffs. "Well, I'm not very tolerant," she says, picking up on this word and ignoring my message. "Like with these gangs around here, I'm not tolerant at all." She lapses into a discussion I've heard from her before, how *they* are coming up from Los Angeles, bringing drugs and crime to our small town, how we cannot let *them* take over our neighborhoods.

My heart clenches up as I listen and then I make an excuse to leave, regretting my involvement in this conversation. Maybe I am the crazy one, I think, with all this talk of tolerance; maybe I am the one who is ignoring the lessons of history.

This disparity of interpretation was evident on a May weekend in 1991, at a hotel in New York where a conference for children hidden during World War II was being held. The first international gathering of its kind, its organizers had hoped as many as five hundred people would attend; fifteen hundred showed up. The "hidden children"—many of whom had learned late in life of the identities of their birth-parents; many of whom were raised as Gentiles and only recently learned that they were born Jews; many of whom, in order to survive, knelt at Catholic altars by day and whispered *Sh'ma Yisrael* into their pillows at night—were ready to come forward, to speak about and to acknowledge their history, and for many it was the first time they spoke about this publicly.

In one workshop, a woman tells of how she watched Nazi soldiers shoot her mother and was told by her father not to cry, for fear of their being discovered; she was a child of ten, forced into hiding on both the literal and the psychological level. A Polish Gentile family took her in, in exchange for money; they used her as a servant in the household and abused her physically and psychologically. This story is horrific and typical and will be repeated in different forms throughout the three-day conference. Her voice shaking, the woman ends by saying, "And what I really want to say is that I hate the Germans, I hate the Poles, I hate the Gentiles, and I always will."

Another woman stands up to speak. Her story, too, is filled with horror. As a child in France, she spent two years in hiding and was then captured and sent to Birkenau—she barely survived and was the sole survivor of her family. "There's something that I don't hear people talking about," she says softly, "and I think it's important. I think we have a responsibility to teach our children not to be bigoted, not to hate. We have to show them by example that human tolerance and understanding begin with me, that racism and bigotry end with me. It has to stop, here and now, with me."

The woman who had her childhood ripped from her, who was forced to use her budding womanhood to bargain with death, who watched her mother die and could not cry out, speaks of her hatred. How could we expect otherwise? She will remind us when we forget, and to her I am grateful. But hatred cannot be the lesson.

I have more questions than answers. How can I put together the pieces of my life, my family's life? What is my place on earth, both literally and figuratively—where do I belong? These are the personal questions. But it is the bigger questions, in the end, that compel me. What are my obligations as a daughter of victims of oppression in its most extreme form? What are my obligations, as a woman and as a Jew, to others of the disadvantaged and oppressed? It is clear that, as Jews, we need to protect ourselves—can we manage to do so and yet avoid the perpetuation of these atrocities on others, especially on those who fall under the governance of Israel? How far can we allow fear to take us, before we are all lost? If it were happening now, here, would I risk my life—and the life of my family—to save another? Would you?

I think of my grandmothers: Miryam, devout and nurturing; Ruchel, independent and rebellious. Who would they be if they lived in my world, faced with the same choices and contradictions? What is the point of religion—of studying history—if not to make us more able to choose to rise above hatred, violence, fear?

In the lobby of the hotel where the conference is held, I stop to look at a bulletin board covered with over five hundred messages. One reads: "HAVE YOU SEEN MY SISTER? I last saw her in a hospital in France in 1942. If you have any information about her, PLEASE call." I move through the lobby, round a corner, and overhear a conversation between two men who work for the hotel, a Black and a Hispanic:

"Man, have you looked at that bulletin board?"

"No."

"You oughta look at that bulletin board—after all this time, people are still looking for lost brothers and sisters. The stuff these people have been through—nobody on earth should have to go through that. Nobody."

Rachel Federman Altman, November 1991

NOTES

1. Interview with Ann Federman, July 31, 1976. Used by permission of Morrie Warshawski and Ann Federman.
2. Ibid.

26

Joan Ringelheim

So much work on women and the Holocaust remains to be done. What has been researched thus far merely touches the surface of a complex and difficult field of study.

JOAN RINGELHEIM

If anyone is the founding mother of women's Holocaust studies, Joan Ringelheim deserves to be among the top contenders for the distinction. Years ago this philosopher and historian was organizing conferences, writing essays, and setting agendas for research in this area. She did so even when critics told her that such concerns were inappropriate or morally questionable because, it was mistakenly alleged, they would distract attention from more important Holocaust issues. Ringelheim wisely persisted, and her efforts show signs of paying off. More attention has been paid to issues involving women and the Holocaust, and it is likely that even more will be paid in the future. Meanwhile, few if any scholars are more knowledgeable about this subject. Whenever she speaks or writes about women and the Holocaust, other students of the Holocaust must take notice.

"Different horrors, same hell"—Ringelheim uses equally potent words to make points related to Myrna Goldenberg's succinct phrase. Underscoring that "surviving is different from living" and that "oppression does not make people better, oppression makes people oppressed," Ringelheim speaks about double jeopardy. *What she means and wants to explore she summarizes effectively in her 1990 essay, "Thoughts about Women and the Holocaust":*

> *Jewish women suffered both as Jews and as women from anti-semitism and sexism in their genocidal forms. More women were deported than men. More women were killed*

373

than men. Women's chances for survival were simply not equivalent to those of men. . . . If anti-semitism were all that mattered, men and women would have been similarly endangered and victimized. Thus, the question is not whether being male or female mattered during the Holocaust. The real question is: How did it matter? It is blind, if not malicious, to subsume and hide women's experiences under those of men when there are significant differences.

In the reflections that follow, Ringelheim defends such claims with empirical data. She also displays a philosophical turn of mind that will keep leading her to reconsider, reevaluate, and revise her own historical research. Far from undermining her basic convictions, however, the continuation of such careful scholarship is likely to advance her thesis that women, especially but not exclusively Jewish women, were indeed in "double jeopardy" during the Holocaust.

A Jewish woman who survived the Holocaust, Ringelheim reports, once remarked to her that "I had two enemies: Nazis and men." Hoping her scholarship can relieve such duress, Ringelheim concludes that "so much work on women and the Holocaust remains to be done. What has been researched thus far merely touches the surface of a complex and difficult field of study." With a contribution that provides not only an ending for this book but also a call for ongoing research and reflection, pioneering scholar Joan Ringelheim leads the way.

Women and the Holocaust:
A Reconsideration of Research

I

Thinking is like the veil of Penelope: it undoes every morning what it had finished the night before.

HANNAH ARENDT, "THINKING AND MORAL CONSIDERATIONS"

Even a cursory look at studies about the Holocaust would indicate that the experiences and perceptions of Jewish women have been obscured or absorbed into descriptions of men's lives. The similarity among Jewish victims of the Nazi policy of destruction has been considered more important than any differentiation, including or especially that of gender. It is not surprising, then, that until quite recently there has been no feminist perspective in Holocaust scholarship.[1]

From Joan Ringelheim, "Women and the Holocaust: A Reconsideration of Research," *Signs: Journal of Women in Culture and Society* 10 (1985): 741–61. Copyright © 1985 by The University of Chicago. Reprinted by permission of The University of Chicago Press. In addition to making minor changes in the original text, Joan Ringelheim has added a postscript and appendices that did not appear in the 1985 edition. The postscript and appendices are copyright © 1992 by Joan Ringelheim and published by permission of the author.

Although the research on women and the Holocaust is only just beginning, it already has taken a problematic and troubling direction. Since my own work has been instrumental in setting this course, I am going to make it my case study for analysis and criticism. Using fragments of stories Jewish women survivors have told me in interviews, I will first recapitulate the assumptions, hypotheses, and categories I have used in my interpretation and then explore what is problematic in this approach. I want to look particularly at the influence of cultural feminism on my own work and to pose myself and others some new questions.

When I began research I assumed that gender must have counted for something and that focusing on women's experience would yield new questions and new data: if you were Jewish, in what ways did it matter whether you were a man or a woman? Did gender cause any difference in policies, actions, or reactions of either the Nazis or those opposed to them? In what ways did sexism function in the racist ideology against Jews and other so-called non-Aryans? Is there, for instance, anything to be seen in statistics about the number of men killed as compared to women, differences among those selected to die, or distinctions in types of work assigned? Did the Nazis prolong and intensify an already existing sexism against Jewish women as they prolonged, intensified, and even elaborated anti-Semitism against the Jews as a whole?[2] In what ways was sexism maintained and intensified under Nazism by the Jews themselves?

Were women's experiences during the Holocaust different from men's in some respects? Were there differences in work, relationships, roles, and in maintenance possibilities or capabilities—that is, in what a person did or tried to do simply to keep going, to make it from day to day?[3] Do women and men possess different maintenance skills? Because of traditional gender roles are women better able to bear conditions of deprivation?

At the initial stages of research, I suggested that traditional attitudes and responses toward women, as well as gender-defined conditions, made women especially vulnerable to abuse of their sexuality and of their maternal responsibility—to rape, murder of themselves and their children, the necessity of killing their own or other women's babies, forced abortion, and other forms of sexual exploitation—in the ghettos, in resistance groups, in hiding and passing, and in the camps. I believed it important, moreover, to explore the claim of some survivors and scholars that women's capacities for enduring the trauma of dislocation, starvation, loss of traditional support structures, and physical and mental abuse were different from and sometimes greater than men's.[4]

These assumptions and ideas shaped the form of an interview schedule with a twofold aim: (1) to recapture the Holocaust experience as a whole, and (2) to establish women's sense of their particular experience within it: what was done to them (their vulnerabilities) and what they did (their resources). I began each of the twenty interviews I conducted with some general questions about life prior to the Holocaust: family background, relationships, education, class, and so on. I wanted the women to start their stories in a way that seemed comfortable, even familiar. I expected to be able to hear their understanding of themselves both as Jews and as women from the narrative structures they devised. I asked further questions when they were needed to clarify or expand an idea, or to raise a topic not yet mentioned. In particular, I asked about those things that seemed related to their lives as women: sexuality, sexual abuse, family, children, relationships, food, resistance, and passivity. I asked questions about choices, decisions, and problems. What did they tell me?[5]

In their descriptions of the tragedy of Jews during the Holocaust, the women interviewed discussed women's particular victimization. They spoke of their sexual vulnerability: sexual humiliation, rape, sexual exchange, pregnancy, abortion, and vulnerability through their children—concerns that men either described in different ways or, more often, did not describe at all.[6] Almost every woman referred to the humiliating feelings and experiences surrounding her entrance to the camp (for my interviewees, this was Auschwitz): being nude; being shaved all over—for some being shaved in a sexual stance, straddling two stools; being observed by men, both fellow prisoners and SS guards. Their stories demonstrate shared fears about and experiences of sexual vulnerability as women, not only about mortal danger as Jews.

Some women remember the ways in which sex was used as a commodity in the ghettos; sexual exchanges for food or other goods involved Jewish men at least as often as, perhaps more often than, they did Nazi authorities. S. spoke of her experiences in Theresienstadt—the so-called model ghetto in Czechoslovakia. She was about twenty: "Women survived partly by brains. I worked in the office, in supply, in the education office. I wasn't doing badly. . . . [Up] to [a certain] point you were autonomous . . . you could lead your own life . . . people could get married. You also survived by your male connections. It was the males who had the main offices, who ran the kitchens. . . . [The] *Judenrat* [was] running [the ghetto and the Jewish men] *used* it. And did they *use* it. *Did* they use it. That was how you survived as a woman—through the male. I was done in by one. I suppose I didn't sleep high enough, to put it bluntly. Because in that society, that was the only way you could survive."

Her experiences with sexual abuse did not end when she was sent to Auschwitz. Once when she was working in *Kanada*, an SS officer approached her as she began to take a nap.[7] He tried to wake her by kicking the bunk on which she was resting. She knew what he wanted (she had noticed him staring at her) and feigned sleep, pushing him away or moaning as if he were part of a dream. S. claimed that he would not have forced her to have sex—he would only have had relations if she agreed because a prisoner could report the SS. In such cases the prisoner had some "power," she said, because it was a crime for an SS to have sexual relations with a Jew. This SS man went away. Another time, S. was not so lucky: she was raped by a prisoner.

At the time of the Warsaw Ghetto, G. was about fifteen years old. She remembered seeing a young SS officer spot beautiful Jewish women, go to their houses, and rape them. Afterward, he would shoot them. He always came prepared with a horse-drawn hearse. Since G. was quite pretty, her mother and cousin made paste from flour and water and put it on her face with the hope that she would be less vulnerable if less attractive. She was afraid but never really "knew if it was better to look prettier or terrible."

About three years later, G. was in a camp near Lublin and Maidanek, and the commandant decided to open up the gates of the men's camp and allow them to go over to the women's. "The men came. I was pretty young then. Strangest thing—so many of these men tried right away to screw. . . . [They were] like a horde of animals. . . . I had this vision for a long, long time—this horde of sick men jumping." She was only watching, and this is all she remembers. It was one of her worst memories from the Holocaust.

Although there are many stories about sexual abuse, they are not easy to come by. Some think it inappropriate to talk about these matters; discussions about sexuality desecrate the memories of the dead, or the living, or the Holocaust itself. For others, it is simply too difficult and painful. Still others think it may be a trivial issue. One survivor told me that she had been sexually abused by a number of Gentile men while she was in hiding, when she was about eleven years old. Her comment about this was that it "was not important . . . except to me." She meant that it had no significance within the larger picture of the Holocaust. But why should ideas about the Holocaust as a whole exclude these women's experiences—exclude what is important to women—and thus make the judgment that women's experiences as women are trivial? These aspects of women's daily lives—vulnerability to rape, humiliation, sexual exchange, not to speak of pregnancy, abortion, and fear for one's children—cannot simply be universalized as true for all survivors.

It would be wrong to suggest that abuse characterized the whole of women's sexual experiences during the Holocaust. Some women speak about heterosexual love relationships, great passions, or small romances in the ghettos, resistance groups, and even in the camps. They also speak of liaisons created out of loneliness, friendship, the need for help, or even the desire to experience sex before one's death.

In sex-segregated camps, as most were, deep friendships occurred among the women that sometimes developed into sexual relationships. Thus far no woman has talked to me about such experiences as her own. S. did say that she knew of lesbian relationships and that "it wasn't an issue; wherever you could get warmth, care, and affection, that was good. That was all that mattered."[8] Her view is not the common one that I have encountered. More often than not those interviewed showed hostility at the question, some associating it with visions of SS women in drag with whips. Attitudes toward lesbian relationships in the camps seem at best ambiguous or ambivalent and require careful study if we are to understand fully relationships and interactions in the camps and elsewhere.

Coping with pregnancy, childbirth, and infant care made Jewish women particularly vulnerable in other ways to physical abuse and mental anguish—whether through abortion by choice, forced abortion, bearing a child, being killed with a child as its actual or supposed mother, bearing a child and not being able to feed it, killing a baby because its cries jeopardized other people or because if the baby were found (at least in Auschwitz) both Jewish mother and baby would be killed.[9] I heard one child survivor say that all adults were enemies to children,[10] but women with children may have been more vulnerable than anyone except children by themselves.

What I am trying to make graphic is the complexity of these Jewish women's lives because of the connections between biology and sexism. There are particular vulnerabilities, such as pregnancy and abortion, resulting from women's biology; others, created by sexism, perpetuate violence against women in the form of humiliation, molestation, rape, and sexual exchange. These vulnerabilities, as well as the sheer terror, degradation, and genocide perpetrated by the Nazis against the Jews, existed for Jewish women in the Holocaust.

Besides their special vulnerability, the other topic that I discussed with the women I interviewed was their special resources. Survivors testify to gender difference in this regard. A number of observers had the impression that women survived better than men, that women "tended to outlive" men, at least in comparable situations.[11] Such perceptions need to be examined.

Study of the Holocaust requires more specific research on the comparative survival rates of women and men than is represented in the sporadic opinions and unrepresentative surveys now available.[12] Without such statistics (and they may never be available) we have only impressions and speculations, a series of questions rather than answers. Were more women killed than men? What was the relation between work and survival? If some sorts of work could save lives, did women and men have similar chances to do it? What was the pattern of food distribution between women and men, among women, and among men—that is, were women eating the same amount as men or sharing their portions more than men did? Are there biological differences to account for the dissimilarities mentioned by survivors and scholars about the effects of starvation?

Some of the differences perceived do appear as transformations related to gender: starving transformed into communal sharing of recipe stories; sex into food, rather than the reverse; rags into clothes; isolation into relationships or surrogate "families." Women were able to transform their habits of raising children or their experience of nurturing into the care of nonbiological family. Men, when they lost their role in the protection of their own families, seemed less able to transform this habit into the protection of others. Men did not remain or become fathers as readily as women became mothers or nurturers. Do women apply and modify previous gender roles more easily than do men?[13]

The so-called trivial, everyday activities of which the women speak constitute the necessary but not sufficient conditions for their survival. "Women's work"—activities centering around food, children, clothing, shelter, social relations, warmth, cleanliness—may be regarded as the only meaningful labor in a time of such dire necessity. It is only with such trivial—and often trivialized—concerns that life among the oppressed becomes possible. And it is important to look at what this means both to women and to men whose relationship to necessity has traditionally been quite different in European as well as other cultures.

Because of the different material conditions and social relations that characterize their lives, women are able to create or recreate "families" and so provide networks for maintenance that may be related to survival rates. Awareness of such responses (and of such variables as class, age, and nationality) is crucial to understanding the lives of the women.[14] Excerpts from the following three interviews give you some preliminary sense of the ways in which a few women have spoken about the importance of relationships to their survival.[15]

Rose

Rose, from a poor family, was born in Hungary in 1919. She was trained as a hairdresser and was deported to Auschwitz in March 1942. After a year on an outside demolition crew, she began work in the sauna, cutting the hair of the incoming prisoners. "There were mountains of dead bodies outside of the barracks which were picked up by trucks every morning. If you had to go to the bathroom [diarrhea was rampant and getting to the latrine difficult], then you went to the bathroom on top of them. Didn't think twice about it. You had no feelings. [Yet] I knew a young girl from Holland, Eva, who was brought to Block 25 [a kind of holding pen for women going to be gassed]. Eva was fifteen or sixteen and got diarrhea which was enough for them to take you away. Took her to Block 25 and I knew where she was going to go. . . . I sneaked there and took her something to eat. . . . My heart was aching for her. You know, here I was walking over dead bodies and it didn't bother me, but it bothered me to see a young girl like this go and nothing I could do for her. There was still feelings. . . . I couldn't cry too much. . . . I felt so bad for her and when you got close to these barracks in Block 25, you can't imagine what you saw in there. Just can't imagine—half-crazy, laid on top of one another, lost their minds . . . horrible."

At about the time Rose got her job in the sauna [1943], Rollie came to Auschwitz from Greece with two sisters. The youngest, Teresa (Rollie's favorite), got sick and died. Rollie was beside herself and wanted to commit suicide. Rose met her. "If it wasn't for me, she wouldn't be alive. We helped each other. We had to cling . . . you had to have somebody. We helped each other. She considers me her best friend, her mother, her father, everything. . . . I considered her as my daughter [Rose was then twenty-four; Rollie was eighteen]. This I felt for her. I was sheltering her. . . . When I had typhus, all I wanted was an apple. Who can get an apple there? [Rollie] sold her bread to exchange for an apple that I should get it."

A small incident. In the chronicle of concentration camp horrors, it may even appear to be minuscule. For Rose, it is only small because it takes a short time to tell. It is an emblem of life for her: "That time you don't think what kind of relation; you just think, I got somebody here I can talk to, somebody close by. That's all what you think about. . . . I fought going off my mind. I thought of taking my life [going to the electrified wires that surrounded the camp and forgetting] the whole thing. But . . . I gotta live. This woman told me, I'm gonna be free, I'm gonna go to America to see my father. . . . [That] gave me a lot. . . . Got Rollie here and she's still a baby—this was how I was thinking about her. Can't do that [commit suicide or lose her mind]. You know, there was always something that was stopping me. Now here was little Eva, she goes in Block 25 and I just want to see her once more—was always something that I say 'No, I'm not gonna do that.' Didn't let myself go."

Rose gave her own reasons for the way in which women kept themselves and others going, and explained what it meant that they did so: Women were "picking each other like monkeys [for lice]. . . . Never remember seeing the men do it. The minute they had lice they just left it alone; the women have a different instinct. Housewives. We want to clean. . . . Somehow the men, . . . the [lice] ate them alive. . . . [During roll call] the women holding each other and keeping each other warm. . . . Someone puts their arm around you and you remember. . . . Can you imagine how much it meant to us over there! Men were crouching into themselves—maybe five feet apart [Rose demonstrated how the men she saw put their arms around their own bodies, rather than around the next person for warmth]. . . . I think more women survived. . . . As much as I saw in Auschwitz, the men were falling like flies. The woman was somehow stronger. . . . Woman friendship is different than man friendship you see. . . . We have these motherly instincts, friend instincts more. If two or three women are friends they can be closer than two or three men. [Men] can be nice to each other, talk to each other, have a beer with each other. . . . But that's as far as it goes, you know? But that's what was holding the women together because everybody had to have somebody to lean on, to depend on. The men, no . . . the men didn't do that. Men were friends there too. They talked to each other but they didn't, wouldn't, sell their bread for an apple for the other guy. They wouldn't sacrifice nothing. See, that was the difference."

Susan

Susan was born in Vienna in 1922 and moved to Czechoslovakia in 1938 with her mother and father. She was deported to Theresienstadt in 1942 and to Auschwitz in January 1943. In the first month there she worked as a typist in the political department. She was sent back to the regular prison population because one of the women in her group was caught passing food and the entire group was punished for it. Susan got typhus soon after returning to the regular camp population.

She had become part of a group of Jewish women from Berlin, and "without them, I wouldn't have gotten through this illness. They helped me through a good eight days of 103–4 degree temperature. . . . I remember like today, every morning standing in roll call, standing close, braced—walked out with their arms under me. These women supported me physically . . . emotionally and spiritually. I was supposed to go to the hospital block [this usually meant death] and my blockleader (*Blockälteste*) Ilka, with whom I had established a relationship, let me stay in the barracks for a day while she covered for me. This was my day of crisis. Without this protection, I would have died. . . . Always part of some group of women for whom you went through fire. . . . Maybe it was egotistical. You knew your group cared for you. . . . It was the reciprocity that kept you alive and going."

I asked if one needed affection: "Oh yes. Yes, you did, oh yes, you did. Women amongst each other . . . for warmth, for feeling of someone caring. That you needed. Most basic point, it kept you warm if you were cuddled. Yes, we were affectionate. Even later in *Kanada*[16] when we were quite comfortable . . . you slept four in a bunk next to each other; sure you cuddle up every so often—that was quite natural. That was not out of the ordinary. When people let themselves go, they also lost touch with other people."

Groups were formed in *Kanada*: "It was a different sort of friendship than in outside *kommandos*. There, it was a matter of survival. Don't know what men did. From what I read, it was not [the same]. The only way you had it with men [was] if they were communists or part of religious groups. . . . There was less of a need for support in *Kanada* because we could get necessities."

So in *Kanada*, the women formed different groups made up of people sharing the same interests or with people who thought alike. In Susan's opinion, these friendships among like-minded people, instead of groups united for maintenance, were possible because death was not imminent in this situation. Friendships here seemed more relaxed and were formed not out of sheer necessity but instead out of mutual sympathy for each other.

Judy

Judy is the youngest of these women. Born in 1929 in Hungary, she came to Auschwitz when she was fifteen, in May 1944. Unlike Rose and Susan, she arrived with her family. They were separated on arrival. Judy was the only one who survived.

She was in Auschwitz for about nine months. She did speak of friendships with the girls in her bunks—she was in a barrack with about one thousand fifteen-year-old girls. She "mothered" those in her bunk whose education and experience were different from hers. She told them stories from such books as

Gone with the Wind and *My Son, My Son*, and from Deanna Durbin and Shirley Temple movies.

In November, she was sent on a transport to a labor camp, Guben, near Berlin. She was "brought to work in a factory soldering electrical equipment. The conditions were better here. Only fifty people to a room. Each bunk had two or three people. Each person received a blanket. They slept on a wooden board, with no mattress or pillow."

That first evening, she had just fallen asleep when someone came into the room and turned on the lights: " 'Is there anyone here from Uzhorod [her hometown]?' It was Emu, the sister of a childhood friend, [who was looking for her sister]. Even though I was not her sister, there was excitement and from that moment I had somebody and that meant everything to me . . . meant life to me."

Emu was there with her sister-in-law, Rosie. They were between ten and twelve years older than Judy. Emu worked in the kitchen and Rosie in the clothing warehouse. "I became attached to both of them. . . . I got a coat right away from Rosie. . . . [Emu] always had an extra potato or two for me. She would see to it that I got the thicker part of the soup, not the liquid. Every so often, she would have an extra piece of bread which I joyously took back to my room and then shared with the few who were around me who didn't have that fortune as I did. I felt extremely lucky because of the friendship of these two women. They were very devoted, very caring, very kind and . . . good to me."

Her hope and strength were building. She thought the war would be over soon. However, they were evacuated to Bergen-Belsen on a death march. It was cold and snowing; they had no water or food. Judy wanted them to leave her: "I was weak and my feet were blistered and bleeding. But they wouldn't let me go, they dragged me when I couldn't walk, and stood close by when the guards were near so they wouldn't see me." Somehow they managed. "I ate snow off of the person's shoulder in front of me or pulled frozen roots from the ground."

Judy is simply taken into the lives of Emu and Rosie; there are no discussions, no negotiations. They seem to trust each other in what they do with and for each other. It is part of their practice. Is it partly because they were not total strangers? They do not *ask* Judy to go on; they simply do not let her fall. The acts push and sustain. It is not the will to live that gets Judy through; it is a practice, a set of behaviors between one and the others.

They finally arrived at Bergen-Belsen. Rosie had taken some jewelry with her from Guben for possible bartering. They stuffed the pieces in their mouths as they went through the showers. Judy said that conditions were awful. They slept on the floor. They hardly had any food and "no sanitation . . . people dying by the minute. We were given one meal a day. Often there was no bread. . . . Eventually [there were] lice everywhere. [We were] continually and totally infested by lice [which] carried the typhus germ."

They each got typhus. Rosie was first. "We would drag her to where we could manage to get a little water . . . keep her supported between us, walking, so she's not lying down all the time. Tried to wash her face and slap her face gently. [Tried] to breathe life into her. Somehow these two ladies found a source . . . [and traded] their jewelry for aspirin, some food, sugar cubes, extra pieces of bread. . . . Every time they acquired an extra bite of food they would share it with me as if I was a one-third partner. That was the most amazing thing. I just couldn't believe that. . . . It wasn't mine at all. [Yet] they never even considered not sharing.

"After Rosie got better, Emu got very sick. . . . She developed huge welts—spotted typhus. She was very bosomy and had welts underneath her bosom that were festering. . . . I remember Rosie lifting her breast and me blowing on it to air it, to try to help this . . . to just lift it away from the wound so that the wound would reach some air. . . . We would force feed her and she would say, 'I can't swallow it. Let me die. I can't live anymore. I can't get up.' 'No! You can. You've come this long, and you're not going to go now. You can and you have to and you will.' Just the way they did on the death march for me. . . . We were encouraging this way in Bergen-Belsen."

Judy also got sick. Emu and Rosie did what they could to keep her alive. They still had a piece of jewelry. "They traded it for some cheese and bread. [We] shared it in honor of my sixteenth birthday. It was some sixteenth birthday under those kinds of conditions." Judy was sick for a few days: "I was shivering and my teeth were shaking. I was sure I was not going to live. Someone burst into the room and said, 'All our guards are gone. English soldiers are all over the place.' . . . I couldn't walk. My friends dragged me outside into a sunny, spring, day. Liberation, April 15, 1945, about 1:00 P.M. I took this day as my new birthday."

Obviously Rose, Susan, and Judy survived because the Nazis did not kill them, and they were liberated. Ultimately, survival was luck. But that tells us very little if we want to find out about their maintenance strategies and how these strategies relate to their survival. "Luck" does not tell us how they committed life in a world meant for death. In other words, they survived because the Nazis did not kill them; but they lived (trying to be human) because of what they did. Surviving is different from living.[17]

While other things may have been needed in order to keep going—inside work, extra food, cleanliness, willingness to risk, physical and psychological strength—friendships and relationships are central to the stories of Judy, Susan, and Rose.[18] An important clue to these women's understanding of how they carried on, such acts of friendship also suggest questions that need to be asked of others about their experiences. These women recognized that isolation and separation were created by the Nazi system in the camps. They also knew that, if strength mattered, if it was even possible, it could only exist with others. In their "families" they created the possibilities for material and psychological strength. Their relationships—their conversations, singing, storytelling, recipe sharing, praying, joke telling, gossiping—helped them to transform a world of death and inhumanity into one more act of human life.

II

What I propose . . . is very simple: it is nothing more than to think what we are doing.

HANNAH ARENDT, *THE HUMAN CONDITION*

The language and perspective in Part I recapitulate some of the research I had written up before May 1984, when I came to see serious problems in my work arising at least in part from my unconscious use of cultural feminism as a frame through which to view Jewish women survivors.[19] Cultural feminism informed the assumptions posited, hypotheses created, and the conclusions reached, and I have come to believe that the perspective it gave must be changed.

Politically cultural feminism can be associated with the breakup of the New Left and the deradicalizing of feminism in the early 1970s; since then, it has been reflected in the work of many involved in women's studies and feminist theory. While I cannot give a complete historical analysis of cultural feminism in these few pages, I can attempt to show what cultural feminism is about, how it has affected my work, how it may reflect liberalism, and why it poses a significant problem for us as feminists.

Cultural feminism was a reaction against at least two views: (1) radical feminism's position that women are an oppressed class, and (2) the position of both New Left politics and radical feminism that personal liberation is impossible without widespread social change. The reaction shifted the territory of liberation from an insistence on the need for changing material conditions to a belief in changing the inner life, consciousness, culture, and so on.

Brooke, an early 1970s feminist critic of cultural feminism, called it "the belief that women will be freed via an alternate women's culture. It leads to a concentration on lifestyle and 'personal liberation,' . . . [and it] is an attempt to transform feminism from a political movement to a lifestyle movement." Cultural feminism thus disavowed the radical feminist position that "the locus of oppression . . . is not culture but power, men's class power."[20] To posit liberation as personal turns the politics of revolution away from the belief that genuine liberation must deal with power first and foremost and not with culture—with changing material conditions, not simply changing hearts and minds.

While those who originally espoused cultural feminism may have thought and even intended that women would rise up and revolt once their consciousness was changed, the result was something else again. The putative politics of revolution turned into a politics of accommodation for individual and personal solutions. Sheila Rowbotham points out that the tendency is "towards preoccupation with living a liberated life rather than becoming a movement for the liberation of women."[21] This political shift to cultural feminism both supported and was supported by an inward turn of women's studies toward a focus on consciousness, women's culture, gender differences, and so on.

Cultural feminism developed not simply as a tactic for battling the antiwoman line in a sexist world,[22] but as a way to detour around it without violent revolution; without confronting the state, family, marriage, or organized religion; and without eliminating institutions intent on keeping women in their place. This detour became a new strategy and ideology. While some may consider cultural feminism to be synonymous with feminism, the two terms cannot serve as substitutes for one another. Rather, cultural feminism substitutes a political activism that was risky and offensive for another that, accidentally or not, conveniently disallows risk. Certainly, feminism is safer if it is cultural rather than political.[23]

The "liberation" that cultural feminism invokes is from women's past. From that recollection comes the discovery or development of a separate women's culture and community based in turn on the belief that women and men are in some sense radically different. Such recollection, goes the claim, can create (and this is true) a positive class consciousness as well as (and this is questionable) a genuinely different society. Proponents offer biological or cultural explanations, alternately, for gender differences, but embedded in both is the judgment that the feminine or the female is superior to the masculine or the male. Thus, cultural feminism overthrows a theory of masculine superiority for its opposite rather than standing such an idea on its head or throwing it out the window.

On these terms, cultural feminism celebrates woman—her values, art, music, sexuality, mothering. In her article "Female Nationalism," Ti-Grace Atkinson succinctly characterizes cultural feminism as "the search for a *mythical history*, the *cult of femaleness*, the *glorification of motherhood, naturalism*, and *separatism*, [so that] female consciousness [became] the source and arbiter of world reality."[24]

While women's consciousness, "herstory," culture, and so on, became the standard by which to understand and judge the world, there was confusion about whether the quintessential woman—the most typical or representative woman—was to be a woman of the past or a new woman of the future. The confusion resolved itself in a psychoanalytic mode: the past is the future. Then struggles arose about which woman of the past would serve as the model. The result was that we did not emerge with a consciousness, let alone a politics, that produced genuine solidarity with all women, though we did advance different claims to superiority. Lesbian separatism may be the most important example politically and motherhood the most egregious expression of the kinds of chauvinism (even nationalism) that developed.[25] The struggles within the women's movement have been "resolved" by cultural feminists who superficially claim the universality of women's culture, "christianized" into the love of women.

Cultural feminists share with liberals a belief in individual solutions as well as in values of individuality, autonomy, and self-determination. Liberals maintain that we are all human beings and, if we but acknowledge this and act out our humanity, the world will change. What counts are our human similarities; thus differences and the structures that established the possibilities for some of those differences are not crucial. If we change ourselves, the world should change. First things first. Liberals say that their discourse includes everyone, and they mean that they are concerned about white Anglo-Saxon Protestants; cultural feminists say that they consider all women, but they refer only to lesbians, and/or mothers, and/or straight women, and/or S/M lesbians, and/or university women, and/or middle-class women, and/or women against pornography, and/or any number of others. While cultural feminists speak about a kind of universal woman, in fact they privilege some women over others. This imitation of, or connection to, liberalism is hazardous. And so, the face of the enemy has become each other; the focus is no longer on men and their institutions—least of all, on the male state. Indeed, with cultural feminism these institutions have become irrelevant or redeemable. Meanwhile the very "femininity" that seemed oppressive earlier in the women's movement has now been made sacred.

Can we so blithely reclaim and make right what has caused so much oppression without some careful scrutiny of our motives and politics? Can Jews reclaim the language of "kike"; or lesbians, "dyke"; or blacks, "nigger" without retaining some of the negativity that infests and infects the oppressors' use of those words, let alone the institutions of which such language is only a part? Even more, can values, ways of life, and skills be reclaimed as if they have not arisen within an oppressive situation? And do they become free of oppression or of its effects simply because we would like them to be so? Such uncritical valorization allows us to retain old patterns without having to believe they are negative.

Thus, cultural feminism entrenches us in a reactionary politics of personal or lifestyle change, in liberation of the self. What about solidarity with other women? With other feminists? Ann Oakley is right when she says that while not all solidarity with women demonstrates feminist consciousness, "there can be no feminist consciousness without female solidarity."[26] And if female solidarity is to have political import, there must be an active, progressive movement.

The valorization of oppression damages not only our politics but our research. We want to justify our valorization of such beliefs and practices so much that our critical faculties become quiescent when we discuss these questions. The claim of female superiority is not at issue so much as the nature of gender differences and the kind of woman who best exemplifies them. What does all this mean for our research strategies? We must resolve not to use research either to valorize oppression or to blunt or negate its effects. To excavate women's past, to begin to know and understand what has been "hidden from history," does not mean that we use that "herstory" as a model for women's liberation. Our task must be to contribute to a strategy for changing, not simply reinterpreting and obfuscating, women's lives.

The archaeological perspective that we have had on women's culture must be reexamined. Why do we take this point of view? How do we want to use it? Against what are we fighting? What new world are we making? Does our work sustain or even reinforce oppression? Are we articulating ways to understand and combat oppression? How does our work further the liberation of women? And if it does not, in what sense is it feminist?

Political and philosophical or conceptual errors are not far apart from each other. Analysis of my own work on women and the Holocaust has to turn on a critique of both my political and my philosophical perspective on the material and on the world. My use of cultural feminism as a frame (albeit unconsciously) changed respect for the stories of the Jewish women into some sort of glorification and led to the conclusion that these women transformed "a world of death and inhumanity into one more act of human life." It was important, perhaps even crucial for me to see choices, power, agency, and strength in women's friendships, bonding, sharing, storytelling, and conversations in the camps and ghettos, in hiding and passing. And indeed, there are inspiring stories and people, moving tales of help, devotion, and love. However, they describe incidents and are not at the center of the Holocaust. They need to be put into perspective.

The Holocaust is a story of loss, not gain. After all, most Jews were killed in Europe. In addition, one-fourth to one-half of the Gypsy population was killed. Perhaps 10–15,000 homosexual men were killed. The list goes on. Even if we can find differences—even if women did maintain themselves better than men—how is this a real gain? We need to look critically, moreover, at the many ways in which women maintained themselves; their strategies were not always positive, and so a most difficult question has to be asked: "what have the victims wrought?"[27]

It is interesting to look at differences between women and men. It is even interesting to see, if we can, whether women maintained themselves either better than or—perhaps more accurately—differently from men. However, the discovery of difference is often pernicious because it helps us to forget the context of these supposed strengths—oppression—and to ignore the possibility that they may be only apparent. To suggest that among those Jews who lived through the Holocaust, women rather than men survived better is to move toward acceptance or valorization of oppression, even if one uses a cultural and not a biological argument. Oppression does not make people better; oppression makes people oppressed. There is no sense in fighting or even understanding oppression if we maintain that the values and practices of the oppressed are not only better than those of the oppressor but, in some objective sense, "a model [for] humanity and the new society."[28] This is not to say that there are no differences between men and women in the ways that they relate to institutions or in their values. It *is* to question our interpretations of the conceptual and political import of such differences.

My attempt, then, to emphasize friendships among women in the camps gives a false or misleading impression that oppression is only external and not internal as well. Why the silence about the internalized oppression of the Jewish women survivors? To avoid another dimension of the horror of the Holocaust or of oppression in general? In the work represented in Part I, I seemed to be saying that in spite of rape, abuse, and murder of babies; in spite of starvation, separations, losses, terror, and violence; in spite of everything ugly and disgusting, women bonded, loved each other. Rose said: "That's what was holding the woman together." Must we not ask, How many women? At what cost? For how long? Under what conditions?

"Can you imagine what it meant," Rose said to me, "to have affection in spite of the dirt, disease, stench?" I do not doubt that it meant a great deal. It is not that the statement is necessarily false but that the focus on friendship, affection, and so on distorted our understanding of a larger situation in which that experience may have played only a small role. The bonding was limited and exclusive. It was not a bonding against the enemy in solidarity with women. Did the terror of isolation and death *not* affect the women because they bonded? Perhaps these friendship stories cover a deeper and more troubled story of intrigue, bitterness, hurt, pain, and brutality. What else happened in the groups? Between the groups? The talk about friendship allowed those of us who heard the stories to admire these women, even to receive some peace and comfort. It helped to lessen the terrible surrounding sounds of the Holocaust. This "woman-centered" perspective and the questions it addressed were misguided.

Perhaps it was the only way I could have begun. Perhaps this emphasis on something like achievements was a necessary stage. On the other hand, perhaps it was too frightening to look at women and the Holocaust without having a way out. It is only human, even for a feminist, to look for something that will make the horror less horrible or even negligible. We have a need for the appearance of order as well as for real order; and when that need arises from a desire for solace or peace in a disturbed world (or from the belief that structural change in society is either impossible or too risky), we can be misled.

Yet if the perspective and questions were wrong, the work is not useless. It needs rather a different political and philosophical context. Different questions must be asked of the survivors—different interpretations made of their replies. To reconstruct the research on women and the Holocaust, we must begin with new questions:

1. What does oppression do to us? What is its process and effect? What is the price of survival? Of oppression? Can anything good come out of oppression?

2. Is women's culture liberating? How can it be if it was nourished in oppression? Can we ever forget the price we pay as oppressed women? Should we? How does a belief that we can *survive* oppression affect our determination to *fight* oppression? If we glorify "the feminine" from a presumably feminist perspective, how do we avoid valorizing oppression in order to criticize or organize against it? Are we unwilling to confront the damage of oppression— how it has killed us? How we kill each other? If sexism makes women better able to survive, why get rid of it? Does suffering make us better people? If these questions make sense, then are there real dangers in the work of Mary Daly, Carol Gilligan, Nancy Chodorow, Adrienne Rich, Dorothy Dinnerstein, and others who begin from a position of difference and end with the judgment (or at least do not deny the judgment) that women—in values, skills, and, some suggest, even in biological makeup—are superior to men? In sum, does cultural feminism, in spite of itself, glorify the oppression of women? To what extent does cultural feminism, with its emphasis on women's values, skills, and so on, contribute to this kind of perspective and itself become part of the problem we have to solve as feminists? What are the "forces of interested ignorance" in the women's movement, in feminist theory, in women's studies?[29] Does "gender pride" or the apparent need for "gender pride" get in the way of the truth?[30] How break this dangerous alliance between trying to understand oppression and needing to mythologize our strengths in oppression or in spite of it? How envision a liberated future without an appeal to an oppressive past?

3. Do we lie in order to survive, no matter what the level of oppression?[31] Do the women survivors of the Holocaust lie? Engage in self deception? Bad faith? Just not tell the truth? Mythologize in order to keep surviving? Does the women's understanding of themselves during the Holocaust differ from what happened? How do the survivors deal with life having been such a ghastly disappointment because of the Holocaust? How live with themselves unless they transform the story? Is the story they tell less about the Holocaust than about present suffering over the past and the attempt to survive its memory? Is the only possibility for survival of any kind the creation of some "cover story" for an individual or a people? How often do survivors say things because they have a sense of obligation to their group, as women or as Jews? Are there patterns to these transformations? Do we have the right as researchers to uncover this story? An obligation? How do we as researchers transform the stories we hear? How should we?

4. Is it a methodological and theoretical mistake to look at women and the Holocaust from the vantage point of their difference from men rather than from that of oppression? Why do many women survivors believe they survived better than men? Does it have to do with the reality of the Holocaust or with

women's return to traditional roles and expectations afterward? Is it the only thing to hold onto in a world that pays so little attention to them either as women or as survivors? Why do men believe that women survived better?

5. Were women's friendships in the camps really as crucial, in a positive sense, as those interviewed say? Is there more to the story than the women are likely to report no matter what questions are posed? Are these groups more like a form of tribalism than a form of friendship—exclusive, competitive, damaging to self and others? How much depends on context, position, class, language? How much exploitation is there in these groups? How does sharing really occur in camps? In ghettos? In resistance groups? What does it mean that the women use the term "family" to describe their groups? If biological family loyalties were often a hindrance to the survival of individuals during the Holocaust outside the camps, to what extent did families—surrogate or biological—hamper women in the camps? Why is it important for us to believe that these friendships or relationships were so central to their stories? What is at stake for us?

6. What is resistance? Is anything an oppressed woman does an act of resistance? Is survival resistance? What if a person kills herself? Does suicide then become resistance? If suicide is sometimes an act of resistance, is it always so? Is dying resistance? Is courage resistance? Is singing on the way to the gas chamber resistance? Is maintaining the Jewish religion resistance? Is stealing resistance? Is hiding resistance? Escape? Is helping resistance? Is sabotage? Is killing the enemy resistance? See how the term becomes neutralized—worse, destroyed. Such slippage in language suggests that all Jews became heroes or martyrs and all women heroines. Can that possibly make sense of what happened? Do descriptions of the lack of active or armed resistance against the enemy (either by the Jews or women or others) have to lead us not only to defend what they did but also to glorify it, to make of it what it was not? And so we reach what has become a common feminist position: Survival is resistance. Certain values, described as feminine virtues, may get some women through but do not seem to offer most women the resources for fighting the enemy—for genuine resistance. They do not, that is, push one to "cripple or damage" or stop the enemy—or at least to try.[32] Manipulation of the system is not resistance, even though it can mean survival. Do women know more about the manipulation of systems than about resistance to systems? What is the relationship between manipulation and survival? If we believe that survival is resistance, we may end up with the notion that armed or active resistance is not a priority or that it stands on equal footing with living through the Holocaust in any way possible.[33] Is survival a good no matter what the cost? What do we say about cooperation or even collaboration for survival? What about sexual exchanges for food or protection? Is the term "resistance" supposed to describe a kind of heroism about almost anything and anybody? The phrase "resistance is survival" is a mystification in response to which at least one final question can be posed: What do we say about the dead?

7. What does the transformation of female gender roles really mean in the face of the oppression and genocidal murder perpetrated during the Holocaust? Is our ability to transform ourselves a liability—or are only certain kinds of transformations liabilities? Did any genuine transformations actually take place? Do women become "liberated" in the process of these transformations in sex-segregated circumstances? or merely more deeply embedded in these roles? How did these transformations affect their lives after the Holocaust?

8. Did anyone really survive the Holocaust?

9. How be true to the material given me by those I have interviewed? How be true to the women? What does that mean? What are my obligations as a woman? As a Jew? As a historian? As a philosopher? As a feminist?

10. What are the political effects or consequences of studying women and the Holocaust? What is the philosophical yield?

These questions and the critique out of which they come not only have enabled me to see where I have been but also show me in what direction I need to move.

> *Comprehension . . . means the unpremeditated, attentive facing up to, and resisting of reality—whatever it may be.*
>
> HANNAH ARENDT, *THE ORIGINS OF TOTALITARIANISM*

Institute for Research in History
New York City
1985

POSTSCRIPT

When this paper was completed, I turned my attention to the issue of women's survival. I focused on one of the more prominent questions from my previous work: Did women survive better than men? I might have tried to analyze this question from the perspective of whether women were better survivors in some qualitative way during and after the Holocaust—that is, better equipped to withstand the terror, torment, starvation beatings, loss, etc., than men. However, the pursuit of such a question seemed at best premature unless another issue was tackled; namely, were more Jewish women than men actually killed during the Holocaust?

This question is important because it is death which defines the Holocaust. Without the killing operations, there is no Holocaust. The Nazi genocide was neither haphazard nor arbitrary; it was a killing operation which not only selected Jews, among others, to be killed, but also distinguished among Jews. Jews were not a mass of undifferentiated persons to the administrators of this process. At the very least, they were Jewish men, Jewish women and children. Deportations lists distinguished by sex; death lists often identified people by sex as well as so-called crime; the death camps and concentration camps were usually sex-segregated. Jewish women were singled out in this process as women, just as Jewish men were singled out as men.

The Nazis were not the only ones to differentiate Jewish women and Jewish men. The Jews themselves did so. Even after 1941, it was common to believe that men were in danger, not women or children. Irene Eber wrote of a conversation she heard between her father and uncle in Poland:

> Reuben thought that [in Poland] men were in greater danger than women—the Germans were already rounding them up in the streets and sending them to work in the Pustkow camp. Father seemed to agree with Uncle Reuben, "Deep down the Germans are civilized," he said. "They would not harm women and children."[34]

Believing this meant that all kinds of decisions were made which put women and children in even greater jeopardy than they already were. Women were often the largest population available for the various killing operations after many men had emigrated or been evacuated or been taken into forced labor. Women and children often suffered a killing rate faster than that of men because the Nazis had even less use for Jewish women than for Jewish men. All in all, genocide was not neutral about gender. Gender was a coordinate in the process of destroying the Jewish populations.

There seemed to be enough justification for targeting Jewish men in the Nazis' antisemitic and racial propaganda. Consequently, when the decision was made to kill Jews, it did not seem necessary to put out any special reasons for the killing of Jewish men. This was not the case when it came to Jewish women and children. Himmler's statements are revealing:

> When I was forced somewhere in some village to act against partisans and Jewish commissars . . . then as a principle I gave the order to kill the women and children of those partisans and commissars too. . . . Believe you me, that order was not so easy to give or so simple to carry out as it was logically thought out and can be stated in this hall. But we must constantly recognise what kind of a primitive, primordial, natural race struggle [*Rassenkampf*] we are involved in.[35]

> We came to the question: what about the women and children? I have decided to find a clear solution here too. In fact I did not regard myself as justified in exterminating the men—let us say killing them or having them killed—while letting avengers in the shape of the children . . . grow up. The difficult decision had to be taken to make this people disappear from the face of the earth.[36]

Jewish women were to be killed as Jewish women not simply as Jews—women who may carry and give birth to the next generation of Jews. Although all Jews were to be killed, Jewish women's death and survival rates were dependent upon two obvious descriptions: Jewishness and femaleness. Jewish women were not necessarily linked to the sort of antisemitism which targeted Jewish men, e.g., the so-called Jewish World Conspiracy. But women were, of course, connected to the race struggle of National Socialism because they carried the next generation of Jews. For precisely the reason that women were distinguished from men and racism was directed at Jewish women as women, it is necessary to look at the figures which indicate how that Nazi-identified "race struggle" was played out in the process of destruction against the Jews.

The population and deportation records of certain ghettos offer evidence that more Jewish women were deported than men and may have been murdered in greater numbers than Jewish men in the killing centers. While we have some certainty about the totals of Jewish dead—at least the range is argued between 5.1 and 6 million—we have practically nothing in the way of estimates of the dead by gender. These figures have not been available from death camp records. (Recent work about Auschwitz by Franciszek Piper, however, may eventually offer some substantial information about the victims by gender.) The problem with the available camp records is that only those who entered the camps as prisoners were registered. Those who were immediately killed were never registered. Consequently, any attempt to figure out death rates by gender must include earlier killing operations (the *Einsatzgruppen*) and population and deportation records. There are not many records from the vast majority of *Einsatzgruppen* operations and ghettos that indicate killing rates by gender. But there are enough significant examples to warrant analyses and some conclusions.

The ghettos (or, as some say, ghetto camps) were a kind of intermediate stage in the genocidal process—somewhere between normal life and the death camps. The ghettos were places where many Jews died of disease and starvation. But primarily, they were the places from which Jews were transported to death camps. These transports were peopled with deportees rounded up at random by the Nazis or selected by the Jewish Councils. Perhaps 10% of those deported to Auschwitz became members of the camp population. In other death camps—Belzec, Treblinka, Sobibor and Chelmno—virtually all those transported were killed immediately. Only a handful of Jews survived. The deportation figures from the ghettos provide an important part of the equation in trying to estimate loss by gender. Another part of the equation comes from an investigation of the displaced persons camps. From the available records of the displaced persons camps, estimates of survivors by gender are possible.

Although I cannot go into extensive detail about my findings concerning the numbers of victims by gender, I can offer a summary that I hope will be illuminating.

Women survivors have a clear memory that there were many more men than women in the displaced persons camps. Although the United Nations Relief and Rehabilitation Agency (UNRRA) figures do not indicate the wide disparity of the anecdotal evidence, nevertheless there are differences. Figures for the Jewish population in the displaced person's camps in 1946 (January) show that 40% of the population was female and 61% was male; in 1947, 44% was female and 56% was male.[37]

SELECTED POPULATION FIGURES FROM CONCENTRATION CAMPS AND D.P. CAMPS BY GENDER

	Female		Male	
TOTAL POPULATION				
WVHA				
January 1945	28%	(202,674)	72%	(511,537)
UNRRA				
October 1945	38%	(244,787)	62%	(399,292)
UNRRA				
January 1946	41%	(237,165)	59%	(344,736)

	Female		Male	
JEWISH POPULATION				
UNRRA				
January 1946	39.5%	(12,210)	60.5%	(18,695)
1947	43.6%	(52,004)	56.4%	(67,150)

The deportation of more Jewish women to the death camps and their murder upon arrival are at least parts of what probably accounts for the fact that fewer Jewish women populated these displaced persons camps.

The *Einsatzgruppen* operations also offer some evidence on this issue. It has been estimated that over 1.3 million Jews were killed in the mobile killing operations. One report from Strike Group A, Strike Commando 3, operating in parts of Lithuania and Latvia, lists the killing of a significantly large population—137,443 killed between June and November 1941, of which 135,837 were Jews. Between June and August 1941, 43% of those killed were not identified by sex. Thus it is impossible to make any claims about sex differentials during those months of the operations of Strike Commando 3.[38] However, in more detailed figures about the next few months, important differences begin to emerge. Of the Jews killed between September and November 1941, 43.85% (35,683) were women; 28.17% (22,923) were children; and 27.15% (22,096) were men. Altogether women and children made up 72% of those killed between September and November 1941. Although this report represents only 10% of the total number of Jews killed in the *Einsatzgruppen* operations, there are indications from other documents and scholarly analyses that the adult population available was predominantly female. And it was this population, together with children and the elderly, who were most victimized by the mobile killing operations.[39] Such figures are not conclusive by any means, but they do give pause.

Another revealing document concerns a March 1943 transport to Auschwitz from Berlin. Nazi Germany's *Wirtschafts-Verwaltungshauptamt* (Economic-Administrative Main Office; WVHA) record reads: "Berlin shipment arrived 5 March 1943. Total 1,128 Jews. Qualified for work 389 men (Buna) and 96 women. Killed 151 men and 492 women and children. . . . Berlin shipment arrived March 7, 1943. Total 690. . . . Qualified for work 153 men and 25 [protective custody prisoners] (Buna) and 65 women. Killed 30 men and 417 women and children."[40] While 25% of the male population was killed, 84.9% of the women and children, or perhaps more accurately, women with children, were killed. As transports from the ghettos to the camps are investigated, it will be found that this Berlin transport was by no means an anomaly. Indeed, it makes sense that in the Jewish population being destroyed by the Nazis, women and children would be among the least valuable to keep alive even for a little while. Whatever skills women might have, their "biological skills" could never be useful for the Nazis. As mothers of future generations of Jews, Jewish women held particular danger for National Socialism. One example hardly creates a pattern. However, between this Berlin transport and the *Einsatzgruppen* operation previously cited, patterns seem to emerge. It makes sense, then, to look at deportations from the ghettos to fill in more information.

After the 1939 invasion of Poland, ghettos were established by the Nazis to concentrate and exploit the Jewish populations. Once the decision was made to kill Jews en masse and the open-air killing operations proved inadequate to the task, the ghetto served additional purposes. It was the institution in which the Jewish population was decimated by disease and starvation, the institution from which primarily male Jews were sent to slave labor camps, and the institution that became the central conduit to the death camps. Within the ghettos the Nazis established Jewish Councils to serve as a link with the occupants of the ghetto.[41]

These Councils proved to be tragic alliances of perpetrator and victim: in many instances the organizational structures that tried to help Jews survive ended up helping the Nazis to destroy Jews. For survival, the councils had divisions of "health, welfare, and supply"; for destruction, there was "the Central Bureau, the Registration and Records Office, and, above all . . . the police."[42]

The structure of the ghetto and the decisions of the leaders (almost entirely male) put certain groups more at risk than others. If survival was at best only a possibility for some, then for the majority it was no possibility at all. Women may well have been the majority of the population at the bottom of the hierarchy. And if women did not die as quickly as men did in the ghetto, the deportations changed that balance. Jewish policy in the ghettos was predicated on privilege of one sort or another (money, status, profession, skills). This policy, along with established patterns in the Jewish community, made it less likely that women would be among the privileged in the ghetto except through their relationships with men.

The policy that produced work certificates was not implemented on the basis of merit or the economic needs of the ghetto. Other priorities took precedence. People who had money or its equivalent were able to buy work certificates; such "people" were usually men. Women who were not attached to men of some means or position had little or no chance, nor did the poor of either sex. The Jewish police in the Warsaw ghetto "believed that the participation of Jews in the [deportations] would make it possible to limit its scope, prevent harm from befalling people who 'deserved to be protected,' and, above all, avoid the prospect of the Germans' taking direct action, which might result in infinitely greater harm."[43] Thus, ghetto leaders made systematic choices that harmed those least able to protect themselves in order to save "the best." The ancient idea of salvaging a remnant of the Chosen People died a hard death, and there were certain requirements for that remnant. Between these requirements and Nazi orders for the deportations, Jewish women were simply in a worse position than men.

The Lodz ghetto was established in April 1940, and it lasted four years and four months—longer than any other ghetto. The most extensive statistical documentation about conditions in the ghettos comes from Lodz.[44] At the beginning of 1941, the female population of Lodz numbered 83,391; by the end of the year it had reached 92,703. In January 1941, the male population was 70,870; by the end of the year, it was 69,978. By December 1941, women were 57% of the population in Lodz and men were 43%. In 1941, the male mortality rate from disease and starvation was one and a half that of women: an average 12.28 women died each day, and an average 19.06 men—a 2:3 ratio.[45] In 1942, the average daily mortality rate was 19.6 for women and 33.1 for men.[46] Thus, while death rates rose for both sexes, the female-male ratio remained approximately the same: 2:3. Obviously, the higher mortality rates for men partially explain the greater number of women in Lodz. In addition, there were more women in the transports from the east to Lodz, which also kept the ratio of women to men consistently higher.

In 1941, the Nazis began the so-called resettlement policy, shipping Jews to various extermination camps in Poland.[47] In 1942, the total number of deportees from the Lodz ghetto to the death camp at Chelmno was 71,485. In the ghetto records, 34,181 are identified as women; 20,990 are identified as men. A closer analysis of these figures reveals that there were probably a total of 61.9% (43,749) women and 38% (26,863) men on the transports.[48]

Women had been approximately 57% of the ghetto population at the end of 1941. Of the total number of deportees from Lodz in 1942, 62% were women and 38% were men.[49] Thus women from Lodz were sent to the death camp at Chelmno in a percentage higher than their representation in the ghetto population, men in a percentage lower.

It has been suggested that the greater number of women among the elderly might account for this disparity in the transports to the extermination camps.[50] In the transports of May 4–15, 1942, 57.8% were over fifty years old, and most of these were women (67.9% or 4,291); 32% (2,022) were men. The age distribution in two other 1942 transports is quite different. The majority of people in the January and February–April transports were under fifty. In the January transport, only 11% of the total deported were over fifty; in the February–April transports, 18% of those deported were over fifty. Significantly, in the January transports, women between the ages of fifteen and forty-nine were 37% of the total deported, while men were 24%; in the February–April transports, women between the ages of fifteen and forty-nine were 38% and men 19% of the total deported from Lodz.[51] Thus, while the hypothesis that the sex discrepancy can be partially accounted for by the larger percentage of elderly women in the population is a good one, old age alone does not explain why more women were transported except in May. Furthermore, in each of the 1942 transports women of childbearing age (fifteen to forty-nine) were sent in numbers almost twice that of men of the same age: 19,369 women and 10,180 men. These are the same women who not only could bear children, but already had children of their own. They were clearly some of the most useless persons to the Nazis and in that category were to be killed immediately. For all intents and purposes the death camps of Chelmno, Treblinka, Sobibor, and Belzec allowed no opportunity to escape death. These places differed from Auschwitz, which was both a death camp of tremendous proportions and a labor camp with many prisoners. In Auschwitz there was at least some chance for someone to escape the first selections for the gas chambers. However, this was not the case for women with children in Auschwitz either, unless the mother or caretaker was willing to separate from the child or children.

In these Lodz ghetto deportations the percentage of women deported within each age group was significantly higher than the percentage of men. In the fifteen- to forty-nine age group, 66% of those deported were women, 34% were men; in the twenty-to-forty-nine age group, 69% were women, 31% were men; in the twenty-to-twenty-nine age group, 70% were women, 30% were men.[52] It is very clear that women, no matter of what age, were chosen for deportation at a higher rate than men in the Lodz ghetto.

The following table sums up the female/male population distribution on each transport from Lodz in 1942:

Transport	Males	Females
January	42.4%	57.5%
	(4,231)	(5,740)
Feb/April	37.7%	62.29%
	(12,847)	(21,226)
May	33.5%	66.49%
	(3,657)	(7,257)
TOTALS	20,735	34,223
	38%	62%

Women formed the majority of the population (both the indigenous and refugee populations) of the Lodz ghetto, and they were chosen for deportation in greater numbers and percentages than their representation in the population: overall, 62% of those transported were women and 38% were men. Gender differences must be a critical factor in the analysis of the transports.

There are far fewer statistics for Warsaw than for Lodz. However, in those that are available, the numerical pattern is similar: there are more women than men in the population; fewer women than men die in the ghetto of disease;[53] more women are available for deportations; and more women are sent to the camps. Statistics that parallel the figures from Lodz emerge from the Warsaw ghetto: 59% of those deported were women and 41% were men. At the beginning of 1942 there were more women than men in the ghetto by a ratio of 4:3.[54] After the deportations, the ratio was reversed: of the total female population prior to deportation, 7.4% remained; of the men, 12.6%. Only in the ten- to twenty-nine age group were there slightly more women left than men (6,844 women and 6,034 men).

Prior to the Warsaw deportations in 1942, women were 57.2% of the population; afterward they were 44%. Prior to deportation, men were 42.7% of the population; afterward they were 55.9%. In all, 92.5% of the total female population and 87% of the total male population were deported.[55]

It is important to note that despite the similarity in the figures, the situation in Warsaw was different. The pattern of deportations was much more random. Here the Nazis simply emptied and murdered nearly the entire population in Treblinka within a matter of months. The Jewish Councils in both Lodz and Warsaw cooperated with the Nazis in hopes of saving some Jews. In Warsaw this attempt to cooperate did not work at all because the Nazis made vast roundups in the ghetto and only 9.6% of the population remained at the end of the deportations in 1942. In Lodz almost 50% of the population remained after the deportations of 1942. The circumstances of each ghetto were different. Yet even considering the terrible overall death toll, women seemed to be targeted in these deportations in greater numbers than men.

There are similar figures from at least one other ghetto. In Theresienstadt, the so-called model ghetto in Czechoslovakia, 54% of the population— 61,003 out of 130,952—was over sixty-one years old between 1941 and 1944. Women composed the majority of those in this age group.

According to H. G. Adler there were 101,758 people in the ghetto in 1942. Women over sixty-one were 34.4% (34,984) of the population and men over sixty-one were 19.1% (19,449).[56] As a whole, women made up 59.9% of the total population and men 40.1%. At no time did men outnumber women on the transports to Auschwitz.

The following tables break down the transports into Theresienstadt and the transports from Theresienstadt to Auschwitz by sex and age.

TRANSPORTS INTO THERESIENSTADT
1941–44

Age	Male	Female
0–14	3,783	3,622
15–45	15,137	18,993
46–60	11,558	16,854
61–	22,048	38,955

DEPORTATIONS OUT OF THERESIENSTADT TO AUSCHWITZ
1942–44

Age	Male	Female
0–14	2,569	2,437
15–45	12,867	14,327
46–60	9,367	12,903
61–	8,653	17,060

In 1942, 38.3% (16,807) of those deported were men and 61.6% (27,064) were women. In 1943, 44% (7,520) of those deported were men and 55.9% (9,548) were women. In 1944, 47.4% (9,129) of those deported were men and 52.56% (10,115) were women. Among the population over sixty-one years old, 66% of those deported were women, 33.6% were men.

Since more women populated the ghettos and these ghettos in the east were also the transit points to the death camps, it simply must be acknowledged that given the Nazi view of women in general and their particular view of Jewish women, more Jewish women were murdered than Jewish men in these first selections in the death camps. There were many more camps for men than for women—camps which offered some possibility for survival. The usual assumption is that, since there were more camps for men, men of all groups were the primary victims. It may be that more men ended up in the camp system, but that does not mean that fewer women were sent into that system. It may mean that more women were killed at the outset. In two small labor camps the figures tell an important story. Oskar Schindler in Poland created what amounted to a labor camp that saved Jews. When the figures are looked at, it is easy to see why women had less of a chance to survive than men. There were 200 women and 1,000 men on Schindler's list. In another labor camp, Debica, there were 10 women and 300 men. None of these numbers can make us sanguine about the possibilities for either Jewish women or Jewish men to survive. But they add to the growing impression that Nazi policy allowed for the possibility of more Jewish men than Jewish women to survive; and that the Jewish Councils, either through ignorance or acknowledgment of the situation, decided to save Jews—which often meant the saving of Jewish men.

The numbers begin to show a stark and disturbing reality. It can no longer be doubted that being male or female mattered during the Holocaust. Sexism attended antisemitism during the Holocaust, as it attends all forms of racism and, of course, exists even where there is no racism. Antisemitism, racism, and sexism were not separated in the theory of the Nazis or in their practice—nor was sexism absent from the responses of the Jewish community. Sexism, the division of social roles according to biological function, placed women at an extreme disadvantage during the Holocaust. It deprived them of skills that might have enabled more of them to survive. At the same time, the group that was supposed to protect them—men—was not able to do so.

It was the search about numbers of victims by gender that framed the research following the publication of my earlier article in *Signs*. It also helped to drive the themes for my recently drafted but as yet unpublished book, *Double Jeopardy: Women and the Holocaust*. So much work on women and the Holocaust remains to be done. What has been researched thus far merely touches the surface of a complex and difficult field of study.

Washington, D.C.
1992

NOTES

The research for this article was partially supported by a Kent Fellowship, Wesleyan University, and an American Council of Learned Societies Fellowship. Parts of this article were written for the conference "Communities of Women" sponsored by *Signs* and the Center for Research on Women at Stanford University, February 1983, and the Sixth Berkshire Conference on the History of Women, June 1984. I want to thank the following people for reading versions of this article, for listening, criticizing, and supporting the work: Pamela Armstrong, Marylin Arthur, Mary Felstiner, Joy Johannessen, Sally Hanley, Esther Katz, Eva Fleischner, Susan Cernyak-Spatz, Irene Eber, Nancy McKenzie. I especially want to thank Ti-Grace Atkinson, whose honesty, insight, and friendship helped me to see, to cut through a wall I was up against, *and* to continue.

1. The first conference on women and the Holocaust took place in March 1983 at Stern College. It was funded by the New York Council for the Humanities and sponsored by the Institute for Research in History. See *Proceedings of the Conference, Women Surviving: The Holocaust*, ed. Esther Katz and Joan Miriam Ringelheim (New York: Institute for Research in History, 1983) (hereafter *Proceedings of the Conference*). See Joan Miriam Ringelheim, "The Unethical and the Unspeakable: Women and the Holocaust," *Simon Wiesenthal Annual* (1984): 69–87; "Communities in Distress: Women and the Holocaust" (Institute for Research in History, 1982, typescript); "Resources and Vulnerabilities" (Institute for Research in History, 1983, typescript); and "Thoughts about Women and the Holocaust," in *Thinking the Unthinkable: Meanings of the Holocaust*, ed. Roger S.

Gottlieb (New York: Paulist Press, 1990), pp. 141–149. See also Sybil Milton, "Women and the Holocaust: The Case of German and German-Jewish Women," in *When Biology Became Destiny: Women in Weimar and Nazi Germany*, ed. Renate Bridenthal, Atina Grossman, and Marion Kaplan (New York: Monthly Review Press, 1984), pp. 297–333, and "Issues and Resources," in *Proceedings of the Conference*, pp. 10–21; Vera Laska, ed., *Women in the Resistance and in the Holocaust* (Westport, Conn.: Greenwood Press, 1983); and Marlene Heinemann, "Women Prose Writers of the Nazi Holocaust" (Ph.D. diss., Indiana University, 1981); Myrna Goldenberg, "Different Horrors, Same Hell: Women Remembering the Holocaust," in *Thinking the Unthinkable*, pp. 150–166; Claudia Koonz, *Mothers in the Fatherland* (New York: St. Martin's Press, 1987); Gisela Bock, *Zwangssterilisation im Nationalsozialismus, Studien zur Rassenpolitik und Frauenpolitik* (Opladen: Westdeutscher Verlag GmbH, 1986); Konnilyn G. Feig, *Hitler's Death Camps* (New York: Holmes & Meier, 1981), pp. 133–190.

2. See Gisela Bock, "Racism and Sexism in Nazi Germany: Motherhood, Compulsory Sterilization, and the State," *Signs: Journal of Women in Culture and Society* 8, no. 3 (Spring 1983): 400–421.

3. I decided to use the term "maintenance" rather than the more customary "survival" because whether one survived or was murdered was determined by the Nazis or by one's fate (that is, luck), whereas "maintenance" was determined by the victims, to some degree.

4. Originally formulated in 1981. See Ringelheim, "The Unethical and the Unspeakable," p. 84.

5. Unless otherwise indicated, the subsequent quotations are from my interviews with Jewish women survivors. I have done twenty-eight interviews with twenty women. Most of the interviews were three hours long; a few lasted between six and ten hours. They were all in English. For the purposes of this article, I have culled some fragments to illuminate issues and concerns. For clarity, I have sometimes added words or explanations in brackets.

6. Twelve out of twenty of the survivors interviewed mentioned fear of rape, feelings of sexual humiliation, or instances of sexual exchange. Two of the twenty said they were raped. Another said she was almost raped.

7. *Kanada* was a section of the *Effektenkammer*, storehouse for the valuables—clothes, jewelry, and so on—of the prisoners who entered Auschwitz. Those who worked there were considered an elite *Kommando* (work crew).

8. See also *Proceedings of the Conference*, pp. 73–74, 141–42; Milton, "Women and the Holocaust," pp. 315–16.

9. See Ringelheim, "The Unethical and the Unspeakable," pp. 74–75, 78, and "Resources and Vulnerabilities," p. 20; and *Proceedings of the Conference*, pp. 40–41.

10. Yaffa Eliach, "The Holocaust and the Family" (paper presented at Lehigh University, March 1984).

11. Elmer Luchterhand, "Social Behavior of Concentration Camp Prisoners: Continuities and Discontinuities with Pre- and Postcamp Life," in *Survivors, Victims, and Perpetrators*, ed. Joel Dimsdale (New York: Hemisphere Publishing, 1980), p. 273.

12. See Alexander Donat, "Jewish Resistance," in *Out of the Whirlwind*, ed. Albert H. Friedlander (New York: Schocken Books, 1968), p. 62; Leonard Tushnet, *The*

Uses of Adversity: Studies of Starvation in the Warsaw Ghetto (New York and London: Thomas Yoseloff, 1966), p. 27; Milton, "Women and the Holocaust" (n. 1 above), pp. 307–8, and "Issues and Resources" (n. 1 above), pp. 15–19; Raul Hilberg, ed., *Documents of Destruction: Germany and Jewry 1933–1945*, (Chicago: Quadrangle Books, 1971), pp. 40–41; Germaine Tillion, *Ravensbrück* (New York: Anchor, 1975), pp. 39, 230; and Lucjan Dobroszycki, ed., *The Chronicle of the Lodz Ghetto* (New Haven, Conn.: Yale University Press, 1984), p. lvii and passim.

13. See Ringelheim, "Communities in Distress" (n. 1 above), pp. 35; 43, n. 27; *Proceedings of the Conference* (n. 1 above), p. 176.

14. See Ringelheim, "The Unethical and the Unspeakable" (n. 1 above), p. 80.

15. The interviews with Rose and Judy took place in May 1982. Susan was interviewed in August 1979. I have had subsequent conversations with Judy and Susan. Again, the quotations are from these interviews unless otherwise stated. Ten among the seventeen other women survivors interviewed (1981–84) also spoke of relationships with other women as being significant.

16. See n. 7 above.

17. See Ringelheim, "Communities in Distress" (n. 1 above), pp. 33–34.

18. These categories were worked out in a conversation with Susan Cernyak-Spatz and Pamela Armstrong in August 1982. See also Milton, "Issues and Resources" (n. 1 above), pp. 17–19, and "Women and the Holocaust" (n. 1 above), pp. 311–15.

19. I first was made aware of these problems when I read the English (unpublished) version of Ti-Grace Atkinson's "Female Nationalism" ("Le Nationalisme feminin," *Nouvelles questions féministes* 6–7 [Spring 1984]: 35–54). Subsequent discussions with Atkinson about cultural feminism, feminist theory and politics, philosophy, and women and the Holocaust demonstrated that the impasse I had reached had much to do with my unknowing adherence to cultural feminism.

20. Brooke, "Retreat to Cultural Feminism," in *Feminist Revolution: Redstockings of the Women's Liberation Movement* (New York: Random House, 1975), pp. 79, 83.

21. Quoted in Ann Oakley, *Subject Women* (New York: Pantheon Books, 1981), p. 310.

22. Cultural feminism may have had its roots in the pro-woman line. See Carol Hanisch, "The Personal Is the Political," in *Feminist Revolution* (n. 20 above), pp. 204–5.

23. Since the cultural feminist position has few, if any, points of conflict with the establishment, the government can more easily adopt or adapt it as a cheap substitute for real change. Cultural feminism is endorsed and supported because it poses no threat.

24. Atkinson (n. 19 above), pp. 35, 53.

25. See ibid.

26. Oakley, p. 278.

27. Hope Weissman in a letter to the author, June 1984.

28. See Barbara Burris, "The Fourth World Manifesto," in *Radical Feminism*, ed. Anne Koedt, Ellen Levine, and Anita Rapone (New York: Quadrangle Books, 1973), p. 356.

29. Sandra Harding, "Philosophy and History of Science as Patriarchal Oral History"

(University of Delaware, Department of Philosophy, 1982, typescript). She used the phrase about science, not about feminists.

30. Suggested to the author in a letter from Mary Felstiner, July 1984.
31. See Adrienne Rich, *On Lies, Secrets, and Silence: Selected Prose, 1966–1978* (New York: W. W. Norton & Co., 1979), p. 189: "In the struggle for survival we tell lies."
32. Suggested by Raul Hilberg in "Bibliography and the Holocaust" (paper presented at the Scholar's Conference, New York City, April 1981).
33. Compare Ringelheim, "The Unethical and the Unspeakable" (n. 1 above), p. 75–81.
34. Irene Eber, "Mrs. Steiner's Daughter," p. 2 of an unpublished manuscript. Irene is a survivor who hid in a chicken coop for two years after leaving her family because she believed that the Nazis would kill everyone. Of course gender is not the only factor. While lists do not show economic class differentiation, there is a good deal of anecdotal evidence that indicates wealthier Jews were able to provide themselves with possibilities to keep going and ultimately survive in ways that poorer Jews could not. Although difficult to accept, it is not really surprising.
35. From Bradley F. Smith and Agnes F. Peterson, eds., *Heinrich Himmler: Geheimreden 1933 bis 1945* (Frankfurt: Propylaen, 1974), p. 201. I am grateful to Gisela Bock for pointing this out to me. See her paper, " 'Equality,' 'Difference' and 'Inferiority': Motherhood, Antinationalism and Gender Relations in National Socialist Racism," *Maternity and Gender Policies: Women and the Rise of the European Welfare States*, ed. Gisela Bock and Pat Thane (New York: Routledge, 1991).
36. From Smith and Peterson, eds., ibid., p. xxx.
37. United Nations Relief and Rehabilitation Agency (UNRRA) Archives, Pag. 4/3.0.11.0.1.1, Box 4, January 1947. "Monthly Report of Chief of Operations, All the Allied Zones," January 1947, p. 10. Between 1946 and 1947, the Jewish population in these camps rose as the other population groups fell.
38. Hilberg, ed., *Documents of Destruction*, pp. 46–57. See also Raul Hilberg, *The Destruction of the European Jews*, 3 vols., rev. and def. ed. (New York: Holmes & Meier, 1985), 1:273–390. For more information see Appendix E.
39. See Hilberg, *The Destruction of the European Jews*, 1:295; *The Einsatzgruppen Reports: Selections from the Official Dispatches of the Nazi Death Squads' Campaign Against the Jews*, compiled by Yitzhak Arad, Shmuel Krakowski, and Shmuel Spector (New York: Holocaust Library, 1987): "September 21, 1941: Operational Situation Report USSR 90—Einsatzgruppe B"; *The Einsatzgruppen Reports*, unpublished version, p. 223. From report dated: October 9, 1941: "Operational Situation Report USSR 108, Einsatzgruppe B." See also Sybil Milton, "Women and the Holocaust: The Case of German and German-Jewish Women," in *When Biology Became Destiny: Women in Weimar and Nazi Germany*, ed. Renate Bridenthal, Atina Grossman, and Marion Kaplan (New York: Monthly Review Press, 1984) pp. 325 and 301, n. 23: Jewish women were "unable to emigrate and obtain visas in the same numbers as single Jewish men." . . . "Thus the census of April 1939 recorded respectively 123,104 female Jews and 90,826 male Jews in Germany. The comparatively large number of Jewish women meant that more German-Jewish women than men were deported and murdered after October 1941." This means that 57.5% of German-Jewish population were women; 42.45% were men. Cf. Christopher Browning, *Fateful Months: Essays on the Emergence of the Final Solution* (New York: Holmes & Meier, 1985),

Chapter 2, "Wehrmacht Reprisal Policy and the Murder of the Male Jews in Serbia," pp. 39–56; Philip Friedman, "Social Conflicts in the Ghetto," in *Roads to Extinction: Essays on the Holocaust*, ed. Ada June Friedman (New York: The Jewish Publication Society of America, 1980), pp. 142–44.

40. Benjamin B. Ferencz, *Less Than Slaves* (Cambridge, Mass.: Harvard University Press, 1979), p. 27. Ferencz refers to Leon Poliakov and Josef Wulf, *Das Dritte Reich und die Juden* (Berlin: Arani Verlag, 1955), p. 198, citing *Documents from Central Jewish Historical Commission* (Lodz: N. Blumenthal, 1946), p. 110.

TABLE 1

SUMMARY OF BERLIN TRANSPORT: MARCH 1943

Total Population			Men Killed	Men "Work"
Men	723	(40%)	181 (25%)	542 (74.9%)
			Women/ *Children Killed*	*Women "Work"*
Women/Children	1,070	(59.6%)	909 (84.9%) 84.9%	161 (15%) 15%
Protective Custody	25		No information	
TOTALS	1,818		1,090	703

41. See Yehuda Bauer, *They Chose Life* (New York: American Jewish Committee, 1973); Hilberg, *The Destruction of the European Jews*; Lucy Dawidowicz, *The War Against the Jews* (Holt, Rinehart and Winston, 1975), and Isaiah Trunk, *Judenrat* (New York: Stein and Day, 1977).

42. Raul Hilberg, *The Destruction of the European Jews*, 1:232–33. It should not be forgotten that many ghettos functioned only for a short time and with no organizational structure. Also it must be noted that this view of the Jewish Councils is not universally held. See note 41 for bibliography on this.

43. Yisrael Gutman, *The Jews of Warsaw, 1939–1943: Ghetto, Underground, Revolt* (Bloomington: Indiana University Press, 1982), p. 208.

44. See Lucjan Dobroszycki ed., *The Chronicle of the Lodz Ghetto* (New Haven: Yale University Press, 1984); and *Lodz Ghetto Collection*, Document 58, YIVO Institute for Jewish Research.

45. Hilberg, *The Destruction of the European Jews*, 1:269, n. 307. Also see p. 1:268–69 for a more general statistic: in 1938, the monthly average death rate in Lodz was 0.09%; in 1941, 0.63%; and in 1942, 1.49%. This information can also be found in the *Lodz Ghetto Collection*, Document 58, p. 23.

46. Hilberg, *The Destruction of the European Jews*, p. 1:269, n. 307. See also *Lodz Ghetto Collection*, Document 58, p. 24. The population most devastated by disease and starvation were men and women 46 years and older, especially men over 60. Women died at a slower rate, except for 1940 when women over 60 had a higher mortality rate than men. In *The Uses of Adversity* (New York: Thomas Yoseloff, 1966), p. 23, Leonard Tushnet states that the caloric intake in Warsaw was 1,500 calories for the *Judenrat*, less than 1,000 for the workers and professionals, and 300 for others; see also pp. 60–62. Isaiah Trunk, *Judenrat* (New York: Stein and

Day, 1977), pp. 356–382, has different caloric figures: Council members, 1,665; artisans, 1,407; shopworkers, 1,225; and the general population, 1,124. See also *The Warsaw Diary of Adam Czerniakow*, ed. Raul Hilberg, Stanislaw Staron, and Josef Kermisz (New York: Stein and Day, 1979), p. 57.

47. See Hilberg, *The Destruction of the European Jews*, 3:1219–20. Hilberg calculates that out of the estimated 5.1 million Jews killed during World War II, 2.7 million Jews were killed in 1942. This means that in 1942 alone, the Nazis killed 53% of all the Jews killed during the Holocaust. According to Hilberg's calculations, by the end of 1942, 76% of the Jewish population marked for extermination had already been killed or had died.

48. The figures are derived from *The Chronicle of the Lodz Ghetto*, pp. 127, 132, 139–140, 157, 194. The statistics from the Jewish Council do not indicate the gender breakdown for the deportations in September 1942. Using the September death rates for men (608) and women (466), as well as the drop in the male and female population from September to October, I arrived at the estimates for the deportations bracketed in Appendix B, Table 1. One question that needs to be considered: Why does the percentile of men and women remain so consistent throughout the 1942 deportations?

49. *The Chronicle of the Lodz Ghetto*, pp. 14, 22, 107–309. See also *Lodz Ghetto Collection*, Document 58, pp. 7, 23, 42. The figures in these two sources are somewhat different.

50. A discussion with Raul Hilberg in August 1985 led me to explore this possibility.

51. See Appendix B, Table 2.

52. Population and deportation figures by age-group are in Appendix B, Table 3.

53. The death rate in the Warsaw ghetto was generally 1% per month after August, 1941. Total deaths recorded in the Warsaw ghetto were approximately 82,624. See *The Warsaw Diary of Adam Czerniakow*, p. 60; and Hilberg, *The Destruction of the European Jews*, 1:268–269. See also Myron Winick, ed., *Hunger Disease, Studies by the Jewish Physicians in the Warsaw Ghetto* (New York: John Wiley, 1979), p. 35. See Appendix D as well.

54. Gutman, *The Jews of Warsaw, 1939–1943*, p. 270.

55. The chart below summarizes some of the population and deportation totals by sex in Warsaw in 1942. See Appendix D, Table 2, for more detail by age and sex.

TABLE 2
1942 WARSAW

Sex	Total Pop.	Total Deported	% of Total Deported	% of Deportees from Total Population	Population After Deportation
Male	157,610	137,673	41.3%	37.3%	19,937
	42.7%	41.3%			55.9%
Female	211,292	195,596	58.6%	53.02%	15,696
	57.3%	58.7%			44%
TOTALS	368,902	333,269	99.9%	90.32%	35,633

56. These and subsequent figures on Theresienstadt are from H.G. Adler, *Theresienstadt* (Tübingen: J.C. Mohr-Paul Siebeck, 1960), pp. 42–43.

APPENDICES

Appendices A, B, and C have been derived from the Lodz Ghetto Collection, Document 58, YIVO Institute for Jewish Research, and Lucjan Dobroszycki, ed., *The Chronicle of the Lodz Ghetto* (New Haven, Conn.: Yale University Press, 1984). Appendix D has been derived from Yisrael Gutman, *The Jews of Warsaw, 1939–1943: Ghetto, Underground, Revolt*, trans. Ina Friedman (Bloomington: Indiana University Press, 1989), pp. 62–65; Myron Winick, ed., *Hunger Disease: Studies by the Jewish Physicians in the Warsaw Ghetto* (New York: Wiley, 1979), p. 35; and Adam Czerniakow's report to Heinz Auerswald, dated February 12, 1942 (Polen 365e, p. 563), see Raul Hilberg, *The Destruction of the European Jews*, 3 vols., rev. and def. ed. (New York: Holmes & Meier, 1985), 1:269, n. 307 and 3:1225. Appendix E has been derived from Raul Hilberg, ed., *Documents of Destruction: Germany and Jewry 1933–1945* (Chicago: Quadrangle Books, 1971), pp. 46–57.

Appendix A
Population and Death
in the Lodz Ghetto

TABLE 1
POPULATION AND DEATHS IN THE LODZ GHETTO: 1941

Date	Total population	Female pop. (deaths)		Male pop. (deaths)	
Pre-1939	250,000				
May/40	163,172				
1941					
Jan.	154,261	83,391	(419)	70,870	(805)
Feb.	152,791	83,010	(395)	69,781	(668)
Mar.	151,628	82,615	(370)	69,013	(659)
Apr. 7	150,436	82,243	(379)	68,193	(572)
May	148,547	81,794	(395)	66,753	(604)
June	146,682	81,390	(382)	65,292	(548)
July	145,858	81,057	(319)	64,801	(548)
Aug.	144,997	80,831	(375)	64,166	(601)
Sept.	144,467	80,561	(326)	63,906	(439)
Oct.	143,800	80,278	(280)	63,522	(364)
		[Transports in: 13,906]		[Transports in: 9,129]	
Nov.	159,505	90,323	(409)	69,182	(519)
Dec. 1	163,623	93,101	(432)	70,522	(599)
Dec. 31	162,581	92,603		69,978	

Derived from the Lodz Ghetto Collection, Document 58, pp. 7, 23. See also Hilberg, *Destruction of the European Jews,* 1: 268–69.

TABLE 2
POPULATION AND DEATHS IN THE LODZ GHETTO: 1942

Lodz 1942	Total population	Female pop. (deaths)		Male pop. (deaths)	
Jan. 1	162,681	92,703	(704)	69,978	(1,803)
Feb. 2	151,001	86,284	(745)	64,717	(1,128)
Mar. 1	142,079	81,250	(833)	60,829	(1,411)
Apr. 1	115,102	65,008	(722)	50,094	(1,116)
May 1	110,806	62,738	(710)	48,068	(1,068)
June 1	104,470	59,176	(754)	45,294	(960)
July 1	102,546	58,495	(798)	44,051	(1,227)
Aug. 1	101,259	58,039	(726)	43,220	(1,012)
Aug. 30	105,131	60,043		45,088	
Sept. 1	105,961	60,408	(466)	45,553	(608)
Oct. 1	89,446	50,374	(332)	39,072	(474)
Nov. 1	88,727	50,069	(292)	38,658	(397)
Dec. 1	88,036	49,774		38,262	
1942 TOTALS	[av. pop. 112,865]		(7,171)		(12,084)

Derived from Dobroszycki, ed., *The Chronicle of the Lodz Ghetto*, pp. 14, 22, 107–309. See also the Lodz Ghetto Collection, Document 58, pp. 7, 23, 42. The figures in these two sources are somewhat different.

Appendix B
Population and Deportation in the Lodz Ghetto

TABLE 1

POPULATION AND DEPORTATION IN THE LODZ GHETTO: 1942

1942	Population Female	Males	"Resettlement" Females	Males	Totals
Jan. 1	92,703	69,978	5,750	4,253	10,003
Feb.	86,284	64,717	4,267	2,758	7,025
Mar. 1	81,250	60,829	15,420	9,267	24,687
April 1	65,008	50,094	1,476	873	2,349
May 1	62,738	48,068	7,257	3,675	10,914
June 1	59,176	45,294			622
July 1	58,475	44,051			7
Aug. 1	58,039	43,220			
Aug. 30	60,043	45,088			
Sept. 1	60,408	45,553		174	174
Betw. Sept. 1–7 estimated deportations:			[9,568	5,873]	15,685
Oct. 1	50,374	39,072			
Nov. 1	50,069	38,658			
Dec. 1	49,774	38,262	11	8	19
TOTALS			34,181	20,990	
			[+9,568]	[5,873]	
			43,749	26,863	= 70,612
			61.9%	38%	
				Uniden. 873	
					71,485

Derived from Dobroszycki, ed., *The Chronicle of the Lodz Ghetto*, pp. 127, 132, 139–140, 157, and 194. See also the Lodz Ghetto Collection, Document 58, pp. 17–19. There are some differences in the figures between these two texts. The statistics from the Jewish council do not indicate any gender breakdown for the deportations in September 1942. Using the September death rates for men (608) and women (466), as well as the drop in the male and female population from September to October, I arrived at the estimates for the deportations bracketed in this chart.

TABLE 2
AGE AND SEX OF EACH SET OF TRANSPORTS IN 1942

LODZ 1942
JANUARY 16–29 TRANSPORTS

Age	Male	Female	Total (M/F)	% of Total Deportation
50+	418	637	1,055	10.58%
15–49	2,414	3,725	6,139	61.56%
0–14	1,399	1,370	2,769	27.77%
TOTALS	4,231	5,740	9,971	99.91%
%	(42.4%)	(57.5%)		

LODZ 1942
FEBRUARY 22–APRIL 2 TRANSPORTS

Age	Male	Female	Total (M/F)	% of Total Deportation
50+	2,163	3,987	6,060	18%
15–49	6,486	13,038	19,524	57%
0–14	4,198	4,291	8,489	25%
TOTALS	12,847	21,226	34,073	100%
%	(37.7%)	(62.29%)		

LODZ 1942
MAY 4–15 TRANSPORTS

Age	Male	Female	Total (M/F)	% of Total Deportation
50+	2,022	4,291	6,313	57.8%
15–49	1,280	2,606	3,886	35.6%
0–14	355	360	715	6.55%
TOTALS	3,657	7,257	10,914	99.95%
%	(33.5%)	(66.49%)		

TABLE 3
POPULATION AND DEPORTATION BY SEX AND AGE

LODZ GHETTO 1942 FEMALES

Age/ Total Pop.	Population Females	Deportation Females
50+	20,477	8,825
35,220	58%	66%
15–49	71,273	19,369
124,037	57%	66%
20–49	44,948	15,764
73,464	61%	69%
20–29	14,863	4,746
22,974	65%	70%

LODZ GHETTO 1942 MALES

Age/ Total Pop.	Population Males	Deportation Males
50+	14,743	4,603
35,220	42%	34%
15–49	52,764	10,180
124,039	43%	34%
20–49	28,516	7,181
73,464	39%	31%
20–29	8,110	2,023
22,974	35%	30%

TABLE 4
DEPORTATION BY DATE, SEX, AND AGE: LODZ, 1942

Age	DATE JAN. 16–29		DATE FEB. 22–APRIL 2		DATE MAY 4–15	
	Male	*Female*	*Male*	*Female*	*Male*	*Female*
80–91	2	2	4	15	5	13
70–79	9	16	134	257	202	312
60–69	102	150	790	1,368	1,073	1,886
50–59	305	469	1,235	2,257	742	2,080
40–49	492	867	1,558	3,381	469	1,276
30–39	585	1,088	1,550	3,755	314	651
20–29	573	1,001	1,174	3,332	276	413
15–19	764	769	2,204	2,570	221	266
10–14	656	668	2,168	2,209	175	211
5–9	534	460	1,526	1,560	118	108
–4	209	250	504	522	62	41
	4,231	5,740	12,847	21,226	3,657	7,257
TOTALS:	9,971		34,073		10,914	

FINAL TOTAL: 54,958

Derived from the Lodz Ghetto Collection, Document 58, 17–19.

TABLE 5

PERCENTAGES FOR EACH AGE GROUP TRANSPORTED IN 1942

Ages	FEMALES		MALES	
	% / *numbers*		% / *numbers*	
50+	66%	(8,825)	34%	(4,603)
15–49	66%	(19,369)	34%	(10,180)
20–49	69%	(15,764)	31%	(7,181)
40–49	69%	(5,524)	31%	(2,519)
30–39	69%	(5,494)	31%	(2,449)
20–29	70%	(4,746)	30%	(2,023)
15–19	53%	(3,605)	47%	(3,189)
–14	50%	(5,952)	50%	(6,021)

PERCENTAGES OF THE TOTAL DEPORTED BASED ON
KNOWN AGE AND SEX (54,958)

Age	Female	Male
50+	16%	8%
15–49	35%	19%
20–49	29%	13%
30–39	10%	5%
20–39	9%	4%
20–29	9%	4%
15–19	7%	6%
–14	11%	11%

Appendix C
Employment in the Lodz Ghetto

TABLE 1

EMPLOYMENT DISTRIBUTION ACCORDING TO AGE AND SEX
JULY 12, 1940

	MALES				FEMALES			
Age	(%Emp.)	Emp.	Unemp.	Totals	(%Emp.)	Emp.	Unemp.	Totals
under 8		0	(10,711)	10,711		0	(10,115)	10,115
9–14	(1%)	115	(9,487)	9,602	(.007%)	67	(9,064)	9,131
15–19	(51%)	3,684	(3,600)	7,284	(35%)	2,826	(5,252)	8,078
20–25	(97%)	5,653	(159)	5,812	(65%)	5,521	(2,919)	8,440
26–35	(99%)	11,312	(80)	11,392	(53%)	8,106	(7,274)	15,380
36–45	(99%)	10,030	(47)	10,077	(33%)	4,444	(8,885)	13,329
46–60	(99%)	10,709	(38)	10,747	(19%)	2,590	(10,805)	13,395
60+	(99%)	5,547	(55)	5,602	(10%)	726	(6,545)	7,307
TOTALS	(66%)	47,050	(24,177)	71,227	(29%)	24,316	(60,859)	85,175

Derived from the Lodz Ghetto Collection, Document 58, pp. 4–5.

TABLE 2
EMPLOYMENT BY OCCUPATION AND SEX: LODZ 1940

PARTIAL LIST

Occupation	Male	Female	Total
Laborer	6,535	4,792	11,327
Baker	962	25	987
Construction worker	76	0	76
Bookbinder	217	47	264
Office of trade employee	5,548	2,541	8,092
Hairdresser	495	281	776
Hatter	385	405	790
Salesperson	7,887	1,678	9,565
Plumber	29	0	29
Furrier	29	9	38
Teacher	27	543	570
Corset maker	16	232	248
"Packer"	288	0	288
Tailor/laundress	6,302	8,682	14,984
Shoemaker	2,456	4	2,460
Knitter	141	339	480
Carpenter	1,125	0	1,125
Watchmaker/engraver	193	0	193
Weaver	4,068	1,849	5,917
Stocking maker	2,679	2,078	4,757
Dentist	21	40	61
Dental technician	39	9	48
TOTALS	39,518	23,554	63,072

Appendix D
Population and Death
in the Warsaw Ghetto

TABLE 1
POPULATION AND DEATH RATES: WARSAW 1941–42

Dates	Population	DEATHS Female	Male	Children	Totals
1941					
Jan.	380,740	350	454	94	898
Feb.		378	587	58	1,023
Mar.	445,337	641	838	129	1,608
April		709	1,206	146	2,061
May	442,337	1,111	2,536	174	3,821
June	439,309	1,321	2,614	355	4,290
July	431,874	2,101	2,809	640	5,550
Aug.	420,116	2,249	2,592	719	5,560
Sept.	404,300	1,907	2,196	442	4,545
Oct.		1,803	2,511	402	4,716
Nov.		1,939	2,452	410	4,801
Dec.		1,737	2,183	446	4,366
1942		Population	Population		
Jan.		211,292	157,160		5,123
Feb.	368,902				4,618
Mar.					4,951
April					4,432
May	400,000				3,636
June					3,356
July	335,514				3,672
TOTALS		16,246	22,978	4,015	73,027
Aug.–Dec. 1942					9,597
TOTALS					82,624

TABLE 2

DEPORTATION OF THE POPULATION OF WARSAW BY
AGE AND SEX: 1942

Age	Sex	Population Before Deportation	% sent	Population After Deportation
0–9	Male	25,759	99.0	255
0–9	Female	25,699	99.1	243
10–19	Male	35,238	93.8	2,183
10–19	Female	39,790	94.3	2,263
20–29	Male	19,747	80.4	3,851
20–29	Female	36,041	87.3	4,581
30–39	Male	29,155	76.9	6,748
30–39	Female	40,892	88.28	4,791
40–49	Male	21,128	79.6	4,319
40–49	Female	30,652	91.6	2,564
50–59	Male	14,758	86.3	2,019
50–59	Female	20,812	95.54	928
60–69	Male	8,881	96.0	353
60–69	Female	12,335	98.8	143
70–79	Male	2,553	98.8	30
70–79	Female	4,361	99.7	—
80–	Male	287	100	—
80–	Female	603	100	—
unknown	Male	59	—	179
	Female	107	—	148
TOTALS	Male	157,610	87.4	19,937
	Female	211,292	92.6	15,696

Derived from Gutman, *The Jews of Warsaw,* pp. 270–71, and corrected by the author.

Appendix E
Mobile Killing Unit Operations,
Lithuania, and Latvia, 1941

THE VICTIMS OF STRIKE GROUP A, STRIKE COMMANDO 3

	Men	Women	Children	Unident.	Totals
Sept.	11,464	17,849	11,402	665	41,380
Oct.	7,817	13,647	10,346		31,810
Nov.	2,815	4,187	1,175		8,177
TOTALS	22,096	35,683	22,923	665	81,367
	27.15%	43.85%	28.17%		

Derived from Hilberg, ed. *Documents of Destruction*, pp. 46–57.

Suggestions for Further Reading

Aaron, Frieda W. *Bearing the Unbearable: Yiddish and Polish Poetry in the Ghettos and Concentration Camps*. Albany: State University of New York Press, 1990.

Arendt, Hannah. "The Concentration Camp." *Partisan Review* (July 1948).

———. *Eichmann in Jerusalem: A Report on the Banality of Evil*. New York: Viking, 1963.

———. *The Origins of Totalitarianism*, new ed. New York: Harcourt Brace Jovanovich, 1973.

Bar-On, Dan. *Legacy of Silence: Encounters with Children of the Third Reich*. Cambridge, Mass.: Harvard University Press, 1989.

Browning, Christopher R. *Ordinary Men: Reserve Police Battalion 101 and the Final Solution in Poland*. New York: HarperCollins, 1992.

Cernyak-Spatz, Susan. *German Holocaust Literature*. New York: Peter Lang, 1985.

Des Pres, Terrence. *The Survivor: An Anatomy of Life in the Death Camps*. New York: Oxford University Press, 1976.

Eckardt, A. Roy, and Alice L. Eckardt. *Long Night's Journey into Day: Life and Faith after the Holocaust*, rev. and enl. ed. New York: Holocaust Library, 1987.

Eliach, Yaffa, ed. *Hasidic Tales of the Holocaust*. New York: Oxford University Press, 1982.

Epstein, Helen. *Children of the Holocaust: Conversations with Sons and Daughters of Survivors*. New York: Penguin, 1988.

Ezrahi, Sidra. *By Words Alone: The Holocaust in Literature*. Chicago: University of Chicago Press, 1980.

Fine, Ellen S. "Women Writers and the Holocaust: Strategies for Survival."

Reflections of the Holocaust in Art and Literature. Edited by Randolph L. Braham. New York: The City University of New York, 1990.

Fiorenza, Elizabeth Schussler, and David Tracy, eds. *The Holocaust as Interruption*. Edinburgh: T. & T. Clark, 1984.

Fleischner, Eva, ed. *Auschwitz: Beginning of a New Era?* New York: KTAV, 1977.

Goldenberg, Myrna. "Different Horrors, Same Hell: Women Remembering the Holocaust." *Thinking the Unthinkable: Meanings of the Holocaust*. Edited by Roger S. Gottlieb. New York: Paulist Press, 1990.

Haft, Cynthia. *The Theme of the Nazi Concentration Camps in French Literature*. The Hague: Mouton, 1973.

Heinemann, Marlene E. *Gender and Destiny: Women Writers and the Holocaust*. Westport, Conn.: Greenwood Press, 1986.

Ka-Tzetnik 135633 (Yehiel Dinur). *House of Dolls*. London: Granada, 1982.

Klepfisz, Irena. *A Few Words in the Mother Tongue: Poems Selected and New (1971–1990)*. Portland, Ore.: The Eighth Mountain Press, 1990.

Lamont, Rosette C. "Charlotte Delbo, A Woman/Book." *Faith of a (Woman) Writer*. Edited by Alice Kessler-Harris and William McBrien. Westport, Conn.: Greenwood Press, 1988.

Langer, Lawrence L. *The Age of Atrocity: Death in Modern Literature*. Boston: Beacon, 1978.

Lipstadt, Deborah E. *Denying the Holocaust: The Growing Assault on Truth*. New York: Free Press, 1993.

Rich, Adrienne. *An Atlas of the Difficult World: Poems 1988–1991*. New York: Norton, 1991.

Ringelheim, Joan. "Thoughts about Women and the Holocaust." *Thinking the Unthinkable: Meanings of the Holocaust*. Edited by Roger S. Gottlieb. New York: Paulist Press, 1990.

———. "The Unethical and the Unspeakable: Women and the Holocaust." *Simon Wiesenthal Center Annual* 1 (1984).

Rittner, Carol, and John K. Roth, eds. *Memory Offended: The Auschwitz Convent Controversy*. New York: Praeger, 1991.

Roiphe, Anne R. *A Season for Healing: Reflections on the Holocaust*. New York: Summit Books, 1988.

Rosen, Norma. *Accidents of Influence: Writing as a Woman and a Jew in America*. Albany: State University of New York Press, 1992.

Sachs, Nelly. *O the Chimneys: Selected Poems, Including the Verse Play, ELI*. New York: Farrar, Straus and Giroux, 1967.

Sichrovsky, Peter. *Born Guilty*. Translated by Jean Steinberg. New York: Basic Books, 1988.

Spiegelman, Art. *Maus: A Survivor's Tale*. 2 vols. New York: Pantheon, 1986, 1991.

Epilogue
DIFFERENT VOICES

Somewhere amid the forests of Bohemia a birch tree
bends its golden hair toward a reddish ruin.
In mourning, hands clasped at its chest.
And yet the bluebells dance around its feet,
And colored cow-wheat smiles upon the powerless dungeon
tower, while grasses idle mournfully on buried
walks.
Bright coppers flutter past the fallen, sunlit walls of
vanished generations.

GERTRUD KOLMAR

As one excavates what Ida Fink called "the ruins of memory," certain images and persons, events and phrases, become emblematic of women and the Holocaust. There is Lulu, that "practical woman" who helped Charlotte Delbo survive Auschwitz when she thought "none of us will return." There is the blanket that Sara Nomberg-Przytyk received from a caring woman during a freezing evacuation from Auschwitz. Or one might recall Theresa Stangl, wife of Treblinka's commandant, or Magda Trocmé, who saved Jews from the fate that Nazi Germany intended all of them to have. One thinks, too, of Myrna Goldenberg's "different horrors, same hell," four words that sum up what women experienced during the "Final Solution." Gertrud Kolmar's question—"You hear me speak. But do you hear me feel?"—is heard and felt as well.

Epitomizing what happened to women during the Holocaust, another episode with power to grip memory in those ways occurred in Auschwitz–

421

Birkenau on June 25, 1944. In a two-sentence paragraph, awesome not only
for what it says but also for the questions its silence contains, Danuta Czech,
the keeper of the *Auschwitz Chronicle*, describes the event:

> Empty children's strollers are taken away from the storerooms of the personal
> effects camp, known as "Canada," which is located behind Camp B-IIf between
> Crematoriums III and IV. The strollers are pushed in rows of five along the path
> from the crematoriums to the train station; the removal takes an hour.[1]

Although Czech states the facts without commentary, one can surmise what
went on. Some of those baby carriages had arrived with Hungarian Jewish
mothers. They had been permitted to bring that equipment along—all the
way to the gas chambers—to prolong the deception that made murder simpler. True, sometimes children were born in Auschwitz–Birkenau; some even
lived long enough to have numbers tattooed on their frail bodies. But most
mothers and children, especially Jewish ones, could not keep their lives, let
alone their strollers, in that place. Having no utility, mothers and children
usually disappeared in fire and smoke. German efficiency, however, could not
let their empty prams be wasted. They had value. So off the carriages went,
first to "Canada" and then to the train station in the camp's official five-row
formation. Probably they were headed to Germany, where there were still
mothers, raising children for the Reich, who could use them.

Czech says simply that the strollers were pushed to the train station. The
removal, she adds, took about an hour. Her *Chronicle* does not say how long
that hour took, but an Italian Jewish woman named Giuliana Tedeschi reflects
on that question. Part of a transport of 935 Italian Jews who reached
Auschwitz-Birkenau on April 10, 1944, she was one of the 80 women and 154
men who did not go directly to the gas.[2] Those women were tattooed with
numbers ranging from 76776 to 76855. Tedeschi's was 76847.

She was the wife of an architect and the mother of two children, but as a
woman in Birkenau, Tedeschi was alone, at least until she made friends with
some of the other prisoners. Her moving memoir, *There Is a Place on Earth: A
Woman in Birkenau*, not only recalls and records the horrors that surrounded
her, but also repeatedly draws attention to those human relationships that
helped her to survive. With a remarkably sensitive and insightful feminine
touch she describes, for example, how much it meant to discover "Zilly's
hand, a small, warm hand, modest and patient, which held mine in the
evening, which pulled up the blankets around my shoulders, while a calm
motherly voice whispered in my ear, 'Good night, dear—I have a daughter
your age!' And sleep crept slowly into my being along with the trust that hand
communicated, like blood flowing along the veins."[3]

A feeling and a need for connectedness, for relationships with others, perme-
ates Tedeschi's book. Zilly comforted her when she was overcome by a wild
desperation. Also there was Olga, the woman who became her soulmate:

I came across Olga one day and we hid ourselves away together in a corner of the hut. I suddenly felt I would be able to speak to her and she would understand. I spoke about the Dionysian sense of life and she of the spirit and the body. My pupils lost themselves in the whites of her eyes. The huts disappeared, we forgot the barbed wire, and an unbounded liberty of spirit intoxicated us beyond any limit imposed by human bestiality. We decided to be friends.[4]

There were moments of reprieve, but in Birkenau friendship meant sharing and resisting the limits that were imposed by human bestiality. As Tedeschi would learn, that bestiality involved children's strollers.

There had been times in the camp when, at least comparatively speaking, Sundays were days of rest. During Tedeschi's time, however, that tradition had been abolished, and special Sunday tasks were assigned. Sometimes she had to work along the railroad tracks that brought the Hungarian Jews to Birkenau during those late spring and summer days of 1944 when the Third Reich was collapsing but the gas chambers were operating at full and frenzied capacity. Close up, she saw the transports unload. She knew what the new arrivals did not, that death was imminent for all but a few. She also associates these Sundays with a smell:

> ... The whole camp was gradually pervaded by a smell that only we old hands could recognize, the smell that haunted our nostrils, that impregnated our clothing, a smell we tried in vain to escape by hiding away inside our bunks, that destroyed any hope of return, of seeing our countries and children again—the smell of burning human flesh.[5]

Sundays could make Tedeschi feel "morally destroyed, physically exhausted; the awareness of our impotence humiliated us, the instinct to rebel choked us."[6]

June 25, 1944, was a Sunday. That day Tedeschi was one of fifty women who turned right when she went through the gate from her part of the camp. Ordinarily her work column went left, toward Birkenau's main gate and the road that led beyond. But on this particular Sunday the route was different. It led in the direction that most of the Hungarian Jews took only once. Up ahead, at the end of the rail spur, were Crematoriums II and III. It might be their turn, some of the women thought, but they were directed on, turned right again, and followed a path through the birch trees from which Birkenau took its name.

The path led to another crematorium. "The women went in through the big door," Tedeschi recalls, "and stood in the hall."[7] There death met them—not directly but in the form of fifty empty baby carriages. The Germans ordered them to push these strollers to safekeeping. Tedeschi says the distance was two miles; Czech says the removal took about an hour. Neither far nor long—even to push a child's stroller—on any normal Sunday, but for Giuliana Tedeschi,

June 25, 1944, was a Sunday she would never forget. Nor in all likelihood could any woman who experienced it as Tedeschi did.

Fear for their own lives "drained away," Tedeschi writes, "yet each face was stamped with a grimace of pain." And here is how her description of "this place on earth" continues:

> The strange procession moved forward: the mothers who had left children behind rested their hands on the push bars, instinctively feeling for the most natural position, promptly lifting the front wheels whenever they came to a bump. They saw gardens, avenues, rosy infants asleep in their carriages under vaporous pink and pale blue covers. The women who had lost children in the crematorium felt a physical longing to have a child at their breast, while seeing nothing but a long plume of smoke that drifted away to infinity. Those who hadn't had children pushed their carriages along clumsily and thought they would never have any, and thanked God. And all the empty baby carriages screeched, bounced, and banged into each other with the tired and desolate air of persecuted exiles.[8]

The accounts of Danuta Czech and Giuliana Tedeschi are close but not identical. Czech does not say who pushed the children's strollers. Giuliana Tedeschi says that women were assigned the task and that her company's strollers came directly from a crematorium. Neither report mentions that men got stroller duty, but perhaps they did, for the fifty carriages mentioned in Tedeschi's report were by no means the only ones that reached Birkenau. More of them can be seen in Lili Meier's *Auschwitz Album*, and there is at least one woman survivor whose testimony at the Nuremberg trials said sometimes there were hundreds, sometimes even a thousand, children's carriages that arrived during a day's work in Birkenau.[9] If men got such assignments, their feelings would be no less important than those of Giuliana Tedeschi and the other women she describes. But Tedeschi's report, a woman's testimony, is certainly one about Sunday, June 25, 1944, that needs to be heard and felt.

Was it an accident that women in Birkenau were assigned to move those baby carriages, a journey whose yearning and pain, grief and hopelessness, so far exceeded the hour and two miles that it took? It is hard to think so. Far more likely the mentality that created Birkenau would have reasoned precisely: "Who better than women—Jewish especially, mothers even—to move empty baby carriages from a crematorium to safekeeping for the Reich?" That possibility was a real limit imposed on Tedeschi and her sisters by human bestiality.

The Holocaust leaves behind heartbreaking memories and images—so many they cannot be counted. But none symbolizes more poignantly the plight of women during the Holocaust than the one offered by Giuliana Tedeschi: a Jewish woman prisoner pushing an empty baby carriage in Birkenau. In that vision, the unrelentingly cruel calculation of the "Final Solution's" impact on women—theft, enslavement, and murder—is reflected in ways that no words can express, let alone forgive and redeem.

"There is a place on earth," Giuliana Tedeschi's memoir begins, "a desolate heath, where the shadows of the dead are multitudes, where the living are dead, where there is only death, hate, and pain."[10] As the women in Birkenau went to get the children's carriages from the crematorium on that June Sunday in 1944, Tedeschi recalls that the birch trees she passed were still elegant, though at the time "none of the women was aware of the wood, of the birds singing, of the rustling leaves, the whiteness of the bark, the blue of the sky."[11] Perhaps Gertrud Kolmar had seen—and not seen—those same trees some months before. It was not them she wrote about, of course. By the time she reached Birkenau, her writing and her life were finished. But earlier she had thought of birch trees, too, and she imagined one of them bending "in mourning" toward a ruin. If trees can mourn, Birkenau's birches must be among the saddest of them all.

While some women wrote about their Holocaust experiences soon after 1945, there has been a new outpouring of women's memoirs in the last decade.[12] Writing memoirs or giving oral histories much more recently, these women—at least to some extent—have been able to move beyond the past, to establish new families, to get on with living their lives. What impels them to revisit that shattering past and to testify nearly fifty years after the end of World War II and the Holocaust?

Each woman is different, and yet it seems that those who are still writing or speaking after Auschwitz share a deeply felt need—especially as they grow older—to ensure that the past which engulfed their families and friends will not be forgotten. To remember that "there is a place on earth" cannot restore what was lost, but the Holocaust is forgotten at our peril. Remembering it can be a warning and a shield for the future.

This book has provided occasions for women to speak for themselves about the Holocaust and its consequences. Drawing attention to memoirs and reflections that emphasize the distinctive conditions faced by Jewish and non-Jewish women, it also has explored some of the distinctive ways in which women have responded to the Holocaust then and now. As women's voices have reflected on women's experiences during and after the Holocaust, we hope that *Different Voices* has increased understanding that will benefit men as well as women.

Birkenau stood in the very heart of Western civilization, within easy reach of the great universities, cathedrals, and institutions of European culture. In that "place on earth" so many of Western culture's humanizing promises failed. "Birkenau," says Giuliana Tedeschi, "existed to suffocate hope and annihilate logic, to provoke madness and death."[13] Listening to her voice and to the voices of her Holocaust sisters, can we hear them feel? Surely we must.

NOTES

1. Danuta Czech, *Auschwitz Chronicle 1939–1945*, trans. Barbara Harshav, Martha Humphreys, and Stephen Shearier (New York: Holt, 1990), 652.
2. See ibid., 608.
3. Giuliana Tedeschi, *There Is a Place on Earth: A Woman in Birkenau*, trans. Tim Parks (New York: Pantheon, 1992), 9–10.
4. Ibid., 10.
5. Ibid., 90.
6. Ibid., 89.
7. Ibid., 94.
8. Ibid., 95.
9. See Peter Hellman, *The Auschwitz Album: A Book Based Upon an Album Discovered by a Concentration Camp Survivor, Lili Meier* (New York: Random House, 1981), 38. Although *The Auschwitz Album* identifies her only as S. Szmaglewska, it is likely that this woman is the Polish author of early memoirs about Birkenau, which, unfortunately, have long been out of print. See Seweryna Szmaglewska, *Smoke Over Birkenau*, trans. Jadwiga Rynas (New York: Holt, 1947) and *United in Wrath* (Warsaw: "Polonia" Foreign Languages Publishing House, 1955). Szmaglewska's testimony at the Nuremberg Trials can be found in *Trial of the Major War Criminals before the International Military Tribunal* (Nuremberg: 1947), 8:317–23. In this testimony, Szmaglewska, who says she was in Birkenau from October 7, 1942, until January 1945, is identified as Severina Shmaglevskaya. For another reference to the baby strollers in Auschwitz, see Rudolf Vrba and Alan Bestic, *I Cannot Forgive* (New York: Grove Press, 1964). With help from the camp resistance, Vrba, a Slovakian Jew, escaped from Auschwitz in the spring of 1944 and reported what was happening there. Before his escape, he worked in "Canada," the storehouse area in Auschwitz-Birkenau.
10. Tedeschi, *There Is a Place on Earth*, 1.
11. Ibid., 94.
12. In addition to Giuliana Tedeschi's superb book, one also thinks of Judith Magyar Isaacson's *Seed of Sarah: Memoirs of a Survivor* (Urbana: University of Illinois Press, 1990) and Liana Millu's *Smoke Over Birkenau*, trans. Lynne Sharon Schwartz (Philadelphia: The Jewish Publication Society, 1991). It is interesting that Millu's book borrows the title of one of the earliest Holocaust memoirs to be published by a woman. See n. 9 above for more detail.
13. Tedeschi, *There Is a Place on Earth*, 138.

Glossary

Aktion (also **Action; Round-up**): Raid against the Jews, often in a ghetto; the primary purpose was to gather victims for deportation to the Nazi concentration and extermination camps.

AK: *Armia Krajowa*, or Polish Home Army.

Appell (also **Zählappell**): Roll call in the camps.

Arbeitführers: Work leaders.

Aryan: The original purpose of the term was to designate and classify an Indo-European language group. The Nazis used the term to mean a superior, white Nordic heroic race, but, in fact, the term has no biological validity as a racial term.

Aufseherin: Work supervisor.

Blockälteste (f.), **Blockältester** (m.), **Blockältesten** (pl.): The barracks supervisor; a male or female prisoner functionary who was responsible for the prisoners in his/her barracks during roll call, for the distribution of food to inmates, and for order in the barracks.

Blocksperre: A curfew during which prisoners were not permitted to leave their barracks.

Blokowa (also **Blokhova**): Female supervisor of a block of barracks in a Nazi concentration or extermination camp. **Sztubowa** were assistants to the *blokowas*.

Boit'l: A small sack or packet; something similar to a pocket.

Canada (also **Kanada**): The depot where the personal effects stolen from the inmates were stored. It was called "Canada" because to the prisoners Canada represented unlimited abundance. Initially the goods were stored in five barracks; ultimately there were thirty such barracks.

Capo (also **Kapo**): A male or female prisoner functionary appointed by the SS; chief of a work battalion or some other branch of a concentration camp such as a kitchen or "hospital." Capos often were drawn from the criminals among the camp inmates.

Death March: Forced marches of concentration camp inmates (mostly Jews) from places like Auschwitz to camps inside Nazi Germany. These occurred near the end of World War II as the Third Reich was collapsing and the German army was in retreat.

Deportation: The transportation or "resettlement" of Jews from Nazi-occupied countries to labor, concentration, and death camps in other parts of occupied Europe.

Einsatzgruppen: Mobile killing units of the SS and SD attached to the *Wehrmacht*. Their official tasks were to wipe out political opponents and seize state documents. They carried out mass murders, primarily of Jews in German-occupied areas in the USSR and Poland. **Einsatzkommandos** were "special action" commandos that were subunits of *Einsatzgruppen*.

Final Solution: In German *Die Endlösung der Judenfrage in Europa*—"the final solution of the Jewish question in Europe"—a Nazi euphemism for the physical extermination of European Jewry.

FKL: *Frauenkonzentrationslager* or women's concentration camp.

Forarbeiterin: Work foreman.

Generalgouvernement (also **General Government**): Refers to an area of Poland occupied by Germany but not incorporated into the Third Reich. An administrative unit under the command of Hans Frank, it included five districts: Galicia, Cracow, Lublin, Radom, and Warsaw.

Gestapo: An abbreviation for *Geheime Staatspolizei* or the Secret State Police of Nazi Germany. The Gestapo, under the command of Heinrich Himmler, was a branch of the SS that dealt with political opponents through the use of terror and arbitrary arrest.

Haftling: Concentration camp prisoner.

Judenrat (Jewish Council): Council of Jewish leaders established on Nazi orders; the *Judenrat* was an administrative unit set up in each ghetto by the German occupation forces to organize and administer the ghettos.

Judenrein: A German term meaing "pure" or "clean" of Jews. It was the goal of the Nazi "Final Solution" or the Holocaust.

KL, KZ: *Konzentrationslager* (concentration camp).

Kommando: Work crew; labor battalion in the concentration camp.

Kristallnacht (also **Crystal Night,** or **Night of the Broken Glass**): Refers to the night of November 9–10, 1938, when the Nazis in Germany and Austria smashed, burned, and looted Jewish homes, synagogues, and businesses.

Lager: Camp.

Lagerälteste: Within the hierarchy of the camp, the highest rank that could be obtained by a prisoner; often translated as "camp elder."

Lebensborn (Fountain of Life): SS association established in 1935. Its main tasks were to facilitate the adoption of "racially appropriate" children by childless SS couples and to encourage the birth of "racially sound" children.

Lebensraum (Living Space): One of Hitler's goals in World War II was to gain "living space" for Germans in the East. **Lebensraum** was a principle of Nazi ideology and foreign policy, expressed in the drive for the conquest of territories, mainly in Eastern Europe.

Mensch: Human being.

Mischlinge: Nazi term for persons having one or two Jewish grandparents.

Musulmans (also **Muselmänner**): Persons in the camps who were at the absolute end of their physical and psychological resources; they are on the verge of death from starvation and exhaustion; the "living dead."

National Socialism: The political and social philosophy of Hitler and of Germany from 1933–1945. National Socialism meant dictatorship and included the philosophy of racism as its rationale. German fascism was called National Socialism.

Nuremberg Laws: Two laws issued in September 1935 that furthered the legal exclusion of Jews from German life: the "Reich Citizenship Law" removed Jews' citizenship; the "Law for the Protection of German Blood and Honor" prohibited Jews from engaging in marital and other relations with Germans ("Aryans"). The laws made antisemitism part of Germany's legal code.

Pogrom: A violent attack on Jews by non-Jews. Such attacks included rape, murder, and the looting and destruction of Jewish property.

Pulverraum: Gunpowder room.

Rassenschände: Nazi term for sexual contact between an "Aryan" and a Jew; racial defilement.

Revier: The infirmary or camp "hospital." Located in a separate section of the camp, surrounded by barbed wire, it lacked medicine, hygiene, and sanitation.

RSHA: *Reichssicherheitshauptamt*, the Reich Security Main Office, a Nazi administrative office formed in September 1939.

SA: *Sturmabteilung* or Storm Troopers; until 1934 the elite, left-oriented paramilitary corps of the Nazi party.

Selection: The decision by the Nazis in the camps about who would live and who would die. The decision was made by SS doctors on the basis of a prisoner's outward appearance. Only those who could work were kept alive.

Shtetl: Yiddish word meaning a small, predominantly Jewish village in Eastern Europe. During the Holocaust, thousands were destroyed and their inhabitants murdered on the spot or deported to Nazi concentration camps.

Shul: Synagogue.

Sonderkommando: Special Jewish crews, living and working in isolation, forced by the Nazis to work in the gas chambers and crematoria.

SS: *Schutzstaffel* or "Protection Squad." Originally, the elite guard who protected Hitler. Headed by Heinrich Himmler, the SS became an efficient organization that controlled the concentration, labor, and death camps. The SS included elite combat troops (Waffen SS) as well as secret police (Gestapo).

Tish'a B'Av: The ninth day of the month of Av, a fast day to commemorate the destruction of the Temple in Jerusalem.

To Organize: A camp term meaning to steal, buy, exchange, or somehow get hold of some article necessary for survival. It also meant to acquire a thing that was needed without wronging another prisoner. Sometimes it meant getting at the storehouses and distributing some article of daily need to others without being caught.

UNRRA: United Nations Relief and Rehabilitation Administration, an organization established in 1943 that aided millions of displaced persons in postwar Europe.

Wehrmacht: The German army (as distinguished from the SS).

WVHA: *Wirtschafts-Verwaltungshauptamt*, Nazi Germany's Economic and Administrative Main Office, an SS "ministry." Branch D was responsible for running the concentration camps, although Branch C (Works and Buildings) and Branch W (Economic Enterprises) also had direct interests in the camps.

Zugang (s.), **Zugänge** (pl.): A newcomer to camp, to the *revier*, or to the barracks; a group of newly arrived prisoners before they lost the attributes of "free men and women." Such people usually did not understand the conditions into which they had been delivered and were often exposed to especially vicious bullying.

ZOB: *Zydowska Organizacja Bojowa*, the Jewish Fighting Organization established in the Warsaw ghetto on July 28, 1942.

Zyklon B: A commercial name for hydrogen cyanide, whose pellets turned into a lethal gas as soon as they were exposed to air. This pesticide was used in the Euthanasia Program and especially in the gas chambers at Auschwitz–Birkenau. Supplies of *Zyklon B* for Auschwitz–Birkenau were handled by the Tesch and Stabenow Company and DEGESCH, a firm controlled by I. G. Farben.

Index